Cultural Anthropology

Eugene N. Cohen
Edwin Eames

Baruch College, The City University of New York

Cultural Anthropology

Little, Brown and Company
Boston   Toronto

To Helen, Robert, and Michael
and
Phyllis, Mona, David, and Lori

Library of Congress Catalog Card No. 81–81413
ISBN 0–316–149918

9 8 7 6 5 4 3 2 1

Hal

Published simultaneously in Canada
by Little, Brown & Company (Canada) Limited

Printed in the United States of America

ACKNOWLEDGMENTS

The authors gratefully acknowledge permission to use material from the following sources.

Alan Beals, from *Being an Anthropologist: Fieldwork in Eleven Cultures,* edited by George D. Spindler, p. 38. Copyright © 1970 by Holt, Rinehart and Winston, Inc. Reprinted by permission of Holt, Rinehart and Winston and George D. Spindler.

Jean L. Briggs, abridged from "Kapluna Daughter," in *Women in the Field,* edited by Peggy Golde, published by Aldine Publishing Co. (1970). Reprinted by permission of Jean L. Briggs.

Robbins Burling, abridged from "Language Development of a Garo and English Speaking Child," in *Word* (1959) vol. 15, no. 1. Reprinted by permission of Johnson Reprint Corporation.

A. W. Cardinall, from *In Ashanti and Beyond,* reprinted by Greenwood Press, Westport, Conn. (1927).

William C. Clarke, abridged from *People and Place: Ecology of a New Guinean Community,* University of California Press (1971). Reprinted by permission of the publisher.

Henry F. Dobyns, Carlos M. Medrano, Mario C. Vasquez, abridged from *Saturday Review* (Nov. 3, 1962). Copyright © 1962 by Saturday Review. All rights reserved. Reprinted by permission.

Acknowledgments continued on page 428.

To the Instructor

We decided to write this introductory text when we found that, using existing texts, it was difficult to motivate our students without skimping on important concepts. From our more than three decades of teaching experience we have noticed that students responded favorably to ethnographic accounts based upon fieldwork. Therefore, a fundamental feature of our presentation is the integration of ethnographic data with analysis throughout the text to clearly — and interestingly — document the scientific process that is the basis of the anthropological study of human behavior.

Carefully abridged ethnographic accounts written by professional anthropologists, as well as original and unpublished ethnographic data from the authors' own field research, begin each chapter. These accounts introduce students to the basic scientific material of cultural anthropology and to its technical vocabulary. We chose ethnographies that reflect the divergent and world wide interests of cultural anthropologists. These range from descriptions of the subsistence patterns of a New Guinea Highland tribe (Chapter 3) to the study of female impersonators in the United States (Chapter 13), from the dedication of a bridge in South Africa (Chapter 2) to the celebration of a birthday party for a bridge connecting New Jersey and Pennsylvania (Chapter 2). In addition to standard ethnographies, historical sources have been tapped for their descriptions. An account of the encounter with the Buganda king by a British traveler more than one hundred years ago opens Chapter 7, and a description of a Maori revolt against British authority a century ago introduces the topic of social change (Chapter 12). In Chapter 5 we have selected an unusual format, a play script to begin the chapter. This play, based upon an actual incident in the lives of a group of Tlingit Indians, introduces the importance of kinship in an innovative way. Language and culture (Chapter 11) begins with a description of language acquisition by a fieldworker's son who accompanied him to a tribal area of India.

These opening ethnographic accounts are the basis for the general discussion in the chapter. From Chapter 3 on, a tripartite division — ethnography, contextual analysis, and comparative perspective — takes the student from specific data to generalization and theoretical construct. For instance, Chapter 10 begins with a description of child rearing among the Ngoni. Their socialization techniques are then discussed in the context of the history of Ngoni migration and military domination. In the comparative section various socialization techniques are then described, generalizations are derived, and theoretical explanations are explored. This model parallels the process of moving from ethnography to generalization characteristic of the discipline.

Our initial enthusiasm for the ethnographic approach has been heightened by the responses of students and colleagues to earlier versions of this text. Students' comments and criticisms as well as those of professional reviewers have had an impact upon this final version. We believe the changes based upon their responses make this one of the best volumes available for an introductory course in cultural anthropology.

We have provided a broad coverage of the field while at the same time incorporating a variety of approaches to enhance the effectiveness of the text. Included are an extended discussion of anthropological methods of research and analysis, a systematic presentation of the mutual interplay of theory and data, an emphasis on anthropology's contribution to an understanding of the modern world, and a focus on the human as well as the institutional aspects of life.

Since fieldwork is the foundation of ethnographic description, we have provided students with a glimpse of both the human and scientific aspects of this singular method of data collection. In Chapter 1 a variety of personalized fieldwork accounts provide insight into the many problems encountered while doing fieldwork. Using the material provided a student can be taken from the initial steps of defining a research problem and obtaining funds to the completion of the fieldwork.

Theoretical explanations are among the most important contributions of anthropologists to the understanding of human behavior. Throughout the text theoretical explanations of particular aspects of behavior are developed. Chapter 2 provides explanations of the various theories current in anthropology. Using the incest taboo and the way different theories explain its universality, we are able to document the varied approaches of the current major theoretical positions held by cultural anthropologists. By focusing on fieldwork and theory early in the book, we feel that students will be better able to appreciate the scientific underpinnings of cultural anthropology. In our later discussions of subsistence, marriage and the family, kinship, war, origin of the state, and mental illness we present various theoretical positions and critically evaluate them. In teaching, however, we have found that students are often bewildered by abstract theoretical explanations that are not solidly moored in concrete empirical data. Therefore, we have tried to attain a balance of theory and data — that combination that will most clearly convey meaning to students. For example, Chapter 8 takes a complex arena of human behavior — religion — and subjects it to a sustained and systematic theoretical position derived from the work of Victor W. Turner. Taking the theoretical position he developed to explain the religious practices and beliefs of the Ndembu people of Central Africa, we show its utility and value in explaining the religious beliefs and practices of other cultures; from this one specific application, we hope students will see the usefulness of theory in enlarging our understanding of human behavior.

Specific sections of the text are designed to illustrate the anthropological contribution to an understanding of the world we live in. Our contemporary world is to a significant degree the consequence of five hundred years of European colonial hegemony. In Chapter 12 we explore colonialism not as an isolated historical interlude, but as the framework within which the social structure of our planet has been transformed. Social change, for Western culture as well as for tribal and peasant cultures, is presented within the context of the colonial experience. Among the most serious problems facing our time is the question of war. Interest in war as a social and cultural phenomenon has recently emerged in cultural anthropology, and this new interest is reflected in our extensive treatment in Chapter 6. We find it perplexing that although marriage and family are given extensive coverage in cultural anthropology, the question of divorce is rarely discussed in introductory textbooks. As the number of divorces per year in the United States approaches the two million mark, it seems incumbent upon cultural anthropologists to make their findings available to a wider audience. We do this in Chapter 4. In order to understand the modern world, material from American and Western society has been included as well as the more traditional data from tribal and peasant society.

Although cultural anthropologists recognize the human aspects of their discipline, this side of cultural anthropology is rarely described to the introductory student. An entire chapter, Chapter 9, describes the variety of ways in which people enjoy themselves. In addition to topics such as food, sex, and games, actual recipes that can be tried by students are included in this chapter. The humanistic component of cultural anthropology is introduced throughout the text as well.

There are four parts to the text: Part I, "The Uniqueness of Cultural Anthropology," introduces the unique manner in which cultural anthropologists collect and analyze data about human behavior in diverse cultural settings. Part II, "Dimensions of Social Behavior," looks at the ways in which people in different cultures order their lives. "Learning the System," Part III, explores the processes of acquiring culture and how cultures change. In Part IV, "Retrospect and Prospect," we look at cultural anthropology within the context of a changing world. By beginning with data collection and analysis we provide a foundation for understanding and evaluating the substantive findings of the field. By concluding with a view of the future of cultural anthropology, we are able to identify its enduring qualities as a scientific and humanistic inquiry into the human condition.

Within the text specific teaching aids are used to enhance its effectiveness. Key terms and important concepts are italicized in the text for easy reference. Each chapter concludes with a world map indicating the location of all groups discussed in that chapter. In addition maps on the inside front and back covers show the locations of all peoples discussed in the

text. Maps provide information that students should acquire as part of their introduction to cultural anthropology. Each chapter ends with a concise summary and a list of the key terms introduced. The terms are listed in the order in which they appear within the text, thus providing a skeleton framework for chapter review. Definitions of terms and concepts can be found within each chapter and in the comprehensive glossary at the end of the book. An annotated suggested readings list at the end of each chapter provides readily available material that students can use as a starting point for information about specific areas of anthropological work. A reference bibliography at the back of the book identifies the sources used in writing the text. It can be used by those students wishing to explore more advanced topics in anthropology or who are given assignments requiring reading and research.

An instructor's manual has been prepared to accompany the text. It contains more than 700 test items. We believe that the enthnographic emphasis of the text can be strengthened through the use of ethnographic films. Therefore, we include in the manual a selected and annotated list of films to supplement each chapter.

Acknowledgments

Writing a text book is neither a simple nor easily accomplished task, and we were fortunate in having had the assistance of many friends, colleagues, and co-workers. We would like to acknowledge the aid and encouragement of our colleagues at Baruch College, in particular Norman W. Storer, Chairman of the Department of Sociology and Anthropology, Larry Arno and the staff of the Audiovisual Center, and Harold Iverson and the staff of the library. Virginia Lotz, secretary of the Department of Sociology and Anthropology, cheerfully assumed the responsibility for the numerous details related to the writing of this text. Avrama Gingold and Sandra Dean not only typed and retyped several versions of the manuscript, but also offered editorial suggestions and comments. Particular thanks are owed to Ceal Holzman who, in her capacity as research assistant, provided bibliographical material, film reviews, library research, and critical evaluations of our writing.

A number of our colleagues have been very helpful in supplying photographs. William Bascom, Gerald Berreman, Alan Beals, Robbins Burling, Paul Doughty, Raymond Firth, James Gibbs, Robert Glasse, Paul Hocking, Anthony Leeds, Lorna Marshall, Esther Newton, Lisa Peattie, Arnold Pilling, Victor W. Turner, and Eric Wolf generously shared their photographs with us. Our only regret is that we could not use all of the photographs they supplied.

We are grateful to the following people who reviewed portions of the manuscript or helped us obtain specific materials incorporated in the text: Ruth Almstedt, San Diego State; Sandra Barnes, University of Pennsylvania; William Bascom, University of California at Berkeley; Roger Basham, College of the Canyons; Peter Bertocci, Oakland University; Jean Briggs, Memorial University, Newfoundland; James Gibbs, Stanford University; Walter Goldschmidt, UCLA; Michael Harner, New School for Social Research; Mary Hyatt, Baruch College; Selma Koss-Brandow, Trenton State; Mervyn Meggitt, Queens College CUNY; Anthony Mendonca, Community College of Allegheny County; Salo Weindling; and Daniel Yakes, Muskegon Community College. The editorial staff at *National Geographic* and Elizabeth Meyerhoff deserve our special thanks for providing the photograph used for the front cover. Particular appreciation is owed to James Gibbs who reviewed an earlier version of the manuscript and stayed with our project until completion. We must also include that large number of anonymous individuals who critically reviewed the manuscript. We did not always agree with their reviews, but a considerable number of their suggestions found their way into our text and we do appreciate the effort and thought they gave our work.

Writing is only the initial step in producing a finished book. Between the authors and the final product stand a large number of individuals whose time and professional input are an absolutely necessary ingredient. The staff at Little, Brown contributed a level of interest and competence that converted a manuscript into a textbook. Jane Aaron and Garret White were extremely helpful in initiating and supervising the project. Janet B. Welch, developmental editor, took what was often an unwieldy manuscript and transformed it into an integrated teaching tool. Almost every page of the text reflects her professional skill and involvement. Cynthia Chapin, book editor, was responsible for establishing a production schedule and keeping us to it. Thanks are also due Laurel Anderson, photo researcher, Frances Garelick, copyeditor, and Andrea Pozgay, permissions editor. Barbara Anderson and Billie Ingram, editorial assistants, handled the myriad details that are always part of producing a book.

Our wives, Helen and Phyllis, gracefully accepted the madness associated with writing this text. Missed dinners, lost weekends, interminable phone conversations, and houses littered with papers, files, typescript, and books were tolerated with good humor and understanding. Finally, we must acknowledge the help, albeit anonymous, of our students whose criticisms and comments of earlier versions of the text were important contributions to its final form.

To the Student

A basic challenge you'll face in an introductory anthropology course is becoming familiar with what appears to be a bewildering variety of tribal and peasant groups. Cultural and social groups are to cultural anthropology as elements are to chemistry; they are the real-life material whose behavior researchers observe and record. From these observations come the fundamental theories that you'll study in this course. To help you become familiar with these many groups, we've included a world map at the end of each chapter that shows the name and locations of the groups discussed. We hope these maps will be helpful as you review the text.

All scientists use words that have special meaning within each scientific discipline; for example, *calorie,* which to most of us is something to count, has a technical meaning — a unit of heat — to a chemist. Anthropologists, too, use a special, technical vocabulary. In the text, we have alerted you to an anthropological term or concept by italicizing it and providing the anthropological definition. You'll also find lists of these key terms at the end of each chapter and a glossary at the back of the book that should help you review new terms.

In the vocabulary of cultural anthropology there is one term — *tribe* — that is not only widely used, but also defies a clear-cut and universally accepted meaning. It would be impossible to write a text in cultural anthropology without using the words *tribe* and *tribal.* What do they mean, and how do we use them? Many anthropologists use the term *tribe* to refer to a particular level of political organization, usually defined as simple and lacking complex institutions. Other definitions of this term stress the lack of a written language and emphasize kinship relations as basic attributes. In this text, we use the terms *tribe* and *tribal* to refer to groups having a particular means of making a living and obtaining food: *hunters and gatherers* who hunt wild animals and gather vegetable foods growing in the wild, *gardeners* who grow their own food, but use a simple technology without the use of plows or draft animals, and *pastoralists* who tend herds of domesticated animals. Our usage is primarily *economic* and differentiates *tribal* people from *peasants* who are farmers using plows, draft animals, and fertilization techniques that permit continuous cultivation.

Brief Contents

Contents

Part II Dimensions of Social Behavior 79

Chapter 6 War and Law   173

Chapter 7 Power and Political Organization: Head Man, Chief, and King   203

List of Ethnographies

Introduction

Anthropology is a scientific discipline that takes as its subject matter human beings and human behavior. Traditionally, it has been divided into four major fields: *physical anthropology, archaeology, linguistics,* and *cultural anthropology.* Together these four branches constitute the total discipline of anthropology often called *general anthropology.*

Physical anthropologists study human biology, describing the genetic and physical characteristics of humanity. They also investigate the origins of the human species. The search for the physical remains — fossil bones and teeth — of our ancestors is a central activity in physical anthropology. Through the work of the late Louis Leakey in East Africa the search for our human ancestors is probably that aspect of anthropology most familiar to the general public. His research in East Africa revolutionized our knowledge about the antiquity of human origins.

Archaeologists study humanity's past by excavating, or literally digging up, the physical remains of past cultures. These remains can range from buried and forgotten cities to small and broken pieces of pottery. Usually, no written records exist that describe these past cultures or ways of life. Therefore, archaeologists must reconstruct them from the remains, or artifacts, that are uncovered. Certainly, the most well-known archaeological discovery was the excavation of the tomb of Tutankhamen, a pharaoh of ancient Egypt.

Linguistics is the scientific study of language. Recording the numerous nonwritten languages spoken by tribal people and analyzing their grammatical structures occupies a major place in linguistic anthropology. Linguists also investigate the biological and physical bases of human speech and the possibility of language capacity among nonhuman primates. A specialized field of study in linguistics, historical linguistics, investigates the relationships between separate languages. Thus, linguists are able to show that languages as diverse as Sanskrit, Greek, Latin, Persian, English, Russian and ancient Hittite are all descended from a prehistoric and now extinct language called Indo-European.

Cultural anthropologists study all aspects of human behavior and thought. Describing the varied customs, manners, and ways of life of different groups all over the world is a basic task of this branch of general anthropology. In addition, explaining and understanding human behavior is an important goal for cultural anthropologists. For these reasons cultural anthropology is often classified as a social science, sharing close ties and common interests with sociology, psychology, political science, economics, and history.

What ties these diverse subfields of anthropology together? Primarily it is their interest in the human condition. From their different perspectives and approaches they illuminate the problems of our origin, history, and behavior. Cultural anthropology and archaeology share an interest in the history and development of human culture. What the cultural anthropologist observes directly, the archaeologist infers indirectly from the artifacts uncovered in the process of excavation. Physical anthropologists and cultural anthropologists share overlapping concerns. The cultural anthropologist often turns to the findings of physical anthropology to ascertain the physiological and biological framework of human behavior. Attempting to deterine the impact of language upon behavior and thought, cultural anthropologists use the specialized research and theories developed by linguists.

It is from the integration of these different branches that anthropologists develop a *holistic* or integrative view of humanity. This view incorporates the biological, historical, and cultural dimensions of the human condition. Cultural anthropology is unique among the social sciences. Not only does it bring to the study of humanity an awareness of the historical and biological aspects of our behavior, but it is distinctive in terms of the breadth of its subject matter and its methods of research and analysis.

Traditionally, cultural anthropology was defined as the study of non-Western tribal people. This dimension differentiated cultural anthropology from the other social sciences that took as their subject matter literate civilizations and Western society. Although many people still view anthropology as the study of tribal people, more and more anthropologists have shifted their interest to the study of modern society. Today, you are as likely to find an anthropologist doing research in New York City as in the islands of the South Pacific. Thus, the emphasis on the study of non-Western tribal people no longer defines cultural anthropology.

Over the years, the significance and relevance of cultural anthropology have been debated and widely discussed. When cultural anthropology was defined as the study of tribal people, it was suggested that such study would provide insight into our own past. As anthropologists direct their attention to the study of American and Western society, they can perhaps provide a significant understanding of our own behavior and institutions. In 1979, Andrew Young, then the United States Ambassador to the United Nations, presented a posthumous award to Margaret Mead, one of the most illustrious figures in anthropology. In presenting this award, he said, "It would be wonderful to have some anthropologists sitting in our National Security Council. . . . Such representation . . . might help the United States better understand social and cultural changes at a time when we are hard-pressed to make sense of these mammoth forces that confront us." (1979).

Part I

The Uniqueness of Cultural Anthropology

Cultural anthropology is one of several disciplines grouped together as social, or behavioral, sciences. All of the social sciences take as their subject matter human behavior, but cultural anthropology has two dimensions that make it unique: the manner in which anthropologists collect data and the approaches they use to analyze their data.

Fieldwork, the basic data collecting technique used by cultural anthropologists, involves living with people in order to study their behavior. For the cultural anthropologist, living with people means participating in their everyday activities and developing close ties with them. Thus fieldwork is a research method that is unique in combining scientific and human aspects. Chapter 1 begins with personal accounts by four anthropologists describing their field experiences. These accounts are drawn from work with Australian natives, Eskimo in the Arctic, Melanesians on a South Pacific island, and a Black gang in a Chicago ghetto. Drawing upon this material, as well as upon other fieldwork accounts, the scientific and human components of anthropological research are explored in the remainder of Chapter 1.

In Chapter 2 we begin with two accounts — the dedication of a bridge in South Africa and a birthday party for a bridge connecting New Jersey and Pennsylvania — to illustrate one approach to understanding anthropological data: contextual analysis. Witchcraft — the belief in the power of the evil — is the basis for presenting another fundamental anthropological approach: the comparative, or cross-cultural, method. It is these types of analyses, contextual and cross-cultural, that distinguish cultural anthropology from the other social sciences. In contemporary cultural anthropology different theoretical positions are used to comprehend human social behaviors. To illustrate the key principles of these theories, we describe how each of them explains the same widespread human custom, the prohibition of sexual relations between relatives — the incest taboo.

The cultural anthropologist obtains information by going directly to the people. Here Richard Lee talks to a San man about edible foods that make up the diet of these hunting and gathering people.

Chapter 1

The Anthropological Enterprise: Fieldwork

Almost all anthropologists would agree that understanding human behavior is the goal of cultural anthropology. The study of human behavior in anthropology includes both the exotic and the ordinary. It ranges from the study of faraway and unknown people with strange and unfamiliar customs to the ordinary and everyday institutions of our own society.

Not only is the subject matter of anthropology vast and varied, but anthropologists disagree, sometimes vehemently, on the meaning, purpose, and direction of cultural anthropology. These arguments need not concern us at this point, but they do raise the question: what are the distinctive and defining characteristics of *cultural anthropology?*

We believe that cultural anthropology has several distinctive characteristics. One of these characteristics is *fieldwork.*

The Experience of Fieldwork

Fieldwork is the basic method used in cultural anthropology to learn about human behavior. In order to understand human behavior, anthropologists immerse themselves in the lives of the people they study. Anthropologists attempt to learn, think, feel, and act another way of life. Broadly speaking, fieldwork as a method involves long-term residence with the people of

Questioning informants and recording their responses is a basic data-gathering technique used by fieldworkers. Allan Holmberg's informant is an Indian in the highland region of Peru.

another culture, learning and using *their* language, and establishing social relations with them. It also involves the tedious and time-consuming procedures of recording observations, keeping detailed notes, and participating in everyday activities. At the same time, an anthropologist must stay fed, housed, clothed, and maintain emotional and physical health in what are often difficult circumstances.

An important aspect of fieldwork is *participant-observation.* This involves participating physically and even emotionally in a different culture while at the same time observing it scientifically. Fieldwork is both a human and a scientific experience, and it is central to cultural anthropology.

Learning how to do fieldwork, doing fieldwork, and understanding what it involves are difficult, for the methods are imprecisely defined. One anthropologist, Ivan Karp, in writing about fieldwork (1976), states that one sign of a professional anthropologist is constant complaints about the poor training anthropologists receive for doing fieldwork. Undoubtedly, an older generation of anthropologists emphasized theories and concepts in teaching anthropology. Rarely did they describe how to establish a social relationship, obtain information about an individual's sex life, or discover some bit of political gossip. No better statement of this problem can be found than in the account given by one of the finest fieldworkers in anthropology, E. E. Evans-Pritchard, who sought advice about doing fieldwork from the eminent anthropologists of his day:

That charming and intelligent Austrian-American anthropologist Paul Radin has said that no one quite knows how one goes about fieldwork. Perhaps we should leave the question with that sort of answer. But when I was a serious young student in London [in the 1920s] I thought I would try to get a few tips from experienced fieldworkers before setting out for Central Africa. I first sought advice from Westermarck. All I got from him was "don't converse with an informant for more than twenty minutes because if you aren't bored by that time he will be." Very good advice, even if somewhat inadequate. I sought instruction from Haddon, a man foremost in field-research. He told me that it was really all quite simple; one should always behave as a gentleman. My teacher, Seligman, told me to take ten grains of quinine every night and to keep off women. The famous Egyptologist, Sir Flinders Petrie, just told me not to bother about drinking dirty water as one soon became immune to it. Finally, I asked Malinowski and was told not to be a bloody fool. So there is no clear answer, much will depend on the man, on the society he is to study, and the conditions in which he is to make it (Evans-Pritchard 1976:240).

Fifty years ago Haddon told Evans-Pritchard that fieldwork was quite simple, "one should behave as a gentleman." John Middleton, a contemporary anthropologist with extensive fieldwork experience in Africa recently wrote "The basic requirements for fieldwork are good training and good manners" (Middleton 1970:225). Why is it that fieldwork, the basic method in anthropology, still appears as a mysterious enterprise (Cohn 1980:200–201)?

An important reason is that the cultural anthropologist, unlike the researcher in the so-called "hard sciences," works with and studies other human beings. The involvement of the anthropologist goes beyond the experimental procedures of psychology or the limited and sometimes anonymous questionnaires, interviews, and samples used in sociology. Fieldwork is full-scale immersion in daily and nightly living with a group of people whose behavior, beliefs, habits, customs, and manners are usually strange, often bewildering, and many times physically and emotionally difficult and disturbing.

Fieldwork is intensely personal and to some extent each field research experience is unique, as are anthropologists themselves. There are vast differences among people from different cultures, and there are differences among individuals in the same culture as well. In addition, social, political, and historical circumstances vary from place to place and over time, and they too add a unique dimension to fieldwork. These factors are among the more prominent reasons why anthropologists have been so vague about how to do fieldwork. In the field each anthropologist must forge, individual by individual, the human links of relationship that constitute the true basis of field research in modern cultural anthropology.

In order to provide a basis for understanding how fieldwork is accomplished and, we hope, to communicate the flavor of the field experience, we present in the next section of this chapter personal accounts by anthropologists about their own fieldwork experiences.

Fieldwork Among the Tiwi

In the middle 1920s, C. W. M. Hart was a student of A. R. Radcliffe-Brown at the University of Sydney in Australia. Radcliffe-Brown, who was one of the dominant figures in anthropology at this time, specialized in the study of Australian tribal groups. Under the impact of European settlement in Australia, many tribal groups had either been destroyed or had suffered severe cultural disruption. A few isolated groups escaped this fate. One such group was the Tiwi, who lived on two islands, Melville and

Bathurst, located twenty-five miles from the northern coast of Australia. Because little was known about these people, Radcliffe-Brown assigned Hart to study them. Except for a mission station, there were no white settlements on the islands. Hart decided to live with the most isolated and traditional Tiwi group.

On the way to the islands Hart met a Tiwi man named Mariano, who became an interpreter and guide for Hart during his field research. Hart's account of his fieldwork from 1928 to 1929 gives a vivid picture of what fieldwork was like among an isolated tribal group more than fifty years ago.

Tiwi men returning from a successful hunt. Like these men, Hart hunted to obtain his own food.

I arrived at the Mission more or less under his [Mariano's] sponsorship. Looking back now, I cannot see that anybody else in the whole tribe would have been nearly so useful as he was. For intelligence, reliability, and capacity to objectively analyze and explain his own culture he could not be faulted. Until I could learn the language for myself I simply had to keep him.

Fieldwork among the Tiwi in 1928–1929 was not difficult provided that the fieldworker was young, healthy, undemanding of personal comfort, and unmarried. Living with the Malauila and Munupula [the most untouched Tiwi bands] meant, of course, living pretty close to nature. It surprised me, who had no boy-scout background, how little in the way of manufactured objects one needed. Sneakers, a hat, and a pair of shorts were all the clothing necessary; a shotgun to kill wallaby and wild fowl and plenty of shells for it; pencils and notebooks; soap and toothbrush (even towels were optional); pipe and tobacco; a camera and plenty of film. These seemed to be the only essentials, except that for an Australian, tea and sugar had to be added. The heaviest and bulkiest item of all [was] an endless supply of native twist tobacco, a currency that took one everywhere and opened all doors.

Blankets were not necessary; the Tiwi on chilly nights sleep between two small fires which can be kept burning all night with twigs that you take to bed with you, and provided you do not roll, the fires give warmth and keep the mosquitoes away. The native food was perfectly adequate and usually abundant, and by lending my shotgun to a native hunter I was able on most days to contribute my share to the total food production of the household with which I was living. One of the objects thankfully left behind was a razor, since beards were prestige symbols for the Tiwi. Older and important men carried luxuriant beards, the bushier the more admired. For a man without a beard to expect to be taken seriously in Tiwi culture was quite simply tactless and anthropologists should avoid [that]; otherwise they are no different from tourists.

After a few weeks on the islands I also became aware that they [the Tiwi] were often uneasy with me because I had no kinship linkage to them. This was shown in many ways, among others in their dissatisfaction with the negative reply they always got to their question, "What clan does he belong to?" Around the Mission, to answer it by saying "White men have no clans," was at least a possible answer, but among the pagan bands like the Malauila and Munupula such an answer was incomprehensible — to them everybody must have a clan, just as everybody must have an age. If I had a clan I would be inside the kinship system, everybody would know how to act toward me, I would know how to act toward everybody else, and life would be easier and smoother for all.

How to get myself into the clan and kinship system was however quite a problem. Even Mariano, while admitting the desirability, saw no way of getting me in. There did not seem much hope and then suddenly the problem was solved entirely by a lucky accident. I was in a camp where there was an old woman who had been making herself a terrible nuisance. Toothless, almost blind, withered, and stumbling around, she was physically quite revolting and mentally rather senile. She kept hanging round me asking for tobacco, whining, wheedling, snivelling, until I got thoroughly fed up with her. As I had by now learned the Tiwi equivalents of "Go to hell" and "Get lost," I rather enjoyed being rude to her and telling her where she ought to go. Listening to my swearing in Tiwi, the rest of the camp thought it a great joke and no doubt egged her on so that they could listen to my attempts to get rid of her. This had been going on for some time when one day the old hag used a new approach. "Oh, my son," she said, "please give me tobacco." Unthinkingly I replied, "Oh, my mother, go jump in the ocean." Immediately a howl of delight arose from everybody within earshot and they all gathered round me patting me on the shoulder and calling me by a kinship term. She was my mother and I was her son. This gave a handle to everybody else to address me by a

kinship term. Her other sons from then on called me brother; her brothers called me "sister's son"; her husband (and his brothers) called me son; and so on. I was now in the kinship system; my clan was Jabijabui (a bird) because my mother was Jabijabui.

From then on the change in the atmosphere between me and the tribe at large was remarkable. Strangers were now told that I was Jabijabui and that my mother was old so-and-so and when told this, stern old men would relax, smile and say "then you are my brother" (or my son, or my sister's son, or whatever category was appropriate) and I would struggle to respond properly by addressing them by the proper term.

How seriously they took my presence in their kinship system is something I never will be sure about. However, toward the end of my time on the islands an incident occurred that surprised me because it suggested that some of them had been taking my presence in the kinship system much more seriously than I had thought. I was approached by a group of about eight or nine senior men all of whom I knew. They were all senior members of the Jabijabui clan, [and] I called them all brother or mother's brother. It turned out that they had come to me on a delicate errand. They were the senior members of the Jabijabui clan and they had decided among themselves that the time had come to get rid of the decrepit old woman who had first called me son and whom I now called mother. As I knew, they said, it was Tiwi custom, when an old woman became too feeble to look after herself, to "cover her up." This could only be done by her sons and her brothers and all of them had to agree beforehand, since once it was done they did not want any dissension among the brothers or clansmen, as that might lead to a feud. My "mother" was now completely blind, she was constantly falling over logs or into fires, and they, her senior clansmen, were in agreement that she would be better out of the way. Did I agree also? I already knew about "covering up." The Tiwi, like many other hunting and gathering peoples, sometimes got rid of their ancient and decrepit females. The method was to dig a hole in the ground in some lonely place, put the old woman in the hole and fill it in with earth until only her head was showing. Everybody went away for a day or two and then went back to the hole to discover, to their great surprise, that the old woman was dead, having been too feeble to raise her arms from the earth. Nobody had "killed" her, her death in Tiwi eyes was a natural one. She had been alive when her relatives last saw her. I had never seen it done, though I knew it was the custom, so I asked my brothers if it was necessary for me to attend the "covering up." They said no and they would do it, but only after they had my agreement. Of course I agreed, and a week or two later we heard in our camp that my "mother" was dead, and we all wailed and put on the trimmings of mourning. Mariano thoroughly disapproved and muttered darkly that the police in Darwin should be informed, but I soon told him that this was Jabijabui business and since he was not Jabijabui, it was none of his affair (Hart 1970:145–147, 149–154).

Life in Lesu

In 1928–1929, the same years that Hart was living with the Tiwi, Hortense Powdermaker began her residence in the village of Lesu, on the Melanesian island of New Ireland in the South Pacific.

At that time there were two great figures in British anthropology, Radcliffe-Brown and Bronislaw Malinowski. Powdermaker was a student of Malinowski and originally had planned to work with an isolated tribal group in New Guinea. The Australian government was anxious about the potential problems a female anthropologist might have in the field and "suggested" the island of Lesu as the site for her research.

Few accounts by anthropologists explore their inner-most thoughts about their field experiences. Powdermaker provides a rare account of the feelings and emotions that are part of anthropological field research in her book, *Stranger and Friend* (1966), from which the following account is taken.

This was my first night in Lesu alone. As I sat on the veranda of my thatched-roofed, two-room house in the early evening, I felt uncertain and scared, not of anything in par-

Men of Lesu gossiping and working on the beach. Powdermaker herself was not allowed to participate in such activities, but she was allowed to take this photograph.

ticular, but just of being alone in a native village. I asked myself, "What on earth am I doing here, all alone and at the edge of the world?"

I had arrived two weeks earlier, accompanied by the Australian government anthropologist and a young English anthropologist. They had generously offered to help me get settled in Lesu. Their help in setting up my housekeeping was invaluable. The introduction by the government anthropologist was good because he was known to the natives through his occasional patrols, and he was well liked.

Both men supervised the finishing of my house, the building of a privy, the making of a primitive shower, adding a room to the cookhouse for a servant's bedroom, and all the other details of settling in. Ongus, an Australian-appointed chief, was a well-built, intelligent-looking man, obviously in command as he directed the unloading of my boxes and bales and the finishing of my house. During these first days, I was busy unpacking and settling in.

My real contacts were limited to the two anthropologists; we talked about anthropology and gossiped about anthropologists. I was still primarily in my own modern world.

A day or two later, my anthropologist friends left me to return to their own work. As I waved good-bye I felt like Robinson Crusoe, but without a man Friday. That evening as I ate my dinner, I felt very low. I took a quinine pill to ward off malaria. Suddenly I saw myself at the edge of the world, and *alone.* I was scared and close to panic. When I arrived I had thought the place was lovely. Everything seemed in harmonious accord: the black natives, the vividness of the sea and of the wild flowers, the brightly plumed birds, the tall areca palm and coconut trees, the delicate bamboo, the low thatched-roofed huts, the beauty of the nights with the moon shining on the palm trees. But now the same scene seemed ominous. I was not scared of the people, but I had a feeling of panic. Why was I here, I asked myself repeatedly.

Then came the day when Ongus called all the people to assemble in front of my house. They stood or squatted on the ground, men separately from women, as I told them why I was there. My people at home, I said, knew nothing about Lesu and had sent me to find out about their customs. When I went home, I would tell them all I had learned and write it in a book.

The next day I began, with Ongus's help, to make a diagram and census of the village. On the diagram I marked every house with a number and wrote the names of the people who lived in it, their sex and kinship to each other, and if they were related to next-door neighbors. The diagram also contained the position of the men's house, the cemetery, the cook houses, a mission church, bush which had not been cut down, and the boundaries and names of the fifteen small hamlets into which the village was divided. I described also the interior of the thatched-roofed huts, and noted their cleanliness and the fact that they were, apparently, used only at night for sleeping and during the rains.

Most activities, except, of course, sexual relations, were carried on outdoors, a boon indeed for a field worker who lived in the middle of the village. Nothing was too small to escape my notebook: how women held their babies; the way two adolescent boys walked with the arm of one thrown casually around the shoulders of the other; a man putting powdered white lime on his hair to cleanse and beautify it, and so on ad infinitum. The census was a useful way of starting, particularly as I was diffident about beginning. Taking the initial plunge is never easy. Why bother people with impertinent questions, was my first unanthropological reaction. But the census was relatively impersonal, easily understood, and very specific.

After breakfast I frequently worked on the veranda of my house with a male informant; genealogies, language, magical spells, speeches made the previous day at a feast, and other aspects of native life were the topics. A short nap followed a light lunch. In the afternoons I often strolled through the village and joined a group of women as they sat on the ground preparing the taro to be baked. Other times, several of my women friends came to see me. They sprawled on the floor of the veranda, telling jokes, talking about themselves, or gossiping about others. An elderly woman told of her youthful sexual episodes and how she led on one man for quite a time before surrendering. These intimate tales of extra-marital sex life were told without embarrassment and to the accompaniment of much laughter. Much of the data about the women's private lives came in this casual manner and I had a sense of real understanding, when unaided, I saw the point of their jokes. During these gay, friendly visits, I generally did not take out my notebook, but wrote after they went home what the women had told me.

After I had been in Lesu for about three months, I was given a place in the kinship system. It happened at a large gathering of women who had just finished their communal preparations for a big feast. An elderly woman from my hamlet suddenly announced that I was her daughter. The next day my "mother" sent me a large bunch of bananas, and a day or so later I reciprocated with a small gift. I was pleased with having a native "mother," but did not fool myself that I was really part of a Melanesian clan. It was rather that my Melanesian friends liked me and this was their symbolic way of expressing it.

Relations with the men were a bit more formal. I did not sit in the men's house or on the beach listening to them talk and gossip. But there was no problem in getting good male informants. Anyone I asked was glad to come and work with me.

My life and native life seemed to consist mainly of endless repetition: rising with the sun every day; going to little feasts and big ones, to mortuary rites and other ceremonies; working with individual informants on genealogies, language, magical spells, economic and other aspects of the social structure; listening to folk tales and myths; strolling through the village; chatting with the women when they were at leisure; writing notes continuously and typing them later; taking photographs and developing them; and so on and on.

The lack of seasons contributed to the monotony. There were only two — the rainy and the dry. The rainy season was sometimes quite uncomfortable. Fortunately, I had a strong raincoat and boots with me. One evening when the rains had been particularly heavy, tiny insects, which came with them, were attracted by the light of my lamp and swarmed all over the place. As I ate dinner, they crawled down my back, entered my mouth when I opened it, and drowned in the coffee cup. They did not sting or bite, but were a most uncomfortable pest. Only one escape was possible: to crawl into bed under the mosquito canopy. Other times, wearing my last piece of clean underwear, I wondered if the sun would ever shine again and permit washing and drying. It always did and was so strong and hot that everything — the ground as well as my clothes — dried quickly and I forgot the inconvenience of the last torrential downpour.

Sometimes I was discouraged. How could I ever get data on all the topics in my long outline? To "crack" a strange culture, never taking anything for granted, to ferret out relationships between customs, to dig out the system of kinship from many genealogies, to understand the social structure, to learn a language which had never been recorded, was decidedly not easy. Less than halfway through my stay in Lesu, I conveyed some of my impatience and discouragement to Ongus. Looking at me quizzically, he asked if I expected to know everything in four or five moons?

Probably the most monotonous part of my life in Lesu was the food. Breakfast consisted of a papaya, bacon, fried sweet potatoes, bread, marmalade, and coffee. Once in a while I had an egg. Lunch was light: tea and cheese with bread. For dinner there was usually fresh fish or a bird the cook had shot. Once in a while I was lucky enough to have a lobster fresh from the sea. This menu was varied with tinned frankfurters, the only canned meat I had with me which I liked. Dessert was a papaya, pineapple, or banana, all available in abundance. On a special occasion, such as my birthday, I opened a bottle of olives for dinner.

My health remained good, although I lost considerable weight. I enjoyed being almost continuously outdoors and became acclimatized more quickly to the tropical heat than I had to the damp coldness of London winters. I took my five grains of quinine every night and never suffered from malaria, even though it was all around me. But sometimes, in spite of good health and the steady accumulation of data, the monotony, which I could not change, was very oppressive.

A member of my family sent newspapers, which arrived at least four months late. I could not have been less interested in most of the news, which appeared not to have changed since I left home.

The New Yorker and *Punch* were sent to me by two friends. What really interested me was their advertisements, which lifted me right out of Lesu. Pictures of beautiful cut glass goblets permitted me to forget tempo-

rarily my worn enamel cup. I was torn between the "car of cars," a Cadillac, and a small sport car, "so easy to handle in Picadilly traffic," and was oblivious to the fact that the next day I had to walk five miles to another village. From the advertisements I conjured up a society to which I had never belonged, and it provided a fantasy escape from Lesu.

The morning of my departure came. My Lesu friends stood without speaking in a circle around the truck. They wept openly. I felt terrible, torn by ambivalent feelings. I was truly fond of my Lesu friends and was much upset at the severing of ties with them; yet I was desperately eager to leave the island and go home. I wanted to cry, but I didn't. I stood silent, and then told my friends that I would never forget them. Hastily, I climbed into the truck and was off (Powdermaker 1966:51–53, 60–61, 76, 81, 94–99, 102, 122).

The Vice Lords, an Urban Gang

The field research of Hart and Powdermaker represents traditional anthropology, but R. Lincoln Keiser's experience represents a recent development in anthropology. Keiser, a white anthropologist, studied a Black gang in the Chicago ghetto in the early 1960s.

Keiser's account points up the problem of doing anthropological research in urban America. His fieldwork could not be isolated from the history of Black-White conflict and hostility in America. If his work was different in this respect, his story also reveals the broad similarities common to the enterprise of fieldwork.

Establishing relationships was difficult. No one, much less a White, can go into an area inhabited by a club and initiate a research project. Very careful and time-consuming ground work has to be done. It is necessary to make contact with influential members of the group and to gain their trust before one can begin serious work. I approached this prob-

A group of Vice Lords outside their recreation center.

lem through the means of a job. I was offered employment with the Social Service Department of what was then the Municipal Court of Chicago, and was assigned as a court caseworker to Boys' Court North. Its jurisdiction included the Lawndale area of Chicago's west side Black ghetto, and the court dealt with members of three large fighting clubs — the Egyptian Cobras, the Roman Saints, and the Vice Lords. The court caseworker's job consisted of counseling individuals referred by the court; thus I became acquainted with members of these three groups.

My role as caseworker conflicted in some ways with my role as anthropologist. As a caseworker my primary purpose was to help the people referred to me make the kind of adjustment to the urban world that would prevent their coming into conflict with the rules and enforcement agencies of predominantly White, middle-class Chicago. As an anthropologist, however, it was crucial to try not to judge behavior relative to my own values, much less to change it. Since my primary

responsibility was to the role of caseworker, I was seriously limited in the use of my "clients" as anthropological informants. In spite of these difficulties, I was able to gather some basic material.

In order to conduct further research, I had to establish relationships outside the court context. I was told about a woman who had taught in a West Side school, and who had become close friends with several Vice Lords. I contacted her, and she agreed to introduce me to Sonny, one of the Vice Lords she knew. At the time I met Sonny, I also met another Lord called Goliath. In the next year Sonny, Goliath, and I went to parties together, met in bars, and visited each other's homes. During this time I also met a few other members of the club and collected several life histories. Goliath and I got along especially well, and in the course of the year became quite good friends.

At the beginning of the summer I approached Goliath with my plan. I would rent an apartment in the ghetto, and Goliath would live with me rent free. In return he would introduce me to the leaders of the Vice Lords, and give assurance that I was not a police spy. Goliath agreed, and the plan was initiated.

At the beginning of the summer Goliath introduced me to Tex, Bat Man, and Shotgun, three of the most important leaders of the 15th Street Vice Lords. Through Goliath I approached these older individuals who had become the leaders of the [Vice-Lords]. I explained that I wanted to write a book about the Vice Lords, and offered to share any royalties with the group. The proposal was put before the club in a meeting, and the majority of members gave their approval. This legitimized my position in the eyes of the other club members, and the rest of the summer I concentrated my research on the corner of 16th and Lawndale.

Adjusting to living conditions was nowhere near as difficult in my Vice Lord research as it was in my study of a mountain village in Afghanistan where conditions were similar to those usually encountered by anthropologists working in non-Western societies. I lived in an apartment that, although dingy, had hot and cold running water, a bathroom, and a stove and refrigerator. However, there were some differences that took some adjustment on my part. The greatest of these was getting accustomed to living with the possibility of robbery and ambush. Goliath took many precautions in choosing an apartment that had a well-lighted entrance and well-lighted hallways. We kept a .45 pistol in the apartment, along with several wooden clubs. Goliath always put a match in the door jamb before we left so that he could tell if anyone had forced open the door while we were gone and might be hidden in the apartment when we came back. At night he put boards and empty cans in front of the windows and doors so that if someone tried to break in, he would make so much noise that

we would be awakened. These were precautions that any sensible person took. It turned out they saved me possible trouble and injury. Early one morning a man forced his way into our apartment through a window. He knocked over the board we had set up and awakened me. I was waiting for him with a two-by-four (Goliath had spent the night with a girlfriend and had taken the .45 with him), and when he saw me, he turned around and went back out the window.

The [methods] I used are standard in anthropological fieldwork: I did participant observation and conducted interviews with informants. For me, participant observation consisted of observing behavior while hanging out on the streets, going to bars, attending parties, visiting friends and relatives, and simply driving about the West Side with members of the club. As a participant observer I was involved in the first stages of one actual gang fight, and was part of the preparations for another that never materialized. My presence in the neighborhood was legitimized by me being "the man who is writing the book." People knew what I was doing there, and why I was doing it. But I could never fully participate in the life of the streets. For one thing, not everyone accepted me to the same extent. For some, the fact that I was White seemed to cause little difficulty. In conversation, Vice Lords often call one another "nigger" in a joking manner. When "nigger" was used in conversation by a person who did not know me very well, often he would turn and say, "Oh, excuse me," as if he had insulted me. One time when this was said, a friend of mine answered, "That don't make no difference, Jack. The man's a nigger just like us, only he's white. He's a white nigger." Others had such strong antagonisms that they were unable to be friends with me. They tolerated my presence, but for the most part ignored me. Finally, there were some individuals who could not control their hatred toward Whites, and in a few instances it boiled into the open aimed at me. When this happened, I simply walked away.

One of the greatest difficulties in my Vice Lord research was handling my emotional responses. On the streets of the ghetto I was functionally an infant, and like all infants, had to be taken care of. I did not know what was, and what was not, potentially dangerous; and I did not understand the significance of most actions and many words. For example, one afternoon while I was standing on 15th Street with a group of Vice Lords, a young man in his early twenties walked up and started yelling that he was a Roman Saint, and was going to "whup" every Vice Lord he found. It was obvious by the way he talked and acted that he was mentally deranged. One of the Vice Lords said, "The dude's crazy, Man! He ain't no Saint. Leave him alone." Suddenly a dead-pan look came over the young man's face. Abruptly he turned from us, and walked down an alley that was directly opposite from where we were standing. Very calmly, and with no show of speed, every Vice Lord in the group walked away, out of a line of possible fire. Suddenly I found myself standing alone, looking down the alley at this fellow. Tex came up and pulled me to the side. He said, "Man, the dude get to the end of the alley, he liable to get his jive together and burn you down (pull out his gun and shoot you)!" Besides feeling stupid, I did not know whether to be afraid or not. The fellow reached the end of the alley, turned the corner, and was gone. The extent of my helplessness had been made quite clear.

This feeling of helplessness was very difficult for me to handle. In the early part of my research it often made me feel so nervous and anxious that the events occurring around me seemed to merge in a blur of meaningless action. I despaired of ever making any sense

out of anything. Vice Lords sensed my feelings and I could see it made some people uncomfortable. This increased the difficulty of gaining the rapport necessary to carry out successful research.

I also had emotional responses to events that stemmed from my own value system. How to handle these responses was another source of difficulty. There were certain aspects of Vice Lord life that I found personally distasteful. They made me upset and uneasy. Although intellectually I felt my values were not demonstrably superior, I still could not stop my emotional reactions. These reactions often made it difficult for me to retain objectivity. More important, I was never completely sure if Vice Lords sensed my reactions, and in turn reacted to them. Thus I was not always certain if my feelings affected the events I was trying to observe. Although I tried to control my responses as much as possible, I am still not sure how successful I was. Undoubtedly some bias crept into my observations, and probably certain events I was trying to observe were changed in subtle ways in response to my emotional reactions (Keiser 1970:226–229, 234–235).

An Eskimo Daughter

Our previous accounts describe how anthropologists live with the people they study, developing and maintaining social relationships. In Jean Briggs's fieldwork establishing close and intimate social relationships was essential to her research. Instead of merely living with an Eskimo group, Briggs was adopted as a daughter by an Eskimo family, acting the role of an Eskimo daughter.

She selected for research a remote group of Eskimo, the Utkuhiksalingmiut who live in Chantrey Inlet, just north of the Arctic Circle, and her account begins with her introduction to and contact with this group.

Chantrey Inlet. This forbidding environment was the setting in which Jean Briggs did her research. Briggs lived in an igloo much like this one.

I arrived in Chantrey Inlet at the end of August 1963 on the plane that the Canadian government sent in once a year. I had with me letters of introduction from the Anglican deacon and his wife in Gjoa Haven, Eskimos from the eastern Arctic who served as missionaries not only to the Anglican Eskimos in Gjoa Haven, but also to the Utkuhiksalingmiut. The letters said that I would like to live with the Utkuhiksalingmiut for a year or so, learning the Eskimo language and skills: how to scrape skins and sew them, how to catch fish and preserve them or boil the oil out of them for use in lighting and heating the winter iglus. They told the people that I was kind and that they should not be shy and afraid of me: "She is a little bit shy herself"; and assured them that they need not feel — as they often do feel toward kaplunas [white people] — that they had to comply with my every wish. They said, finally, that I wished to be adopted into an Eskimo family and to live with them in their iglu as a "daughter."

In many ways Briggs became an active member of her Eskimo family. Her Eskimo father treated her like his daughter, used the Eskimo kinship term daughter for her, and expected her to obey him without question.

Briggs inevitably recognized that her role as Eskimo daughter and her role as anthropologist were in conflict. When her family moved, for instance, she insisted that they take her equipment and field notes. Her father pointed out that these materials overloaded his dog sled and should be left behind. Although a good Eskimo daughter would never argue with her father, Briggs insisted upon taking these items with her. This role conflict was the cause of serious tension between Briggs and her Eskimo family.

In addition, her upbringing as an American female created problems. Unlike an Eskimo daughter, she was unwilling to be silent; she spoke out and she expressed anger. Her getting angry, even though it was to defend the interests of the Utkuhiksalingmiut, brought on a crisis in her relationship with the group.

Briggs was never wholly acceptable to her Eskimo family. She could not become a "daughter" as they understood the role. Even so, after she left Chantrey Inlet they wrote to say that while they had not thought they would care, in fact they did miss her.

The crisis was brought about by the visit to Chantrey Inlet of a party of kapluna sports fishermen. Every July and August in recent years Chantrey Inlet has been visited by sportsmen who fly up to the Arctic for a week's fishing. Every year the sportsmen ask permission to borrow the Eskimos' canoes. These canoes were given to the Utkuhiksalingmiut by the Canadian government after the famine of 1958 and are indispensable to the economy of the Eskimos. Originally there had been six canoes, one for each of the Utkuhiksalingmiut families, but by the time I arrived in Chantrey Inlet only two of these remained in usable condition.

The first parties that came asked, through me, if they might borrow both canoes, and the Utkuhiksalingmiut, who for various reasons rarely if ever refuse such requests, had acquiesced, at some cost to themselves. They sat stranded on the shore, unable to fish; unable to fetch the occasional bird that they shot on the water; unable to fetch a resupply of sugar for their tea from the cache on the nearby island; and worst of all, perhaps, unable to visit the odd strangers who were camped out of sight across the river. Ultimately these kaplunas left and were replaced by another group, which asked to borrow only one canoe. But relief was short-lived; trolling up and down the unfamiliar river in the late twilight, the kaplunas were unfortunate enough to run the canoe on a rock and tear a large hole in the canvas, whereupon they returned that canoe and announced to the men through sign language that, since the boat was unusable, they were now obliged to borrow the other: Inuttiaq's [Briggs's Eskimo father]. When I arrived on the scene, the kaplunas were attaching their outboard to the canoe, as Inuttiaq and the other Utkuhiksalingmiut men watched.

I exploded. Unsmilingly and in a cold voice I told the kaplunas' guide that if he borrowed the second canoe we would be without a fishing boat; that if this boat also was damaged, we would be in a very difficult position. Then, armed with the memory that Inuttiaq had earlier, before the arrival of this party of kaplunas, instructed me in vivid language never again to allow anyone to borrow his canoe, I told the kaplunas that the owner of that second canoe did not wish to lend it.

The kapluna guide was not unreasonable; he agreed at once that the loan of the boat was the owner's option. Slightly mollified, I turned to Inuttiaq who stood nearby, expressionless like the other Utkuhiksalingmiut. "Do you want me to tell him you don't want to lend your canoe?" I asked in Eskimo. "He will not borrow it if you say you don't want to lend it."

Inuttiaq's expression dismayed me, but I didn't know how to read it; I knew only that it registered strong feeling, as did his voice, which was unusually loud: "Let him have his will!"

That incident brought to a head months of uneasiness on the part of the Utkuhiksalingmiut concerning my volatility. I had spoken unbidden and in anger; that much the Eskimos knew. The words they couldn't understand, but it didn't matter; the anger itself was inexcusable. The punishment was ostracism. So subtly was it expressed, however, that I didn't at first realize my situation. I would have continued to think that my difficulties were all of my own imagining had I not come into possession of a letter that Allaq's [Briggs's Eskimo mother] father, Pala, had written to the deacon, Naklirohuktuq, the day after the kaplunas left. Pala had intended to send it out on the plane that was to come and pick up the schoolchildren. Fearing that when the plane finally came, he would forget the letter, he had given it to me to hold along with my own correspondence. The letter was in syllabics, of course; in an amoral spirit I decided to read it, to test my skill in reading Eskimo. I did not anticipate the contents: "Yiini [that was my name] lied to the kaplunas. She gets angry very easily. She ought not to be here studying Eskimos. She is very annoying; she scolds more and more and gets angry easily. Because she is so annoying, we wish more and more that she would leave."

I was not at all sure that Inuttiaq would invite me to move in with his family again as he had done the year before, but I need not have worried; his hostility did not take such a crass form. However, the quality of life in the iglu was in striking contrast with the previous year. It was as though I were not there. If I made a remark to Inuttiaq or Allaq, the person addressed responded with his usual smile, but I had to initiate almost all communication. If I offered to fetch water or make tea (which I seldom did) my offer was usually accepted, but no one ever asked me to perform these services. My company was anathema; nevertheless people still took care to give me plentiful amounts of the foods I liked best, to warn me away from thin ice, and to caution me when my nose began to freeze. The Utkuhiksalingmiut saw themselves — and wanted me to see them — as virtuously solicitous, no matter what provocations I might give them to be otherwise. Allaq's sister expressed this ethos of concern explicitly in a letter to Ikajuqtuq [the deacon's wife], in Gjoa Haven: "Because she is a kapluna and a woman, we have tried to be good to her here, and though she is sometimes very annoying . . . we still try to help her."

It was at the end of August that the incident with the kapluna fishermen occurred, and it was the end of November before I was finally able to explain myself to the Utkuhiksalingmiut. I had wanted from the beginning, of course, to confront them with an explanation of my behavior, but I had feared that such un-Eskimo directness would only shock them the more. Instead, I had written my version of the story to Ikajuqtuq, had told her about my attempt to protect the Utkuhiksalingmiut from the impositions of the kaplunas, and had asked her if she could help to explain my behavior to the Eskimos. My letter went out, along with Pala's, in September. Unfortunately there was no way in which Ikajuqtuq could reply until the strait froze in November, enabling the men to make the long trip out to Gjoa Haven to trade. But when Inuttiaq finally went out, he brought back from the deacon and his wife a response that surpassed my expectations. Inuttiaq reported to his family: "Naklirohuktuq says that the kaplunas almost shot us when Yiini wasn't there." The exaggeration was characteristic of Inuttiaq's lurid style of fantasy. He turned to me: "Did you write that to Naklirohuktuq?" I denied it — and later, in Gjoa Haven, Naklirohuktuq denied having made such a statement to Inuttiaq — but I did confirm the gist of Inuttiaq's report: that I had tried to protect the Eskimos. I described what it was that I had written to Ikajuqtuq, and I explained something of the reasons for my anger at the kaplunas.

The effect was magical. The wall of ice that had stood between me and the community suddenly disappeared. People talked to me voluntarily, offered me vocabulary, included me in their jokes and in their anecdotes of the day's activities; and Inuttiaq informed me that the following day he and I were going fishing. Most heartwarming of all is the memory of an afternoon soon after the men had returned. The iglu was filled with visitors. I [was] bent over my writing, and I paid no attention until suddenly my mind caught on the sound of my name: "I consider Yiini a member of my family again." Was that what Inuttiaq had said? I looked up, inquiring.

"I consider you a family member again," he repeated. His diction was clear, as it was only when he wanted to be sure that I understood. And he called me "daughter," as he had not done since August. (Briggs 1970:21, 34–38).

These fieldwork accounts vary widely in time, place, and situation, but all of them provide an introductory glimpse into some of the particular problems and unique situations faced by anthropologists in the field. In this section our purpose is to bring together these field experiences to provide a more general picture of fieldwork.

The Development of Fieldwork

Cultural anthropology as a recognized discipline is a little over one hundred years old. Fieldwork as the fundamental mode of research emerged only at the beginning of the twentieth century. In nineteenth-century anthropology, fieldwork was relatively unknown and unimportant. Instead of gathering and collecting data directly, nineteenth-century anthropologists depended on descriptions of tribal people written by missionaries, explorers, administrators, and travelers. Anthropologists of the nineteenth century were not overly concerned with the description and analysis of particular cultures. They directed their efforts toward reconstructing the cultural history of humanity. Immersion in the particular nuances of a single culture, the essence of fieldwork, was not seen as vital in this broader problem of understanding human history.

A milestone in the emergence of fieldwork was the Torres Strait Expedition of 1898–1899. This expedition, under the leadership of the British anthropologist A. C. Haddon, surveyed the native cultures of the southeastern coasts of New Guinea. It was an important step in the evolution of fieldwork, because it brought anthropologists into direct contact with tribal people. Nevertheless, many aspects of modern fieldwork, such as long-term residence and competence in native languages, were still absent.

While Haddon and other members of this expedition were orienting British anthropology toward fieldwork, Franz Boas was developing a similar approach for American anthropology. In both cases a major stimulus was the fear that tribal cultures were being irreversibly changed under the influence of Western culture, imperialism, and political control. Anthropologists feared, in fact, that many tribal cultures would disappear entirely before they could be studied.

Boas, who was educated as a geographer in Germany, accompanied an expedition to the Canadian Arctic in 1883. As part of this expedition he spent many months living with the Eskimo. As a consequence of this experience Boas turned to anthropology and later was regarded as the founding father of American anthropology. In addition to his experience among the Eskimo, Boas worked with American Indian groups, especially the Indians of the Northwest Coast of America. Under his guidance, a number of American anthropologists turned their attention to the study of American Indian tribes. Boas organized the Jesup North Pacific Expedition in 1897, which was designed to investigate the relationships between the peoples of northeastern Asia and the Indian and Eskimo groups in northwest America. The primary goal of Boas and his students was to describe the cultures of American Indian tribes before they were placed on reservations. As a result, American anthropologists did most of their work with older Indian informants who had direct experiences of the traditional tribal way of life before the reservation.

Under the influence of Haddon and Boas, anthropologists began to close the gap between themselves and the objects of their research: tribal people. This development culminated in the experience of Bronislaw Malinowski in the Trobriand Islands of the South Pacific. Instead of short-term survey type fieldwork, which had been developed during the Torres Strait expedition, Malinowski studied a single culture, the Trobriand Islanders, for over three years, from 1914 to 1918.

Malinowski's continuous residence with these people, his total immersion in their culture, and his mastery of their language gave him an unparalleled insight into the nature of Trobriand culture. In a series of widely read volumes, published in the 1920s and 1930s, the complexity and intricacy of Trobriand tribal life were revealed. His research enshrined fieldwork as the basic method in cultural anthropology for gaining understanding of an alien culture. All of the fieldwork accounts cited in this chapter are the intellectual descendants of Malinowski and his predecessors.

Scientific Aspects of Fieldwork

Fieldwork is more than an adventure among exotic people. It is a scientific enterprise designed to gather accurate and reliable data about the behavior of human beings in different cultural settings. Anthropologists believe that such information can enable us to understand why people do what they do.

Training, funding, and orientation of research are essential elements in the preparatory stage preceding fieldwork. Once in the field, anthropologists use a variety of techniques designed to obtain accurate and detailed information about human behavior.

Preparing for the Field

The fledgling fieldworker requires graduate training in anthropology. Such training is designed to familiarize the student with the existing literature in anthropology and with the theories and methods of modern anthropology. For the veteran fieldworker graduate training may have been years before, but it is assumed that any professional anthropologist will stay abreast of new developments in the discipline.

For an earlier generation of fieldworkers, such as Hart and Powdermaker, field research often meant a venture into the unknown. Little was known about the Tiwi or the people of Lesu. A voluminous literature already existed on the Eskimo, and before going into the field, Briggs undoubtedly familiarized herself with much of this information. Contemporary fieldworkers find that training and familiarity with the ethnographic literature are necessary foundations for modern fieldwork.

Doing fieldwork is costly. Expenses include transportation to and from the field, living costs (clothing, housing, food) while in the field, the purchase of equipment such as cameras and tape recorders, and goods to be given to friends and informants. A typical budget for eighteen months of fieldwork for an anthropologist in the 1980s would be approximately $20,000. Patterns of funding also have a significant impact on the direction of anthropological research.

Many of the early observers of tribal life were well-to-do travelers who could afford to visit remote areas of the world. Missionaries and colonial administrators, important sources of anthropological data before the emergence of professional fieldworkers, were supported by missionary societies and colonial governments.

Prior to World War II (1939–1945), there was little financial support for anthropological research. Boas and his students studying North American Indian tribes required minimal funding as their research did not involve costly travel or lengthy residence in the field. Not until the conclusion of World War II did anthropological fieldwork receive generous support. At that time, various agencies of the United States government and private foundations began to support anthropological research at a significant level.

The Fulbright program, suggested by Senator Fulbright of Arkansas, used money owed to the United States government by foreign governments to support a research and teaching program for American teachers and researchers in foreign countries. Anthropologists quickly took advantage of this program, and much of the fieldwork in the 1950s and 1960s was supported under this program.

In addition, other government agencies, especially the National Science Foundation (NSF) and the National Institute of Mental Health (NIMH), supported anthropological fieldwork. Private foundations, like the Ford, Rockefeller, and Carnegie foundations, also supported fieldwork by anthropologists. These agencies and foundations were interested in international problems and funded research that expanded the number of Americans with overseas experience and knowledge. Availability of funds for overseas research shifted the majority of American anthropologists away from American Indian studies to studies of other non-Western people.

In the 1970s the funding of anthropological research experienced a major reorientation. Many private foundations became interested in domestic concerns and were no longer interested in supporting overseas anthropological research. Governmental agencies also shifted their priorities away from supporting overseas fieldwork. As one of the administrators at NIMH said, "We are no longer interested in having American dollars spent in other parts of the world." This inward-looking approach has continued into the 1980s, and as a result fewer funds are available for overseas anthropological research.

In the early fieldwork period represented by Hart and Powdermaker, an anthropologist might select a group to study simply because very little was known about them. Whatever was learned about the Tiwi or the people of Lesu could be looked on as a contribution to knowledge in and of itself. Today there are very few "unstudied" or "untouched" groups left. For this reason many contemporary field studies are based on theoretical problems instead of studying the entire way of life of a people or culture. Margaret Mead's classic work, *Coming of Age in Samoa* (1928), is a good example. This work is not a full description of Samoan culture, but rather an account that focuses on adolescent girls in Samoa. Mead followed up this fieldwork in Samoa with work in New Guinea that emphasized the differences in sex and gender roles in three different tribal groups (1935). Mead's future work reflected her continuing interests in the problems of women and growing up in society.

An example of *problem-centered research* is the work of Allan Holmberg among the Siriono, a tribe in eastern Bolivia, South America (Holmberg 1950). Holmberg wanted to study a group in South America that had difficulty obtaining sufficient food to meet its needs. He researched the existing literature on Latin American tribes and found references to the Siriono that indicated that they lived under conditions of food deprivation. The Siriono therefore met his specific requirements for problem-centered research.

Mead's concern with the problems of women and growing up in society are research questions that can be investigated in any cultural setting. Holmberg's research on food deprivation can be studied only in societies where such conditions occur. Thus there are research problems that can be explored in any society and other problems that are more limited.

Although contemporary research is increasingly problem centered, in many cases the most significant results of fieldwork are still derived from unanticipated situations that reveal significant elements of the culture of the people being studied. Most anthropologists recognize the constraints of a rigid research design and for this reason try, despite what they have promised on their funding applications, to keep their research projects and interests open and loose. Many times the particular opportunities of a field situation will determine the focus of research.

In the Field

An anthropologist going into the field faces a number of immediate problems. These may include the locale to be studied, making initial contact, and beginning to learn the language. Once research begins, anthropologists have available a variety of research methods that are used for gathering accurate data on human behavior.

Choosing a site. For an anthropologist going into the field the most difficult and anxiety-producing situation is the decision about the specific locale for research. Not only does the anthropologist experience anxiety in making this decision initially, but the anxiety may continue afterward. "Is this the right place for the research?" anthropologists ask themselves. Few know precisely which community or group they will study. What factors and considerations lead an anthropologist to choose a specific place to study?

Sometimes an anthropologist can specify the exact research site before going into the field. One of the authors, Edwin Eames, for example, did his initial fieldwork in an Indian village that was part of a research program developed by Cornell University. As a graduate student at Cornell and as a member of the Cornell research program, Eames was expected to do his research in this Indian community.

At the other extreme are anthropologists who have no clear notion about the specific locale of their research. Julian Pitt-Rivers, who did fieldwork in southern Spain (Andalusia), indicates that he chose the village of Alcala for fieldwork, "because I was invited into the *casino,* the club, and given a drink more promptly there than in any other place I had been" (Pitt-Rivers 1961:2).

On the other hand, Laurence Wylie, who wanted to study a French village, first consulted volumes of government statistics to find an "average" region and then spent one month driving twenty-five hundred miles in a single French district before deciding on a village to study. Despite this rational decision-making procedure, Wylie admits that an important consideration in making the final decision was finding suitable housing for his family (1957:viii–ix).

A somewhat more exotic solution to this problem is reported by an anthropologist and his wife in the New Guinea Highlands. They had visited a number of tribal communities to determine a group suitable for investigation. While the researchers were making up their minds about which group to study, one of the tribal groups decided *they* wanted to be studied. On their own, the group built their version of a European dwelling and literally kidnapped the anthropologist and his wife, informing them, "this is the place we want you to stay."

Not all site selection procedures are as unusual as this example. However, there is probably not a single country in the world that does not have scholars or university personnel with anthropological training and interests. It is not only good manners, but also enormously helpful, to contact such individuals, who may be important in the process of site selection. Perhaps the best advice about site selection was received by one of the authors, Eugene Cohen, who was told by an Italian anthropologist to pick a community he liked: "You are going to be there for two years and you might as well enjoy where you are and what you are doing."

Although anthropology may be problem oriented in its research today, it is still concerned with the study of human behavior. Therefore, wherever a group of human beings live together there is a site suitable and appropriate for anthropological investigation. Every human community is in its own way an experiment in living and the proper subject of anthropology.

Getting started. Selecting the exact locale for study and making initial contacts with the group to be studied are often intertwined. In each fieldwork account described in this chapter, *contact persons* are named as initial linkages between the anthropologist and the community. Sometimes these contact persons are members of the community, and at other times they are not. Whatever the case, their importance cannot be overemphasized.

Hart admits that without Mariano fieldwork among the Tiwi would have been impossible. Is it possible to conceive of Keiser's fieldwork without the aid of Goliath? For Briggs, the Eskimo Anglican deacon Naklirohuktuq served not only to introduce her to the group she studied initially, but was also vital in resolving her crisis with her Eskimo family.

There are numerous kinds of first contact situations and we cannot cover all of them. Certainly one of the most unusual situations was Allan Holmberg's "contact" with the Siriono. According to what he had read and heard about these natives of eastern Bolivia, they were a very suspicious and hostile group. With the aid of a Siriono assistant whom he had met at a missionary station, Holmberg located a camp of these nomadic people. Holmberg and his assistant entered the Siriono camp in the late afternoon when most of the men were sleeping. They entered the camp naked, the usual state for the Siriono, speaking Siriono loudly, and carrying meat that they knew the Siriono craved. The suddenness of their entrance into the camp startled the Siriono, and before they had time to reach for their weapons Holmberg and his assistant were in their midst. The Siriono, torn between their desire for meat and their fear of strangers, opted for the meat. Holmberg was then able to work out a deal with the Siriono; they would let him stay with them and in return he would kill animals for them with his shotgun.

Most anthropologists would agree that without a good contact fieldwork would be ex-

tremely difficult if not impossible. The importance of a good contact is not merely to gain an introduction. Although suspicion may not be a cultural universal, a good number of groups are suspicious and wary of strangers. The contact, either explicitly or implicitly, vouches for the "credentials" of the anthropologist. For the anthropologist, it is a foot in the door. After that it is up to the anthropologist to establish and maintain a set of social relationships, to survive physically and emotionally, and to do the research.

Language and time. Compared to research in other social sciences, anthropological research is unusual. An anthropologist may spend as much as two years in a community that may number no more than a few hundred people or sometimes even less. Why is so much time required to comprehend the customs and manners of such a small group?

Anthropologists are not mere collectors of data; they attempt to comprehend the society they are studying. Even the smallest community has a complex culture, and understanding requires time.

Part of understanding a society is learning the language of the people being studied. By learning their language, by observing as wide a range of behavior as possible, and by intensive questioning, the anthropologist begins to unravel and understand the often confusing scenes of everyday life in another society.

Learning the language is often a first step in developing close and friendly social relationships with individuals. Members of most societies are pleased when an outsider takes the trouble to learn and use their language. An anthropologist who attains complete fluency in another tongue is rare; but in fact, the grammatical mistakes and mispronunciations often serve to reduce the authority and dominant position often accorded to the apparently well-to-do and powerful outsider. Anthropologists frequently mention how they become the butt of jokes that are based on their linguistic inadequacies and how in turn this jesting can become the basis for developing close relationships with individuals.

Language is a crucial guide to understanding a culture. Anthropologists are intensely interested in determining how people in another culture see, think, talk, and organize their perceptions of the world. In many contemporary definitions of culture, emphasis is placed on the categories used by a population. These categories are frequently referred to as maps or blueprints for behavior. Only through the acquisition of language can an anthropologist begin to understand how these maps are organized.

Participant-observation. An essential component of all fieldwork is participant-observation. Fieldworkers participate in as many activities as possible while observing and recording events. By participating in everyday activities, the fieldworker obtains direct access to and experience of behavior in another culture.

It is the combination of participant-observation, language competence, and long-term residence that is the basis for obtaining accurate and reliable data. As a long-term participant-observer, the anthropologist becomes a familiar and accepted part of the environment. In effect, the distance between the anthropologist and the human beings who are being studied is minimized, and becomes a relationship between human beings. Under such conditions, it is unlikely that the individuals being studied will either fabricate stories about their cultural behavior or assume a formal and stilted pose designed to please outsiders and strangers. Deception is also difficult to maintain for any extended period of time.

To participate effectively means that the fieldworker has to acquire a minimal understanding of another culture. Even events that seem simple — having a drink, feasting, and gossiping, for example — are based on cultural rules. Participation means social interaction and to participate successfully requires that the anthropologist learn the correct behavior for that particular culture. Observation and recording require the researcher to be conscious of what is being learned.

Participation varies from fieldworker to fieldworker and from culture to culture. Briggs pushed participation to the point of membership in an Eskimo family; Keiser, although he lived with the Vice Lords, did not participate in

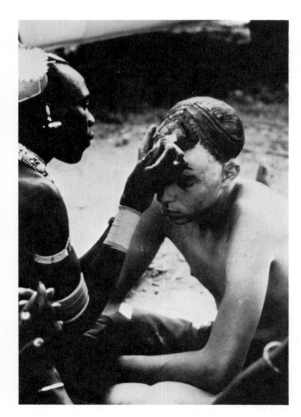

Anthropological fieldworker having his hair and face decorated in traditional fashion by a Pokot man (East Africa) in preparation for participation in a Pokot ceremony.

all of their activities and in fact found many of them disturbing to his own cultural values. When Hart hunted and moved with the Tiwi, when Powdermaker gossiped with her Lesu female friends, and when Keiser "hung out" with the Chicago Vice Lords, they were all participant-observers.

Informants. Fieldworkers can participate in and observe behavior, but they do not always understand what they are doing or seeing. An integral part of anthropological research is the use of informants. *Informants* are persons knowledgeable about their own culture who are both willing and able to articulate and communicate their knowledge to the anthropologist. They may communicate their knowledge for money, for love, or for reasons that are not clear, but without informants most anthropology could not be done at all.

There are many reasons why informants are important. Many areas of social and cultural knowledge in most cultures are known only by specialists. These persons may include religious practitioners, midwives, storytellers, and political leaders. In order to obtain information about these areas of knowledge, the fieldworker must find and work intensively with such experts. Some aspects of life are not observable through participant observation, and data about myths, religious beliefs, historical lore, and genealogy, for example, must be recorded from informants. In addition, the anthropologist may be excluded from participation in and observation of certain activities, and some events and ceremonies may not occur during the period of fieldwork residence. Informants provide an interpretation of the culture that the fieldworker cannot obtain through participant observation. In all of these cases and for all of these reasons, informants are an essential research tool.

The issue of the informant is complex, because in the anthropological enterprise the informant is a true partner. Very often the quality of anthropological research depends upon the nature of the relationship between the anthropologist and the informant.

This situation is illustrated in the following account by Raymond Firth of his major informant, Pa Fenuatara, on the island of Tikopia in the South Pacific (1960:5–6).

Pa Fenuatara's knowledge of economic and allied matters more than matched his skills. In some ways he was, if not the best informed, at least the most systematically minded Tikopia in respect to ritual affairs. His knowledge of Tikopia belief extended over a wide range. In

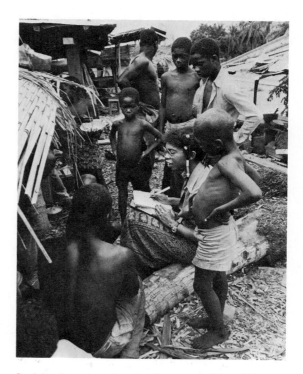

Studying the arts and crafts of a group in West Africa, an anthropologist uses the mainstay of anthropological fieldwork — pen and notebook — while working with informants.

1928–1929, apart from meeting him in a great number of public contexts, I recorded having about two dozen full-scale discussions with him, each lasting for half a day or over an evening. In these we covered an immense number of topics, ranging from magic formulae to help in handling a canoe at sea, to attitudes towards death and the afterworld of the spirits.

He was particularly lucid in talking about human relationships and found generalization easy. My book on Tikopia kinship owes much to his explications of the meaning of obligations in the [kinship] system and of variation in behavior. He was himself a family man, having at the time I knew him two sons and four daughters. Gentle and kindly in his treatment of them, he was able to recall in detail their childhood speech and behavior which he delighted in discussing with me.

Roles and role playing. Fieldwork accounts document the importance of social relationships between the fieldworker and the people studied. In fieldwork an anthropologist develops a network of informants, friends, and acquaintances. This network of social relations becomes a set of information pipelines. In the course of daily life, gossiping, talking, playing cards, drinking, hanging out, helping with a harvest, telling stories, and simply being with people become the basic means for collecting information and for understanding what is going on. In this seemingly innocuous and informal manner the anthropological field enterprise is pursued.

Thus the anthropologist is not only a research instrument but also a social actor playing many and varied roles with the group being studied. Briggs as a daughter, Hart as a clan member, and Keiser as a friend portray the typical roles adopted by fieldworkers.

Many anthropologists make conscious attempts to avoid being cast in roles considered to be undesirable in the field. The usual list includes missionary, administrator, government official, and boorish Westerner. These roles are familiar even to the most isolated cultures, and they carry with them undesirable and negative images.

The most desirable situation is for the fieldworker to assume a role that fosters acceptance and access to information. Malinowski claims to have achieved this level of relationship with the Trobriand Islanders. He described his relationship with the Trobriand Islanders as follows:

> The natives saw me constantly every day, they ceased to be interested or alarmed, or made self-conscious by my presence, and I ceased to be a disturbing element in the tribal life which I was to study. In fact, as they knew that I would thrust my nose into everything, even where a well-mannered native would not dream of intruding, they finished by regarding me as part and parcel of their life, a necessary evil or nuisance, mitigated by donations of tobacco (1961:7–8).

This Malinowskian image of the nosy, but accepted, researcher is an idealized one, that most fieldworkers would like to attain.

In explaining their presence to the people being studied, anthropologists of an earlier generation defined their role as students of tribal life. They claimed that after they returned home they would tell their people what life in this community was like. This tactic was used by Powdermaker, and although it was apparently accepted by the people of Lesu, we do not know to what extent this definition was understood. In anthropology there is now considerable controversy about the adequacy of the explanation given by anthropologists to the people they are studying.

A variety of roles can be adopted by fieldworkers in different research situations. It may be that this multiplicity of potentially useful roles is basic to the problem raised at the beginning of this section, the complaint about the lack of training anthropologists receive in order to carry out field research. What the complaints really stem from is the lack of training for a clear-cut research role in the field. It is clear from our presentation that very little can be done to resolve this problem. Each anthropologist has to carve out the roles that fit a particular place, time, situation, and society.

Research techniques. Complicated equipment and research instruments are not characteristic of anthropological fieldwork. In the early days of fieldwork a pencil and notebook were the basic instruments for recording data. Recently tape recorders, movie cameras, and even minicomputers have been taken into the field, although notebooks and pencils still remain important.

Powdermaker describes how she used a census to begin her research. Censuses and maps are among the most basic research techniques used by anthropologists. They bring a fieldworker into contact with a large number of people, they usually involve the recording of neutral information, and they make the fieldworker a familiar object in the environment. Maps and censuses can be used as the basis of sampling a population (see Figure 1.1). In addition, genealogies and life history materials are collected by almost every fieldworker. Genealogies provide information on the kinship and marital dimensions of a community. Life histories are biographical accounts of individuals. They provide insight into personal experience and historical events. For the fieldworker they are vehicles for assessing the impact of culture on an individual's life.

Recording information is a central activity for every fieldworker, and traditionally, it has meant taking notes and writing down conversations and interviews. Verbatim note taking provides a high level of accuracy and completeness, but sometimes field workers may find that note taking is either impossible or disturbing to informants. Powdermaker describes

this kind of situation when she participated in women's gossip. Information that is recorded at a later time may be less complete and contain inaccuracies.

Most fieldworkers keep a daily diary or log, which provides chronological information about the climate, events, experiences, and all the activities of the fieldworker. It may also be used by the fieldworker to record and express private and personal feelings. As far as we know, few diaries have ever been published. The most famous is Malinowski's diary, which was discovered after his death and published some years ago (Malinowski 1967). It reveals that Malinowski, during his stay on the Trobriand Islands, was deeply disturbed by personal and emotional problems.

Other notes are kept in a field notebook. After the initial recording of information, notes are typed and organized by topic and subject matter. As the fieldwork continues the volume of data grows at a rapid rate. To control this growing body of information and to make it usable, fieldworkers develop a system for organizing and retrieving data. Such a system is useful for defining the areas for further investigation.

Cameras are common instruments in anthropological research. Some anthropologists specialize in photography in fieldwork, which is known as visual anthropology. Visual anthropology encompasses a wide range of photographic techniques ranging from the production of full-length ethnographic films by a fieldwork team to the analysis of photographs taken by informants supplied with photographic equipment by the field researcher.

Tape recorders are particularly important in the collection of linguistic data, music, songs, folklore, and mythology, for which accuracy and completeness are essential. Some anthropologists use tape recorders to record their field notes as well as interviews and conversations with informants.

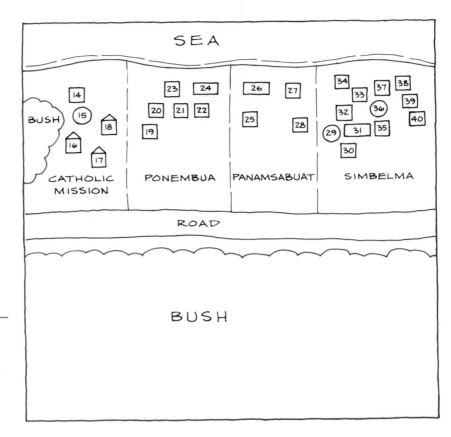

Figure 1.1
Map of Lesu village hamlets
drawn by Powdermaker as
part of her census and mapping research techniques.
The house marked X in the
hamlet of Penguli is where
Powdermaker lived.

A recent development, portrayed in the work of Napoleon Chagnon with the Yano-mamo, is the use of minicomputers in the field. Computers are most useful in long-term research when the investigator is making additions to an already existing body of information. The computer storage of Yanomamo genealogical information has been an important part of Chagnon's research.

Validity and reliability. Every scientific endeavor must be concerned with the validity and reliability of its data. *Validity* is defined as the accuracy or truthfulness of information obtained. *Reliability* is the degree to which different researchers or research techniques would obtain similar information. Perhaps these complex scientific issues can be illustrated from our common experience. Instructors in most academic institutions must give grades to their students. In most cases tests are the basic methods for determining grades. Both students and instructors frequently recognize that tests may be imperfect instruments that do not really tap all the knowledge acquired by students. To the extent that tests do not tap this knowledge, they are *invalid.* If a student scores in the same range on a series of tests, however, we assume the tests are a *reliable* measure of that student's knowledge. Grades are important, of course, and we all hope that the instruments used to determine them are both valid and reli-

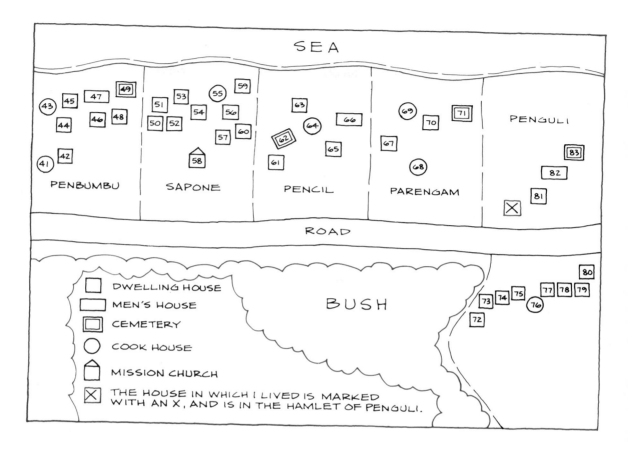

SEA

47 49 53 55 59 51 54 56 63 69 71 PENGULI
45 43 46 48 50 52 57 60 62 64 66 70 83
44 41 42 58 61 65 67 68 82 81
PENBUMBU   SAPONE   PENCIL   PARENGAM

ROAD

BUSH

☐ DWELLING HOUSE
▭ MEN'S HOUSE
▱ CEMETERY
○ COOK HOUSE
⌂ MISSION CHURCH
☒ THE HOUSE IN WHICH I LIVED IS MARKED WITH AN X, AND IS IN THE HAMLET OF PENGULI.

80 77 78 79 73 74 75 76 72

able. In a similar fashion, we hope that the research techniques used by anthropologists produce valid and reliable information.

One of the major criticisms of nineteenth-century anthropology is that its conclusions were based on the writings of untrained observers such as travelers, explorers, and missionaries, whose knowledge of tribal society was limited and frequently biased. Although fieldwork is an improvement over the haphazard observations of nineteenth-century writers, it also has problems of validity and reliability. Since the anthropologist is the basic instrument of data collection, biases based on theoretical preconceptions and closely held personal and cultural values may threaten the validity of data.

In addition, the age, sex, religion, and race of a fieldworker may subtly influence and distort observations and information gathered from informants. Thus Powdermaker enjoyed informal and familiar gossip relations with Lesu women that were not possible with Lesu men. Keiser confesses that some Vice Lord activities were profoundly disturbing to him and influenced his perception of their behavior.

Sources of bias are not limited to the fieldworker; lying and misinformation are problems sometimes faced by fieldworkers. Chagnon in his work with the Yanomamo Indians of Venezuela eventually discovered that his informants were deliberately giving him obscene and incorrect names for their deceased ancestors.

They found it hilarious to hear Chagnon repeat these obscene utterances; in addition, the Yanomamo have a cultural prohibition against using the names of deceased relatives. Chagnon had to repeat his genealogical study after discovering what the Yanomamo had done (1968:10–16). This specter of misinformation haunts every fieldworker.

Recognition of these multiple sources of bias has led fieldworkers to develop techniques to counteract them. Theoretical biases can be countered by good training and flexibility of research design. Cultural and personal biases are difficult to deal with, but awareness of them may lessen their distorting influence. As a stranger and outsider, the fieldworker approaches another culture with the benefit of cultural objectivity, lacking the emotional commitments that distort the views people have of their own culture. Because each person takes his or her own culture more seriously than any other culture, it is difficult for most individuals to view their own objectively and dispassionately. Anthropologists assume that the fieldworker, as a member of one culture, can observe behavior in a different culture with greater objectivity. The fact that Keiser, like the Vice Lords, was a member of American society may have led to his difficulties in dealing with his own feelings while doing fieldwork with this group. Many anthropologists argue that the personal and cultural biases of the anthropological observer are to some extent compensated for and corrected by the fact of cultural and emotional distance from the culture being studied.

Long-term residence and cultural familiarity become major ingredients in controlling bias and misinformation. Cross-checking information with a variety of informants is another technique used by fieldworkers to investigate an informant's validity and reliability. Since many fieldworkers study populations that have previously been studied, they are able to compare their findings with other materials. The emergence of significant discrepancies between sets of data becomes a signal for reassessing information.

Over the long run problems of validity and reliability are significantly reduced when the fieldworker becomes an accepted figure in the community. Once this occurs, many anthropologists discover that certain individuals are strongly motivated to help them by providing accurate and truthful information. Informants used by Powdermaker and Keiser saw themselves as helping the researchers write their books. It seems improbable that these informants would deliberately lie to them.

Most of the techniques we have described are designed to improve the validity of data. Reliability, however, poses a more difficult problem. A second anthropologist may study a community that has already been investigated and discrepancies may emerge in the course of the second study. Such differences in the same community could be the result of change rather than incorrect or invalid data. Since most fieldwork is carried out by a single investigator in a single community and at a particular period of time, it becomes difficult, if not impossible, to repeat the original study and arrive at the same results. Reliability thus remains a difficult and intractable problem in anthropological research because there is no way of duplicating the circumstances of the original research.

The anthropologist as the research instrument. Unlike the chemist and physicist, who have laboratories, the psychologist, who uses a one-way mirror, or the sociologist, who uses a questionnaire, the anthropological fieldworker has few sophisticated research instruments. One reason for this difference is the perception held by most anthropologists about the role of the human being as a scientific observer. Anthropologists regard the trained observer as an important research instrument. This is in contrast to the other social sciences, in which research instruments are designed to compensate and correct for the inherent biases of the human observer. Although some technical devices have been introduced into anthropological fieldwork, the fieldworker is still seen as the basic recording and observing instrument in anthropology. Anthropologists believe that an intelligent and well-trained individual can objectively observe and record human behavior. The assumption underlying this approach is that the only way to record another culture is to live it, learn it, and understand it.

Human Aspects of Fieldwork

To many nonanthropologists, the idea of spending an extended period of time living in a remote and isolated area of the world may appear to be inherently dangerous. Among these sources of danger are animals; the supposed potential of non-Westerners, especially tribal people, for violence; and disease.

How dangerous is fieldwork? Dangerous animals seem to be a minimal threat to the fieldworker. The frightening image of ravenous crocodiles, stampeding elephants, and hissing cobras appears to be overdone.

Despite the fact that fieldwork has been carried out among some people renowned for cannibalism and headhunting, few anthropologists have been killed while doing fieldwork. Once again the image of the hostile, spear brandishing native reflects Hollywood more than reality. Anthropological fieldwork in previous decades was carried out in areas under European colonial domination. The peace imposed by European colonial authority provided a relatively safe environment for anthropological field research. Unlike the trader, plantation owner, missionary, or government official, the fieldworker was more interested in learning about kinship terms than making money, saving souls, or collecting taxes. In contrast to most Europeans, the anthropological fieldworker

was not seen as engaging in directly exploitative behavior. For this and other reasons, most anthropologists probably have very little to fear from the people they are studying.

Based upon the accounts of fieldwork in this chapter, Chicago in the 1960s was a more dangerous place in which to do fieldwork than Lesu, Australia among the Tiwi, or the Arctic. In many ways, living in contemporary American society appears to be more dangerous than residing among people whom Western society has labeled as the essence of the "primitive savage."

Disease is a constant threat in some fieldwork situations. Malaria, dysentery, hepatitis, and parasitic infections are common diseases in many parts of the world, especially tropical areas. Fieldworkers, like other residents of these regions, are exposed to these diseases. Where preventive measures are available, anthropologists use them. When Eames went to India in the 1950s he took the following immunization shots: cholera, smallpox, tetanus, typhoid, paratyphoid, and bubonic plague. Powdermaker noted that her daily dose of quinine kept her free from malaria. Despite these precautions, many fieldworkers suffer from disease and illness. However, few anthropologists die from diseases contracted in the field.

Although fieldwork may not be physically dangerous, the fieldworker faces many problems. Some of these are related to the everyday aspects of survival, while others are psychological and emotional.

Meeting Basic Needs

Housing, food, and sanitation are among the most immediate physical needs that an anthropologist in the field must satisfy. It is generally necessary to change established behavioral patterns and adapt to different ways of satisfying these needs. Although sex is not an immediate need in this sense, it can become a difficult problem in various ways, both physi-

Variety of housing used by anthropologists in different field settings. Top: Brush shelter of the type used by Hart among the Tiwi. Bottom: Tent Malinowski occupied while doing fieldwork in the Trobriand Islands. Right: A stone house built and lived in by anthropologists working on the Vicos Project in Peru.

cally and emotionally. The manner in which these needs are satisfied has an impact on the course of fieldwork.

Housing. Most fieldworkers adopt the housing available in the society they study. Hart camped out with the Tiwi, Powdermaker had a house built for her. Briggs and Keiser moved into existing housing, the first into an iglu and the other into a dingy ghetto apartment. Housing is not merely a matter of having a place to sleep and eat. It may have a continuing impact on the per-

sonal and emotional life of the fieldworker as well as on the research itself.

Evans-Pritchard notes that when he lived with the Nuer he could look out of his tent and see the everyday life of the people (1940:14–45). Housing patterns of many groups who live in tropical and semitropical climates reflect this kind of environment, and consequently much of their daily life is both visible and public. This factor is certainly of enormous aid to an anthropologist using the technique of participant observation, although of course the reverse of this situation is that the anthropologist is also open to public view, As Evans-Pritchard writes (1940:15), "The chief privation was the publicity to which all my actions were exposed, to performing the most intimate operations before an audience in full view of the camp."

Availability of housing may have a very important impact on site selection, as in Wylie's decision about which French village to study. An important decision must be made about whether to live alone as Powdermaker did or to move in with a family as Briggs did. In either case this decision may determine the research network of friends and informants that becomes available to the fieldworker.

Food. Anthropological fieldworkers depend on locally available food. Rarely can fieldworkers bring all of their own food with them. In the rural and tribal areas of the world where most anthropological research takes place, the food pattern that is familiar to most of us is either absent or found in the most limited manner. Fieldworkers therefore have to work out some kind of accommodation to the food patterns of the societies where they work. This adaptation includes obtaining, preparing, and consuming local food.

Hart hunted with the Tiwi and apparently had no difficulty in obtaining or consuming food. Holmberg not only hunted for his own food, but supplied the Siriono as well. Briggs and Powdermaker entered the local exchange system, and Keiser bought his food in local stores. Although some anthropologists, like Hart and Holmberg, may be directly involved in obtaining their own food, usually someone else obtains and prepares food for the fieldworker.

Anthropologists often have sufficient funds to purchase food and to employ servants to procure and prepare their food. Hiring servants is not simply a matter of the anthropologist's superior economic position. Most societies lack American kitchen technology, and the processes of procuring food and preparing meals can be both difficult and time-consuming.

Alan Beals's account of how he and his wife attempted to set up housekeeping in Gopalpur, a South Indian village, is a good example of the problems involved in setting up housekeeping without servants.

To Gopalpur we brought stoves, cooking utensils, typewriters, and other equipment we were sure would not be available. Our plan was to live totally without servants, depending upon locally available food supplies and vitamin tablets. As soon as we had arrived in the garden house, I unpacked our equipment and began getting the stove ready to boil water. The Gauda [village headman], his servants, and some twenty important persons from the village gathered around to watch the lighting of the primus stove and to give me such helpful advice as they could. With an air of great coolness, I began assembling the parts. Accustomed to carrying out the business of living in complete privacy, the steady flow of advice soon broke my nerve. My hands began to tremble, my face flushed, and the stove became more and more obdurate. With an air of confidence, Kanamma (Mrs. Connie) [Beal's wife] seized a pan and went to the creek to obtain water. With a quick glance at the other ladies to see what they were doing, she dug a shallow hole in the sand, waited for the dust to settle and began to scoop water into her pan. Somehow, the water trickled away between her fingers and the little water that reached the pan turned out to be full of dirt. A seven-year-old child came over and filled Kanamma's pan.

In a surprisingly short time, we were painfully aware that we had achieved an almost legendary reputation for incompetence. We could not get water, we could not make fire. We seemed totally unable to get food or prepare it properly once we had it. Already exhausted by such simple tasks as getting water, Kanamma was in no shape to scrounge around for foodstuffs or to endure the routines of cookery that involved six to eight hours of hard work on the part of highly skilled local women. Within a few days, we were begging the Gauda to find us a servant (Beals 1970:38).

Many times the monotony of the diet is a major complaint of the fieldworker, and this criticism is especially striking in Powdermaker's account. Very few societies enjoy the variety of foods available in American society. This problem is not only technological, but in many societies there is also a basic unwillingness to try new and different foods even when they are available.

An additional problem derives from foods that the fieldworker may find repulsive. Strange and sometimes repugnant food — for example, grubs, monkey meat, and assorted insects — may become important in fieldwork if they are part of the hospitality and feasting activities of the people being studied. The basis of fieldwork is establishing social relations, and in a majority of societies the development and maintenance of friendly relations are often associated with feasting and eating together. Thus fieldworkers may spend considerable time eating with the group being studied. Unless special arrangements have been made beforehand, it is not unusual for fieldworkers to be presented with foods that may make them queasy.

A delightful story that has been told for some years in anthropology — and we hope it is a true story — concerns a famous anthropologist who was a guest of honor at a feast held by the group he was studying. The main course of the meal was a whole roasted sheep. After the sheep was cooked the host leaned over and deftly removed one of the sheep's eyeballs with his knife, proudly presenting it to their resident anthropologist. There was nothing he could do but accept, and so he popped the eyeball into his mouth and swallowed it. His hosts were immensely gratified. They had never before seen a European eat an eyeball, and they immediately removed the second eyeball and offered it to their honored guest. At this point the anthropologist, who was having a hard time holding down the first eyeball, raised his hand and said, "No, among my people it is not polite for the guest to take all the most delicious foods," and he insisted that his host must eat the other eyeball. The host did so with obvious relish. Perhaps this is what Middleton means when he advocates good manners for the field researcher.

Sanitation. Outside of the industrial world and the urban centers of the developing nations, flush toilets are not frequently found. During fieldwork every anthropologist faces problems of sanitation and disposal of body wastes.

Robert Dentan complained that while he was studying the Semai of the Malay rain forest he could never defecate in private. The Semai used rivers for this purpose, and every time Dentan went to the river, one or two men would offer to join him. Dentan feared that by rejecting this form of Semai hospitality he would offend them and ruin his relationship with them (Dentan 1970:105).

When Eames went to the village of Galipur, he brought a large supply of toilet paper with him. Like most villagers, he used the nearby fields for urination and defecation. It soon became apparent from the trail of toilet paper left behind which fields he was using. He failed to realize, however, the problems he was creating for the villagers by using toilet paper. One of his informants told him that anyone stepping on the toilet paper became ritually polluted and had to purify himself. Toilet paper, unlike feces, was not quickly and directly absorbed into the ground. Although he did not mean to, Eames began to create a major problem for the residents of Galipur, a problem that threatened to have a negative effect on his research. As a consequence he was forced to make a difficult change in one of his most basic behavioral patterns and give up the use of toilet paper.

In the area of sanitation, the problem is adaptation to a different pattern of behavior. Anecdotal accounts about sanitation traded by anthropologists in gossip sessions indicate that although they adapt successfully, this process involves both anxiety and uneasiness. Such is the impact of culture on human behavior.

Sex. An aspect of the human side of fieldwork that is rarely mentioned is the anthropologist's sexuality. While this issue, we assume, confronts every anthropologist in the field, most personalized accounts avoid this topic, giving the impression that field research involves an extended period of abstinence. Because of the lack of evidence, it is impossible to determine the degree to which abstinence is the behavior of the lone or lonely researcher. The fieldworker's sexual activity, or inactivity, has implications for the effectiveness of field research; it is not merely a personal problem.

Our impression is that the usual advice given to novice anthropologists going into the field is to avoid sexual involvement with members of the community being studied. Seligman so advised Evans-Pritchard before his fieldwork in Central Africa. It is difficult to say if this advice is based upon moral and ethical grounds or on a scientific and research basis.

There are several factors involved in this issue. In some societies premarital and extramarital relationships are frowned upon. In such cases the anthropologist may encounter serious difficulty, if not real danger, if there is an attempt to develop sexual relationships. In some instances the single male researcher may be viewed with suspicion and is told directly or indirectly to stay away from the women. This happened to John Beattie in his fieldwork in Bunyoro in East Africa (Beattie 1965:16).

In many societies like the Tiwi the role of the unmarried adult female is unknown. Thus the female anthropologist may occupy an ambiguous and perhaps confusing role that may make her research efforts difficult. Powdermaker faced this problem on Lesu, and she solved it by explaining that she had been married and had divorced her husband for reasons that were also grounds for divorce in Lesu. The female anthropologist may be subject to the sexual advances of local males. There are unsubstantiated rumors and innuendoes, in fact, that in some communities female anthropologists have been sexually exploited as part of the price of informant cooperation. The truth of these stories is exceedingly difficult to determine.

Sexual activity for the single anthropologist (male or female) can also be a problem in societies that are either sexually permissive or sexually open. In some societies it is assumed that the anthropologist will set up a sexual liaison as a matter of normal human activity. In other situations the male anthropologist may be offered access to women as part of a hospitality pattern or because it is part of a *machismo*, or masculinity, pattern of behavior. Finally, sex may be offered as part of a scheme to manipulate the anthropologist. Colin Turnbull reports that this type of scheming occurred while he was working with the Pygmies of Central Africa. A non-Pygmy chief in a neighboring village thought he could cement his relationship to the Pygmies by giving his daughter to Turnbull, who was living with the Pygmies (1962:143–144). Turnbull felt he could neither accept nor reject this offer, and thus he worked out a complicated scheme that did not involve any sexual behavior.

Beyond the purely psychological and pleasurable aspects of sex, we must consider the advantages, disadvantages, and problems of sexual activity between the researcher and members of the community being studied. Establishment of a sexual relationship may permit the fieldworker to gain information about areas of behavior considered to be secret or private. In sexually permissive societies such a relationship may operate to validate the fieldworker as both normal and human, thus establishing the fieldworker as a reliable and trustworthy person in whom the community members can confide. On the other hand, a fieldworker may occupy a powerful position, economically and politically, in relationship to the group being studied. The use of wealth and position to establish a sexual relationship must be viewed as a particularly nasty form of exploitation.

Sexual involvement with particular members of a community may lead to suspicion and resentment from other members of the community. Many accounts about fieldwork stress the important and helpful role of "stranger" or "outsider" that the anthropologist enjoys. Such a role may give the anthropologist access to different and often competing groups without raising suspicions. As an outsider it is also possible to ignore and evade many rules and customs that would be demanded and expected from a full-fledged participating member of the community. The intimacy of a sexual relationship may begin to erode this vital "stranger role," and thus interfere with the purpose of the research.

Husband-wife teams in the field might reduce some of these problems. In societies that are concerned with the chastity of their women, the married male anthropologist may appear to be less threatening than a single male. Husband-wife teams, however, have problems as well.

David Reisman and his wife did fieldwork among the Fulani of West Africa. He found that being married created difficulties in his relations with Fulani men. The Fulani expected married men to pursue extramarital affairs avidly. When Reisman refused to participate in these affairs, he used the fact that he was married as an excuse. Fulani men did not accept this as a valid reason. Some believed that Reisman was overly dominated by his wife, but the majority felt that Reisman found Fulani women unattractive. Either interpretation of Reisman's behavior could have created a barrier between Reisman and the Fulani (1971:602–613).

Little has been written about the strains, sexual and other, that married couples may endure in the field. Robert Dentan, whose wife accompanied him into the field, reports that one of their greatest difficulties was in obtaining privacy. He writes (1970:104–105):

> We found it inhibiting, for example, when trying to indulge in a little connubial bliss in our creaky house, when Uproar, our next door neighbor, would shout jokingly, "Hey, what are you two doing in there?"

Emotional Well-Being

Powdermaker's account provides a clear illustration of the feelings of anxiety, depression, and even helplessness encountered by the fieldworker. These experiences are known to every field researcher. These feelings begin at the initiation of fieldwork and may continue throughout the entire course of the research. The very nature of anthropological research requires that individuals consciously remove themselves from the world they have known,

moving from a condition of certainty to one of uncertainty.

An additional anxiety-producing factor is the realization that the fieldworker's future career depends upon the successful completion of the research. As fieldwork proceeds, most anthropologists realize that even in a period of two years there is no way of obtaining data on every aspect of a culture. The difficulty, if not the impossibility, of acquiring complete data can produce recurring bouts of anxiety and panic.

The first few weeks of fieldwork may be the most difficult and disturbing period. During this time contacts must be initiated, the rudiments of the language acquired, and the sorting out of impressions begun. If anything operates to reduce feelings of panic and anxiety, it is time and the emergence of individual social relationships. All of the field experience accounts reveal this process. These social relationships serve not only as vital sources of information, but also become the basis for the satisfaction of emotional and psychological needs for the fieldworker. Without them it is doubtful that most researchers could carry on their work for any extended time.

The importance of human relationships with members of the group studied is seen in the deep and intense feelings that many anthropologists develop toward the group. This attitude is frequently reflected in their reference to the group studied as "my people," "my village," "my tribe."

In spite of physical and psychological problems faced by every fieldworker, fieldwork is an emotionally rewarding experience. Some of the sources of personal fulfillment are summarized by Walter Goldschmidt in his appraisal of fieldwork as a ritual of initiation into the anthropological tribe.

> Consider the most important ritual in the culture of anthropology, its initiatory rite: the

Field Trip. It involves the familiar theme of death and rebirth, with its prescribed year or longer in the bush.

The field experience is inevitably an intense one. Among the sources of this intensity are the following: the establishment of an intimate bond and mutual dependency between investigator and subject, the sharing of personal crises, including physiological events (births, illness, death), the acquisition by the neophyte of at least sectors of the behavior of those studied, a sense of encapsulation in this exotic world, and an inevitable recognition of the interrelatedness of all things that take place. No other social scientist — indeed no other scientist — has this intimate relationship with the subject of his study. No historian, however much he would like to, lives with the people he studies. The economist analyzes the market, not the marketplace, let alone the buyers and sellers. The sociologists classically interpose an instrument between themselves and their subjects. We not only live in our villages and tribes, but even as we complain of the lack of privacy and the flies, we boast that we were inducted into a clan and address our subjects by the proper kin terms. This characteristic anthropological involvement is certainly the great source of our intellectual strength. (Goldschmidt 1977:294–295).

Problems of Contemporary Fieldwork

Fieldwork as we have described it has remained relatively the same for the last half-century. There have been a number of specific changes, however. As a method of research it has become more finely tuned in technique, and greater attention is now paid to the collection of numerical, statistical, and biographical data.

Today practitioners of field research must deal with constraints and considerations unknown to an earlier generation of fieldworkers. When Malinowski was doing his fieldwork in the Trobriand Islands, Powdermaker her work in Lesu, and Evans-Pritchard his research among the Nuer, it was sufficient to be introduced to the people being studied by representatives of the colonial regime.

In recent decades, however, many areas of the world that were the natural habitat of the anthropological fieldworker have been closed. Many new nations in Africa and Asia see anthropologists, particularly European or American anthropologists, as remnants of a painful colonial era. Perceiving them as representatives of neocolonialism, they may deny them entry. Turnbull, in the introduction to his volume on the Ik of East Africa (1972), notes that he had planned initially to study a tribal group in India, but eventually realized that the Indian government was unwilling to give him permission to do the research.

Officials in many Third-World governments are very suspicious of anthropologists who want to do research in their countries. They may place constraints upon the researchers, telling them where they can go and whom they can talk to, and they may demand access to all the data collected. Government officials may make the conditions surrounding fieldwork so difficult that the researchers may decide to abandon their study. Governments can refuse permission for anthropologists to enter their country.

In addition to these problems, there is the controversial issue of ethics in anthropology. Over fifty years ago Malinowski published a book entitled *The Sexual Life of Savages in North-West Melanesia* (1929). Although contemporary anthropologists would shudder at the use of the term "savages," more importantly the title and subject matter of this volume reveal that Malinowski did not expect his Melanesian informants to read his account of their sexual lives. In other words, Malinowski did not consider the impact of his volume on the lives of his subjects.

This situation was not true for Oscar Lewis. Lewis, who is best known for his work on the culture of poverty, published an account of urban poverty in Mexico City (1961). His description of urban poverty, which is as accurate, we trust, as Malinowski's account of Melanesian sexuality, received a critical, if not hostile, reception. The Mexican press became visibly disturbed by his portrayal of Mexican life, and they denied the validity and objectivity of his description. Lewis was threatened with legal action, and efforts were made to discover his informants.

The point of this episode is clear. Today, informants and other interested parties are able to read ethnographic reports about themselves and of their country and people. Anthropologists are not opposed to critical evaluations of their work, but they are dismayed by criticism that may be political rhetoric, naive forms of nationalism, or based on a heightened sensitivity to self-images. Such attacks and threats on anthropology develop a "chilling atmosphere." Areas of research, specific problems, and particular findings may be ignored or hidden in order to avoid personal and professional problems as well as problems for informants.

In the course of field research many anthropologists collect information about individuals that can be either embarrassing or even dangerous if it is made public. We know of an anthropologist who was given information by individuals about their participation in a series of political assassinations. Because he feared that this information could be used by the government to prosecute his informants for murder, the anthropologist who gathered the data made arrangements that the information would not be published. Even though most anthropological information is not as dramatic as this data, anthropologists wish to protect the confidence of their informants and have an ethical responsibility to do so. The protection of informant privacy is threatened by some governments that have demanded, as part of the permission to do research, that the fieldworker turn over a complete copy of all data collected.

In the era of Malinowski, Hart, and Powdermaker, the issue of ethics was not considered important. Anthropologists were rarely, if ever, attacked in public for their findings, and colonial regimes either supported or were disinterested in their research. Under such conditions, it was possible to define the anthropological fieldworker's purpose as one of pure science. The chief obligation was the collection of accurate information. From their writings anthropologists of an older generation appeared to be sympathetic to the problems of tribal peoples in a changing world, but in reality questions of loyalties, obligations, and choices did not exist.

Today a relevant ethical issue is the question, for whom is the anthropologist working and for what purpose? Some anthropologists still defend the role of the so-called uninvolved scientist, the investigator of human behavior. At the other extreme are anthropologists who perceive their role as activists and advocates for the people they study. Since the communities usually studied by anthropologists are both poor and politically impotent, these people can be defined as both oppressed and exploited. This ethical position taken on the side of the poor and the oppressed places such anthropologists in opposition to established authority.

Between these two extreme positions is that ill-defined middle ground where anthropologists attempt to be anthropologists while at the same time recognizing their obligations and support for the people who, in the truest sense, have been their partners in the anthropological enterprise.

Summary

Fieldwork is a hallmark of cultural anthropology. It involves long-term residence, acquisition of native languages, and participation in the daily lives of the people being studied. It is the major method of collecting data on human behavior in different cultures.

In order to illustrate some of the dimensions of fieldwork, the experiences of anthropologists working under different conditions have been presented. These accounts vary from research in traditional and isolated tribal societies to research in urban America. Despite the differences in time, place, and situation, there are common elements in all of the accounts.

Fieldwork is a scientific enterprise. It developed at the beginning of the twentieth century and became a way of bringing the researcher into direct contact with the people being studied. As a scientific research method its goal is to obtain valid and reliable information. Participant observation and the use of informants are the major research methods used by anthropologists in the field. In recent years photography, tape recorders, and minicomputers have been added to the traditional techniques of the fieldworker.

Training and funding are necessary requirements for successful fieldwork. Fieldwork has been traditionally viewed as the collection of data about all aspects of a culture. As data accumulated, problem-oriented research designs began to determine the direction of anthropological research.

Fieldwork is unique in that the anthropologist is used as a research instrument. As a result fieldwork has human as well as scientific elements. In the course of fieldwork the anthropologist must face and resolve physical and psychological problems, many of them unanticipated, including housing, food, sanitation, sex, anxiety, and depression.

Fieldwork, because it depends so much on the establishment of close social relationships, is often a source of emotional fulfillment for anthropologists. This intensity of feeling is rarely duplicated in any other discipline and gives to cultural anthropology a unique dimension.

At the present time, constraints have been placed upon fieldwork that did not exist in the past. Postcolonial governments view foreign fieldworkers with suspicion, and in addition, many ethical questions and responsibilities have emerged that were not relevant for an older generation.

Key Terms and Concepts

fieldwork/field
    research
participant-
    observation
problem-centered
    research

contact person
informants
validity
reliability

Suggested Readings

Bowen, Elenore Smith. *Return to Laughter.* Garden City, N.Y.: Natural History Press, 1964. *Elenore Smith Bowen is the pseudonym of a well-known anthropologist. This is a delightful account of how one anthropologist adapted to life in an African village.*

Casagrande, Joseph B., ed. *In the Company of*

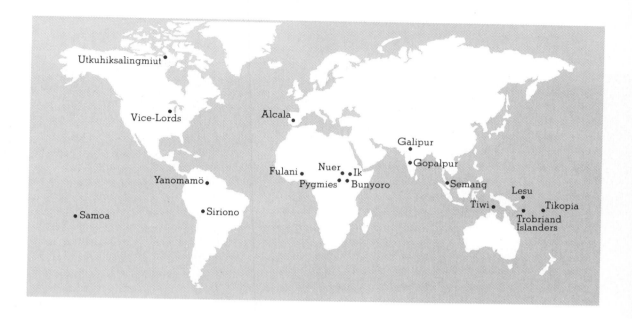

Man. New York: Harper & Row, 1960. *Twenty biographical portraits of anthropological informants. Written about individuals who were important to anthropologists during their field research, these accounts describe the unique relationship of anthropologist and informant.*

Foster, George, Thayer Scudder, Elizabeth Colson, and Robert V. Kemper, eds. *Long-Term Field Research in Social Anthropology.* New York: Academic Press, 1979. *In this volume, fourteen case studies describe the development and contributions of long-term field research, where data is gathered on the same group over an extended period of time.*

Golde, Peggy, ed. *Women in the Field: Anthropological Experiences.* Chicago: Aldine, 1970. *Twelve women anthropologists describe their experiences during fieldwork. Useful in documenting cross-cultural attitudes toward women. A more extensive account of Briggs's relationship with her Eskimo family is included.*

Henry, Francis, and Satish Saberwal, eds. *Stress and Response in Fieldwork.* New York: Holt, Rinehart and Winston, 1969. *Explores the problems and stresses anthropologists undergo during fieldwork.*

Rabinow, Paul. *Reflections on Fieldwork in Morocco.* Berkeley: University of California Press, 1977. *A introspective portrayal of Rabinow's experiences with his Moroccan friends and acquaintances. He presents fieldwork not merely as a research technique but as a cultural activity central to the definition of cultural anthropology.*

Spindler, George D., ed. *Being an Anthropologist: Fieldwork in Eleven Cultures.* New York: Holt, Rinehart and Winston, 1970. *Eleven first-hand accounts of fieldwork, including the complete reports by Hart and Keiser about their field experiences.*

Spradley, James P. *Participant Observation.* New York: Holt, Rinehart and Winston, 1980. *A complete discussion of the most fundamental research method in cultural anthropology.*

Chapter 2

The Anthropological Approach: Context, Comparison, and Theory

As you read in Chapter 1, fieldwork is the basis for data collection in cultural anthropology. Generally speaking, anthropological data can be presented in two ways: ethnographic accounts and comparative presentations.

Many fieldworkers present their data in a form called an *ethnography*, which is a description of the way of life of a particular people. An ethnography is not only a catalog of customs and behaviors observed during fieldwork, but it also attempts to explain and understand observed behavior, and understanding requires interpretation. In many ethnographies interpretation is accomplished by using a contextual framework. Contextual frameworks can vary; for example, understanding family organization in terms of economic demands is one form of *contextual analysis*. Whatever the framework, contextual analysis usually explains data for a particular group or community by relating the data to a wider setting.

A second approach to the presentation of anthropological data is comparing ethnographic data from a number of different cultures. Understanding human behavior derives not only from contextual analysis, but also from *cross-cultural analysis*. The analysis of large masses of cross-cultural data points to the similarities and differences in human behavioral patterns. These two modes of analysis along with fieldwork make cultural anthropology unique among the social sciences.

In applying these different analytic methods to ethnographic data, anthropologists have developed a variety of concepts and theoretical approaches. Although many concepts and theories have changed throughout the history of anthropology, the concept of *culture* has remained central to the discipline of anthropology. Numerous attempts have been made to define culture and its relationship to other anthropological concepts. More than a quarter of a century ago, in 1952, A. L. Kroeber and Clyde Kluckhohn surveyed the anthropological literature for definitions of culture and found more than 150 of them. For many anthropologists this multiplicity of definitions reduced the usefulness of culture as a concept, but culture still remains a central tool in anthropological thinking. It is hardly possible to write a text in anthropology without using the term culture. In its most widely used sense, culture refers to the way of life of a particular group of people — their distinctive manners, customs, beliefs, and material possessions.

Margaret Mead in native dress during her fieldwork in Samoa from 1925–1926. Her work in Samoa forced anthropologists and psychologists to reassess their view that adolescent revolt against parental authority is a universal pattern of behavior.

Contextual Analysis

As we saw in Chapter 1, Bronislaw Malinowski was an important figure in the development of modern fieldwork. His work among the Trobriand Islanders from 1914 to 1918 remains a model of ethnographic research. In addition to establishing basic rules for doing fieldwork, Malinowski developed a mode of analysis that was basically contextual. He viewed all aspects of Trobriand life and culture as constituting an integrated and interrelated unit. He concluded that to understand a particular facet of Trobriand culture, such as magic or inter-island trading, it was necessary to understand their complex interrelationships with other institutions in Trobriand life. His description and analysis of Trobriand Island life as a web of interrelated and intertwined customs and institutions constituted a major breakthrough in understanding human society. Although certain aspects of Malinowski's particular form of contextual analysis are no longer used, the recognition that different aspects of a culture are interrelated remains a general principle in anthropology.

Contextual analysis goes beyond the mere cataloging of events and behavior and attempts to understand human behavior. The following three accounts illustrate different types of contextual analysis and how they explain human activity.

The Opening of Malungwana Bridge

In 1938 Max Gluckman was doing fieldwork among the Zulu of South Africa. As a participant-observer, he attended a bridge-opening ceremony held in a Zulu reserve (a rural area set aside by the South African government for the Zulu). This ceremony is described by Gluckman in the following excerpt. Gluckman does not merely report the event; he analyzes this small-scale event in an attempt to comprehend the complicated nature of Black-White relations in South Africa. To Gluckman, what happened at the bridge-opening ceremony was only a small part of the larger South African social system, and it must be understood in that context.

On January 7th [1938] I awoke at sunrise and with [chief] Matolana and my servant, Richard Ntombela, prepared to leave for Nongoma, to attend the opening of a bridge in the neighboring district of Mahlabatini. At the hotel in Nongoma we separated, the Zulu to breakfast in the kitchen at my expense, and I to a bath, and then breakfast. I sat at a table with L. W. Rossiter, Government Veterinary Officer (G.V.O.) for the five districts of Northern Zululand. He also was going to the opening of the bridge as, like myself, he had a personal interest in it since it was built under the direction of J. Lentzner of the Native Affairs Department Engineering Staff, a close friend and old schoolfellow of both of us.

The significance of a ceremonial opening of the bridge was that it was the first bridge built in Zululand by the Native Affairs Department under the new schemes of Native development. It was opened by H. C. Lugg, Chief Native Commissioner for Zululand and Natal (C.N.C.). It is built across the Black Umfolosi River. The Black Umfolosi rises rapidly in heavy rains (sometimes twenty feet) and becomes impassable; the main purpose of the bridge is to enable the Mahlabatini magistrate to communicate with part of his district, which lies across the river, during slight rises of the river. It also makes possible access to the Ceza Hospital, which is famous among Zulu for its skill in midwifery.

Where the road forks to Ceza, the Mahlabatini magistrate had posted a Zulu in full warrior's dress to direct visitors. On the branch road we passed the car of Chief Mshiyeni, Regent of the Zulu Royal House, who was driving from his home in Nongoma district to the bridge. The Zulu in [our] car gave him the royal salute and we greeted him.

The bridge lies between fairly steep banks. When we arrived, a large number of Zulu [were] assembled on both banks (at A and B in sketch map); on the southern bank, on one side of the road (at C) was a shelter where stood most of the Europeans. They had been invited by the local magistrate, and included the office staff; the magistrate, assistant magistrate, and court messenger from Nongoma; the district surgeon; missionaries and hospital staff; traders and recruiting agents; police and technical officials; and several Europeans interested in the district. Many were accompanied by their wives. The Chief Native Commissioner and Lentzner arrived later, and also a representative of the Natal Provincial Roads Department. The Zulu present included local chiefs and headmen and their representatives; the men who had built the bridge; Government police; the Native Clerk of Mahlabatini magistracy; and Zulu from the surrounding district. Altogether there were about twenty-four Europeans and about four hundred Zulu present.

Arches of branches had been erected at each end of the bridge and across the one at the southern end a tape was to be stretched which the Chief Native Commissioner would break with his car. At this arch stood a warrior in war-dress, on guard. The G.V.O. and I were caught up in conversation with various Europeans while our Zulu joined the general body of Natives. Matolana was welcomed with the respect due to an important adviser of the Regent. When the Regent arrived, he was given the royal salute and joined his subjects, quickly collecting about himself a small court of important people. The Chief Native Commissioner was the next to arrive: he greeted Mshiyeni and Matolana. He then went round greeting the Europeans.

About 11:30 A.M. a party of the Zulu who built the bridge assembled at the north end of

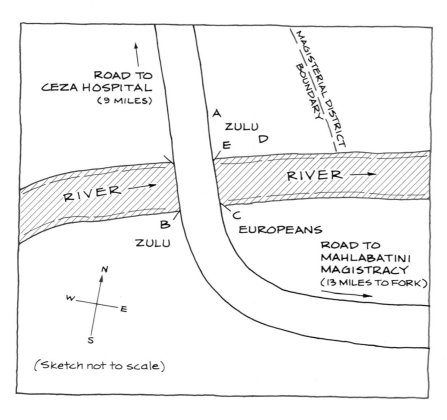

Zulu cross the bridge to welcome the C.N.C. and Regent. Note man in war dress on guard; men's clothes; notice in English.

the bridge. They were not in full war dress but carried sticks and shields. The important Zulu were nearly all dressed in European riding clothes, though the King wore a suit; common people were in motley combinations of European and Zulu dress. The body of armed warriors marched across the bridge till they stood behind the tape at the southern arch: they saluted the Chief Native Commissioner with the Royal Zulu salute, *Bayete,* then they turned to the Regent and saluted him. Both acknowledged the salute by raising their right arms. The men began to sing the *ihubo* (clan song) of the Butelezi clan (the clan of the local chief, who is chief adviser of the Zulu Regent). Proceedings now opened with a hymn in English, led by a missionary from Ceza Swedish mission. All the Zulu, including the pagans, stood for it and removed their hats. Mr. Phipson, Mahlabatini magistrate, then made a speech in English, which was translated into Zulu, sentence by sentence, by his Zulu clerk,

Mkhize. He welcomed everybody and specially thanked the Zulu for assembling for the opening; he congratulated the engineers and Zulu workmen on the bridge and pointed out the value it would be to the district. Then he introduced the C.N.C. The C.N.C. (who knows the Zulu language and customs well) spoke first in English to the Europeans, then in Zulu to the Zulu, on the theme of the great value of the bridge; he pointed out that it was but one example of all that Government was doing to develop the Zulu reserves. The representative of the Provincial Roads Department spoke shortly and said that his Department had never believed a low-level bridge would stand up to the Umfolosi floods, though they had been pressed to build one; he congratulated the Native Affairs engineers on the present bridge, which though built at little cost had already stood under five feet of flood water; and added that the Provincial Department was going to build a high-level bridge

Warriors, singing the *ihubo*, lead the cars back. Note man chanting with his stick lifted; in left foreground, next to policeman, is an *induna* in the military garb much favored by Zulu.

on the main road. The final speech was by the Regent Mshiyeni, in Zulu, translated sentence by sentence into English by Mkhize. Mshiyeni thanked the Government for the work it was doing in Zululand, said the bridge would enable them to cross the river in flood time and would make it possible for their wives to go freely to the Ceza Hospital to have their children; he appealed to the Government, however, not to forget the main road where the river had often held him up and to build a bridge there. He announced that the Government was giving a beast to the people and that the C.N.C. had said that they must pour the gall [animal stomach fluid] over the feet of the bridge according to Zulu custom, for good luck and safety for their children when crossing the bridge. The Zulu laughed and clapped [at] this. The Regent ended and was given the royal salute by the Zulu who, following the Europeans' lead, had clapped [after] the other speeches. The C.N.C. entered his car and, led

by warriors singing the Butelezi *ihubo,* drove across the bridge; he was followed by the cars of a number of other Europeans and of the Regent, in haphazard order. The Regent called on the Zulu for three cheers (hurrahs, Zulu *hule*). The cars turned on the further bank, and still led by the warriors, returned; on the way they were stopped by the European magisterial clerk who wanted to photograph them. All Zulu present sang the Butelezi *ihubo.*

The Europeans went into the shelter and had tea and cake. A woman missionary took some outside to the Regent. The local Zulu had presented the Regent with three beasts and these, as well as the Government beast, were shot on the northern bank by him and his *aide-de-camp* amid great excitement. The Regent ordered Matolana to select men to skin and cut up the cattle for distribution. The Regent withdrew to a nearby copse (D on the sketch) to talk with his people and drink Zulu beer, of which large quantities were brought for him. He sent four pots, carried by girls, to the C.N.C. who drank from one pot and kept it; he told the carriers to drink from the others and then give them to the people. This is proper according to Zulu etiquette.

The C.N.C. and nearly all the Europeans went away; most of the Zulu had assembled on the northern bank. There they were divided, roughly, into three groups. At the copse (sketch map, D) was the Regent with his own and local *indunas* [chiefs], sitting together, while further off were the common people. They were drinking beer and talking while they waited for meat. Just above the river bank at A (sketch map) were groups of men rapidly cutting up three beasts under Matolana's supervision; they were making a great noise, chattering and shouting. Behind them, further up the bank, the Swedish missionary had collected a number of Christians who were lined up singing hymns under his direction. In their ranks I noticed a few pagans. Lentzner got two warriors to pose on either side of him for a photograph on his bridge. Singing, chattering, talking and cooking continued till we left; I passed from group to group except for the hymn singers, but most of the time I talked with Matolana and Matole, the Butelezi chief, whom I met that day for the first time. Matolana had to stay to attend on the Regent and we arranged that the latter should bring him to the Nongoma meeting. We left with Richard and the veterinary office-boy. The gathering at the bridge was to last all day. (Gluckman 1940:2–8).

This account represents a specific development in fieldwork methods. Instead of reporting generalized descriptions, the field researcher records details that are important in understanding social life. Placing individuals within a social setting represents a fine tuning of anthropological field methods. Gluckman's

interest is not confined to the bridge ceremony as an isolated event, but instead as a social situation that delineates the social principles of South African society in 1938.

According to Gluckman, the dominant feature of the South African social system is the relationship between Blacks and Whites. The major themes of this relationship are separation, domination, opposition, and cooperation. Gluckman notes that he was not allowed to eat with his Zulu friends and informants. The sketch map of the bridge ceremony clearly indicates the physical separation of the races. Although the Zulu Regent is accorded the respect due nobility, he is not invited to share food with the whites. A missionary lady brings tea and cakes to him.

White domination is both political and economic. Africans represent a majority of the population, but they are ruled by a much smaller number of Europeans. This imbalance is noted by Gluckman, as twenty-four Europeans and about 400 Zulu attended the ceremony. Europeans planned and developed the bridge, and Zulu laborers built it. European domination over the Zulu is part of South African history and social structure. Zulu men in traditional battle dress are a reminder of the great Zulu armies and empire before their defeat by the British and the Boers (Dutch settlers) in the nineteenth century. In the ceremony at the bridge the Europeans have a shelter but the Zulu do not. Europeans speak first and are followed by the Zulu Regent, who speaks last. At the beginning of the ceremony, Zulu warriors salute the Chief Native Commissioner (C.N.C.) before they salute their Zulu Regent.

Along with the major themes of separation and domination, Gluckman introduces the theme of cooperation. The two groups come together at the ceremony to dedicate the bridge. This occasion is one instance of Black and White cooperation. It does not mean that they share the same interests or the same cultural values, but rather a mutual intersection of interests. The Zulu want the bridge to get to the hospital, and the Europeans desire it in order to develop a more efficient administration and to show an interest in Native Development Schemes. The fact that Zulu and European share and respect a number of each other's customs is another facet of cross-racial cooperation. Pagan Zulu show respect to Christian hymn singers. The C.N.C. calls for a Zulu ritual designed to keep the bridge safe for Zulu children, and there is a mutual exchange of beer, meat, tea, and cakes.

In this excerpt, the theme of opposition is not noticeable; in the remainder of his account, however, Gluckman notes that the various Zulu officials who congratulate the Europeans for building the bridge, and whose position in the administration is dependent upon Europeans, voice strong opposition to other government policies. He recorded at a meeting held later on the same day that Zulu men voiced their displeasure at government policies about the care of cattle and wages paid for labor. Gluckman notes that "the severity of European domination is increasing." Zulu opposition occasionally erupted in "riots and assaults on police officials which are forcibly repressed." Gluckman concludes that the South African social system is permeated by social contradictions that flow from this pattern of Black-White relations. There appears to be no basis for the political or social resolution of these differences; instead there is an increasing use of force to maintain the system as it lurches from one crisis to another.

The ability to see relatively simple events as a reflection of a much larger and complex social system is an advantage of contextual analysis. Such an analysis may reveal the political and social dynamics that are the context for these events. In a manner comparable to Gluckman's analysis of the bridge dedication ceremony, Edwin Eames and Howard Robboy analyzed the thirty-ninth birthday party held for the Tacony-Palmyra Bridge that connects Pennsylvania and New Jersey over the Delaware River. Eames and Robboy relate participation in the Tacony-Palmyra bridge party to the context of localized bureaucratic and political conditions.

The Tacony-Palmyra Bridge Birthday Party

On Wednesday, August 14, 1968, an intriguing, and we believe, unique social event occurred in the interterritorial region between Pennsylvania and New Jersey: this was the celebration of the thirty-ninth birthday of the Tacony-Palmyra Bridge, a span crossing the Delaware River which connects the northeastern portion of Philadelphia and the area midway between Camden and Trenton, New Jersey. The significance of the event is attested to by the extent of participation: an estimated three thousand people came to celebrate this particular occasion, according to local newspaper accounts.

DESCRIPTION OF THE EVENT

The birthday party was officially called for 11:30 A.M. on Wednesday, August 14, 1968, by a local radio announcer named Bill Bircher. As one drove toward the bridge on this particular occasion he was confronted with a long line of traffic. To distinguish those who were arriving to celebrate the birthday party from those who merely wanted to use the bridge to get from Pennsylvania to New Jersey or vice versa, listeners of Bircher were instructed earlier in the day to approach the bridge with their headlights on. As a Bircher listener, following instructions, neared the bridge, the driver was waved over to the side of the road where space was provided for the parking of cars. Bridge policemen took care of this traffic detail.

Approaching the center of the span by walking along the pedestrian roadway, provided on the side of the bridge, the observer was struck by the mass of humanity milling about and asking, "Where is Bill Bircher?" Keeping amused by pointing out and commenting upon some of the costumes worn and signs brought along for the occasion kept many from becoming impatient. Finally, about 12:15 P.M., Bill Bircher arrived in a jeep following a contingent from one of Philadelphia's best-known high school bands, the Cardinal Dougherty High School Marching Band. To accommodate this group and Bircher, one lane of traffic was closed. Everybody pressed in on Bircher and surrounded the jeep which had brought him over from the New Jersey side. As many as could, shook his hand and exchanged greetings with him. By now the crowd was at its maximum and the bridge officials kept the lane which they had opened for Bircher and the band off limits to vehicular traffic.

As Bircher led the crowd in the singing of "Happy Birthday, Dear Bridge," the mood of the crowd changed to one of real involvement and active participation. During the second rendition of the song, both accompanied by the band, a fireboat appeared beneath the bridge and shot a stream of water up to the center. As the singing ended one of the participants handed Bircher a bottle of champagne which was consumed by those closest to him.

At this point Bircher introduced the head of the authority which runs the bridge: he expressed the bridge's appreciation for their attendance. Next the first person to drive over the bridge when it was opened in 1929 made a speech indicating how happy he was to be able to take part in this wonderful celebration. (Since he was 78 years old we would imagine that he was, indeed, happy to be there.)

After this spurt of speeches Bircher collected all the presents which had been brought for the bridge and showed them to the crowd. Several birthday cakes made their appearance and were quickly consumed. Finally, Bircher announced that free Cokes would be served on the New Jersey side of the bridge. By this time many of the older celebrants were tired and left, while the younger ones went for the Cokes. The feeling of involvement demonstrated by the rise of conversation between strangers was impressive during the entire period of the celebration.

The sequence of events described here lasted for about forty-five minutes from the time of arrival of Bircher and is based primarily upon the observations made by Robboy. (Eames and Robboy 1969).

By using participant-observation and a follow-up questionnaire, as well as questioning participants, Eames and Robboy collected data about reasons for attending this bridge party. Although people gave many reasons, the following statements were common: "it's a homey bridge," "it's the poor man's bridge," "it's not like those big bridges which are controlled by City Hall," "it's a bridge which lets us go across free on Christmas and New Year's Day," "it's the little man's bridge."

Analysis of these responses and the event itself required an explanatory framework that viewed the bridge party within a larger social context. The tone and quality of many of these remarks led Eames and Robboy to suggest that the comments represented feelings of opposition, antagonism, separation, and powerlessness, stemming from the eroding social, economic, and political position of the people who came to this event. Largely drawn from the white lower-middle-class and skilled worker categories, this population experiences a vague feeling of estrangement, helplessness, and economic difficulty in the face of bureaucratic, economic, and political forces that they see as unresponsive to their needs. Eames and Robboy interpreted this event as a form of *oblique social protest.* Oblique social protest is defined as opposition to established authority that does not use direct and violent forms of confrontation and conflict. This form of protest is eminently suitable for a group whose values do not support violent attacks upon the establishment. This mode of contextual analysis uses a theoretical position to explain observable behavior.

The Nuer: Structure, Time, and Ecology

One of the classic ethnographic studies is Evans-Pritchard's study of the Nuer (1940). The Nuer of Evans-Pritchard's study number about 300,000 and live in the Republic of the Sudan in East Africa. Evans-Pritchard describes them as aggressive cattle-herding nomads, primarily concerned with increasing the size of their herds. A major factor in increasing their herds is their ability to successfully raid their tribal neighbors, the Dinka. For Evans-Pritchard, this relationship between the Nuer and the Dinka is an important basis for his understanding of Nuer life and customs. His interpretation assumes a timeless quality as the Nuer raid the Dinka and the two groups maintain a fixed relationship of raider (Nuer) to raided (Dinka). His analysis assumes that this relationship has always existed and always will exist. In some ways Evans-Pritchard uses the Nuer view of their social universe as part of his analysis. The following Nuer myth explains and justifies the Nuer relationship to the Dinka and illustrates how Evans-Pritchard also assumes this unchanging and timeless relationship between Nuer and Dinka.

As far as history and tradition go back, and in the vistas of myth beyond their farthest reach, there has been enmity between the two peoples. Almost always the Nuer have been the aggressors, and raiding of the Dinka is conceived by them to be a normal state of affairs and a duty, for they have a myth, like that of Esau and Jacob [in the Old Testament Book of Genesis], which explains it and justifies it. Nuer and Dinka are represented in this myth as two sons of God who promised his old cow to Dinka and its young calf to Nuer. Dinka came by night to God's byre [cattle pen] and, imitating the voice of Nuer, obtained the calf. When God found that he had been tricked he was angry and charged Nuer to avenge the injury by raiding Dinka's cattle to the end of time. (Evans-Pritchard 1940:125).

Evans-Pritchard did his fieldwork with the Nuer in the late 1920s and early 1930s. Subsequently other fieldworkers also studied these people. Based on these later descriptions as well as Evans-Pritchard's numerous writings on the Nuer, Aidan Southall has challenged Evans-Pritchard's static view of Nuer-Dinka relations (1976:465–491).

Southall avoids the nonhistorical and timeless approach characteristic of Evans-Pritchard's world. Southall no longer describes the Nuer and Dinka as timeless tribal entities with clear and fixed boundaries. Instead he defines his contextual arena in terms of two dimensions — time and ecology. Southall postulates a large population occupying a large region suitable for a cattle economy, which is further subdivided into smaller geographical segments. Southall assumes that some time in the past, perhaps as much as 2000 years ago, the Nuer and Dinka constituted a single population in terms of language and culture. One segment of this population occupied a rich zone favorable for cattle herding. In time both the people and cattle in this favored zone increased in number and eventually exceeded the capacity of the land to maintain both human and animal populations. As a consequence the people in this zone moved into other geographical zones in their search for land, pasturage, and water. By attacking outward, they set in motion the scenario of raider and raided that began to differentiate the population of the entire region into Nuer (raider) and Dinka (raided), a process that continued for the next 2000 years.

According to Southall, the split between Nuer and Dinka is not fixed. The Nuer conquer and incorporate the Dinka, who in turn become assimilated as part of the Nuer. The Nuer attacked by the people behind them become part of the Dinka in the eyes of their attackers and conquerors. Southall cites evidence showing that the largest conquering Nuer tribe is, in fact, of Dinka origin (Southall 1976:467).

Although Southall's analysis is speculative and based upon a reconstruction of history, it adds a new dimension to contextual analysis. He writes, "The dominant vogue in social anthropology has ... shifted from the synchronic [timeless] study of structural relations between groups ... to an interest in process [history] and individuals, ... striving to find ... frames of reference within which all three dimensions can be seen as integrated and meaningfully related" (Southall 1976:488).

Contextual analysis is fundamental to the understanding of human behavior. Malinowski introduced contextual analysis by emphasizing cultural interrelationships. Gluckman's analysis looks at a particular event within the context of a wider social order, whereas Eames and Robboy develop their analysis within a theoretical approach. Evans-Pritchard's work represents a major trend in British anthropology that focuses upon social structure. Southall's analysis adds the dimensions of history and ecology, and his work represents a growing trend in contemporary anthropology to incorporate within its structure new dimensions of context and contextual understanding.

Comparative Analysis

Contextual analysis is usually limited to a single cultural unit. As scientists who are interested in generalizing about human social behavior, anthropologists must compare human behavior across the boundaries of particular cultures. Most anthropologists agree that comparative analysis is a necessary element of cultural anthropology.

In moving beyond contextual analysis, the comparative or cross-cultural approach parallels the experimental techniques used in the hard sciences such as physics or chemistry. Anthropologists are able to develop hypotheses, control variables, and develop tests to accept or reject hypotheses. Given the vast array of ethnographic data, anthropologists can draw upon these materials to construct and test hypotheses. Other anthropologists can duplicate the testing of these hypotheses. Cross-cultural analysis thus meets one of the basic standards of the scientific method — the ability to test and retest hypotheses.

Controlled Comparison: Witchcraft in Four African Societies

Controlled comparison attempts to retain as much contextual detail as possible while comparing different cultural groups. The cultural groups chosen for controlled comparison share many cultural and social features, but it is the minor differences that are crucial to the analysis. Controlled comparison involves a relatively small number of groups usually drawn from the same region.

S. F. Nadel did fieldwork in four African societies: two in West Africa (Nigeria) and two in East Africa (The Republic of the Sudan). Nadel's fieldwork in these four African societies was the basis for constructing and testing a hypothesis about the significance of witchcraft. The two societies in West Africa, Nupe and

Gwari, shared a number of social and cultural similarities, as did the two societies in East Africa, the Mesakin and the Korongo. Each pair of societies was similar in language, social organization, economic system, and religious beliefs and organization. They had differences in both witchcraft beliefs and practices. Nadel attempted to understand these differences by using the method of controlled comparison. He believed that if he could understand the reasons underlying these differences, he might be able to understand in a more general sense the meaning and function of witchcraft in human society.

The Nupe and Gwari of West Africa believe that some people have the ability to injure or kill other people by supernatural means. Among the Nupe, *only women* are accused of being witches, whereas among the Gwari *both sexes* can be accused.

Why should the Nupe and Gwari, two similar societies, each select a different group to accuse of witchcraft? According to Nadel, tension between men and women in Nupe society explains this difference. Nupe women, unlike Gwari women, operate as petty traders. This economic base allows Nupe women to control greater economic wealth and power than their husbands. At the same time these women have greater opportunities to engage in extramarital affairs; in fact, many women traders operate as part-time prostitutes. Nupe women also avoid having children because they believe it will interfere with their trading activities. None of these circumstances is found in Gwari society. Nupe values, according to Nadel, however, do not support or justify either the dominant economic position of women or promiscuity, prostitution, and abortion. On the other hand, Gwari women do not have the economic or sexual opportunities available to Nupe women and are unable to challenge the culturally accepted economic and sexual dominance of men. Ac-

cording to Nadel, this discrepancy between *what is* and what men *think ought to be* causes tension in Nupe and is the basis for the witchcraft accusations made against Nupe women by Nupe men (Nadel 1952:18–29).

Based on this initial comparison, Nadel derived a *frustration-aggression hypothesis.* This hypothesis states that individuals who believe that their legitimate and culturally supported interests are being frustrated will develop expressions of aggression. An accusation of witchcraft is one form of aggression, from Nadel's point of view. Thus Nupe women, violating the cultural expectations of Nupe society, frustrate the interests and the feelings of Nupe men. Nupe men retaliate by accusing women of being witches. Nadel subsequently extended this frustration-aggression hypothesis to the two cultures he studied in East Africa: the Korongo and the Mesakin.

Although the Korongo and the Mesakin are neighboring societies and share many cultural similarities, a major difference exists between them. The Korongo have no witchcraft beliefs at all, whereas among the Mesakin the fear of witchcraft and witchcraft accusations are widespread. Why does this difference exist, and can the frustration-aggression hypothesis help to explain it?

Nadel found that both of these societies link property rights and the enjoyment of life to their concept of age. One difference between the two societies is their conception of what age means to men. Among the Mesakin men are forced to become "old men" at about the age of 25. Men of this age, therefore, must relinquish all pleasurable behavior such as wrestling, spear throwing, and living an adventurous life guarding the cattle. Among the Korongo men give up these same activities gradually and become "old men" at about the age of fifty.

These general patterns, however, are acted out between particular individuals. In both of these societies males inherit property from their mother's brother(s). A man usually requests a portion of his inheritance before the death of his mother's brother, and such a request is a clear signal of the increasing age of the "older man."

Among the Mesakin such requests can be made when the mother's brother is in his middle twenties. He is supposed to turn all his property over to his nephew at that time. He loses control over his cattle, which are not only valued goods, but also the basis of the Mesakin way of life. If a man loses his cattle and property, he relinquishes his power and prestige and becomes an "old man." Refusal to hand over property and power to nephews is interpreted by the nephews as a denial of their manhood. The contradictory demands of Mesakin life thus produce tension and conflict within the system. A result is the widespread fear and accusations of witchcraft between a nephew and his mother's brother in Mesakin society.

Although the Korongo have a similar pattern, its impact is spread out over a period of 25 years. A man is not expected to relinquish everything at once and thus be thrust abruptly into old age. The demands of Korongo society do not produce tension and conflict between nephews and their mother's brothers. According to Nadel's hypothesis, the legitimate behavior of one person does not frustrate the legitimate interests of another person. Nadel concludes that his data support a frustration-aggression hypothesis for witchcraft accusations.

Statistical Comparison: Witchcraft in Fifty Societies

An advantage of controlled comparison is the use of context for the analysis. Nadel places his discussion of witchcraft within the fabric of social life in each of the four societies. Two problems develop from the controlled comparison

approach, however. First, we can ask how representative of *all* societies are the few societies selected, and second, how far can we generalize from such a small sample?

These problems have led to the development of large-scale *statistical comparison* and analysis in anthropology. Large-scale cross-cultural comparisons go back to the origins of anthropology. In the middle of the nineteenth century both Lewis H. Morgan and Edward B. Tylor based their reconstructions of the evolution of human culture on a sample of more than 300 societies.

About forty years ago systematic cross-cultural comparison was stimulated by the development of the *Human Relations Area Files*, or *HRAF*. Led by George P. Murdock, a number of anthropologists at Yale University developed a classification scheme *(Outline of Cultural Materials, OCM)* that is used as the basis for organizing material in HRAF. OCM is a classification system for ethnographic data consisting of more than 800 cultural categories and definitions. All the relevant data for a single culture are gathered and coded in OCM categories. Over 1000 societies have been classified in this way.

At its inception HRAF was organized as an alternative to tedious library research. Relevant ethnographic data are selected for each culture chosen, ranging from full-length ethnographies to shorter descriptive articles. Each selected source is coded according to the OCM outline and is reprinted on file slips. Each coded file slip is then placed in its proper place in the file, which means that a single file category, for a single society, contains all the information on that file topic from all the sources selected.

Today HRAF is an enormous data bank easily accessible to anthropologists interested in doing large-scale statistical cross-cultural comparison. In recent years HRAF data have been computerized. For a cross-cultural researcher, anthropological data for over a thousand societies are available from a computer terminal, thus making large-scale statistical research a reality.

Some anthropologists have been critical of HRAF and its use. They argue that *cross-cultural statistical* comparison results in a lack of context. Critics claim that the researcher who selects a large number of societies for statistical cross-cultural comparison will probably be unfamiliar with most of them and therefore will lack the special sense of cultural understanding gained during fieldwork. Classifying material under OCM topic headings also removes material from its particular cultural context. Critics argue that cultural activity that has

meaning in terms of a specific culture now derives meaning from a category definition.

Despite these criticisms many valuable studies have been based on information from the HRAF data bank. One of the earliest studies was done by Beatrice Whiting, who selected fifty societies to test a hypothesis based on her study of the Paiute Indians of Nevada (1950).

Whiting discovered that among the Paiute, individuals who deviate from approved behavioral norms are often accused of being witches. She developed the hypothesis that in societies like the Paiute, which lack centralized political means of controlling behavior, witchcraft accusations serve as an alternative means of control. In order to test her hypothesis about the purpose of witchcraft, she selected a sample of fifty societies. Half of them lacked centralized authority, whereas the other half had some form of central authority. The two groups were then compared on the basis of the importance of

---

Witchcraft beliefs vary according to society and period. For most Americans the Wicked Witch of the West illustrates how witches look and act. In present day America there are a large number of practicing witches, some of whom present themselves in the traditional form.

Witchcraft and political authority		
	Witchcraft important	*Witchcraft unimportant*
No central authority	24	1
Central authority	11	14

(Source: Revised from Whiting 1950: 85)

witchcraft in the society. A much higher percentage of societies with *no centralized authority* were also societies in which *witchcraft was an important social phenomenon.* She also found that witchcraft occurred in some societies with centralized political authority. The data, however, were analyzed statistically to show that the probabilities of such a relationship between witchcraft and the lack of centralized authority could not have occurred as a result of chance. This statistical analysis tended to support her hypothesis about the social control purpose of witchcraft.

The Anthropological Framework: Basic Concepts

An anthropologist requires tools for describing human behavior in a simplified fashion. We call these tools concepts — abstractions from concrete reality. Terms such as clan, witchcraft, centralized political authority, and oblique social protest are concepts. Concepts are, however, more than shorthand ways of describing reality. They become the basis of analysis and theory building in cultural anthropology as they do in every other discipline (Pelto 1970:10–11). Clarity of concepts is a fundamental requirement for the development of analysis and interpretation. Many of the controversies that develop between anthropologists are about the meaning and definition of concepts.

Although not all anthropologists agree completely about the exact meaning of the concepts used in the discipline, certain concepts in anthropology are basic to an understanding of what anthropologists do. Among these concepts are: ethnocentrism, cultural relativism, status, role, norm, culture, and society.

Ethnocentrism and Cultural Relativism

Unlike many other disciplines that trace their roots to the ancient Greeks, cultural anthropology is more a child of the European Age of Discovery and Age of the Enlightenment (fifteenth to seventeenth centuries). The ancient Greeks and Romans, aware of diverse peoples on their borders, considered themselves superior to these people, whom they called barbarians. Distinguishing themselves as "civilized" people and all others as "barbarians" is an indication of their *ethnocentrism* (Honigman 1976).

Ethnocentrism is the belief that one's own way of life or culture is both superior to that of others and the most normal way of living for all human beings. An ethnocentric attitude is also based on the assumption that a person's own culture can be used as a basis for measuring and evaluating behavior in other cultures. Thus the American practice of monogamy (marriage of one man to one woman) is assumed by many Americans to be the best and most normal form of marriage. Other forms of marriage may be evaluated as inferior, abnormal, savage, weird, strange, or immoral. When Eugene Cohen described the dating practices of American girls to older women in the Italian village he studied, all of these women were shocked and commented that American girls are like prostitutes. If ethnocentrism is pervasive, no fieldwork can be pursued effectively because the fieldworker's belief in the superiority of his or her own culture would prejudice the perception of other peoples and their cultures.

With the discovery of non-Western people

Bare bosoms were acceptable in traditional Samoan culture, but the Christian missionaries in Samoa equated nakedness with sinfulness. Based on this ethnocentric view, they insisted that converts wear proper European dress. These two Samoan girls — properly clothed — attended the mission school.

in the 1500s, a new view of other people emerged. Many prominent Europeans felt that Europe had much to learn from the non-Western peoples they had contacted. Instead of the concept of the "barbarian," by the mid-eighteenth century some European intellectuals had developed the idea of the "noble savage." This concept interpreted the behavior and customs of non-Western tribal peoples as admirable and even instructive in comparison to the "fettered and overcivilized" humanity of Europe.

Despite this favorable attitude, many other Europeans remained ethnocentric in their attitude toward tribal customs. A British army officer who served in West Africa in the nineteenth century was asked about the manners and customs of the people living there. His answer, "manners none, customs filthy," is a prime example of ethnocentrism.

Ethnocentrism is not a Western monopoly; it is characteristic of much of humanity. Every group appears to assume its superiority over others. An example of non-Western ethnocentrism is found in the novelist Aubrey Menen's account of his Nayar [India] grandmother's view of the "dirty English."

She had never met the English but she knew all about them. She knew they were tall, fair, given to strong drink, good soldiers and that they had conquered her native country. She also knew that they were incurably dirty in their personal habits. She respected them but wished they would keep their distance. It was very much the way that a Roman matron looked upon the Goths.

My eldest uncle had been to England for

two years and he spoke up for the English. He said that while the Hindus were undoubtedly the most civilized race on earth and had been civilized a thousand years before the English, nevertheless, the English were now the masters of the Hindus.

Her chief complaint was that the English were so dirty. When my grandmother asked if, like decent people, they took a minimum of two baths a day, my uncle, who could not lie to his mother without committing a disgraceful sin, said that, well no: but a few took one bath and the habit was spreading. He could go no further than that. But he added that my grandmother should remember that England had a cold climate. This she loyally did, and when she discussed the matter with me, she was able to treat the matter lightly, as one does the disgusting but rational liking of the Eskimos for eating blubber.

As for the question of eating, she did not have the expected prejudices. She did not think it strange that the English ate ham and beef. The outcaste hill-tribes who made the family straw mats and cleaned the latrines ate anything. She was not disturbed, either, about their religion, because my uncle assured her that they had practically none. Their manners, however, she abominated. If she did not mind them eating meat, she considered their way of eating it beyond the pale of decent society. In my family home, each person eats his meal separately, preferably in a secluded corner. The thought that English people could sit opposite each other and watch each other thrust food into their mouths, masticate, and swallow it, made her wonder if there was anything that human beings would not do, when left to their own devices.

She deplored the plumbing of every other nation but her own. She would often say to me, "Never take a bath in one of those contraptions in which you sit in dirty water like a buffalo. Always bathe in running water. If you have servants to pour it over you, that's best. But otherwise you must stand under a tap or pour water over yourself. A really nice person does not even glance at his own bath water, much less

sit in it." Here she would laugh to herself, while my uncle translated; not an unkind laugh, but a pitying one, as she thought of the backwardness of the white man's bathroom (Menen 1953:26–28, 32–33).

Today some anthropologists suggest that ethnocentrism has beneficial consequences, particularly for groups that have been traditionally oppressed and powerless. Ethnocentrism is viewed as one basis for social cohesion and group pride. Menen's account of his grandmother's view of the English can be seen as one means of maintaining the integrity of Nayar Indian culture under colonial rule. This consequence of ethnocentrism has been recognized for some time. Anthropologists recognize that the integrity of Zuni culture (southwestern United States) rested upon the Zunis' suspicion, dislike, and negative view of white culture. Ethnocentrism is probably normal for all people. When growing up individuals not only learn the customs of their culture, but also see them as normal and even superior to the practices of other cultures.

Modern cultural anthropology denies the validity of ethnocentrism, which establishes one form of behavior as a universal standard for normality. Fundamental to contemporary cultural anthropology is *cultural relativism.* The cultural relativist approach states that every culture must be understood in terms of *that* culture, which means that there are no better cultures or worse cultures, only different ones.

Cultural relativism is not a moral position or philosophical justification for any kind of behavior. Relativism is a basic position necessary for the development of cultural anthropology. A relativist approach allows us to understand why a particular behavior occurs in a society, even if it offends our own sense of morality.

We can see an example of relativism in studies of Eskimo life, in which female infanticide (the killing of female infants) used to be practiced. A relativist position forces the anthropologist to look at the total system of Eskimo society and culture in order to understand this custom. One contextual explanation relates the practice of infanticide to the scarcity of food in the Arctic. Infanticide is a mechanism of population control guaranteeing that the population does not outrun the food supply. Such understanding does not imply approval. Relativism does not mean that anthropologists discard their own set of cultural or moral values, but rather merely suspend their use as a basis of evaluative and scientific judgments.

Role and Status

Although ethnocentrism and relativism are basic concepts related to the practice of anthropology, concepts such as role and status are shared with other social sciences. A *role* is a set of behavioral expectations that goes along with a particular position in a society. The position is usually referred to as a *status.* Comprehension of the ideas of role and status is the first step in understanding the reality of human behavior. Each field account in Chapter 1 involves the concept of role. There are a variety of roles played by the anthropologist and by the people themselves. In the course of daily social life everyone plays a multitude of social roles.

Let us begin with a set of simple positions or statuses. Being female, or an uncle, working as a bartender, or being seventeen years old are positions or statuses in American society, and each is associated with a set of expected behaviors or roles. When we play these roles we are expected to act in particular ways. To a great extent, growing up in any society consists in learning the roles and their appropriate behaviors.

Being an anthropologist in the field is like growing up. In this situation growing up in another society is learning and understanding the roles of another culture, which is not always an easy task. The problem is that the same status

or position may be found in many societies, although the roles or behavioral expectations may be very different. This is evident in the account by Jean Briggs. She found that the behavioral expectations (role) of a daughter, a status found in both Eskimo and American cultures, were not the same.

Another approach to understanding the meaning of role is to look at the rights and obligations linked to a status in society. This idea of rights and duties is clearly seen in Hart's relationship to his Tiwi "mother." Other Tiwi men, in asking Hart's permission to cover up his mother, were recognizing that as her son and as a member of her clan (his status) he had a right to take part in this decision. He had a role to play. Mariano, a Tiwi, *but of a different clan,* had no such right and was told that it was none of his business.

This idea of appropriate role behavior and rights and obligations is illustrated in the way that Tiwi men wanted to know Hart's clan, age, and marital status. These factors were significant dimensions of a man's position for the Tiwi, and had to be known before they could figure out how to behave toward him. Americans act exactly the same way. Aside from the obvious clues we immediately observe when we meet someone for the first time, most of us try to find out what a person does for a living, which defines that person's status position. Once the status is known, we are reasonably good anthropologists in figuring out what kind of person we are dealing with and what role behaviors are appropriate. For the Tiwi all men must have clans; for Americans all persons must have an occupation.

In Nadel's analysis of witchcraft he does not focus on individuals, but rather on the roles of Nupe "men" and "women" and of Mesakin and Korongo "nephews" and "uncles." In his analysis he refers to the appropriate ways that individuals with these statuses are expected to behave. Nadel claims that the inconsistency and the contradictions involved in role playing generate witchcraft accusations.

By using the concept of role, an anthropologist can go beyond the unique and idiosyncratic behavior of individuals in a society. Role and status are organizing concepts that emphasize shared patterns of behavior.

Another dimension of status is the degree to which it is *achieved* or *ascribed*. An *achieved status* is earned through individual effort. An *ascribed status* is acquired through birth or through a natural process, such as aging. In Gluckman's analysis, the two key statuses — Zulu and European — are ascribed statuses. The Chief Native Commissioner, for example, knew both Zulu customs and language, but no Zulu would mistake him for another Zulu.

The distinction between achieved and ascribed statuses is more important than merely characterizing societies by how status is conferred. Because so much of human behavior revolves around status and status relationships, understanding how statuses are obtained gives us an appreciation of the processes of a society. Americans pride themselves on being an achievement-oriented society. Our folklore about men born in log cabins who become president is one aspect of how we think about achievement in our own society. Some statuses in American society are based upon ascription, however, although we may fail to recognize this fact. We have laws regulating drinking, driving, and voting that are based solely on age. In some societies, such as India, ascribed occupational statuses (barber, priest, leather worker) are openly recognized. In twentieth-century America, ascribed statuses strike us as being unfair and undemocratic, and therefore they are not openly recognized.

The investiture of Prince Charles as Prince of Wales is an example of a status ascribed by birth and inheritance. The graduate from college is an example of status achieved through individual merit and effort.

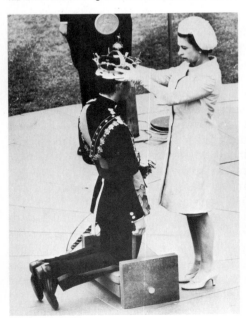

As new occupations develop positions are often filled on the basis of achievement. Over time, however, these positions develop aspects of ascription; that is, birth and parents become more and more crucial in obtaining these statuses. We can see this development on a small scale in the Hollywood film industry. When the film industry first developed, talent and achievement were important considerations, although it is certainly true that Black Americans did not have the same opportunities for stardom as whites. Today, however, a list of well-known Hollywood stars would include the sons and daughters of the previous generation of film stars. Do they really have more talent and merit than outsiders, or do they have occupational advantages derived from their accident of birth, not shared by the rest of us?

Norms

Norms are rules that define and regulate behavior. They indicate what should and should not be done and what must and must not be done. Norms set standards and define proper and improper role behavior.

Determining norms is one of the most fundamental tasks of the cultural anthropologist. The fieldworker faced by strange and unfamiliar behavior has to determine which behavior is idiosyncratic and which is based on norms.

When Eugene Cohen was doing his Italian village study, he noted that a family living across the street from him did not speak to him while he was in the community. He did not know whether their failure to greet him was the result of something he had done, whether they were just strange and unfriendly people, or whether another reason accounted for their behavior. He later discovered that in this community people who have had a dispute with someone avoid the company of the other person and no longer speak to each other. He was living with a family that had had a dispute with the family across the street, and they were merely follow-

ing the general norms for the situation. Because he did not initially recognize this norm, Cohen caused the family some embarrassment by trying to initiate conversations with them. He was, in fact, engaging in improper role behavior.

Another difficulty in determining norms is that in response to questions from the anthropologist, informants may state a general rule regarding how things *ought* to be done even though very few people may actually follow such a norm in their behavior. At the same time we must recognize that people violate rules, and that rules and behavior change over time. Finally, an anthropologist may observe a pattern of behavior, a rule, that is not always recognized or verbalized by the people being studied.

Cohen was told often that the ideal pattern in the village he studied was for a girl to move into the household of her husband's family after marriage. By checking actual household records, he discovered that only a minute percentage of households were organized in this fashion. He also found, by comparing past and present marriages, that older people preferred to marry someone who had grown up with them in the community, whereas younger people wanted to marry someone from outside the community. Here we have an example of rules that are changing. It was also clearly observable that women did not go to the village cafe. When Cohen asked if women were not allowed to go into the bar, everyone laughed and stated that if they wanted to, women could go to the bar, but that they just did not want to do that. Although it was not a formally recognized norm, female avoidance of bars was an informal norm of this community.

Society and Culture

Society as used by many anthropologists refers to a group of people living in a defined territory, speaking a common language, and having a common identity. Another related definition of society is that it consists of an organized system of roles and statuses. For the latter definition, neither a common language nor a common identity is an essential element. Gluckman, for example, conceived of South Africa as a society in which various cultural and linguistic groups were linked together by social relationships. Thus in South Africa the various tribal groups, varied European groups, and other ethnic groups were linked together in an organized political and economic system.

British anthropology, more than American anthropology, focuses on the analysis of society and social relations. As a result of the emphasis on society and social relationships, British anthropology is called *social anthropology.* A. R. Radcliffe-Brown, who was a major figure in British anthropology, referred to social anthropology as comparative sociology that had as its goal the study of the organization of society.

In traditional anthropology when tribal groups can be studied as distinct and well-defined units, the first definition of society as a distinct group is useful. Thus anthropologists speak about Tiwi society, Navajo society, and Lesu society, all of which are characterized by a common language, a defined territory, and a common identity. As anthropologists began to study more complexly organized groups and to recognize the importance of larger political units, the definition of society as an organized system of statuses and roles became more useful. This is especially true for complex political and economic systems, characterized by occupational, language, cultural, and social class differences.

In contrast to British social anthropology the concept of culture is emphasized in American anthropology, and most American anthropologists refer to themselves as *cultural anthropologists.* At the beginning of this chapter we introduced a general definition of culture as the way of life of a particular group of people, but there are other definitions of culture that many anthropologists find useful.

Some definitions emphasize the normative characteristics of culture. This approach stresses the idea that culture operates as a set of rules regulating and guiding behavior. In this definition culture is a design for living (Kluckhohn and Kelly 1945:97).

In contrast to definitions of culture that relate it to particular groups, anthropologists also define culture as a distinctly human quality. In this usage culture does not refer to a specific pattern of culture or way of life, but rather to the capacity of the human species to invent different ways of life to solve the problems of human survival. The earliest systematic definition of culture, offered by Edward B. Tylor in the nineteenth century, stressed the idea that culture is *acquired* by a person as a member of society. This definition of culture, as well as all subsequent definitions, recognizes the social rather than the biological roots of culture. According to this position, which is fundamental to cultural anthropology, the cultures of particular groups and their distinctive ways of life cannot be explained on the basis of the biological makeup of the population. In cultural anthropology the biological uniformity or similarity of humanity is stressed, instead of the differences.

The recognition of this position leads to the fundamental anthropological problem: how can we explain the diversity of human culture in the face of human biological uniformity? One possible answer to this question is that culture is humanity's basis for survival. Culture is an adaptive mechanism, and the different cultures of the world may represent cultural solutions to varied environmental conditions. For many anthropologists this adaptive nature of culture is a vital characteristic.

Problems of Conceptual Meaning

This text defines the major concepts in cultural anthropology in a simplified manner. It avoids some of the controversies of definition and meaning. Concepts are abstractions from reality, and the reality observed by anthropologists is much more complex than the simplified conceptual vocabulary used in anthropology. Conceptual meaning is a problem in all scientific disciplines. For the anthropologist it becomes a more difficult problem because of the tremendous diversity of human behavior.

The terms tribe and society as used by anthropologists remain fuzzy, ill-defined, and controversial concepts. This problem of meaning can be illustrated in the work of Evans-Pritchard and Southall. In the view of Evans-Pritchard there were in the Sudan two distinct tribal societies, Nuer and Dinka. Southall questions this assumption and looks at the categories of Nuer and Dinka as fluid and changing labels. Anthropologists continue to be uncertain about the reality that the term tribe supposedly describes.

A further example of the problem of meaning can be illustrated by examining the *couvade*.

The couvade. An unusual behavioral pattern associated with childbirth and reported for a number of different societies attracted particular attention in the nineteenth century. This was the couvade. At the birth of a child the father is treated as if he had given birth. In some instances he even imitates the birth process itself. Usually the man rests, avoiding hard or hazardous labor, and is given special foods and considerable attention after the birth of his child. The following excerpt describes this custom as practiced by the Witoto Indians of South America.

> The mother presents the newborn child to the father and on the following day resumes her usual labors in the fields, returning only at night to suckle the infant. The father, however, rests for a week or more in his hammock, observing certain dietary regulations and receiving congratulatory visits from his friends. His couvade — as this simulation by the father of the

mother's rôle in childbed is called — endures until the infant's navel has healed, during which time he must not eat meat, hunt, or even touch his weapons (Murdock 1934:464).

Allan Holmberg in his work with the Siriono of Bolivia notes that these people had special customs surrounding childbirth. He describes them as follows:

> For about three days following childbirth the Siriono family undergoes a series of observances and rites which we may loosely term the couvade. These rites are designed to protect the life of the infant and to ensure its good health. [The parents] are restricted in various ways. Except for satisfying the calls of nature they do not move outside the house. They stay close to their hammocks, and are subject to a number of food taboos. Neither jaguar nor coati [a tropical forest mammal similar to a racoon] is eaten lest the infant break out with sores all over its body; paca [a tropical forest rodent] cannot be eaten or the infant may lose its hair; papaya cannot be eaten lest the infant become a victim of diarrhea.
>
> More important than the abstinence from certain foods is the carrying out of certain other practices that must follow the birth of every baby. On the day after the birth both parents are scarified on the upper and lower legs with the eyetooth of a rat or a squirrel. Usually the father is scratched first. He stands by his hammock during the operation. The person doing the scarifying squats down and makes long scratches on the outside of the upper legs from the hips to the knees and on the back and outside of the lower legs from the knees to the ankles. The mother then undergoes the same operation, usually at the hands of her husband.
>
> The parents stay close to their hammocks on the day following the birth, the father resting and the mother attending the infant. They do little cooking themselves but are fed by other members of the extended family (Holmberg 1969:180–181).

What Holmberg calls a Siriono couvade differs in a number of significant aspects from

Among the Waiwai tribe (Guiana, S. America) a father cares for his child while his wife continues her household work preparing cassava. As part of the couvade, this man is not permitted to hunt.

the traditional definition of this custom. The Siriono include the mother in the childbirth rites and apparently do not treat the father as if he had given birth to the child. There is no hint of imitation in his behavior.

More recently Harriet Kupferer (1965:99–102), in a review of the uses of the term couvade, notes that it is being used very loosely to describe many different forms of behavior associated with pregnancy and birth. She feels that this wide usage is reducing the usefulness of the concept to describe a particular pattern of behavior. She suggests that a distinction should be made between imitative behavior by the male that is only role playing and behavior based upon genuine psychosomatic illness in which the father actually feels the pains of the birth process. For Kupferer, the key element in the couvade is the fact that the imitative behavior performed by the man is part of a socially acceptable role he plays. What Kupferer has done, in effect, is to single out a particular ele-

ment in the couvade, imitation, and subdivide it into two types: role playing and real illness.

In addition, the couvade may have very different meanings for participants (insiders) and observers (outsiders). This distinction between the insider and outsider view of behavior is an important idea in contemporary anthropology. Anthropologists refer to it as the *emic* (insider) versus the *etic* (outsider) point of view. Holmberg gives us two different interpretations of the Siriono couvade. He reports that the Siriono firmly believe that without these observances and taboos, the infant's life and health would be threatened. He advances his own argument, however, that the couvade establishes and defines the social ideas of fatherhood and motherhood. The first interpretation, drawn from the Siriono, is an *emic* definition of the couvade. The second definition, Holmberg's interpretation, is an *etic* definition of the couvade.

To complicate this description, there are different etic and emic interpretations of the couvade. Nineteenth-century anthropologists interpreted the couvade as a reflection of the shift from a female-dominated society *(matriarchy)* to a male-dominated society *(patriarchy)*. Holmberg's etic interpretation, in contrast, identifies the socially beneficial purposes of the couvade, that is, the contribution it makes to the maintenance of Siriono culture. Other etic interpretations might focus upon food taboos associated with pregnancy and childbirth and suggest that they are mechanisms for distributing important food resources within the society. Anthropologists influenced by psychological and psychoanalytic theory could interpret the couvade in terms of sexual identity: males envious of females taking this opportunity to play out their fantasies and unconscious wishes.

If outsider interpretations differ, so do emic, or insider, interpretations. Evidence for this position can be found in Holmberg's account of a man who refused to participate in the Siriono couvade. His motivation was not to threaten the well-being of the child, and, in fact, he cut the child's umbilical cord, another part of the Siriono couvade, in order to prevent the infant's death. His refusal to participate in the other parts of the couvade ritual was directed at the mother of the child. As Holmberg writes, "He [Eoka, the man involved] repeatedly told me that he had divorced this woman and that he would have nothing more to do with her" (1969:187). We could conclude from this statement that in Eoka's view, which was an emic perception, participation in the couvade legitimizes a relationship to a woman rather than protecting the newly born infant.

The couvade illustrates some of the difficulties faced by anthropologists in their conceptual formulations. A cross-cultural perspective introduces the difficulty of defining the behavioral context of a concept. The meaning of behavior, as well as different emic and etic views, also poses difficulties in clearly defining anthropological concepts.

Anthropological Theory

Over the years anthropologists have developed different and often competing theories designed to explain the fundamental nature of culture, society, and human behavior. It is necessary to understand these theoretical approaches in order to comprehend what anthropology is all about. The differences among theories often reveal the fundamental premises of anthropological thinking. Theoretical formulations may be stated as high-level abstractions and are frequently difficult to comprehend. We will attempt, therefore, to convey the essential principles of various anthropological theories by focusing on a single complex of behavior, the incest taboo.

The Meaning of Theory

A theory consists of a number of principles, concepts, and generalizations designed to organize and explain the multitudinous findings of research. Every scientific discipline contains a body of knowledge obtained by various research methods. In cultural anthropology the basic research method is fieldwork. Beyond the research data gathered from fieldwork are hypotheses, concepts, and generalizations. Both Nadel and Whiting offer alternative hypotheses about witchcraft; however, these are hypotheses, not theories. A fully developed anthropological theory has to explain an entire range of human behavior and identify fundamental processes in culture, society, and behavior.

In addition to integrating research findings, theory can point us in the direction of new research that will either sustain or alter the basic propositions of the original theory. Because theory ultimately rests upon research findings, further research usually requires the alteration or replacement of existing theory.

We can illustrate the corrective influence of research on theory with the work of Malinowski and Gluckman. Malinowski is generally recognized as a major figure in a theoretical approach called *functionalism.* A principle of his brand of functionalism is that the parts of a culture are not only related, but are also well integrated into a consistent cultural system. A consequence of Gluckman's work with the Zulu of South Africa was the recognition that societies are in fact characterized by internal conflict and inconsistency. Gluckman's study as well as many others has forced anthropologists to abandon Malinowski's initial formulation about the well-integrated nature of human society. This is only one example of how research alters or replaces theoretical formulations.

The Incest Taboo: Variety in Explanation

Many anthropologists consider the incest taboo a universal norm found in every human society. Although recent data on brother-sister marriage in ancient Egypt (Hopkins 1980:303–354) have led some anthropologists to question the universality of the incest taboo, the majority of anthropological theoreticians assume its critical importance in the development of human culture. For this reason, theories of culture and society attempt to explain the incest taboo, and the explanations become a convenient device for presenting the key principles of particular theoretical systems in anthropology.

Most anthropologists define the *incest taboo* as the prohibition of sexual relations between designated relatives, but it must be remembered that incest prohibitions and marriage prohibitions are different. In India marriages are not supposed to occur between individuals from different castes, and in the United States, there used to be laws prohibiting interracial marriages. These restrictions are not incest prohibitions.

The anthropological definition is broad and relatively nonspecific. The reason why this definition is so broad is that incest prohibitions are applied to a wide and varied range of relatives in different societies. In its most universal form,

however, the incest taboo applies to three potential sexual relationships: mother and son, father and daughter, brother and sister.

Evolutionary theory. The theory of evolution as applied to the origin and development of societies and social institutions was first developed in the middle of the nineteenth century. Nineteenth-century evolutionary theory was an attempt to understand worldwide cultural diversity in terms of history, time, and development. An underlying assumption of this theory was the rationality of humanity and belief in the progressive development of human culture. An eminent American evolutionary anthropologist, Lewis H. Morgan, argued that human society had developed through a series of three fixed stages, from savagery to barbarism to civilization. Important evolutionary theorists in England such as Sir James Frazier and Edward B. Tylor wrote books that traced the progressive evolution of human institutions.

Cultural evolutionists of the nineteenth century sought to explain the diversity of human culture known to them at the time without using a theory of inherent biological differences. They recognized the diversity of human culture and classified this diversity in terms of evolutionary stages. The theories were, however, unclear as to why particular cultures had not attained a higher stage of cultural development. To account for this difference in cultural attainment, they retreated, on occasion, to vague arguments about racial differences in mental and cultural capacity (Harris 1968:129–130, 137–141).

The most famous and influential approach to the interpretation of the incest taboo according to evolutionary theory is in the work of Edward B. Tylor. He concluded that the incest taboo, by forcing marriage *outside* of the familial unit, provides the basis of alliances between otherwise separate and potentially hostile groups. Alliances based upon marriage have survival advantages. Tylor's interpretation was summed up in his famous and often-quoted aphorism, "Marry out or be killed out" (1889:267). The incest taboo thus becomes the essential ingredient for converting isolated groups into a society. For Tylor and other evolutionists the incest taboo is the invention of society; they consider it an innovation that drove the machine of human cultural progress.

A twentieth-century cultural evolutionist, Leslie White, shares this view. The following quotation from his work is a clear presentation of the role of the incest taboo as the basis of human society and cultural evolution.

> Cooperation between families cannot be established if parent marries child; and brother, sister. A way must be found to overcome the centripetal tendency with a centrifugal force. This way was found in the definition and prohibition of incest. If persons were forbidden to marry their parents or siblings they would be compelled to marry into some other family group — or remain celibate, which is contrary to the nature of primates. The leap was taken; a way was found to unite families with one another, and social evolution as a human affair was launched upon its career. It would be difficult to exaggerate the significance of this step. Unless some way had been found to establish strong and enduring social ties between families, social evolution could have gone no farther on the human level than among the anthropoids (White 1949:316).

A growing recognition of the limitations and inadequacies of nineteenth-century evolutionary theory developed between 1890 and 1910. As a theory it lost support among almost all anthropologists and its rejection appeared both complete and final. By the 1940s and the 1950s, however, new varieties of evolutionary theory appeared. Although these theories share a number of basic orientations with evolutionary theory of the nineteenth century, there are significant differences. Modern evolutionary theories in cultural anthropology are much more restricted and limited in what they try to explain. One variety of *modern evolutionary theory* (general evolution) is primarily concerned with the evolution of political and economic institutions over time. Adherents of *multilinear evolutionary theory,* on the other hand, have primarily concerned themselves with explaining the emergence and similarity of cultural developments in comparable world regions.

Unlike nineteenth-century evolutionary theorists, modern evolutionary theorists emphasize environmental conditions and make greater use of accurate ethnographic data. Contemporary evolutionary theorists reject the simplistic idea of progress and fuzzy notions about racial differences that were part of nineteenth-century theorizing. They do, however, share the essential principles of cultural evolution that development takes place in sequential stages characterized by a growth of culture from simple to complex.

Julian Steward, founder of the multilinear evolutionary approach (1955) using primarily archaeological data, compared stages of cultural growth in the centers of civilization in the New World (the Americas) and in the Old World (Europe, Asia, and Africa). He concluded that the movement toward civilization in these separate regions proceeded along the same evolutionary lines, from rural village to urban center and from simple band to complex civilization.

General evolutionists have attempted to establish sequences of development, or laws of cultural growth, particularly for politics and economics. In economics they trace cultural development from subsistence patterns based upon hunting and gathering to the large-scale production of food and goods (see Chapter 3). In politics the origin of the state, an organized political entity, is seen as marking a fundamental shift in the evolution of political forms (see Chapter 7).

For much of the Western World Leviticus in the Old Testament defines those kin who fall under the ban of the incest Taboo. Although other cultures may define kin differently, the core relationships—mother and son, father and daughter—are universally taboo.

6 No man shall approach a blood-relation for intercourse. I am the LORD.
7 You shall not bring shame on your father by intercourse with your mother:
8 she is your mother; you shall not bring shame upon her. You shall not have intercourse with your father's wife: that is to bring shame upon your father.
9 You shall not have intercourse with your sister, your father's daughter, or your mother's daughter, whether brought up in the family or in another home; you shall not bring shame upon them. You shall not have inter-
10 course with your son's daughter or your daughter's daughter: that is to bring shame upon yourself. You shall not have intercourse with a daughter
11 of your father's wife, begotten by your father: she is your sister, and you shall not bring shame upon her. You shall not have intercourse with your
12 father's sister: she is a blood-relation of your father. You shall not have
13 intercourse with your mother's sister: she is a blood-relation of your mother. You shall not bring shame upon your father's brother by approach-
14 ing his wife: she is your aunt. You shall not have intercourse with your
15 daughter-in-law: she is your son's wife; you shall not bring shame upon her.

Tráſla.Grc.lrr.cū interp.latina.

Tráſla.B.Piero:

Ʒer.Heb.   Leui.   Ca.xviij.Priīua.heb.

Functional theory. A very different attempt to explain society and culture is found in the variety of theories termed *functionalist.* Unlike evolutionists who are concerned with discovering *laws of cultural growth and development,* functionalists are primarily concerned with explaining the *laws of cultural maintenance and continuity.* Where the evolutionists try to explain the perplexing diversity of cultures, the functionalists merely accept cultural diversity as a given quality of social reality. This perspective of functional theory led to its basically nonhistorical bias.

Bronislaw Malinowski, one of the founders of functional theory, provided an interpretation of the incest taboo that stressed its functional role in the maintenance of society.

> In any type of civilization in which custom, morals, and law would allow incest, the family could not continue to exist. At maturity we would witness the breaking up of the family, hence complete social chaos and an impossibility of continuing cultural tradition. Incest would mean the upsetting of age distinctions, the mixing up of generations, the disorganization of sentiments and a violent exchange of roles at a time when the family is the most important educational medium. No society could exist under such conditions. The alternative type of culture under which incest is excluded, is the only one consistent with the existence of social organization and culture (Malinowski 1927:251).

Malinowski states two major points: The family is a basic human social institution that the incest taboo preserves; and if no incest taboo existed roles within the family would be confused and lead to social disruption and disintegration. Although Leslie White's explanation of the incest taboo bears a superficial resemblance to that of Malinowski, the two interpretations are vastly different. For White the existence of the incest taboo forces *alliances* between existing families and thus promotes

cultural growth. For Malinowski the existence of the incest taboo permits the *existence* of the family and hence of society.

Malinowski's interpretation of the incest taboo is extended by functional theorists to society and culture at large. Functional theorists select a given item of culture or society and relate it to the larger cultural and social system. The underlying premise is that the functional purpose of social and cultural activities is the *maintenance* and *survival* of both the social system and the human beings living in the system. Functional theory is more concerned with the interrelations within a culture or society at a specific time, rather than with historical changes or cultural origins.

At present functional theory has fallen into disfavor among many anthropologists. In attempting to understand how societies maintain themselves, functionalists often found themselves trapped in a difficult theoretical position. Functional analysts often appeared to be arguing that everything that existed in a culture served a necessary and required purpose, and the result was a theoretical image of society as a coherent and consistent system. Overemphasis on social coherence and consistency made the study and understanding of social and cultural change difficult, if not impossible, from a functionalist perspective. The key principles of functionalism were unable to encompass the reality that societies are neither coherent nor static.

Ecological theory. *Ecological theory* assumes that human beings, their cultural system, and the entire physical environment exist as a single *ecosystem.* But it does not mean that the physical environment (climate, terrain, and existing animal and plant life) is the single most powerful determinant of human behavior. Rather, an ecological approach stresses the interplay, mutual intersection, and feedback of the many components (human, cultural, environmental) in the total system. Ecologically oriented anthropologists tend to emphasize the part of culture that provides the material basis for human sustenance. Other aspects of culture and society are seen as responding to these basic requirements, but they in turn also have an impact upon these fundamental aspects of human existence.

In 1959 Mariam Slater offered an ecologically oriented explanation for the origin of the incest taboo (1959:1042–1059). Her argument is based on the hypothesis that early human societies, equipped with a simple technology, were limited in food production. The consequences of this simple technological system were reflected in birth rates, death rates, life expectancies, and the intervals between births. She argues that the culmination of these demographic factors led to a situation in which potential sexual and marital partners within the nuclear family *were not available.* Thus incest could not occur. Mothers and sons, fathers and daughters, and even brothers and sisters would be so far removed in age that they would not be suitable mates. In addition, because of low life expectancies parents would die before their children reached sexual maturity. She concludes that the incest taboo operated without a cultural statement of the taboo. As technology improved the demographic constraints upon incest were removed. She contends, however, that other aspects of the culture had by now become enmeshed in this pattern of nonfamilial matings, and this new pattern became the basis for establishing the incest taboo as a cultural pattern and norm. What had been an ecologically based pattern of behavior (nonoccurrence of incest) was now transformed into a culturally defined and based pattern of behavior, the incest taboo.

Ecological theory in anthropology begins with the premise that certain material conditions of life must be met if human beings are to survive. Marvin Harris, a major figure in eco-

logical theory, says that "reproductive pressure, intensification [greater food production], and environmental depletion would appear to provide the key for understanding of family organization, property relations, political economy, and religious beliefs, including dietary preferences and food taboos" (1977:xi). Harris attempts to explain such diverse aspects of human culture as Yanomamo female infanticide, Hindu prohibition of cow slaughter, Jewish and Muslim pork taboos, tribal warfare, Aztec cannibalism, and the origins of capitalism on the basis of ecological theory. For ecologists, the diversity of human society and culture is a result of the complex interplay between history, culture, environment, and population.

Mentalist theories. A continuing interest in anthropological theory is to unravel the thinking process of homo sapiens. For some anthropologists the attempt to understand how individuals from another culture think has been a central problem. In contemporary anthropology the idea that culture may reflect fundamental properties of the mind or that culture is a derivation of unconsciously held mental rules has gained a number of adherents. Lévi-Strauss, a French anthropologist who was trained in philosophy, is the founder and proponent of a theoretical school of anthropology called structuralism. *Structuralism* is an attempt to go beyond cultural diversity and uncover the basic structure of the human mind. A parallel theory is *cognitive anthropology,* which is an attempt to discover the mental maps or rules in people's minds that determine their behavior. Because both of these theories focus on human thinking and consider culture essentially as a mental construct, they are generally called mentalist theories.

Understanding Lévi-Strauss's theoretical work is difficult. He is an erudite scholar who writes in a complicated and convoluted manner, characterized by puns, allusions, double entendres, and poetic license. In addition, translations of his work from French may not always reveal the true meaning of his complex thoughts.

An understanding of structuralism may be gained from the explanation of the following quotation about the incest taboo from Lévi-Strauss's work:

> The primitive and irreducible character of the basic unit of kinship, as we have defined it, is actually a direct result of the universal presence of an incest taboo. This is really saying that in human society a man must obtain a woman from another man who gives him a daughter or sister (1949:46; Harris 1968:495).

Central to an understanding of Lévi-Strauss and this quotation is the recognition that his primary goal is to explore the conception of the basic structure of the human mind. For him human thinking is basically binary, that is, thinking in pairs; and the only way to think in pairs is to oppose and contrast things. Thus there is night:day; up:down, male:female, raw:cooked, and most importantly, nature:culture. Culture, for Lévi-Strauss, is order, classification, and structure; nature is random, unclassified, and nonorganized. The incest taboo is the means for transforming "brutes" into culture-bearing humans. Incestuous matings are part of nature, not culture.

This is what Lévi-Strauss means when he speaks of the basic unit of kinship being the direct result of an incest taboo. For Lévi-Strauss the basic unit of kinship is the exchange of women between recognized kin units. Such recognition and exchange could not occur until humanity had developed a sense of order and classification. Recognition of *my* kin group as opposed to *another* kin group, therefore, illustrates binary thinking and must coincide with the concept of incest and its prohibition. Based on this form of exchange, between opposed

and contrasting categories, more complex forms of kinship organization are constructed. Despite their diversity they all reflect their origin in elementary binary forms of exchange.

In all the aspects of culture investigated by Lévi-Strauss—cooking, mythology, kinship—the goal is to begin with cultural diversity and move toward the unveiling of their elementary structures. In all cases these elementary structures reflect the binary structure of human thought.

The major premise of cognitive anthropology is that culture exists in the minds of cultural actors. Various terms such as blueprints, templates, mazeways, and cultural grammars have been advanced to conceptualize the assumed organization of culture in people's minds. Here diversity is not only characteristic of cultural systems, but is also characteristic of individuals within a society. Each individual may represent a unique strand of culture. This position assumes a certain degree of overlap between the "blueprints" contained in the minds of people rather than identical blueprints in the minds of people in a particular culture.

These blueprints are assumed to be the basis for human behavior. It is impossible, however, to observe directly what exists inside the human mind. Cognitive anthropology therefore depends upon inference, frequently using linguistic materials for analysis. Cognitive anthropologists are emicists. Although they do not deny the validity of observed material, they criticize attempts to use the categories of the observer (etic interpretations) as the sole basis for analysis.

Attempts to understand the systematic rules that underlie human behavior are not merely exercises in esoteric anthropology. Knowledge, information, and technical skills gained in the cognitive analysis of human action may come to occupy a position of practical importance. The skills of computer programmers and computer language experts are similar to the skills needed in cognitive anthropology. In order to construct a computer program or language, the programmer must first develop a set of systematic and sequentially organized set of instructions or rules. Any mistakes or omissions in such a program or language destroy its usefulness. In a sense the cognitive anthropologist attempts to construct a program that controls and explains the complex actions of human beings in certain situations. If cognitive anthropologists can crack the code of human thought, it should be possible to translate this code into a set of computer instructions. Thus in the future in theory it might be possible for computers to create culture.

Biocultural theory. Interest in the biological basis of human behavior has been stimulated in recent years by advances in genetics, primate studies, and numerous fossil finds related to human evolution. In one sense we are returning to a fundamental issue, for in *biocultural theory* the extent to which the biological inheritance of humanity expresses itself in particular cultural patterns is examined.

The role of biology in explaining human behavior has been an important issue in modern anthropology. In the nineteenth and twentieth centuries many people, mostly non-anthropologists, assumed that biological differences in racial inheritance could explain differences in behavior as well as indicate that various racial groups had different capacities for cultural creativity. These "racist" ideologies were widespread and popular, and their followers generally argued that Nordic whites — blue-eyed blonds — were biologically and culturally superior to everyone else and that Oriental and Black populations were markedly inferior.

Modern American anthropology, under the leadership of Franz Boas, attacked these racist theories. The essential point of his attack was that race and culture were unrelated and inde-

pendent phenomena and that biological makeup could not be used to explain the existence of particular cultural behaviors. By mid-century this position was widely, if not completely, accepted within anthropology, the other social sciences, and the biological sciences.

Although anthropologists denied any connection between race and culture, they recognized that the capacity of human beings to create culture has a biological base and that the human species is the product of an evolutionary line of development. These positions, however, did not constitute a biologically based theory of culture. In 1975 Edward O. Wilson, a professor of zoology at Harvard University, presented such a theory (1975). Known as *sociobiology,* its theorists argue that human social and cultural behavior has a biological base and is transmitted genetically. Sociobiologists argue that human behavior, especially marital practices and kinship systems, can be explained on the basis of human biology and the contribution they make to the genetic survival and continuity of a population.

Sociobiology has stirred a controversial debate among anthropologists. Although a number of anthropologists have become fervent supporters of sociobiological theory, many other anthropologists are disturbed by the emergence of this type of biology in cultural anthropology. In 1978 Marvin Harris, a critic of sociobiology, and Edward O. Wilson had a controversial debate about the usefulness of sociobiology in explaining human cultural behavior. The following remarks about their different interpretations of the incest taboo indicate the dimensions of this debate as well as the sociobiological interpretation of the incest taboo as a custom that avoids genetic damage.

MARVIN HARRIS: To place the incest taboo under genetic control flies in the face of an awful lot of evidence concerning the very high rate of incest. Social workers report as many as two million cases a year. The question is why, as far as I know, has there been no society that has developed rules which would have promoted incest? I think there is a cultural reason rather than a genetic one.

EDWARD WILSON: I don't believe that. The evidence shows that there are compelling genetic reasons to avoid incest. Furthermore, a strong predisposition originates in early development to avoid incest automatically, so that even if a society tried to overcome the inhibition culturally it would probably run into a very strong built-in psychological resistance from its members. And if any society succeeded, it would reap quite a wreckage in terms of genetic defects.

MARVIN HARRIS: Yes, I would agree with that. But the wreckage that would occur would be fed back on the cultural level, not on the genetic level.

Presumably, the reason we don't have societies which insist on a rule of incest mating is perhaps because it was tried in the past and proved to have very deleterious consequences, some of which were genetic and many of which were psychological. I can't see the necessity for having a gene that controls whether or not you are going to have incest.

EDWARD WILSON: Except that there are apparently programmed learning rules — what some psychologists called prepared learning. The brother-sister incest inhibition rule, based on the automatic avoidance of sexual relations among people who have grown up together during the first six years following birth, appears to be an example of such a learning rule that is both automatic and irrational. Whenever you find a strong and irrational disposition to learn one thing as opposed to another, it's reasonable to suppose that evolution has built in a safeguard beyond mere rational calculation at the fully cultural level.

MARVIN HARRIS: If that safeguard is there, it would seem to be quite weak because it has to be backed up by very strong cultural rules, penalties and sanctions. I find it hard to believe that there is a set of genes that defines the limits of mating for humans, given the fact that we have such tremendous variety of sexual behavior and of mating activities and marriage forms. (Harris and Wilson 1978:13).

The Role of Theory

Theory is a reduction of reality into an abstract and simplified set of principles, and, ideally, these principles should explain and illuminate a variety of disparate data. Theories, we hope, point in the direction of further research. Theories are not unchangeable; they require refinement and reformulation. The variety of theories in anthropology is testimony to the power and productivity of research methods and modes of analysis that supply the ultimate foundation for theory building in anthropology: past, present, and future.

Summary

Contextual and cross-cultural approaches are fundamental modes of analysis in anthropology. Contextual analysis attempts to place behavior in terms of a wider cultural and social setting; it flows directly from the field research experience. Anthropologists recognize that the understanding of human behavior depends upon its analysis in a wide range of cultural settings. As a result the comparative or cross-cultural approach is basic to the development of general principles of human behavior.

There are varieties of contextual analysis. In the work of Gluckman as well as that of Eames and Robboy, a single event is placed within the context of a larger social system. Evans-Pritchard sees Nuer life within the context of Nuer–Dinka hostility. Southall adds the dimensions of geography and history to his contextual analysis.

There are two basic forms of cross-cultural comparison: controlled comparison and statistical comparison. Controlled comparison seeks to understand minimal differences among a small number of similar societies. This approach is illustrated by the work of Nadel on witchcraft accusations in four African societies.

Large-scale statistical studies are not a recent innovation in cultural anthropology. Development of the HRAF data bank has created an organized system of data retrieval that facilitates such studies. Whiting's study of witchcraft in fifty societies exemplifies the use of large-scale statistical approaches to test hypotheses.

Concepts are essential tools in anthropological analysis. Cultural relativism operates as a corrective to ethnocentrism and constitutes the basis for an objective and scientific study of human behavior in diverse cultural settings. Role, status, and norms are concepts designed to organize observations of human behavior. They permit analysis to go beyond individual and idiosyncratic activities. These concepts become the basis for understanding the rules that govern human behavior.

Although anthropologists may disagree about the definitions of culture and society, these terms are major and important conceptual ideas in anthropology. To some extent these controversies also reflect changing research interests and emphases. At one time the idea that human groups were organized into well-defined and distinct tribal groups permitted the definition of society as a group of people sharing a common territory, language, and identity. Recognition that political and economic systems may include people of diverse linguistic and cultural backgrounds caused a redefinition of society as an organization of statuses and roles.

Culture can be used to refer to the total way of life of a particular group of people. Seen as a unique characteristic of the human species, culture guides and constrains human behavior and is the major element involved in humanity's adaptation to the diverse environments of this planet. It is the very breadth of anthropological interests that provides one of the most difficult problems faced by anthropologists: the problem of meaning. The couvade, a set of behavioral patterns associated with childbirth in a number of societies, is used to illustrate this problem. Problems of meaning have two dimensions: controversy over the behavioral content of a custom on a cross-cultural basis and competing interpretations about the function and purpose of a custom. Not only do anthropologists offer a variety of explanations for a particular pattern of behavior, but members of a single culture may differ in their own understanding of particular events.

Anthropological theories are attempts to construct a highly abstract system of principles to explain and understand all human behavior. Scientific theories are based on data, and therefore the accumulation of additional ethnographic information has resulted in the demise of older theories and the appearance of new ones. Perhaps the most significant aspect of theories in anthropology is the different basic assumptions they make about the purpose of explanation and the position of humanity on the planet. To evolutionary theorists human culture is a history of advancement and development. Functional and ecological theorists perceive humanity as one element in a complex interrelation of material and social circumstances. Opposed to this view are structuralists and cognitive theorists, who see human culture as the expression of our mental capacities and organization. Finally, there are biocultural theorists, who seek to understand the biological basis and roots of human nature. One strand of this approach, sociobiology, suggests that cultural practices are designed to guarantee the flow of genes over time.

It is an arguable question whether or not

these basic premises, which lie at the heart of anthropological theories, can be verified or invalidated by the usual procedures of science. Often they reflect a philosophy or intuition about the human condition. We must recognize that at our present level of understanding, the complexity, diversity, and variability of human behavior and culture are so great that support, in one way or another, can be found for most anthropological theories. Thus it appears clear that the future of anthropology will be characterized by the emergence of a succession of new theories as well as the reworking of older, traditional ones.

Key Terms and Concepts

ethnography
contextual analysis
cross-cultural
   analysis,
   comparative
   method
culture
oblique social protest
controlled
   comparison

frustration-
   aggression
   hypotheses
HRAF (Human
   Relations
   Area File)
statistical
   comparison
ethnocentrism
cultural relativism

role
status
achieved status
ascribed status
norms
society
couvade
emic
etic
functionalism
incest taboo

modern evolutionary
   theory
multilinear
   evolutionary theory
functional theory
ecological theory
structuralism
cognitive
   anthropology
biocultural theory
sociobiology

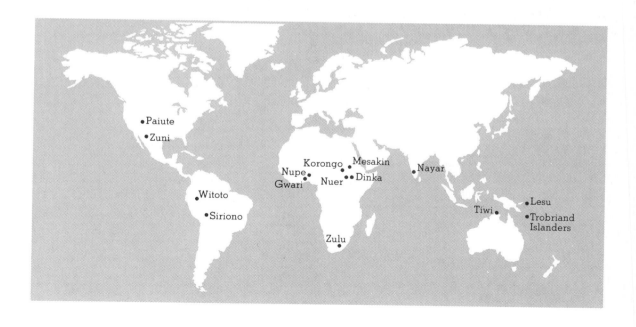

Suggested Readings

Evans-Pritchard, Edward E. *The Nuer: A Description of the Modes of Livelihood and Political Institutions of a Nilotic People.* Oxford, 1940; rpt. Oxford: Oxford University Press, 1969. *This study of the Nuer is an ethnographic classic. Evans-Pritchard analyzes the political institutions of this stateless society within the context of Nuer kinship, their pastoral economy, and the terrain on which they live.*

Garbarino, Merwyn S. *Sociocultural Theory in Anthropology: A Short History.* New York: Holt, Rinehart and Winston, 1977. *A brief overview and introduction to theory in cultural anthropology.*

Harris, Marvin. *The Rise of Anthropological Theory: A History of Theories of Culture.* New York: Crowell, 1968. *A comprehensive history of anthropological theory written from a cultural materialist perspective. His interpretation of the history of anthropology is both provocative and controversial, but his work is always worth reading.*

Hatch, Elvin J. *Theories of Man and Culture.* New York: Columbia University Press, 1973. *Introduces and explains the ideas and theories of ten major figures in anthropology.*

Malefijt, Annemarie D. *Images of Man: A History of Anthropological Thought.* New York: Knopf, 1974. *An introductory history that focuses on the major figures in the emergence of cultural anthropology.*

Pelto, Pertti J., and Gretel H. Pelto. *Anthropological Research: The Structure of Inquiry,* 2nd ed. Cambridge: Cambridge University Press, 1978. *A comprehensive introduction and survey of research methods. The authors also discuss theory building in anthropology, statistics, hypothesis testing, and using computers.*

Part II

Dimensions of Social Behavior

Cultures are diverse, but people in all cultures face some similar problems: making a living, living with others, exercising and reacting to power, relating to the world of the supernatural, and enjoyable life beyond the mere routines of existence. Through field-work and contextual and comparative analysis, anthropologists have accumulated an impressive store of knowledge about the way peoples in many cultures cope with these issues. In this part, these common problems are explored.

In Chapter 3 we start by examining how a group in New Guinea makes a living, and then look at how people in other societies obtain their food. Chapter 4 begins with a description of marriage and family among the Tiwi of Australia and a contrasting view of marriage in a small village in India; the remainder of the chapter deals with how people in different cultures choose mates, solemnize their choices, and set up households. Chapter 5 opens with a dramatization of a murder case in which kinship plays a crucial role; then kin terms, kin and nonkin groups, and kin-based behaviors in many cultures are compared. In Chapter 6 we focus on war and law, looking first at warfare among the Mae Enga of New Guinea. Chapter 7 covers the topics of power and political organization, and starts with a British explorer's account of his meeting with a Buganda king. In Chapter 8 we present a description of a Hindu religious festival and a recounting witchcraft among the Badyaranke of Senegal; the rest of the chapter further explores the realm of the supernatural. Chapter 9 introduces some important and frequently ignored components of the human condition involving eating, drinking, and making merry — the enjoyment of life.

From birth, children are incorporated into an ongoing cultural system. In the Greek Orthodox tradition baptism marks the official introduction of a child into the culture, with its emphasis on ritual, structure, and male dominance.

Chapter 3

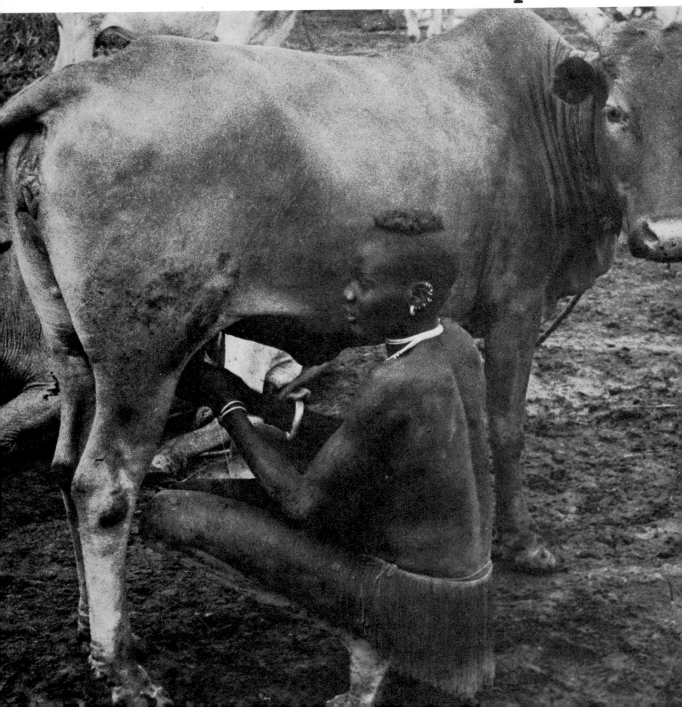

Making a Living

In our society when we need food we buy it at a supermarket, for few of us are directly involved in producing or distributing the food that we eat. For people living in tribal or peasant societies, however, the phenomena of supermarkets and the purchasing of food are absent. People in these societies obtain their food directly through their own efforts.

Production of food is accomplished through a complex network of techniques, technology, resources, and work activities called a *subsistence system*. Anthropologists recognize five major types of subsistence systems: *foraging* or *hunting and gathering, horticulture* or *gardening, pastoralism* or *herding of animals, agriculture* or *peasant farming*, and *industrialism* or *factory production* and *mechanized agriculture*.

One of the major events in the development of subsistence systems was the emergence of a *domesticated food economy*. This system involved the cultivation of plants and the transformation of wild animals into tame creatures supplying milk, meat, hides, skin, and bone. Understanding the dynamics of this development is of major anthropological interest.

Subsistence systems can be distinguished by the various fundamental characteristics that relate to obtaining food. A foraging society is built around the search for food. In a horticultural or gardening society the need for land and fertilizer for growing food is of central importance. Pastoralists search for pasture for their herds, and this quest gives rise to a distinctive way of life. Peasant farmers generally live in a condition of scarcity. Access to land and attempts to gain an equitable distribution of what they produce have been salient dimensions of peasant life for thousands of years. Even though industrial society has an enormous productive capacity, there are still periods of inflation, recession, and economic insecurity. Many of the social and political movements that occur in industrial societies are reactions to these events. Employment and jobs are critical for people living in industrial society.

In our society we are unable to get along without money because money and prices are the mechanisms we use for the distribution of the goods and services of our economy. In other societies people are able to get along very well without money, and in this chapter we look at the principles that underlie these other systems of exchange and distribution.

Today women in American society are defining a new relationship to the economic system for themselves. They are no longer content with the roles of housewife and mother, and therefore they are demanding participation in productive activity. Cross-cultural investigation of the role of women in different subsistence systems indicates considerable variation in their productive roles. This investigation illuminates the factors that influence the economic position of women.

Cattle herding is one of the major forms of subsistence found in the world. Nuer women milk the cows that are herded and guarded by men.

The Bomagai-Angoiang: Gardeners of the New Guinea Highlands

In the history of subsistence activities human beings survived for more than a million years as foragers or hunters and gatherers; they hunted animals, fished, and gathered the wild foods that nature provided. Only during the last 12,000 years have people begun to grow food rather than collect it. In this chapter we describe the various modes of subsistence human groups practice, and we also describe the shift in human subsistence activities from gathering to growing and the consequences of this change. Although present-day hunters and gatherers may resemble the initial stage in human subsistence activities, today they constitute only a minute percentage of the world's population. In addition, surviving foraging groups occupy geographical zones that are characterized by harsh, uninviting, and often severe climatic conditions such as deserts, arctic regions, and jungles. In the past hunters and gatherers occupied not only all the habitable zones of the earth, but also areas rich in animal and food resources. Because most contemporary hunters and gatherers live in areas that are poor in natural resources, however, they are not likely to reflect the activities of past foraging societies accurately.

At the present time horticulture or gardening is a more widespread subsistence pattern than hunting and gathering. Gardeners are found in Africa, the mountain zones of South and Southeast Asia (India to the Philippines), New Guinea and the islands of the Pacific, and portions of South, Central, and North America. Contemporary fieldwork in tribal societies is usually done among horticultural populations.

The Bomagai-Angoiang of highland New Guinea, described by William C. Clarke (1971), are in many ways typical of most gardening societies. An understanding of this society provides insight into a pattern of subsistence activities characteristic of the vast majority of tribal societies.

Four important aspects of the Bomagai-Angoiang horticultural system are described in the following account by Clarke. Included are:

1. the productive unit and the sexual division of labor
2. the daily pattern of work activities
3. clearing forest for a garden
4. crop variety

THE PRODUCTIVE UNIT AND THE SEXUAL DIVISION OF LABOR

The married pair or, among unmarried adults, some male-female combination is the basic productive unit among the Bomagai-Angoiang. The male is responsible for clearing forest and building fences around the garden plots. Men also plant some of the crops, do at least a little of the weeding, and work in the gardens at specifically masculine chores. The expectation is, however, that women will do the steady work of planting, maintaining the garden, and providing a daily supply of vegetable food for their male partners, children, and the domestic pigs.

THE DAILY PATTERN OF WORK ACTIVITIES

Kunbun is a young, energetic married man about twenty-three. Kunbun's wife, Rameka, has one child, an infant boy.

In June 1965 Kunbun had two gardens in operation. Rising near dawn [Rameka] begins her day slowly by feeding her baby and putting wood on the embers in her hearth. She eats either food already cooked and stored overnight in leaves or else tubers cooked that morning on the hearth. After she has eaten, if it is sunny, Rameka joins a group of women

Rameka in her garden. The bag on her lap serves as a cradle. The bag to her right she fills with food as she combines harvesting with weeding.

sitting outside at her hamlet or the nearby hamlet gossiping, making thread or net bags, and picking lice from each other's heads. After an hour or so of sitting in the sun, she gets ready to leave the hamlet with her digging stick and two net bags, one a cradle for her baby, the other a carryall for garden produce. The walk to Garden 1 takes half an hour, that to Garden 2, nearly an hour. In the gardens she works at weeding and harvesting. Light weeds she pulls up by the roots and lays on stumps, rocks, or logs to dry; heavier weeds she pries out with her dibble or cuts with the bush knife she sometimes carries. She harvests concurrently with weeding; as she moves about the garden, she gradually fills the net bag, digging up a sweet potato here and taking a handful of greens there. Frequently she stops to rest and play with or feed her baby. When Kunbun is in the garden he weeds and harvests, too, but seldom for as

long a time as Rameka. Between two and three in the afternoon Rameka starts home with her baby and the net bag, now full of tubers, greens, and other produce weighing at least twenty or thirty pounds. On the way home she may pick up some firewood from [a] tree felled earlier by Kunbun so that it would dry. When she reaches the hamlet, she lays aside her burdens and fetches water if necessary or sends a young boy for it. Then together with Kunbun and others she begins the preparation of the day's main meal.

Kunbun's days are less regular. He may do other garden tasks for himself or clansmen. He may go on a collecting trip. He may loaf. He may set out to do one thing and end up doing another, as when he comes across a feral [wild] pig and takes up the hunt. On his way home he often collects firewood, too, or gathers fern leaves, bananas, and sugar cane to take to the hamlet (Clark 1971:30,129).

Felling a tree. Including the building of the scaffold, the operation took about 40 minutes.

CLEARING FOREST FOR A GARDEN

From January to June, three Bomagai-Angoiang men, Nakemba, Kong, and Man, clear forest in order to make a garden. Clarke's diarylike presentation of this work activity conveys the physical labor and social organization involved in this undertaking.

January 10, 1965. Nakemba began clearing in old secondary forest. By clearing he will establish rights to the unclaimed plot, which is covered with forest at least forty years old. The initial clearing consists of slashing with a bush knife or pulling up the undergrowth of ferns, bushes, and saplings by hand.

January 24. There has been still more clearing of underbrush. Several thousand square feet are now clean of growth under the canopy of the high trees.

February 9. Today for the first time large trees were felled on this plot. Nakemba, Kong, and Ndinga (a young bachelor) came to do the work. The plot will belong to Nakemba, Kong, and Man; Ndinga came simply to help. As the three men worked at felling, other men who passed stopped to help for half an hour or so. This was not, I think, from a sense of obligation but because they very much enjoy the excitement and accomplishment of felling trees. After about two hours of work, ten large trees had been felled and an area of from two to three thousand square feet, opened to sunlight. Then felling was over for the day, and Nakemba, Kong, and Ndinga went to work piling debris against trees or on small scaffolds of sticks to dry.

Nakemba, Kong, and Ndinga left the plot about three in the afternoon. Before he went, Nakemba planted several stem cuttings of sugar cane in the tract which had been opened to sunlight only a few hours before.

March 1–15. In this period several thousand more square feet of undergrowth and trees were cut down by several men. There was also more planting of sugar cane [and] manioc.

March 16–May 12. During this interval clearing and felling continued spasmodically until, by May 12, the opened tracts had coalesced into a single plot of at least two acres. Also by May 12 the three owners had designated "marks" dividing the garden into three parts. Nakemba planted in his sugar cane, manioc, taro, [and] bananas. His female garden partners will plant sweet potatoes later.

May 17. Today, Togma, a widow who is one of Man's garden partners, began burning in her section of Man's part of the plot. She heaps some of the leaves and small pieces of wood that litter the ground onto the piles of trash gathered earlier by the men. After a pile is burning well, she spreads the burning material and ash over the surrounding ground with her digging stick. Concurrently with the burning, Togma plants sugar cane and bananas.

May 19. Nakemba's wives are burning trash and planting sweet potatoes and taro in Nakemba's part of the garden. The small, separated fires do no harm to the crops already planted and in some cases already sprouting. Man's wife is planting and burning in her husband's part of the garden.

May 28. For the past week planting and burning have been going on almost every day. Togma as well as Man's half-sister, Man's wife, Kong's mother, Kong's bride, and Nakemba's wives have all taken part, each in her own section except for Kong's bride who works with his mother. Yams and taros have predominated in the planting.

CROP VARIETY

To convey the nature of a Bomagai-Angoiang garden, I will summarize an actual [walk through] a five-month-old garden. From the fence at the edge of the garden the ground is invisible beneath a continuous cover of crop vegetation. To enter the garden is to wade into a green sea. To walk is to push through irregular waves of taro and to step calf-deep in the cover of sweet potato vines. The ground

of the first 3 [feet] is covered with sweet potato. Rising out of the mass of vines [is] a taro plant. In the next segment the *tukaya* sweet potato is mixed with the *alepun* variety. Together they cover the ground solidly.

Fifteen feet into the garden, one encounters a 7-foot banana plant around whose base there spreads the cover of sweet potato vines that extends continuously from the fence. In the next segment is still more sweet potato, as well as a not-before-encountered variety of taro, another kind of weedy fern, and the sprouting stump of a *Ficus* [fig] species, 7 inches in diameter. Then comes a banana plant, followed by the stumps of two trees felled to clear the plot. Beyond the stumps [is] a spreading, vaselike cluster of sugar cane. The garden continued with successive variation to its farthest edge. The heterogeneity of species and varieties within such a garden extends to individuals of the same variety of a single species. Of two taros of the same variety side by side, one may be waist high and luxuriant, the other knee high and stunted — the difference being caused by variation in the richness of the soil, in the vitality of the planting stock, and in the length of time since planting, which may vary by weeks.

An Analysis of Bomagai-Angoiang Subsistence

Subsistence activities among the Bomagai-Angoiang can be analyzed in a variety of contextual frameworks: evolutionary, historical, ecological, and functional. Each framework provides insight and understanding into this aspect of Bomagai-Angoiang culture. Although the subsistence techniques of the Bomagai-Angoiang might appear to be ancient, backward, inefficient, and a time-consuming means of making a living, this impression is incorrect.

The cultivation of food crops and the raising of domesticated animals are one of humanity's recent inventions. Our humanlike ancestors roamed the East African plains more than 2 million years ago, and modern homo sapiens emerged 40,000 to 50,000 years ago. Given this time perspective, the domestication of crops and animals, which took place only 10,000 to 12,000 years ago, is a recent innovation.

Growing food and keeping pigs in the highlands of New Guinea are even more recent, beginning not more than 1000 to 2000 years ago. Sweet potatoes are an important crop for the Bomagai-Angoiang and other highland New Guinea tribes. Sweet potatoes, which apparently are of South American origin, may have been introduced into New Guinea by Spanish explorers in the sixteenth century. Another possibility is that sweet potatoes were introduced into this area of the Pacific even earlier. Whatever the case, the movement of peoples, like the Bomagai-Angoiang, into the highlands of New Guinea was probably based upon sweet potato cultivation. This food crop flourishes in the ecological setting of the highland area. Thus the subsistence practices, settlement patterns, social organization, and warfare activities characteristic of highland New Guinea cultures may be a consequence of the recent migration of people into this ecological zone.

Bomagai-Angoiang garden practices cannot be dismissed as backward and inefficient. Clarke's account shows that simple tools are used efficiently in this environment. He concludes that the Bomagai-Angoiang "... have created from the natural elements of their environment a habitat they understand and can manipulate so that it gives them subsistence" (Clarke 1971:191). Unlike our society, the Bomagai-Angoiang have developed a balanced relationship with their environment that avoids destroying and despoiling the basis of their existence. A group of about 150 people survive on a little more than 36 acres of cultivated land. This represents less than 3 percent of the land available to the Bomagai-Angoiang for food production. Cultivation of only a small segment of the available land is a part of a larger horticultural cycle. When cultivated plots are abandoned they slowly become covered in forest, and eventually they are used for gardens again. The entire cycle may take forty years.

Clarke notes that the population has been kept down by epidemic diseases and warfare. The introduction of modern medical practices and outside political control are eliminating both of these population control devices. Future population increases may require bringing more land into production, but living standards will probably not improve. Cultivating more land may, in fact, lead to a decrease in nutritional quality and greater ecological disturbance and destruction. Extending the cultivation of land beyond the 2 to 3 percent now used would not allow the full regeneration of abandoned plots into forest. The extension of cultivation could destroy the delicate balance between cultivated plots and available forest for future generations. In addition, wildlife, a source of protein for the Bomagai-Angoiang, could be depleted as a result of more extensive cultivation.

Clarke's account of a walk through a Bomagai-Angoiang garden illustrates a central element in horticultural societies: the incredible mixture of different crops within the garden. This type of cultivation contrasts dramatically with modern agricultural practices of cleared fields and separate plots for separate crops. Mixed cultivation has beneficial consequences for the soil, one of which is the resistance of crops to disease, and it also provides a continuous supply of different crops for the Bomagai-Angoiang.

Bomagai-Angoiang subsistence practices, as well as those of many other horticultural groups, seem to be well adapted to the environment. The system depends upon the availability of large blocks of unused land, sufficient time for forest to grow back, a stable population, and crops adapted to this particular environment. Protein derived from hunting wild animals and from domesticated pigs raised by the Bomagai-Angoiang supplement the largely carbohydrate diet of vegetable foods. In fact, the Bomagai-Angoiang feed a portion of their sweet potatoes to pigs, thus converting starchy food to high-grade protein. Any significant change in one or more of these factors could easily upset the ecological balance achieved by the Bomagai-Angoiang. Horticulture is in many ways an admirably designed and efficient system for making a living in what are otherwise difficult and demanding environments.

Bomagai-Angoiang subsistence practices are related to other aspects of their culture. As Clarke notes, there is no ownership of forest land, and an individual acquires title to a plot of land by clearing it. When a garden plot is abandoned all rights to it are relinquished. The lack of developed notions of private ownership of land is related to the horticultural pattern of Bomagai-Angoiang subsistence. Fields are used for short periods of time, and little investment and no improvements are made in such fields.

The requirements and organization of the labor force among the Bomagai-Angoiang also reflect the needs of their subsistence system. Men are primarily involved in cutting down trees and clearing the land. Women help burn over the area of dry trees and foliage and plant crops. Responsibility for mulching, weeding, and harvesting is also in the hands of women. As a result of this division of labor, the productive unit is a man, his wife, and his female gardening partners. One aspect of this horticultural system is that women are able to combine subsistence activities and child-rearing responsibilities. The important role of women in the Bomagai-Angoiang subsistence system and the sexual division of labor appear to be typical of most, if not all, horticultural societies.

Modern society prides itself on the development and use of "labor-saving devices." Do Bomagai-Angoiang men and women engage in exhausting and continuous labor? Apparently they do not. Clarke estimates that the average cultivator spends approximately 1200 hours of garden work per year, which is approximately twenty-three hours of work per week. Clarke's description of the daily work activities of Kunbun and his wife Rameka shows that their day is controlled neither by rigid work schedules nor by a boss. Their days are punctuated, in fact, by periods of leisure, loafing, and intermittent work activities. Similar patterns have been noted for other gardening societies.

By contrast the average worker in modern industrial society puts in many more hours of work. With a work week of forty hours, the average American spends approximately 2000 hours a year at work, and this figure does not include commuting time, shopping, moonlighting on second jobs, overtime, and other subsistence-related activities. In modern industrial society the daily pattern of life is subordinate to the demands of the job, rigid work schedules, the separation of work and leisure activities, and the demands of superiors. Such features are not characteristic of Bomagai-Angoiang economic life.

Subsistence in Comparative Perspective

A comparative view of subsistence systems requires the consideration of several different frameworks. From an evolutionary perspective, the development of various subsistence systems can be interpreted as humanity's continuing response to the needs for productivity in the face of an expanding population. From this perspective the domestication of crops and animals was a revolutionary innovation. In addition to considering subsistence systems in relation to their evolutionary development, we can analyze them in terms of functional consequences. In tribal and peasant societies, almost the entire adult labor force is involved in the primary production of food. For this reason many social scientists consider subsistence to be a fundamental institution in human society. Thus, understanding the basic dimensions, needs, and dynamics of each mode of subsistence permits recognition of the functional consequences and correlations of these varied modes of making a living. At the same time the comparative study of subsistence systems provides the basis for understanding specific problems. One problem, for example, concerns the principles of exchange and distribution found in human society. An understanding of the social and economic context of different principles of exchange permits some understanding of the changes that are now occurring in Western industrial society. Another problem

that can be viewed on a comparative basis concerns the role of women in economic life. Again, a comparative perspective indicates some of the important factors behind the economic role allocated to women in various societies.

Evolutionary Development of Subsistence Systems

Hunting and gathering as a means of subsistence was an eminently successful way of life. Hunters and gatherers spread across Africa, Europe, Asia, and Southeast Asia, and eventually foragers, the ancestors of American Indians, penetrated across northeast Siberia and the Bering Strait into the New World. At the present time, however, only a minuscule percentage of the world's population subsists as foragers (Figure 3.1). Carleton Coon, an anthropologist who studies hunters and gatherers, says, "Today a scant quarter of a million hunters are left, no more than .003 percent of

Figure 3.1 Location of recently extinct and contemporary hunting and gathering people. (Recently extinct groups are shown in capital letters.)

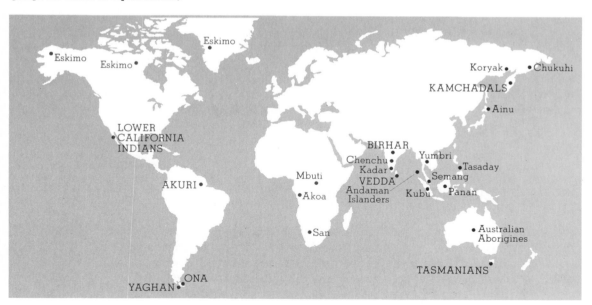

mankind. Ten thousand years ago they numbered about 10 million, 100 percent of the earth's population" (1971:xvii). Why did this pattern of subsistence, which lasted for so long, come to an end?

Mark Cohen is an anthropologist who has considered some of the reasons for the demise of foraging and the emergence of plant and animal domestication (1977). Based on an extensive survey of archaeological and anthropological data, Cohen concludes that gradual population growth among hunters and gatherers began to undercut their way of life. They needed new sources of food and intensified techniques of production to feed their growing population. This need for additional food was the basis of the domesticated food economy that began 10,000 to 12,000 years ago. An alternative and supplementary possibility is that hunting technology and techniques became so efficient that animal resources, especially large game animals, were depleted. Thus the increasing efficiency of hunters may have undercut hunting as a *primary* subsistence activity. Given the depletion of large game animals, many foraging groups had to depend upon gathering wild foods and hunting small game. According to Cohen, archaeological evidence records this shift away from big game hunting to fishing, small game hunting, and dependence on wild vegetation about 15,000 years ago (1977).

Although archaeologists and cultural anthropologists have not determined the exact circumstances giving rise to the cultivation of crops and the raising of domesticated animals, this new mode of production, emerging about 10,000 to 12,000 years ago, began to supplant foraging, becoming the dominant mode of production throughout the entire world. Domestication of plants and animals occurred in a limited number of localities during a relatively narrow time span. Among these localities the Middle East, Africa, Southeast Asia, South

America, and Meso-America (Mexico–Central America) were important. Domestication apparently occurred independently in each area. From these centers of origin the domesticated food economy spread throughout most of the world. Increases in population and the necessity for acquiring new and fertile land were the basis for this expansion.

The initial phase of cultivation probably resembled many of the characteristics found among Bomagai-Angoiang cultivators. Relatively low populations, large blocks of land, much of it unused, and the necessity of shifting gardens and settlements as soil fertility declined were basic dimensions of this productive technique.

In certain favored environments it was possible to develop a more intensified mode of production dependent upon the plow, irrigation, animal power, and more efficient use of human labor. This complex development, referred to as plow agriculture, originated about 5000 years ago. Agriculture as a subsistence system is more productive than simple gardening. Through the intensive use of available land, it is possible to support larger populations and to create permanent settlements. The "high civilizations" of the ancient world were dependent on this mode of production. Using Cohen's thesis, it can be argued that population increases that occurred under a horticultural subsistence system became the basis of the development of agriculture as a more intensive version of the general pattern of domestication.

In many parts of the world, especially in arid and grassland areas, agriculture was not a viable alternative. In these ecological zones pastoralism, the herding of domesticated animals, became the basis of a new subsistence system. Pastoralism represented the adaptation of one part of the generalized pattern of domestication to marginal areas.

Only within the last two centuries has a new mode of production appeared — industrialism.

This mode of production, which emerged in Europe, harnessed new sources of energy to the production process. It resulted in a tremendous increase in productivity. Initial sources of energy, such as coal and steam, were rapidly replaced by oil, gas, and electricity, and many now advocate the use of nuclear and solar power to run the industrial machine. Application of industrial technology and mechanization to the production of food resulted in enormous increases in productivity, with a consistently declining number of people required to produce food. In contrast to all other subsistence systems, only a small proportion of the total labor force in an industrial society is involved in the production of food.

The complex network of circumstances underlying the emergence of industrialism is not completely understood. In the sixteenth century, the Spanish conquistadores pillaged the Aztec and Inca empires; the gold and silver that poured into Europe in the following centuries played a role in the emergence of this new mode of production by supplying capital for commercial and industrial ventures. Population expansion also played a significant role in this development. Beginning in the seventeenth century the population of Europe steadily increased. Importation into Europe of crops originally domesticated by American Indians, such as corn and potatoes, was an important basis for this growth in population. Used for both human and animal consumption, these crops could be grown on marginal soils, and the expanded food supply that resulted may have been an important basis for the population increase. In addition, depletion of forest resources in the eighteenth century played a role in the search for alternative sources of energy, especially coal.

Taken together, increasing wealth, population growth, and depletion of forest resources for energy purposes may have accounted for the development of this new and intensified mode of production. One consequence of the Industrial Revolution has been an additional increase in the population of the world. Thus population growth, which may have played a crucial role in the emergence of industrialism, is still a factor in the drive toward increased productivity and the discovery of new sources of energy.

Functional Consequences of Subsistence Systems

Each subsistence system can be distinguished by the resources it uses as well as its technology. Societies that utilize these systems are not identical, and variations within each system can be recognized. Each subsistence system, however, has a related set of characteristics that are direct consequences of its resource base and technology.

Foraging

Vegetable foods growing wild and wild animals are the resource base of foragers. The amount of rainfall and sunlight ultimately determines the quantity of food available to them. Although foragers are limited in their ability to increase the amount of available food, some techniques for expanding the food supply are available. Development of more efficient hunting methods and tools may initially add to the food supply by increasing the number of animals killed. Such efficiency may prove disadvantageous in the long run, however, by eliminating the animals that are the basis of the hunting system. Another technique that may expand the food supply is the practice of burning bush and grass. Grass and bush fires may increase the edible wild foods available to foragers as well as encourage the growth of foods eaten by the wild animals they hunt. Aside from these techniques, however, foragers basically live on the bounty of nature.

A fundamental variation within the foraging

San woman using a digging stick, which is the basic implement used by food gatherers.

pattern is the distinction between hunting and gathering. There were groups, especially the Eskimo of the Arctic, who depended solely upon hunting large land and sea animals (whales, seals, walrus, caribou). The Shoshone Indians of Nevada, Utah, and eastern California, in contrast, relied almost exclusively upon gathering wild foods and catching small animals. Unlike the harsh and cold environment of the Arctic, the Shoshone Indians lived in a dry and desertlike country that provided them with little in the way of abundant animal food resources. They lived primarily upon nuts, seeds, roots, and berries. Grasshoppers, an important item in their diet, were dried and ground into an edible flourlike paste. In addition, they supplemented their diet with rats, mice, gophers, ants, larvae, snakes, and lizards. From descriptions of the Shoshone Indians, it appears that almost everything that could be eaten was on their menu (Coon 1956:46–61). Some foraging societies combine hunting with gathering. Australian tribal groups hunted kangaroo and wallaby and gathered wild vegetable foods and larvae. Foraging as a subsistence system is adaptable to a variety of ecological zones and resource bases.

In many ways the technology used by foragers reflects the variations in their ecological circumstances and resource bases. Some general equipment found among most foragers includes knives, spears, clubs, bows and arrows, traps, and digging sticks — implements that resemble broom handles with a point, used primarily for digging out roots and subterranean parts of plants. Specialized equipment includes blowguns, boomerangs, nets, harpoons, ostrich egg water containers, and poisons. Blowguns used in Southeast Asia and South America are suitable for hunting in areas of heavy jungle. Ostrich eggs, which serve as water containers, are used by the San of the Kalahari Desert to store and carry water in this arid region. Boomerangs, essentially a further refinement and development of clubs for throwing, were used as hunting implements by Australian aborigines who did not have bows and arrows. Harpoons were used by the Eskimo to hunt and kill large sea animals. The essential element of a harpoon is its detachable spearhead. When a sea animal is struck, the spearhead sinks into the flesh of the animal and separates from the spear shaft. The head is attached to a float so that after the animal flees Eskimo hunters can, by spotting the float, retrieve the dead animal.

As the use of the harpoon indicates, Eskimo technology is ingenious and specialized. Their technology can be seen as an example of human cultural adaptation to a difficult and demanding environment. Their technology includes not only harpoons with detachable heads, but also ingenious traps, skin-covered boats or kayaks, snow goggles (the Eskimo version of sunglasses), sledges, and tailored and sewn clothing made from animal skins.

One of the fundamental characteristics of hunters and gatherers is their acute awareness and knowledge of the environment in which they live. Terrain, climatic conditions, the habits of animals, and patterns of vegetation growth are part of the store of knowledge of these people. Ability to distinguish and locate edible foods and sources of water are well-developed capabilities found among gatherers. Although many European explorers sickened and died in these areas because they were unable to find food or water, the indigenous inhabitants survived with little difficulty.

Because they must search for food and water, foraging societies are nomadic. The seasonal availability of vegetation and animals means that foraging groups must coordinate their migrations and habitation sites with the cyclical and seasonal movements of animals and the growth cycle of plants. Hunting and gathering in a single area will deplete the available resources, and migration to new areas is required. Thus the lack of fixed habitation and settlement sites is one characteristic of the foraging pattern, although nomadic movement is not an invariable consequence of foraging. Given a substantial food resource base, foragers may settle in a single place, build permanent settlements, and develop complex social systems.

A prime example of such development was found among the Indian tribes of the Northwest Coast of North America. Blessed with predictable and abundant supplies of salmon, land animals, sea mammals, and wild vegetation, these groups developed complex societies — large settled communities, substantial wooden plank houses, and a complex political and social rank system (see "Stand-in for a Murderer," Chapter 5).

A continuing controversy among anthropologists is the degree to which foraging is a difficult and insecure way of making a living. In the past anthropologists viewed hunters and gatherers as living on the edge of survival. John Marshall's film "The Hunters," which is about the San of the Kalahari Desert of southern Africa, conveys the impression that hunting provides the basis for subsistence and that it is a tough, arduous, and uncertain activity. Summing up the literature on the San as part of a survey of hunting cultures, Elman Service (1966:100–101) characterizes them as "... a hungry people, their habits oriented around a constant struggle for food and water. Vegetable foods are rare most of the year, as is grass and water ..., hence the [San] is almost constantly migrating."

Recent research by Richard Lee (1968) among another group of San, the Dobe, describes the overwhelming importance of wild vegetable foods in their diet. Between 60 and

80 percent of the food acquired by the Dobe is wild vegetable foods gathered by women. Lee indicates that the predictable harvest of wild foods, especially mongongo nuts, provides an adequate and nutritional diet for these people, as well as permitting a significant amount of leisure time. Lee estimates that the Dobe devote sixteen to nineteen hours a week to acquiring food. On the basis of this finding, Lee suggests that the usual interpretation of hunters and gatherers as forever on the brink of starvation and hunger is not correct.

Horticulture

A key element in horticulture is the use of trees and foliage as a source of fertilizer. A consequence of this practice is the need for large areas of forested land. This aspect is well documented in the account of the Bomagai-Angoiang. A field must be cleared, trees felled, and foliage cut down. After being allowed to dry and then burned, trees and foliage constitute the source of fertilizer. Such practices are referred to as *slash and burn* or swidden cultivation.

A crop may be grown in the same field for about three or four years, sometimes even less. After this period of time the crop yield declines due to a loss of chemicals, such as nitrogen, in the soil, and the amount of labor time required to weed the garden increases (Figure 3.2).

For the Bomagai-Angoiang this cycle of plot use is even shorter, less than two years. Abandonment of the field and the clearing and cultivation of a new plot of forest land are responses to these production and labor curves. In order to maintain this system large areas of land are needed, with the vast majority of it remaining uncultivated. The example of the Bomagai-Angoiang is typical. There is a ratio of one acre of cultivated land to forty acres of uncultivated (fallow) land. This practice allows the cutdown forest to regenerate itself in order to provide future fertilizer for food production. For the Bo-

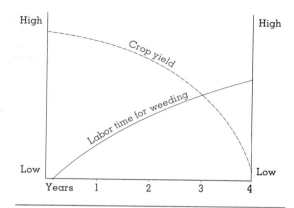

Figure 3.2. Crop yields and labor for weeding in horticulture.

magai-Angoiang the complete cycle may take up to forty years. In other ecological areas and where different crops are grown, the total cycle may be shorter, averaging eight to fifteen years.

Because fertilization is such a significant factor in horticulture, some societies have developed alternative and supplementary sources of fertilizer. Manure and composting are the most common supplementary techniques for fertilizing garden plots. Composting is the use of decayed organic matter (food wastes, grass, leaves). Some groups living in river and stream valleys depend upon the deposit of fertile silt from floods to enrich their soil. Any level of success will operate to improve the productivity of the entire system.

Horticultural societies encompass a wide range of subsistence patterns. A fundamental distinction can be made between seed crops and root crops, for example. The major seed crops are wheat, barley, rice, oats, millet, sorghum, corn, and some vegetables. The major root crops are potatoes, yams, taro, manioc, and sweet potatoes. Seed crops require greater soil nutrients for successful growth. For this reason seed crops use up available soil nutrients at a faster rate than do root crops. The length of time required for the regeneration of a field, therefore, is greater when seed crops are cultivated than when root crops are grown. These two different crop complexes have an impact on settlements and population.

Under seed crop cultivation there is a greater likelihood that settlements and fields will be abandoned for long periods of time. With root crop cultivation, on the other hand, permanent village sites can be maintained. Even though garden sites are shifted, they can be put back into production within a reasonable time. This characteristic of root crop cultivation may help to explain why densely populated permanent village communities occur throughout West Africa, where root crops are grown.

Although root crops have decided advantages, seed crops also provide some benefits. Seed crops provide a high protein food in comparison to the high starch and carbohydrate content of root crops. In addition, the products of seed crop cultivation can be more easily stored, thus providing a food surplus.

Compared to foraging economies, horticultural systems provide greater food productivity, and this increase in food resources can support large populations. The small village is typical of many horticultural societies, and many horticultural societies rarely develop beyond a village form of political and social organization. Under favorable conditions, however, horticulture can give rise to complex political, social, and economic institutions. The Maya civilization of Mexico and the great kingdoms of West Africa are examples of complex cultures built upon horticulture.

Pastoralism

Pastoralism is a subsistence system based upon herds of domesticated animals. The systematic butchering of animals for meat is not a common practice among pastoralists. Instead,

Table 3.1. Pastoral regions and animals herded

Pastoral region	Major animal herded
Africa	Cattle
North Africa–Middle East	Camel, sheep, goat
Mediterranean	Sheep, goat
Central Asia–Tibet	Horse, yak, cattle
Siberian Tundra	Reindeer

Note: This table indicates only the *major* animal herded in each region. Many pastoral societies herd a variety of animals if it is possible for them to do so.

milk, cheese, butter, and blood are the mainstays of the diet.

Pastoralism is found in the arid and grassland regions of Africa, Asia, and Europe that are unsuitable for nonmechanized agriculture. The great homeland of the pastoral societies stretches from Mongolia through Central Asia, the Russian Steppes, the Middle East, the Mediterranean, and Africa. Within this wide geographic zone a variety of animals have been herded, but five regions can be distinguished on the basis of the major animal or animals herded (see Table 3.1).

Whenever anthropologists write about pastoralists they always associate them with nomadism because the provision of water and pasturage for their animals requires migration. In these societies the movement of people and their animals is one of the most dramatic events in their lives; for example, the Bedouin of Arabia may travel as much as 1000 miles in a year. In Central Asia the summer months are the occasion for movement up the mountain slope into high altitude pastures, and although the distance covered is short, the variation in climate and altitude is extreme. Part of the drama of these migrations is that vast herds of animals and large numbers of people move from one place to another. An entire society is on the march.

Many pastoral peoples have an almost obsessive interest in their animals; for example, cattle to the Nuer of the Sudan are like members of the family. Each animal has a personal name and men are called by the names of their cows. Nuer men compose poems in honor of their favorite animals. Evans-Pritchard recorded the following "cattle poem."

I. The wind blows *wirawira;*[1]
   Where does it blow to?
   It blows to the river.
   The shorthorn carries its full udder
      to the pastures;[2]
   Let her be milked by Nyagaak;
   My belly will be filled with milk.
   Thou pride of Nyawal,
   Ever-quarrelling Rolnyang.[3]
   This country is overrun by strangers;
   They throw our ornaments into the river;
   They draw their water from the bank.[4]
   Blackhair my sister,
   I am bewildered.
   Blackhair my sister,
   I am bewildered.
   We are perplexed;
   We gaze at the stars of God.[5]

2. White ox good is my mother
   And we the people of my sister,
   The people of Nyariau Bul.
   As my black-rumped white ox,
   When I went to court the winsome lassie,
   I am not a man whom girls refuse.
   We court girls by stealth in the night,
   I and Kwejok

Nyadeang.[6]
We brought the ox across the river,
I and Kirjoak
And the son of my mother's sister
Buth Gutjaak.
Friend, great ox of the spreading horns,
Which ever bellows amid the herd,
Ox of the son of Bul
Maloa.[7]

(Evans-Pritchard 1974:46–47)

Evans-Pritchard once complained that no matter how he began a conversation with Nuer men, it ended in talking about or describing cattle (1940:18–19). In a similar fashion, Donald P. Cole, who lived with and studied the Al Murrah Bedouin of the Empty Quarter of Arabia, noted the intense identification of Al Murrah men with their camels. They gave them names, made up poems and songs about them, and told endless stories about them (1975:27).

This obsession indicates a balanced relationship between human beings and their animals. If human beings need the animals for sustenance, the animals are no less dependent upon people for water, pasturage, and protection from predators. Neither could survive without the other. Such a mutually beneficial relationship is called a symbiotic relationship.

The care and protection of animals frequently requires aggressive behavior on the part of pastoralists. Warfare, raiding, and combat are not only common but also highly valued activities. Raiding may be the most effective way of securing animals. In the past whenever pastoral nomads came into contact with settled cultivators, the advantages fell to the pastoralists. Pastoralists value their way of life and its cultural values over that of the cultivator or peasant.

From the earliest records of Middle East

[1] Literally 'My wind'. The singer runs against it and seems by so doing to add to its strength. This is the north wind which blows at the time of rich pasture when the cows give plenty of milk: hence the connection between the first three lines and those which follow them.
[2] The cow has refused to suckle its calf or to be milked before going to graze.
[3] Nyagaak is the sister of the poet. Pride (*gweth*) is the dance-name of a girl, Nyawal. Rolnyang is a youth's ox-name.
[4] The strangers are Government forces. The reference to drawing water from the bank is obscure.
[5] Blackhair is a girl's name. The Nuer are perplexed by foreign invasion and the last line is a prayer to God to help them in their adversity.

[6] The ox referred to in the first and fourth lines is the poet's ox. Kwejok is a friend, whose mother is Nyadeang.
[7] Buth is the birth-name of a friend whose ox-name is Gutjaak. The poet, who is a son of Bul Maloa, addresses his ox as his friend in the final lines.

A Rendille woman of East Africa loads the family residence into a camel. Ability to move about is vital to pastoral nomads.

cultures up to modern times, the pastoralist hovered on the fringes of agricultural society as predator, challenger, threat, and on occasion as overlord. The most extreme example was that of the Mongol Empire of the thirteenth century, whose mounted nomads spread from China to Eastern Europe, attacking the urban societies of India and the Middle East. Perhaps no pastoral group had such an impact on world history as the Bedouin of Arabia. In the seventh and eighth centuries, Bedouin tribesmen made up the armies that spread Islam throughout the Middle East, North Africa, and Iran.

In order to maintain and protect their herds, pastoral nomads must obtain information about all aspects of the environment. They require full knowledge of the physical environment, climate, rainfall, waterholes, trails, passes, caves, and pastures, as well as infor-mation about other groups in the area and instances of disease, drought, and raiding. Observers of pastoral nomads have noted the widespread emphasis upon hospitality. The stranger as an individual poses no threat and is frequently an important source of information.

Until recently the pastoral nomad, especially the mounted nomad, enjoyed a dominant political position in relation to settled cultivators. Nomads had both strategic and tactical superiority. Prior to European colonial expansion, luxury products, such as spices and silks, were taken by caravans across the grasslands and deserts that were home to the pastoral nomad. Tribute and payment to nomads as "caravan guards" were important parts of the pastoral economy. In the last hundred years the declining importance of the caravan trade and the military superiority of national armies have threatened pastoralism as a way of life.

In the Sahel of West Africa recent droughts have wiped out large numbers of animals and forced pastoral tribesmen into towns and refugee camps. Some anthropologists have argued that the obstacles nomads faced in crossing political frontiers coupled with the drought were major factors in the destruction of the animal herds.

In other parts of the world national governments are attempting to turn pastoralists into settled ranchers who produce meat, dairy products, and hides for national and international markets. Both political and economic circumstances are eroding the traditional practices of pastoralists. Traditional pastoralism will probably survive, although in a diminished and altered form from the classic pattern that emerged thousands of years ago.

Agriculture and Peasant Farming

Until the 1930s, most anthropologists studied tribal groups — foragers, horticulturalists, and pastoralists. In 1930, Robert Redfield published a study of a Mexican peasant community, Te-

Plowing a field in Collefiore, Italy. Use of plows and animals for labor is characteristic of peasant agriculture.

potzlan. A few years later he collaborated with Alfonso Villa Rojas in studying another peasant village in Mexico, Chan Kom (1934). These ethnographic accounts of peasant villages opened the study of peasant cultures throughout the world by anthropologists. Today, as well as at the time of Redfield and Villa Rojas's study, peasants represent the majority of the world's population. They are found in Japan, China, Southeast Asia, India, the Middle East, North Africa, the Mediterranean, Eastern and Western Europe, and Latin America.

Agriculture is the basic productive activity in *peasant society.* Basic technological features of peasant agriculture are the use of the plow and work animals. Animal manure is available as a source of high-quality fertilizer. This combination of technology and manure permits intensive cultivation and greater food productivity. Plows and animal power enable peasants to cultivate areas and soils beyond the technological capabilities of horticulturalists.

Agricultural communities often develop irrigation and terracing techniques, which lead to continuous cultivation and very high levels of food production. For this reason land in a peasant community is a scarce and valued resource. A combination of high population and valuable land leads, among other things, to the concept of private, individual, family, or group ownership of land. Individual cultivators invest large amounts of time, effort, and resources in clearing, fertilizing, preparing, plowing, and irrigating the soil.

When Redfield studied the residents of Tepotzlan he described them as peasant proprietors. After looking at the same village twenty years later and consulting landholding records from the 1920s when Redfield did his research, Oscar Lewis (1951) concluded that

Men in Galipur, India use a basket to irrigate fields. Irrigation in peasant agriculture permits intensive cultivation and greater productivity.

over half the population were in fact laborers who owned no land. These people worked in the fields of landowners. Subsequent research in peasant communities throughout the world has validated Lewis's picture of the peasant community as one in which groups have differential access to productive land. This differential access to land makes the peasant community a stratified society in which individuals and groups vary greatly in terms of their economic, political, and social positions. In contrast to peasants, there is little *social stratification* among foragers, horticulturalists, and pastoralists.

In many peasant villages land is owned by absentee landlords who frequently reside in urban centers that are centers of political domination. Rulers living in cities extract a portion of the peasants' production through taxation, rent, or tribute. This percentage of peasant produc-

tion serves as the economic base for the urban center. Looked at from the peasant point of view, the process consists of exploitation and confiscation.

In most peasant villages there are marked social and economic differences between landless laborers, small peasant owners, and large landowners. In urban centers there is an even greater social differentiation between people at the top and people at the bottom. Elites made up of rulers, administrators, intellectuals, religious specialists, and military officials constitute a privileged class. At the other extreme are groups like scavengers, sweepers, beggars, and criminals (Eames and Goode 1973).

A basic requirement in a horticultural society is a reserve of available but uncultivated land. In peasant society the comparable component of the system is a reserve of cheap and available labor. Thus many peasant societies contain large numbers of unemployed and underemployed masses who can be used when needed, especially during the vital grain harvest season.

Industrialism

Less than two centuries ago Western Europe moved from an agrarian society based largely on animal and human power to an industrial society based on fossil energy: coal and oil. Factories were built bringing together workers, machines, and sources of energy. This resulted in the production of goods on a scale unimaginable in a peasant or horticultural society. Previously goods in limited quantities were produced in peasant households or by individual craftsmen. English weavers in the eighteenth century were an example of this shift from artisan production to factory production. As skilled craftsmen before the advent of industrialism, weavers enjoyed a favored economic position. They owned spinning wheels, looms, and textile dyes, and produced cloth in their own homes (cottage industry). With the emergence of textile factories and the centralization of production, weavers were displaced as producers of woolen cloth. The highly skilled and independent weavers sank into poverty. Factory owners hired women and children with no particular skills to run the factory looms at low wages.

While factories were emerging in cities a corresponding revolution was taking place in the countryside. Farming was becoming mechanized; landowners replaced peasants with machines and small work crews. Although the production of food increased, the need for labor decreased. Hordes of dispossessed and unemployed country folk flocked into the cities. Some were fortunate in obtaining factory employment, whereas others lived in urban squalor and poverty. During the early decades of the Industrial Revolution millions of people

worked and lived under conditions that Marvin Harris suggests no member of a tribal society would find livable (1977:183). At the beginning of the Industrial Revolution, for example, factory hands worked sixty to ninety hours a week and young children worked in mines and factories.

Outside of the industrializing nations many tribal and peasant people were transformed into poorly paid wage laborers. In Central Africa, for example, copper mines employed thousands of African tribesmen. Throughout the tropical and semitropical regions of the world,

Ten-year-old girl working in a New England textile mill around 1900. Until the outlawing of child labor, the exploitation of children as low-paid factory hands was characteristic of early industrialism.

plantations and commercial agricultural ventures were established to produce commodities for the export market. Cotton, rubber, sisal, tea, coconuts, and sugar were grown by an emerging class of poorly paid laborers or rural proletarians.

One of the major consequences of the Industrial Revolution was to change the way in which most people make a living. In peasant and tribal societies most people make a living by engaging in what we call primary production, that is, producing their own food and making most of their material goods. The transformation of populations from largely self-sufficient producers of food and goods into individuals dependent upon others for their basic needs sets industrialism apart from all other subsistence systems. Individuals in industrial society sell their labor and use their wages to purchase food and manufactured goods. Employment and jobs are basic to industrial society. In industrial society many of the ideological and political movements of today can be interpreted as instruments for protecting job and wage security. Emergence of unions, capture of the state apparatus and bureaucracy by a political party or faction, job tenure, attempts to reduce unemployment, minimum wage laws, controls on imports, and the attraction of socialist philosophies with their promise of worker control are all indications of this overriding concern with economic security in modern industrial society.

Principles of Economic Exchange

Although in tribal and peasant societies individuals make their own material goods and produce most of the food they require, exchange of goods, food, and services is an important and vital part of economic and social life in every society. Anthropologists identify three principles of economic exchange: reciprocity, redistribution, and market exchange.

Reciprocity, a form of gift exchange, has a number of defining elements. Parties to a reciprocal exchange have a relationship to each other that is reinforced through the exchange system. Often the flow of goods involved in reciprocal exchange follows the lines of other social relationships such as kinship, family, and band membership. The essential element in these exchanges is balance. Receiving a gift places the recipient under an obligation to return something of equivalent value. Although reciprocity is found in every subsistence system, it is the predominant form of exchange in most foraging societies.

Reciprocal distribution of goods is a way of maintaining equality between individuals, a marked tendency in foraging societies. The better hunters usually distribute their catch to all other members of the group. Many hunting groups have complex sets of rules governing the sharing and distribution of food. Because most hunting-gathering groups are small, reciprocity defines the boundaries of a group. The famous Scandinavian explorer-anthropologist Knut Rasmussen describes the social basis of reciprocity among the Eskimo as follows:

> People living together in a hunting camp feel closely attached to one another in many ways. They mostly have a strong feeling that they cannot manage singly but need one another's help in the daily hunting. Therefore the men call their hunting companions, "those with whom I live on the firm ice," an expression that has come to mean: "the one with whom I have sought refuge." The thought is always this: "If I do not catch anything, I will surely get food for myself and my family from the others in the camp." The moral is of course: "I expect you to do for me what I do for you." (Coon 1956:125).

Probably the most famous example of reciprocity is the *Kula ring* of the Trobriand Islands described by Bronislaw Malinowski (1922) (Figure 3.3). Malinowski discovered that the

Trobriand Islands were one part of a complex trading system that incorporated a number of different island societies in Melanesia. Men on one island had trading partners on other islands, and men in these trade relationships exchanged Kula valuables — armshells and necklaces. An armshell could be traded only for a necklace, and a necklace could be exchanged only for an armshell. These valuables were not for everyday use, nor could they be kept and owned once and for all by any one individual. Kula valuables circulated slowly among the trading partners, and based on their particular age, history, and previous owners, the necklaces and armshells brought prestige and renown to the men who acquired them.

The Kula was a true reciprocal system. Although individuals attempted to make the best deals possible, the items exchanged were likely to be of equivalent value. As the Kula ring makes clear, reciprocity is not restricted to the exchange of utilitarian goods and food supplies.

Redistribution is a form of exchange in which goods and services are brought to a central authority who then redistributes them in terms of political, economic, and familial relations. Redistribution occurs in societies where differences in rank and power are present. Thus it is generally absent from foraging societies, but occurs widely in horticultural, pastoral, peasant, and industrial societies. Although redistribution is a form of economic exchange, it is closely associated with the exercise of political power and political relations. The payment of taxes in American society is a painful

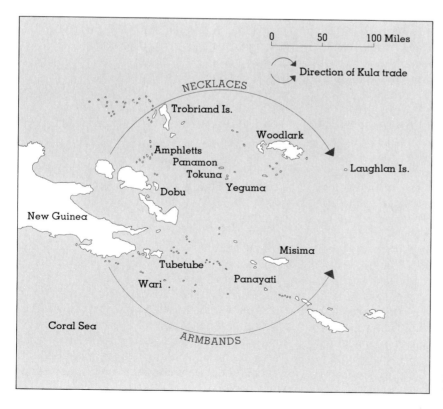

Figure 3.3
The Kula ring.

example of redistribution and its political ramifications. The taxes we pay to various governmental bodies are returned to us through a variety of governmental activities. Schools, highways, social security checks, and a host of government programs are a few of the returns of government to the people. Exchange, however, may not be balanced. Some taxpayers pay far less in federal taxes than they receive in benefits from the federal government, and others receive less than they pay. It is the prerogative of the central authority to redistribute goods, services, or taxes according to criteria it establishes.

Market exchange is based on supply and demand. Each party to a transaction, the buyer and seller alike, attempts to gain the "best deal." Unlike redistribution, market exchange does not involve a political element nor, like reciprocity, is it embedded in a network of other social relations. Ideally, a buyer and a seller agree on a mutual exchange value, which is their sole relationship. Although money, defined as a universal medium of value and exchange, facilitates market exchange transactions, it is not a necessary ingredient.

In our society, market exchange permeates most aspects of our lives. Although most people think of markets as physical places for buying and selling, market exchange is actually a principle, not a place. Most Americans live by selling their labor in the labor market, which is the mechanism through which the cost of labor is established. The demand for workers with certain qualifications and skills may increase their worth (wages) in the labor market. Oversupply or falling demand for certain occupational categories, on the other hand, will seriously depress the worth of these workers and their opportunities for employment.

Markets are a prevailing form in industrial society, and together with money they dominate our cultural landscape. Often pure market exchange controlled solely by supply and demand is a fiction rather than a reality. Governments may control prices or the supply of goods. Workers seek job security and employment opportunities; the capitalist investor seeks market and money security. Monopolies and price fixing thus become techniques of undercutting what economists call the free market, where the laws of supply and demand along with price competition are supposed to operate.

Economic Exchange in Two Peasant Societies: Galipur and Collefiore

In many societies all three principles of exchange may be found. This is especially true in peasant communities. In order to illustrate the cultural forms of these principles, we compare Collefiore in Italy and Galipur in India.

The Italian village, Collefiore, studied by Cohen, has a population of 750 people and is first recorded in written documents in 950 A.D. Galipur, in India, studied by Eames, has a population of about 600 people. It is 300 years old and traces its origins to another village, still in existence, that originated 500 years ago.

In Galipur the Thakurs, a specific caste group, are the major landowners. Other groups, like potters, barbers, and ironsmiths, are obligated to provide goods and services to a group of Thakur families. In return for these goods and services, the Thakurs reciprocate by supplying grain at the time of harvest or by providing arable land for cultivation. Within this system, called *jajmani,* artisans may also exchange goods and services with each other. Thus a potter provides clay pots to a barber family, and in return the barber cuts the hair of the male members of the potter family. The hereditary and noncompetitive nature of this system has fascinated many anthropologists. These reciprocal obligations are inherited and become the means for exchanging many economic goods.

An example of redistribution. An Indian chief in Venezuela supervises the regular distribution of food to the members of the village.

In Collefiore there is an informal system for the reciprocal exchange of labor. At the time of the wheat harvest men are needed to bring in the grain as quickly as possible, and many of the sharecropper peasants, who are either unwilling or unable to hire and pay for labor, agree to help each other in the harvest. A man who aids his neighbor thus expects his neighbor's help in turn. There is no payment for this work, although the man whose grain is harvested distributes wine to the work crew.

Sharecropping is a basic part of the agricultural system in both Galipur and Collefiore. In such a system a landowner leases his land to a peasant family. The harvest is usually divided in half, with 50 percent going to the landowner and 50 percent to the peasant. Sharecropping is a form of redistribution. The landlord receives a portion of the harvest from "his" peasants. The landowner's share of the harvest may be redistributed within the community by supporting poor families and subsidizing religious festivals. The greater share of the landowner's harvest is sold in markets, whereas the sharecropper peasant uses his portion for subsistence.

Peasant communities as part of a larger society provide economic resources for other segments of the society. Governments, both local and national, tax peasant communities.

A market in the city of Shillong, Assam, India. Sale of surplus food in markets is common in peasant society.

This taxation may take the form of labor service, a percentage of the crop, or taxes paid in money. Such resources support the political and administrative elites. Some resources, however, are returned or redistributed to the peasant community in a variety of forms. This redistribution may include roads, military and police forces, irrigation and land reclamation projects, and education and health services. The peasant in the countryside has historically been the foundation for the urban and political elites of agrarian civilization, and traditionally the balance of payment between the city and countryside has been more favorable to the city.

In spite of the role of reciprocity and redistribution within in the village economy, market exchange occupies a place of importance. Galipur villagers produce melons as a cash crop, not as an item for their own consumption. Melons, along with other surplus foods, are taken to nearby urban centers for sale. The prices for melons and other foods for sale fluctuate greatly, reflecting supply and demand. In times of food shortage prices skyrocket,

whereas food surpluses lower market prices. Galipur is located about a mile and a half from a rural market center. Twice a week merchants come to this market with their goods, and villagers walk to the market so that they can purchase cloth, bangles, salt, tobacco, and other objects not available in the village. Some villagers purchase goods from the same merchant week after week, which implies that even market exchange involves a network of social relationships. In Collefiore stores sell mass-produced items and serve as an outlet for local food produce. Once a year Collefiore has a market fair, where local and traveling merchants set up stalls in the village square.

In American society we usually buy goods at a fixed price. In Galipur and Collefiore, however, as in most peasant societies, bargaining and haggling over prices are central to market behavior. The function of bargaining which is, according to experienced bargainers, one of the joys of market behavior, is to deny the pure buyer-seller relationship and connect it in part to a social, as well as an economic, exchange. It appears as if the participants prefer to see their exchange for individual gain as part of a socially approved form of reciprocity.

Economic Exchange and Subsistence Systems

Although all three principles of exchange are found in most subsistence systems, there appears to be a relationship between the type of subsistence system and the dominant form of distribution. As the production of food and goods increases, there is a shift away from reciprocity to redistribution and market exchange.

Reciprocity appears to be especially compatible with the limited food productivity of many foraging and horticultural societies. In these societies there is an emphasis upon equality and a limited development of specialized political and economic institutions.

As the production of food increases, however, there is a corresponding growth in social, political, and economic complexity. This complexity invariably implies major differences in social rank, class, political, and economic power. Under these conditions redistribution develops as a dominant type of exchange.

In peasant society the peasant community often exhibits all three principles of exchange. One reason for the maintenance of reciprocity in the peasant village is a lack of money or other economic wealth to purchase goods and employ labor. Reciprocal sharing and cooperation thus avoid the depletion of scarce resources. Reciprocity also maintains and reinforces social relationships within a small community. Redistribution and market exchange become principles that link peasant villagers to their superiors and to the larger society. From the perspective of the peasant community, this linkage serves to drain away surplus production and maintain village scarcity.

Industrialism has meant vast increases in productivity and wealth. In the early stages of industrialism market exchange became dominant, which can be seen in the conversion of land and labor into commodities that could be bought and sold. Fluctuations in a free market economy, however, threatened everybody in the system — workers, bankers, and factory owners. A cycle of financial panics and economic depressions appeared to be part of the free market system. This situation was intolerable; capitalists attempted to protect their investments, and workers wanted to protect their jobs. For a variety of reasons, everyone thus began to tinker with the system in an attempt to control these disruptive elements. Devices such as monopolies, price controls, unions, and government subsidies reflect political power and political realities rather than the operation of a free market economy.

The incredible productivity of industrial technology has raised the standard of living in industrial nations, but it has also exaggerated the economic and social differences within society. Such vast differences have been the basis for ideological movements that seek to narrow or do away with economic and social differentials. In these political and ideological movements the major mechanism for achieving this result is government redistribution. The socialist slogan, "from each according to his ability, to each according to his needs," expresses the idea that the function of government is to extract from us what we can contribute and guarantee that we will all have our needs satisfied. In the last half of this century many nations have moved toward redistributive economic systems, and it is likely that this principle of exchange will come to dominate industrial society.

Women and Men and the Subsistence System

The activities of women in subsistence systems vary widely. In some societies women are intimately involved in the production of food; in other societies women do not take part in productive activity but concentrate on domestic chores and child-rearing responsibilities.

In most foraging societies based primarily upon hunting, women play a minor role in the acquisition of food. In predominantly gathering societies, however, women are often the primary producers of food. As Richard Lee discovered, Dobe San women gather and prepare most of the food consumed. In his research with Australian hunter-gatherers in the Gibson Desert of Western Australia, Richard Gould found that gathering by women was so efficient and productive that it gave the entire group abundant time for leisure (Gould 1969).

Women are also a significant element in horticultural systems. A Bomagai-Angoiang man has an available labor force that includes not only his wife, but also a set of female garden partners. Men fell trees and clear underbrush, and women plant, weed, harvest, and take care of pigs. The Bomagai-Angoiang are relatively typical of most horticulturally based societies. Because women are responsible for much of the time-consuming horticultural activities, men devote their time to other pursuits: hunting, loafing, or taking part in war.

In pastoral societies women play a reduced role in food production. Most pastoralists consider the care and herding of domestic animals as the primary responsibility of men, with the tasks of milking and the preparation of dairy foods belonging to women. Defense and raiding, which are a part of the total pastoral pattern, are exclusively male occupations.

An example of how the *sexual division of labor* affects those in a pastoral society is found among Tibetan nomads. Robert Ekvall found that among Tibetan pastoral nomads men are exclusively responsible for raiding, a technique used to increase the size of their herds (1968). Women, on the other hand, are exclusively responsible for milking the animals and for preparing dairy products.

A consequence of plow agriculture is the *decreasing* importance of women in production and the *increasing* involvement of men in productive activity. In Galipur high-status (upper-caste) women do not perform economic functions outside the household, and they are expected to remain within the confines of the house. This pattern is also found in the Mediterranean. Low-status (peasant) women, both in Collefiore and Galipur, work alongside men in many of the agricultural activities. Women are less involved in major economic activities outside the home in direct proportion to their class position, however.

The economic role of women in Western society is both complicated and confusing. Women and children were employed in factory production during the early phases of industrialism. During the nineteenth century, however, middle- and upper-class women rarely engaged in productive labor outside the home. Removing upper-class women from direct economic activity and restricting them to domestic and social affairs became an ideal in Western society.

In the nineteenth century male beliefs about the inherent inability of women to perform any kind of work competently justified, to men, the noneconomic role of women. Thus the first typists were men, because men considered typing too complicated for women. As the industrial and commercial economy grew certain occupations became defined as female occupations — telephone operators, receptionists, typists, nurses, secretaries, and schoolteachers. While the expansion of the commercial economy brought middle-class women into the labor force, working-class women had always been employed in certain manufacturing jobs, especially in the textile and garment trades.

The rigid distinction between men's occupations and women's occupations was maintained during most of the twentieth century. Even the large-scale employment of women in defense industries during World War II was a temporary and expedient interlude. The postwar economy saw a return to occupational segregation by sex. Only within the last two decades has occupational discrimination based on sex been seriously questioned and changed. To a great extent the attack on sex discrimination in the economy has been spearheaded by the entrance of middle-class women into the labor force. The previous cultural patterns in which the middle-class female fulfilled her destiny as homemaker, housewife, and mother have been denied and discarded by our present society.

Variations in the productive role of women may be related to the incompatibility of productive activity with child-rearing responsibilities. Rameka, Kunbun's wife, brought her baby with her while she worked, weeded, and harvested in the garden. Rameka could harvest and hold her child; she could stop working to breastfeed the baby, and she could even put him down somewhere in the garden without any fear for the infant's safety. It would be difficult to picture a similar pattern of child care under the conditions of hunting wild game, engaging in pastoral raiding, plowing fields, or working in a factory or office. Although this thesis of female incompatibility with productivity appears to be reasonable, it may be a social myth that justifies an existing cultural pattern in our society.

Removal of women from direct production may reflect status and prestige considerations rather than the incompatibility between child rearing and productive labor. Economic considerations may account for the absence of middle- and upper-class women from the labor force. Until recently it was possible for a single wage earner, who was usually male, to support a family unit. Changing economic conditions, especially for the middle classes in America and Europe, have made the maintenance of this pattern more difficult. From this perspective we arrive at the conclusion that middle-class women are entering the labor force in increasing numbers for economic reasons.

Other factors have also facilitated the movement of women into the labor force. The invention of effective contraceptive devices and the development of alternative child care institutions have removed the most constraining obstacles to female participation in work outside the home. Employment of women has also been stimulated by an ideological movement stressing the capacity and capability of women to participate in all areas of modern life.

Summary

In the course of human history several major events occurred that fundamentally shifted the way in which people make their living. For most of human history people were directly dependent upon what nature provided, and these people, known as foragers, inhabited almost every part of the planet. Foragers exhibited a wide range of cultural adaptations to particular environmental settings. They did, however, manifest several common characteristics: low population, small settlements, systems of reciprocal exchange embedded in a network of social relations, and nomadism. Unlike the usual views of such people, recent evidence indicates that foragers did not spend a great deal of time in acquiring food and that they did not continually hover on the brink of starvation.

The Bomagai-Angoiang represent a fundamental change in human economy. Mark Cohen has argued that increasing population pressures among foragers, which occurred 10,000 to 12,000 years ago, were the major cause of the domesticated food economy. In contrast to foragers, horticulturalists and pastoralists have large populations and the village becomes the basic form of settlement. Under favorable circumstances this economy can begin to support more complex political and social institutions.

Simple agriculture, in a limited number of suitable environments, developed into the peasant society. In such societies we find the emergence of urban centers that become the locale of political domination and elite cultural traditions. Peasants cultivate the land and provide the economic basis of the agrarian society. Much of their production is expropriated by the political and urban elite. Peasant villages are relatively large in size and geographically fixed. There is a stratified class system within the peasant village as well as throughout the entire society.

Industrialism may have been a response to a growing population, for its major characteristic is an enormous increase in productivity. People have shifted their basic way of making a living from direct food production (primary production) to wage labor. A small segment of the working population provides all the food consumed by the rest of the population. Vast differences in wealth and power, social inequality, urban sprawl, and unimaginable material prosperity are some of the consequences of industrialization. Unlike the Dobe San hunter or the Bomagai-Angoiang cultivator, industrial workers work longer hours and until recently labored under unspeakably poor conditions. It is a strange paradox that poverty and squalor as well as wealth and opulence are associated with industrial society.

A somewhat simplified view of making a living under different subsistence systems can be summarized as follows:

1. Foragers search for available wild foods and animals.
2. Horticulturalists search for land and fertilizer resources.
3. Pastoralists search for water and pasture.
4. Peasants seek a more equitable distribution of land and of the food they grow.
5. Workers in industrial society search for job security, while capitalists seek financial gain and market security.

Distribution and exchange of goods and services are part of every economic system. In Western society money and market exchange are the major mechanisms used to distribute products of the economic system, while in other societies reciprocity and redistribution are the major techniques for distribution. Although these three principles, market exchange, reciprocity, and redistribution, may be found in most societies, they tend to be associated with particular subsistence systems. Foragers generally use reciprocity, while redistribution is common in horticultural and pastoral societies. Peasant societies use all three principles of exchange, although within the peasant community reciprocity and redistribution are of primary importance.

In modern industrial society market exchange becomes a dominant principle, converting land and labor into commodities that can be bought and sold. Market exchange in early industrial society appears to have been associated with severe economic dislocation, panics, and depressions. As industrial society matures redistribution may come to play a more important role in the exchange of goods and services. For many social critics redistribution is seen as an economic mechanism designed to guarantee financial and employment security.

In contemporary Western society women are demanding access to economic and productive activities. A comparative analysis of the role of women in economic affairs reveals their importance in foraging and horticultural societies. With the exception of purely hunting economies, women usually produce most of the food consumed in these two subsistence systems. In pastoral, peasant, and industrial societies, women's activities are largely centered around domestic life and child-rearing. In industrial society, however, the exclusion of women from direct economic activity was largely the province of upper- and middle-class women, whereas lower-class women have historically been employed in menial and poorly paid labor. There is no direct biological reason for the exclusion of women from primary productive activity. It is possible, however, that economic activities in pastoral and peasant society are incompatible with child-rearing demands. In contemporary society the development of effective contraceptive devices, the emergence of day-care centers, and economic necessity have combined to bring millions of middle-class women into the labor market.

Key Terms and Concepts

subsistence system
foraging/hunting
    and gathering
horticulture
pastoralism/herding
agriculture/peasant
    farming
industrialism/factory
    production
slash and burn

domesticated food
    economy
peasant society
social stratification
reciprocity
Kula ring
redistribution
market exchange
sexual division of
    labor

Suggested Readings

Belshaw, Cyril S. *Traditional Exchange and Modern Markets.* Englewood Cliffs, N.J.: Prentice-Hall, 1965. *An introductory survey of exchange and market systems. Discusses the modernization of traditional economies.*

Cohen, Mark N. *The Food Crisis in Prehistory: Overpopulation and Origins of Agriculture.* New Haven, Conn.: Yale University Press, 1979. *A comprehensive presentation of the hypothesis that*

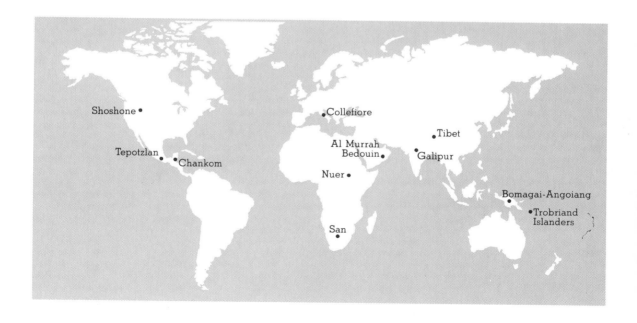

population growth and population pressure on food resources among hunters and gatherers was the fundamental factor in the origin of a domesticated food economy.

Coon, Carleton S. *The Hunting Peoples.* Boston: Atlantic-Little, Brown, 1971. *One of the foremost experts on hunters and gatherers describes adaptations of the foraging pattern to different environments. Includes an excellent description of the material technology of hunting and gathering.*

Kessler, Evelyn S. *Women: An Anthropological View.* New York: Holt, Rinehart and Winston, 1976. *An anthropological interpretation of the status and role of women in various cultures. Especially valuable for the material on women in different economic and subsistence systems.*

Netting, Robert M. *Cultural Ecology.* Menlo Park, Calif.: Cummings, 1977. *Discusses and analyzes foraging, pastoralism, and cultivation from the perspective of cultural ecology.*

Service, Elman R. *The Hunters,* 2nd ed. Englewood Cliffs, N.J.: Prentice-Hall, 1979. *A survey of hunting and gathering groups that contains short ethnographic descriptions of foraging societies.*

Wallace, Anthony F. *Rockdale: The Growth of an American Village in the Early Industrial Revolution.* New York: W. W. Norton, 1980. *Using letters, diaries, records, and other documents, Wallace recreates the social history of a small Pennsylvania milltown during the early years of the Industrial Revolution.*

Wolf, Eric R. *Peasants.* Englewood Cliffs, N.J.: Prentice-Hall, 1966. *A short survey of the economic, social, and religious aspects of peasant society.*

Chapter 4

Mating, Marriage, Family, and Household

As students of human behavior in all of its diverse forms, anthropologists recognize that marital and familial systems reflect human ingenuity and inventiveness. Influenced by the ethnocentric values of Victorian prudery in which people viewed the values of their society as superior to the values of any other society, nineteenth-century cultural anthropologists were titillated by the sexual and marital customs of tribal people. Sexual permissiveness, plural marriage, bride-price, and marriage by capture, customs often found in tribal society, were engrossing topics that were related to preconceived notions of European cultural development and tribal backwardness.

In contrast to this view modern anthropologists see the variety of marital and household forms as fundamental institutions in the social organization of society. Through these institutions basic economic functions are frequently pursued, and, in addition, the care and upbringing of children are undertaken, primary responsibilities of the human family.

Marriage and Family in Two Societies

A single ethnographic example could hardly do justice to the full range of marriage and family systems found in human society. Obviously the two examples presented do not exhaust the total range of such forms, although they do provide a detailed view of how human cultures can differ in regard to these basic institutions. One example, drawn from the peasant village of Galipur in India, illustrates marriage, family, and household organization that is common in peasant societies. The other example, the marriage system of the Tiwi of Australia, illustrates a tribal marital system that is strikingly different from both the system found in America and the system in Galipur.

Tiwi Marriage

In Tiwi society most married men have many wives. Two basic norms in Tiwi culture contribute to this phenomenon: all females must be married, and men below the age of twenty-five cannot marry. Hart and Pilling (1960) describe how the system operates and its relation to other aspects of Tiwi life.

Marriage ceremonies are a means of maintaining tradition. In Mexico a newly married couple in formal dress leaves the wedding in a horse-drawn carriage that identifies them with the past.

MARRIAGE BY BETROTHAL

In aboriginal times there was no concept of an unmarried female in Tiwi ideology, no word for such a condition in their language, and in fact, no female in the population without at least a nominal husband. Their own explanation of this unique situation was connected with their beliefs about conception and where babies come from. [They] believed that a woman becomes pregnant because a spirit has entered into her body. Since any female was liable to be impregnated by a spirit at any time, the sensible step was to insist that every female have a husband *all the time* so that if she did become pregnant, the child would always have a father. As a result of this logical thinking, all Tiwi babies were betrothed before or as soon as they were born; females were thus the "wives" of their betrothed husbands from the moment of birth onward. For similar reasons, widows were required to remarry at the gravesides of their late husbands, and this rule applied even to ancient hags who had already buried half a dozen previous husbands in the course of a long life.

Their cultural insistence that all females of every age be married resulted in unusual features of the domestic situation. No compulsory marriage was required or expected of males. Hence, the total female population, but only part of the male population, was married. This permitted, indeed required, a high degree of plural marriage. The men who held the right to betroth — namely, the fathers of the female babies — bestowed them, generally speaking, where some tangible return was to be anticipated. Put bluntly, in Tiwi culture daughters were an asset to their father, and he invested these assets in his own welfare. He therefore bestowed his newly born daughter on a friend or an ally, or on somebody he wanted as a friend or an ally. Such a person was apt to be a man near his own age

or at least an adult man, and hence perhaps forty years or so older than the newly born baby bestowed upon him as a wife. The father might bestow an infant daughter on a man who had already bestowed an infant daughter upon him, thus in effect swapping infant daughters. A father looking for a suitable male upon whom to bestow his infant daughter's hand might decide to use her as old-age insurance — in which case he selected as her future husband, not one of the older adult men, but a likely looking youngster "with promise"; that is, a youth in his late twenties or thirties who showed signs of being a good hunter and a good fighting man, and who was clearly on his way up in tribal power and influence.

No Tiwi father ever thought of bestowing an infant daughter upon any male below the age of at least twenty-five. This meant that a youth of twenty-five had his first wife betrothed or promised to him at that age but had to wait another fourteen years or so before she was old enough to leave her father's household and take up residence and marriage duties with him. By this time he was about forty. An age gap between husband and wife at least as great as this was a necessary and constant result of the Tiwi betrothal system.

As in our own culture, where the first million is the hardest to make, so in Tiwi the first bestowed wife was the hardest to get. If some shrewd father with a daughter to invest in a twenty-year-old decided to invest her in you, his judgment was likely to attract other fathers to make a similar investment. As a result, for *some* Tiwi men, the arrival in residence of the first wife was quickly followed by the arrival in residence of a second, third, fourth [and] perhaps half a dozen between his late thirties and his late forties as his various betrothed wives reached the age of puberty and joined his household, and from then on he was practically certain to accumulate still more wives as later bestowals grew up and as he was able to invest the daughters borne by his first crop of young wives in transactions which brought in a later crop.

But while [betrothal] was the most prestigeful form of marriage and the only respectable way in which a man could obtain a *young* wife, there were other ways of setting up a household.

WIDOW REMARRIAGE

To become "a big man" a Tiwi had, among other things, to accumulate a lot of wives. A rising star who accumulated by bestowal seven or eight wives by his middle forties and then died, merely left a lot of widows to be redistributed at his graveside. Hence, the largest number of wives ultimately accrued to the successful man who lived longest, since he was likely to gather up at least a few of the widows of each of his contemporaries or seniors as they predeceased him.

There was thus a close correlation between increasing age and the number of wives a man had, and the largest households belonged to a few surviving old men in each

A seventy-five-old Tiwi man and the youngest of his four wives, who is thirty-three years old. Working in front of their house, the two are shaping spears for sale to the tourist trade.

band. The two conditions, therefore, which were necessary to accumulate a large household were (1) to attract prospective fathers-in-law to invest their infant daughters in you while you were a young man, and then (2) to live long enough to reap the dividends. The longer you lived, the more dividends would accrue to you from one source or another, provided you started off right by attracting betrothals in your twenties and thirties.

But what about the unimpressive young men, the "noncomers," who somehow failed as young men to attract any prospective fathers-in-law to invest an infant daughter in them? It would appear as if a young Tiwi male overlooked or ignored by all fathers of bestowable female daughters had no alternative except permanent bachelorhood. Doubtless Tiwi fathers, as a class, would have regarded this as an ideal situation and would have said that permanent bachelorhood was a proper fate for such friendless and hence useless young men, but no social system of such rigidity has ever been discovered by anthropologists. Tiwi fathers were able rigidly to control the marriages of their infant daughters, but they were not able to control with the same rigidity the remarriages of their own widows, and it was widow remarriage that supplied the loophole in the system, or the cultural alternative that took care of young men.

A girl of fourteen who entered into residence with her first husband when he was fifty was likely to be left a widow by him within the next fifteen years, and even if she remarried a man of the same age as her first husband, she could easily be widowed for the second time while still herself a comparatively young woman. The situation may be illustrated by the concrete case of one of Turimpi's widows, an ancient crone (in 1930) named Bongdadu. Born about 1865, she was betrothed at birth to a powerful old man named Walitaumi who was

at least the same age as her father. He died while she was still a child and well before she was old enough to join his household. Her betrothal was then reassigned, so to speak, to Walitaumi's half-brother, Turimpi, then in his early forties. About seven years later, she joined Turimpi's household as a blushing bride of fourteen, her husband then being close to fifty. In the next twenty years she became Turimpi's most prolific wife and bore numerous children, three of whom, Antonio, Mariano, and Louis, all born between 1883 and 1900, were men of importance in Tiwi politics in 1930. Around 1900, when Bongdadu was still only about thirty-five, she passed to M. and was his wife until his death around 1925. By this date, Bongdadu was over sixty and had borne ten children, four of whom died young. Not unnaturally, she was beginning to approach the hag or crone stage of Tiwi womanhood. Nonetheless, she had to remarry, but by now all of the people who might have claimed any rights of bestowal in her were long since dead, her eldest sons were adult men of some importance and able to protect their mother's interests, and clearly she was unlikely to produce any more children. Her chief value was as a food producer and housekeeper and female politician, roles for which she had been well trained in her long years as wife of Turimpi.

In 1925, then, Bongdadu, widowed three times already, married as her fourth husband one Dominico, a man of no importance whatever, as was shown by the fact that at this time he was nearly forty and had not been able to attract even one bestowed wife. He had, however, already married one widow, so that his marriage to Bongdadu gave him a second wife, also, of course, a widow. This marriage is of further interest when we discover that Antonio, Mariano, and Louis, the main sons of Bongdadu by a previous marriage, had some influence in arranging this marriage of their mother to a contemporary and satellite of theirs, and that a year or two before, Antonio had married the ancient mother of Dominico when *she* became a widow. In other words, Antonio and Dominico had married each other's mothers. Earlier, we mentioned the practice of fathers swapping their daughters within the infant bestowal system; here we find sons swapping their mothers within the widow remarriage system.

HOUSEHOLDS AND SUBSISTENCE

Households were primarily autonomous food-producing and food-consumption units. A household made its own decisions, camped where it saw fit to camp, moved on when the food quest made it advantageous or necessary to move on. A large household was a complete community in itself, with the old man as executive director. He laid down the daily, weekly, and monthly work and travel schedules for the women, the young men, and the children.

The Tiwi themselves had no doubt about the close relationship between plural marriage and good eating. "If I had only one or two wives I would starve," the head of a large household once told the missionary who was preaching against plural marriage, "but with my present ten or twelve wives I can send them out in all directions in the morning and at least two or three of them are likely to bring something back with them at the end of the day, and then we can all eat." This was a realistic appraisal of the economic situation and it is to be noted that he put the emphasis on the food obtained by the women gatherers rather than that supplied by the male hunters. Based on the observations of 1928–1929, it would appear that the Tiwi ate pretty well, especially in the larger households. Kangaroo and other marsupials, and lizards were very plentiful, as were fish and turtles and wild geese. But all these were extras or dividends; the staple everyday foods were the vegetable foods gathered day after day in apparently unending quantities by the women.

Compulsory marriage for all females, carried out through the twin mechanisms of infant bestowal and widow remarriage, resulted in a very unusual type of household, in which old successful men had twenty wives each, while men under thirty had no wives at all and men under forty were married mostly to elderly crones. This unusual household structure was the focal point of Tiwi culture. It linked together in an explicable unity the kinship system, the food-gathering system, the political and prestige system, the seniority system, the sexual system, and the legal-moral-religious system of the tribe. Or perhaps all these should be labeled as subsystems under the household structure, the master system which unified them. (Hart and Pilling 1960:14–20, 29–30, 33–34).

Marriage and Family in Galipur

Tiwi marriage customs may be extreme, but they point up the fact that in a majority of human societies custom and social norms control and guide mate selection and marriage. Choice of marital partners in many societies is considered too important to be left up to young people; in such systems marriages are arranged by parents or relatives. An example of such a system is found among the peasantry of rural India. The following account is based upon Eames's fieldwork in Galipur.

MATE SELECTION

There are several elements that are important in unraveling the complex system of marriage in village India. All marriages must take place between members of the same caste. Individuals from the same village, however, cannot marry each other and must obtain mates from other communities. Marriages *within* a defined group are called endogamous. Thus marriages in India are caste endogamous. Marriages that take place *outside* of a defined group are termed *exogamous.* In India there is also village exogamy. Marriages are arranged by elderly male relatives of the two people to be married. Marriage is monogamous and traditionally divorce is unknown. Widows cannot remarry, although widowers are allowed to do so.

Villagers explain village exogamy by claiming that people brought up in the same village are too closely related to marry. Caste endogamy is such a strong cultural value that marriage outside of a person's caste is unthinkable. Anthropologists see caste endogamy as one basis for maintaining the existence of this ancient institution.

Most village girls, shortly after the onset of puberty, are married to boys about three or four years older. The male kinsmen of the prospective spouses are responsible for arranging the marriage, and the future husband and wife do not see each other until the marriage ceremony is performed. From the arranger's point of view it is much more important to arrange the marriage with a suitable *family* than with a suitable spouse.

Such arrangements are, as might be expected, a matter of extreme importance and delicacy. Not only is the future of a son, daughter, niece, or nephew at stake, but also the future and reputation of the family. For upper-caste families the determination of a *dowry* (money and goods paid to the groom's family) is an essential element in the negotiations. There is a delicate balance that must be reached in dowry negotiations. If a family's daughter is involved, it is essential for the family to send along a "proper" dowry with her. The higher the dowry, the greater the reputation of the family and the greater value they place upon their daughter. Too high a

dowry, on the other hand, threatens the future economic viability of the family. Selling land or borrowing money for the dowry may sometimes be necessary, but it is avoided if possible. Although a boy's kinsmen wish to obtain as high a dowry as possible, they recognize the financial strain that is being placed upon the girl's family.

Very early in the negotiation process an astrologer is called in. This Brahmin (priest-astrologer) casts the horoscopes of the two people who are to be married and determines whether or not their future will be happy. From discussions with these astrologers it appears as if their recommendations are based on the relative strengths of the astrological configurations of the two people. If the girl's configuration is stronger or more dominant than the boy's, the recommendation is that the marriage should not take place. Another function of the astrologer is to set the date for the actual marriage ceremony. Usually the date set for the ceremony is during the hot summer months of April, May, and June, when agricultural activities are minimal.

MARRIAGE CEREMONY

The marriage ceremony usually takes place in the girl's village. The boy is accompanied to his future wife's village by a party composed of male kinsmen and members of other caste groups who are closely tied to the groom's family through the jajmani system (see Chapter 3). These people include a Brahmin (priest), Nal (barber), and Kumhar (potter), and sometimes these marriage parties of villagers contain as many as sixty to seventy men. Rarely do women accompany the groom. Ceremonies usually last several days, and the girl's family is responsible for providing food, shelter, and entertainment during this period. As part of the ceremonial cycle the groom is brought to the girl's house by his male relatives. He is then pushed into a room in which all of the girl's female relatives have assembled. The women taunt him, insulting him and his manhood, and they warn him that he must treat his wife well. After enduring this highly abusive female language, he is told to leave but to remember that he must treat his wife well and with dignity.

The culmination of events related to the marriage occurs when the girl, fully veiled, is led from an enclosed canopy to her husband-to-be. His loincloth *(dhoti)* is knotted with her sari and they are led seven times in a counterclockwise direction around a fire. After this the couple is led back to the bride's house, where a special room has been cleaned and set aside for them. Participants in the wedding party stand outside the house and sing songs and shout encouragements while the couple are supposed to consummate the marriage sexually.

Hindu wedding ceremony in Madras, India. Guests and relatives look on while a Brahmin performs the ceremony.

On the following day the girl accompanies her husband and his marriage party as they return to his village. While she is departing the bride is expected to wail and scream, and indeed one of the most heartrending, though ritualized, scenes in an Indian village is the departure of a newly married girl. At her husband's house she is introduced to all of his female relatives, who have been anxiously awaiting her arrival. Her mother-in-law, sisters-in-law, and her husband's female cousins all greet her, and from this time on her home is with her husband and his relatives.

FAMILY AND HOUSEHOLD

The ideal household in India goes beyond the small nuclear family of a husband, a wife, and their children which is very familiar in American society. In India a boy stays home and his wife joins him, and they live together under the authority of an older male, usually the father of the boy. As each daughter marries she leaves her home to live with her husband and his family in the husband's village. The head

of the household *(malik)* is the oldest living male in the household. He is supposed to make all of the major decisions affecting the well-being of the household. His female counterpart *(malikin)* controls the female segment of the household, and she determines the chores that are to be done by the women.

Behavioral patterns among the women are fixed by custom. A mother-in-law, who is usually the malikin, has almost absolute control over her daughter-in-law's activities. Newly married girls are expected to remain within the confines of the house during the day, and if a newly married girl leaves the house at night to take care of her elimination needs, she is accompanied by her mother-in-law and a sister-in-law, who stand on either side of her. As a result of this seclusion, most of the newly married girl's social relationships and everyday interactions are with the female members of her husband's family — the wives of her husband's older brothers and his younger unmarried sisters. To a large extent she is competing with the wives of her husband's brothers for the favor of the mother-in-law, and this competition may last for a very long time.

Custom also dictates that a husband and wife maintain a formal and distant relationship with each other. In public they have no physical contact, and a wife is not even supposed to initiate a conversation with her husband; she can only respond to his initiation of a conversation. She is supposed to obey and revere him. Villagers say that she should be like the mythological figure, Sita, who walked through fire in order to show her fidelity to her husband, Ram. It is apparent, however, that this ideal is rarely achieved. Wives can be heard arguing with their husbands, and it is not unusual to hear of women who have physically abused their husbands. Many of the norms that require formality between spouses

are relaxed over time. As a husband and wife live and grow old together, their relationship can and does become much less formal.

Several other males are a significant part of a married woman's household — her father-in-law and brothers-in-law. A married woman is supposed to avoid the presence of her father-in-law at all times. When he enters a room or the courtyard of the house, she is required to leave his presence, and she must never converse with him directly. With her husband's younger brothers, on the other hand, she maintains a joking relationship. They can tease each other and interact very informally.

What actually happens in daily life, however, may vary considerably from these ideal patterns. A Brahmin woman in Galipur, for instance, had earned a reputation for being a very aggressive person. One day her father-in-law appeared wearing a bandage. His daughter-in-law apparently had become angry at him and had attacked him with a shoe. This abuse was doubly insulting because he was the local village priest, and for a priest any contact with leather, which represents the hide of the sacred cow, is considered a degradation of his ritually pure Brahman status. In order to avoid her attack, this elderly man had run out of the house and had injured himself in his haste to avoid her wrath.

Although newly married females join a new household unit, males remain in their households from the time of birth. Fathers and sons have a formal relationship with each other, and a son is supposed to show respect for his father, who must be obeyed without question. The oldest brother is the potential future head of the household, and he is supposed to be treated by his younger brothers in much the same way that the father is treated.

The lack of warmth and spontaneity in the

relationship between a boy and many of his male relatives is made up for in his relationship with the female family members. Mothers and sisters are fundamental figures in the boy's emotional world. A very close, warm, and affectionate bond is developed between a mother and son, and a sister and brother. Much of the tension in the relationship between a mother-in-law and daughter-in-law can be traced to this mother-son relationship. The intrusion of the daughter-in-law is frequently resented by the mother-in-law as a potential and real threat to her relationship with her son. Everyone recognizes that over time many of the restrictions placed on the husband and wife relationship will be relaxed and the husband will turn to his wife rather than to his mother for affection, comfort, and advice.

Brothers are expected to protect and care for their sisters throughout life. Even after a sister marries and leaves the household, her brothers are committed to her welfare. This commitment carries over to her children and is the basis of a very close relationship between a boy and his mother's brother. Every year there is a ceremony called *Rahska Band,* in which brothers are supposed to visit their sisters no matter where they live. Brothers bring gifts and sisters tie strings around their brothers' wrists. For several weeks after this ceremony men can be seen proudly displaying these brightly colored strings tied around their wrists.

An Analysis of Tiwi and Galipur Domestic Life

Perhaps the most striking similarity between Tiwi and Indian marriage customs is the relative lack of control women have over their own marriages. Although an elderly Tiwi woman may have some voice in her remarriage, her sons have the major decision-making authority when she remarries. The inability of Tiwi and Indian women to control their own marital destinies is a reflection of the basic authority patterns vested in men in both of these societies. This pattern, which is called *patriarchal,* is common throughout the tribal and peasant societies of the world.

Women in these societies are not completely subservient or without authority. Older Tiwi women and Indian married women enjoy responsibility and authority in the operation of the female side of the household unit. For the Tiwi woman this authority goes far beyond the usual domestic concerns and includes the gathering of wild foods required by a Tiwi household for its sustenance.

Mate Selection

The most basic rules for mate selection are *endogamy* (marriage within a defined group) and *exogamy* (marriage outside of the defined group). Among the Tiwi groups of relatives, called clans, are the exogamous units, and the entire tribe, isolated on their island home, is the endogamous unit. Similar rules of endogamy and exogamy operate for Indian marriages. In rural Indian villages people are required to marry within their own caste (caste endogamy), but the marriage partners must come from another village (village exogamy).

One consequence of the rules of exogamy and endogamy is the requirement that marriages must take place between members of different families and different social groupings. This point has generated different theoretical positions and controversies in anthropology. One view — *alliance theory* — holds that exogamy creates alliances between different and potentially competitive groups. This phenomenon can be seen among the Tiwi, since bestowals carried out by men operate as a means of establishing and cementing political ties between males.

An alternative approach — *descent theory* — views marriage as a recruitment institution, concerned with the cultural and biological continuity and maintenance of the social group over time. Rules of endogamy appear to emphasize this position. Endogamous rules keep wealth, property, access to particular occupations, and political power within the confines of a select group. Caste endogamy, as found in India, preserves the occupational and social integrity of the various caste groups. The rare examples of brother-sister marriage among the Inca, Hawaiian, and Ptolemaic Egyptian royal families are usually interpreted as extreme forms of endogamous marriage restricting kingship and queenship to a single family line.

Alliance and descent theories explain different elements of marital systems. Alliance theory emphasizes exogamy and relations between groups; descent theory emphasizes endogamy and the maintenance and continuity of a social group. Because all societies have rules for both exogamy and endogamy, alliance and descent theories complement each other.

Family and Household

There are major differences between the Tiwi and Galipur marital systems. Although some Tiwi men have more than twenty wives, an Indian man can have only a single wife at a time. A Tiwi woman must remarry when she is widowed; an Indian woman cannot remarry. Spouses in an Indian village are generally close in age, while age differences between Tiwi spouses are basic to the entire system.

Part of the explanation for these and other differences can be found in the economic roles of women. The Tiwi are a hunting-gathering society, and although hunting is important, the gathering of wild foods by women is essential to Tiwi subsistence. Tiwi women constitute the basic productive unit of Tiwi society. This situation is not true for Indian women. In Galipur men work at the essential economic tasks of food supply, services, and material production, and the basic role of women is largely domestic.

There is a relationship between economic factors and household composition in these societies. Tiwi households consist of an older man, his wives, and their children — a two-generational unit. Households in Galipur are frequently three-generational units, consisting of related males, grandfathers, fathers, and sons, as well as their spouses.

In both societies women leave their homes to live with their husbands after the marriage ceremony. In the Tiwi system men establish their own independent households when they marry for the first time, and they subsequently add more wives to this household. In an Indian community a group of men remain in the village and their wives join them. Indian men do not, as a rule, establish independent households when they marry. Their young age at marriage accounts for this in part. Indian men and women marry at about sixteen, an age when no couple is in a position to establish an independent household. Tiwi men, by contrast, marry late, and once they are married to an older woman they have the basis for setting up an independent household.

Despite these cultural differences, Tiwi and Indian households are institutions that serve similar functions and needs. They are basic production and consumption units, and are responsible for the care and training of children.

These systems illustrate two of the many kinds of marital systems found among the cultures of the world. Other societies have their own forms of marriage and family structure that serve biological, psychological, and cultural needs.

Mating, Marriage, and Household in Comparative Perspective

Marriage is the basic building block in the organization of society. It establishes a set of social relationships that develops into family and household systems. Marriage itself, however, is based upon mating and mate selection practices.

Mating

Mating, in its most basic sense, refers to the sexual union of a couple; and societies vary greatly in the degree of sexual freedom they permit. Although sexual compatibility may be a basis for marital choice in our society, it is not necessarily the basis of marriage in other societies. Selection of a mate is a culturally defined process, and the rules governing the selection of mates vary widely from one society to another.

Permissiveness and Constraint in Human Sexuality

No society allows a person to have complete sexual access to everyone who might be re-garded as a potential sexual partner. Nor can a society be so sexually restrictive as to threaten its biological survival. Not only does the incest taboo restrict sexual access, but there are also other rules, customs, and norms limiting sexual behavior.

In Galipur both boys and girls are sexually restricted. Girls are expected to be virgins at marriage, and the postmarital sexual behavior of women is also closely controlled. As in many other male-dominated societies, the sexual restrictions placed upon females in Galipur do not apply equally to men. There are sexual outlets outside of marriage for men in Galipur, although they vary according to caste position. All men have the opportunity to visit brothels in nearby urban areas, and within the village, men of the higher castes have access to women of lower castes. In fact, many sexual restrictions are relaxed for lower-caste women, who may have affairs with upper- and lower-caste men. This behavior reflects the sexual aspect of the social inequality of the caste system. Women of the higher classes are the only ones that are

Two Muria boys in front of their Ghotul.

truly restricted. This pattern of sexual restriction of upper-caste and upper-class females is not uncommon in highly stratified societies and was characteristic of American society in the latter part of the nineteenth century and in the early part of the twentieth century. Although Galipur is sexually restrictive when compared to many other societies, there is flexibility in the system and alternatives are provided in what would otherwise be a system of rigid restraints. Such loopholes are common in many societies, especially in those that attempt to restrict a drive as basic as sex.

Sexual patterns found in Galipur are generally characteristic of many villages in India. Within the subcontinent of India, however, there are numerous tribal groups that have very different patterns of sexual activity. One such group is the Muria of Central India (Elwin 1947). Among the Muria, boys and girls leave their parental homes at about the age of six and become members of a village dormitory *(ghotul)*. They live and work together, are supervised by older members of the ghotul, and eventually establish sexual liaisons in the ghotul.

As part of the mate selection process the ghotul utilizes an extreme form of premarital sexual freedom and experience. In one type of ghotul boys and girls are required to have a variety of sexual partners. No two individuals are allowed to cohabit for more than three consecutive nights, for the Muria believe that limiting the frequency of sexual activity with one partner keeps a girl from becoming pregnant. When a girl does become pregnant she leaves the ghotul and marries.

Among the Muria sexual activity is an accepted basis for mate selection. Galipur marriages, in contrast, are not based on premarital sexual activities. In Western societies sexual attraction has frequently been the basis of mate selection. At present sexual compatibility based upon premarital sexual relations is becoming the basis of mate selection in American society. Whether or not this practice leads to an improvement in marital stability and compatibility is not known.

Mate Selection

Mating patterns are obviously related to marriage, but because anthropologists are primarily concerned with the more permanent aspects of social relations, they tend to focus on marriage instead of mating. *Marriage* is the *socially recognized* union of two or more individuals who are usually, but not always, of the opposite sex. This definition suggests one of the basic dilemmas of anthropology: the difficulty of developing a definition that will fit the widely varied practices of human societies. We have defined this term very generally, because more specific definitions of marriage have been questioned on the basis of particular practices in many societies. This definition identifies public or social recognition as the basis for distinguishing marriage from other types of sexually based unions. Factors such as the number of individuals in the relationship and the functions of the unit have been so varied that they cannot be used as defining characteristics of marriage cross-culturally.

All societies have rules that regulate marriage. Marriage, it would appear, is much too important an issue in society to be left to random choice. Even in societies in which individuals are left free to choose their own marital partners there are still rules, either explicit or implicit, that both limit and narrow marital choices. In American society race, ethnicity, religion and social class are important constraints on marital choice. We have defined some of the general rules governing marital choices — endogamy and exogamy — however, even more precise marriage regulations exist.

Cousin marriage. One of the most precise patterns of marital selection is cousin marriage. Approximately 30 percent of all societies in the

Mating in an age of telecommunication. Video dater Candi talks with interviewer about her ideal date while closed circuit TV camera records the interview. Candi is one of several hundred men and women who are meeting by first seeing each other on video tape.

In American kinship usage no distinction is made between cross and parallel cousins; both are classified as first cousins. In many societies, however, cross and parallel cousins are distinguished, which is reflected in different kin terms for them. The Yanomamo of the Amazon, for example, use the term *hebaraya* to include siblings (brother and sister), father's brother's daughter and son, and mother's sister's son and daughter (parallel cousins). The term *suaboya*, which can be translated as wife, refers to a female cross-cousin (mother's brother's daughter, father's sister's daughter), and the term *heriya* classifies both male cross-cousins and brothers-in-law together (Chagnon 1974:222–233).

In understanding cross-cousin marriage systems it is important to know that parallel cousins are often classified as siblings; that is, as brothers and sisters; while cross-cousins are classified as members of another kin group. In the example of the Yanomamo, who have a cross-cousin marriage system, the same kin term is used for brothers, sisters, and parallel cousins. As a system for selecting mates, cross-cousin marriage goes beyond arranged marriages, for certain categories of individuals are defined as potential spouses.

Mate selection in all human societies is guided and controlled by a variety of principles, rules, and group membership requirements. In Galipur caste and village membership are crucial determinants of marriage; in other societies membership in discrete kin groups or categorization as a cross- or parallel cousin is the significant factor in marital choice. In American society, even though there are no explicit rules governing the choice of mates, the majority of marriages take place between members of the same racial, religious, ethnic, and social class groups. From an anthropological perspective it appears that marriage in American society is largely endogamous within these groups.

world have rules that define cousins as the proper and preferred mate. In its most usual form a male is expected to marry his mother's brother's daughter (MoBrDa) or his father's sister's daughter (FaSiDa). These are his cross-cousins. *Cross-cousins* are the children of siblings of the opposite sex. A few societies, especially in the Middle East, prefer marriage between a man and his father's brother's daughter (FaBrDa) or parallel cousin. *Parallel cousins* are children of siblings of the same sex.

Marriage

Despite the diversity of marital practices, several common forms of marital union are widespread. One way of distinguishing marital unions is by the number of spouses involved. Three forms can be distinguished on this basis: polygyny, polyandry, and monogamy. An extremely rare form of marriage, group marriage, is occasionally mentioned in ethnographic descriptions.

Polygyny

Polygyny is the marriage of a man to two or more women at the same time. In a study of more than 850 societies, Burton Pasternak found that 83 percent were polygynous (Pasternak 1976:62; Murdock 1967).

Polygyny is generally practiced by only a small percentage of men in those societies in which it is the most accepted form of marriage. Some societies, however, have arrangements that permit a large number of polygynous marriages. The Tiwi are a good example of a society in which most marriages are eventually polygynous. Widespread polygyny among the Tiwi is achieved by the operation of two cultural rules: younger men are not permitted to marry, and all females must be married. Polygyny could result from frequent warfare leading to high death rates among men, or the importation of women from outside the society to increase the number of potential spouses.

Why is polygyny preferred by so many societies? Pasternak offers the following explanations:

1. Dominance over others and constant sexual urges are innate biological characteristics of males.
2. Unbalanced sex ratios in favor of females brought about by high levels of male mortality through warfare, violence, and dangerous male occupations.
3. An answer to male sexual frustration and deprivation caused in those societies that prohibit sexual relations with a wife for considerable periods of time after the birth of a child (Pasternak 1976:63–64).

Although limited support and evidence can be found for each explanation, no comprehensive answer for the prevalence of polygyny is available. The description of Tiwi polygyny and the discussion in Chapter 3 of the productive role of women in foraging and horticultural societies, however, suggest that polygyny may provide a basis for organizing women into a productive labor force. Tiwi polygyny, and the important role of women in gathering and horticultural activities, would seem to support this argument. Thus it is possible to conclude that in some foraging societies and in many horticultural societies the more wives a man has the better off he may be.

Polyandry

At the other extreme *polyandry,* the marriage of one woman to a number of men at the same time, is one of the rarest forms of marriage. Of the socieites surveyed by Pasternak, less than one percent preferred polyandry as a form of marriage. This form of marriage is even less explainable than polygyny. A cultural pattern that appears to be associated with polyandry is a surplus of men and a shortage of women in a population. In some instances this population imbalance may be related to the practice of killing female babies (female infanticide). Female infanticide leads to an unbalanced sex ratio in the population, and with considerably more men than women, polyandry is a form of marriage that becomes possible.

One of the earliest ethnographies in anthropology described the Toda of South India (Rivers 1906), among whom the practice of polyandry was prevalent. The usual form of marriage among the Toda was *fraternal polyandry,* in which a woman married a man and immediately became the wife of all his living brothers, as well as brothers yet to be born. All of them lived together, and she was the sexual partner of all the brothers who were her husbands.

Female infantcide was widely practiced among the Toda, and the preponderance of men in the population was undoubtedly basic to the polyandrous system. It is not clear why the Toda practiced female infanticide. Instead of being used as a form of population control, the practice of female infanticide may have been related to the minimal and unimportant economic role of women in Toda society. However, cultural values may also play a key role in determining marital preferences. The Indian government prohibits female infanticide among the Toda, and this has resulted in a more balanced sex ratio. Polyandry has remained, however, and has become an interesting form of group marriage, in which a group of brothers, instead of sharing one wife as in earlier times, now share two or more wives.

Monogamy

Monogamy, the marriage of one man to one woman at the same time, is the marital form with which Americans are most familiar. Not only is it considered normal, but it is also defended by legal codes that define other forms of marriage (bigamy) as illegal and punishable. Monogamy, however, is the preferred form of marriage in less than 20 percent of the 850 societies sampled by Pasternak. Whether or not it is preferred, monogamy is the form of marriage found in most societies. The practice of monogamy in otherwise polygynous societies can be illustrated by the norms governing marriage in Islamic countries. According to the Koran a man is allowed to have up to four wives at the same time, although the Koran also stipulates that a man must be able to maintain such a

Toda bow-giving ceremony. One of the woman's husbands gives her the ceremonial bow to acknowledge that he is the father of her unborn child and all her succeeding children. The ceremony is related to the pattern of Toda polyandry that was practiced in the recent past.

household economically and to treat each wife with equal favor. Under these conditions of economic and cultural constraints, few Muslim men are able to have more than one wife. A recent study of Muslim Bedouin in Israel, however, indicates that the percentage of plural marriages is increasing, and it appears to be a consequence of a general increase in available wealth, thus permitting a larger number of Muslim men to support polygynous households (Kressel 1977:441–458).

Nayar and Nuer Marriage

Ethnographies contain accounts of what may be considered exotic and rare types of marriage. Although these forms of marriage are few in number, they demonstrate the wide range of marital arrangements created by various societies. These unique forms, which probably originated because of particular, if not peculiar, circumstances, allow anthropologists to observe more clearly the determining factors at work. Perhaps by understanding the particular and unusual we may gain some insight into the general and typical.

The Nayar: Visiting and ritual husbands.
Kathleen Gough (1959:23–24), who did fieldwork among the Nayar of southwestern India, used data from this group to challenge some traditional anthropological concepts of marriage and family. Compared to the vast majority of human cultures, the Nayar certainly appear to be atypical.

A Nayar woman has two different kinds of husbands: a ritual husband and one or more visiting husbands. A ritual husband is acquired at puberty in a marriage arranged through a woman's brother or maternal uncle. This marriage is marked by ceremonial observances. The couple spends three days together; they may or may not have sexual relations; and at the end of the three days the ritual husband returns to his own household. Afterward the couple

have few mutual obligations; they do not reside together, they do not cooperate economically, and there is little likelihood of any continuing sexual relationship. A wife's only obligation is to mourn her ritual husband at his death.

After the ceremony with the ritual husband a Nayar woman acquires a visiting husband or husbands. No ceremony marks this relationship. Gough estimates that the average Nayar woman has between five and eight visiting husbands. Visiting husbands are really visitors; they do not live with their wives nor does the relationship involve economic cooperation as either producers or consumers. A visiting husband has the right to spend the entire night with his wife, provided no other visiting husband has arrived before him. According to Nayar custom a man leaves his spear outside the door of the wife he is visiting as a signal to other visiting husbands. At sunrise the visiting husband must leave; if he remains beyond this time he is forced to pay a fine to his wife's kin.

Unless a woman has both a ritual and a visiting husband, her children are not considered legitimate. To legitimize the birth of a child one or more of the visiting husbands must give gifts to the mother and pay the midwife for her services. It could be argued that these gifts and payment constitute a wedding ceremony, for the male-female union is publicly recognized and acknowledged in this way. From an ethnocentric perspective the only unusual aspect of this wedding ceremony is that it occurs at the birth of a child.

In Nayar society children live with their mother and her blood relatives. Nayar households are composed of people who are related through blood or kinship rather than marriage ties. Women live with their brothers and sisters, their own children, their sisters' children, and their daughters' children. Males are primarily responsible for the economic maintenance of their sisters and their sisters' children.

A significant historical reason for the Nayar

pattern of marriage was the employment of Nayar men as mercenary soldiers, which required them to spend many of their adult years serving in armies throughout southern India. Thus the long-term absence of men from their villages and the organization of households along kinship ties may be crucial ingredients in the emergence of this unique marriage system.

The Nuer: Woman marriage and ghost marriage.

In some societies marriages are permitted between members of the same sex. Among the Nuer a barren woman is married as a "husband" to another woman, who becomes her wife. This wife is impregnated by a male, but her female husband is considered the "father" to the children. In the Nuer kinship system children belong to the father's kin group, and this unusual form of marriage is a vehicle for recruiting children into that kin group. Thus by taking the role of husband a woman can also accomplish the male function of adding to her father's kin group.

Marriage as a means of recruitment (descent theory) is seen in another unusual Nuer marriage: ghost marriage. A Nuer man can marry a woman on behalf of the spirit of his deceased brother and any offspring will be considered the children of the deceased man. This manipulation of marriage is useful in organizing and controlling factors such as continuation of a family name, inheritance of property, or succession to office.

The Marriage Bond

Marriage can be defined as a socially recognized union. One way in which marriage becomes socially recognized is through public ritual and ceremony, and in addition, economic exchanges frequently accompany marriage. Ceremonies and economic exchanges solidify the marital union.

Ceremony. When a Nayar visiting husband gives gifts at the birth of a child and pays for the midwife, this public proclamation of his relationship with the woman and child could be interpreted as a marriage ceremony. Marriage ceremonies show considerable variation cross-culturally. For the Siriono, a marriage takes place when a man moves his hammock alongside the hammock of his selected wife. Although this ceremony is limited in ritual, it is still a publicly recognized act. A minimal ceremony is described by Murdock for the Witoto of the Amazon basin of South America in which a Witoto husband merely "licks tobacco" with the father of the bride at the time of the marriage (Murdock 1934:46).

As the following excerpt indicates, weddings among the Haida Indians of British Columbia involve a lengthy ceremony and exhibit many characteristics found in a number of societies.

The wedding takes place at the home of the bride in the presence of the immediate relatives of both parties. The groom sits on a mat in the seat of honor behind the fireplace, and the bride is escorted to his side. After speeches by the men of both families, the mother and sisters of the groom exchange presents with the clanswomen of the bride, and the girl's father gives his new son-in-law a slave, a canoe, a "copper," or some other valuable present. At a feast following the wedding the clanswomen of the groom shower the bride with clothing, household utensils, and other practical gifts. The young couple live for an entire season in rotation at the homes of the groom's sisters, where they are lavishly entertained. They then take up their residence with the bride's father, unless he is dead or the groom is himself a house chief. A man scrupulously avoids his mother-in-law and shows great deference in the presence of the male relatives of his wife (Murdock 1934:251).

A Haida wedding ceremony does not seem very unusual to us. It shares traits found in American weddings such as the giving of gifts and useful household utensils, feasting and celebration, and a honeymoon. Not all wedding ceremonies, however, follow this familiar form of feasting, exchange of vows, and gift giving.

In traditional Samoan culture a high value was placed on the virginal status of the chief's daughter. As part of the wedding ceremony a princess had to submit to a public defloration as proof of her virginity. Girls who failed this test were clubbed and stoned, often to death, by their outraged relatives (Murdock 1934:74). This practice did not apply to all Samoan girls, for commoners were expected to participate in premarital sexual activities.

Dowry System

For the Haida, the people of Galipur, and for Americans, weddings are marked by the exchange of gifts. In many societies the practice of gift giving develops into the exchange and transfer of valuable property between the kin of the married couple. There are varied forms of exchange at marriages, and the purpose and meaning of the exchange have been areas of debate in anthropology.

Descriptions of marital exchanges indicate that the flow of goods and property is often one-sided. In Galipur the bride's family is required to give a considerable amount of money to the groom's family and jewelry and new clothing to the bride, and they also must pay the wedding expenses. A system in which the major gifts go from the bride's family to the groom's family is called a *dowry system*.

The dowry system is found extensively in Europe and Asia. In traditional European society both royalty and peasantry negotiated marriage contracts that contained provisions for a dowry. Remnants of a dowry system in American society may be found in the custom of the "hope chest" and the tradition of having the bride's family pay for the wedding expenses.

Dowry payments may be analyzed as an economic contribution by the bride's family designed to establish a new household unit. In peasant Europe newly married couples usually establish their own households, and the dowry, along with a man's inheritance, provides an economic basis for the new household. Status and social mobility are also integral parts of a dowry system. Ernestine Friedl, in her study of a rural Greek village, clearly shows that the dowry system can be used to obtain a good marriage for a daughter (1964:65–66). The competition for townsmen as husbands for village girls, for example, had driven up the dowry from $3000 in the early 1950s to $4500 by the late 1950s. In traditional Chinese society the prestige function of the dowry is evident. During the wedding ceremony the bride hides behind a curtain, but the items that make up her dowry are in plain view for everyone to inspect, admire, and evaluate. Families attempt to look as good as possible, of course, by providing elaborate and expensive dowries.

The burden of providing a dowry for a daughter is one aspect of the dowry system. When Eames inquired in Galipur who was the poorest family in the community, a man with five daughters was identified. Although this man was a substantial landowner, his future obligations to make five dowry payments, one for each daughter, was seen as dissipating his economic resources.

In addition to economic and status considerations, dowries may also operate in the political sphere, which was especially true in the heyday of European nobility. If a noble family had no male child, their daughter would inherit their land. When she married the land was part of her dowry and became the property of her husband. It was in this manner that John of Gaunt married, in 1359, Blanche of Lancaster, the heiress of vast land holdings, and became

Among the Berber people of North Africa, bridewealth is measured in terms of amber and bronze necklaces such as the one worn by this girl.

Bride-price. In many societies the reverse flow of goods occurs—from the groom's family to the bride's family. This form of marital exchange is termed *bride-price* and has been the source of a continuing controversy in anthropology. Bride-price payment is prevalent among the tribal peoples of the world, and recent surveys have found that it is especially common in African societies (Kressel 1977:441; Goody and Tambiah 1973).

Europeans, especially missionaries, first interpreted and condemned this practice as a form of wife purchase. They thought that natives considered women to be little more than property to be sold to the highest bidder. Anthropologists were not as negative in their views of bride-price; they frequently interpreted it as a means of validating the father's right to future offspring. This view of the bride-price is called a progeny price interpretation. Another interpretation explains the bride-price as compensation to the bride's family for loss of her economic and domestic services.

Bride-price payment may be a source of marital stability, for such payments involve the groom and his kin who contribute to the payment. The bride's family usually disburses the payment as bride-price for their own male kinsmen. The kin of a married couple have a major interest in keeping a marriage together because divorce requires the return of the bride-price.

Perhaps one of the most surprising developments in the anthropological interpretation of bride-price is the emergence of a position closer to the old missionary view. Based on recent work in East Africa, Walter Goldschmidt (1974) suggests that bride-price in the group he studied is a technique of downgrading females and treating them as a form of property.

An alternative to bride-price is suitor service, when the groom and his family are unable to make the required payment. A familiar example of suitor service is the biblical story of

the Duke of Lancaster. A more complicated, but similar, transaction can be found in the marriage of Eleanor of Aquitaine. Eleanor was first married to Louis VII of France, and as her dowry she received the provinces of Aquitaine (Guienne, Gascony, Poitou). When her marriage to Louis VII was later annulled, she retained control of these provinces. She then married Henry, the Duke of Anjou, who became King of England as Henry II. The dowry land in France that Eleanor brought with her when she married Henry became one of the fundamental causes for the Hundred Years War between England and France.

Jacob, who agreed to work seven years for his father-in-law in order to marry Rachel. When the actual marriage took place Jacob's father-in-law, Laban, substituted his older daughter, Leah, for Rachel. Jacob had to work an additional seven years for his father-in-law in order to marry Rachel (*Genesis* 29:20–26).

Dissolution of Marriage

Marriages often end in divorce, and any consideration of marriage must deal with its dissolution and termination. Galipur and the Tiwi are examples of two very different approaches to this problem. In rural India no divorce is allowed, whereas for the Tiwi, death, rather than divorce, terminates the marriage.

Divorce. In the vast majority of societies a marriage that is not working can be terminated. In a recent cross-cultural study of divorce it was found that in 97 percent of a representative sample of societies divorce is permitted and that in about seven out of ten socieites divorce is relatively easy (Whyte 1978:211–237). Reasons for divorce, the divorce rights of men and women, and the frequency of divorce, however, vary widely from society to society. Major reasons for divorce fall into four major classifications: the inability of the couple to get along with each other, economic problems, sexual adjustment problems, and childlessness.

Difficulties in interpersonal marital relations include quarreling, nagging, mistreatment, and cruelty. Survey figures on divorce indicate an interesting differential pattern for males and females. Reasons for divorce such as nagging and quarreling are used primarily by males. Females, on the other hand, are permitted to obtain divorces for cruelty and mistreatment (Murdock 1950:145–201).

In most tribal and peasant societies the household is a basic economic unit. In such societies laziness and nonsupport are potential

reasons for divorce. In our own society during the Great Depression of the 1930s the probabilities of divorce increased when a man lost his job. A clear tribal illustration of the economic aspects of marriage occurred when Holmberg tested his hypothesis about the economic basis of polygyny among the Siriono. He trained a relatively incompetent Siriono hunter to use a shotgun for hunting. Within three months this man had three wives, but he realized that when Holmberg left, taking the ammunition with him, his ability to maintain a household of three wives would disappear. In response to this problem the man left his group and obtained wage employment at a nearby plantation, and as a result was able to keep two of his wives.

One of the most frequently cited reasons for divorce is sexual infidelity and adultery. A number of societies also permit divorce for either sexual impotence or unwillingness to engage in sexual relations.

In all human societies the bearing of children is considered part of the human condition. The Ashanti of Ghana, in West Africa, may be extreme, but hardly atypical, in their attitude toward barrenness and sterility. "A barren woman is looked upon with pity not unmixed with scorn. She feels an outcaste. The lot of a childless man is equally hard. However rich he may be he feels that there is something seriously lacking about him if he is sterile" (Fortes 1950:262).

In addition to considering the general reasons for divorce that affect all societies, we can look at specific causes for divorce in a single society. Among the Muria of Central India, for example, the men and women advance different complaints. Men accuse their wives of not cooking for them or of not taking care of them. Women, on the other hand, accuse their husbands of drunkenness and lack of family support. A number of couples claim that they simply cannot get along together. Sexual impotence is also a problem recognized by the Muria. They have a proverb explaining divorce and desertion: "As soon as the penis weakens, the vagina runs to the jungle" (Elwin 1947:636).

Divorce and social structure. It is difficult to determine from the cross-cultural data whether divorce rights are equal for men and women, or if one sex has greater rights and access to divorce. We have descriptions of societies where the women clearly enjoy superior rights and ease in divorce, and yet there are also many societies where men enjoy superiority in divorce rights. On the basis of a cross-cultural study made more than twenty years ago, George Murdock claimed that in three out of four societies the sexes appeared to have fairly equal prerogatives in obtaining a divorce (1950). From a recent study, however, it appears that the ethnographic information about women's divorce rights is unclear and that it is not known if divorce rights are shared equally by men and women in most societies (Minturn, Grosse, Haider 1969).

How prevalent is divorce? Ethnographic data indicate that societies vary in their rates and frequencies of divorce. At one extreme are the small number of societies that do not permit divorce at all. In some societies there are very low rates of divorce, 10 percent or less, while in other societies 60 to 100 percent of all marriages may end in divorce. An example of a society with a high divorce rate is the Kanuri of Bornu in West Africa. Marriage is very brittle among the Kanuri, and 80 to 90 percent of all marriages end in divorce. An individual Kanuri may experience as many as eight or nine divorces (Cohen 1967:44–55).

Differences in the frequency and rate of divorce in various societies have led some anthropologists to suggest a relation between divorce and social structure. More than twenty years ago Max Gluckman (1950:190–192) suggested that societies tracing descent through the male line (patrilineal) tend to have low divorce rates, while societies tracing descent through the female line (matrilineal) tend to have high divorce rates. A recent cross-cultural survey of sexual behavior by Minturn, Grosse, and Haider appears to confirm this hypothesis. They found that divorce is easier and the divorce rate higher in societies that are matrilineal (Minturn, Grosse, Haider 1969:308; Gibbs 1964:160–170).

In American society divorce has been easier to obtain over the last half century, and both the frequency and rate of divorce have been increasing. This increase may reflect the growing equality of the sexes in American society and the movement away from a social and legal order that was weighted in favor of a male-dominated marriage system. Assuming that this analysis is valid, social critics who interpret the rising American divorce rate as the decline of the American family are not correct. If divorce is related to social structure, as the social structure changes so also will the rate and frequency of divorce. In other words, each social structure may have its own normal divorce rate.

Death: Widowhood and remarriage. Divorce is the voluntary dissolution of marriage; death is an involuntary termination of marriage. The Tiwi are extreme in this regard, for death is the only way in which their marriages can be terminated. Many societies have specific rules about the remarriage of widows and widowers. In Tiwi society widows are immediately remarried, and the concept of "widow" does not exist. In contrast to the Tiwi, Galipur provides an opposite approach, for widows are not allowed to remarry.

In societies in which remarriage is either permitted or required, the question becomes: what arrangements, if any, are made? Although in a number of societies, such as our own, there is no special provision for remarriage of surviving spouses, many societies do offer preferred solutions. Among the provisions for remarriage are the levirate and the sororate.

In the *levirate,* which is a widely practiced custom, a woman marries her dead husband's brother. In a sample of 159 societies, 70 percent practiced as well as preferred the levirate (Murdock 1949:29). This custom is mentioned throughout the Old Testament, and one of the most interesting references is found in the story of Onan. According to the Bible, Judah's firstborn son married a woman named Tamar, but he was slain by the Lord for his wickedness. Judah then ordered his second son, Onan, to marry Tamar in order to raise children for his brother, which, of course, resembles the Nuer practice of ghost marriage. Onan refused to marry Tamar, and, as the Bible states, he spilled his seed upon the ground. The Lord was displeased by this action, and Onan was slain for this violation of Israelite custom (*Genesis* 38:6). Orthodox Jews still observe the custom of the levirate. A younger brother must either marry his older brother's widow or renounce his rights to her, and, if he does neither, she cannot remarry.

In the *sororate,* which is the reverse of the levirate, a man marries his deceased wife's sister. This custom is not as common as the levirate, but it is reported to occur in about 60 percent of a sample of 159 societies (Murdock 1949:29). The levirate and the sororate are not the same custom, and if a society permits one it generally prohibits the other. In orthodox Judaism the levirate is permitted and the sororate prohibited. Both customs are practiced by the Siriono, however. They carry these customs even further and practice what is known as "anticipatory levirate and sororate." Among the Siriono a younger brother is allowed sexual access to both his brother's wife and wife's sister. A woman, conversely, is permitted sexual relations with her husband's brother and her sister's husband. Because marriage may occur between these relatives in the case of a

spouse's death, it makes sense to the Siriono to establish a sexual bond prior to marriage.

Several explanations have been advanced for the levirate and the sororate, and one of them concerns the dependency of children. Death destroys a family unit, and in tribal economies it may be difficult for a surviving spouse with children to maintain the family as an economic and household unit. Remarriage between people who are already related restores the familial unit with a minimum of adjustment.

Other explanations derive from the interpretations of alliance and descent theories. An explanation based on alliance theory suggests that once a relationship has been established between two kin groups through marriage, the levirate and the sororate maintain the alliance established by the previous marriage. The Nuer forms of woman marriage and ghost marriage as well as the Old Testament account of Judah and his sons support explanations derived from descent theory. In these situations the levirate and sororate operate as recruitment devices designed to provide heirs and descendants for individuals and organized kin groups.

Family and Household

Although wedding ceremonies are among the more dramatic events observed by an anthropological fieldworker, it is the relationship established after the marriage ceremony that is significant for both individuals and for society. Whether we focus on alliance or descent theory, the social significance of marriage is the creation of household and family units. Among some groups in modern American society there has been a tendency to downplay, if not criticize, the nuclear family. In tribal societies, however, the importance of the family cannot be sufficiently emphasized. The following statement by an aged Pomo Indian of California to the anthropologist, Burt Aginsky, indicates not only a tribal perspective regarding the family, but also the Indian's view of the family in white society.

> An old Pomo Indian once said to me: What is a man? A man is nothing. Without his family he is of less importance than that bug crossing the trail. A man must be with his family to amount to anything with us. If he had nobody else to help him, the first trouble he got into he would be killed by his enemies because there would be no relatives to help him fight. No woman would marry him because her family would not let her marry a man with no family. He would be poorer than a newborn child; he would be poorer than a worm, and the family would not consider him worth anything. It is the family that is important. In the white ways of doing things the family is not so important. The police and soldier take care of protecting you, the courts give you justice, the post office carries messages for you, the school teaches you. Everything is taken care of, even your children, if you die; but with us the family must do all of that (Aginsky 1940:43–44).

A difficulty in discussing the concepts of *family* and *household* is the failure to convey clearly the distinction between the two units. This distinction can be drawn sharply by asking two questions: who are the members of my family? Who lives with me? For many of us the answers to these two questions would be very different. Most Americans would include within their family married brothers and sisters who are not living with them. Families are not necessarily residential units; households are residential units. This section discusses those factors that give rise to a variety of household units.

Joint and Independent Households

Understanding begins with classification, and in order to bring some sense of order to the great variety of household units found in human societies, anthropologists find it useful to dis-

tinguish between two general types of households: joint and independent. In American society the expected process is for a newly married couple to establish a household independent of their respective parents. In many societies newly married couples do not establish an *independent household*, but instead become part of an already existing household unit, thus creating a *joint household*.

Formation of a household depends on a variety of rules regarding the postmarital residence of a newly married couple. Three major rules of postmarital residence are currently found throughout the world: patrilocal, matrilocal, and neolocal. In *neolocal residence* a married couple lives *apart* from the parents or other relatives of the respective spouses. In *patrilocal residence* a married couple lives *with* or *near* the parents of the groom, whereas in *matrilocal residence* the married couple lives *with* or *near* the parents of the bride.

Patrilocality is the most common of these three rules in residence. In slightly more than half of the societies in the world patrilocality is the basic rule of postmarital residence. In an additional quarter of the societies, the matrilocal rule of postmarital residence is followed. In a small proportion of societies, one of twenty, the neolocal rule of residence is usual, and in the remaining 15 percent of the world's societies, various other types of residence rules are practiced.

The neolocal rule of residence, which is the preferred pattern in American society, leads to the establishment of an independent household. The independent type of household found in American society is often called *nuclear family;* it consists of a married couple and their children. Often the nuclear family is used as a conceptual equivalent for the independent household. Independent household units are not, however, necessarily small or monogamous. Tiwi households consist of a man, his numerous wives, and their dependent offspring,

Three generations of this Middle Eastern family share a residence. When a son marries, his wife comes to live in his parents' home.

and because some Tiwi men have more than twenty wives, these independent households may number more than forty people. Upon the death of the married man, his household dissolves. His wives are redistributed to other men and to other households. This characteristic of *impermanence* is fundamental to the independent household.

Rules of patrilocality and matrilocality are basic to the formation of joint households. Patrilocal and matrilocal residence rules, however, do not always lead to the development of joint households, for more than common residence is required. Besides coresidence, cooperation and coordination of a wide range of activities are necessary. Such joint households are basic units of economic production, distribution, and consumption, and in addition domestic chores, such as cooking and child care, are shared by members of the household.

In many circumstances common residence

can be found without a joint household. Cohen found in his study of Collefiore that in some cases a newly married couple lived patrilocally, occupying a single room in the house of the husband's parents. However, the couple purchased their food separately, cooked it on their own gas-fired stove, and ate apart from the groom's parents. They formed an independent household, despite the fact they lived in a room in a house occupied by the parents of the husband.

The Siriono are usually classified as matrilocal because when a man marries he moves his hammock alongside that of his wife, who lives with her mother, father, sisters, and unmarried brothers. There is, however, no economic cooperation among them; they do not obtain, prepare, or consume food together and they operate as independent households. For the Siriono the matrilocal rule of residence does not lead to a joint household.

The Curvilinear Hypothesis

What are the conditions that lead to the emergence of joint and independent households? The *curvilinear hypothesis* has been suggested by cross-cultural survey data (Winch and Blumberg 1972:898–920). This hypothesis states that a high proportion of joint households tend to be found in societies with a domesticated food economy. These societies can be classified at an intermediate level of social complexity. At one end of the curve are societies with simple subsistence systems (hunting-gathering technologies) and at the other end of the curve are complex industrial urban societies. In both types of societies independent households predominate (Figure 4.1).

Why does this relationship between the level of social complexity and the type of household exist? The usual explanations may be listed as follows:

1. In domesticated food economy the food supply is stable enough and large enough to support a joint household. Most contemporary foraging people live in environments that are poor in resources. Thus a limited technology coupled with a limited resource base restrict these people to supporting small and independent households.

2. Tribal economies based on domesticated food systems lack a machine technology and depend on human power for most of the work and energy required. Organization of people into joint households may be an efficient means of mobilizing individuals into effective labor groups.

3. Landholding in a domesticated food economy may operate to hold a group together because this economic resource is vital to the entire group.

4. Emergence of independent households in

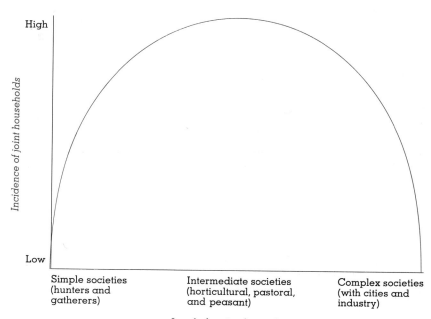

Figure 4.1.
Relationship between joint households and level of societal complexity.

Source: Pasternak, Prentice-Hall, 1976.

Incidence of joint households

High

Low

Simple societies (hunters and gatherers)

Intermediate societies (horticultural, pastoral, and peasant)

Complex societies (with cities and industry)

Level of societal complexity

urban industrial society may reflect the ability of small nuclear families and independent households to support themselves in a money economy.

5. A common feature of foraging societies as well as industrial societies is a high degree of geographic mobility. In hunting-gathering societies nomadic movement is often necessitated by economic conditions: the search for food. In urban industrial society geographic mobility is extreme. The mobility of households in urban society is undoubtedly related to shifting economic and employment opportunities and the ability of small household units to earn sufficient income for their financial support.

Households and Other Residence Rules

In addition to the three major rules of residence, there are a variety of residence rules practiced by a small number of societies that often lead to different kinds of household units. One such residence rule is termed *avunculocal.* According to this rule the married couple lives with or near the groom's maternal uncle. This form of residence is associated with matrilineal descent systems and may lead to an avunculocal joint family. In matrilineal descent systems a man inherits position and property from his maternal uncle. Avunculocal residence may be one way of bringing together individuals who are kin and share, own, and eventually inherit the same property.

In some societies a married couple is permitted wide options in choosing their place of residence. Although this rule is technically termed *bilocal,* once the couple decide where they will live, their residence then follows one of the other residence rules. An unusual variation of the bilocal rule is found among the Dobuans of the South Pacific, where a married couple alternate their residence yearly. One year is spent in the wife's village (matrilocal) and the next year is spent in the village of the husband's maternal uncle (avunculocal). The reason for this yearly shift is that the Dobuans are highly suspicious, and married couples do not trust each other or the kin of their spouses. By shifting their residence each year perhaps some balance of mutual mistrust is achieved.

Earlier we described the marriage and household arrangements of the Nayar, in which the married couple live apart from each other. This type of residence is termed duolocal, and it is found in a small number of societies. *Duolocal residence* as practiced by the Nayar results in a consanguine household, which means that the household is composed of blood relatives. In these households the family and household are almost identical. In most societies spouses are considered part of a person's family, but not for the Nayar. Robin Fox describes a pattern of duolocal residence among the Irish inhabitants of Tory Island, who marry at a late age. The bond between brothers and sisters is very intense, and therefore after marriage spouses tend to live with their siblings rather than with each other (Fox 1978:157–185).

Households Through Time

Households can be compared cross-culturally in order to understand the varied circumstances that influence their formation. It is also useful to look at households within a society, especially in terms of their development and change over time. This development over time is called process.

In most discussions of household types there is a tendency to treat them as if they were static social units, which of course is far from true. Just as an individual goes through a life cycle beginning with birth and ending in death, so does a household go through a similar process of emergence, growth, maturation, decline, and disappearance. This process is more readily apparent for independent households, but it is equally true for joint households.

For the Indian joint household in Galipur, the process begins when a boy marries and brings his wife into his household. As the wife has children, the household, originally consisting of the husband's father, mother, and other brothers and sisters, expands and becomes a three-generational household unit. As the husband's younger brothers marry, they too bring their wives into the household. At the death of the father certain strains begin to emerge that eventually lead to the dissolution of the joint household. The eldest son is supposed to become the new head of the household and hold the same authority as his deceased father. The younger brothers, however, may not be as willing to accept the oldest brother's authority as readily as they had accepted their father's authority. Differences may emerge, and some of the younger brothers may decide to establish their own households. Because all of the sons inherit equally in their father's estate, all the land and other forms of wealth have to be partitioned among them.

An initial step in the process of household dissolution occurs when the women begin to cook food separately for their own husbands and children. Common cooking and common consumption of food are basic characteristics of the functioning joint household. When the women begin to cook separately it is an indication to everyone that the household, as it is then organized, is in the process of disintegration. Partitioning the house is the next recognized step. Each "new" household occupies a particular section of the house. The final step in the process takes place when separate houses are built for each household unit, with the common estate being subdivided among the brothers.

Male villagers suggest that the basic cause of household dissolution is the inability of the wives to get along with each other. An often-quoted proverb states: "Any number of penises may live together, but no more than one pair of breasts." This proverb and the frequent references by villagers to quarrels among cowives provide a rationale for the dissolution of households that places the blame upon the women rather than the men.

Summary

Ethnographic studies reveal that there is a great range in mating, marriage, family, and household practices. Some of the dimensions of this diversity are illustrated by two examples, the Tiwi and Galipur. Tiwi marriages are polygynous, while Galipur marriages are monogamous. There is a strong prohibition against premarital sexual activity in Galipur. Among the Tiwi this issue is irrelevant, for all females, from infancy to old age, are married. Independent households are the rule among the Tiwi, while joint households are usually found in Galipur.

Attitudes toward sexual activity before marriage vary among societies. Few societies actually condemn premarital sexual activity, and many condone or tacitly approve it. It is generally assumed that premarital mating will lead to the establishment of more permanent unions recognized as marriage. Marriage is a socially recognized union of two or more individuals, usually, but not always, of the opposite sex. Underlying marriage are rules of mate selection. In some societies people have very little control or voice in choosing their marriage partners. Rules of endogamy and exogamy also constrain the choice of mates. Besides the general rules of endogamy and exogamy, more precise rules of mate selection, such as cousin marriage, may be found.

There are several forms of marriage, including polygyny, polyandry, and monogamy. Although plural marriage is preferred in the majority of societies in the world, demographic and economic factors usually result in monogamous marriages for most people in most societies.

In addition to ceremonies at marriage (weddings), in many societies an economic exchange also takes place. When the exchange of goods moves primarily from the groom's family to the bride's family we call it brideprice, and when it moves in the opposite direction we call it dowry. Such exchanges appear to be related to the stability of the marital union.

Marriages are not necessarily permanent unions. Divorce is allowed in most societies throughout the world, and it is not particularly difficult for either spouse to obtain a divorce. Another cause of marital dissolution is death. As a response to death, many societies provide immediate replacement for the deceased spouse through the levirate and sororate.

Households can be distinguished from families. Households are residential and cooperative units, while families are individuals linked by blood or marriage ties. Households are the operative units in society; within these units children are reared and economic and social cooperation takes place.

Households can be classified as either joint or independent. This distinction is based on postmarital residence rules and economic and social cooperation. Joint households are usually found in intermediate level societies, while independent households are found among foraging societies as well as complex societies.

One of the most important characteristics of the household is that it goes through periods of growth and decline. Independent households disappear with the marriage of the children and the death of the parents. Although joint households frequently have longer time spans, they also go through periods of growth, decline, and dissolution.

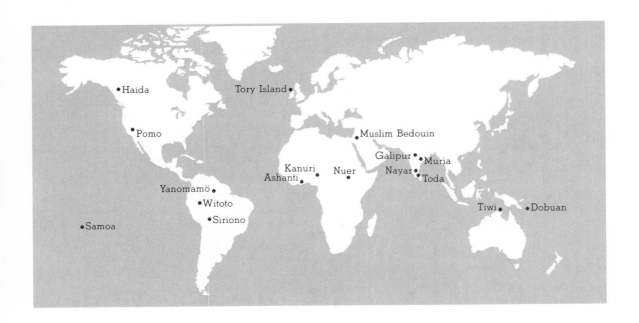

Key Terms and Concepts

patriarchial
endogamy
exogamy
alliance theory
descent theory
mating
marriage
cross-cousins
parallel cousins
polygyny
polyandry
fraternal polyandry
monogamy
dowry system
bride-price
levirate

sororate
household, family
independent
    household
joint household
nuclear family
neolocal residence
patrilocal residence
matrilocal residence
nuclear family
curvilinear
    hypothesis
avunculocal
    residence
bilocal residence
duolocal residence

Suggested Readings

Bohannan, Paul, and John Middleton, eds. *Marriage, Family, and Residence.* New York: Natural History Press, 1968. *A collection of papers on incest, marriage, family, and household that includes a wide variety of social and cultural groups.*

Hart, C. W. M., and Arnold R. Pilling. *The Tiwi of North Australia.* New York: Holt, Rinehart and Winston, 1979. *Full-length ethnographic study concentrating on the Tiwi marital system and its ramifications throughout Tiwi culture. This edition includes a final chapter describing Hart's field experiences with the Tiwi.*

Leibowitz, Lila. *Females, Males, Families: A Biosocial Approach.* North Scituate, Mass.: Duxbury Press, 1978. *Using an evolutionary and cross-cultural approach, Leibowitz examines sex, family arrangements, and the origin of the family, and she challenges the theory that men and women are biologically programmed to behave differently.*

Nimkoff, M. F., ed. *Comparative Family Systems.* Boston: Houghton Mifflin, 1965. *A cross-cultural study of variations in the organization of the human family. Includes studies of the family in tribal, peasant, and complex societies.*

Pasternak, Burton. *Introduction to Kinship and Social Organization.* Englewood Cliffs, N.J.: Prentice-Hall, 1976. *A survey of kinship and marriage. More than half the chapters focus on marriage, incest, the family, and post-marital residence rules.*

Stack, Carol B. *All Our Kin: Strategies for Survival in a Black Community.* New York: Harper & Row, 1975. *Describes kinship among lower-class blacks and emphasizes the usefulness of extended kin networks.*

Chapter 5

Living with Others: Kin and Nonkin

Throughout the ethnographic accounts presented in previous chapters, kinship has been an important element. Until Hart established a kinship linkage with the Tiwi, they really did not know how to relate to him. Clarke in describing Bomagai-Angoiang horticulture relates how Kunbun was aided in clearing forest by men of his own clan; that is, men who were his relatives. Nadel's analysis of witchcraft is based on an understanding of obligations and expected behaviors between kin. In tribal and peasant societies the relationship between individuals, their behavior, and the groups to which they belong are permeated by ties of kinship.

Understanding kinship and kin groups occupies a central position in anthropological studies. In their attempts to understand kinship, anthropologists have developed sophisticated models of kinship systems and a specialized terminology to describe kinship groups and systems.

Kinship is only *one* means of classifying people and defining relations among individuals and groups. Even the smallest band society classifies and categorizes individuals into groups; the complexity of the social world seems to require simplification. Kinship and nonkinship principles are a means of classifying and hence simplifying this complex reality. Labels, such as kin terms, tribal names, and group designations, categorize individuals into an easily learned classification scheme. At the same time labeling and categorizing provide the basis for patterned, repetitive, and predictable social behavior. The organization and classification of human beings into a variety of social groupings are among the defining characteristics of humanity.

Stand-In for a Murderer: A Case of Tlingit Clan Loyalty

"Stand-In for a Murderer" is a dramatization of an actual event that took place more than 150 years ago among the Tlingit Indians of southeast Alaska. The Tlingit are one of many tribes

Nonkin groups serve functions that kin groups do not. For Black Shriners, recruitment is based on commitment to charitable contributions to society as well as membership in a racial ethnic group. Members reinforce their identity with the group by participating in the annual parade.

that make up what anthropologists call the Northwest Coast culture area. The tribes of this culture area (Kwakiutl, Nootka, Bellacoola, Salish, Haida, Tsimshian) are among the best known societies in anthropological literature. These hunting, fishing, and gathering groups live in an area rich in natural resources, and by using these resources they developed complex societies. Material wealth, wooden plank houses, large boats, and a complicated social order of slaves, commoners, and nobles were part of the traditional culture. Nobility was organized in a series of graded ranks. Competition, pride, prestige, and position were continual concerns and, as our story indicates, they were basic motivations for their behavior.

The scene is set in southeast Alaska, some time early in the nineteenth century. The characters of the story are:

DATGAS	*A young nobleman of the Nanyaayi clan.*
DUQDANEK	*The old chief of the Nanyaayi clan.*
KAKAE	*A young nobleman of the Nanyaayi, higher in rank than Datgas.*
HAYIAK	*Another Nanyaayi noble.*

NARRATOR: The Nanyaayi clan of the Tlingit Indians gathered along the Stikine River. The time of the salmon run was at hand.

With spear and gaff they pulled the large, firm, tasty fish from the foaming torrent. The first salmon they caught was treated with the same respect they paid to a chief. A feast was given in its honor to win its forgiveness and good will. Then fishing went on. Some of the salmon was cooked, but most of it was split and hung from the rafters of the huts to dry. The Nanyaayi were happy. They would have food for a long time to come. But then like a storm cloud some news brought by one of their warriors, Datgas, moved a shadow across the vista ahead.

DATGAS: The Kanhaades are here.

KAKAE: Where?

DATGAS: Down the river at the cataracts.

KAKAE: How many?

DATGAS: It is a large band, Kakae, much larger than ours.

KAKAE: Do they come to fight, Datgas?

DATGAS: They have their women and babies with them. They are building huts and setting their Raven crests out front. They have even raised a totem pole.

DUQDANEK: They have come to stay. They have come to take our fishing waters.

HAYIAK: Are their hunting grounds and fishing waters not already vast?

DUQDANEK: The salmon do not fill their rivers as they do the Stikine.

KAKAE: We shall attack them and drive them away! Call the head men. Gather in my sweatroom for a council of war.

DUQDANEK: We are outnumbered, Datgas says.

KAKAE: Bravery and fierceness are better than numbers, Duqdanek. Attack without warning, attack them at night.

DUQDANEK: The Kanhaades is a large and scattered clan.

HAYIAK: Yes, if we ambush those down the Stikine from here and kill them all, that will not end it — only begin it.

DATGAS: Did they not force us to leave our old hunting ground? Do we let them drive us on again?

DUQDANEK: Long ago that was. In peace we have lived many seasons. We are of the same great Tlingit nation, many of their women are our wives —

KAKAE: A cause for war —

HAYIAK: You are young, Kakae, and wish for trophies. But not this time. You are noble and brave; enough trophies will come your way.

DUQDANEK: We shall hold a potlatch, a feast, for the Kanhaades.

HAYIAK: And shame them into leaving our fishing grounds.

DUQDANEK: Gather all your wealth, Hayiak, Kakae, and Datgas. The Kanhaades have given many great potlatches, but this will surpass any of them. Their hosts they will dare not insult further by remaining on our fishing grounds. We shall shame them with great gifts, shame them, shame them. In dark humiliation they will withdraw.

ANTHROPOLOGIST: But what's this? Protection of property by giving it away? Defeating an enemy by giving him a feast? Yes, this is in the pattern of Tlingit culture — and probably the most economic military tactic in the world. For honor comes to those who can outgive their rivals, who can make the greater display of generosity — a game perhaps not unknown to hostesses in our culture. But here among the Tlingit it is a dominant cultural motif: the famous potlatch ceremony, the rival gift-giving. Let's see how it works out.

NARRATOR: The potlatch was arranged. The Kanhaades accepted the invitation of the Nanyaayi, and came wearing their ceremonial costumes and carrying their valuable emblems engraved on copper shields, emblems inherited and emblems won. The Nanyaayi greeted them wearing their finest costumes. Food was piled in great stacks, deer meat, berries, salmon, trout, and wooden boxes full of candlefish oil. There were songs, storytelling, speeches, and much exchanging of gifts. Fur blankets, slaves, cedar-log canoes, and copper shields changed hands, each clan trying to outdo the other in generosity. Gifts were destroyed in the great fires to add to the ostentation. And slaves were killed — to the accompaniment of a chant.

Tlingit men dressed for participation in the potlatch ceremony.

CHANT:

The words of people are now backing down on me, the words of worthless people.

The words of people are now backing down on me, the words of worthless people.

(*A voice cries out in great pain and the chant increases in intensity.*)

The words of people are now backing down on me, the words of worthless people!

The words of worthless people! . . . The words of worthless people, the words of worthless people, the words of worthless people. . .

DUQDANEK: (*Watching the scene of the potlatch ceremony with Hayiak.*) Hayiak, we have given away more than the Kanhaades.

HAYIAK: Yes, Duqdanek, we have shamed them. They have nothing more of value to give away or destroy.

DUQDANEK: They look over at us with sullen eyes.

HAYIAK: They will slink away.

DUQDANEK: Look! Kakae comes out with still another copper shield.

HAYIAK: It is not needed. They are already beaten.

DUQDANEK: Kakae must win grandly; that is Kakae in everything.

HAYIAK: But who is he giving it to? To one of their lesser nobles, Haimas. What is that for?

DUQDANEK: Haimas is small, but his talk has been big. Kakae would shut him up forever.

KAKAE: (*At the scene of the potlatch, taunting Haimas with a chant.*)

Haimas only made a pretense with cedar bark. He made it into copper plates.

Will you come back here?

Do you think we never have feasts, the Nanyaayi?

HAYIAK: That has made Haimas very angry. He is not going to attack Kakae?

DUQDANEK: No, he is going to answer with a song.

HAIMAS: Kakae!

HAIMAS: (*Chanting in reply.*) Kakae, I hate what you say. I hate to have you talk to me — because you have spots all over your face.

DUQDANEK: Oh, grave insult.

HAIMAS: And you look like a slave!

KAKAE: Haimas, I am Kakae, one of the noblest of the Nanyaayi, and for what you have just said, you die!

HAYIAK: Kakae has unsheathed his knife. (*The crowd reacts in fear.*) He has stabbed Haimas! (*The crowd reacts in anger; a voice is heard above the noise.*)

VOICE: Haimas is dead!

HAYIAK: Now there will be a war.

ANTHROPOLOGIST: The enemy was vanquished with gifts. But now another element in Tlingit culture intervenes, for in Tlingit culture wealth and property are measures of status, and status is jealously guarded, and in such a culture there are excesses of pride that endanger the peace and safety. The Tlingit and their neighbors are deeply concerned with face, they are resentful, suspicious, and hostile. Such personality traits seem to the Tlingit to be the very nature of man.

Another aspect of Tlingit culture comes to the fore — the strength of clan organization and clan loyalty.

DUQDANEK: (*The crowd is still angry.*) I must prevent a battle. If I can get between them with my sacred Grizzly Bear emblem —

(*The murmuring grows louder as Duqdanek rushes to reach them.*)

No, no, do not fight, do not fight, Nanyaayi and Kanhaades! There will be retribution! No, no, do not make war! Honor the Grizzly Bear crest and the Wolf crest of the Nanyaayi, and the Raven crest of the Kanhaades! There will be justice!

TSAGUEDI: We honor the Grizzly Bear crest and the Raven crest. If there is justice, we shall not make war.

DUQDANEK: Tsaguedi of the Kanhaades, never have the Nanyaayi failed in justice.

TSAGUEDI: Duqdanek of the Nanyaayi, Haimas who has been killed belonged to the council of chiefs; he was the son of a great chief, Dexhintadeuxe, slain fighting against the Kwakiutl. Haimas was a brave warrior. And the feasts he has given have raised his prestige high.

DUQDANEK: But he is not the equal of Kakae who killed him.

TSAGUEDI: And so we do not ask for the death of Kakae. But the warrior from your clan who is to die must be the equal of Haimas in bravery, wealth, and prestige.

DUQDANEK: The warrior chosen will not dishonor your warrior Haimas. At least he will be the equal of the dead Haimas. We would not dishonor our clan by sacrificing less than you have lost.

NARRATOR: The head men of the Nanyaayi clan and the head men of the Kanhaades clan met to choose the warrior who was to die for the murder of Haimas. The haggling went on for a full day, and not until sundown did they settle on a warrior acceptable to both clans.

DUQDANEK: I shall go to him then and inform him and tell him to prepare.

TSAGUEDI: His death will bring honor to himself, and to the slain Haimas, and to our two clans.

DUQDANEK: So that justice and honor be done to Haimas of the Kanhaades, killed while a guest of our potlatch, you are to die — Datgas. You are to be slain in combat, you are to die a great warrior, Datgas.

KAKAE: Datgas!

DATGAS: Kakae, who slew Haimas, speak!

KAKAE: We have weathered together many storms on the open water, Datgas, and together have hunted along many trails. Back to back we have fought off the Haida, the Kwakiutl, and our Raven clans. But now I have

forced you into a battle alone — to die for your clan.

In songs of the Nanyaayi, and in stories, the name of Datgas will be remembered and handed down.

DATGAS: My fasting begins at this hour. I shall want a while to bid farewell to my brothers and my wife and young ones. I shall speak to the Wolf and the Grizzly Bear. And then I shall be ready.

NARRATOR: The day of the execution. Datgas drew on his ceremonial garments, his Grizzly Bear cloak, and his bear headpiece with eyes and ears of abalone shell. And he stepped forth from his house. His clan were assembled on either side. Across the clearing were the Kanhaades.

Datgas went on at considerable length, as was the custom among the Tlingit Indians, telling of the deeds of his clan and his ancestors and ending with his own history. Then he looked over at the Kanhaades. One of their number in ceremonial robes and with painted face had moved out from the others, a shell-tipped spear in one hand, a knife in the other. This was the man who was to slay him in mock combat — in mock but glorious combat. But before he had come far, Datgas scowled and raised his arm.

DATGAS: Stop! Come no farther! Who is this you send to fight with me? Kaogu! Kaogu, who has fought in but three battles, and in one of which he ran! What emblems can he show me? How much did he pay for his bride? Was it ten blankets and one old canoe? Kaogu! At the only feast he ever gave he was mercilessly shamed! Send me a warrior, a chief — worthy to do battle with me, worthy to claim the death of Datgas!

NARRATOR: Shaking and pale with anger and humiliation. Datgas turned and strode back into his house. The Nanyaayi were proud of their warrior Datgas. This moment would go down in their legends. Datgas was aware of his greatness and he would accept death at the hands of no warrior less noble and brave than himself. So it was to be. So it had always been ordered. The Nanyaayi standing there felt they had taken on new prestige, felt more closely bound together as a clan. They waited with staring black eyes for the Kanhaades to rectify their blunder. The Kanhaades chiefs gathered in council. And Datgas brooded in his house. He had come out to die, but death had come to him in a miserable guise and he had refused it. Now he must prepare again.

DATGAS: I have faced death many times; I can face it once more. But I was prepared to meet it as a friend. Now I cannot. But still I shall go out again — to keep our two clans at peace and maintain the high honor of my clan. Do we not say there is no greater act for a Tlingit Indian? But I shall miss many things.

DUQDANEK: Datgas! Datgas!

DATGAS: My chief, Duqdanek!

DUQDANEK: Datgas, their greatest chief, Tsaguedi himself, has come forward to join with you in combat. He invited you to come.

The highest honor, he says, is due you.

DATGAS: Tsaguedi will fight me?

DUQDANEK: He is confident you are worthy.

DATGAS: I shall go to meet him!

DUQDANEK: Kakae, place the Grizzly Bear cloak on Datgas once more. Hayiak, hand him his spear.

DATGAS: And my knife. The battle of Datgas and Tsaguedi. I go to my glory and my death.

NARRATOR: And so Datgas died. With pomp and circumstance, with head held high, he died in a mock battle with a man of high honor whom he might easily have slain.

ANTHROPOLOGIST: And so Datgas' soul went to the highest heaven, and we learn that Datgas' brave act was inspired by religion as well as by clan loyalty and personal pride. In the Tlingit religion, death in battle was a sacred death that had its reward in afterlife, but Datgas' sacrifice was considered even more sacred. The clan will enshrine this deed as the sacred symbol on its totem pole as inspiration for its future generations. (Peterson 1954:11-17).

An Analysis of Tlingit Kinship Behavior

Homicide is basic to the plot of this Tlingit drama. The events leading up to the homicide show the overriding importance of the *clan* as a fundamental kin unit. This kinship unit is composed of a group of people who trace their ties from a common founding ancestor. One clan encroached upon the fishing grounds owned by another clan, which triggered a state of hostility and potential conflict. The Tlingit, however, have an unusual and unique way of handling such disputes. As an alternative to going to war

a Tlingit clan can challenge another clan to a *potlatch* — a great feast where clans compete in giving away property. The clan that succeeds in giving away the most goods wins. The potlatch can be interpreted as an extreme form of redistribution (see Chapter 3).

In many tribal societies generosity by a tribal leader or important group means prestige and high status. In Tlingit culture the potlatch serves as a mechanism for competition between men and as an opportunity to humiliate opponents. If we recall that values centered on rank and position are important in Northwest Coast Indian cultures and attempt to view their cultures from their own perspectives (not from our own ethnocentric perspective) we will better understand the reasonableness of the potlatch. It is, as they say, "fighting with property."

In this story, a man named Kakae, a member of the clan winning the potlatch, could not be content with merely winning. Motivated by pride, arrogance, a sense of his own importance, and a desire to humiliate an opponent, he taunted and insulted a man, named Haimas, from the losing clan. Insults were exchanged between the two men, tempers flared, a knife was pulled, and Kakae stabbed and killed Haimas. This kind of interpersonal violence and the image of masculinity associated with it are not unusual in American society. What is unusual is the manner in which the resolution of this homicide was handled among the Tlingit.

The police were not called, for there were no police among the Tlingit. The killing and justice for the homicide was the clan's responsibility. The killer had to be executed as retribution and revenge. In this case, however, Kakae was of much higher rank than Haimas, and his execution would not have been a "fair" exchange. Therefore, a stand-in for Kakae had to be found. The stand-in, Datgas, who was equivalent in rank to Haimas, had to die in order to avert further conflict and to provide justice to Haimas's clan. Datgas agreed to be put to death for the good of his clan. His willingness to sacrifice his life is the prime indication of clan loyalty and commitment. In selecting Datgas, clan leaders recognized and accepted collective clan responsibility for Kakae's act.

This account makes clear the overriding importance of the clan in almost every aspect of Tlingit life. It is not only commands loyalty and responsibility, but it is also an economic, military, political, and religious unit.

Kinship in Comparative Perspective

In the comparative study of kinship anthropologists study three major topics: *kinship principles and groups, kinship terminology and systems,* and *kin-based behavior.* Kinship principles underlie the classification of individuals into groups of kin. The different kinds of kin groups found in various societies reflect different kinship principles. Individuals use kinship terms to label, address, and categorize other people. Kin terms are part of a larger system of kinship terminology. Systems of kinship terminology appear to be related to kinship principles. Kin labels do more than identify and categorize people. They usually define appropriate behavior, and many anthropological studies have documented the kin basis of behavior in different cultures.

Kinship Principles and Groups

Both the Tlingit and the Tiwi have clans that are matrilineal; that is, a person belongs to the clan of his or her mother. On the other hand, Bomagai-Angoiang have patrilineal clans; that is, a person belongs to the clan of his or her father. These two principles of descent, matrilineality and patrilineality, constitute one basis for the formation of kin groups.

There are three connected issues in accurately defining these *principles of descent:*

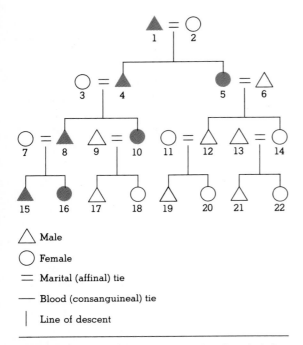

△ Male

◯ Female

= Marital (affinal) tie

— Blood (consanguineal) tie

| Line of descent

Figure 5.1. Patrilineal descent. The colored symbols in this diagram are all related through the male line to a common ancestor. Individuals 15 and 16 trace descent through their father (8), his father (4), and his father's father (1). Although females 5, 10, and 16 are part of this patrilineal group, the children of these women (12 and 14, 17 and 18) are not; they are associated with the patrilineal groups of their fathers, 6 and 9.

1. common ancestor or ancestress
2. line of genealogical descent
3. recruitment, or which group an individual joins

The *patrilineal principle* means that individuals, both male and female, are members of the same kin group if they have a common *male* ancestor, can trace their relationship to each other and to their common ancestor *through males only,* and if they belong to the kin group

of their fathers (see Figure 5.1). The *matrilineal principle* is exactly the same as the patrilineal principle except that the common ancestor is a female ancestress, relationships are traced through females only, and an individual is recruited into the kin group of his or her mother (see Figure 5.2). Because both of these two principles use only *one* side of the family to trace descent, they are called *unilineal.*

Many American students find these principles and the kin groups they establish confusing because of the lack of unilineality in the American kinship system. Americans use a nonunilineal principle that anthropologists call *bilateral.* Instead of tracing relatives through one parental line, we trace relations through *both* the mother's side and the father's side — hence bilateral (literally, two-sided).

We can see the importance of unilineal kin groups and how they operate in terms of inheritance. If you lived in a matrilineal society, you would primarily inherit property from your mother or mother's brother (MoBr). If your society were patrilineal you would primarily inherit property from your father or father's brother (FaBr). A Tlingit man belongs to the clan of his mother and if that clan controls a fishing ground, he obtains the legal right to fish at that fishing ground through his mother. In patrilineal Galipur, a man inherits land, cattle, house sites, and agricultural implements from his father. In our bilateral society, we inherit property from both our father and our mother.

Unilineal Kin Groups

Clans are unilineal kin groups. Anthropologists also distinguish the *lineage* as an important unilineal kin group. Like clans, lineages may be either patrilineal or matrilineal. The differences between lineages and clans are *size* and *generational depth.* Members of a lineage can trace the *exact* genealogical ties that link them to one another and to their founding ancestor or

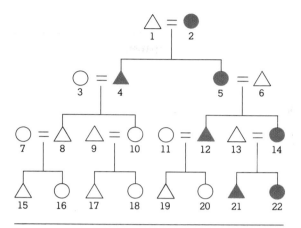

Figure 5.2. Matrilineal descent. The colored symbols in this diagram are all related through the female line to a common ancestor. Individuals 21 and 22 trace descent through their mother (14), her mother (5), and her mother's mother (2). Although males 4, 12, and 21 are part of this matrilineal group, the children of these men (8 and 10, 19 and 20) are not; they are associated with the matrilineal groups of their mothers, 3 and 11.

ancestress, usually five or six generations in the past.

Clan members claim to be kin to each other, but they are unable to document their exact relationships, or their supposed descent from a common ancestor. Often this ancestor is either genealogically remote or may even be a mythical being. In some instances the idea of clan unity is expressed in fictional history or symbols. For example, the Nanyaayi clan of the Tlingit have a grizzly bear crest as a symbol of their clan and a legend of their relationship to the grizzly bear. Since the founding ancestor or ancestress of a clan is further back in generation and time than the founder of a lineage, there are usually more members of a clan than of a lineage.

When clans and lineages are found together, the lineage is a segment or part of the

clan. A lineage is the smallest unilineal unit possible, and the members of a particular lineage are more likely to live close together.

At the other extreme, many societies group their clans into even larger-scale kin units: *phratries* and *moieties.* The Tlingit have about twenty different clans, and a portion of these clans are grouped together as Wolf clans. The remaining clans are grouped together as Raven clans. Membership in the Raven and Wolf groups is matrilineal, and each clan is exogamous. When a society is divided into two such groups, we call the groups *moieties.* When clans are grouped into more than two large units, we call the units *phratries.*

An attribute of unilineal kin groups is the existence of a clearly delineated boundary between kin and nonkin. Kin groups such as clans, lineages, moieties, and phratries are known as *corporate units.* They are collective bodies with a clearly defined membership that establishes a boundary between kin and nonkin; they also have continuity over time. Individuals are born into such groups and eventually die, but the kin group continues. It is the twin attributes of boundedness and continuity that permit such groups to acquire key social functions.

One of the universal functions of unilineal kin groups is the control of marriage. Lineages, clans, phratries, and moieties are usually exogamous groups. When the potential conflict between the Nanyaayi and the Kanhaades became apparent, a Nanyaayi chief noted that one reason for avoiding conflict was the fact that some Nanyaayi men had married Kanhaades women.

Unilineal kin groups like clans and lineages are found in approximately 60 percent of human societies (Pasternak 1976:103). In attempting to explain this prevalence of unilineal kin groups, anthropologists have advanced two basic arguments, one economic and the other military-political.

Proponents of the economic explanation

argue that unilineal kinship is an effective and simple technique for mobilizing individuals into productive work units. This is particularly important in societies with simple technologies. The choice of kinship system, whether patrilineal or matrilineal, could be explained on the basis of different economic and ecological necessities. Thus peasant societies that depend upon the intensive labor of a group of men are patrilineal, while horticultural societies where women perform basic productive tasks are often matrilineal.

Some anthropologists claim that the challenge of warfare, which requires effective and reliable fighting units, may be met by developing strong patrilineal groups that can be mustered for collective military action. In societies where phratries and moieties exist, related clans also have a kinship basis for establishing alliances and large-scale military units. One

anthropologist, Marshall Sahlins, has argued that if lineage groups link up into larger-scale units they can constitute an effective, expansionary, and predatory military force (1961).

Another function of unilineal kin groups is the provision of mutual aid as well as access to resources. If a fight breaks out between two Nuer men, for example, onlookers do not inquire who is right or wrong. They ask which man is their kinsman and go to his aid. Research among Chinese restaurant workers in London indicates that they work together in clan groups. In establishing a new restaurant clan members negotiate exclusively among themselves. Owners of restaurants are expected to employ newly arrived members of their clan (Watson 1974:201–222). In Central Africa, men residing in urban areas for long periods of time can return to their tribal homes and lay claim to a plot of farmland owned by their lineage. The Yanomamo of South America, described as an intensely warlike society, will go to war to avenge the death of a fellow lineage member.

Turn of the century family reunion — a gathering of the kindred to celebrate the Fourth of July

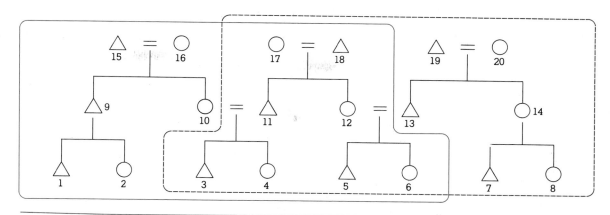

Figure 5.3. Bilateral descent. In this system the kindred is individual-centered, has no clearly stated boundary, and membership overlaps because individuals can belong to any number of kindreds. A simplified portrayal of a kindred is shown here. The solid line encloses the kindred of Individual 3 and includes his sister (4), his parents (10, 11), his uncle and aunt (9, 12), his cousins (1, 2, 5, 6), and his grandparents (15, 16, 17, 18). The dashed line encloses the kindred of Individual 6 and includes her brother (5), her parents (12, 13), her aunt and uncle (11, 14), her cousins (3, 4, 7, 8), and her grandparents (17, 18, 19, 20).

In American society, hiring an unqualified relative is considered to be a particular form of corruption called nepotism. In kin-based societies, hiring kin is considered to be the observance of a highly valued pattern of behavior. Kin loyalty overrides matters of qualification and competence.

Nonunilineal Kin Groups

About 40 percent of all societies are nonunilineal. This category includes several subtypes: bilateral, ambilineal, and bilineal or double descent.

The Bilateral Kindred. *Bilateral kinship* is characteristic of American society. The kinship group that emerges from the bilateral principle is the *kindred*. An essential element of a kindred is that it consists of a group of kin tied together by a single individual who can trace a relationship to every other member of his or her kindred. Thus a person's kindred consists of members of his or her immediate family, with aunts and uncles, first cousins, grandparents, nieces and nephews, and relatives acquired through marriage. Unlike the lineage or clan, a kindred has no founding ancestor, and there is no clearly defined boundary defining its members. Kin relations are traced through both sides of the family, through both males and females, and include relatives acquired through marriage. A kindred has no continuity over time, and it lacks the symbolic representations of unity and loyalty that are so prominent in clan and lineage systems (see Figure 5.3).

In describing a kindred anthropologists sometimes refer to it as an ego-centered group, for each individual in a kindred links together a different set of relatives. Siblings (brothers and sisters) share the same kindred relations until they marry. At the time of marriage they add to their kindred the relatives they acquire through marriage. After marriage although their kindreds overlap they are no

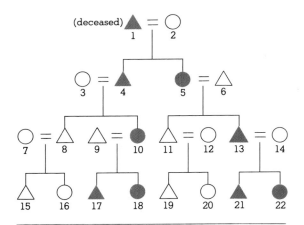

Figure 5.4. Ambilineal descent. Members of an ambilineal descent group—a ramage—trace their descent from a common ancestor through either the male or female line. Common residence often determines the membership of a ramage. In this diagram the members of the ramage (4, 5, 10, 13, 17, 18, 21, 22) live together and claim descent from Individual 1, the founding ancestor. Note that descent goes through both male and female descent lines.

longer exactly the same. Thus a significant feature of kindreds is that an individual can belong to a number of such groups.

Kindreds cannot perform the same functions as unilineal kin groups. A kindred cannot provide common ownership of property, collective military activity, joint economic ventures, and mutual aid. An individual may select a limited number of relatives from his or her kindred who can perform some of these functions. The inability of the kindred to function as a corporate unit may help to explain the importance of the nuclear family and independent households in bilateral systems.

We must not assume that bilaterality is found only in industrial and urban society. As noted in Chapter 4, independent households, neolocality and bilaterality are found extensively in hunting and gathering groups.

The Ambilineal Ramage. Ambilineality differs from unilineal descent in that descent from the founding ancestor can be traced through *either* the male or female line or both. This principle leads to a corporate descent group, which has a founding ancestor as well as continuity over time. The members of this kin group, called a *ramage,* are all related to each other, and it is possible to establish a clear boundary between ramages. The effective ambilineal kinship unit frequently is also a residential or joint household group. Residence thus becomes the basis of establishing group boundaries as well as membership (see Figure 5.4).

Bilineal Descent. In a small number of societies both patrilineal and matrilineal principles are used: an individual belongs to the patrilineal clan or lineage of the father *and* to the matrilineal clan or lineage of the mother. These two different descent groups often control different areas of behavior and property. This principle is known as *bilineal,* or *double, descent.*

An example of such a system is found among the Yako of Nigeria, as described by Daryll Forde (1950:289–332). The Yako recognize both matrilineal and patrilineal descent groups, or lineages. Fixed property – house sites, farms, and groves of trees – is controlled by the patrilineage and inherited through the patrilineal line. Male members of a patrilineage live together in compounds and village clusters, cooperating in work activities. Members of a matrilineage are scattered, but they recognize a strong kinship bond involving ritual activity and financial obligations. Moveable property – cattle, currency, furnishings, and food stocks – is inherited through the matrilineal line.

Aborigines of Australia also have a complicated bilineal kin system involving marriage sections. A major function of the Australian bilineal descent system is to control marital choice through membership in a marriage section. At the same time an individual belongs to a large number of kin groups that cross linguistic and tribal boundaries. An individual, because of these varied kin group ties, thus has access to a variety of hunting areas and food resources.

Kinship Terminology and Systems

In any kinship system relatives are classified and organized by kin terms. A *kin term* refers to the label or name applied to a particular relative. It must be distinguished from a *kin type,* which defines a particular status or position. "Mother's brother" is a kin type, as is "father's brother." In the American kin terminology system we use a single kin term, "uncle," for these two kin types. Other societies may have a different kin term for each of these two kin types.

In certain kinship systems a variety of kin types are classed together under the same term. We call this usage *classificatory kinship.* It is the notion of blood relationship, or consanguinity, between the members of a clan and lineage that fosters classificatory kin terms. Thus, a biological sister and other females of an individual's kin group may be called by the same kin term. We may loosely translate such a kin term as "classificatory sister." For an individual using this kin term, however, the significant element is that the females called "sister" are all females of the kin group and should be treated in much the same way.

There are a number of different ways in which classificatory kinship terms are used. A common procedure in unilineal societies is to place mother (Mo) and mother's sister (MoSi) together under a single kin term. In our own bilateral system we put FaBr and MoBr and FaSiHu and MoSiHu under the single term "uncle." Our kin term "cousin" classifies a number of different kin types under a single kin term. Anthropologists have discovered that the kin term classifications found in human society

Table 5.1. Kinship terminology type, descent system, and frequency

Descent System			
Unilineal		Nonunilineal	
Type	Percent	Type	Percent
Iroquois	25	Hawaiian	32
Omaha	10	Eskimo	16
Crow	8		
Sudanese	8		

Reprinted from *Cross Tabulations of Murdock's World Ethnographic Sample* by Allan D. Coult and Robert W. Habenstein by permission of the University of Missouri Press. Copyright 1965 by the Curators of the University of Missouri.

use consistent and logical principles in their organization. This finding enabled anthropologists to classify kin terminological usages into six kinship terminological systems.

The six kinship terminological systems distinguished by anthropologists are named after the specific tribal groups or regions where they are found. Table 5.1 lists each type of system, its relationship to a descent system, and the percentage of societies in which the terminology system is found.

These systems may be either extremely classificatory or the opposite, extremely particularizing. A *particularizing system* is a system in which there are separate kin terms for the various kin types. A classificatory system is one in which a few kin terms are used for many different kin types.

Sudanese System

The most *particularizing kinship terminological system* is *the Sudanese system* (see Figure 5.5). In this system every kin type — mother, father, mother's sister, mother's brother, father's sister, father's brother — and every kin type in the same generation — brother, sister, father's brother's children, father's sister's children, mother's sister's children, mother's brother's children — is designated by a separate term.

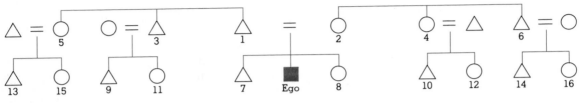

△ Male

◯ Female

▪ Ego (central point of diagram)

= Marital (affinal) tie

___ Blood (consanguineal) tie

Symbols with the same number are referred to in the same way by Ego.

Figure 5.5. Sudanese kinship terminology. Each kin relationship is referred to by a different term.

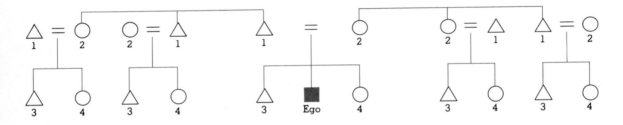

Figure 5.6 Hawaiian kinship terminology.

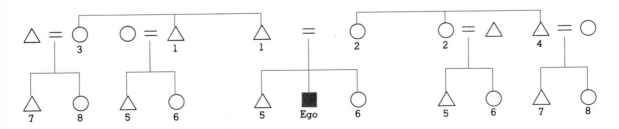

Figure 5.7. Iroquois kinship terminology.

Sudanese systems are found in patrilineal societies with complex political and social institutions. Sudanese kin terminology permits the distinction and separation of kin within a larger unilineal unit. Many anthropologists suggest that if differences in occupation, wealth, and social class are important, this particularistic organization of kin permits the expression of different behavioral patterns among separately labeled kin types. This type of distinction allows recognition of social, economic, and political differences.

Hawaiian System

At the other extreme is the *Hawaiian kin terminological system,* which is extremely classificatory (see Figure 5.6). This system is sometimes called generational because the terms reflect only generational and sex differences. In the parental generation the same kin term is used for father, father's brother, and mother's brother, and another term is used for mother, mother's sister, and father's sister. In the same generation a single term is used for sister and *all* female cousins and another single term for brother and *all* male cousins. Hawaiian terminology is associated with either bilateral or ambilineal descent. Robert Murphy (1967: 169–170) suggests that Hawaiian kin terminology is a kind of nonsystem. It recognizes kin relations, but does not specify the exact role behavior of such relations or to what group kin may belong. Hawaiian kinship terminology and ambilineal descent are often found together. The characteristic shared by Hawaiian kin terminology and ambilineal descent is flexibility, and it is evidence of the consistency between different parts of a total kinship system.

Iroquois System

The most common unilineal system is the Iroquois. This system may be found in association with either patrilineal or matrilineal descent (see Figure 5.7). In the *Iroquois kinship system*

the father and the father's brother are called by the same term, but a different term designates the mother's brother. Mother and mother's sister are called by the same term, but the father's sister is distinguished by a different term. In the same generation father's brother's children and mother's sister's children (*parallel cousins*) are called by the same term used for both brothers and sisters. Different terms are used for *cross cousins* — mother's brother's children and father's sister's children (see Figure 5.8).

This kin terminology system reflects the importance of unilineal kin groups. It classifies people who are members of an individual's own lineage and identifies people belonging to other lineages.

Omaha System

The *Omaha system* is also associated with unilineal descent, but it is specifically related to patrilineal descent (see Figure 5.9). In the Omaha system a person uses the same term for the males (mother's brother, mother's brother's son) in his or her mother's lineage. In addition, the same kin term is used for a person's mother, mother's sister, and mother's brother's daughter — the females in the mother's patrilineage. The distinctive feature of Omaha kinship terminology is that individuals of *different generations* and *ages* are referred to by the *same* kin term.

Crow System

The *Crow system* is the mirror image of the Omaha system (see Figure 5.10). Like the Omaha system, the Crow system is associated with unilineal descent, but it is related to matrilineal descent. In the Crow system individuals in the father's matrilineage are grouped together. All males in the father's matrilineage — father, father's brother, father's sister's son — are called by the same kin term, and there is a single term for father's sister and father's sister's daughter, the female members of the ma-

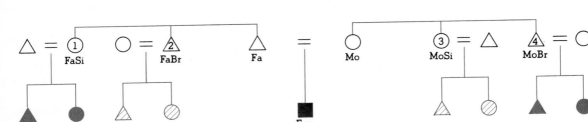

Figure 5.8. Cross and parallel cousins. Ego's cross-cousins are the offspring of ego's father's sister (1) and ego's mother's brother (4). Ego's parallel cousins are the offspring of ego's father's brother (2) and ego's mother's sister (3).

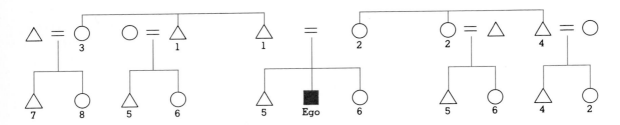

Figure 5.9. Omaha kinship terminology.

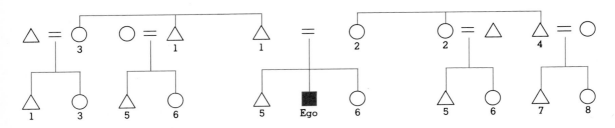

Figure 5.10. Crow kinship terminology.

trilineage. As in the Omaha system, individuals of different ages and generations are referred to by the same kin term.

Anthropologists do not agree on any single explanation of the Omaha and Crow kinship systems and why such important principles of kin classification as age and generation difference are ignored in these two systems. A possible explanation is that the importance of lineality and lineage membership overshadows these other principles of kin classification.

Eskimo System

Americans are most familiar with the *Eskimo kin system* because American kin terminology is classified as Eskimo in type (see Figure 5.11). In the Eskimo terminological system, father is distinguished from father's brother and mother's brother, who are classified together as "uncle"; mother is distinguished from mother's sister and father's sister, who are classified together as "aunt." Brother and sister are distinguished from cousins, who are classified together. The essential element of this terminological system is that lineal relatives — direct ancestors and descendants — are distinguished from collateral or indirect relatives. Lineal relatives are directly related to an individual through ascent or descent and include father, mother, brother, sister, son, daughter, and grandparents. Relatives such as mother's brother, father's brother, father's sister, mother's sister, and their children are collateral

relatives, and they are not directly related to an individual through ascent or descent. Robin Fox (1967: 259) suggests that in Eskimo kinship systems, the nuclear family — composed of lineal kin — is important; like an onion, we surround the core (nuclear family) with concentric layers of collateral kin. The Eskimo terminological system reflects the absence of unilineal descent and the importance of the nuclear family as a separate unit.

Kinship and Behavior

Because behavior in tribal and peasant societies is based largely on kinship, a basic understanding of why people behave as they do is often linked to their kinship system. If there are similar kinship principles and systems, there may also be broad areas of similar behavior. Avoidance relations, such as occur between a marriage partner and in-law of the opposite sex, joking relations, and the relationship to the mother's brother are behavior patterns that are systematically linked to variations in kinship systems.

Avoidance Relations

An *avoidance relationship* is exactly what the term suggests: a person must avoid a particular relative. If it is impossible for them to avoid each other, they must not talk to each other. Usually the person in the junior status avoids the older and higher ranked individual. In addi-

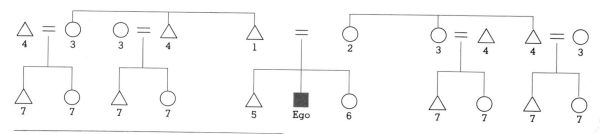

Figure 5.11. Eskimo kinship terminology.

tion, avoidance is most usually found between individuals of the opposite sex, of different generations, and between individuals from families linked by marriage. A Galipur girl must avoid her father-in-law and her husband's older brothers. Navajo men must avoid the presence of their mothers-in-law. Navajo believe that violation of the avoidance taboo will result in supernaturally caused blindness (Aberle 1961: 149–150). A fieldworker among the Navajo noted that while he was talking to a male informant, the informant suddenly disappeared behind a *hogan* (house). A few moments later a woman passed by them. After she had gone, the informant reemerged and explained that the woman was his mother-in-law. This pattern of avoidance is particularly intriguing in light of the Navajo pattern of matrilocal residence. A man does not live in the house or hogan of his wife's parents, but instead builds a hogan for himself and his wife very close to the residence of his wife's parents. The usual anthropological explanation for this avoidance relationship is that it avoids potential conflict between mother-in-law and son-in-law, but it also gives the mother-in-law power over her son-in-law since she can, for example, force him to leave his hogan immediately by simply entering it herself.

Father-in-law avoidance in Galipur also prevents potential conflicts between kin who reside within the same household. Before entering his house an older man who may have avoidance relationships with some female members of his household pauses and coughs. All the females in the household can recognize his cough, and the women who are supposed to avoid him will leave the central courtyard and withdraw to the women's quarters or draw the upper parts of their saris over their faces before he enters the house.

Based on this description of avoidance, a person might ask, why was the Brahmin woman described earlier in the presence of her father-in-law, and why was she allowed to attack him with a leather shoe? In special situations and over time this avoidance pattern may be disregarded. In the case of the old man, he was a widower, the marriage of his son and daughter-in-law had taken place a long time ago, and the daughter-in-law had given up all pretense of avoiding her father-in-law within the household unit. She was criticized for behaving this way as well as for many of her other actions, but no one could or would do anything about her behavior.

Another example from an Indian village of the discrepancy between what should be (ideal culture) and what is (real culture) can be seen in a woman's avoidance of her husband's older brothers. An anthropologist working in an Indian village was told by a number of male informants that they had never seen their younger brother's wives. The anthropologist subsequently took pictures of these women. He then showed his male informants a photograph of a woman who was *not* the younger brother's wife and said, "Here is a picture of your younger brother's wife." In every case the men denied that the person was their younger brother's wife, and they were, in fact, able to select the correct woman from the collection of photographs, disproving the rule of total avoidance in that society. This example also indicates how an anthropologist in the field must check on the verbal statements made by informants.

For the Galipur pattern of avoidance a very different explanation is used from the explanation for the Navajo pattern. In Galipur it may be suggested that since the father and older brother are in such dominant positions over the woman's husband and the woman herself, the avoidance taboo hinders any possibility of sexual involvement between a woman and her father-in-law or her older brother-in-law. Usual explanations for Navajo avoidance patterns stress the possibility of potential conflict between son-in-law and mother-in-law, but perhaps the avoidance of sexual contact is present there, too. In many Southwestern Indian folk tales, in fact, the coyote is a trickster figure and in some stories has sexual relations with his mother-in-law. Although the Navajo who listen to these stories react hilariously, the sexual aspect of the story may reveal some of the deeper dynamics of this avoidance pattern.

Murdock's survey of avoidance patterns in a sampling of 137 societies indicates that avoidance of the mother-in-law is the most common pattern. More than 80 percent of the societies in his sample required either avoidance or extreme respect between a man and his mother-in-law (Murdock 1949:279). Father-in-law avoidance as found in Galipur is the second most common pattern. It is an expected form of behavior in slightly less than half of the societies in Murdock's sample (1949:279).

Joking Relations

Joking relationships are the opposite of avoidance relationships. People involved in joking relationships are expected to be familiar and informal, teasing and joking with each other. Very often the joking revolves around sexual activities, but it may also express abuse and veiled hostility. Unlike the avoidance relationship, it is difficult to generalize which relatives will be involved. In some societies relatives who call each other brother and sister may joke with and tease each other, but in other societies it may be a man and his mother's brother, or individuals related by marriage.

One of the most common patterns of joking is found between a man and his wife's sisters and a woman and her husband's brothers. This pattern especially is associated with the levirate and the sororate. In many societies before the death of a person's spouse an individual may initiate sexual relations with the spouse's siblings. Murdock suggests (1949:281–282) that the joking relationship may act as a basis for establishing a sexual liaison.

In Galipur a married woman is commonly expected to carry on a joking relationship with one or more of her husband's *younger* brothers. If there is no younger brother in the household, a parallel cousin (father's brother's son) may be used as a substitute. In this patrilineal system a HuFaBrSo is called "brother-in-law" and is treated in much the same manner as an actual brother-in-law. A girl and her younger brother-in-law may tease each other about all aspects of life, including sexual activities. A boy may say to his sister-in-law that her husband has told him that his wife is a very poor sex partner and he (the husband) will have to visit a brothel to satisfy his sexual needs. She might respond by saying that while she was drawing water at the village well, she heard some girls say that he was one of the ugliest boys in the world and also probably impotent, although they were not likely ever to find out. In both of these situations, the boy and girl knew that they were being teased because an older brother would never confide such intimacies to a younger brother, and a young married girl would never be allowed to remain by herself at the village well and listen to the gossip of the local unmarried village girls.

In describing the Tikopia, Raymond Firth indicates that men who stand as "brother" to each other enjoy a joking relationship that includes the exchange of obscene insults (1936). Even chiefs are not exempt from this custom, and they, too, can exchange obscenities with commoners. He recounts an incident in which a chief encountered a common brother and epithets such as "You are the big testicle" flew back and forth between the two men to the accompaniment of hilarious laughter (Firth 1936:189–190).

The Mother's Brother

Where matrilineality is the basic principle of kin affiliation and inheritance, it is frequently a man's mother's brother rather than his father who controls property and other valued goods. This pattern is found among the Tlingit, Mesakin, and Korongo (see Chapter 2). Thus although women may be central figures in tracing

Little boy enjoying the company of his mother's brother. This kinship relationship is a very close one in Yanomamo society.

relationships and focal points of kin organization, they are subordinate to men politically and economically. In a matrilineal system, a man is heir to his mother's brother's wealth.

As Malinowski noted for the Trobriand Islanders, this inheritance pattern frequently establishes a situation of conflict between a boy and his mother's brother. In dealing with this phenomenon among the Trobriand Islanders, Malinowski suggested that the resentment which a boy feels toward his mother's brother was similar to that which Freud said existed toward the father in his analysis of the Oedipus complex in Western society. With this material, Malinowski demonstrated that Freud was incorrect in his suggestion that the Oedipus complex was based solely on sexual conflict between son and father over access to the mother-wife. Trobriand Island boys, both overtly and in their dreams, showed great fondness for their father and great hostility, even hatred, for their mother's brother. Based on this evidence, Malinowski suggested that the mother's brother's role as disciplinarian, authority figure, and eventually the person from whom the boy inherits was the basis for the hostility between these two kinsmen. This is a celebrated example of the use of anthropological data to demonstrate that a supposedly universal and inborn human behavioral pattern (the Oedipus complex) is controlled by culturally defined patterns of inheritance, authority, and descent.

Students unfamiliar with a matrilineal system frequently ask, "What happens if the mother has no brother?" This question in part reflects the Eskimo–American kinship system, which is characterized by an absence of unilineal descent groups. In matrilineal societies a lineage must contain a number of older men. From the perspective of a young boy in a lineage, all these older men are his mother's brothers — that is, men of his mother's generation. They are his *classificatory* mother's brothers.

In patrilineal societies where the mother's brother does not exercise these rights over his nephews, there is a literal reversal of kin behavior and meanings. Instead of appearing as an authority figure to his nephews, the mother's brother in patrilineal society emerges as a warm, indulgent, playful, and nurturing individual. This type of relationship can be seen in the accompanying photograph of a Yanomamo man playing with his nephew (SiSo). This man was a visitor from another village that was at war with the village where his sister lived. Despite the state of hostilities and the possibility and danger of being attacked and killed, he took time to play with the child, his sister's son.

In patrilineal societies the mother's brother, who can sometimes be defined in classificatory terms as any male in the mother's lineage, is a close relative, but he is *not* a member of the nephew's clan or lineage. This relationship means that he has little authority or control over his nephew and that the two kin do not come into conflict over property or inheritance. In patrilineal societies the two kin (MoBr and SiSo) can enjoy their relationship without being concerned that the other person is actually interested in self-gain. The importance of understanding this relationship is that it provides an excellent example of how kinship operates to generate a specific and widespread pattern of behavior.

Fictive Kinship

Although most kin terms are used to describe people related by blood or marriage, there are situations where kin terms can be applied to nonkin. The use of kinship terms between nonkin usually implies behavior that closely resembles that of actual kin. This usage is called *fictive kinship*.

Many people have aunts and uncles who are not really their aunts and uncles. Frequently they are friends of their parents who are very close to the parents and whom they have been taught to call aunt and uncle. It is apparently too

awkward and cumbersome to call them Mr. and Mrs., and it would be too familiar to call them by their first names. Using kinship terms solves this dilemma.

There are many ways in which we use fictive kinship. Certain social movements and religious orders use such terms freely. Blacks often refer to each other as "brother" and "sister." In the Catholic Church priests are called "father," nuns "sister," and monks "brother." Fraternal organizations also tend to use the kinship terms of "brother" and "sister." Kin terms for the expression of political relationships were immortalized by George Orwell in his use of the term "Big Brother" for the dictator of *1984* society, and Americans use the term "Uncle Sam."

Another significant form of fictive kinship is the *godparenthood complex.* Found in the Mediterranean, Europe, and Latin America, godparents are fictive kin acquired at the time of birth or baptism. Godparents may be kin who reaffirm the kinship ties between themselves and the child. Frequently the child's parents select the godparents, and in this manner link nonkin to the family unit. Generally godparents are supposed to care for their godchildren, especially if they are orphaned. In addition, they are supposed to guide them, help them in times of need, and provide gifts on ceremonial

Baptism is the ceremony that ties together godparent and godchild. In the United States, the major obligation of godparents is to provide a second family in times of distress and need.

occasions. In some Mediterranean communities, the establishment of a godparent link at baptism is extended to all members of the respective families. Thus young and unrelated boys and girls in the two families can now call each other "brother" and "sister," and they also observe an incest taboo.

Although the general functions of the godparenthood complex may be similar, particular ethnic groups in American society show a number of interesting differences in their use of godparents. Research with Hispanic and Black students in New York indicates that over time godchildren begin to assume responsibility for their godparents. As their godparents age, Black and Hispanic godchildren help them in times of illness, providing transportation and performing other chores for them. Jewish students, on the other hand, indicate that nonkin godparents become unimportant for them after childhood. A special feature in the Jewish godparent tradition is that among Orthodox Jews only boys have godparents.

Nonkin Groups

Early anthropologists argued that tribal society was essentially, or entirely, based on the ties of kinship. Although kinship plays a vital role in these societies, groups can be based on other kinds of social principles. The most important principles are age and sex. As the tribal world undergoes change, new nonkin groups, associations, and networks emerge and become increasingly important in the social world of these people.

Age and Sex Groups

In Nadel's comparison of the Mesakin and the Korongo of East Africa (Chapter 2), he notes that both societies have *age-grades,* which means that men of approximately the same age are placed together in the same group. Men in a particular age-grade group in these societies participate collectively in spear-throwing contests and wrestling and live together in the cattle camps. For those two societies both age and sex were used as organizing principles.

A specialized nonkin group based on age and sex was the Zulu *impi,* the basic military unit of Zulu society. Upon reaching manhood, men of the same age joined an impi. These men, who were warriors, lived in special military barracks. As the anthropologist Max Gluckman described it:

> Shaka, head of the Zulu tribe, organized a nation out of all the tribes he had subjected. His chief interest was in the army and he made whole-time warriors of his men; he developed the idea of regiments formed of men of the same age, and quartered them, for most of the year, in large barracks built in different parts of his country. They trained there for war, herded the king's cattle and worked his fields. The men were forbidden to marry till the king gave them permission, as a regiment, to marry into a certain age-regiment of girls. (Gluckman 1940a:26).

While the Zulu adapted the age-grade into a military unit, the Nyakyusa of Southern Tanzania organized age-grade villages. "Villages consist not of kin, but of age-mates" (Wilson 1950:111). Monica Wilson describes how boys ten to eleven years old begin to build huts at some distance from the village of their parents. They are joined over time by younger boys, until a group covering a span of about five years in age is formed. These boys marry and bring their wives to the village. As their children are born and grow up, their sons repeat the process, moving away to build villages inhabited by age-mates (Wilson 1950:111).

In Chapter 4 we described the village dormitory (*ghotul*) of the Muria, an age-based group. Boys and girls join the dormitory at the age of six and remain there until marriage. Ghotul members not only live together, but also work as a common group.

Sex has also been used as a basis for group formation. The institution of the men's house in Melanesia is one of the best examples

A men's house in New Guinea. These large structures are used exclusively by men for meetings, feasts, and ceremonial occasions.

of a *sex-based group.* In some societies women may form exclusive groups for particular purposes. In West Africa, for example, religious and secret societies of women have been described. These groups of women may exercise considerable power, and one anthropologist commented that few men would dare penetrate into an area controlled by such a group of women. Although males dominate in military activity and organization, a military unit of women warriors was established in the nineteenth century by the king of Dahomey in West Africa. They were assigned to protect the life of the king, who was also their husband. Reports indicate that they were excellent fighters (Burton 1864).

Ethnic Groups and Associations

Throughout the tribal world the emergence and growth of urban areas bring together diverse and varied populations. In this urban context new groups that are based on nonkinship principles develop. These nonkin principles include a shared culture and language as well as common tribal membership and a common occupation and economic position.

The idea that a group of people share a common tribe, culture, and language is often linked to vague notions of blood relationship. When all these factors are taken together, they define a group of individuals as a distinct people. Social scientists call such groups *ethnic groups.* Feelings and sentiments of ethnic identity are among the most powerful principles of group formation, and ethnic groups are found all over the world.

Some anthropologists interpret the emergence of ethnic identity among tribal people in urban areas as a means of making sense out of the complexity and diversity of urban life (Berreman 1972; Gluckman 1961; Mitchell 1974). Many other researchers have identified the economic and political advantages of ethnic solidarity. Abner Cohen's study of the Hausa people in the city of Ibadan in Nigeria (West Africa) revealed how their economic success in the cattle trade strengthened their sense of ethnic identity. As a consequence of their ethnic solidarity, the Hausa in Ibadan exercise political power that protects their economic position (Cohen 1969).

Associations are organized groups. Different principles can be used to organize associations, but the use of ethnicity as a principle of associative organization and membership is very common. Kenneth Little (1965) describes the emergence of voluntary associations among urban migrants in West Africa. These formally organized associations based on tribal membership meet on a regular basis and elect officers. The primary concern of these associations is to improve their rural-tribal homeland. A great portion of their activity is devoted to fund raising for community projects.

Tribally based associations may also perform ceremonial and mutual aid functions for their members. In this sense the urban associations assume some of the functions and obligations performed by organized kin groups in their traditional tribal culture.

Not all associations among tribal people are based on ethnicity and shared cultural origins. A. L. Epstein studied the trade union movement among the thousands of African workers employed in the copper belt region of Zambia (1958). Because the workers were drawn from all over Central Africa and represented scores of different tribal groups, the European mine administrators assumed that the most logical way to organize the African labor force would be in terms of tribal membership. Thus they instituted a system of Tribal Elders to represent the interests and welfare of the African workers.

Beginning in the 1930s and continuing into the 1950s, however, labor unrest and strikes

Puerto Ricans in the United States are politically concerned about the future status of Puerto Rico. For these paraders ethnic and political concerns unite to form a common bond.

occurred among the African workers in the copper belt. Surprisingly, the workers expressed a great deal of hostility toward the Tribal Elders. Eventually the African Mineworkers Union emerged and demanded the abolishment of the Tribal Elder system. According to Epstein, this development indicated the growing unimportance of tribal membership in an industrial setting. Occupational categories — clerk, unskilled laborer, underground miner — and income differences instead become the new basis for organization and association.

Social Networks

Ethnic affiliations and formal associations are not the only means of establishing relationships in urban areas. In the fluctuating and transient world of the city, individuals develop social relations with a wide variety of people. These people include neighbors, fellow workers, members of the same religious group, fellow tribesmen, and people from different tribes.

These individually based sets of linkages are referred to as *social networks*. Networks may be defined as groups of people that a person knows and interacts with in a particular way. The members of a social network are often unknown to each other, and they are linked together by the person who has a set of relations with each of them. Their membership is fluctuating, uncertain, and ambiguous.

Studies of social networks have indicated their utility in a wide range of social situations. Bette Denich (1970:133–148), in her study of rural to urban migration in Yugoslavia, found that social networks were mobilized by migrants in obtaining employment and housing. A. C. Mayer, in his study of a local election in a small Indian town, shows how social networks were mobilized by politicians to obtain votes (1966:97–122). Many studies of the poor in the United States and Latin America indicate the use of network relations in maximizing limited

resources and in obtaining access to jobs, welfare, and medical services. In all these instances, individuals have used any available combination of kin, neighbors, friends, fellow workers, and ethnic affiliations and associations to secure their desired goals.

An excellent example of a network that illustrates the use of traditional kin usages in a changing urban setting is A. L. Epstein's description of the experiences of an African man named Chanda who lives in the town of Ndola in Zambia. Epstein had Chanda record the people he met over the course of a few days and how he related to them. The following account is a small excerpt from the diary that Chanda kept.

> It was shortly after noon when Chanda left off work. He decided to do a little shopping in town. On the way to town, he met a woman who had just arrived in Ndola on the bus from Fort Rosebery. She was of his own tribe, a Lunda of Kazembe, and he greeted her.
>
> After some further conversation, in which they exchanged news of friends and acquaintances, Chanda bade the woman farewell and set off again on his bicycle. Near the Government Offices he ran into his friend Thompson. Thompson at this time was having an extramarital affair with a girl called Paula who was Chanda's classificatory sister. As they greeted one another a co-worker of Thompson called out to ask if he [Chanda] were going home, but Thompson replied that he had met his "brother-in-law" who would persuade his girlfriend [Paula] to be nice to him. "You have to keep in with your brother-in-law if you are to have a good 'friend'," he added.
>
> Returning home later, and passing by the Beer Hall, [Chanda] ran into a number of close kinsmen who had just arrived in Ndola from home. They were talking to Crawford, an official of the African National Congress. Chanda knew Crawford very well, but now he learnt that they were also kinsmen, for it soon emerged in the course of the introductions that Crawford was Chanda's classificatory father, although

they were of different tribes and came from different parts of the country. Neither had known previously of the relationship, and now they both expressed their pleasure in its discovery. "So you are related to Francis, my brother-in-law here," Crawford exclaimed. "You know," he went on, "Francis' sister is married to my own brother. Now it is good that our relationship is revealed today. That is why we get on so well together. It is the blood of kinship. Very fine, indeed."

The following afternoon, a Sunday, Chanda dressed up properly to watch the football match between teams from Ndola and Mufulira. But at the entrance to the ground he met his sister-in-law [Alice] and her husband Robert on their way to the Beer Hall together with another elder sister of his wife. Robert then invited Chanda to accompany them to the Beer Hall.

At the Beer Hall they found seats and immediately Chanda found himself being introduced to a large number of people whom Robert addressed as brother, maternal uncle and so on. Together they all set to drinking the large supply of bottled beer which Robert had provided. All present seemed to be growing increasingly drunk. Alice asked Chanda, who tended to become intoxicated rather quickly, why he was drinking so little and sat there so

quietly. Chanda replied that he was perfectly all right; he was afraid to say much lest in an unguarded moment he let something slip which might give offence to his freshly introduced affines [in laws]. A Bemba woman sitting nearby agreed, and said it was always wise to watch one's step when drinking with one's inlaws (Epstein 1969:80–81, 87–88).

The most striking feature of Chanda's account is his wide range and use of kin terms to designate and classify many of the people he meets. Even strangers are quickly incorporated into Chanda's kinship network. These kin linkages then become a means of defining appropriate behavior. So inclusive is Chanda's use of kinship terms that individuals from different tribes are converted into familiar and traditional kin categories. Although Chanda's wide use of kin terms would appear to reflect the continuing influence of traditional tribal culture in the urban area, it is actually the use of traditional categories in an entirely new setting. Some basis, no matter how slender, is used to establish a relationship. This relationship, along with all the other relationships an individual maintains, becomes a social network that an individual can use for a variety of purposes.

Summary

Kinship is a major means of organizing and mobilizing human beings into effective social groups, designed to carry out a multitude of functions. We have described the principles underlying kinship, the kinds of groups that are formed on the basis of these principles, kinship terminology, and the behavioral consequences of kinship.

Most societies in the world develop kinship groups on the basis of a unilineal principle of descent: matrilineality or patrilineality. These principles lead to the formation of bounded and corporate kin groups: clans and lineages. Where these groups exist, they play a vital role in the fabric of society. Such kin groups usually control marriage, exercise economic and political power, and organize religious activities. Individuals belonging to clans and lineages identify with them and hold strong loyalties to them. The account of "Stand-In for a Murderer" is a classic example of kinship loyalty.

Many societies use nonunilineal instead of

unilineal principles of descent. Nonunilineal principles – bilateral, ambilineal, and bilineal – lead to the formation of different kin groups, such as kindreds, ramages, and combinations of matrilineal and patrilineal groups.

Kin terms have received considerable attention in the development of kinship studies in anthropology. The variety of kin terms found in human society can be reduced to a small number of principles and systems. The six kinship classifications recognized by anthropologists are related to descent principles and to certain types of economic activity.

When different kin terms are used behavioral expectations are found to differ as well. Despite the similarity of kin types (father, mother's brother, and so on), the behavioral content differs from one society to another. There are some widespread similarities in kinship-based behavior, however. Three major areas of kin-based behavior are the relationships of avoidance, joking, and the mother's brother.

In many societies kinship terms and behavior are extended to nonkin, which we call fictive kinship. A common pattern of fictive kinship found in European, Mediterranean, and Latin American societies is the godparent complex.

Despite the emphasis on kinship in tribal society, there are numerous instances of groups based on nonkin principles. Age and sex are the most common principles for the formation of such groups. In many urban and developing areas nonkinship principles – common tribe, language, culture, occupation – give rise to ethnic groups and associations. In addition, individuals develop their own social networks using any combination of kin and nonkin principles.

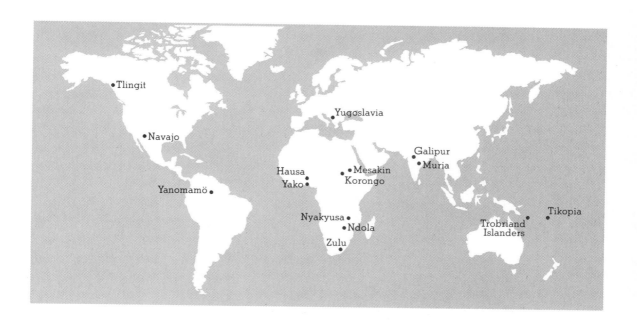

Key Terms and Concepts

clan
potlatch
patrilineal descent
matrilineal descent
unilineal descent
bilateral descent
lineage
moiety
phratry
kindred
ambilineal descent
ramage
bilineal/double
    descent
kin term
kin type
classificatory
    kinship
    terminology
particularizing
    kinship system
Sudanese kinship
    terminology

Hawaiian kinship
    terminology
Iroquois kinship
    terminology
parallel cousins
cross cousins
Omaha kinship
    terminology
Crow kinship
    terminology
Eskimo kinship
    terminology
avoidance
    relationship
joking relationship
fictive kinship
godparenthood
    complex
age-grades
sex-based group
ethnic groups
associations
social networks

Suggested Readings

American Ethnological Society, and John W. Bennett. *The New Ethnicity, Perspectives from Ethnology: Proceedings.* New York: West, 1975. *A collection of papers that focuses on the problem of analyzing the meaning of ethnic consciousness in the contemporary world.*

Bott, Elizabeth. *Family and Social Network: Roles, Norms and External Relationships,* 2nd ed. New York: Free Press, 1972. *This pioneering study of family life in London introduces the concept of social network. Includes a clearly presented comparison of middle- and working-class Londoners.*

Fox, Robin. *Kinship and Marriage.* Baltimore: Pelican, 1968. *A comprehensive presentation of kinship and marriage that goes beyond the introductory level.*

Keesing, R. M. *Kin Groups and Social Structure.* New York: Holt, Rinehart and Winston, 1975. *A thorough introduction to kinship, descent, and kin terminologies. Keesing makes extensive use of short ethnographic cases as examples.*

Pasternak, Burton. *Introduction to Kinship and Social Organization.* Englewood Cliffs, N.J.: Prentice-Hall, 1976. *A short introduction to kinship and marriage. Chapter 9 is especially valuable for its clear discussion of kinship terminology.*

Schusky, Ernest L. *Variation in Kinship.* New York: Holt, Rinehart and Winston, 1974. *A concise and readable introduction to kinship.*

Chapter 6

War and Law

Combining a discussion of war and law in a single chapter may appear to be peculiar and unjustified. Most of us are taught that war is brutal, unjust, and the breakdown of the rule of law. Law is associated with justice, peace, and the application of the sense of reason to the affairs of individuals. There are, however, links between war and law, for both are concerned with the ordering of social relations. In addition, war and law both represent aspects of coercive power, and as aspects of power they are a segment of a larger realm of human activity called politics.

Politics is the organization and exercise of power in society. Power and politics involve decision making, control over the behavior of others, access and control over resources, and the definition of group goals or public policy. One major aspect of politics is organization and government, a topic discussed in Chapter 7. This chapter is concerned with two of the most important aspects of the political process: war and law.

Anthropological interest in the study of war is a relatively recent development. Although many of the best studied tribal groups, such as the Nuer of the Sudan, the Zulu of South Africa, the Plains Indians of the American West, and the Maori of New Zealand, are well known for their fighting and military capabilities, until recently few anthropologists attempted to develop a general understanding of warfare in human society.

An important stimulus for this new interest in the anthropology of war was the conflict in Vietnam (Fried, Harris, Murphy 1968). Many anthropologists were against the Vietnam war, and from their opposition there emerged the general question of the origin, purpose, and impact of war in human society. Anthropologists turned to descriptions of warfare among tribal groups in order to understand it. In effect, anthropologists used a comparative and cross-cultural approach to place modern warfare within the context of human warfare.

Fighting and violence are not uncommon in human society. Such activities are classified in three ways: feuding, raiding, and warfare. Although the lines distinguishing these three types of violence are often fuzzy, their central elements can be conceptually identified.

Feuding is an activity that involves individuals and their supporters and is likely to involve members of the same social group. Revenge for prior wrongs appears to be the major impetus for feuds, and a continual cycle of reciprocal killings makes it difficult to bring feuds to an end. The well-known Hatfields and McCoys of American folklore represent this type of fighting. The Sicilian vendetta, a deadly dispute between families that supposedly goes down through the generations, is another example of feuding.

Raiding is more organized than feuding

American soldiers in World War I charge out of their trench into no man's land.

Devil Anse Hatfield (seated) and his family. One of the most famous feuds of American history was between the Hatfields and the neighboring McCoys. The feud endured for several decades and finally ended in 1891 when a Hatfield married a McCoy.

and is often directed at outside groups. Its major object is not revenge, but rather the acquisition of plunder and booty. Raiding is common among pastoral people, who find it a convenient and efficient way of increasing their herds of animals at the expense of others. Raiding is rarely a sustained activity; the objective is to seize booty and escape. Guerrilla bands, pirates, and bandits who suddenly swoop down on their surprised victims represent this traditional form of violence.

Warfare is a more sustained and organized form of fighting that involves armed and organized combat between recognized groups. A significant proportion of the population usually takes part in combat or in support of the fighting. The objectives of warfare are varied. In some cases revenge and plunder are the goals of combat, and in other cases annihilation of the enemy, access to and control over land and resources, and conquest of a population may be involved. Wars have also been fought on the basis of political and religious ideologies. This reason for warfare, however, appears to be rare in tribal societies.

Warfare as we have defined it is not universal. Groups like the San of the Kalahari Desert, the Semai of the Malay Peninsula, the Tasaday of the Philippines, and the Pygmies of the Ituri Forest in Central Africa do not engage in war. It may even be suggested that violence of any kind is unknown to these people. Thus feuding and raiding are also not universal.

If warfare is not universal, then how widespread is it? Unfortunately, anthropologists cannot answer this question with any degree of accuracy. One reason why the answer is elusive is the suppression and prohibition of native warfare by colonial administrators in the eighteenth, nineteenth, and twentieth centuries. As a consequence, anthropologists doing fieldwork in the twentieth century were usually unable to observe native forms of warfare. Warfare in the Amazon Basin and New Guinea represent isolated instances where colonial and national administrations were not able to suppress these activities.

Although colonial rule suppressed native warfare in most parts of the world, some evidence indicates that early contact with Europeans fostered and generated intense and destructive warfare in a number of tribal societies. European firearms also intensified the brutality of tribal warfare. Trade and competition for access to European goods stimulated intertribal warfare. In North America in the eighteenth century, for example, Iroquois and Huron Indians fought to control the fur trade. In West Africa the slave trade contributed to the emergence of highly organized African states, and these states used warfare and raiding to maintain the flow of slaves. Europeans often enlisted native peoples in their wars. In North America conflict between the French and the British (the French and Indian Wars of 1754–1760) involved the establishment of Indian allies on both sides of this conflict. In South Africa the development of the warlike Zulu empire in the early nineteenth century may have been brought about by European settlement. European settlements blocked the expansion of small African tribes seeking new lands for their gardens and fresh pastures for their cattle. Because they were unable to spread out, these tribes fought each other in a ruthless and bloodthirsty series of wars that eventually gave rise to the Zulu empire.

Some anthropologists see a connection between modes of subsistence and warfare, suggesting that warfare did not become an important part of human culture until the domestication of plants and animals 12,000 years ago. This position assumes that population pressure and surplus food production are basic to the emergence of war.

Opponents of this interpretation point out a number of problems. Warfare is not unknown among foraging groups. Among the Plains Indians of North America raiding and warfare were central to their culture. For the Indian tribes of the Northwest Coast of America, warfare and raiding were well-developed cultural patterns. Perhaps these examples may be seen as exceptional cases. The Plains Indians had horses and the Northwest Coast Indians, although foragers, had abundant food supplies. However, the foraging tribes of Australia, considered to be among the most technologically simple groups known, engaged in feuding, raiding, and warfare.

W. Lloyd Warner, who studied an Australian tribal group, says that "warfare is one of the most important social activities of the Murngin and surrounding tribes. Without it, Murngin society as it is now constituted could not exist" (1958:155). The Murngin of North Australia distinguish six varieties of fighting and warfare, ranging from brawls to all-out war. All-out wars take place on a regional basis and involve a number of clans. Such wars are preceded by protracted provocations and killings that eventually generate a war hysteria. Once the Murngin decide to go to war they say, ". . . that this is a spear fight to end spear fights, so that from that time on there will be peace for all . . ." (Warner 1958:173).

Absence of warfare among some foragers is not conclusive evidence for the emergence of warfare with the development of the domesticated food economy. Although the technology of warfare has progressed and modern wars are fought on a worldwide scale involving large populations, the technological development of weapons and increases in the scale of warfare must not be confused with the evolution of warfare as a culture pattern. Human beings fight for a variety of reasons. In fact, the Murngin justification for warfare seems to be a caricature of the commitment of modern society to war as national defense. In terms of tactics, strategy, destructiveness, and involvement, tribal wars and contemporary wars are often similar. An all-out war leading to the death of fifteen men was as devastating for the Murngin as was the death of millions in the two European world wars.

Warfare Among the Mae Enga of New Guinea

One of the regions in the world where tribal warfare still occurs is Highland New Guinea. Mervyn Meggitt, in his account of the Mae Enga, provides a description of native warfare that in many ways parallels warfare in Western society (1977). The Mae Enga are a Highland New Guinea group with a total population of 30,000. They are horticulturalists and pig herders who live in clan-based villages containing 300 to 400 people. Although these patrilineal clans are grouped into higher-level kinship units (phratries), the clan is the basic political, economic, and social unit of the Mae Enga. It is the war-making body.

Warfare is a serious business to the Mae Enga. It is highly organized and under the direction of fight leaders. The Mae Enga have developed strategic and tactic maneuvers much like the maneuvers used in contemporary warfare. Unlike hit and run raiding, Mae Enga wars often bog down into protracted wars of attrition. Such combat involves long periods of nervous boredom, punctuated with moments of terror, ambush, and attack. In many ways the description of their warfare is reminiscent of trench warfare during World War I (1914–1918). In a Mae Enga war, when a stalemate develops both sides attempt to recruit allies to throw fresh troops into the battle, which often tips the scales in the favor of one side. Often such a development shatters an enemy's will to resist, and defeat and rout are the consequences.

Mae Enga warfare is not without serious cost. Death and destruction of property are invariable accompaniments. Meggitt provides figures showing that more than one-third of all male deaths among the Mae Enga occur as the result of warfare. Such casualty rates are staggering. To provide a comparison, in four years of intensive combat in World War I France lost about 10 percent of its adult male population.

The following account drawn from Meggitt's description of the Mae Enga depicts the dimensions of their warfare in terms of weaponry, leadership, strategy, tactics, and the cost of conflict.

WEAPONS

The Mae armory of offensive weapons is limited, comprising primarily the axe, the spear, and the bow. Bows are usually made from the strong wood of the black palm. The bow itself is about five feet long. The "bowstring" is a narrow strap of flexible bamboo or rattan. The whole is, for the novice, very difficult to bend. In the hands of an Enga it discharges an arrow with tremendous initial force, and at close range can drive the arrow through a half-inch pine plank.

Mae men greatly prize barbed [arrow] heads made from black palm, because these do severe damage and are difficult to withdraw. Some Mae manufacture [an] arrow from a slender bamboo tube, which is sharpened

and given a longitudinal channel with keen edges. They may also stud the channel with slivers of broken glass.

A more common fighting arrow among the Mae is one whose head is a leaf-shaped blade of bamboo. The edges are razor-sharp and, when they encounter bone, tend to explode into their component fibers and spread out to cause infection. The Mae spear is generally made of black palm. When thrown in the Enga overarm fashion, the spear has an extreme range of about fifty yards, but it can be thrown accurately only about thirty yards.

Men may go into battle carrying a spear in the right hand and bow and arrows in the left, in which case they quickly hurl the spear at the end of a darting, weaving run, then drop back as they fire arrows. More often the spear is employed as a stabbing weapon at close quarters, especially in ambushes. In battle, spearmen, who usually number only about a tenth of the force, carry shields and move together as a tight front line, keeping close to protect one another's flanks. Their archers fire over and around them.

A Mae Enga warrior holding a stone axe fashioned in the traditional manner.

LEADERSHIP

Presumably as a consequence of social training and cultural expectations, most Mae men are tolerably competent warriors. Among the Mae no one goes berserk or runs amok under fire. Men do not go into battle determined to die facing suicidal odds, either to prove a point of honor or to shame their clansmen. On the contrary, every man hopes to survive to fight another day. Fight leaders [are] found in each clan.

The Mae recognize that the bravery, self-confidence, and skill in fighting which distinguish the hero are not always accompanied by the intelligence and experience requisite to the successful deployment of armed forces. For a man to be accepted and followed in battle as a fight leader, his own confidence in his ability to kill opponents does not suffice; his clansmen must be confident that his commands will be the right ones, that he can use the terrain and the available warriors to the best advantage, that he can perceive and capitalize on changing circumstances in the flow of combat, and that he can assess the morale of the enemy group. Accordingly, a fight leader is more than his title suggests. His task is to employ his forces effectively to produce a material victory. To this end, then, the fight leader divides his time during a battle between performing exemplary actions in the front line and assessing the total situation from the rear.

STRATEGY AND TACTICS

Accounts of actual invasions and discussions with experienced Mae warriors suggest that in general the overall strategy intended is informed by principles common to all successful military campaigns — speed, secrecy, and the propitious concentration of strength. With these requirements in mind, the organizers make the critical strategic decision, namely, on which section of enemy territory their warriors will converge. That choice, together with the number of men they have at their command, governs subsequent decisions on the size and disposition of units, the manner of their entering the combat area, and the action they take once there. Nevertheless, as the Mae well know, strategy planned by one side in the privacy of the men's house does not always prove appropriate once the battle begins. Then the fight leaders' experience and personal bravery are crucial, for these men must make constant tactical judgments to meet the rapidly changing circumstances of combat, as well as provide the steadying influence that heartens men confused by sudden shifts of fortune in the field.

Let us take first the simplest case of a clan, initially without allies, that invades its neighbors' territory without warning. Given that the population of a Mae clan is around 300–400, we can estimate that the average attacking force at the start comprises about 100 warriors, and the defenders about the same.

Divided into two or three smaller groups to facilitate their silent movement in the darkness to the clan border, they take up their stations in readiness for the predawn onslaught. This is necessary because of the local terrain, whose slopes not only tend to be naturally uneven but also are encumbered with deep garden ditches, sturdy fences, and groves of trees. For a force to try to move as one through these obstacles at night could be disastrous. To get into position for the assault quietly, rapidly, and more or less simultaneously, the bodies of men keep to tracks carefully chosen by the fight leaders to converge on the appropriate place of assembly.

Then all the columns converge to form a shallow phalanx, four or five ranks deep (of which the first may comprise men armed with spears and shields), and firing arrows as they go, charge the oncoming defenders, preferably downhill for impetus. If they are able to overrun the opposing line, the invaders split up again into tight columns, each of which mops up the small, disorganized enemy clusters, using axes to dispatch any wounded they overtake.

The invaders press their assault, pursuing and killing any opponent they see, and they try to sweep across the clan domain to force the survivors to flee into the forest or the territories of neighboring clans. If the assailants can achieve this goal on the first day, they have won a complete victory, and there is little to prevent their holding most or all of their opponents' land.

The ideal response to such an incursion, assuming that the defenders can at once mobilize a substantial body of warriors, is for them to get to the invaders before these can complete their initial killing and arson, and to try to pin them down and surround them. The invading columns, however, put out flanking units precisely to guard against encirclement. And in any case the odds are against the defenders' mustering enough men in time to form a circle sufficiently strong or deep to hold their opponents.

A more feasible and more common tactic is for enough defenders to reach the invasion point before the invaders are ready to make their concerted rush deep into the victims' territory. Here the defenders oppose the enemy phalanx with their own, which then, fighting strenuously against superior strength, drops back as slowly as possible to allow the remaining clansmen (as well as allies) time to join the combat. The main danger now facing the defenders is that the longer the delaying action continues, the more opportunities the larger invading force has to break their front or to outflank them. Accordingly, when the fight leaders in the retreating group believe they have sufficient reinforcements and the terrain and cover are suitable, they attempt, by "refusing" their own center, to trap the invaders.

At its simplest this maneuver merely requires that, as both wings of the defenders' company withdraw slowly, the men in the center drop back more quickly, as if the enemy center is too much for them. As the overconfident attackers press forward to exploit their apparent advantage and push into the concavity created by the yielding defenders, their own men, first at the center and then on the wings, are increasingly exposed to heavy crossfire from archers on the defenders' wings. The attackers, moreover, are too crowded to deploy freely their greater numbers and fire power. If the defenders' wings can hold steady and maintain the pressure, they have a chance to close the trap and subsequently to take the invaders in the rear.

When, as is commonly the case, a surprise attack does not achieve decisive results by nightfall of the first day, the invaders withdraw to safe positions and throw out patrols. If the intended victims have put up an unexpectedly vigorous resistance and kept the attacking forces from penetrating any distance into the disputed territory, and especially if numerous allies have come to the defenders' aid, counsels of caution may prevail. The aggressors retire inside their own border and partially demobilize, while maintaining strong scouting parties and posting sentries at the border to detect and delay any counterattack or retaliatory raids. Then, if within the next few weeks neither group initiates further large-scale military action, all parties assume the war is, for the time being at least, ended.

A more likely outcome, however, given Mae intransigence and the aggressors' explicit desire for more land, is for their leaders to press for a continuation of overt hostilities, arguing that, since they have already occupied some of the enemy's territory, it is worth pursuing the struggle and risking more deaths in the reasonable hope of retaining possession of their present gains. Moreover, as experienced warriors know, if from a vantage point within the enemy domain they maintain pressure on their opponents, they are in a better position to exploit any weakness in the defense and thus to seize more of the coveted land.

Such a unilateral decision pushes both groups into a war of attrition that may continue for weeks, even months. Whatever the duration, the course of events is much the same — periods of comparative inaction punctuated by sporadic raids intended to unsettle the opponents and by larger engagements aimed at forcing them to give ground. The situation also becomes very much a war of nerves.

It usually happens that early in the war, a belt of several hundred yards on either side of the antagonists' common border is laid waste. All the houses there are burned, fences destroyed, pandanus and other valuable trees felled, and gardens torn up or trampled into mud. This area becomes the main field of combat. By day small parties of scouts (with about four to six men), exploiting what cover remains, patrol there to keep a constant watch for any untoward activity among the foe and, most important, to detect the arrival of potential enemy allies, because this may presage a renewed attack. Similarly, the men who are not guarding the borders but discussing military and political plans do so in shelters set high on the slopes, from which they can observe the enemy's movements and oversee their own women who are working in the gardens. Meanwhile, the parties at the front remain ready to snipe at warriors who incautiously emerge from cover and approach too closely.

Days, sometimes weeks, may pass in this manner, with increasingly tired and edgy warriors taking turns patrolling by day and standing sentry by night. The slightest unexpected noise (or indeed a prolonged silence) sends the armed men out into the darkness to scour the paths leading to the disputed area or to the borders with unfriendly clans to check on their sentinels. It is small wonder that Mae men speak with real feeling of the great strain they undergo at such times, of the combination of anxious boredom and physical exhaustion that oppresses them, and of the frequent overwhelming urge that seizes them to do something to stimulate action, however ill-advised. It is then that the more restless and hardy warriors plan risky nocturnal raids deep into enemy territory, hoping to burn houses in the "safe" areas and so intimidate their opponents, as well as to relieve their own frustrations.

The course of large-scale combat that occurs within a protracted war is markedly affected by the impossibility of a true surprise attack, for both sides are at all times mobilized. The invaders have little opportunity to implement the preferred tactic of striking alternately with columns and phalanx. Instead, they attack in small columns, protected by flanking scouts, in order to sustain mobility as they engage in turn the rapidly converging units of the defenders.

If the terrain permits, both sides may form extended skirmishing lines, each trying to outflank and roll up the other. Or one line may employ the technique of "striking alternately," continually rushing the other only to fall back quickly when the opponents stiffen their resistance and charge in turn. The men keep this up until their leaders judge that the enemy is tiring and losing coordination, while at the same time enough of their own warriors or allies have come up to exploit this weakness. Then they direct this fresh reserve group at the center of the enemy's slowing line in the hope of shattering it.

Given the fragmented and opportunistic nature of this kind of battle, it is clear that military planning alone is unlikely to achieve a decisive outcome if the groups are fairly evenly matched. The only factor that can tilt the balance at this juncture is marked numerical superiority, especially if it is represented by the appearance of a contingent of enthusiastic and ably led allies who can coordinate their tactics with their hosts'.

Thus, when a large and capably led party of allies arrives in the heat of battle to find their "brothers" tired and hard pressed, they may tell them to fall back in apparent confusion, drawing the confident enemy with them, and then quickly to open their ranks so that the body of fresh warriors can charge through to surprise and scatter the opponents. On occasion this maneuver can sharply change the flow of combat and enable the rested home force to rally sufficiently to take the enemy's flank and so make a decisive push that ends the conflict.

THE IMPACT OF WAR

Statistics indicate that on the average about two men are killed on each side in such intergroup hostilities. At first sight this may suggest that Mae warfare does not take an unduly high toll. When, however, we note both the mean size of a clan (350–400 members — that is, at most about 100 men), the frequency with which a clan goes to war, and the higher losses it may suffer, the figures assume a different complexion. On the one hand there is

Causes of Death Among a Sample of Mae Enga Men
Before 1950

		Cause of death			
	Old age	Illness or accident	Warfare	Unknown	Total
Number	38	64	91	68	261
Percent	14.6	24.5	34.8	26.1	100

the immediate impact that the deaths of five to ten active warriors in an engagement have on a clan — a couple of such encounters and the group is in serious trouble *vis-à-vis* rapacious neighbors. On the other hand, one must consider the consequences over a period of time of the steady drain on manpower that even lower casualty rates may have. The table [above] summarizes the stated causes of death of men before 1950. The ratio of male deaths attributable over time to warfare is substantial — at the least of the order of 25 percent of all male fatalities. In short, the frequency of overt hostilities among Mae groups

significantly determines the pattern of male mortality.

To summarize, it appears that traditional modes of Mae warfare, both in their nature and in their frequency, take a relatively high toll of men's lives, and many of the victims are bachelors, cut off before they have children. In addition these death rates have direct political repercussions in that they can quickly and radically erode the fighting strength of a clan and leave it open to the incursions of more fortunate neighbors. Casualty rates among women and children immediately attributable to Mae warfare are very low.

What of the indirect influence of the physical dislocations that accompany serious or prolonged fighting? We simply do not know how many infants and old people succumb to pneumonia in these flights, how many refugees are drowned when trying to cross boulder-strewn torrents, how many already sick and weak people die because food supplies are interrupted. These less obvious costs of war, I believe, accumulate significantly through time (Meggitt 1977:54–57, 64, 66–68, 83, 88–92, 94–98, 108–112).

The Context of Mae Enga Warfare

The 30,000 Mae Enga people live in small clan villages, containing 300 to 400 people. These clan communities are the sovereign political units of Mae Enga society. The physical proximity of so many separate communities provides a fertile arena for bickering, dispute, and antagonism that flares into warfare on occasion. Each clan community has common borders with a number of other communities. Disputes over boundaries, attempts to expand clan borders, and the formation of alliances against common enemies are important factors in the genesis of Mae Enga fighting. Lacking any level of political organization beyond the clan community, the Mae Enga are doomed to an unending cycle of clan warfare. Their inability to organize on a political basis beyond that of the sovereign clan community creates the setting within which Mae Enga warfare occurs.

Part of Mae Enga warfare consists of sophisticated tactics, strategy, and command structure. They have welded a relatively simple technology of spears, bows and arrows, shields, and knives into an effective and well-led military force that may, in fact, be unusual in the tribal world. The development of Mae Enga military science may be explained in historical terms. If we assume a social-political environment of continually warring clans, the Mae Enga have had a long exposure to organized combat. It appears reasonable to expect that with a long history of fighting, elements of their strategic, tactical, and command structure would undergo an evolutionary development toward greater efficiency and effectiveness.

Among the Mae Enga, as well as among many other horticultural groups, women have primary responsibility for the production of food. The relationship between this feature of Mae Enga economic life and their warfare should be apparent. Men are able to spend their time in protracted military activities without disrupting the food supply. The ability of the Mae Enga to absorb significant levels of male casualties may be related to this relative lack of importance of men in the work of day-to-day food production.

When Meggitt asked the Mae Enga why they fight, their answer was for land. Meggitt quotes the Mae Enga as saying, "We must have the land . . . to feed our people and our pigs. The land is the basis . . . of everything important in our lives. A clan whose territory is too small cannot expect to survive" (Meggitt 1977:182).

Although the Mae Enga offer an economic and ecological explanation for their warfare,

Meggitt notes that it is impossible to determine objectively the reality and validity of this reason. He suggests that the perception of adequate land is culturally determined. Thus, the Mae Enga view of a land shortage may not reflect objective reality, but rather a culturally defined standard of well-being. The implication of Meggitt's view is important. It means that the usual environmental arguments that an objectively determined level of land or food shortage will automatically trigger fighting and warfare are questionable. He states that groups have an image of what is a desirable level of land and food and that this emic view may bear very little relationship to actual circumstances.

Conflict over land is not the only source of hostilities among the Mae Enga. The conclusion of any particular Mae Enga conflict is the potential beginning of another round of hostilities. Although compensation is paid for deaths in battle, past losses fester in the minds of kin. Added to other disputes and bad feelings between clans, eventually they are likely to trigger another round of fighting. Even victorious allies may fall out over the division of the spoils of war. These disputes can become the basis for future hostilities between previous allies. Revenge and greed thus become important ingredients in the causes of Mae Enga warfare.

Warfare in Comparative Perspective

As we can see in Meggitt's account of Mae Enga warfare, most principles of military science used by any army or well-organized fighting group are known and used by the Mae Enga. Surprise, mobilization, command structure, logistics, and tactics are all part of their military activities. These elements of war, however, belong in a comparative study of military science rather than in a cross-cultural discussion of the anthropology of war. Anthropologists are generally more interested in the reasons for warfare than in an analysis of the principles underlying successful military action. For this reason the comparative analysis in this chapter focuses on theoretical positions advanced to account for warfare in human society. The question these theoretical positions seek to answer is basic: why is there warfare?

Theories of Warfare

Renewed anthropological interest in warfare has generated a variety of explanatory theories that may be grouped under four headings: human nature, functionalist, ecological, and political. In discussing these theories we will attempt to assess and criticize them. Although no single theory at this time provides an adequate explanation of warfare, theoretical attempts to explain warfare are an essential element in furthering the understanding of all this potentially destructive aspect of human behavior.

Human Nature, Aggression, and War

Proponents of *human nature theories of aggression* find the sources of such behavior within the biology of the human species. They claim that aggression is an inborn and natural tendency of humanity that expresses itself in violence, fighting, and war. It has frequently been noted that human beings are exceptional in their willingness to attack and kill members of their own species.

Konrad Lorenz, a student of animal behavior, advanced a biologically based theory of human aggression (1966). Aggression, according to Lorenz, evolved as part of the process of natural selection, providing an adaptive strategy for human survival and reproduction. Dominance, attack, and aggression within the human species provided a stable social order, the emergence of competent leadership, and a dispersal of the population in proper balance to available resources. Aggression, according to this theory, is an innate and spontaneous component of the human condition.

Lorenz believes that human aggression did not threaten the total survival of the species, for defeat and death were outweighed by the advantages for survival of the fittest. As human beings developed a terrifying technology of destruction, culture unfortunately outran biol-

ogy. Lorenz argues that unlike other animal species, humanity has no built-in inhibitions that prevent the expression of violence. Thus, the technology of war, harnessed to our innate aptitude for aggression, now threatens survival of the entire species. Lorenz sees few opportunities for controlling this innate tendency toward aggression. At best, he suggests various substitute forms of aggression, such as sports, to act as outlets and harmless diversions for this inborn fury.

Robert Ardrey, a popular writer, has set forth a theory of human aggression and warfare that also rests on innate biological propensities. Ardrey suggests that as our primitive ancestors moved on to the African grasslands millions of years ago they became carnivorous (meat-eating) hunters (1964). As killers of animals, wallowing in the blood of their prey, they developed a lust for blood and taste for aggression. In *The Territorial Imperative* (1966), Ardrey adds to this scenario the idea of an instinct for territorial defense and gain. His view presents an image of human beings as hunter-killers defending their own territory and attacking the territory of others. His view of humanity is, if anything, more dismal than that of Lorenz. He believes that human beings are not simply naked apes, but also nasty brutes.

Two criticisms can be made of human nature theories. Lorenz's theory is based on the study of animal species and is then generalized to the human species. The validity of this type of analogous reasoning can be questioned. A second criticism is that Lorenz is primarily concerned with spontaneous aggression instead of planned and controlled aggression that is characteristic of warfare. Much of the same criticism can be made of Ardrey's work.

For the adherents of the human nature explanation of warfare, there is little distinction between aggressive behavior and warfare. Warfare is seen as only one form of aggression, standing alongside such behavior as murder, suicide, competition, rape, brawling, assault, and stealing. Many anthropologists see warfare as a distinctive form of human activity primarily related to political and social structures. It may involve murder, rape, plunder, and destruction; however, murder, rape, plunder, and destruction do not imply warfare.

The human nature approach to warfare has acquired a wide following, which may result in part from the inadequacies of nonbiologically based theories of human behavior. Such theories have been dominant in anthropological thinking, for almost half a century, and most of the recent theories of warfare have been based on a cultural, rather than a biological, interpretation. Yet an understanding of warfare is still imperfect. The explanatory limitations of these nonbiological theories have driven one cultural anthropologist, C. R. Hallpike, to write (1973:459):

> Because sexual gratification, love of prestige and power over others, and envy of those who have these advantages, are some of the strongest forces in human nature, men enjoy killing other men. The human race has evolved few more definitive means of proving one's superiority over an enemy than by battering him to death and eating him, or by burning his habitation, ravaging his crops and raping his wife. The tortuous explanations advanced by academics for the prevalence of violence in primitive societies in some cases disclose their lack of knowledge of human nature.

Functionalist Theories of Warfare

Functional theory has long occupied a place of importance in anthropological thinking, and many functional theorists believed they could discover the central purposes of warfare. W. Lloyd Warner's statement that Murngin society could not exist in its present state without warfare is a typical example of a classic functionalist approach. Functionalists assume that any social activity, including war, found in a society operates to maintain the continuity of that society.

Connected to the idea that warfare contributes to the continuity of a society is the assumption that social unity and solidarity within a group are consequences of conflict between groups. Social theorists like Georg Simmel (1955) and Lewis Coser (1956) have advanced the proposition that conflict with an outside group can lead to internal unity and social cohesion.

This notion of social cohesion as a byproduct of warfare and conflict must be understood within the framework of functional theory. For functional theorists a central question concerns the problem of how a society maintains itself over time. They suggest that aggression or defense against outsiders intensifies internal unity by diminishing the importance of internal conflict and dispute.

Proponents of a parallel formulation with psychological overtones see warfare as a tension-reducing mechanism for people in society. In this approach it is assumed that living in society generates tension and frustration and that warfare becomes a means for releasing these feelings upon an outside group. It is believed that without such a release tension and frustration would increase and either begin to incapacitate people psychologically or be directed toward members of one's own group.

Malinowski gave an alternative functionalist explanation of tribal warfare. He considered native warfare as a form of sport that contributed to the maintenance of native life by providing opportunities for exercise, courage, and amusement. In a survey of Malinowski's contribution to anthropology, Ian Hogbin quotes the following as typical of Malinowski's attitude toward tribal warfare (1957:249).

> Native warfare causes little damage and has the merit of providing a wide field of physical exercise, the development of personal

courage, cunning, and initiative, and the sort of dramatic and romantic interest, the wider vision of possibilities and ideals, which probably nothing can replace. In the Trobriand Islands . . . in a big war, where a couple of thousand warriors took part, the total casualties might amount to half a dozen killed and a dozen wounded. . . . And such a war afforded excellent amusement, exercise, and development of personal qualities to a large number of men for several weeks. . . . Thus, the establishment of peace and safety is by no means an unmixed blessing, and it is always deeply resented by the natives themselves. The governments ought to have left the milder forms of fighting . . . so as not to unman the natives completely.

Malinowski, however, did not extend this idea to the two world wars, which he interpreted as utterly destructive (Malinowski 1960:216).

Some anthropologists follow Malinowski's approach in minimizing the deadly and destructive consequences of tribal war. "Dead Birds," a film about the Dani of New Guinea, describes their pattern of *ritual warfare.* This film and the ethnography of these people (Heider 1970) testify to the spontaneous and exuberant aspect of Dani ritual warfare. Karl Heider, who did fieldwork with the Dani, writes (1970:111, 129):

> Though battles are fought as part of the [ritual phase of] war, the sportive element in them seems to be very strong. There is a good deal of joking, even across enemy lines. Except

Dani warfare. Lines of Dani warriors oppose each other in combat.

for one or two tense moments, no one was ever in real danger of being overrun by an advancing enemy line.

Battles are casual. Often during the noonday heat both sides simply withdraw and sit in groups, smoking, talking, and resting for a while before resuming hostilities. Once, late in the afternoon, fighting ceased altogether and both sides sat on comfortable rocks hurling insults at one another, picking out certain of the enemy by name. A choice remark would be greeted by both sides with roars of laughter.

The sportive aspect of ritual war is certainly important. Dani adults have no organized sports, and there are few amusements except conversation. There can be no question that Dani men find the battles great fun.

Ritual war is only one phase in a larger cycle of Dani war. Ritual fighting, which takes a small toll in deaths, may continue for years, although at some point the cycle of ritual war can break out into truly destructive war. In a nonritual war, which is planned in great detail and aided by allies, a group of Dani may make a sudden and surprise attack on another group. If the attack is successful, as such tactics often are, the results for the defeated group can be catastrophic. The fatalities of men, women, and children may run into the hundreds, villages may be destroyed, and the survivors may become refugees fleeing for their lives (Heider 1979:103–105).

Functional theories of war suffer from the same shortcomings as functional theories explaining other aspects of human behavior. These theories basically begin with the premise that no matter what exists in a society, it must contribute positively to that society. If no specific function can be determined, the general function of societal and cultural maintenance and continuity is assumed.

Although social solidarity may be a consequence of war for contending groups, for the defeated group it may have the opposite outcome: destruction and disintegration. Another problem related to social solidarity as a function of warfare is determining the boundaries of the unit that benefits from war. Mae Enga fight Mae Enga; Dani fight Dani. Any attempt to develop an integrated and unified Dani or Mae Enga tribe is shattered by warfare within these groups. The assumed beneficiaries of war-induced cohesion are small Mae Enga and Dani clans that live with the continual threat of attack. Theories of social unity and solidarity fail to specify why these small groups rather than larger groups should be the units of social cohesion. Even though living in society may induce tension among many individuals, the tension-reduction theory fails to specify the exact linkage between the release of tension and warfare. A logical extension of this theory is that societies without warfare lack the internal tensions required to motivate warlike activity. Such a conclusion seems highly improbable. Both of these explanations fail to specify why warfare, rather than competitive sports, national ceremonies, witchcraft accusations, and the use of internal scapegoats, should be the mechanism for social solidarity and tension reduction.

War as fun may be applied to Trobriand war with minimal casualties or to a Dani ritual war. The same explanation, however, cannot be applied to the type of warfare described by Meggitt for the Mae Enga or for the nonritual phases of Dani warfare. In this type of warfare large segments of the population face disruption and death. Casualties are high, crops and food resources are destroyed, homes are plundered and burned, and the defeated population is dispersed. Ritual warfare and limited forms of combat such as medieval jousting constitute a small segment of warlike activity. Most warfare is serious, and interpretations of warfare as merely fun cannot be seriously entertained.

War canoes, used to transport large numbers of fighting men from one part of New Zealand to another, were an integral part of Maori warfare. British soldiers considered the Maori to be the fiercest adversaries they encountered.

Ecological Theories of Warfare

Ecological theories emphasize population, environment, subsistence, and technology as parts of an entire system called the ecosystem. According to ecological theory warfare becomes a means of maintaining these parts of the system in balance. When the population increases, technology changes, the environment becomes degraded, or subsistence is threatened, warfare may become one way of reestablishing the relationship between these factors. Warfare may reduce or disperse the population; it may halt the degradation of the environment; and it may bring new land or forest areas into the subsistence system.

Two decades ago Andrew Vayda (1961) developed an ecological explanation of warfare. Using historical data on the Maori of New Zealand, Vayda interpreted their incessant warfare in terms of population pressure on available forest and land resources.

Drawing upon the insights provided by Vayda, Marvin Harris developed a more complex and sophisticated ecological explanation relating warfare and population (1977:31–54).

Harris distinguishes between warfare in highly organized state societies and in tribal societies. He claims that in state societies political conquest and economic plunder are major goals of warfare. However, these *are not* the goals of warfare in tribal society.

Basic to Harris's formulation, as well as to that of Vayda, is the assumption that human populations tend to increase beyond the capacity of the environment to support the population. The ultimate consequence of warfare in tribal societies is to keep population growth as low as possible and to maintain low population densities. Thus warfare maintains a favorable ratio of human beings to available resources.

Harris believes that warfare and combat deaths *do not* significantly reduce the potential of future population growth directly. He observes that the fertility and population growth of a human society depend upon the number of females of childbearing age. Male deaths in combat have little to do with the birth rate, and data from a variety of tribal societies indicate that few females are killed as a direct result of warfare. Therefore, how does warfare lead to population control?

Harris answers that warfare is an exclusively male occupation that glorifies masculinity and men. Women are devalued and considered unimportant. One consequence, according to Harris, is the differential treatment of male and female babies. Male children are desired, nurtured, and cared for, but female children are not. In the extreme application of this differential, female infanticide, the killing of female babies, is practiced. Using data for the warlike Yanomamo Indians, Harris points out their extremely unbalanced juvenile sex ratios, ranging from 148 to 460 boys for every 100 girls. Such distortions can come about only through female infanticide.

Harris applies his explanation of warfare to the Yanomamo. The Yanomamo are experiencing both population growth and territorial expansion. Warfare is intense, continuous, and female infanticide is common. Harris argues that the introduction of metal tools and new food plants — plantains (a tropical banana-like fruit) and bananas — resulted in a population explosion that began about a century ago. This increase in the population led to a greater demand for protein-rich meat. More people had to be fed, but the increasing production of starchy bananas and plantains did not meet their need for protein. There was a need for protein-rich meat that could be acquired only through hunting. Thus the land required for hunting had to be extended, and this expansion was accomplished through warfare.

Warfare, according to Harris, disperses the population over a larger area, decreases population density, and increases access to food resources. Increasing food production and population dispersal through warfare, however, cannot keep pace with reproductive pressure and population increase. Female infanticide becomes a means of regulating population and at the same time fostering a sense of masculine aggressiveness required for warfare. In addition, the scarcity of women becomes an always present stimulus for fighting. Harris summarizes the ecological relationship between warfare and Yanomamo population growth as follows:

> I believe it is possible to show that the Yanomamo have recently adopted a new technology or intensified a preexisting technology; that this has brought about a veritable population explosion, which in turn has caused environmental depletion; and that depletion has led to an increase in infanticide and warfare as part of a systemic attempt to disperse settlements and to prevent them from growing too big (Harris 1977:49).

For both Vayda and Harris population pressure on land resources is crucial to their ecological explanation of war. They are unable, however, to measure objectively the level at which a given population density exceeds the ability of the land to maintain that level of population. Harris notes that the importation of steel machetes, plantains, and bananas may have led to a population explosion among the Yanomamo. These imports also led to greater productivity, thus providing a larger, but protein poorer, subsistence base. Once again, however, there is no objective measure of the minimum protein level needed for full nutrition compared to the actual protein intake of the Yanomamo. In addition, the availability of protein from land animals, reptiles, fish, and insects may be greater than Harris recognizes (Beckerman 1979:533–560).

Meggitt notes that the Mae Enga offer an ecological explanation for their warfare: they fight for land. He admits that it is not possible to determine the objective accuracy of their perception of land shortage. Shortage of land appears to be a culturally defined inadequacy rather than a measurable inadequacy. We do not know on what basis the Mae Enga determine that land available to a given clan is inadequate, thus causing this shortage to serve as an impetus to war.

Basic to Harris's population control argument is the institution of female infanticide. The Yanomamo kill female infants, but the Dani and the Mae Enga do not. Thus a general theory of war that links it to female infanticide is not substantiated in those parts of the world where tribal warfare is still practiced.

A Political Theory of Warfare

Warfare involves aggression, but above all it is a political act. For this reason warfare must be understood within a political context. Despite the numerous causes of warfare the actual outbreak of warfare depends on the possession of political independence. A social group must have the political freedom and independence to go to war against another group. Once such groups lose their autonomy and become integrated into a larger political system they lose the freedom to engage in warfare.

Reasons given for violence and war are quite varied. The Dani told Heider they fought to please the ghosts of the dead; the Yanomamo told Chagnon that they fought over women; and the Mae Enga told Meggitt that they fought for land. One of the most pervasive reasons for warfare is revenge. When two contending groups engage in warfare, revenge for losses suffered is more than sufficient to generate new conflicts. Anthropologists have noted that compensation is frequently paid at the end of a war. No amount of compensation, however, can completely erase the scars left by the loss of kin and destruction of a person's property and home. The motives and reasons for warfare could be extended almost indefinitely. What permits the motives for war to find expression in organized conflict is not the disagreement, but rather the *political freedom* that allows dispute, argument, and revenge to be translated into organized armed conflict.

For both the Mae Enga and the Dani outside political control has been basic to the ces-

sation of warfare. When Meggitt first began his work with the Mae Enga, they were outside the jurisdiction of the Australian administration. By the 1960s, however, Australian police patrols and police posts were actively engaged in suppressing Mae Enga warfare. On one occasion the government flew in a police force when large-scale Mae Enga hostilities erupted.

Heider describes a similar situation for the Dani. He notes that by 1961 Dutch and Indonesian pacification programs effectively ended warfare among the Dani. "The Dani knew the power of the police guns and accepted pacification without argument" (Heider 1970:123). Heider assumed that suppression of warfare would lead to a rechanneling of aggression into other areas of Dani life such as suicide or intragroup fighting. He admits that this assumption was wrong. His Dani informants, furthermore, never complained about the suppression of warfare.

In Africa the development of native kingdoms led to the suppression of warfare in areas under their control. This can be seen in the development of the Ashanti state in West Africa and the Zulu kingdom of South Africa. Both states began as small groups that defeated other groups, incorporating them into a larger political unit. Thus, small scale warfare involving clans and local communities, was supplanted by state level warfare.

Throughout human history periods of extended peace have been associated with the exercise of paramount political power. The Pax Romana (Roman Peace) that characterized the first two centuries (first and second centuries A.D.) of the Roman Empire and the Pax Britannica (British Peace) of the nineteenth century were periods of peace because Rome and Britain suppressed warfare in the extensive domains under their control.

We assume that warfare will occur when the opportunity permits it. The crucial question is: what are the circumstances and conditions that inhibit the development of larger-scale political units in many parts of the tribal world? Warfare is a consequence of the lack of political control over potentially warring parties. The inability of many tribal societies to develop beyond local clan and community levels doomed the tribal world to endemic, small-scale, and incessant warfare.

Much of the recent anthropological interest in war emerged as part of the opposition to the Vietnam war and the threat of thermonuclear destruction. Anthropologists hoped that an analysis of tribal war would reveal the roots of this destructive tendency in human populations, and that once known it might be possible to control and reduce the possibility of future conflict. A *political theory of war* relates warfare to political developments and leads, logically, to the conclusion that warfare will not be eliminated until a single dominant worldwide power emerges and enforces a Pax Mundi (World Peace).

Although a political theory of warfare is appealing, there are problems in formulating this kind of explanation. The data required to substantiate this position are not available. Anthropological knowledge of the tribal world prior to European contact is limited. The frequency and extent of war in the tribal world before the sixteenth century are unknown. This theory assumes that societies at low levels of political integration tend to have an increased frequency of warfare. Evidence, however, from some societies with the lowest level of political integration, such as the Eskimo, San, and Tasaday, indicates that they lack warfare.

Pax Britannica (1900). British army officers dictate peace terms to Pathan tribesmen in Northwest India.

A political theory of warfare assumes a theory of political development where some societies expand, thus incorporating previously independent groups. The circumstances underlying the emergence of larger political units is poorly understood by anthropologists. A complete political theory of war therefore remains incomplete until anthropologists fully understand the origin and development of political systems.

Finally, there is a moral rather than an anthropological objection to this theory. This approach could be used as a justification for the imposition of colonial rule that brought peace to the tribal world. It also suggests that peace can be attained only through the imposition of a worldwide despotic power. It assumes that suppression of warfare can be attained only at the price of political freedom as measured by the ability to use organized violence.

Law in Comparative Perspective

War is the attempt of one group to impose its political will on another group. The expression of political control is not limited to relations *between* groups. All societies impose an internal political will on their inhabitants, which is called social control. Social control encompasses a variety of techniques developed to induce conformity to cultural standards of norms of behavior. Law is only one aspect of social control.

Perhaps the most effective form of social control is the *internalization* of the moral codes of the society by an individual. Through upbringing, education, and indoctrination, individuals are expected to internalize the rights and wrongs of their society. As children grow up, they learn what is proper and improper, right and wrong, good and bad. To the extent that a society is able to indoctrinate its moral code into the conscience of individuals, the necessity of applying external means of social control is minimized. For example, most Americans have internalized the incest taboo. The existence of a law that defines incest as a punishable offense is *not* the basis for adherence to this norm. On the other hand, laws stipulating speed limits have not been internalized by most American drivers.

No society is able to rely solely upon internalization of its normative code; other means of

social control must be exercised. Not only is internalization an incomplete process, but also in most societies the rules themselves may be inconsistent and do not cover every possible situation. Rules may be open to different interpretations, and in addition, change brings about new situations for which old rules do not readily apply. Some means, therefore, must be available to adjust old rules and develop new ones.

A major problem in legal anthropology is to distinguish those social control mechanisms considered legal or the law from other social control techniques. Another major problem is to consider the legal process in a total social and cultural context. This approach goes beyond identifying legal institutions and how they function. It raises such issues as sources of dispute and deviant behavior in society, strategies used for redress of grievances, and the relationship of law to other institutions in society.

What Is Law?

In complex societies, both modern and ancient, law can be seen as a readily identifiable institution. If we think of *law* in America, we are able to specify its sources, its institutional components, and personnel. We could include the

Constitution, the common law, courts, legislatures, police, lawyers, offenders, judges, prisons, probation officers, and law schools as part of the legal apparatus of our society. In tribal societies comparable institutions and personnel are either absent or found in rudimentary form.

The lack of a readily identifiable body of legal institutions in many tribal societies has made it difficult to define law cross-culturally. A major breakthrough occurred in the 1930s with the work of K. N. Llewellyn and E. A. Hoebel (1941). They suggested that the means of discovering the law in tribal society is through disputes or what they call *trouble-cases*. Based on this approach, a law is a norm of behavior whose violation or breach brings about a response by an individual or a group that has a socially recognized right to define guilt, impose punishments, and seek redress. Law is visible only in terms of its violation – when disputes occur and trouble-cases emerge. Using this approach anthropologists began collecting legal case material from many tribal societies. These data led to certain generalizations about law in all societies. The fundamental attributes of law were seen as the use of coercive power, recognized authority, and regularity in the application of sanctions.

Is Law Universal?

Identification of these fundamental attributes of law indicated to Hoebel and other anthropologists that law was universal. In all societies there are people who transgress against accepted ideals of behavior and as a result someone reacts to their behavior.

Leopold Pospisil used his research with the Kapauku of New Guinea to discover universal attributes of law. His attributes parallel the three attributes given above, with the addition that legal decisions confer obligations and rights upon the parties to a legal dispute (Pospisil 1971:81–82).

A different approach has been taken by Max Gluckman; one aspect of his work is the identification of universal legal concepts rather than legal attributes. Based on his work with the Barotse of Central Africa, he suggests that judicial authorities use the concept of the "reasonable man" as the basis for deciding cases. In essence, this position asks what would a reasonable person do in the situation under litigation? The notion of reasonableness obviously, varies from culture to culture.

In one case Gluckman studied, the case of the Violent Councillor, a Barotse village councillor was accused of attacking a man who had a dispute with the councillor's sons. Barotse councillors are supposed to be restrained, controlled, and nonviolent. The councillor defended his violent behavior on the grounds that he was attempting to stop a fight between the plaintiff and his sons. Barotse judges hearing this case found his actions of dragging the fallen plaintiff along the ground as unreasonable behavior for a councillor and found him guilty (Gluckman 1955:83–90).

This case illustrates Gluckman's concept of the *reasonable man* as a means of linking judicial precepts and the circumstances of actual cases. He notes that basic legal precepts are usually couched in ambiguous and general terms. A comparison from our own legal system would be such concepts as reasonable doubt, self-defense, and negligence. These concepts of jurisprudence must be applied to the particular and unique facts of a legal case. Gluckman claims that similar thinking is used everywhere to determine the applicability and meaning of legal precepts to legal cases. The judges' opinion in the case described by Gluckman would have been very different if the councillor had been attacked and had defended himself, or if the plaintiff had been beating the councillor's sons rather than being beaten by the councillor's sons. Under these circumstances the councillor's intervention, no matter how violent, might have been considered reasonable.

Gluckman also proposes that in tribal society the purpose of legal judgment and decision making is not limited to findings of guilt or innocence. He identifies reconciliation and reestablishment of social ties between antagonists as the ultimate goal in these legal systems. This purpose is in contrast to law in complex societies where the goal usually is to assess responsibility and guilt (Gluckman 1955:357–358; 1969:22).

An example of a judicial proceeding with the goal of reconciliation is found in James L. Gibbs's account of a marital dispute he recorded while engaged in research with the Kpelle of Liberia in West Africa. In this case, called the Case of the Outside Wife by Gibbs, a man named Wama Nya inherited, through the levirate, his deceased brother's wife, Yokpo. Wama Nya was already married, and it is clear from the proceedings that his first wife, Yua, resented the presence of Yokpo, the second wife. Wama Nya attempted to divorce Yokpo on the grounds of adultery and drive her out of his house. She went to court and countered his allegations of adultery with counterclaims of assault and insult.

In the informal hearing a full expression of all issues and bad feelings is allowed. The court, or moot, as Gibbs calls it, assesses blame among a number of individuals and imposes minor fines, but it is primarily concerned with the reconciliation of the parties involved.

> Wama Nya, the complainant, had one wife, Yua. His older brother died and he inherited the widow, Yokpo, who moved into his house. The two women were classificatory sisters. After Yokpo moved in, there was strife in the household. The husband accused her of staying out late at night, of harvesting rice without

A paramount chief among the Kpelle of Liberia settling a dispute. The defendant's mother pleads for her son in a case heard on the porch of the chief's house.

his knowledge, and of denying him food. He also accused Yokpo of having lovers and admitted having had a physical struggle with her, after which he took a basin of water and "washed his hands of her."

> Yokpo countered by denying the allegations about having lovers, saying that she was accused falsely, although she had in the past confessed the name of one lover. She further complained that Wama Nya had assaulted her and, in the act, had committed the indignity of

Apache woman with mutilated nose. Among the Apache, men had the legal right to punish adultery committed by their wives. Cutting his wife's nose was just one sanction an Apache man could use.

removing her headtie, and had expelled her from the house after the ritual hand-washing. Finally, she alleged that she had been thus cast out of the house at the instigation of the other wife who, she asserted, had great influence over their husband.

Kɔlɔ [Kawlaw] Waa, Town Chief and quarter elder, and brother of Yokpo, was the mediator of the moot, which decided that the husband was mainly at fault, although Yua and Yokpo's children were also in the wrong. Those at fault had to apologize to Yokpo and bring gifts of apology as well as local rum for the disputants and participants in the moot (Gibbs 1963:3).

Gluckman characterizes tribal societies as *multiplex,* which means that individuals are linked to each other by varied and multiple social ties. Yokpo and Yua were not only cowives, but also classificatory sisters, and Yokpo was the sister of the moot mediator. In *complex societies* individuals are linked to each other through single or *simplex* ties. Reestablishing social relations between disputants in a complex society is unnecessary because they have little need for each other. In America, an employee who sues an employer may never see the employer again and can seek employment elsewhere.

Law, Norms, and Social Control

Law is not the only means of external *social control.* On an individual basis people who violate *norms* may be subject to informal negative *sanctions.* These sanctions may include gossip, ridicule, ostracism, insults, and threats. There are also positive sanctions that reward conformity to society's standards, such as privileges, statements of approval, granting of honors and awards, and the esteem of a person's peers.

Certain norms in every society can be ignored with no fear of punishment. An individual engaged in such behavior may be considered strange, eccentric, independent, or just "doing their own thing." Colin Turnbull (1962), who did fieldwork among the Ba Mbuti Pygmies of the Ituri Forest, describes one man, Cephu, who was a loner. His unwillingness to take part in ceremonies and his desire to live somewhat apart from the main camp were tolerated as peculiar and eccentric traits. Nothing was done in response to this behavior. But when Cephu placed his own hunting net in front of the nets set up by the other hunters, he received the full impact of Pygmy legal retribution. A meeting was held, his actions were denounced, and he was excluded from the camp for a specified time. This was a norm he could not violate because it was a legal norm.

In considering this particular case it is apparent that the Pygmies have at least two major categories of norms. Some are legal norms and others are social norms, which may or may not have sanctions. This kind of distinction is found in all societies. Thus it can be seen that although law as defined by Hoebel and Pospisil may be found in all societies, it represents only one part of the vast array of social rules, regulations, and techniques devised to enforce conformity and compliance.

Law as Process

European colonial rule not only ended tribal warfare, but it affected legal systems as well. Colonial governments established legal mechanisms for settling disputes and resolving conflicts, and often these European legal codes and institutions were grafted onto native systems of traditional law.

The emergence of new nations throughout the non-Western world has meant the incorporation of tribal groups into national political and legal systems (Nader and Todd 1978; Collier 1975). As a result the search for law and legal institutions becomes less important in contemporary legal anthropology. In addition, the view of law as having the primary function of social control and "cleaning up messes" has been supplanted by a broader and more dynamic perspective. Laura Nader, an anthropologist specializing in legal anthropology, illustrates this new development:

> The law has many functions. It serves to educate, to punish, to harass, to protect private and public interests, to provide entertainment, to serve as a fund-raising institution, to distribute scarce resources, to maintain the status quo, to maintain class systems and to cut across them, to integrate and disintegrate societies — all these things in different places, at different

times, with different weightings. Law may be a cause of crime; it plays, by virtue of its discretionary power, the role of definer of crime. It may encourage respect or disrespect for itself (Nader and Todd 1978a:1).

Recognition of the multiple functions of law and of the dynamic aspects of law has led to the posing of new questions and research interests. Among them are two major areas: the sources and meanings of conflict and dispute and the use of the legal system.

Sources and Meanings of Conflict

In explaining war some theorists assumed the existence of an innate human tendency for aggression and violence. Comparable ideas have been advanced to account for individuals who violate legal norms. At one time physical anthropologists interested in criminal behavior believed that they could identify criminal types by measuring head shape and body form. Contemporary physical and cultural anthropologists reject this position and generally believe that the sources of crime are found in society itself.

In nations with a variety of cultural groups there may be different and competing social norms, and following one set of norms may bring an individual into conflict with national legal codes. For Sardinian shepherds, for example, stealing sheep is an act of manly valor, but it is considered theft by the Italian legal system (Ruffino 1978:222).

Early students of law in anthropology interpreted legal systems as a means of resolving disputes and maintaining social harmony. Cooperation and reconciliation were seen as desirable goals and as the ultimate purpose of the legal system.

More recently, however, research has focused on the role played by the legal system in maintaining differential power relationships in society. This view has been primarily extended to the analysis of law in complex and stratified societies where differences in power, privileges, and wealth are clearly evident. This relationship of law, power, and social privilege can be seen in a film of a Kpelle court case made by Gibbs. The film, "The Cows of Dolo Ken Paye," documents a dispute based on social, economic, and political differences.

In the Kpelle community that Gibbs studied well-to-do farmers keep cattle. These animals are allowed to forage for food, and despite precautions they sometimes wander into the rice fields of less prosperous farmers and destroy their rice crops. The dispute described in the film arose when a cow belonging to a well-to-do farmer, who was also a chief, was slashed and eventually died.

The cow was attacked because it had invaded a rice field of one of the poorer farmers and was destroying the crop. The cow's assailant was not known at first, and the film documents the procedures used by the Kpelle to discover the guilty person. Gibbs notes that although this particular dispute was resolved through a process of ordeal with a hot knife and a confession by the guilty person, the underlying causes of these disputes continue. Well-to-do farmers continue to keep cattle and allow them to forage at large, where they can invade the rice fields of less prosperous farmers.

As the film unfolds it becomes clear that the well-to-do farmers who keep cattle are also the chiefs who adjudicate disputes. The result is a conjunction of economic, political, and judicial power. In this specific case, the town chief's cow was killed. This chief appealed in turn to a higher level chief, the paramount chief, to find the guilty person and to deliver a judicial decision. In adjudicating the dispute, the paramount chief defended his interests as well as the town chief's interests, not only as political leaders, but also in terms of their economic position as affluent farmers with cattle. When the guilty person was discovered and confessed, he was told by the paramount chief that he should have

brought the case to court if he had any damage claims against the town chief's cow instead of acting on his own.

In the case of Dolo Ken Paye's cows, we see more than a resolution of a dispute. As a social institution the law reflects economic and power relations and operates to maintain these relations. A Kpelle chief's position is both difficult and contradictory. On the one hand, he claims to be a father to his people; on the other hand, the political and legal system that he controls defends his position as a member of an economic elite whose activity is often injurious to the poorer members of the society.

A recent trend in anthropology is to analyze the function of law in complex societies as an instrument for the maintenance of social inequality, and this orientation can also be used in the analysis of dispute settlements in many tribal societies. In Chapter 4 the Tiwi marital system was described; it was pointed out that an older man's monopoly of women is basic to their marriage system. When a young Tiwi man goes against this authority by openly seducing an older man's wife, he is challenged to a spear duel by the older man. The younger man, who is physically capable of defeating the older man in this type of combat, must allow himself to receive a slight flesh wound. If he is unwilling to allow himself to be injured and thus embarrasses the older man by showing his greater physical prowess, other older men will come to the aid of their age-mate and spear the younger man to death. These duels go beyond resolving adulterous disputes; they sustain the privileged position of older men and the structure of Tiwi society.

A very complex problem concerns the relationship between law and social change. Law is usually perceived as a conservative element in human society. This is especially evident in contemporary society because technological and cultural changes occur more rapidly than changes in the law. Medical technology, for instance, has forced the courts to consider the legal definitions of death, life, and motherhood. Test tube babies and babies born from the implantation of fertilized human eggs into women raise legal issues regarding legitimacy and motherhood.

Law does not have to be a conservative force in society; it can bring about changes in society that have far-reaching consequences for the social order. In the 1980s we are still experiencing the impact of the historical *Brown* v. *Topeka* decision made by the Supreme Court in 1954 that outlawed racial segregation in education. This decision has caused profound societal, political, and educational changes in American life. In urban school districts busing to achieve racial integration continues to be a political issue. In India the constitution adopted in 1951 prohibited discrimination against anyone based on caste. Subsequent legislation in India also set aside a percentage of government positions for members of low castes. In the late 1970s the government of Mrs. Gandhi instituted throughout India a birth control program backed by the threat of government force. Opposition to this legally based form of birth control was widespread and became one factor in the downfall of her government.

Uses of the Legal System

Many recent studies show that people institute legal proceedings for many reasons. One pervasive reason is to seek revenge and to inflict injury or damage upon an adversary.

During his research in Colliefiore, Cohen documented the following court case. A villager accused a traveling wool salesman of violating a section of the labor law regarding the recording of work done by the salesman's clients. This man was brought to trial, found guilty, and fined about $50. When examining this seemingly minor offense further, Cohen discovered that the traveling salesman had had a love affair with the sister-in-law of the man who brought the charges against him. The accuser in this case used the law to punish the man who had insulted the honor of his family.

Other studies have shown similar reasons for instituting legal proceedings. Not only do clients have a variety of reasons for bringing legal action, but legal practitioners — lawyers, judges, prosecutors — also may use the legal system as a source of monetary return, publicity, and political ambition.

It is obvious that not all aggrieved individuals resort to the legal system for redress of wrongs and attainment of justice. In many societies people harbor deep suspicions about the impartiality of the legal system. Not only can a legal claim be met with a counterclaim, but also almost everywhere the pursuit of justice is expensive. Thus, cost is an important reason for avoiding legal proceedings. The considerations weigh most heavily on the poor, the illiterate, and the uneducated. In American society one of the most effective developments in the antipoverty legislation of the 1960s was the establishment of neighborhood legal services for the poor.

Avoidance of legal involvement by people with grievances takes one of two forms: "lumping it" — that is, deciding to do nothing — or seeking alternative paralegal or illegal means of redress and revenge (Nader and Todd 1978a:9). *"Lumping it,"* where a person with a grievance fails to complain or seek legal aid, is widespread in American society. Many women fail to report cases of rape, for example, because of shame, fear of publicity, and insensitive handling by the police and judicial authorities. Other reasons for "lumping it," may involve the expense of going to court or fear of retribution. A growing tendency in American society, as well as other societies, is to use other means of redressing wrongs, such as demonstrations, publicity, talk shows, and political pressure. There is also an increasing use of illegal means to resolve disputes. This may occur because a legal system is difficult and costly to use, or because the establishment of national legal codes and systems makes no allowance for subcultural variations. Thus arson, property damage, theatening phone calls, and murder become alternative methods of seeking redress and revenge.

War and Law in Mae Enga Society

In the middle 1950s Meggitt was still able to observe Mae Enga warfare. Shortly thereafter, under the influence and pressure of the Australian administration, the Mae Enga turned from war to litigation to resolve interclan disputes. Substitution of litigation for warfare occurred rapidly. As Meggitt notes, "The Mae . . . were willing to put up their axes and bows and to try the new system. Litigation appeared to them to be a useful way of achieving their ends, one that economized on time, energy, and blood and would allow them to get on with their all-important gardening and exchanges without

The assistant district commissioner reviews the police force recruited from the native New Guinea population. The Australians used such patrols to attempt to suppress warfare among the Highland tribes.

the interruptions posed by war" (Meggitt 1979:118). Missionaries and armed Australian police patrols were also effective in suppressing warfare.

This peaceful substitution of law courts and litigation for the field of battle lasted about ten years. By the end of the 1960s Mae Enga warfare had reemerged as a means of resolving land and boundary disputes. The resurgence of warfare indicated the inability of the court system imposed by the Australians to deal with the fundamental basis of interclan disputes: arguments over land. An advantage of traditional Mae Enga warfare was the inability to achieve a final settlement. Unless a group was totally defeated and dispersed, they could always regroup and attempt to undo the decisions of a previous war. Thus losers could eventually counterattack and regain lost land; winners in a war could reopen a conflict and attempt to gain more land. Courts did not operate in this way; decisions were made, boundaries drawn, land titles assigned, and as far as the courts were concerned the dispute was settled. The Mae Enga did not agree with this system, and after a decade of litigation, they began to abandon the courts. Exacerbating this situation was a steady growth in Mae Enga population that made

access to land even more important than in the past. In addition, the introduction of cash crops, such as coffee, made land an even more valuable and scarce resource. Because they were unable to press further claims to land through the court system, the Mae Enga reverted to war as a means of obtaining more land and defending the land they had gained.

The total situation has altered, however, for both the Australian government and the newly independent government of Papua, New Guinea, are engaged in suppressing tribal warfare. Thus a Mae Enga war today may be halted long before a military decision is reached.

There seem to be two basic alternatives to this situation. More effective national power may be able to eliminate open warfare among Mae Enga clans, although as long as the problem of land remains unsolved assassination, murder, and small-scale ambushes can be expected to be used as means of resolving conflicts and disputes. Alternatively, the courts may adopt a more flexible approach in settling Mae Enga land disputes. The courts may become more flexible in regard to appeals, counterclaims, and the reopening of cases, and therefore this approach may become a new technique for adapting a system of law to the realities of Mae Enga life.

Summary

Warfare is a common but not universal phenomenon in human society. It can be distinguished from feuding and raiding. Feuding is motivated largely by revenge, involves small segments of a population, and tends to occur within a group. Raiding is primarily directed toward the acquisition of plunder and booty. Warfare is organized combat involving a significant proportion of the population and occurs between sovereign political groups. Although the technology of warfare shows evolutionary development, warfare as a cultural pattern appears on every level of social and political complexity.

An area of the world where tribal warfare has been widespread is New Guinea. Beginning in the 1950s, Mervyn Meggitt was able to observe the warfare of the Mae Enga over a period of 20 years. His description of their warfare reveals surprising parallels between war in tribal society and war in modern society. Despite Meggitt's detailed description of Mae Enga warfare, he is unable to specify the causes of war in this society. Even their own ecological explanation is not susceptible to objective validation.

In the comparative study of war, anthropologists have generally focused on the question of why people fight. A variety of theories have been advanced to account for war. Among them are human nature, functional, ecological, and political theories.

Human nature theories see violence, aggression, and warfare as innate characteristics of humanity. In Lorenz's view, aggression evolved as part of human evolutionary development and served a useful purpose. Now, however, the technology of warfare threatens the very existence of the human species. For Ardrey human aggression is rooted in the blood lust that was developed by ancient hunters, allied to the alleged human instinct for territory. In most human nature explanations, no distinction is made between individual aggression and the collective organized activity called war.

Functionalist theories assume that warfare plays an important role in the maintenance and continuity of a society. Warfare may provide social cohesion and psychological release of tensions. Malinowski interpreted warfare as a form of sport, play, and amusement providing diversions for the boredom of tribal life. Interpretations of ritual war share this view. Functional interpretations of warfare can be criticized for taking an overly positive view of the beneficial consequences of fighting for social solidarity and continuity. There is also a tendency in functional theory to confuse ritual warfare with other and more destructive forms of warfare.

Ecological theories conceptualize warfare as one part of a larger ecosystem consisting of population, technology, resources, and environment. Warfare is often interpreted as a means to keep these factors in a working equilibrium. Vayda and Harris see the role of population pressure as crucial. For Harris population pressure and the problem of maintaining a suitable diet and standard of living trigger warfare, female infanticide, and an ethos of masculinity that maintains populations in equilibrium with their resources. It is not possible, unfortunately, to develop clear and objective measures of population pressure, land shortage, and protein deficiency in order to evaluate and assess ecological interpretations of warfare. Lacking these indices, ecological theories remain intriguing, but unproven.

Political theory links warfare to political development. War is a consequence of contending sovereign powers and may be the mechanism for the creation of larger-scale political entities. This theory avoids an explanation of the origins of war and merely relates it to other aspects of society. Although warfare is now viewed as potentially destructive to the entire planet, in the past it appears that many societies found warfare a convenient and useful means of solving problems and resolving disputes. Whatever the cost in life and property, many people thought the benefits outweighed the disadvantages.

Conformity to cultural standards, or social control, is found in all societies, and law is one form of social control. The problem faced by anthropologists interested in law is distinguish-

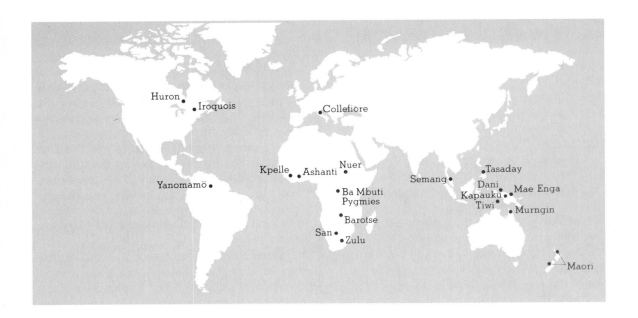

ing law from other types of norms. Llewellyn and Hoebel suggest that legal norms are revealed in "trouble-cases." This distinction is especially useful in tribal societies, for legal institutions and personnel are not easily recognizable in these societies. The study of these "trouble-cases" indicates that law has several fundamental components: coercive power, recognized authority, and regularity.

In his study of law in tribal society, Gluckman identified universal concepts of jurisprudence used by judges to define the facts of particular legal cases. In addition, Gluckman distinguished the purpose of tribal law — reconciliation — from law in complex society — findings of guilt or innocence.

Anthropological interest in law has shifted recently to a concern with legal processes. This concern has focused on the sources of conflict and dispute in society and how the legal system operates and is used. It also raises a fundamental issue about power in society. Are power and the maintenance of the social order used for the general good or are they controlled and used for the benefit of the favored few?

Key Terms and Concepts

feuding	law
raiding	trouble cases
warfare	coercive power
human nature	reasonable man
theories	multiplex
of aggression	relationships
functional theories	complex societies
of warfare	simplex
ritual warfare	relationships
ecological theory of	social control
warfare	norms
political theory of	sanction
warfare	lumping it
internalization	

Suggested Readings

Bohannan, Paul, ed. *Law and Warfare: Studies in the Anthropology of Conflict.* Austin, Texas: University of Texas Press, 1976. *A series of readings on conflict and law in human society. Contains complete accounts by Gibbs on the Kpelle moot and by Gluckman on the judicial process of the Barotse.*

Chagnon, Napoleon A. *Yanomamo: The Fierce People.* New York: Holt, Rinehart and Winston, 1977.

Ethnographic case study of the aggressive and warlike Yanomamo.

Harrison, Robert. *Warfare.* Minneapolis: Burgess, 1973. *A brief overview of different theories of warfare. Useful as an introduction to warfare studies in anthropology.*

Meggitt, Mervyn. *Blood Is Their Argument: Warfare Among the Mae Enga Tribesmen of the New Guinea Highlands.* Palo Alto, Calif.: Mayfield, 1977. *Meggitt's complete ethnographic study of war and peace among the Mae Enga.*

Nader, Laura, and Harry F. Todd, Jr., eds. *The Disputing Process Law in Ten Societies.* New York: Columbia University Press, 1978. *The form, strategies, and resolutions of disputing are considered cross-culturally.*

Otten, Charlotte M., ed. *Aggression and Evolution.* New York: Wiley, 1973. *A wide-ranging collection of articles that consider the issue of aggression in genetic, biological, and cultural terms. Includes material on aggression among nonhuman primates.*

Pospisil, Leopold J. *The Ethnology of Law,* 2nd ed. Menlo Park, Calif.: Cummings, 1978. *A systematic introduction to legal anthropology by a leading expert. Combines a general overview of the anthropological analysis of law with a formal analysis of land tenure law among the Kapauku people of New Guinea.*

Chapter 7

Power and Political Organization: Head Man, Chief, and King

In contemporary American society "doing your own thing" is an expression that is popular. In reality few of us in America, or elsewhere, are able to do our own thing. We are constrained by laws, responsibilities to others, economic limitations, and especially by political control. The ability to control behavior is central to all political systems; this is political power.

Jean-Jacques Rousseau (1712–1778), an eighteenth-century French philosopher, believed that although the emergence of political control meant material improvement for humanity and the establishment of law and order, it also shackled humanity to inequality and unending labor. Political control subjected the majority of people to the will of the politically dominant. He stated his view succinctly: "Man is born free, and everywhere he is in chains." A recent anthropological version of Rousseau's position is Marvin Harris's statement that the development of highly organized systems of political control is the transformation of human beings from freedom to slavery (1977:81–82).

A very different view of political control is found in the writings of the sixteenth-century British philosopher Thomas Hobbes (1588–1679). In his view, without government there is a state of anarchy. He wrote, "The condition of man [in a state of nature] is a condition of war of everyone against everyone. . . . no art; no letters; no society and which is worst of all, continual fear and danger of violent death; and the life of man, solitary, poor, nasty, brutish, and short" (*Leviathan,* 1958, Chapters 4, 13). Hobbes argued that the restraints of political control are fundamental in the transformation of humanity from a state of barbaric anarchy to a state of civilized life.

Rousseau and Hobbes looked at the nature of humanity differently. For Rousseau people were inherently good. For Hobbes they were inherently nasty. From their different conceptions of humanity's original nature, they developed two opposing views of government and political power. For Hobbes the governmental use of political power functioned to restrain humanity's animal impulses and made life safe; for Rousseau the imposition of government shackled humanity with inequality and misery and protected the economic interests of the politically dominant class. Despite their divergent views, both of them, as political philosophers, recognized the crucial view of power in human affairs.

In political terms, power includes manipulation of people, control of resources, the making and influencing of decisions, the ability to punish and reward, and the exercise of coercion or force. Power is organized and exercised in various ways in different societies. This

Germany under Hitler represented a state with extreme centralized power. The youth brigades organized by Hitler were an essential part of the control mechanism used by state authorities.

diversity in the organization and exercise of power is the major theme of this chapter.

The first ethnographic example, Buganda, portrays a political system in which the organization and use of power are extreme. In Buganda power is centralized, vested in a single authoritative ruler, and exercised in an absolute manner. The leader, the Buganda king, or Kabaka (his royal title), controls the lives, property, and behavior of his subjects and rules despotically. Buganda is one type of political system, a state. In other state systems power is also organized and centralized, but it may not be exercised in such a despotic and capricious fashion. In addition, there are many societies where power is neither centralized nor vested in a single leader; these are called stateless societies. The example of Buganda is used because it is extreme, illustrating the basic role of power in political organizations.

Buganda: A Despotic Kingdom

Throughout precolonial Africa there were many different kinds of indigenous kingdoms, but by the end of the nineteenth century, European colonialism effectively limited and eventually eliminated the power of native monarchs. In the postcolonial period newly independent African nations continued this trend. In this century anthropologists thus have little chance of observing an independent African king using the complete sovereignty of his office. A little over a century ago the British explorer John Hanning Speke was able to observe an African kingdom before it came under colonial rule. He was the first European to enter the sovereign kingdom of Buganda[1] in what is now the nation of Uganda.

Speke was not an anthropologist; he was an explorer searching for the source of the Nile, and it was for this reason that he entered Buganda. He was an acute observer, however, and his description of Buganda political life appears to be both valid and reliable. Speke's description of Buganda life records the visible manifestations of kingly power in its most despotic form.

State systems, such as Buganda, involve the organization and exercise of coercive power. In most state political systems the exercise of force by political authorities is often masked and muted. By using legal formalities, economic power and pressure, and the fear of arrest and execution, political leaders do not always indulge in the everyday practice of open physical violence. In contrast the Buganda king Mutesa I, from Speke's description, used power in its rawest and most virulent form. His control appears to have been total, and his exercise of power despotic.

THE KING'S PALACE

The king sent his pages to announce his intention of holding a levée [a formal reception held at a monarch's court] in my honor. I prepared for my first presentation at court, attired in my best, though in it I cut a poor figure in comparison with the display of the dressy

[1] Various prefixes attached to the stem "Ganda" form different words with different meanings:

Buganda means the kingdom or country of the Ganda.

Baganda means the Ganda people.

Luganda means the Ganda language.

Muganda refers to an individual Ganda.

Uganda is the Swahili equivalent of Buganda (Murdock 1934:508).

Speke at Mutesa's court (1862). Speke with his second-in-command, Grant, has an audience with Mutesa I. Baganda courtiers prostrate themselves before the King in deference to his power and authority.

Waganda.[2] They wore neat bark cloaks resembling the best yellow corduroy cloth, crimp and well set, as if stiffened with starch, and over that, as upper cloaks, a patchwork of small antelope skins.

The palace or entrance quite surprised me by its extraordinary dimensions, and the neatness with which it was kept. The whole brow and sides of the hill on which we stood were covered with gigantic grass huts. Lines of huts were joined together, or partitioned off into courts, with walls of the same grass. It

is here most of Mtésa's three or four hundred women are kept, the rest being quartered chiefly with his mother, known by the title of N'yamasoré, or queen-dowager.

The first court passed, I was even more surprised to find the unusual ceremonies that awaited me. There courtiers of high dignity stepped forward to greet me, dressed in the most scrupulously neat fashions. Men, women, bulls, dogs, and goats were led about by strings; cocks and hens were carried in men's arms; and little pages, with rope turbans, rushed about, conveying messages, as if their lives depended on their swiftness, every one holding his skin cloak tightly round him lest his naked legs might by accident be shown.

This, then, was the ante-reception court, in which musicians were playing and singing on large nine-stringed harps, accompanied by harmonicons.

[2] Speke uses a *W* instead of a *B* for the initial sound of the prefix. He also spells *Mutesa* without the *u* — *Mtesa*.

MEETING THE KING

The mighty king was now reported to be sitting on his throne in the state hut of the third tier. I advanced, hat in hand, with my guard of honor following. Here I was desired to halt and sit in the glaring sun; so I donned my hat, mounted my umbrella, a phenomenon which set them all a wondering and laughing, ordered the guard to close ranks, and sat gazing at the novel spectacle. A more theatrical sight I never saw. The king, a good-looking, well-figured, tall young man of twenty-five, was sitting on a red blanket spread upon a square platform of royal grass, incased in tigergrass reeds, scrupulously well dressed in a new mbŭgŭ [bark cloth cloak]. The hair of his head was cut short, excepting on the top, where it was combed up into a high ridge, running from stem to stern like a cock's comb. On his neck was a very neat ornament — a large ring, of beautifully-worked small beads, forming elegant patterns by their various colors. On one arm was another bead ornament, prettily devised; and on the other a wooden charm, tied by a string covered with snakeskin. On every finger and every toe he had alternate brass and copper rings; and above the ankles, half way up to the calf, a stocking of very pretty beads. Every thing was light, neat, and elegant in its way; not a fault could be found with the taste of his "getting up." For a handkerchief he held a well-folded piece of bark, and a piece of gold-embroidered silk, which he constantly employed to hide his large mouth when laughing, or to wipe it after a drink of plantain wine, of which he took constant and copious draughts from neat little gourd-cups, administered by his ladies in waiting, who were at once his sisters and wives.

The king loaded one of the carbines I had given him with his own hands, and giving it full-cock to a page, told him to go out and shoot a man in the outer court, which was no sooner accomplished than the little urchin returned to announce his success with a look of glee such as one would see in the face of a boy who had robbed a bird's nest, caught a trout, or done any other boyish trick. The king said to him, "And did you do it well?" "Oh yes, capitally." He spoke the truth, no doubt, for he dared not have trifled with the king; but the affair created hardly any interest. I never heard, and there appeared no curiosity to know, what individual human being the urchin had deprived of life.

THE KING'S POWER

I was enabled to enlarge the list of topics on which it is prohibited to the Waganda to speak or act under pain of death. No one even dare ever talk about the royal pedigree, of the countries that have been conquered, or even of any neighboring countries: no one dare visit the king's guests, or be visited by them, without leave, else the king, fearing sharers in his plunder, would say What are you plucking our goose for? Neither can any one cast his eye for a moment on the women of the palace, whether out walking or at home, lest he should be accused of amorous intentions. Beads and brass wire, exchanged for ivory or slaves, are the only article of foreign manufacture any Mganda can hold in his possession. Should any thing else be seen in his house — for instance, cloth — his property would be confiscated and his life taken.

I was now introduced to the company present. Usungŭ and Kŭnza, executioners, rank very high, enjoying the greatest confidence with the king. Kŭnza, the executioner, begged as a great favor that I would plead to the king to spare his son's life, who was ordered out to execution on the last levée day.

I have now been for some time within the court precincts, and have consequently had an opportunity of witnessing court customs. Among these, nearly every day, incredible as it may appear to be, I have seen one, two, or three of the wretched palace women led away to execution, tied by the hand, and dragged along by one of the body-guard, crying out, as she went to premature death, "Hai minangé!" (Oh my lord!) "Kbakka!" (My king!) "Hai n'yawo!" (My mother!) at the top of her voice, in the utmost despair and lamentation; and yet there was not a soul who dared lift hand to save any of them, though many might be heard privately commenting on their beauty.

To-day occurred a brilliant instance of the capricious restlessness and self-willedness of this despotic king. At noon, pages hurried in to say that he had started for the N'yanza [pond, river, or lake], and wished me to follow him without delay. I started off in a hurry, leaving every thing behind, and walked rapidly through gardens, over hills, and across rushy swamps, when I found the king dressed in red, with his wakungŭ [court attendants] in front and women behind, traveling along in the confused manner of a pack of hounds, occasionally firing his rifle that I might know his whereabouts. He had just, it seems, mingled a little business with pleasure; for noticing, as he passed, a woman tied by the hands to be punished for some offense, the nature of which I did not learn, he took the executioner's duty on himself, fired at her, and killed her outright.

It is the duty of all officers, generally speaking, to attend at court as constantly as possible; should they fail, they forfeit their lands, wives, and all belongings. These will be seized and given to others more worthy of them, as it is presumed that either insolence or disaffection can be the only motive which would induce any person to absent himself for any length of time from the pleasure of seeing his sovereign. Tidiness in dress is impera-

tively necessary, and for any neglect of this rule the head may be the forfeit. The punishment for such offenses, however, may be commuted by fines of cattle, goats, fowls, or brass wire. All acts of the king are counted benefits, for which he must be thanked; and so every deed done to his subjects is a gift received by them, though it should assume the shape of flogging or fine; for are not these, which make better men of them, as necessary as any thing? The thanks are rendered by groveling on the ground, floundering about and whining after the manner of happy dogs, after which they rise up suddenly, take up sticks — spears are not allowed to be carried in court — make as if charging the king, jabbering as fast as tongues can rattle, and so they swear fidelity for all their lives.

In consequence of these salutations, there is more ceremony in court than business, though the king, ever having an eye to his treasury, continually finds some trifling fault, condemns the head of the culprit, takes his liquidation-present, if he has any thing to pay, and thus keeps up his revenue.

No one dare stand before the king while he is either standing still or sitting, but must approach him with downcast eyes and bended knees, and kneel or sit when arrived. To touch the king's throne or clothes, even by accident, or to look upon his women, is certain death. When sitting in court holding a levée, the king invariably has in attendance several women, evil-eye averters or sorcerers. They talk in feigned voices raised to a shrillness almost amounting to a scream. They wear dried lizards on their heads, small goatskin aprons trimmed with little bells, diminutive shields and spears set off with cockhackles, their functions in attendance being to administer cups of plantain wine. To complete the picture of the court, one must imagine a crowd of pages to run royal messages;

they dare not walk, for such a deficiency in zeal to their master might cost their life.

THE ARMY

In front of the king, in form of a hollow square, many ranks deep, sat the victorious officers, lately returned from the war; the nobles distinguished by their leopard-cat skins and dirks, the commoners by colored mbŭgŭ [bark cloth cloaks] and cow or antelope skin cloaks, but all their faces and arms were painted red, black, or smoke-color. The ceremonies of this grand assemblage were now obvious. Each regimental commandant in turn narrated the whole services of his party, distinguishing those who executed his orders well and successfully from those who either deserted before the enemy or feared to follow up their success. The king listened attentively, making, let us suppose, very shrewd remarks concerning them; when to the worthy he awarded pombé [plantain wine], helped with gourd-cups from large earthen jars, and to the unworthy, execution. When the fatal sentence was pronounced, a terrible bustle ensued, the convict wrestling and defying, while the other men seized, pulled, and tore the struggling wretch from the crowd, bound him hands and head together, and led or rather tumbled him away.

With the company squatting in a large half circle, or three sides of a square, many deep, before him, in the hollow of which are drummers and other musicians, the king, sitting on his throne in high dignity, issues his orders for the day much to the following effect: "Cattle, women, and children are short in Uganda; an army must be formed of one to two thousand strong to plunder Unyoro. The Wasoga have been insulting his subjects, and must be reduced to subjection; for this emergency another army must be formed, of equal strength, to act by land in conjunction with the fleet. The Wahaiya have paid no tribute to his greatness lately, and must be taxed." For all these matters the commander-in-chief tells off the divisional officers, who are approved by the king, and the matter is ended in court. The divisional officers then find subordinate officers, who find men, and the army proceeds with its march. Should any fail with their mission, reenforcements are sent, and the runaways, called women, are drilled with a red-hot iron until they are men no longer, and die for their cowardice. All heroism, however, insures promotion. The king receives his army of officers with great ceremony, listens to their exploits, and gives as rewards women, cattle, and command over men — the greatest elements of wealth in Uganda — with a liberal hand. (Speke 1864:250–251, 276, 280–284, 290, 310, 326–327, 337–338, 361, 373–374).

The Buganda State in Context: Authority, Ecology, and Despotism

In the decades following Speke's visit the Baganda people were subject to many forces of social change. Christian as well as Islamic missionaries entered the land, and conversion to Christian and Islamic beliefs occurred on a large scale. These decades also witnessed the emergence of internal conflict between newly converted religious factions and contenders for political control. Various European forces entered Buganda and contributed to the growing level of disorder. By the end of the nineteenth century Buganda was incorporated into the British colonial system as part of the protectorate of Uganda. As part of the process of social change, cash crops were introduced, a rail line was constructed connecting the country to the East African coast, trade and commerce developed, and new land laws were introduced. Despite these vast changes the basic patterns of authority in Buganda society remained largely intact. This situation was especially true in regard to the respect and deference paid to the institution of kingly power and the incumbent king or Kabaka, who remained a political figure during the colonial period. After independence in 1962, when Buganda became part of the new nation of Uganda, the Kabaka was deposed and the Baganda people became one of many tribal groups in the new nation.

Audrey Richards, a British anthropologist, studied the Baganda people over a period of twenty years beginning in the 1930s. Despite the incorporation of the kingdom within the British colonial system, the Buganda king still commanded deference from his subjects. Richards's description of Baganda behavior in the presence of the Kabaka is similar to Speke's earlier descriptions.

> Subjects still kneel in the presence of their king. Palace servants do so when speaking to him, and the Kabaka's secretary kneels as he hands His Highness the telephone. The members of the Great Lukiiko [council] go on their knees as the Kabaka enters the council hall (Richards 1964:274).

These patterns of deference, authority, and hierarchy permeated Baganda life. Chiefs controlled their subjects, and fathers ruled their children. Richards notes the following examples of the hierarchical organization of authority and power as she observed them in the 1930s.

> All those living on a lord's estate were his clients or "his men." They owed him extreme deference and respect. It was their duty to call on him frequently; to sit about in his reception hut where they waited to be called to give advice, to receive instructions or to do jobs. El-

derly Baganda will sometimes volunteer to act out scenes as they remembered them at a great lord's court. In such a piece of play-acting, the imaginary peasant or subordinate creeps along the verandah of the lord's house, waiting at the door to be spoken to or even to be noticed. He kneels to greet his superior and agrees with whatever the latter may say. The man acting the lord pays him little attention, or else returns his greetings in a summary fashion.

> Elderly princes or clan leaders often treat the peasants on their estates in a similar fashion today, and it is not uncommon to see the superior continuing to play the board game (mweso) with a friend, while a peasant kneels at a respectful distance, having brought some practical difficulty for solution. The prince usually speaks without looking at the supplicant, or apparently showing any interest in him, and then throws out scraps of advice — often quite sensible advice — in asides between discussions with his opponent over moves in the game (Richards 1964:270–271).

Richards's examples document the extent to which patterns of deference shown to the Kabaka are deeply embedded in the authority patterns characteristic of the Baganda. It is quite possible that in the emergence and development of kingship, modes of authority patterns already existing among the Baganda were used and incorporated into the principle of despotic rule. Even during the colonial period when the power of Buganda kings was diminished, traditional patterns of deference and respect persisted. It is possible that despotic and absolute use of power in the political arena developed out of similar expressions of authority in other aspects of Baganda life and culture.

Conrad Kottak explains the emergence of the Buganda kingdom within the context of ecology and external military problems (1972). The Buganda food economy was horticultural, based on bananas and plantains as staple crops. Since fertile soil and adequate rainfall were characteristic of this ecological zone, these crops could be grown continuously in the same plots. Unlike most horticultural people, who practiced shifting cultivation, the Baganda established permanent fields, settled villages and towns, and supported a dense population. Richards's description of the authority and power of Buganda nobility emphasizes its resemblance to a peasant society with lords, landed estates, and peasant laborers. In contrast to peasant society, however, Baganda women, rather than men, constituted the basic horticultural labor force. This division of labor freed the men to engage in military activities and to provide services to the king and nobility.

Kottak's analysis focuses on two aspects of military activities: defensive and expansive. Hostile pastoral peoples on the borders of Buganda were a continual military threat and required defensive military units. In addition, although plantains and bananas provide an abundant food resource and a base for heavy population density and growth among the Baganda, they do not provide adequate protein in the diet. In order to obtain protein the Baganda people had to control and exploit the fish resources of Lake Nyanza (Lake Victoria). Thus the Buganda state required military forces to control, incorporate, and protect a variety of environments: the lake regions rich in protein and the lands productive in bananas and plantains. According to Kottak these circumstances led to the development of a military capacity for both defensive and aggressive warfare. He believes the Buganda state, being based on military superiority, became a means of linking together different ecological regions.

Despite the appealing nature of Kottak's argument, the issue of the *despotic* nature of the system remains unexplained. Even though Kottak may explain the Buganda state in eco-

logical terms, he fails to explain why despotism emerged in Buganda. In explaining despotism a political rather than an ecological explanation may be preferable. A political explanation assumes that once established, Buganda kingship with its power and privilege became an object of internal competition and contention. Ambitious individuals with an eye to the obvious rewards for successful contenders could threaten the reigning monarch, and Buganda kings responded to real or imagined political threats by the use of terror. Speke reports an example of mistrust and fear: Mutesa I used a mirror to see the faces of his courtiers who stood behind him. The apparent capriciousness of Buganda kings in their use of terror and violence dissolved political opposition and possible conspiracy.

An alternative hypothesis is that despotism is an early or intermediate stage in the evolution of the rules that societies use for the maintenance and transfer of power. In the contemporary world, for example, totalitarian and dictatorial regimes practice terror in the form of purges, mass arrests, the use of secret police, and political assassination. Contemporary state terrorism is obviously similar in purpose and effect to despotic power as it was once exercised in Buganda. Real and potential conspiracies may be eliminated, potential political opposition is neutralized, and the decision-making power of the central authority remains unchecked. Revolutionary and newly established states appear prone to despotic political forms of control. This condition may be related to the lack of formal and agreed-upon rules for the transfer of power to others. If this hypothesis is valid, despotism should disappear as political systems evolve more formal rules for succession and the transfer of political power. Because of the intervention of European colonialism, the Buganda state did not have the opportunity to evolve in this direction.

Political Organization in Comparative Perspective

Anthropologists agree that power is found in all societies but that its use and organization vary. A comparative understanding of power involves examination of three major questions: the components of power, the forms of political organization, and the origin of the state.

Components of Power

Power is not a unitary political phenomenon; it has different dimensions. These dimensions include the degree of centralization of power, the stability of offices over time, and the impact of power on other social institutions. Six components of power can be recognized:

1. political role and office
2. centralization
3. extent of political authority
4. coercive power
5. control of economic resources
6. level of political integration

Political Role and Office

Basic to the classification of political systems is the degree of recognition or definition of a political role. A *political role* is a position in a society in which individuals make decisions, control the means of violence, and rule over followers. In some societies political roles are not evident. In other societies not only are political roles recognized, but also there may be a variety of political roles organized into a political institution. Among the Mae Enga of New Guinea there are a limited number of political roles: Big Men and fight leaders. The Buganda state, in contrast, had a complex political organization with a variety of political positions. The king, or Kabaka, had advisors, generals, official

executioners, appointed territorial officials, and soldiers.

When there are a variety of *political offices* in a system, they are usually organized into a bureaucracy of positions with different levels of responsibility, power, and authority. Among the Kpelle of Liberia the hierarchy of political positions included elders, quarter-elders, town chiefs, and paramount chiefs. In American society the bureaucracy of municipal, state, and

A headman of the Huli tribe of Papua, New Guinea. The Hulis are known as "wig men" because of their habit of wearing wigs made of human hair and decorated with flowers, feathers, grass, and herbs. The massive headpiece of this man indicates that he is their headman.

federal authorities constitute some of the institutions of political authority.

Political roles and positions recognized in a society exist apart from the individuals who occupy these positions. Although individuals remain in power for only a limited time, political offices and their authority continue. The basis and maintenance of power related to a political position may vary. Among the Mae Enga and many other New Guinea tribal groups, the role of Big Man is a recognized political position. A Big Man is a clan leader who is primarily involved in interclan negotiations and alliances; his power is based on influence and persuasion rather than force. When a Big Man dies, however, his network of power relations and authority usually disappears with him. Successors to the position of Big Man have to rebuild their

own political networks, authority, and power base. In more complex societies the power and authority associated with political office remain with the office and often increase. In the history of Buganda the office of king became more powerful as each succeeding monarch added to the power he inherited.

Succession to political office is an issue related to the continuity of political positions. In many societies succession is based on kinship ties and involves inheritance of political positions from deceased relatives. Other rules of succession are election and achievement through individual effort. In many societies rules of succession are vague and ambiguous and are open to differing interpretations. A possible reason for this vagueness is the fear that precise designation of an heir to a political position may pose a threat to the present leader. Even if succession rules exist, the competition for position and power may be so intense that contenders for power often turn to violence, rebellions, civil wars, assassinations, and coups to determine who will rule. Much of

A parade in Red Square, Moscow, marking the fifty-seventh anniversary of the Bolshevik Revolution, depicts the centralization of authority and military power characteristic of the modern nation state.

the history of political systems is a story of violence and bloodshed between contenders for political power.

Centralization

In many societies a single authoritative leader exercises power. In a cross-cultural study of political organization it was found that 63 percent of centralized societies concentrated power in the hands of a single individual (Tuden and Marshall 1972:436–464).

Emergence of *political elites* where power is concentrated and exercised by a small ruling body is a core element in *centralized political systems*. Among the first elements controlled by a central authority are the power to wage war and the right to pass laws. Political elites control many strands of power. An excellent example of this concentration of power is in Gibbs's account of the cows of "Dolo Ken Paye." Kpelle chiefs enjoy political, economic, and judicial power. It is the concentration of power among a ruling elite that has led to the characterization of centralized states as oppressive and exploitative systems designed to benefit the few at the expense of the many. Rousseau, in his interpretation of the emergence of the state, argued that the wielders of power instituted the state in order to protect their privileged economic position.

Centralization of power is often paralleled by geographic centralization. Royal courts, capital cities, and feudal strongholds become the seats of power and the symbolic representations of centralization.

Extent of Political Authority

Centralization and concentration of power are the basis for *political authorities* to extend their control into many domains of life. Institutions and practices, such as marriage, religion, dress, residence, language, and the rearing of children, that are not usually thought of as political institutions may become subservient to the will of political elites. An extreme case occurred under the rule of the Zulu king Shaka. When his mother died Shaka proclaimed a state of mourning for all Zulu and prohibited sexual relations during this period (Walter 1969:153). Few political authorities go to this extreme, but control over the lives and behavior of subjects by political authorities is not uncommon. This type of control has become more common in modern times, unfortunately. In the contemporary world the emergence of totalitarian regimes where many aspects of life are controlled by the state is further evidence of the growing expansion of political power. In tribal and peasant societies totalitarianism is relatively uncommon, although it is not unknown. Its rarity may be the result of limited technology and the lack of political ideologies that justify totalitarian rule.

Coercive Power

Coercive power is the ability to reward and punish others. Its most extreme form is shown in Speke's description of Mutesa I's control over the life and death of all of his subjects. Power is ultimately based on the control of military and police forces – the means of violence. One way in which such power can be concentrated is by disarming the major portion of the population while maintaining control over armed and specialized military and police forces. In medieval Europe small numbers of mounted and armored knights controlled large populations of disarmed peasants. Another technique is to gain control over specialized and superior weapons used by well-organized and trained military or police forces. Although Americans may have the right to carry and own weapons, civilian weapons cannot challenge the weaponry controlled by the government.

The use of coercive and often violent power is found in every society. Even in simple foraging groups, such as the Eskimo and tribal groups in Australia, the approved use of violence against deviants and offenders is found. Political systems can be classified in terms of the centralization and exercise of coercive power. In societies that are classified as stateless, the legitimate use of violence is not centralized in a single political office or institution but is found throughout the society. To many anthropologists the monopoly over the means and exercise of violence and coercive power by a centralized political authority is the defining dimension of a state system.

Control of Economic Resources

Control of economic resources is crucial to the emergence and maintenance of complex political systems. Economic resources provide the elite not only with a privileged way of life, but also with the means of supporting a political apparatus whose primary function is administrative and supervisory.

Control over the economic resources of a society is exercised through a variety of techniques in different political systems. These techniques include taxation, payment of tribute by enslaved populations, labor service owed by ordinary people, fines paid to the judiciary, and confiscation or state ownership of property. Political and economic power are often intertwined. Concentration of economic resources in the hands of the few may lead to the acquisition of political power by these same individuals. From this perspective political power may be viewed as the attempt to safeguard economic privileges and resources; although from another perspective power is often seen as a means to acquire wealth and property.

Some of these arguments about political and economic power can be illustrated by examples from American politics. Why did the Rockefellers and Kennedys seek political office? One answer could be their wish to safeguard their wealth, or, alternatively, that such individuals may feel a sense of obligation to participate in the political process. Political figures like Lyndon Johnson and Richard Nixon, meanwhile, entered politics lacking great economic resources, although eventually they did acquire wealth and property.

Level of Political Integration

An essential part of any political system is the *level of political integration;* that is, the degree to which its various units are integrated into a larger political system. At one extreme are isolated and autonomous communities that do not link into higher levels of political integration. In many band societies the autonomous unit often resembles a joint household or large family. Whatever power exists is restricted to this localized and small group of people. At the other extreme are large-scale and highly integrated systems that bring together diverse tribal, linguistic, and cultural groups under the control of a single paramount power.

Forms of Political Organization

By using these components of power it is possible to develop several types of political classifications. An evolutionary and historical classification developed by Elman Service (1962) defines a spectrum of political organization from simple to complex. Along this continuum, four major types of political systems are recognized: bands, tribes, chiefdoms, and states. This movement from simple to complex involves not only the level of political organization, but also the extent and use of power.

Over forty years ago Fortes and Evans-Pritchard (1940) suggested a twofold classification distinguishing *state systems* from *stateless systems.* This classification also focused upon the level of political organization and the use of power. In state systems a complex and centralized political institution develops that organizes and controls

A San band in camp. No badge or symbol of office identifies the headman of the band. San headmen receive no show of deference from band members and they exercise almost no political power.

the use of power. In stateless systems there is a relative lack of centralized political institutions that exercize the exclusive use of coercive power. Political power and its use are spread throughout the society. Although many anthropologists find these classifications useful, there are problems in using them. The boundary distinguishing tribes from chiefdoms is often difficult to determine, and the two-part system developed by British anthropologists may be too general, failing to distinguish major forms of political organizations. We recognize, instead, three major types of political organization: simple, intermediate, and complex. In many ways this classification resembles the division used in the curvilinear hypothesis that relates social complexity to household type.

Simple Political Organization

Simple political organizations are clearly distinguishable from intermediate and complex political systems by a single component: level of political integration. Groups that are not incorporated into a larger political unit represent simple political organization. This does not mean that simple forms of organization are identical, for they vary in terms of the other components of power.

A classic example of a simple political organization is that of the San people of South Africa. For these nomadic foragers the basic community is a band. Members of a band live and work together, and each band has a recognized leader or headman.

Lorna Marshall, in a detailed analysis of the headman role among the !Kung group of San, documents the extremely limited power of this position (1967:15–43). A headman neither rules over nor directs the activities of other members of the band. He is not called upon to resolve disputes, and he has no exclusive control over economic resources. One of the characteristics of the San is their lack of warfare. Lorna Marshall refers to them as the "harmless people." They tell no tales of warriors or battles, and they have no tradition of violent conflict. Tikay, a headman, pointed out that fighting is very dangerous, "Someone might get killed" (Marshall 1967:17).

To a large extent the image of the San as a harmless people without warriors or rulers is often generalized to all simply organized societies. The San have become an ethnographic example of Rousseau's idealized vision of "man in a state of nature" is which the inherent goodness of humanity is allowed untrammeled expression. It is questionable, however, whether the San actually represent a survival of an ancient society in which freedom, equality, peace, and simple democracy were practiced.

San pacifism, in fact, may be a consequence of violent encounters between the San and the Dutch settlers (Boer) in South Africa centuries ago. Conflict between these two groups was common and continuous, and the San raided Boer cattle herds and attacked Boer settlements. In response the settlers organized mobile fighting groups, called commandos, which raided the San and inflicted severe casualties on them. Eventually their defeats at the hand of the Boers forced the surviving San into the inhospitable stretches of the Kalahari Desert.

A very different view of politics in simple societies emerges from Hart and Pilling's account of the Tiwi. Like the San, the Tiwi live in autonomous and nomadic foraging bands. Unlike the San, however, Tiwi political organization is complex, and power is in the hands of older men who enjoy a privileged position. Older Tiwi men defend their privileged position with coercive power. Fundamental to the Tiwi political system is male control over

women and their productive labor. Young unmarried men who attempt to subvert the power of older men by openly seducing their wives are challenged to duels. A young man who fails to allow an offended husband to wound him harmlessly in a duel is attacked and killed by a group of older men.

Although simple levels of political organization have usually been associated with nomadic foraging bands, many horticultural societies fail to establish political units that go beyond clan communities or autonomous villages. This type of organization is amply demonstrated by the Mae Enga and the Yanomamo. In both groups local communities are sovereign political units that enjoy the privilege of making war.

A fundamental characteristic of simply-organized societies is their diversity in relation to the organization and use of power. The essential characteristic of simple forms of political organization is their lack of political integration into larger territorial units.

Intermediate Levels of Political Organization

Unlike simple political systems, *intermediate forms of political organization* cannot be distinguished from more complex political systems by a single criterion. Within this form of political system the various components of power are combined in different ways.

Nuer: Warriors Without Rulers. From the perspective of political thinkers such as Hobbes, the Nuer pose a classic political problem. These pastoral nomads of the Sudan number approximately 300,000 and are divided into numerous tribes and clans. Although the Nuer claim to recognize themselves as a distinctive and separate group, they do *not* constitute a political unit. Warfare, fighting, and feuding between Nuer tribes and clans are common. They do not exist, however, as Hobbes postulated, in a state of anarchy and war of all against all. The fundamental question for anthropologists is how this society maintains a semblance of social order without police, courts, judges, chiefs, or headmen.

Patrilineal lineages are the basic units of Nuer society. Every Nuer is able to trace a kinship relation to every other member of the lineage. In addition, separate lineages can be connected by myths and traditional genealogical links. Evans-Pritchard (1940) analyzed the political aspects of Nuer lineages and their interrelationships. Members of the same local lineage, he discovered, were close kin, and such blood ties were sufficient to inhibit lethal fighting. Members of related lineages felt they had similar kinship obligations. Although this tie may not have been sufficient to prevent violent disputes, when such disputes did occur, as they often did, the ties of kinship were strong enough to avoid open warfare. Disputes of this nature were resolved through mediation and compensation by the persons directly involved. No third parties were able to impose their political will.

More distantly related Nuer lineages did fight and engage in warfare, and in some ways these activities marked the boundary of a Nuer "tribe." Within a tribe disputes were frequently resolved by mediation and compensation; between tribes disputes resulted in warfare. In his analysis Evans-Pritchard indicated how the operation of Nuer kinship relations resulted in the inability of one contending group to dominate or overpower another group. Kinship made allies of enemies when the occasion demanded it. Warring Nuer tribes would come together either to attack a more distantly related Nuer tribe or the nonrelated Dinka. Nuer political organization is fluid rather than fixed. Depending upon the situation and the kin relations of the parties involved, a Nuer political unit can range from a small local lineage to an entire tribe made up of distantly related lineage groups. At no place in this shifting hierarchy of political units is there a specialized political authority or leader.

The person with status closest to a leader is the leopard-skin chief. Such chiefs are essentially ritual specialists and rarely occupy important lineage positions in the communities where they reside. They act as mediators in disputes between related individuals. Their role as mediators without power is illustrated in Evans-Pritchard's account of how disputes are handled among the Nuer.

> As soon as a man slays another he hastens to the home of a leopard-skin chief to cleanse himself from the blood he has spilt and to seek sanctuary from the retaliation he has incurred. As soon as the kinsmen of the dead man know that he has been killed they seek to avenge his death on the slayer, for vengeance is the most binding obligation of kinship. It would be great shame to the kinsmen were they to make no effort to avenge the homicide. By living with the [leopard-skin] chief as his guest the slayer has asylum, for the chief is sacred and blood must not be shed in his homestead.
>
> While the slayer is at the chief's home the avengers keep watch on him to see if he leaves his sanctuary and gives them a chance to spear him. This state of affairs may go on for some weeks before the chief opens negotiations for settlement with the dead man's people. The chief first finds out what cattle the slayer's people possess and that they are prepared to pay compensation. He then visits the dead man's people and asks them to accept cattle for the life. They usually refuse, but their refusal does not mean that they are unwilling to accept compensation. The voice of compromise is supported by the bias of custom. Nevertheless, the close kinsmen must refuse to listen to it till the chief has reached the limit of his arguments, and when they give way they declare that they are accepting the cattle only in order to honor him and not because they are ready to take cattle for the life of their dead kinsman.
>
> It might be supposed that the [leopard-skin chief] has a position of great authority, but

A Nuer leopard-skin chief wearing his symbol of office. Such chiefs have little political power, but they act as mediators in disputes.

this is not so. He has no judicial or executive authority. It is not his duty to decide on the merits of a case of homicide. He has no means of compelling people to pay or to accept blood cattle. He has no powerful kinsmen or the backing of a populous community to support him. He is simply a mediator in a specific social situation and his mediation is only successful because community ties are acknowledged by both parties and because they wish to avoid, for the time being at any rate, further hostilities. (Evans-Pritchard 1940:152–153, 172, 174).

One of the restraints on the emergence of centralized coercive authority among the Nuer

is that the same weapons are available to all Nuer men. They own spears and clubs that can be used against anyone who attempts to violate their rights or gain power over them. Nuer men pride themselves on their fighting ability and their unwillingness to subordinate themselves to anyone. This characteristic of Nuer life underlies their disputes and the means for resolving them. Among the Nuer there are many reasons for disputes and ill feelings, including their cows, watering rights, adultery, or borrowing objects without permission. When a Nuer man believes that his rights have been violated, there is no authority to whom he can go. He must rely upon himself and the aid of his kin. As Evans-Pritchard indicates (1940:151), the Nuer are sensitive and take offense easily. When a man is wronged or feels that he has been wronged he challenges his adversary to a duel, which must be accepted. This is the only way of settling a dispute, and a man's courage and his sensitivity to any violation of his rights are his only protection against aggression.

Nuer men consider themselves equal to all other Nuer and superior to all other human beings. This sense of egalitarian and democratic individualism underlies the Nuer political system. In the following excerpt this feeling of equality and egalitarianism and the Nuer's disdain for authority and hierarchy are clearly evident.

That every Nuer considers himself as good as his neighbor is evident in their every movement. They strut about like lords of the earth, which, indeed, they consider themselves to be. There is no master and no servant in their society, but only equals who regard themselves as God's noblest creation. Their respect for one another contrasts with their contempt for all other peoples. Among themselves even the suspicion of an order riles a man and he either does not carry it out or he carries it out in a casual and dilatory manner that is more insulting than a refusal. I was once discussing the

Shilluk [a neighboring people] with a Nuer who had visited their country, and he remarked, "They have one big chief, but we have not. This chief can send for a man and demand a cow or he can cut a man's throat. Whoever saw a Nuer do such a thing? What Nuer ever came when someone sent for him or paid anyone a cow?" (Evans-Pritchard 1940:182).

From Evans-Pritchard's account of the Nuer we can observe the dynamics of politics in a society without rulers. Violence and the threat of violence are part of the political system. The expression of violence is restrained by the ties of kinship. We have noted that bands resemble large families. Societies based on lineages, like the Nuer, are internally more complex but still rely on kinship principles as the basis for political organization and activity.

Cheyenne: Peace Chiefs and War Chiefs.

As a form of political organization the *chiefdom* represents a level of political specialization greater than that found in simple political organizations or groups based on kinship like the Nuer. Chiefdoms may vary from relatively uncomplicated forms of political organizations to more complex systems that could be considered emerging states. Two such examples are the Cheyenne of North America and the Mandari of the Sudan.

It is impossible for someone to have grown up in American society without having been exposed to the Hollywood version of the American Indian chief. The model of the chief is usually drawn from the buffalo-hunting and horse-riding Plains Indians, such as the Sioux, the Crow, the Cheyenne, the Arapaho, or the Pawnee. A Hollywood Indian chief is most often depicted as a war leader primarily concerned with eliminating the white man. Plains Indian political organization, however, was more complex than that depicted in Hollywood films. Unlike the Nuer, who have no chiefs, the Cheyenne had many chiefs. An analysis of their po-

litical organization will help to explain the complexity of political organization in intermediate level society.

The Cheyenne were a Plains Indian society dependent upon buffalo hunting. In contrast to many foraging groups like the Siriono, the San, and the Eskimo, the Cheyenne were organized into a single tribal unit with recognized leaders.

Before the intrusion of the white man, the plains of North America contained numerous contending tribal groups, all dependent upon herds of wild buffalo for sustenance and material resources. Horses introduced by the Spanish were basic to the successful exploitation of these wild buffalo herds. A consequence of this environmental and ecological situation was chronic intertribal warfare as tribes jostled each other for space, access to buffalo herds, and horses. Thus raiding, warfare, and hunting were vital activities of Cheyenne life.

In the middle of the nineteenth century the 4000 Cheyenne were organized into ten main bands. They had, however, a strong sense of being Cheyenne, and the bands were integrated into a larger political entity: the Cheyenne tribe. A major concern of the Cheyenne was maintaining order within the tribal unit. This was largely the responsibility of a council of Peace Chiefs, as well as the military societies.

A council of forty-four Peace Chiefs represented the centralized authority of the Cheyenne tribe. Each band elected a minimum of four Peace Chiefs to the Council of Forty-Four for ten-year terms. The Council's major concern was the well-being of the Cheyenne people. Identified with the cosmic and supernatural order, the Council of Peace Chiefs had ritual and ceremonial powers that they used to enhance the integrity and success of the Cheyenne people.

Because Cheyenne culture emphasized individual bravery and aggressive skills, a continual fear was the eruption of violence within the tribe. The Council of Forty-Four restrained this tendency toward internal aggression. E. A. Hoebel, an anthropologist who studied the Cheyenne, recorded sixteen cases of homicide within the tribe over a period of forty years, a figure that he assesses as a measure of relative success in inhibiting internal violence (1978:54). In the few cases of recorded homicide, ostracism and exile were the punishments meted out by the Council of Forty-Four. A Cheyenne who murdered another Cheyenne was considered to have transgressed against the fundamental principles of Cheyenne life.

The council members in many ways acted as role models in Cheyenne life, rather than as wielders of coercive power. A Peace Chief was expected to be even tempered, and nothing

was supposed to make him lose control of himself. This trait was sometimes taken advantage of by other men, who would run away with a Peace Chief's wife. Instead of the usual aggressive response that signaled recognition of a grievance, a Peace Chief smoked his pipe and ignored the incident. One chief's way of demonstrating his calmness in the face of having his wife taken by another man was to say, "A dog has pissed on my tepee" (Hoebel 1978:44).

Another aspect of power held by the Council of Forty-Four concerned its role in war and peace. Warfare was not a centralized activity in Cheyenne life. For young men, raiding and warfare were important activities. Raiding was a way for a young man to acquire herds of ponies, and bravery and success in fighting were considered to enhance an individual's reputation. Raids could be organized by individuals without the consent of the Council. When the Cheyenne were engaged in hostili-

Cheyenne council. Chief Two Moons addresses the Council of Forty-Four, a major political institution of Cheyenne society.

ties with the United States government, in fact, the inability of the Council to restrain individual acts of violence against white settlers repeatedly led to reprisals against the tribe by United States military forces.

The Council of Forty-Four shared political power with the military societies led by War Chiefs. Military societies were fraternities of young men drawn from the various Cheyenne bands. Many raiding and warfare parties were organized and carried out by members of a military society. In this activity they were the military arm of the Cheyenne tribe. They were also involved in policing the buffalo hunt, for Cheyenne buffalo hunting was a collective activity. A specific date for the beginning of the hunt was decided by the Council, and anyone who violated this schedule and went hunting alone before the opening date was punished by the military society. In this context the military society operated as a police arm of the Cheyenne tribe.

In many ways the Cheyenne had rudimentary aspects of a complex political system. They had recognized political institutions and offices, continuity in office, some degree of hierarchy, exercise of coercive power, and territorial unity. Despite these factors centralized control was minimal. Control of the buffalo hunt was shared by the Council of Forty-Four and the military societies. These political institutions did not obtain wealth through taxes or tribute and, in fact, a member of the Council was required to be generous and give away goods to his people. The diffusion of power and the lack of centralized coercive power in all aspects of Cheyenne life made the Cheyenne political system an intermediate system.

Mandari: Chief Without Power. Another example of an intermediate political system with many characteristics of a complex state is found among the Mandari of the Republic of the Sudan (Buxton 1958). The Mandari, who number approximately 15,000, are divided into various sovereign and separate chiefdoms. Each chiefdom occupies a defined territory with recognized and defended boundaries.

A Mandari chief, called a *Mar,* inherits his office through the patrilineal line. He is a member of what the Mandari refer to as "the landowning clan." This clan traces its ancestry through genealogical myths to a common mythical ancestor. A chief's descent from this mythical founder is the basis for his ownership of the land and for his right to become chief.

At the death of a Mar, a council of elders helps select the new Mar. The council of elders acts as an advisory body to the Mar as well as deciding who the Mar's successor will be. Ideally, the chosen successor is the dead man's son or younger brother who must, however, have the characteristics deemed essential for a Mar. When a new Mar is chosen, he must undergo a complicated installation or inaugural ceremony.

A Mar is responsible for his people, and he leads them in offensive warfare and raiding. He acts as a judge in disputes, and he also "feeds" his people.

> Mandari say the *Mar* were "good," indicating by this they mean strong, rather than of good moral attributes. A "bad" *Mar* was one who was weak, who could not feed his people, and was defeated in war. Mandari think of the *Mar* as belonging to the people, as well as acting as their ruler, "he is our *Mar*, we put him there so that he can talk and we can eat (off) him."
>
> The *Mar* gives judgments within the chiefdom. *Kutuk na mar,* the "mouth" of the *Mar,* meaning his utterances, is said to be given by God, and for this reason people hear him. The *Mar* crystallizes and expresses the views of the elders after general discussion when people came for help over settling their cases. (Buxton 1958:80–81).

The Mar's responsibility to feed his people

works on several levels. As a religious and ceremonial leader he is expected to perform the ceremonies and sacrifices designed to guarantee the fertility of the land and the well-being of people and cattle. He owns most of the cattle in the chiefdom, and young people care for his cattle and work in his fields. Resources controlled by the Mar are redistributed by him to his followers. He is expected to assist people in need and to provide food and entertainment for the council of elders. In order to attract followers a Mar distributes gifts to individuals from other chiefdoms.

The chiefdoms of the Mandari may be viewed as emerging states because they have some dimensions of a state system. A chief represents centralized authority, and his council members occupy recognized political offices that are hierarchically organized. Rules of succession maintain the continuity of political office. In addition, each chief rules a defined territory, exercising some authority in the lives of his people.

A Mandari chiefdom is defined as an intermediate political system because it lacks coercive power. Although a Mar judges disputes, he does not enforce his judicial decisions. Enforcement is left to the individuals involved in the dispute. He does not control a military or police force; defense of the chiefdom is not his responsibility and is left to the segments of the community concerned. Although he is supposed to control wealth, he lacks any coercive means of extracting tribute or taxes, which is a significant limitation on his political and economic power.

Complex Political Organization

Almost half of the 184 societies Tuden and Marshall surveyed were state systems, including kingdoms, confederations, and empires (1972:45). Although state systems are often defined as centralized systems, there is considerable variation in their complex political organization. Rules of succession may vary, they may or may not have advisory bodies, and kinship may compete with nonkin principles as a basis for political office. In addition, the use of coercive power may be unrestrained, or coercive power may be controlled and constrained by various means.

One of the most common state systems in the non-Western world is the preindustrial *kingdom*. Not all kingdoms operate in the despotic manner described in the Buganda example, for many formal and informal devices exist to limit the unrestrained exercise of power. Once a state system emerges, the maintenance of political integrity becomes a major problem. These two factors — restraint in the growth and use of despotic power and maintenance of the state system — are central to the analysis of the Swazi kingdom of South Africa.

Swazi: A State System. The Swazi, numbering approximately 250,000, are organized into a complex kingdom. Although the present-day kingdom emerged about 200 years ago, the idea of Swazi kingship can be traced to the sixteenth century. Today the Swazi inhabit an area called Swaziland, an independent state. Aidan Southall, in a survey of postcolonial African states, identifies Swaziland as one of the few surviving monarchies on the African continent (1974:157). Swaziland today covers an area of 6700 square miles, slightly less than the state of New Jersey. In the nineteenth century, however, before the Swazi kingdom was brought under European control, it covered an even larger area. The description of traditional Swazi political life is drawn from the work of Hilda Kuper, who did her fieldwork among the Swazi in the 1930s when it was still possible to record many features of the traditional kingdom.

Military conquest was basic to the founding of the Swazi kingdom. Traditional Swazi history tells of the migration of a patrilineal clan named the Dlamini, who settled in present-day Swaziland and conquered the indigenous inhabitants. Through success in warfare and diplomatic marriages, the Swazi kings extended their rule and established a strong monarchy.

Warfare was an essential ingredient in the establishment of the Swazi kingdom. During the eighteenth and nineteenth centuries, the Swazi were involved in conflicts with the Zulu Empire, and refugees from Zulu conquests were incorporated into the Swazi kingdom. Zulu attempts to conquer the Swazi were severely hampered by the mountainous terrain, which permitted well-organized Swazi military forces to use hit and run guerrillalike tactics against the Zulu regiments. These military activities were an important factor in the development of centralized political institutions among the Swazi.

In the traditional Swazi kingdom the king and queen mother, who lived in separate communities or homesteads, shared power. For this reason Kuper characterizes the Swazi as a dual monarchy with the sharing of power and privilege acting as a check on the rise of despotic absolutism. Kingship was restricted, as it is today, to the Royal Clan, the Dlamini, who conquered the area (Kuper 1963:7,30).

The king and queen mother controlled legislative, executive, administrative, and religious power. They exercised their power through a complex political structure. As judge of the highest court, only the king could impose the death penalty, but the queen mother could offer sanctuary to individuals appealing for protection. Military regiments were under the control of the king, but military commanders lived in the queen mother's homestead, the Swazi capital. The king controlled economic resources, but the queen mother could rebuke the king in public for wasting national resources. Supernatural forces were essential to the health and well-being of crops, cattle, and people, and these forces were controlled by the king and queen mother. Most ritual was as-

King Sobhuza II reads a proclamation to the Swazi people on the first anniversary of independence. Princess Alexandra and other Britishers represent the former colonial power in the area.

sociated with the king, but the queen mother controlled the ritual related to rain magic. By requiring that the king and queen mother live in different communities, the Swazi minimized the possibility that they could combine their power. In addition, the king and queen mother had their own royal courts. Competition between these courts probably operated to inhibit the emergence of a single, all-powerful ruler (Kuper 1963:30).

There were two councils: an inner council composed of the senior princes and a general council composed of representatives from the general population. Every Swazi male could attend the meetings of the general council. The two councils advised the king and queen mother and also acted as a check on their power.

State systems present a facade of strength, power, and established authority. Behind this facade are forces that threaten the unity and integrity of the state and the position of the political elite. Territorial dismemberment and internal conflict can tear apart the fabric of political unity. Swazi kings, like all other state rulers, faced these potentially disruptive forces and developed a variety of techniques to maintain their power and the unity of the political system. Economic controls, administrative organization, military power, ritual observances, religious ceremonies, and rules of succession were some of the means that enhanced the territorial and political integrity of the Swazi kingdom and the power of Swazi kings.

A Swazi king was the owner of the land. The land he allocated to his subjects reverted back to royal control when it was abandoned. Not only was this land a source of the king's wealth, but it also gave subjects who received land a stake in the maintenance of the kingdom.

Additional sources of wealth came from the king's ownership of vast cattle herds and garden lands. These economic resources, combined with plunder and booty from war, were important contributions to the economic base of the kingdom. By redistributing these resources the king supported his soldiers, court, advisers, and other dependents. Once again, a stake in the maintenance of the system is apparent. The recipients of the king's generosity were the political elite, the aristocracy of the Swazi kingdom. Whatever differences and interests divided the members of this political elite, their common interest in maintaining their privileged economic position served as a check against the continual eruption of internal conflict and attacks on the kingship itself.

Division into territorially based districts was the basic form of administrative structure in the Swazi kingdom. Each district was small in territory and population, ranging from four to twenty square miles and from 100 to 2000 people. The small size of the districts limited the power base of district chiefs and their potential threat to the king. Of the approximately 150 districts, more than half were ruled by royal princes, and the remainder were ruled by commoners appointed by the king. Both the princes and the commoners owed their allegiance to the king.

Prior to European control, the Swazi were militarily expansive. Newly conquered lands were brought into the administrative structure of the kingdom, and royal princes and successful generals became district chiefs. The ability to "pay off" potential rivals for power by making them district chiefs reduced the possibility of internal dispute and rebellion, and was another means of maintaining the integrity of the Swazi state.

Another means of integration for the Swazi state was the development of military regiments made up of men of the same age who were drawn from a wide variety of kin groups. The earliest Swazi kings developed this institution, which cut across the ties of kinship, as a way of breaking up kin-based military units. Kuper suggests that members of these age-based regiments developed closer relationships with each other than with their kin of a different generation.

Swazi military regiments performed many functions, such as protecting outlying border areas and guarding the king's household. Regiments also served as standby army and police force. The emergence of military forces expanded the coercive power of Swazi kings and maintained the integrity of the kingdom.

A military-police force is an instrument of state power and unity. It has, however, the potential of becoming a threat to the ruler, and throughout history ambitious generals and disgruntled soldiers have engaged in palace revolts, coups d'etat, and royal assassinations. Swazi rulers protected themselves against these potential dangers in a variety of ways. Royal princes, who were legitimate heirs to the kingship, were given command of very limited military forces. Age regiments were commanded by commoners who had no legitimate rights to the kingship. In addition, the commander-in-chief of the soldiers resided in the queen mother's homestead away from the troops who were quartered in the king's homestead.

The Swazi kingdom did not rest solely upon force — the spears of the age regiments. Like many other state systems, the Swazi developed an ideological and symbolic system to legitimize and justify both the political system and the political elite. In describing the founding of the kingdom, Swazi traditional history constituted one basis for the legitimacy of Swazi rule: they were the conquerors. Kingship also rested upon religious ritual and symbols. "The Lion," "The Sun," "The Milky Way," "Obstacle to the Enemy," "The Bull," "The Inexplicable," and "The Great Mountain" were phrases used by the Swazi to praise their king (Kuper 1963:29). These flattering titles simultaneously described the virility and strength of both the king and the nation.

The king and queen mother performed religious ceremonies to insure the fertility of the soil and the well-being of the Swazi people. Association of political power and position with cosmic and supernatural forces is a common theme in political systems. Nuer leopard-skin chiefs are sacred, the Cheyenne Council of Forty-Four represents cosmic forces, and the Mandari Mar speaks with the voice of God when making judicial decisions. Among the Swazi an annual ritual of kingship links the queen mother and king to the great powers of nature.

Perhaps the greatest threat to the maintenance of the Swazi kingdom occurred when a reigning monarch died. Succession to office and the transfer of power provided an opportunity for the emergence of disruptive forces. Recognizing that precise designation of an heir posed a threat to the ruler, Swazi kings did not specify their successors, and rules of succession were vague and ambiguous. After the death of a king the inner council selected a new king from a group of eligible candidates. Specifically excluded from this category was the first-born son of the king's first wife. Eligible candidates for the kingship were sons born to the king's many wives. Because a king could have as many as forty wives, the number of claimants might be very large. As Robbins Burling notes in a study of political succession, "A threat of violence hung over almost every royal Swazi succession" (1974:23). Designation of a precise heir was avoided in order to reduce the possibility of rebellion and disruption during a king's lifetime. Absence of clear succession, however, provided a fertile arena for competing claimants who might decide the issue by conflict and civil war. This possibility was always a threat to the unity and integrity of the Swazi kingdom.

State systems like the Swazi and Buganda exhibit all six components of power in a well-developed manner. Political office develops into a large and differentiated political institution. Succession to office may be ambiguously defined, but the achievement of power becomes restricted to political elites. Power becomes concentrated in a small ruling group. The homesteads of the king and queen mother among the Swazi and the capital of the Kabaka are geographical centers of power that also represent the centralization of power. Unlike headmen and chiefs in intermediate societies, the heads of state systems begin to extend their rule into other institutions of the society. Although they are limited by their lack of technological sophistication, totalitarian systems are not unknown in non-Western state systems.

The penetration of political power into the social fabric of a society is based to a significant degree on the monopoly of coercive power enjoyed by ruling elites in complex political systems. Coercive power makes it possible for elites to control economic resources and to defend their privileged position. Emergence of specialized military forces not only enforces the political will of rulers, but also supports physical expansion of complex political systems and the incorporation of smaller political units into a large and integrated state system.

Development of Political Systems: Origin of the State

Although anthropologists do not agree on a comprehensive and complete evolutionary sequence of political systems, it is clear that simpler forms of political organization precede the development of more complex forms. State systems emerge out of nonstate systems.

We know from the archaeological record that state systems first emerged at least 5000 years ago in Mesopotamia (present-day Iraq). The circumstances leading to the growth of centralization and the ever-widening role of co-

ercive power in human society are not known or understood in detail, however. In surveying the research on the origin of state systems, one anthropologist concluded ". . . state origins are not yet understood, even in the most minimal sense" (Wright 1977:386). Anthropologists as well as other social scientists nevertheless continue to offer theories explaining the emergence of state systems. Robert Carneiro, who recently advanced a theory of state development, classifies theories of state origins into two types: voluntaristic and coercive (1970).

All *voluntaristic theories* rest on the idea that a population of politically autonomous individuals or groups came together in order to form a state. They came together rationally and voluntarily in order to obtain the advantages of a larger political unit. Jean-Jacques Rousseau presents such an idea in his theory of the Social Contract. In the United States Constitution the opening phrases reflect this voluntaristic notion of state origin. Carneiro claims that the basic flaw in these theories is the lack of a single historical instance of an autonomous political unit voluntarily yielding its sovereign power.

Coercive theories are based on the position that force, not rationality, is the basis for state formation. Carneiro, an adherent of the coercive view, suggests that "war lies at the root of the state" (1970:734). Warfare among the Mae Enga, the Cheyenne, the Mandari, and the Nuer, however, has *not* led to state formation. Carneiro recognizes that warfare alone is not a sufficient explanation for the emergence of a state. He adds the idea of *circumscription* to war as one of the significant conditions underlying state formation. By circumscription Carneiro means the presence of physical boundaries that severely limit the geographic expansion of a population and society.

Carneiro begins his political scenario of state formation by contrasting Peru and the Amazon Basin. There is a long historical tradition of warfare and a domesticated food econ-

George Washington and the other leaders of the American revolution drew up the Constitution that has remained the guiding force in American government. Rousseau's notion of the social contract is frequently considered to have been related to this event.

omy in both areas. While the Amazon is an area of unbroken and open terrain, in Peru conditions are quite different. The coastal region is a desert area divided by numerous rivers that flow down from the Andes mountains, and the Andes contain numerous and distinct upland valleys. In the Peruvian area, valleys and upland basins are fertile regions circumscribed by mountains, desert, or sea. In a position similar to Mark Cohen's thesis of population growth and productive intensification (Chapter 3), Carneiro argues that a domesticated food economy implies a continual process of population increase and pressure on resources. One of the ways in which such pressure can be alleviated is to intensify and increase the level of production. According to Carneiro this op-

tion has its limits, and consequently fertile land becomes a valuable and scarce resource. The result is warfare as groups compete for access to land. In areas such as the Amazon with its vast expanse of open terrain, one consequence of warfare is the dispersal of the population over a large area. In physically circumscribed areas, like the Peruvian mountain and river valleys, population dispersal is not possible. As one group conquers another group, it dispossesses the conquered of their land and exterminates them. In this continual process of warfare, dispossession, and extermination a point is reached, according to Carneiro, when conquerors subjugate a defeated group rather than exterminate them. Conquered groups are allowed to remain on the land, but at the price of political subordination and exploitation by the victors. Payment of tribute to the political overlord signifies the birth of the state.

A central question in Carneiro's theory is why subjugation is substituted for extermina-

Even in modern Communist China large forces of laborers are needed to build the irrigation works required for successful cultivation. Obviously such labor must be organized and controlled by other members of the society.

tion. It is not clear what conditions surround the victor's decision to enslave rather than eliminate a conquered group.

Not all anthropologists accept this militaristic explanation of the emergence of the state. Kottak's explanation of the development of the Buganda kingdom describes an example of state formation without circumscription as an important variable. Kottak links together population, defense against external enemies, and the need to incorporate different food resource areas as conditions leading to the emergence of the Buganda state. Kottak's argument is useful in that it presents an explanation for the emergence of state systems in physically noncircumscribed areas. It also points out that trade and the control of needed resources may be crucial factors in the emergence of state systems.

An alternative thesis presented by the historian Karl Wittfogel (1957) focuses on state systems in Asia. Wittfogel advances a *managerial theory of the state.* Food production in these Asian societies depends upon irrigation projects such as dams, canals, dikes, and terraces. Such water or hydraulic projects require coordination, organization, and supervision of large masses of workers by a managerial and administrative elite. This elite develops into a political bureaucracy protecting its projects while exercising despotic control over the peasant masses. Wittfogel's theory may not have universal applicability, but it identifies the important administrative and supervisory role of the state, as well as the social inequality first identified by Rousseau as an integral part of the state.

Whatever the thrust of a particular theory regarding the origin of the state, three related elements appear to be universally present: (1) political elites controlling economic resources; (2) political elites using coercive power; and (3) whenever the opportunity arises, political elites expanding their territorial possessions.

Summary

Power, the ability to control group behavior, individual people, and resources by the imposition of will is characteristic of all societies. Political organization refers to the way in which power is organized and utilized. Cross-culturally, human societies show considerable variety in their forms of political organization.

The Buganda kingdom as described by the British explorer Speke in the nineteenth century is an example of despotic and absolute power. The arbitrary and capricious use of power by an individual despot underlines the impact of this power upon the lives of his subjects. Buganda society was organized on the basis of subordination and superordination, and the organization of Buganda political institutions may be seen as reflections of these more general patterns of the culture. A theory combining ecological, subsistence, and military factors set forth by Kottak seeks to explain the emergence of the Buganda state. Kottak leaves unanswered the problem of Buganda despotism, which may be rooted in the lack of political mechanisms for the orderly transfer of power. When seen from this perspective, the Buganda king appeared to be frightened and sought to neutralize potential opposition and conspiracy through the use of terror.

Political organizations vary, and political systems may be understood comparatively on the basis of a combination of power components and their organization. Components of power are political office, centralization, extent of political authority, coercive power, control of economic resources, and level of political integration.

Even though simple forms of political organization vary, all of them are distinguished by the absence of political integration above the level of the band and local community. Inter-

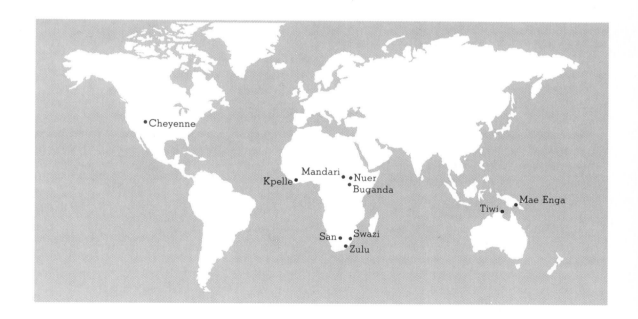

mediate political systems may possess some or all of the components of power, but the absence of centralized coercive power is diagnostic of this level of political organization. Complex systems, or states, exhibit all six components of power organized into effective political institutions.

The origin of state systems is of continuing interest to anthropologists. Although many different theories have been advanced, coercive theories recognizing warfare and population pressure are the current favorites. At the heart of these arguments is the recognition that at some time in human history it became advantageous to subjugate and exploit people rather than to expel and exterminate them. Subjugation and exploitation thus became the basis for the origin of the state, and from this perspective Rousseau triumphs over Hobbes in his explanation of state origins.

Key Terms and Concepts

political role/office
political elite
centralized
    political system
political authority
coercive power
level of political
    integration
state systems
stateless systems
simple political
    system

intermediate
    political system
chiefdom
complex political
    system
kindgom
voluntaristic
    theories
coercive theories
circumscription
    theory
managerial theory

Suggested Readings

Burling, Robbins. *The Passage of Power: Studies in Political Succession.* New York: Academic Press, 1974. Cross-cultural study of the transfer of power from one individual or group to another. Includes material on the Swazi and the Baganda, but focuses primarily on complex societies past and present.

Cohen, Ronald, and Elman R. Service, ed. *Origins of the State: The Anthropology of Political Evolution.* Philadelphia: Institute for the Study of Human Issues, 1978. A collection of papers that examine the difficult problem of understanding the beginnings of the state. Includes an essay on the possibility of a one-world mega-state emerging in the next century.

Fried, Morton. *The Evolution of Political Society: An Essay in Political Anthropology.* New York: Random House, 1968. An introduction to political anthropology that uses an evolutionary approach to political organization.

Hoebel, E. A. *The Cheyennes: Indians of the Great Plains,* 2nd ed. New York: Holt, Rinehart and Winston, 1978. A concise but well-rounded ethnography of this famous Plains Indian tribe. Cheyenne religion, social organization, subsistence, war, and personality are described.

Krader, Lawrence. *Formation of the State.* Englewood Cliffs, N.J.: Prentice-Hall, 1965. A brief introduction to the origin and evolution of the state.

Kuper, Hilda. *The Swazi: A South African Kingdom.* New York: Holt, Rinehart and Winston, 1963. An ethnographic case study of the Swazi. Swaziland is one of the few examples of a pre-colonial state that has maintained its traditional pattern of kingship.

Walter, Eugene V. *Terror and Resistance: A Study of Political Violence.* London: Oxford University Press, 1972. A readable and fascinating analysis of the use of terror in the Zulu state. Walter argues that the random use of violence and terror by Shaka, the Zulu king, maintained the integrity of the Zulu empire.

Chapter 8

The Power Out There: The World of the Supernatural

No form of human behavior has been more intriguing to anthropologists than religion: the belief in various forms of supernatural power and beings. Rituals, magic, witchcraft, trance states, and spirits are all part of this arena of human belief and behavior. Beliefs about the supernatural and behavior associated with these beliefs are common characteristics of human culture.

In the history of anthropology there have been periods when tribal religion was considered an important and controversial object of study. This was true in the late nineteenth century. Nineteenth-century cultural evolutionists were particularly interested in the origin and development of religion and they developed theories that emphasized the evolution of religious beliefs. In writing about what they called "primitive religion," theorists of the nineteenth century set forth a variety of interpretations, none of which was entirely satisfactory. Some theorists saw primitive religion as an attribute of the childlike thinking of primitive people. Others saw primitive people as lacking knowledge about many aspects of life and so inventing supernatural beliefs and stories to explain natural phenomena. In contemporary anthropology such ideas as primitive religion and primitive people are no longer considered meaningful labels.

The early theorists made an important contribution, however, for they distinguished the supernatural from the natural. Although they incorrectly assumed that tribal people were ceaselessly occupied with the supernatural and were unable to distinguish the natural from the supernatural, this distinction remains useful for anthropological analysis. *Supernatural* is a useful term for distinguishing the beliefs and practices that constitute religion. Thus anthropologists frequently define religion as any belief in the supernatural. In his book on religion, Anthony Wallace argues that the defining characteristic of every religion is the *supernatural premise:* the belief "that souls, supernatural beings, and supernatural forces exist" (1966:52).

Recently additional elements have been added to this minimal definition of religion. Religion provides a sense of order and meaning to otherwise inexplicable events and to the hidden forces of nature. An integral part of religion is ritual, the manifestation of belief in symbols, acts, and objects. These elements of religion were incorporated into the view of the French sociologist Emile Durkheim (1858–1917). He saw religion as a set of beliefs or values that served as the basis for social solidarity. In this way believers constituted both a church and a society. From Durkheim's view, in fact, the rituals of a religion provided a means

Various techniques are used to contact the supernatural. In Nepal, Buddhists write their prayers on sheets of paper and hang them from branches, where they look like flags blowing in the wind.

of social integration. He further theorized that the objects of worship, which were usually called deities and spirits, were symbolic representations of the society itself. This sociological view of religion was incorporated into British social anthropology which perceives the integration and cohesion of society as the functional consequences of religious activity and belief.

Addition of these elements to the supernatural premise has fostered the development of such concepts as *secular religions* and *secular rituals.* Thus some political ideologies, although they reject traditional beliefs in the supernatural, may be classified as secular religions. Secular religions manipulate symbols, rituals, sacred objects, and beliefs that provide meaning and order for millions of followers. Many social theorists argue that these secular religions, such as Communism or nationalism, contribute to the social cohesion of large and complex societies.

Love, Hate, and Curing

Beliefs and rituals associated with religion and the supernatural vary widely, and the following ethnographic accounts illustrate the extent of these differences.

The Hindu festival of Holi in a rural Indian village is described in the first ethnography. Despite the fact that the inhabitants of rural Indian villages are divided into separate castes that are unequal in terms of wealth, power, occupation, and prestige, the celebration of Holi is accompanied by sentiments of community love and unity. In addition, during the Holi festival members of the lower castes have power over members of the higher castes. Role reversal and universal love are the major features of Holi.

Hate, rather than love, is the focus of the second ethnography. Among the Badyaranké of West Africa (Senegal) dread of the evil of witches and witchcraft is an ever-present fear. Normal expectations of neighborliness and kin loyalty are denied by the hidden fear that friends, neighbors, and kin are witches — creatures of the night or supernatural beings — engaged in evil and amoral activities.

Illness and health are perennial concerns of all people. Even in American society, where scientific medicine occupies a preeminent position, many people connect religion with health and the cure of illness. This linkage is found in other societies as well. The third ethnography is from rural India; the Nagahar ceremony as practiced in the village of Galipur links supernatural power to the curing of cobra bites.

These accounts not only document the diversity of religious practice and belief, but also identify some common themes found in all religious systems — love and brotherhood, hate and fear, illness and health.

Holi: An Exuberance of Love

In Hindu belief the god Krishna is a central figure and the Holi festival is a celebration devoted to Krishna. Holi is also a calendrical festival taking place at the time of the full moon at the beginning of the Hindu New Year (March–April).

McKim Marriott, who studied the village of Kishan Garhi, describes the festival of Holi and his participation in it. Throughout his account the denial of caste differences, the aggressive behavior of women, expressions of prohibited behavior, and status reversal are dominant motifs.

As it happened, I had entered Kishan Garhi for the first time in early March, not long before what most villagers said was going to be their greatest religious celebration of the year, the festival of Holi. Preparations were already under way.

The adobe houses of the village were being repaired or whitewashed for the great day. As I was mapping the streets and houses for a preliminary survey, ladies of the village everywhere pressed invitations upon me to attend the festival. The form of their invitations was usually the oscillation of a fistful of wet cow-dung plaster in my direction, and the words, "Saheb will play Holi with us?" I asked how it was to be played, but could get no coherent answer. "You must be here to see and to play!" the men insisted.

I felt somewhat apprehensive as the day approached. An educated landlord told me that Holi is the festival most favored by the castes of the fourth estate, the Śūdras [the lowest caste]. Europeans at the district town advised me to stay indoors, and certainly to keep out of all villages on the festival day. But my village friends said, "Don't worry. Probably no one will hurt you. In any case, no one is to get angry, no matter what happens. All quarrels come to an end. It is a *līlā* — a divine sport of Lord Krishna!"

Marriott accepted the invitation to participate in the Holi festival. Unfortunately his recollection of this major religious ceremony was clouded by the effects of a narcotic drink that he was given at the beginning of the festival. At the time of the next Holi festival, however, Marriott avoided taking the narcotic and was able to describe the festival in great detail.

Now a full year had passed in my investigations, and the Festival of Love was again approaching. Again I was apprehensive for my physical person, but was forewarned with social knowledge that might yield better understanding of the events to come. This time, without the draft of marijuana, I began to see the pandemonium of Holi falling into an extraordinarily regular social ordering. But this was an order precisely inverse to the social and ritual principles of routine life. Each riotous act at Holi implied some opposite, positive rule or fact of everyday social organization in the village.

Who were those smiling men whose shins were being most mercilessly beaten by the women? They were the wealthier Brahman and Jāt farmers of the village, and the beaters were those ardent local Rādhās, the "wives of the village," figuring by both the real and the fictional intercaste system of kinship. The wife of an "elder brother" was properly a man's joking mate, while the wife of a "younger brother" was properly removed from him by rules of extreme respect, but both were merged here with a man's mother-surrogates, the wives of his "father's younger brothers," in one revolutionary cabal of "wives" that cut across all lesser lines and links. The boldest beaters in this veiled battalion were often in fact the wives of the farmers' low-caste field laborers, artisans, or menials — the concubines and kitchen help of the victims. "Go and bake bread!" teased one farmer, egging his assailant on. "Do you want some seed from me?" shouted another flattered victim, smarting under the blows, but standing his ground. Six Brahman men in their fifties, pillars of village society, limped past in panting flight from the quarterstaff wielded by a massive young Bhangin, sweeper of their latrines.

Who was that "King of the Holi" riding backward on the donkey? It was an older boy of high caste, a famous bully, put there by his organized victims (but seeming to relish the prominence of his disgrace).

Who was in that chorus singing so lustily

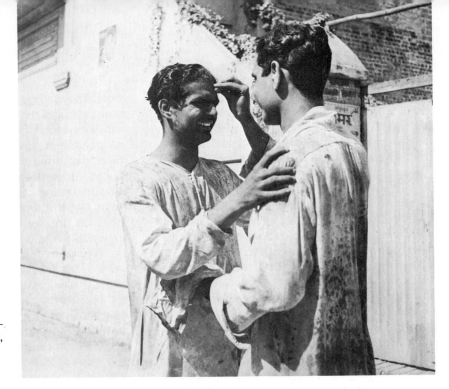

At the end of the Holi festival, one participant daubs another with red dye as part of the festivities.

in the potters' lane? Not just the resident caste fellows, but six washermen, a tailor, and three Brahmans, joined each year for this day only in an idealistic musical company patterned on the friendships of the gods.

Who were those transfigured "cowherds" heaping mud and dust on all the leading citizens? They were the water carrier, two young Brahman priests, and a barber's son, avid experts in the daily routines of purification.

In front of whose house was a burlesque dirge being sung by a professional asectic of the village? It was the house of a very much alive moneylender, notorious for his punctual collections and his insufficient charities.

Who was it who had his head fondly anointed, not only with handfuls of the sublime red powders, but also with a gallon of diesel oil? It was the village landlord, and the anointer was his cousin and archrival, the police headman of Kishan Garhi.

Who was it who was made to dance in the streets, fluting like Lord Krishna, with a garland of old shoes around his neck? It was I, the visiting anthropologist, who had asked far too many questions, and had always to receive respectful answers.

Here indeed were the many village kinds of love confounded — respectful regard for parents and patrons; the idealized affection for brothers, sisters, and comrades; the longing of man for union with the divine; and the rugged lust of sexual mates — all broken suddenly out of their usual, narrow channels by a simultaneous increase of intensity. Boundless, unilateral love of every kind flooded over the usual compartmentalization and indifference among separated castes and families. Insubordinate libido inundated all established hierarchies of age, sex, caste, wealth, and power.

Under the tutelage of Krishna, each person plays and for the moment may experience the role of his opposite: the servile wife acts the domineering husband, and vice versa; the ravisher acts the ravished; the menial acts the master; the enemy acts the friend; the strictured youths act the rulers of the republic.

The observing anthropologist, inquiring and reflecting on the forces that move men in their orbits, finds himself pressed to act the witless bumpkin (Marriott 1966:200–201, 210–212).

Badyaranké Witchcraft

Marriott's description of Holi represents an aspect of religious practice in an exuberant and benevolent form. Krishna, a central figure in the festival, is a supernatural being who represents love, devotion, and communion between people. William S. Simmons's description of witchcraft among the Badyaranké people of Senegal, in contrast, illuminates the malevolent aspects of the supernatural: hate, fear, and suspicion.

THE BEGINNING AND THE END

During my first evening at the village of Tonghia, I watched the Badyaranké women dance and sing. A woman drummed upon a gourd bowl which floated upside down on the surface of a tub of water, while one and sometimes two women entered the circle and danced barefooted. The women were singing, so I was told, about how much suffering there is in the world.

That evening, after the village onlookers had left my doorway and I had finally fallen asleep, a gun discharged close by, jolting me awake. Men with swords and muskets gathered in the compound, talked for a while, then laughed among themselves, and went back to their houses. I later learned that the chief's son, my next door neighbor, had been bothered by a large owl hooting from the top of his roof. He had fired at the bird "with eyes and ears like a man" because it was thought to be a Badyaranké who had come to collect a human life. Despite the owl's appearance coinciding with my arrival, the villagers did not believe this owl to have been me, for although anyone, including an anthropologist, might become an owl, such persons only harm friends, relatives, and neighbors among their own people.

Large owls did not appear in the village again until thirteen months later, on the night before my departure. By this time, I knew the horror that this bird evoked, and I could understand enough of the language to follow what people said. The chief came out of his house wrapped in a blanket, stood in the middle of our compound in the moonlight, and addressed the birds as they hooted from a tree. He said angrily, "If someone dies here I will call Lawalli [a holy man]. You want to start something here again. I know about you. I am the only one who dares to get up and face you." The chief's son then turned a flashlight on the tree and fired his muzzle-loading musket, causing an enormous explosion and a fountain of sparks. Still the birds remained. My assistant, who had patiently been helping me to understand such matters as these during the preceding nine months, first called to me for help. Then he pleaded with two French hunters — from whom I hitched a ride out of the bush — who were spending the night in the village. He asked them to shoot the owls out of the tree, and they obliged by firing several shotgun blasts in the direction of the sounds. Something white fluttered away in the darkness and then all was quiet. The next morning I left the compound for a world where the sounds and movements of the night mean nothing. I explained to the puzzled hunters that the cries they heard were from the throats of restless souls which had flown to the village to announce that a life had come due.

LEARNING ABOUT WITCHCRAFT

I learned of a fifteen year old boy in a nearby village who spoke French. He agreed to come to Tonghia as my interpreter. His most important contribution to my research was unsolicited. One morning I watched him splash some drops of liquid into his hands, lift a baseball cap which he usually wore, and rub the liquid over his head. When I asked what he was doing, he replied self-consciously that he was protecting himself from "the night people." His father had prepared a pink "medicine" to protect him from these individuals — conceivably anyone in the village — who are said to fly from their houses at night in eerie and unnatural forms to kill unsuspecting people. He explained that such "night people" see not only with ordinary eyes, but also with invisible eyes on their cheeks and on the backs of their heads, which are called "the eyes of the night."[1] Some even are said to possess eyes on the tips of their forefingers, which project beams resembling those of a flashlight. These creatures are supposed to revel ghoulishly in graves and to wear the clothing of the dead, acts considered repugnant by any self-respecting Badyaranké.

The subject of night people made everyone so ill at ease that no one wanted to discuss it, even privately. The Tonghia people were willing to explain their rituals and perform them in my presence, to explain the secret lore of male initiation, and to recite folktales for hours, but talk about the beings of the night sky elicited fear and silence. These creatures were so unpleasant and so terrifying that the people preferred not to talk about them (Simmons 1971:1–3, 8–9).

Woko the Witch

Simmons's account shows the Badyaranké as a society permeated by fears of witchcraft. They believe that most misfortunes are caused by witches. Woko was recognized as one of the great witches of Tonghia village, and Simmons

---

[1] The Badaryanké phrase "of the night" means that the thing involved exists only in the invisible dimension of witchcraft.

wrote a biographical sketch of this "creature of the night." Woko causes the death of Fatiba by capturing his soul. It is quite apparent from Woko's biography that witchcraft is a theory of misfortune. Once an individual is identified as a witch, he or she becomes a target for future accusations when other misfortunes strike.

Woko is the most famous witch in the history of Tonghia, and his was always the first name to be volunteered by informants when questioned about witchcraft. His reputation began when he was still a young boy returning with two other boys from arduous labors in the peanut fields near Thies. Woko, Fatiba who was older, and Ngaling who was younger had all worked together as a team and were hiking to Tonghia with their luggage on their heads. Fatiba, a known seer, perceived that the two younger men had tried once and failed to take his soul; they tried a second time during the trek and this time he believed they succeeded. Fatiba was bearing the heaviest part of the luggage, since he was older and stronger; he believed they had concealed his soul in the trunk carried on his head. When they arrived at Tonghia, Fatiba was very sick and said, "If I am dead, these two are responsible."

Ngaling fled, but Woko was tied in the chief's compound and questioned by the elder men; he denied his guilt and was beaten. He was then brought to the ailing Fatiba and ordered by the elders to cure him. Badyaranké believe a soul can be restored by touching the head and body of the victim and by blowing in his ear and on his body. But Woko refused. Then he confessed that he had been sent by his father to kill Fatiba and did not dare cure him. His father said, "Yes, it is true. I have the soul, but it is already dead." Woko and his father were beaten, and two days later Fatiba died. Woko was subsequently attacked by two people with sticks and reportedly attempted suicide. He finally left Tonghia and lived for three years in Gambia.

When Woko returned to Tonghia, he settled peacefully with his father in a new compound. A young girl of the same [matrilineage] as the dead Fatiba fell sick, accused Woko of killing her, and died. Neither the girl nor Fatiba were relatives of Woko, but they came from the same part of the village. When the girl's brother Moussa returned from military service, he tried to shoot Woko; he fled again to Gambia for four years.

While in Gambia, Woko is said to have killed another young man named Sare. Sare had gone to harvest palm wine, and Woko followed him. Sare's younger brother said, "Chase Woko away. He is up to something." Sare said, "No. Let Woko do as he wants." Sare died and Woko is believed to have been responsible. (Simmons 1971:136–137).

Woko later returned to Tonghia, and, according to the information given to Simmons, was suspected of being responsible for at least four more cases of witchcraft death. Eventually Woko left Tonghia and built his own compound.

Nagahar: A Renewal Ceremony

The following account, taken from Eames's notes made during his fieldwork in Galipur, describes the renewal of supernatural curing power. A group of Chamars, leather workers of the untouchable caste, told him about the Nagahar ceremony designed to renew their ability to cure snakebite.

I had heard of these practitioners skilled in curing snakebite victims, particularly those bitten by cobras. In order to renew their curing power, which they called their "poison,"

they had to perform the Nagahar ceremony. At this time they did not have the necessary funds to purchase the paraphernalia needed for the ceremony. Initially, when I tried to question the healers about their activities, they were unwilling to cooperate. Now, however, faced with financial difficulties, they yielded. Thus, some men visited me, the "Amrikan" Sahib, to see if I would finance the ceremony. Intrigued by their initial descriptions, I agreed to finance the event to the tune of 55 rupees, or $11. In addition to obtaining permission to attend the ceremony, I was assured that a careful accounting of all funds would be given.

The importance of the Nagahar ceremony was increased by the fact that the monsoon was beginning and it is during the rainy season that snakebites are most common.

Word rapidly spread through the village that I was sponsoring the Nagahar, and villagers thanked me for funding this ceremony. I began to detect a number of smiles attached to the thanks, that led me to believe that many of the villagers were saying to one another, "We got the 'Amrikan' sucker again." The possibility struck me that many a ceremony as well as a host of other "native" and "traditional" activities would certainly not have taken place if it were not for the stimulus of the affluent American fieldworker.

On the night of the ceremony a sense of excitement pervaded the village. Men brought rope beds (charpoys) from their houses and lined them up in a semicircle in the village center. Two major dirt roads and many of the narrow footpaths that ran through the village intersected at this center. Kerosene lamps were brought and my hurricane lamp was borrowed and placed where the curers would perform the ritual. By 9 P.M. the major curer and his three disciples appeared. Almost all of the adult men in the village were present, seated on the rope beds or squatting on the ground. Later I noticed that many of the older women of the village were squatting or standing beyond the semicircle formed by the men and their charpoys.

The curers built a small fire and poured clarified butter *(ghi)* into the flames, making a sacrificial offering. As the curer and his disciples took their positions at the center and faced the audience, I noticed that they moved in a peculiar way. Questioning those sitting near me, I discovered that the curers had been smoking marijuana *(ganja)*. After performing the ghi sacrifice, the head curer drank a mixture of hashish *(bhang)* and warm milk. Several minutes later he began swaying as if to an inner rhythm. Suddenly he dropped to the ground and began writhing like a snake. A hush fell over the audience; every eye was riveted on him. For approximately ten minutes he continued moving about on the ground imitating the motion of a snake, or *Nag.* I was told that the spirit of Nag had taken possession of his body and it was this possession that renewed the strength of his "poison."

At this point, the curer approached an iron object — the *chappan churi* (fifty-six knives) — that had been placed on the ground. Made of iron, it represented a cobra. The raised part was triangular, like a cobra's head, and it had the eyes and marking of a cobra. The neck extended to the ground where it became an iron shaft ten inches in length. Attached to the end of the shaft were fifty-six razor-sharp knives. This object was used to drive the spirit of Nag out of the curer's body. Timing was important. If the spirit of Nag inhabited his body for too short a period of time, the power of his "poison" would not be sufficiently strong to make it useful in curing. If

A Chamar leather worker who took part in the Nagahar ceremony squats next to the chappan churi used in this renewal ceremony.

the spirit of Nag stayed too long, he would never be able to dispossess the spirit and he would die or go mad.

As the curer approached the chappan churi, convulsions wracked his body. I was told in hushed tones that Nag did not want to leave the body and was causing the convulsions. Finally, in a sudden and frantic move, the curer picked up the chappan churi and began beating his back with it. After a minute of this flogging he dropped to the ground in a state of semiconsciousness. Nobody, including his disciples, dared approach him. Several minutes later, he revived and was carried by his disciples near the fire. Despite the flogging with the razor-sharp knives, there was not a mark or cut on his body. Each of the three disciples then went through a similar state of possession, convulsion, and dispossession. Villagers remained silent throughout the ceremony, passing the clay top of the waterpipe containing a mixture of ganja and tobacco among them.

Next day I interviewed one of the disciples about the ceremony. He could not recall most of the evening's events, but he felt positive that he and his fellow curers could now use their curing power effectively. My conversations with villagers indicated their utmost confidence in the curing abilities of these practitioners. Both practitioners and villagers proudly stated that not a single victim of snakebite who had used these curers had died. I discovered that during the previous five years two individuals who were bitten by cobras, who were not treated by the curers, did in fact die.

I asked the disciple to bring the chappan churi so that I might examine it. Initially he was hesitant, but because I had financed the event he brought it to me. I asked him to demonstrate the technique used to drive Nag from his body. Once again he hesitated, but I persuaded him to hit his back with the chappan churi. The moment it touched his back he began bleeding from the cuts made by the sharp knives. His bloody and lacerated back was an object lesson to both informant and fieldworker of the consequences of intruding into some aspects of the supernatural that are best left unexplored.

Structure and Anti-structure:
The Context of Religious Belief and Behavior

Both evolutionary and functional theories of religion have been criticized by anthropologists as inadequate in explaining religious beliefs and practices. The origins of religion stretch back into the distant and largely unknowable past. Functional interpretations of religion are vulnerable to the general criticism that can be made of all functional positions — they accept whatever exists in a society as being there because it is socially necessary. This explanation was particularly difficult to defend in the case of religious practices — dancing, magic, incantations, prayers, sacrifices, ceremonies and charms — that people believed could bring about solid material benefits such as health, rain, fertility, plentiful harvests, and seaworthy canoes.

Thus ethnographic descriptions of religious beliefs and practices were written, but anthropologists generally avoided the construction of a comprehensive theory of religion. In the last three decades, however, there has been a resurgence of interest in a theoretical understanding of religion. One of the most interesting and promising of the new approaches is the work of Victor W. Turner.

In the 1950s Turner did extensive fieldwork among the Ndembu people in Central Africa. His analysis of Ndembu ritual practices and beliefs was the initial step in developing a wide-ranging theory of the place of religion in human society. Central to Turner's approach is the distinction between *structure* and *anti-structure* (1967, 1968, 1969).

Turner's notion of structure is similar to the concepts of society, social structure, and social order. To Turner structure is an organization of statuses, roles, and norms (see Chapter 2). Previous chapters in this book on making a living, marriage and family, kinship, and politics are all descriptions of structure. The important features of structure for Turner are *hierarchy, classification, differentiation,* and *stability.* Anti-structure, the reverse of structure, is the segment of the world within which statuses, roles, and norms do not exist. Anti-structure exists *outside* structure, *between* structural categories, and *at the bottom* of structure.

Outside Structure

There are several dimensions of *outside structure.* One of these consists of the notion of an invisible world as opposed to a visible world. Various spiritual beings and powers reside in the realm of the invisible. Often this outside invisible world is defined in terms of reversal. Beings of the outside world act in ways contrary to normal human behavior and values. Witches eat human flesh and commit incest, for example; other beings walk upside down, are able to fly, and exhibit shameless and antisocial behavior.

Another dimension of "outsiderhood" is the attribution of special powers to people or groups who live beyond the cultural and social boundaries of the community. It is not uncommon for a group to think of distant societies as possessing mystical, special, and threatening powers. The Kaguru of Tanzania, for example, describe people who live to the east of them as possessing great supernatural power. A somewhat analogous point is made by Gerald Suttles (1968) in his study of a Chicago neighborhood slum. Non-Italians from this slum community believe that all Italians have Mafia connections and will use these connections if threatened. A similar point can be made about science fiction stories in which extraterrestrial civilizations possess tremendous power based upon advanced technology and superior psychic and intellectual capabilities.

Euro-Americans often see tribal people as living in jungles, close to nature, and thus possessing special outsider powers. Seen as communing with nature, tribal people are often thought to lack the neurotic manifestations of urban society and to be sexually free. Anthropologists doing fieldwork with such tribal societies soon discover that the people conceive of their small villages and hamlets as oases of order and culture set in the midst of formless and dangerous bush, the home of supernatural beings and forces. Communing with nature is a cultural notion of Western society.

Strangers often occupy an outsider position and are therefore considered special. Nuer leopard-skin chiefs, the masked Lone Ranger, and Tonto all represent individuals who stand apart and outside the ordinary positions of society. In some instances they may mediate disputes or put things right. The anthropologist, as stranger, frequently finds this outsider role useful in fieldwork. Free to associate with anyone, committed to no particular segment of the community, and uninvolved in the everyday demands of social life, the

The Lone Ranger, masked and unknown, and his Indian companion Tonto, an individual from another culture, represent the anti-structural quality of outsiderhood — the transient strangers who set things right and then ride away.

Between Structure

Cultural systems contain a variety of cognitive maps or blueprints that classify and order the world in terms of norms, categories, and statuses. In certain situations, however, individuals and events may not conform to these cultural classifications.

Social life frequently entails movement from one status to another: boys become men, girls become women, princes become kings, princesses become queens. In the transition from one status to another, anti-structure emerges. In Turner's analysis this period of transition from one status to another is called *liminality*. Liminality means that the individual is stripped of status markers. In the liminal phase of many rituals, which often mark transition, individuals may go naked, are considered asexual, are likened to children, and must be humble and silent; in other words, they lose the attributes of social status. Often individuals assume sacred and holy qualities while in these transitory and liminal states.

In every society some individuals and situations do not conform to status and classification categories. Children who do not follow normal growth patterns, twins who are born when the normal expectation is a single birth, dwarfs, psychotics, and transvestites may fall outside the range of culturally defined normality. In many societies such individuals become sacred or special.

Similar states of betwixt and between occur when situations, people, animals, or plants combine the attributes and characteristics belonging to separate and distinct categories. Among the Kaguru, according to T. O. Beidelman, "Pangolins [scaly anteaters that resemble both fish and mammals] and porcupines [mammals with needles for fur] possess mystical qualities to affect human fertility and hunting prowess. Similarly, unusual or deviant human behavior may bring power ..." (1971:38).

anthropological inquirer may assume a non-threatening and even friendly position with almost everybody.

Teigo Yoshida describes the ambiguous feeling toward strangers held by Japanese villagers. In their view, outsiders possess evil and dangerous mystical powers, but at the same time they are capable of bringing good luck. In traditional Japanese folklore, the outsider may be a god in human guise or a stranger wanderer who rescues the oppressed from unjust authorities. In recent years this theme of the stranger as rescuer has appeared in Japanese television and movies, the most famous of which is *The Seven Samurai* (Yoshida 1981:87–99).

At the Bottom of Structure

Turner suggests that in complex and hierarchically organized societies people at the social and economic bottom, who lack power, property, and prestige, resemble anti-structural entities. Unburdened by property and the selfish motivations thought to be central to the activities of the rich and powerful, these people are often thought of as free spirits. Thus one finds in popular folklore the idea that poor people and enslaved ethnic groups have greater sexual potency, sing and dance better, give free rein to their emotions, and are more willing to share what little they possess. People such as gypsies, untouchables in India, bandits, and prostitutes are frequently assigned these anti-structural qualities.

As we enter the 1980s it is instructive to turn to George Orwell's novel, *1984.* His use of the classificatory kinship term "Big Brother" has already been mentioned. In the tightly controlled, dictatorial society of *1984,* Orwell's hero looks to the uneducated, exploited, and subjugated "proles" as the potential overthrowers of Big Brother's dictatorship and the saviours of humanity.

The Power of Anti-structure

Within anti-structure there are fundamental forces of good and evil, and therefore this realm with its agents and manifestations is viewed with ambivalence. Ambivalence about anti-structure derives from the belief that both desirable and undesirable conditions of human existence are dependent upon anti-structural forces. Every society attributes life, health, success, fertility, justice, and harmony to the benevolent forces of the supernatural world. At the same time the supernatural world, or anti-structure, is the source of human misery: death, illness, failure, sterility, injustice, and discord. Thus the invisible world, strangers, outsiders, the world of witches, creatures of the night,

transitional stages, liminality, inconsistent and deviant states, and subjugated and oppressed people all are imbued with both benevolent and malevolent supernatural power.

Why should anti-structure be the source of wondrous and contradictory powers that we call the supernatural? A complete answer to this question is not available, but the nature of structure and culture suggests certain partial answers. An essential part of a cultural human being is the repression and channeling of basic human drives and urges. Control over fundamental biological and psychological urges and passions is central to humans as cultural beings. From the incest taboo to arranged marriages, the drives of the human species are channeled into socially defined and approved grooves. Such channeling and control can be viewed as a basic source of frustration for the individual. This view, in fact, is central to Freud's analysis of the psychodynamics of human behavior in his book, *Civilization and Its Discontents* (1930).

Turner's view of the same paradox is phrased in social rather than individual terms. Living in a culture and playing the roles demanded by the social order lead to behavior guided by self-interest and a limited recognition of the essential humanity of others. In making a living, getting married, living with kin, and obtaining political and economic power, human beings scheme, manipulate, plot, and even kill for their own interests. To live as a cultural being, or to be human, requires control of basic impulses; to succeed in society requires separation from and limited awareness of the essential humanity of others.

Anti-structure reverses the structural or cultural definition of being human. In anti-structure, unbridled expression of human urges and the full recognition of the humanity of others are essential elements. One basis for the positive and benevolent power of anti-structure, therefore, is the belief that the full expression of basic human drives, outside structure, permits the expression of true humanity. However, continuous and unbridled manifestation of human drives, outside the boundaries and categories of culture, can be viewed as threatening to the very fabric of society. Therefore the ambivalent view of anti-structure, particularly of those concerned with the maintenance of society, is derived from these attributes of anti-structure. The benevolence of anti-structure flows from its liberation of the human spirit from the constraints of culture and society; the malevolent and evil perception of anti-structure springs from its potential threat to the social order and its denial of human beings as cultural beings.

Hierarchy, classification, differentiation, and stability are essential elements of structure. These elements exist in the conceptions people have of their world. Therefore people can conceive of their opposites: egalitarianism, boundlessness, uniformity, and ephemerality. Such qualities can be identified in terms of the three major categories of anti-structure: outside, betwixt and between, and at the bottom. In addition, on certain occasions and at certain times human beings attempt to bring anti-structure into total existence. Turner calls this *communitas,* a group of human beings linked solely by the selfless bonds of humanity. There is neither role playing, status differential, nor sublimation of basic urges. Usually such attempts to transcend the bonds of structure attack and dissolve marriage, property, and power relations.

Religious expression and anti-structure have a basic dilemma built into them. On the one hand, they permit the expression of common humanity undiluted by social and cultural restraints. On the other hand, they deny the cultural and social basis of human existence. Expressions of communitas may appear as anarchy, and their continual expression violates the cultural basis of being human. As Turner notes there is a fundamental notion of ambivalence regarding anti-structure. It is both holy and dangerous. This factor may be why newly

founded cult movements that exuberantly exhibit manifestations of anti-structure — poverty, sexuality, disdain for this world, and opposition to authority — are so often despised and suppressed.

As part of the realm of the supernatural, Holi, Badyaranké witchcraft, and Nagahar can be used to identify some of the specific attributes of anti-structure. At the same time, analysis of these three different cases in terms of Turner's theoretical scheme enables us to penetrate beyond the cultural uniqueness of each case, revealing the underlying uniformities of religious thinking and behavior in human society.

The contextual framework for analyzing these cases is the human condition. It is the restraints of culture that make people human, but by bridling the biological, physiological, and psychological urges common to people, culture denies this common humanity. It is in the uneasy balance and tension between these contending forces that anti-structure, liminality, and communitas emerge as sources of good and evil. All three ethnographic accounts can be analyzed in these terms. In each account there is an attempt to escape and deny the bonds of structure and the social order.

In Hindu religion Krishna is a major deity, and there are many myths and legends associated with his presence on earth. A number of these legends portray Krishna as participating in unbridled sexual activity. It is assumed that any young girl who looks upon his countenance will immediately fall in love with him and offer herself to him. Krishna, in this guise, represents erotic love outside marriage and across caste boundaries. Many of these themes of erotic love and common humanity permeate the festival of Holi.

In previous chapters we have described some aspects of Indian village society. Among them are the importance of caste membership and the subordination and submission of women to men. During Holi caste separation and difference disappear, and women take an active and aggressive role. Behavior during the festival of Holi represents status reversal, which means that individuals occupying high or important positions in village social structure are insulted, humbled, and physically abused by their inferiors, low-caste men and women. For a moment in time the ordinary structure of social life is reversed and disappears, supplanted by communitas.

Witches are antisocial creatures who engage in activities repugnant to Badyaranké concepts of acceptable social behavior. They represent a reversal of the social order. A person's kin, neighbors, and friends can be witches, and the ultimate fear is that these individuals will kill and bring illness in order to steal souls. Thus the fear of *witchcraft* is the fear of the antisocial monster that lurks behind the mask of ordinary human beings.

Several anti-structural elements are present in the Nagahar ceremony. It is significant that low-caste and structurally inferior Chamars possess ritual power. This association between low social status and ritual power is common and is one of the most important generalizations derived from Turner's approach. The use of narcotic drugs in this ceremony is a common feature of rituals that involve contact with the supernatural. While in a trance state an individual is possessed by a supernatural spirit, Nag (snake). This entire ceremony can be seen as an attempt to martial the forces of the supernatural for the benefit of the entire community.

Religion in Comparative Perspective

Turner's theoretical formulation provides insight into the diverse religious beliefs and practices found throughout human cultures. The concepts of structure and anti-structure, outsiderhood, betwixt and between, and at the bottom in their dimensions of good and evil can be used to analyze religious behavior, practices, and beliefs. The wide diversity of beliefs, rituals, and practices in human religions can be divided into three categories:

1. contacting the supernatural
2. controlling and manipulating the supernatural
3. predicting the impact of the supernatural

Contacting the Supernatural

Recognizing the importance of belief in the existence of a supernatural world, how do individuals gain access to this world? Contacting the supernatural world is an essential step in controlling it, if control is conceived as possible. An alternative approach focuses on the intrusion of the supernatural into the ordinary world. Many tribal societies perceive death, infertility, failure, disease, discord, and spirit possession as events caused by supernatural forces. In this context contact refers to how human beings react to such intrusions.

In some societies individuals seek direct involvement in the supernatural. A number of societies have developed techniques that literally propel such seekers into the outside world of anti-structure. These techniques include trance states, infliction of bodily mutilations, fasting, deep meditation, and whipping. One other technique for entering the world of the supernatural is through the use of hallucinogenic drugs.

Hallucinogenic Drugs

A noted researcher in the use of drugs is Michael Harner. Harner did his fieldwork with the Jívaro Indians of the Amazon, who are best known for their practice of shrinking heads taken in headhunting expeditions. He found that the use of hallucinogenic drugs is a central element in Jívaro religion. For the Jivaro the world encountered while under the influence of hallucinogenic drugs is the "real" world.

> The Jívaro believe that the true determinants of life and death are normally invisible forces which can be seen and utilized only with the aid of hallucinogenic drugs. The normal waking life is explicitly viewed as "false" or "a lie," and it is firmly believed that truth is to be found by entering the supernatural world or what the Jívaro view as the "real" world, for they feel that the events which take place within it underlie and are the basis for many of the surface manifestations and mysteries of daily life.

> Thus, within a few days of birth, a baby is given a hallucinogenic drug to help it enter the "real" world and hopefully to obtain help in surviving the hazards of infancy through seeing an "ancient specter." If an older child misbehaves, his parents may administer another, stronger, hallucinogen to enable him to see that the "reality" on which they base their knowledge and authority does indeed exist. Even hunting dogs are given their own special hallucinogen to provide them with the essential contact with the supernatural plane. Finally, entrance into the normally invisible realm is considered so essential to success that the two kinds of leaders in Jívaro society, the outstanding killers and shamans [religious practioners], are the two types of persons for whom hallucinogenic drugs tend to have the most important role. Their achievements are believed by the Jívaro to be directly connected to their ability to enter, and utilize the souls and spirits of, that "real" world (Harner 1972:134–135).

Jívaro shamans are put into direct contact with the spirit world through the use of hallucinogenic drugs. One Jívaro informant describes his direct experience of this outside but "real" world in these words:

> He had drunk, and now he softly sang. Gradually, faint lines and forms began to appear in the darkness, and the shrill music of the *tsentsak,*

A Jívaro shaman prepares the hallucinogenic brew used to bring him into contact with the "real" world.

the spirit helpers, arose around him. The power of the drink fed them. He called, and they came. First, *pangi,* the anaconda, coiled about his head, transmuted into a crown of gold. Then *wampang,* the giant butterfly, hovered above his shoulder and sang to him with its wings. Snakes, spiders, birds and bats danced in the air above him. On his arms appeared a thousand eyes as his demon helpers emerged to search the night for enemies.

The sound of rushing water filled his ears, and listening to its roar, he knew he possessed the power of *Tsungi,* the first shaman. Now he could see. Now he could find the truth. He stared at the stomach of the sick man. Slowly, it became transparent like a shallow mountain stream, and he saw within it, coiling and uncoiling, *makanchi,* the poisonous serpent, who had been sent by the enemy shaman. The real cause of the illness had been found (Harner 1973a:15–16).

The use of drugs to induce hallucinations and to contact the supernatural is known throughout much of the world. In both the Holi and Nagahar ceremonies marijuana is used. Many activities attributed to witches and werewolves in European society now appear related to the use of numerous hallucinogenic substances, including nightshade (belladonna), henbane, mandrake root, and datura (thorn apple) (Harner 1973b:125–150).

One issue raised by the work of Harner and others is the possibility that drug-induced hallucinatory experiences transcend specific cultural settings. Certain commonly reported experiences during drug-induced hallucinations are flying, a sense of joy, visions of serpents and animals, visiting strange places, seeing demons and deities, color imagery intensification, and bodily dissolution and distortion. Perhaps the most interesting experience commonly reported is the disassociation of the body from the spirit or soul. Further research is required to demonstrate if these experiences are the direct consequence of the action of drugs on the nervous system or if the visions are based upon particular cultural traditions.

Hallucinogenic substances lead to vivid experiences of an outside and invisible world in which the separation of body and soul is a central experience. These experiences may reinforce existing conceptions of the supernatural world and the soul. Harner concludes that hallucinatory experiences, rather than dreaming, may be the basis for the universal belief in the supernatural (1973:xiv). Such experiences may have been the origin of religion. This formulation parallels Edward B. Tylor's explanation of religion offered a century ago.

Tylor postulated that a belief in souls or spirits was the origin of religious belief. Tylor claimed that this belief, called *animism,* was used by "primitive" people to explain death and dreaming. Death was explained as the permanent departure of the soul. Departed souls inhabit the invisible world and influence the living. Dreams in which individuals visited strange places and saw themselves and other people were interpreted as the temporary wanderings of the soul.

Spirit Possession

In Galipur there was a man who was periodically possessed by an evil spirit *(bhut).* In this state of possession he had to be restrained forcibly from sexually attacking women in the village. Villagers explained that evil spirits reside in trees and are particularly dangerous at night, and that as a boy this man had urinated on a tree, infuriating the bhut who took revenge by possessing him.

This story, as well as descriptions of the Nagahar ceremony, illustrate another form of contact between humanity and the supernatural: *spirit possession.* Possession of human bodies by spirits is a widely reported phenomenon. A vivid description of possession is presented by Walter and Frances Mischel in their account of Tanti, a Trinidadian woman.

Tanti is a short, powerfully built, heavy-set woman in her middle forties. Her skin color is medium brown, her hair is short and kinky and generally covered by a head tie. Nothing in her behavior when in the nonpossessed state particularly distinguishes her from other Trinidadian women of her age and class. She appears to be a pleasant-mannered, verbal, intelligent, and highly active person.

When the "spirit begins to manifest on" or "catch" Tanti, a dramatic physical transformation takes place. If in a standing position, she staggers, appears to lose her balance, begins to sway (bending her body forward and backward rhythmically), and may fall either to the ground or into the arms of bystanders. Her entire body begins to vibrate, while her arms are either rigid at her sides or stretched out above her. Her feet are planted widely apart and she may lurch back and forth from toe to heel. The vibrations increase in intensity, and somewhat resemble the convulsions of a seizure state. At the same time, she emits deep grunts and groans. Her jaw begins to protrude, her lips pout and turn down sharply at the corners, her eyes dilate and stare fixedly ahead. An expression of masculinity and fierceness envelops her face. She rises from the ground or breaks away from her supporters. She dresses herself, or is dressed by others, in the costume and implements appropriate to the power possessing her. (In this case, as Ogun St. Michael, she

dons a red head-tie and waist-band, and selects a cutlass or sword and bottles of olive oil as her implements.) In the standing position her stomach and pelvis are thrust forward, her head and shoulders are thrown back, legs wide apart, hands on hips. The entire posture is quite rigid. At this point the spectators recognize that full possession by the particular power has occurred. From then on the individual who is possessed, the "horse," becomes identified with the power, and is referred to and treated as such (Mischel and Mischel 1958:249–250).

According to the Mischels, sex and role reversal behavior are salient characteristics of Trinidadian spirit possession. Possession is commonly found among women rather than men; three-quarters of those possessed are women. Possessed individuals exhibit numerous instances of role reversal behavior. Women engage in aggressive masculine behavior and men evidence feminine behavior. During possession some individuals act like

A possessed spirit dancer of the Vishnumurti cult in South India is helped out of a mound of white hot embers into which he leaped. By throwing himself on the embers the dancer has demonstrated the purity of his devotion as well as possession by the deity.

children, wetting and soiling their clothing and speaking unintelligible gibberish. Individuals under the control of a spirit make demands that must be obeyed; onlookers immediately carry out any wish or command. The Mischels claim that possession is related to stress situations and social position and that family and marital discord, court cases, and conflict-producing situations are often preliminaries to possession. In addition, women occupy a subordinate position in Trinidad society, and men and women who become possessed are drawn from the lower classes of Trinidadian society. All of these dimensions testify to the anti-structural aspects of possession.

I. M. Lewis analyzes spirit possession on the basis of controlled comparison. Using material from Africa and India, Lewis hypothesizes that women who occupy subordinate and limited positions and men who occupy low status and despised social categories are prone to spirit possession (1970:308). He argues that spirit possession permits the individual to attain a temporary position of power.

Lewis's generalization linking social status and possession is illustrated by the possession of BaVenda women of South Africa. Spirits from another tribe, the Karanga Shona, invade women, and the women speak in Karanga and become ill. Their behavior resembles the possession state described by the Mischels in Trinidad, where a possessed BaVenda woman dances wildly, falls on the ground, grunts, and eventually the spirit possessing her reveals itself by speaking. The spirit voices demand many symbols of male authority: clothing, food, axes, and spears. All these objects must be brought immediately. A possessed woman is treated and saluted as if she were a chief, and she refers to her husband as "grandchild." Lewis labels this kind of possession a mystically couched feminist movement in which subordinate wives in a male-dominated society can demand and receive deference and respect. They are able to vent their discontent without engaging in open subversions of the social order. Lewis calls it *oblique social protest,* paralleling Eames and Robboy's analysis of the Tacony-Palmyra bridge birthday party discussed in Chapter 2.

Ritual

Anthropologists define *ritual* as repetitive and patterned procedures associated with supernatural beliefs and practices. There are, as we have noted, a number of desirable conditions central to religious practices and beliefs: well-being, health, fertility, good fortune, harmony, and justice. Rituals as a way of contacting the supernatural are techniques designed to maintain well-being or to reestablish it when threatened. An understanding of ritual involves recognizing the themes of anti-structure that flow through them.

One illustration of ritual is a Ndembu ceremony described by Turner. Parts of the ritual are called *chijikijilu* in Ndembu, the same term as that for landmark or beacon hunters use to mark their paths in the bush. As a hunter's landmark chijikijilu connects the known (the settled village) with the unknown (the formless and uninhabited bush) and creates order out of formlessness. In similar fashion ritual connects the known and the unknown; it creates order from disorder and makes visible that which is invisible.

These themes are found in Turner's description of the Isoma ritual, a fertility ritual for women who do not bear live children. Ndembu believe that the reason for infertility is the displeasure of a woman's matrilineal ancestress because of some transgression committed by the infertile woman. Lurking in the background is the possibility that witchcraft is also involved. The fact that a matrilineal ancestress may be causing the death of infants, who in this matrilineal society would belong to the ancestress' lineage, points up the anti-structural themes of Ndembu mystical explanations. As part of the Isoma ceremony a doctor and his assistants go into the bush and prepare a circular sacred site. Construction of this sacred site creates form and structure in the midst of untamed bush. While a doctor collects medicines, his assistants dig two holes connected by an underground tunnel within the sacred enclosure.

Naked, except for a loincloth, the afflicted woman and her husband enter one of the holes. They pass through the tunnel from one hole to another while the woman clutches a white chicken to her bare breasts. In the process they are splashed with medicines, songs of various Ndembu ceremonies are sung, and a red chicken is killed and its blood poured into one of the holes. The couple subsequently return to the village, and the woman is secluded with the white chicken in a hut outside the village. The Isoma actually ends when the woman gives birth to a live child.

Ndembu refer to the husband and wife in the Isoma as being like infants or corpses, and by removing their clothing, the participants lose their status markings. The two holes represent life and death. Medicines are taken from trees and bushes that have attributes associated with life and death. Hot medicines represent death; cool medicines represent life. Among the cool medicines are pieces of trees that have positive attributes. Trees that even elephants are unable to knock down represent strength and endurance. Medicine from a tree with a slippery surface is used, symbolizing the slipping away of the woman's infertility as well as the easy slipping through of a newborn infant. White to the Ndembu represents good fortune, and it may be symbolic of semen. The white chicken is therefore an essential element. Red is the color of blood and may represent killing, which is the death of infants. The red

Ndembu husband and wife participate in the Isoma ritual designed to produce the birth of a live offspring. Blood from a decapitated chicken is poured over the couple by the doctor who leads the ceremony.

chicken that is killed also stands for blood, misfortune, and the grudge of witchcraft that may be, in Ndembu thinking, the root of a woman's infertility (Turner 1969:10–43).

Calendrical and *life-cycle rituals* represent periods of transition. Holi is an example of a

Calendrical rituals such as Mardi Gras often incorporate the anti-structural themes of revelry, suspension of some of the norms that govern social behavior, and concealment of social identity as seen in the masked clowns on this Mardi Gras float.

calendrical rite. It marks the movement from one season or time to another. Often such rituals are characterized by reversal behavior. In Western society Carnevale or Mardi Gras and Halloween are calendrical rituals marked by the approved transgression of the social order. People dress in costume, wear masks, dance in the streets, get drunk, represent outlaws, pirates, demons, and witches, and little children play tricks on authority-holding elders.

Birth, initiation, puberty, marriage, parenthood, and death are all aspects of an individual's life cycle. These events are punctuated by rituals that aid and mark the transformation from one status to another. Rituals that celebrate events in an individual's life cycle are called *rites of passage*.

A basic framework for the analysis of rituals is found in the work of Arnold Van Gennep (1909), who recognized three phases in these ritual dramas: separation, transition, and reincorporation. Separation involves the removal of an individual from his or her usual statuses in society. Transition refers to a state of anti-structure, betwixt and between. Reincorporation is the return of the individual to structure and usually involves a change in status. From this perspective the Isoma can be considered a rite of passage. Husband and wife are removed from their village of residence: separation. Removal of clothing and movement in the tunnel from the holes of life and death inside the sacred enclosure symbolically represent a state of transition. The final incorporation of a woman occurs when she gives birth to a live child and becomes a mother, the definition of womanhood among the Ndembu.

Rituals are a central feature of all religious systems. In contemporary American society the major religions include numerous ritual events.

Some of these events are calendrical (Easter, Christmas, New Year's). Others are life-cycle rituals – baptisms, confirmations, weddings, and funerals.

Control and Manipulation of the Supernatural

In many societies contact is a step toward control and manipulation of the supernatural. Control and manipulation have two major goals: the attainment of *well-being* and the avoidance of *misfortune*. Since these goals are fundamentally important, human beings have invented a multitude of manipulative and controlling techniques. Witchcraft and the evil eye are devices of misfortune; magic is a technique in the service of many goals; curing is a goal achieved by a multitude of techniques. These three areas provide a limited survey of humanity's attempt to harness the power of the supernatural.

Witchcraft and the Evil Eye

Perhaps no aspect of belief and behavior has generated greater interest and more controversy in anthropology than the belief in *witchcraft*, the use of supernatural power for evil purposes. One reason for this interest is the belief shared by many anthropologists that human society is a cooperative and integrated entity. Beliefs in witchcraft, however, generate fear, suspicion, antagonism, and conflict, as illustrated by the Badyaranké. Social theorists who assume social integration and harmony have found it difficult to account for the disruptive and discordant consequences of witchcraft beliefs. Theoretical explanations advanced by Nadel and Whiting (see Chapter 2) are attempts to solve this dilemma by suggesting indirect, but positive, functions for witchcraft. For Nadel witchcraft accusations serve to reduce social and psychological tensions. For Whiting witchcraft accusations are an effective mecha-

nism for social control in simple and intermediate level political systems.

Witchcraft accusations, witchcraft trials, and executions of witches were widespread in European society until the early 1700s. By the middle 1700s European governments no longer recognized the validity and legal standing of witchcraft accusations. Colonial governments prohibited witchcraft accusations and trials in the tribal societies under their control, an extension of the European belief that interpreted witchcraft as an irrational delusion.

In the 1930s Evans-Pritchard published an account of witchcraft beliefs among the Azande people living in the Anglo-Egyptian Sudan (now the Republic of the Sudan) that attempted to explain witchcraft as a logical and consistent belief system rather than an irrational delusion. According to Evans-Pritchard the basic premises of Azande beliefs include the notions that there is no such thing as a natural death, and all events have a particular cause. Based on these assumptions, the entire system of Azande witchcraft beliefs make logical sense (1937). Evans-Pritchard shifts his analysis of witchcraft from an outsider's perspective, attempting to determine its function, to an insider's perspective, attempting to perceive its philosophical consistency. Witchcraft for the Azande, as well as the Badyaranké, is a theory of misfortune. As Evans-Pritchard writes, "Witchcraft participates in all misfortunes and is the idiom in which Azande speak about them and in which they explain them" (1976:19).

In human societies there are basic notions of well-being *and what ought to be*. Unfortunately, the course of social life rarely conforms to these desired states. People become ill, kinsmen fail to meet their obligations, disputes erupt, marital discord emerges, and food supplies may become threatened. These and similar events may be defined as one kind of anti-structure; they are deviations from normal and desired expectations. In the gap between what is and what ought to be, theories of misfortune — such as witchcraft — emerge.

In more than 75 percent of the societies for which information is available, witchcraft beliefs are present. Although the exact nature and content of witchcraft belief systems vary, there appears to be a common core of belief. Witches are people who have the power to injure others. Their actions are often described as the opposite of normal behavior. Flying, engaging in incest and cannibalism, associating with graves and the dead, going naked, and violating other notions of proper human behavior are commonly attributed to witches, who are thought to be driven by antisocial and amoral motives. This attribute of antisocial reversal given to witches is another level of anti-structure. When Woko the witch admits to having captured Fatiba's soul, he is demonstrating this aspect of anti-structure.

The Tiv of Nigeria have a detailed and comprehensive image of witchcraft as it operates in their society (Bohannon 1958). Witches are recruited through a series of human flesh debts. Unsuspecting individuals are fed human flesh. They are now under an obligation to pay back this flesh debt. Through supernatural means they kill a kinsman and invite their fellow witches to the cannibal feast. Witches are thought to be organized into a council. They meet at night, rob graves to eat the corpses, and bewitch people. The power of this council is recognized and feared. Bohannon writes, "Because no one can ever win against the organization [the council of witches], you must [eventually] give yourself to them as a victim because you have no kinsman left to give" (1958:5). Tiv believe that witchcraft power has a physical component, called *tsav,* that grows on the heart. This component can be artificially increased by engaging in witchcraft cannibalism.

Tiv have techniques designed to counter-act evil tsav (witchcraft). Oral traditions and historical records show that Tiv society has been periodically convulsed with anti-witchcraft movements. Using various forms of magical devices — fly whisks, fetishes, medicines, and specially brewed beer — the Tiv believe that they can detect witches and counteract and neutralize the impact of evil tsav.

Integration of witchcraft beliefs into a general system of belief is common. Evans-Pritchard notes this integration for the Azande. The Azande are a very pragmatic and practical people who believe that individuals are responsible for their own actions. A person who lies, commits adultery, or steals cannot claim bewitchment as a defense. On the other hand, death is seen as a consequence of witchcraft. If a man is killed by an elephant, it is obvious to the Azande that the elephant caused the death, but their question is why: why that particular man and that particular elephant came together in that particular place at that particular time. The answer is witchcraft. As the Azande put it, the elephant is the first spear, and witchcraft is the second spear.

Thus far we have considered witchcraft beliefs and accusations as static elements; societies either do or do not have them. Historical data reveal that the level and intensity of witchcraft accusations and fears in any society may vary over time. Some anthropologists and historians have suggested that cycles of witchcraft outbursts are associated with periods of economic and social disruption. Many anthropologists working in urban African towns note that witchcraft accusations increase as a result of the anonymity and disruption of urban life (Mitchell 1965:192-202). Clyde Kluckhohn and Dorothea Leighton (1962:244-245, 252) point out a correlation between increases in witchcraft fears and economic difficulties for the Navajo. In such situations witchcraft again becomes a theory of misfortune.

Witchcraft, however, is only one theory of

misfortune. Belief in the power of the *evil eye* is another explanation of why things go wrong. The evil eye, the look that injures or kills, is thought to be motivated by envy and jealousy (Maloney 1976).

Belief in the evil eye is found in complex peasant societies characterized by inequalities of wealth, power, and prestige (Roberts 1976). In the peasant villages of Galipur and Colle-fiore, where such social and economic conditions exist, no one publicly brags about how beautiful, rich, or well off they are, for fear that such statements would generate envy, jealousy, and the retribution of the evil eye.

In Ethiopia a class of people called *Buda* are thought to possess the evil eye. This group is despised and feared by the politically and economically dominant Amhara people. It is believed that envy is kindled in the heart of a Buda by anyone possessing wealth, power, beautiful children, or good looks (Reminick 1974:279–292).

Lewis's suggestion of oblique social protest may provide an explanation for the belief that the poor and deprived injure the wealthy and powerful. Lewis suggests that the deprived, lacking real power, use indirect means of striking back. If the differential of power and possessions is part of structure, the evil eye, which attacks on the basis of these inequalities, is anti-structure. In complex societies belief in the evil eye becomes a theory of misfortune rooted in the anti-structure of structural inequalities.

Magic

Magic is usually defined as the attempt to control and manipulate the supernatural world through spells, formulas, and rituals. Magic can be used for good (white magic) or evil (black magic). There are two generally recognized principles underlying most magical techniques: *contagion* and *imitation.*

Contagious magic rests upon the assumption that things that have been physically associated with people retain this association after separation. Therefore manipulation and treatment of these separated items will have an impact on the individual from whom they came. Such items usually include nail parings, hair clippings, feces, blood, saliva, and the placenta. When an Apache woman places the placenta of a newly born infant in a tree, it is assumed that as the tree flourishes so will the child. Morris Opler writes:

> The approved method of disposal is to place the bundle in a fruit-bearing bush or tree "because the tree comes to life every year, and they want life in this child to be renewed like the life in the tree." Before final disposal, the bundle is blessed by the midwife. To the tree she says, "May the child live and grow up to see you bear fruit many times" (1941:8).

Imitative magic is based upon the notion that like produces like. An image of an enemy can be destroyed, thus causing the death of that enemy. When an Ojibwa Indian of North America wishes to inflict evil on anyone,

> he makes a little wooden image of his enemy and runs a needle into its head or heart, or he shoots an arrow at it, believing that wherever the needle pierces or the arrow strikes the image, his foe will at the same instant be seized with sharp pain. If he intends to kill the person outright, he burns or buries the puppet, reciting magic words (Frazer 1959:135).

Voodoo combines both principles. A doll image of an enemy is constructed that contains an item that has been in intimate contact with that individual. Destruction of the doll causes pain, illness, or death of an enemy.

Malinowski provided an explanation of magical rituals that many anthropologists still find useful. He claimed that magical rituals emerge as a response to situations of uncertainty and anxiety. He pointed out in his de-

In New Guinea, magic is used to augment wealth. Moss and bark scraped from the center pole of a house fall on wealth objects below, causing them to increase. The shavings are also cooked with vegetables and eaten by men to add to their fertility.

scription of Trobriand fishing practices that although lagoon fishing was not surrounded by magical rites and spells, ocean fishing did have a magical component. He explained this difference by reference to the dangers of ocean fishing and the relative safety of lagoon fishing.

Using this same line of reasoning, George Gmelch has argued that professional baseball players engage in magic and ritualistic behavior (Gmelch 1971). He pointed out that rituals are associated with those aspects of baseball over which players have little or no control: batting and pitching. Gmelch noted that fielding, however, the other major aspect of the game, has little or no associated ritual. Fielding success runs close to 100 percent, but batters and

pitchers have a much lower percentage of success. Any baseball player who hits one out of every three times at bat would be considered a great hitter. Thus when a baseball player comes to bat he often engages in ritualistic behavior. Bats are never crossed over each other; home plate may be approached hesitantly, and batters may tap their bats on the plate a set number of times. Willie Mays, one of the great hitters of modern baseball, always touched third base on his way to the dugout in the hopes of hitting a triple.

Curing

In tribal and peasant societies illness is often attributed to the activities of supernatural forces. One consequence of this theory of disease causation is that cures are also derived from the supernatural realm. Examples of this theory of illness are illustrated in the Isoma and the hallucinatory trance of a Jívaro shaman.

Illness can be thought of as temporarily placing an individual outside of structure. Normal roles and proper modes of behavior are disrupted. In a satire on American health and cosmetic customs Horace Miner (1956) claims that even the slightest deviation from a culturally defined norm of beauty and health categorizes a person as abnormal. People are either too fat or too thin, too short or too tall, their breasts are either too small or too large, and their mouths must attain a halo of cleanliness. In addition, Miner notes that the sick American is taken outside the structure and placed in special shrine establishments (hospitals), where people go to die. Although the American concern with health appears extreme, the Shilluk of East Africa go even further. A Shilluk priest-king is thought to represent the entire community. Thus when a Shilluk priest-king falls ill his condition threatens the moral, physical, and spiritual well-being of the entire population. Their solution is simple: he is put to death.

Not all societies are this extreme. Illness is a condition that can be cured, and a varied set of curing practices are found in human cultures. In a trance state a Jívaro shaman sees the cause of illness, a poisonous serpent in the victim's belly. This is a common technique in the shamanistic diagnosis of disease. For the Yanomamo illness is caused by a *Hekura* (spirit force) sent by an enemy shaman. A Yanomamo curer uses his own Hekura to counteract and expel the spirit. In Galipur a cobra bite is not considered to be induced supernaturally, but it is treated by curers with supernatural powers.

A common curing technique is the extraction of a foreign object from the patient's body. Many North American Indian tribes have specialists known as "sucking doctors," who are experts in removing these illness-causing objects.

Predicting the Supernatural

The workings of the supernatural world are mysterious, and many societies have techniques designed to understand and predict the actions of the invisible world. Divination is the general term used for these practices.

Divination is the reading of the past, present, and future. In some societies animal intestines are read; in other societies figures are drawn on the ground and the subsequent patterns made by animals walking across the figures are the sources of the divination. A complex system of divination has been described for the Yoruba of West Africa by William Bascom (1969).

A Yoruba diviner, with the god Ifa as a source of his inspiration, uses palm nut seeds to cast the future. Sixteen seeds are held first in the right hand and then thrown into the left hand. The seeds that are caught become the basis of the divination. This process, called the casting of the seeds, is assumed to be controlled by the god Ifa. Based upon the casting of

A Yoruba diviner prepares to cast seeds as a first step to the creation of verses that his client will interpret to predict the future.

the seeds, the diviner constructs a diagram drawn from a repertoire of 256 traditional diagrams. Associated with each diagram is a set of verses. The best and most renowned diviners know the greatest number of verses by heart, and Bascom reports that one diviner memorized over 2000 verses.

A diviner is consulted by a client. Clients do not tell the diviner what the nature of their concerns may be. As a diagram emerges the diviner recites verses that are related to the particular diagram. It is up to the client to select the verse that is most appropriate to his or her problem.

Yoruba divination is a closed and logical system. Verses are sufficiently vague that they may cover many situations and be interpreted in different ways. Clients are actually involved in the divination process. Only the client knows the problem, listens to the verses, and selects the verse that is most appropriate.

Part of each divination is the sacrifice of an object or animal to Eshu, who is called the messenger of Ifa. Eshu in turn intercedes on the client's behalf with Ifa, who in turn carries the message of the sacrifice to the high god, Olorun. A diviner receives part of the sacrifice as his fee. Clients consult diviners for a variety of problems, although most commonly their concerns are with death, illness, sterility, failure, and defeat by an enemy. Death versus long life is an essential element in Ifa divination. If death is imminent, if a person has a short life, all other concerns are irrelevant. A person's time of death is fixed and determined. Despite a

divination predicting long life there may be circumstances that can shorten it. Sacrifices are one way of offsetting such misfortune, but if Olorun has ordained a short life, no amount of sacrifice will alter this fact.

It must not be assumed that the Yoruba are resigned to fixed destinies or that they rely on divination to help in all the problems they face. There are several Yoruba proverbs that clearly convey a message of skepticism and pragmatism, for example, "Bravery by itself is as good as magic," "A chief is calling you and you are casting Ifa; if Ifa speaks of blessing and the chief speaks of evil, what then?", "A charm of invisibility is no better than finding a big forest to hide in; a sacrifice is no better than many supporters; and a deity to lift me onto a platform is no better than having a horse to ride away on" (Bascom 1969:119).

Practices and purposes of a Yoruba diviner are similar to practices found in Western society. Horoscopes, palm readings, tarot cards, tea leaves, and crystal balls are all used for understanding and comprehending the invisi-

Tarot card reading is a technique that remains popular among Americans as a key to interpreting the invisible forces that control the present and future.

ble world. Eames has been associated with a research group studying psychics in the New York area, and preliminary results of this research suggest striking parallels to Yoruba divination.

A belief in a deterministic universe is characteristic of both Ifa diviners and American psychics. As one New York astrologer said, "The time and place of birth determine your life. However, these are only broadly determined. There are many areas where you can influence your fate." Thus if a psychic sees illness, the client can be warned and perhaps lessen its impact by taking precautions and early treatment.

It is apparent that psychics tell the client about certain areas of life that they assume are of fundamental concern. These include health, career, interpersonal relations, money, marriage, and family life. It is common after an initial reading to ask clients if they have further questions or problems.

Astrologers, palm readers, card readers, and tea leaf readers read patterns in much the same way as a Yoruba diviner. They share the belief that a greater power controls the particular pattern. An additional parallel is found in the goals of divining in Yoruba and American society. Clients are seeking health, good fortune, success, and harmonious social relationships, and through the divination or psychic reading a client is put in contact with the forces of the invisible world that control these valued conditions.

Practitioners of the Supernatural

Thus far we have described a variety of practices that are used to contact, control, and predict the supernatural. Such practices involve practitioners, people who are specialists in dealing with the invisible world. Just as there are a variety of ritual practices, so also are there a variety of ritual practitioners. They include curers, magicians, witches, diviners, psychics, priests, and shamans.

Anthropologists traditionally distinguish between two major types of religious practitioners: shamans and priests. These positions are usually distinguished on the basis of two dimensions: specialization and organization. *Shamans* are part-time religious specialists who operate as individuals and are not members of organized religious groups. *Priests* are full-time practitioners who specialize in the occupation of religion and who are members of a religious organization. Other practitioners — curers, witches, psychics, diviners, holy men, magicians — are distinguished on the basis of what they do. These criteria are useful, but they tend to mask the essential similarities exhibited by all religious practitioners.

Following Turner's conception of anti-structure and structure, practitioners of the supernatural would be expected to exhibit a variety of anti-structural attributes and characteristics. Outsiderhood, betwixt and between, and at the bottom, or poverty, should all be significant features in the careers of religious practitioners.

Witches represent an amoral and antisocial outsiderhood. Witchcraft beliefs reflect the idea that witches engage in behavior that is the direct opposite of the moral and cultural community. They attack kin and neighbors and they are accused of engaging in incest, cannibalism, and murder.

Among the Amhara of Ethiopia there is the position of magician-healer, the *debtara*. He wanders from place to place, lives a solitary existence, and indulges in sinful and amoral behavior. The characteristics of wandering and solitary existence are well known for holy men, monks, and hermits.

A number of anthropologists have suggested that religious practitioners are frequently stigmatized by physical and personality abnormalities that place them outside of structure. Anthony Wallace states, "The potential shaman is very often a sick human being, suffering from serious mental and physical disorders which spring from or involve profound identity conflict" (1966:145). The Ethiopian debtara is often stigmatized by a physical deformity — withered arms, blindness, hunchback, and dwarfism. Many observers of Siberian shamans have noted the high incidence of epilepsy among these practitioners. Some anthropologists have associated religious practitioners, especially shamans, with schizophrenia, manic depression, and other psychological disorders.

Whether or not shamans are psychologically or physically abnormal remains debatable. In terms of the concepts of structure and anti-structure, however, they represent certain elements of anti-structure. It can be argued that people who commit themselves to the welfare of their fellow beings exhibit an aspect of anti-structure and communitas that sets them apart from the rest of society.

Spirit possession described by the Mischels is an aspect of betwixt and between in which personal crisis, conflict, and stress place an individual in a difficult and uncertain condition. In a study of shamanism among the Ainu of Sahkalin in northern Japan, Emiko Ohnuki-Tierney (1973) discovered that one woman began her shamanistic practices after her daughter had drowned. In a similar way Yoruba diviners often defy the calling of divination until a series of personal crises overtakes them.

In India the ideal for a man is to go through four stages of life:

1. student
2. householder
3. forest hermit
4. wandering beggar (sadhu)

After leaving his home, community, and family, a sadhu wanders around the countryside supporting himself by begging. He loses all prior statuses including caste. He seeks enlightenment and religious inspiration. In Hindu religious belief a man cannot attain religious enlightenment and salvation until he renounces such structural attributes as marriage, family, caste, community, and possessions. An intriguing subcategory of sadhus are the nagas (naked ones). These men are naked when they participate in religious festivals. They are thought to be repositories of fertility, and women attempt to touch their genitals in order to become fertile. Infertile married women visit nagas at night and have sexual relations with them.

One of the most explicit examples of ambiguous status are the half-men half-women of the Cheyenne. Termed berdache by anthropologists, they are true transvestites, men who dress and act like women. They are thought to have great powers, especially for curing, successful warfare, and love magic. They are considered important figures in Cheyenne courtship ceremonies.

Ritual powers are also associated with individuals occupying the lowest and most despised positions in society. In the Nagahar snake ceremony low-caste Chamars obtain supernatural power for curing. In Ethiopia the despised Buda class possesses the power of the evil eye. As I. M. Lewis points out in his comparative study of spirit possession, subordinate women and despised men use ritual and spirit possession to obtain some degree of control over people who dominate them. In these examples we see lowly, ambiguous, and uncertain status (anti-structure) associated with notions of ritual power, fertility, and the supernatural.

Much of the foregoing description may not seem to be applicable to the contemporary full-time religious practitioner in America — priest, rabbi, minister. How do these practitioners represent and manifest anti-structure?

The berdache in plains Indian society was considered to be a powerful person. By combining the attributes of male and female, an individual acquired great supernatural power.

These are full-time religious specialists who are members of organized religious institutions. Unlike the largely individual practitioners of tribal society, they occupy *offices* that have anti-structural attributes. Vows of poverty, celibacy, and special clothing are common features of these offices, setting them apart from the rest of society. Titles such as Father, Sister, Brother, Reverend, and Rabbi (teacher) appear to remove them from the narrow bonds of

structure. They are supposed to epitomize the moral community, and they often are spokesmen for the oppressed, poor, and exploited of the world.

An issue that deserves examination is the gender basis for the recruitment of religious practitioners. Ethnographic examples used in this chapter indicate the preponderance of male religious practitioners. Ifa diviners, Yanomamo curers, Jívaro shamans, Indian sadhus, Ethiopian debtaras, and religious offices in Western society are primarily male occupations. A cross-cultural survey reinforces this view of male dominance of religious statuses. Although popular folklore in Western culture connects females and witchcraft, cross-cultural evidence indicates that in a large majority of societies men rather than women become witches. Shamans, like witches, also tend to be males. In six out of ten societies shamans are either exclusively men, or if a society has both male and female shamans, men enjoy superior shamanistic power (Whyte 1978:215–216).

Structure, Anti-structure, and the Supernatural in Modern Society

Throughout this chapter we have discussed religion in tribal and peasant society. Is the analysis of religion in tribal and peasant society applicable to contemporary American life? We believe that Turner's concepts, developed on the basis of ethnographic fieldwork among a tribal group, the Ndembu in Central Africa, illuminate the religious and supernatural beliefs of contemporary American society.

Earlier anthropologists emphasized the role of the supernatural in defining religion and magic. Both evolutionist and functionalist anthropologists, such as Tylor and Malinowski, followed this position. A view shared by both schools of thought was that aspects of the supernatural — prayer, magic, spells — would surrender their dominance to the growing influence of scientific and rational interpretations of existence.

Malinowski believed that a lack of knowledge about the natural world resulted in magical rituals designed to reduce anxiety and that as scientific knowledge expanded, magical rituals would decline. According to this approach as Trobriand Islanders gained greater knowledge about deep sea fishing and acquired more reliable fishing boats, their anxieties as well as their reliance on magical spells would be reduced. Other anthropologists saw both magic and religion as retreating before rational interpretations of the world. Thus the world of religion and the supernatural would eventually give way to the world of science and the natural.

In contemporary society, however, both magic and religion are flourishing. Beliefs and practices associated with the occult, witchcraft, divining, and belief in the "power out there" have gained wide and growing acceptance. Earlier theories that focused on the supernatural as a defining element in such beliefs obviously provide little help in understanding this resurgence of religious and magical fervor in modern society.

Turner's concepts of anti-structure and structure provide some insight into this phenomenon of modern life. One implication of Turner's approach is that the habits and practices related to the "power out there" will expand in modern society. Modern society is characterized by an ever-increasing emphasis upon structure. The contemporary world has become more complex, more complicated, and the number of roles and role specializations has increased. There is an increasing differentiation and hierarchy of social class and

power and a growing bureaucratization of society. Almost every major social theorist and critic has pointed out the increasing dehumanization of contemporary existence. This view of modern life is expressed by such concepts as "mass society" and "alienation," terms commonly found in literature, social science, and social criticism.

Structure can be defined in terms of anti-structure. Greater complexity, specialization, differentiation, and hierarchy imply the existence of the opposite characteristics. Thus growth in structure implies a corresponding growth in anti-structure. It is no accident that as modern society becomes more complex and complicated, other movements emerge calling for the abolition or total destruction of society, and a return to social simplicity. One kind of development calls the other kind into existence; the vehemence and extremism of many contemporary anti-structural movements correspond to the increasing complexity of modern social structure.

From this perspective the emergence of a bewildering variety of anti-structural social movements in recent years becomes understandable and expected. From social revolutionaries who preach utopia on earth to the inward-looking devotees of consciousness-changing drugs, the message is the same: our essential humanity is achievable only outside of structure. We foresee that as political and economic leaders of nation-states bring more and more of the social order under control, more anti-structural movements based upon liminality and communitas will emerge. These movements will stress disdain of authority, real or symbolic equality, heightened sexuality or denial of sexuality, and their message will be communicated in song, dance, music, drugs, and ritual that transcends the limiting bonds of structure.

Summary

Concepts of structure and anti-structure are useful in understanding the universal belief in the supernatural. Structure refers to the social and cultural dimensions of human existence, norms, statuses, roles, classification, and hierarchy. Anti-structure denotes another model of human existence in which these dimensions do not exist. Anti-structure has three dimensions: outside, betwixt and between, and at the bottom.

Anti-structure is viewed ambivalently: it has a malevolent as well as a benevolent aspect. Situations and individuals manifesting anti-structural attributes may be viewed as sacred and holy or dangerous and evil.

Anti-structure, the power out there, is a release from the constraints and limitations of social and cultural existence, permitting the expression of true humanity. This manifestation of its benevolent aspect is seen in the Holi and Nagahar ceremonies. In both instances denial of caste, religious, and sex differences lead not to social anarchy, but rather to the expression of a common humanity. At the same time anti-structure denies the social and cultural basis for human existence. This malevolent aspect is exemplified in the witchcraft fears of the Badyaranké, who believe that retreat from the many social and cultural obligations of kinship, friendship, and neighborliness implies the emergence of inhuman and antisocial monsters bent upon death and destruction.

In response to this perceived dimension of power for both good and evil, human societies have developed a variety of techniques to contact, control, and predict the effects of the supernatural world. Hallucinogenic drugs, spirit possession, and ritual are only a few of the techniques employed to contact the supernatural. Witchcraft, the evil eye, magic, and curing are techniques used to control the impact of the power out there. Divining attempts to predict

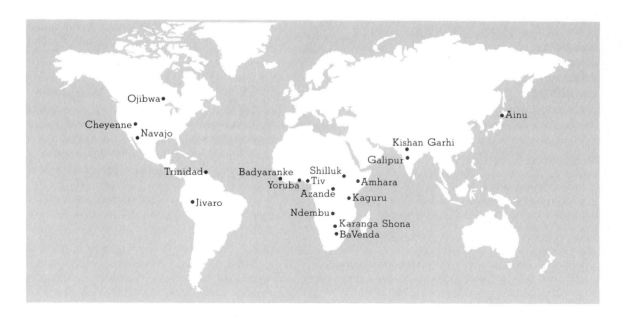

the supernatural and descriptions of Yoruba diviners and New York psychics indicate a fascinating parallel in this cultural activity.

The cast of religious practitioners is long and varied, including shamans, magicians, curers, and full-time religious specialists. All of these practitioners exhibit attributes of anti-structure, which is their badge of office. Outsiderhood, betwixt and between, and at the bottom are the three categories into which practitioners can be placed. In all cases they represent anti-structural elements that remove practitioners from structure.

Turner's approach, based upon his work in Central Africa, testifies to the usefulness of theory in anthropology. Although designed to explain the intricacies of Ndembu religious belief and practice, his ideas are relevant to the analysis of religion in all human societies. Using his concepts, we suggest that the surprising growth of religions and utopian social movements in contemporary society is a consequence of the growing and overwhelming complexity of modern life. Growth of structure implies a corresponding growth in anti-structure. As modern life becomes dehumanized, solace and salvation will be found in the extremes of anti-structural communitas.

Key Terms and Concepts

supernatural
secular religions
structure
anti-structure
outside
betwixt and between
at the bottom
liminality
communitas
witchcraft
animism
spirit possession

oblique social
    protest
ritual
calendrical rituals
life-cycle rituals
rites of passage
evil eye
magic
divination
shaman
priest

Suggested Readings

El Guindi, Fawda. *Religion in Culture*. Dubuque, Iowa: Wm. C. Brown, 1977. A brief introduction that presents Turner's material on ritual and Levi-Strauss's work on myth.

Evans-Pritchard, Edward E. *Witchcraft, Oracles, and Magic Among the Azande*. Oxford, 1937; rpt. Oxford: Clarendon Press, 1976. An abridged version of a classic ethnography of misfortune and magic among the Azande of Central Africa.

Harner, Michael J., ed. *Hallucinogens and Shamanism*. New York: Oxford University Press, 1973. A collection of essays that focus on the use of hallucinogenic substances and their relation to religious beliefs and practices.

Norbeck, Edward. *Religion in Human Life: Anthropological Views*. New York: Holt, Rinehart and Winston, 1974. A concise introduction to the anthropological interpretation of religion. Includes material on rites of passage and religious movements.

Simmons, William S. *Eyes of the Night: Witchcraft Among a Senegalese People*. Boston: Little, Brown, 1971. A complete ethnographic study of witchcraft among the Badyaranké of West Africa.

Turner, Victor W. *The Ritual Process: Structure and Anti-Structure*. Ithaca, N.Y.: Cornell University Press, 1977. The major concepts — structure, anti-structure, liminality, communitas — developed by Turner in his analysis of religion are contained in this volume.

Wallace, Anthony F. *Religion: An Anthropological View*. New York: Random House, 1966. A comprehensive introduction to the anthropological study of religion.

Worsley, Pater. *The Trumpet Shall Sound: A Study of Cargo Cults in Melanesia*. New York: Schocken, 1968. A survey and comparison of millenial cult movements throughout Melanesia.

Chapter 9

The Enjoyment of Life in Society

Cultural anthropology has its roots in a humanistic as well as a social science tradition. It is *humanistic* in the most fundamental meaning of the term — humanity is what anthropologists study. In the process of studying human behavior fieldworkers relate to individual human beings; they come to know the people they study and become enmeshed in their lives. Walter Goldschmidt expresses this essential element about anthropologists when he writes, "No other social scientist . . . has this intimate relationship with the subject of his study. No historian . . . lives with the people he studies. The economist analyzes the market, not the market place, let alone the buyers and sellers. We not only live with our villagers and tribes . . . we boast that we were inducted into a clan and can address our subjects by the proper kin term" (1977:295).

Despite this humanistic orientation, anthropological analysis and presentation often fail to communicate the full range of human activity. Anthropologists find it necessary to organize and present material in terms of institutional areas, such as economics, marriage, kinship, politics, and religion. This orientation is reflected in the organization of this text. Such an organization is necessary because of the impossibility of describing in words the total complexity of social life. In both contextual and comparative analysis, boundaries that define the limits for analysis must be established, because without them analysis is impossible. In a sense, anthropologists have to stop the kaleidoscope of life in order to comprehend and present what is happening.

In presenting anthropology within the confines of a textbook, the danger exists that a distorted view of people in other cultures will be communicated. By emphasizing institutional areas, it may seem that tribal and peasant people are primarily concerned with making a living, getting married, remembering kin relationships, manipulating others for power and profit, and appeasing the supernatural. This impression is a serious distortion of the true situation, because like us, these people exhibit in their own way the joy and exuberance of life and the things that make them laugh and give them pleasure. We are all part of a common humanity.

An earlier view of tribal people that permeated anthropology depicted them as captives of their cultures. In this perspective custom was king and little leeway was allowed for individual expression. A more recent image of many tribal and peasant people portrays them as overwhelmed by poverty and oppression, struggling to survive in a hostile world. It is impossible to deny that individuals are motivated by their own interests, that behavior is

Dancing is just one of the many activities that humans pursue in their leisure time. For these Watusi men, it is a primary source of enjoyment.

controlled by custom, and that poverty and oppression are crosses borne by millions of people. We would argue, however, that despite these conditions people enjoy life. This aspect of human existence must be considered in order to appreciate the entire dimension of the human condition. Too often anthropologists ignore those activities that make people happy.

A Day in Tikopia

One of the devices used in ethnography to communicate a comprehensive picture of community life is the description of a typical day in the life of the people. Such accounts, termed the *daily round,* begin with the earliest activities of the morning and close with the retirement of people for the night. An account of daily life provides a sense of completeness and totality that may be lacking in the analysis of particular institutions, because it shows real people doing the ordinary and everyday things that are the fabric of social life.

Raymond Firth's account of a typical day in Tikopia (one of the Polynesian Islands in the South Pacific) illustrates one of the major points about life in tribal society: work and leisure are intrinsically woven into everyday life. Rigid and overwhelming work schedules do not exist, and activities flow into one another.

Eating, sex, games, and storytelling constitute significant activities in the daily life of Tikopians. As Firth indicates, the height of the day's activities is the afternoon meal. Mornings are primarily devoted to work and obtaining food, although even then individuals are free to allocate their time as they wish. Afternoons and evenings are given over to relaxation, chatting, and playing games. Evenings may involve fishing expeditions or dancing and storytelling. Evening provides the opportunity for the young and unattached to engage in flirtations, intrigues, and lovemaking.

The village wakes early. On a normal day its people throw back their bark cloth blankets soon after sunrise, push aside their thatched doors with a rustle and straggle out into the cool morning air. They stroll down the beach or to the lake shore to attend to the calls of nature and to bathe, performing their toilet in full view, though at some distance from each other. After the toilet they return up the beach and chat about the night's fishing or exchange other gossip. On going back to their houses they find the floor cleared of bedding and the smoldering embers of the fire blown into a flame by someone who has stayed behind — a child, an old person, or a woman nursing a baby. A kit of cold food, remnant of the meal of the day before, is lifted down from its hook and anyone who wishes helps himself. Ends of taro or slices of breadfruit are doled out to the children, who run out munching. Their elders eat indoors. This food is eaten quickly and without ceremony, and soon afterwards the able-bodied members of the household scatter to their work. This varies according to season and to whim; personal choice is allowed great play so long as food is procured. Fishing or work in the orchards absorb the men and some of the womenfolk; others stay behind to look after young children, beat bark cloth, or perform household duties. It may take an hour or more up to the cultivations on the plateau or round the

crests of the hills, so that the workers start early. The morning passes in this way.

At midday the village is inactive and asleep in the hot glare of the sun. Most of its inhabitants are away. Some are still in the cultivations, from which they return home in the early afternoon loaded with taro, breadfruit, or bananas. Others, if the tide allows, are out on the reef — the men with pronged spear or rod and line, the women with their shell-bordered scoop hand nets, sometimes combining in a large fish drive.

As the sun declines from the zenith the place begins to waken. People come in singly or in little groups, nearly everyone bearing some contribution to the forthcoming meal. This preparation and consumption of their food is the chief point of the day's activities, the focus of the energies of each member of the community. Two features of primitive life soon strike an observer who spends much time in close contact with its people. One is

the directness of the tie between a man and his food; each day sees a fresh levy upon nature for the satisfaction of that day's needs, and the individual himself must work and sweat to cull and transform the materials of his desire. Cooperation, exchange and multiform obligations weave the quest for food into a complex social pattern, but the close contact of man with his primary natural resources remains an ever-recurring element. The other feature is the manner in which the provision of food becomes the apex of the day's work. In a civilized environment one is apt to look upon a meal as an interval in the real business of life: a pleasant social relaxation, a gastronomic indulgence, or a conventional interruption for bodily refueling. In a primitive society it may be, as it is in Tikopia, the main daily business in itself. To this the work of the fore part of the day leads up, and after it is over, the time of recreation has come. People in this island community do not arrive home to snatch a meal and return to work; the attainment of the meal itself is the fulfillment of their work. A man may go on with some piece of craftsmanship afterward, but

A work group of Tikopia men move the heated rocks used in cooking in preparation for the main meal of the day.

that is a concession to his personal interest, and is in no way socially dictated. Only during specific tasks, such as the building of a house or a canoe, is the meal regarded as an interval in labor.

Shortly after the return of the people to the village thin columns of smoke waver up from the oven houses as the fires are kindled [and] stone-lined ovens have been filled; in this leisure space of an hour or so people go and bathe, chew betel or sleep. Then the ovens disgorge their burden again, and the welcome sound of the pounding of puddings in their wooden bowls is heard, a sign that the meal will not now be long delayed. Instead of having communal ovens as do some communities, each family in a Tikopia village cooks its meal and consumes it independently of the others; coordination between them is represented by the occasional clubbing together of neighbors when food has to be prepared for a formal presentation. At last the most laggard household has completed its eating and tidied away the remains, and its members begin to stroll off on their various pursuits, or to while away the time before dusk in easy social intercourse.

In the cool of the afternoon as the sun is setting a Tikopia village is a pleasant sight. Groups of men, their work over for the day, are sitting on the sand, chatting, smoking and chewing betel. Everywhere are the children, busy with their play in the dry sand of the upper beach, running around the group of men, or dispersed among them listening to their talk; outside the circle of their elders the crackle of their voices can be heard rising at times to explosive pitch as a quarrel develops, then dying away again as their interest becomes reabsorbed in the affair in hand.

As the afternoon wears toward evening the social side of the village life becomes more evident. Gradually more and more people stroll down from their houses toward the place where the crowd is gathered on the beach, conversation becomes more general, games start among the young men, wrestling [and] practice in the hurling of the *tika* dart. Dusk falls, and deepens quickly into night. If there is no moon and the wind is right, the canoes which have been got ready earlier are pushed out, equipped with torches, nets and paddlers, and then begins the great nightly sweep for flying fish, partly sport but mostly hard work in grim earnest. Much later, at moonrise or at dawn, the fishermen return, weary but full of their night's doings, ready with excuses and not backward with self-praise.

If the moon rides high and full or the surf forbids the launching of the canoes, then the dance is probably instituted, either on the village ground if there is one, or on the open beach, illuminated only by the light from the sky. Dancing does not occur in all the villages simultaneously, but the young people go over to one in the vicinity which has begun to beat its sounding board. There, however, they are accepted as visitors, not as entrants by right. Sometimes a dance is "set up" in a village and "carried" to another village, thus introducing a competitive atmosphere into what is usually an informal proceeding. Normally, married people do not take part in the dance and the field is left clear for the young and unattached. Here is the opportunity for flirtation and intrigue, and from time to time an individual drifts off with some flimsy excuse to join a lover in a canoe shed or empty dwelling. Other young people, losing energy, come back to the house, take food and floor mats with them and go and sit on the sand, to gossip and joke or listen to the recital of some traditional tale. The delight of the Tikopia in *te arara*, yarning, is one of the most characteristic features of their social life, an amusement recognized and stressed by them.

Dancing, games and conversation on the

beach may go on till any hour; there is no conventionally appointed time for retiring, but people trickle off as the desire for sleep comes upon them. And so the day comes to an end (Firth 1936:52–55).

Life and Leisure in Tikopia

In many ways life in Tikopia resembles a tribal paradise as depicted in the writings of Herman Melville and the paintings of Paul Gauguin. These two men, along with many other Europeans, saw Polynesians as enjoying the bountiful fruits of nature without the corruption of civilization. Although Melville and Gauguin may have overstated the ease and pleasure of life in Polynesia, there can be no question that the Tikopians enjoy many advantages that set the stage for a relatively easy existence.

Tikopia is an island formed by an extinct volcano. The rich volcanic soil supports a lush variety of vegetation. The Tikopians recognize 150 different plant species. Traditional food plants include taro, yams, breadfruit, coconut, and sago palm. New plants introduced by Europeans include bananas, sugar, corn, and manioc. In addition, fishing provides an invaluable source of protein. Both saltwater fish from the ocean and freshwater fish from an inland lake are part of their diet.

Climatic conditions are not only conducive to plant growth, but also to the enjoyment of life. Temperatures range from 80 to 85 degrees Fahrenheit throughout the year, rarely going above 90 degrees. Together, temperature and rainfall provide an exceptionally excellent basis for continuous food production. The principal climatic feature of Tikopia is the variation in wind and rainfall. There is a monsoonal or rainy period from October through March, and a dry season of westerly winds from April to September. As a consequence of this climate, Tikopians enjoy an outdoor life with particular emphasis upon bathing and swimming.

At the time of Firth's research the Tikopians numbered approximately 1200 individuals, inhabiting an area of about five square miles. The relationship between population, land resources, and food supply enables the Tikopians to develop a daily round of life that incorporates manual labor with time for extensive leisure. Apparently the Tikopians recognize the delicate balance between population, food, and leisure. They practice coitus interruptus as a birth control technique and in the past have resorted to infanticide and celibacy to keep the population from becoming too large. In the history of Tikopia, Firth notes (1936:415) that when population pressure upon land resources became evident, a section of the population was forced to take their canoes and paddle out to sea. Thus the maintenance of what is often defined as a Polynesian paradise is built upon some cruel practices.

Tikopia is a speck of land set in the wide expanse of the Pacific Ocean. It is hundreds of miles from any larger island, and for most of its history it has been relatively isolated from the rest of the world. Unlike many other peoples in the world, the Tikopians were never subjected to raids and invasions by more powerful neighbors, nor did they attack other groups. Tikopians have had only intermittent contact with Western society. Their physical isolation partly accounts for this, but more important is that they lack resources that are of value to European commercial and industrial interests. As a result, in the 1920s Firth was able to observe a Polynesian society that was still largely untouched by European culture.

For all these reasons Firth summarizes his view of Tikopia in the following words, "In this state of isolation from the outer world, in a home of great natural beauty, adequate in the staple materials for a simple but comfortable existence, the Tikopia have shaped their life" (1936:30).

Enjoyment in Comparative Perspective

Portrayed in Firth's account of life in Tikopia are four major areas of enjoyment: food, sex, games, and storytelling. These are not the only ways in which people enjoy themselves. Warfare, according to Malinowski, Heider, and Hallpike, may be one form of fun in some societies. According to Evans-Pritchard, Nuer men most prefer to spend their time extolling the beauty of their cows in poem and song. Although clearing trees is an arduous and laborious activity, Bomagai men, in Clarke's description, find excitement and a sense of achievement in felling large trees. Hunting activities, from most ethnographic descriptions, also appear to be a source of pleasure as well as excitement for men.

Of all the visual and aural arts, dancing is the most widespread. It is part of the Tikopian daily round and is usually a prelude to sexual encounters. For the Siriono of Bolivia dancing takes place during the course of drinking bouts. On the island of Bali dance is part of ritual dramas that lead to trance states and spirit possession. Dance may be incorporated into sex and marriage, religious rituals, drinking, warfare, as among the Dani of New Guinea, or merely be an expression of fun and enjoyment. Among the Masai of Kenya, for example, young men enjoy leaping up and down into the air. This custom is apparently being duplicated in Great Britain where some of the followers of English rock groups enjoy themselves by jumping up and down during rock concerts.

Music and art are other activities that provide pleasure and enjoyment. The recognition and appreciation of the art production of tribal society are relatively recent. Students of tribal art have usually restricted their interest to three major areas of the world: West Africa, Melanesia, and the Northwest Coast of America. Different cultures in these three areas are well known for their art production, especially wood carvings, including statues, masks, and totem poles. In West Africa metal was also used in artistic production. The traditional approach to tribal art is relatively restrictive. It excludes activities such as Navajo sand paintings, which are erased after a ritual is concluded, and Maori body tattooing. Many anthropologists, however, consider Navajo sand painting and Maori body tattooing as tribal art forms.

The comparative study of music presents another set of problems, for although music is easy to record and define, variations in tonality, scale, rhythm, and melody make comparison difficult. Of all the musical forms singing is the most common. Musical instruments in tribal society are limited to a few basic types, mostly percussion instruments such as drums, tambourines, and gongs.

The sources of human enjoyment are wide and varied. Some activities are very specialized, such as warfare and tree felling. Others, like dance, music, and art, are widespread but difficult to define and describe. We have chosen four areas for cross-cultural comparison: eating and drinking, sex, games and sport, and storytelling. These four areas appear to represent the broadest and most commonly shared pleasures of life.

Food and Feasting

Eating includes both biological and cultural dimensions. The symbolic use of food on special occasions, the painstaking preparation of special dishes, and the various kinds of eating etiquettes observed in different societies prove that human beings are more than caloric intake machines.

Cooking as a characteristic that defines human beings was elegantly stated by the eighteenth-century wit, Dr. Samuel Johnson. James Boswell, his biographer, records his words as follows:

> I had found out a perfect definition of human nature, as distinguished from the animal. An ancient philosopher said, Man was "a two-legged animal without feathers," upon which his rival Sage had a cock plucked bare, and set him down in the school before all the disciples, as a "Philosophick Man." Dr. [Benjamin] Franklin said, Man was "a tool-making animal," which is very well; for no animal but man makes a thing, by means of which he can make another thing. But this applies to very few of the species. My definition of *Man* is, "a Cooking Animal." The beasts have memory, judgement, and all the faculties and passions of our mind, in a certain degree; but no beast is a cook. Man alone can dress a good dish; and every man whatever is more or less a cook, in seasoning what he himself eats (Kuper 1977:v).

Food has symbolic and social meanings in all human societies. Eating together may symbolize social comradeship and social boundaries. In many societies men and women eat separately. Ritual activities usually involve consumption of food that exemplifies the social and gastronomic side of ritual activity. Ethnic foods — soul food, spaghetti and pizza, bagels and lox, tacos and enchiladas — are symbolic representations of ethnicity in American society.

In some societies the sharing of food around a table or from a common pot binds a group of people together. Two Yanomamo villages cement a political alliance by feasting together, a practice duplicated throughout other areas of the world and practiced by modern diplomats.

Food in Galipur

Many basic themes in the cultural analysis of food are illustrated in the following account based upon Eames's research in Galipur. In Galipur food is divided into two basic categories: raw and cooked. Although there is no single term for raw food, food that is not cooked is treated differently. It can be handled, touched, and distributed without reference to caste. Wealthy and high-caste landowners employ low-caste laborers to grow, harvest, and store foods such as wheat and rice. Low-caste work-

A member of the potter's caste, one of the few castes that has the right to assist in the preparation of food in a Brahman household. This caste right is a point of status for potters.

ers, however, cannot cook food for or serve it to higher-caste individuals.

Cooked food is divided into two categories: pukka (real or good) and kacha (second-rate) food. Pukka food is fried in oil; kacha food is boiled in water. Kacha food is considered open to social contamination and can be eaten only when prepared or served by an individual of equal or higher caste. Pukka food, on the other hand, can be prepared and served by someone of slightly lower caste position. In neither case can a high-caste person take or eat cooked food from someone of a very low caste position. As a result of these distinctions, the caste ranking system in Galipur can be described in terms of who prepares food and who serves food. A consequence of the social meaning of food in India is that restaurants in cities advertise the high-caste status of their cooks. Brahmins, the highest as well as the priestly caste, are in great demand as cooks, since anyone can eat food they prepare.

Within the household unit food is cooked and served by women. Men consider this domestic chore to be the exclusive realm of women. This division extends to the etiquette of eating. In the household men and women eat separately and at different times. Women serve the men and eat after the men have finished. Informants in Galipur explain this custom as being based upon respect for men by women, but non-Indians might interpret the custom as domination of women by men.

Eating together by men who are not members of the same household unit is a symbolic representation of their equal caste position. Eating together is, in fact, almost always restricted to men of the same caste. On the few, primarily ceremonial occasions when men from different castes eat together, caste distinctions are still maintained. Higher-caste men sit apart from the others, and the serving of food follows the hierarchy of caste. Upper-caste men eat first, and the food is distributed from higher to lower castes.

Food is an integral part of social and ritual events in Galipur. At the conclusion of religious ceremonies small amounts of food, considered to be blessed, are distributed by the priests. Weddings, funerals, and other life-cycle events are marked by feasting. One of Eames's key informants, Baba, liked to attend ceremonies in which he could indulge his hearty appetite. Other villagers would joke about it and point to his protruding belly as evidence of his recent attendance at a feast. Another informant had been excluded from his caste group for violating caste norms. Several years after he left the village, he returned and sought readmittance to his caste. The caste council demanded that he sponsor a major feast for over 250 members of his caste as the price of readmission. Bringing together a large number of fellow caste members and eating with them was a symbol of his renewed membership in the caste.

Varieties of Food

In addition to the symbolic and social aspects of food, people derive considerable pleasure from the consumption of food that they consider delicacies. Bomagai relish the oil-rich flesh of the cassowary bird, and in some North African societies the eyeball of the sheep is considered a gourmet's delight. For the gourmet of haute cuisine in complex civilizations, the preparation and consumption of food delicacies becomes an art form in itself. This orientation is well developed in French and Chinese cultures, where cooking and eating are both a gastronomic and a gourmet delight. An appreciation of the finer delights of food is not restricted, however, to the jaded appetites of civilized sophisticates.

Aborigines of Australia allow kangaroo meat to decompose until it is covered with a green slime. Isobel White describes the gastronomical quality of this dish, called a whistling steak, as follows:

The delights of feasting and merrymaking are captured by Pieter Brueghel, a Flemish painter of the sixteenth century.

I remember a 10 lb. piece of rump steak that was hanging so long that it swelled up and went perfectly green. In fact, it whistled when you passed it. I yelled out to one of the people to throw it away. He said, "No, we'll take it to the camp and eat it. This is good tucker [food]."

This is what the locals did: they soaked that piece of steak for two days in running water, then they cooked it in the ground oven with leaves around it, as usual, to flavor it. After it was cooked and taken out, it looked so beautiful and smelled so good that I reckoned I would have a little bit of it. It was absolutely marvelous! It was tender and tasty, and provided that you could get over the fact that it had been green, it made a fine meal.

A veterinary friend later told me that it was quite safe to have eaten the "whistling steak."

The bacilli that poison people, he said, are on the meat only when it *first* starts to go off. Once meat goes green *it is not poisonous*. The water and the fire destroyed both the bacilli and the smell (White 1977:219–220).

Perhaps there is no greater measure of the gastronomic ends to which human beings will go to satisfy their palate than the consumption of toxic food. One example is the Japanese taste for the puffer fish (*fugu*). Fugu is quite poisonous, and special techniques have been developed to reduce its lethal effects. Lewis Grivetti gives an account of its preparation and enjoyment:

The Japanese have developed special dietary patterns to satisfy a craving for this [puffer] fish. There are specialty restaurants where *fugu* is served under exceptional public health inspection regulations.

The fish are eviscerated: only the musculature is used for food. The meat is cut into small pieces and soaked in water, which is periodically changed over three or four hours. The flesh is kneaded, and the soaking process attenuates the poison. Afterwards, the meat is sliced in nearly transparent pieces, arranged artistically on plates and served to customers.

Consumers of *fugu* claim to relish the physiological effects of the flesh; reactions range from sensations of warmth, mild paresthesia [abnormal skin sensations such as burning, itching, and tingling] of the tongue and lips, and exhilaration to euphoria. Despite strict governmental controls and regulations governing preparation and serving of *fugu,* up to 470 deaths per year can be attributed directly to eating this toxic food (Grivetti 1978:176).

Recipes from Different Cultures

When compared to most societies Americans have a wide diversity of food cuisines available to them. In the anthropological literature, however, there are examples of foods and modes of preparation that go beyond American cultural pluralism. We offer as a minimal introduction to the cuisines of tribal and peasant people the following carefully chosen recipes. They can be prepared in the American kitchen without much difficulty.

These recipes are introduced because their preparation and consumption may provide a concrete experience with other cultures that cannot be duplicated outside actually living in these societies. They include the three major food elements discussed in Chapter 3: meat, cereal, and root crops.

Tiv Sesame Chicken

Sesame chicken is one of the culinary creations of the Tiv people of Nigeria. It is a special dish prepared for an occasion such as the celebration of the marriage of a man to his first wife.

1 large frying chicken
½ cup sesame seed
salt
½ cup peanut (groundnut) oil
2 or 3 hot red peppers
½ tbsp parsley (optional)
2 large ripe tomatoes
1 lb (450 grams) okra or "spinach"
1 or more large Spanish onions

Use *chile pequeños* or black pepper; cheyenne or white pepper comes out wrong. For a bitter taste, appreciated by Tiv, use mustard greens, beet greens, or spinach well washed. For an oleaginous quality, also much appreciated by Tiv, use lots of okra, broken so that the seeds and "glue" come out in the cooking.

In a deep, very heavy pot (the best is iron lined with porcelain) heat peanut oil and brown chicken. Remove chicken. Crush ½ cup sesame seeds in mortar; brown gently in oil from which chicken has been removed. Remove as much of sesame seed as possible, add to chicken. Take pot from fire and pour off the oil. Add minimal amount of water, just enough to make browning from chicken and seeds into a suspensible mixture. Add layer of sliced and heavily washed vegetables, sprinkle with seasoning and sesame, add layer of chicken. Repeat till vegetables and chicken are used up. If you are using only the one chicken, cook on top of gas stove over the smallest possible flame (with an electric stove use an asbestos pad, or cook in oven). If using several chickens (I've done a casserole of this for twenty people), put in slowest possible oven at about noon. Midafternoon, remove and turn the topmost layers to the bottom. Serve in the evening.

Warnings. Do not add water. It cooks in its own juices, and in using the leaf vegetables one must be very careful not to come up with a thin soup. Do not use a stewing chicken: it becomes unbearably fat. African chicken is a lean and gamy bird (Bohannan 1977:87–88).

Kisir — Turkish Cracked Wheat

Grains of various kinds are perhaps the most widely used food staple. They can be transformed into many different cooked dishes — breads, spaghettis, porridges, pancakes, or the Kisir described in the following recipe.

1 lb (450 grams) cracked wheat, usually obtainable at health or foreign food shops under the labels "Bulghur" or "Labsi"
12 spring onions with tops (or substitute a mixture of white and spring onions)
2 cloves garlic
⅓ cup (100 ml) mild olive oil (or substitute a mixture of strong olive oil with vegetable oil)
2 or 3 chicken bouillon cubes. Note that this is our suggested addition to the recipe and not a part of the dish we were originally taught.
2 pts (1-2 liters) boiling water
2 tsp tomato purée (or substitute tomato sauce or ketchup)
¼ tsp cayenne, if you like pungent tastes, or red pepper, if you don't. Note that the tomato purée and cayenne are a substitute for the liquefied tomato paste and chili pepper pulp found in southern Turkey. The substitution maintains some authenticity because red pepper and cayenne come from the same species as Turkish chili peppers.
black pepper, to taste
salt, to taste
4 to 8 oz. (100–200 grams) parsley, finely chopped. The flat French or Continental-type parsley is preferable if available
⅔ cup (200 ml) lemon juice
3 heads of romaine lettuce (or substitute cos or ordinary lettuce)
3 or 4 lemons, sliced for squeezing over final preparation

Chop the onions using all the green of the tops. Chop the garlic finely. Heat the olive oil slowly in a large pot and sauté the onions and garlic until soft. Boil 2 pints of water in a separate pot. Dissolve the bouillon cubes in a small amount of water in another container.

Pour the cracked wheat into the large pot with the onions and garlic. Mix the wheat until it has taken up all the oil. Pour in the bouillon and the 2 pints of boiling water, completely covering the wheat. Drop in the tomato purée and stir well. Bring the wheat to the boil, cover, and reduce the heat to low.

Cook the wheat until it is soft and fluffy. Be careful not to overcook, as the wheat can become too soft and mushy.

Season the mixture to taste with salt, pepper, and cayenne or red pepper. Pour in the lemon juice to taste. Add the parsley and mix well. Cover and let stand until ready to serve. The flavor deepens the longer it stands.

Prepare a small bowl of romaine (canoe-shaped) lettuce leaves for each person. Chilling the leaves well adds flourish to the occasion and contrasts pleasantly with the steaming wheat. Chilling, however, is our addition to the dish and therefore departs from Turkish authenticity This recipe serves six. (Leach and Leach 1977:62–63.)

Yam recipes. As described in Chapter 3, root crops constitute the second major staple in human diets. They may be prepared in many ways, roasted, boiled, steamed, grated, and fried. The following recipes indicate some of the ways in which these root crops may be prepared. The first two, yam fritters and steamed yams, are from the Yoruba of West Africa. The recipe for yam pudding is from the island of Tikopia in the South Pacific.

Yam Fritters (Ojojo)
Yams are peeled, washed, grated, mixed with pepper, salt, and, if desired, onion, and molded into round balls about the size of a lime. These are deep fried *(din)* in a large pot of palm oil until crisp.

Steamed Yams (Amuyale)
Fresh yams are peeled, grated, mixed with pepper and salt, and molded into small lumps which are rubbed with the palm of the hand, adding water until they become soft but not liquid. They are then wrapped in leaves and steamed *(se)* in a large covered pot. This dish is usually eaten alone, but may be served with palm oil as a sauce (Bascom 1977:84).

Yam Pudding

Yams are roasted and then peeled. They are put in a wooden bowl and pounded until they attain a stiff consistency. Coconut cream is poured over the mixture and it is given a good pounding. According to Raymond Firth, the best way to eat yam pudding is with two fingers, deftly delivering it to the mouth (1936:104).

Alcoholic Beverages

The human ingenuity that transforms a multitude of foods into intoxicating beverages can only be admired. Although not every society produces an intoxicating beverage, the practice is extremely widespread. Usually grains, such as wheat, barley, millet, rice, corn, and sorghum, are fermented. Unusual food items have also been used for intoxicating beverages. The nomads of Central Asia ferment mare's milk into an alcoholic beverage, *kumiss.* Banana wine is consumed by the Baganda. In parts of Polynesia a nonalcoholic, but narcotic, drink, *Kava,* is consumed. Kava is prepared from the root of a pepper plant: people chew the mixture and then spit it into a water-filled bowl. In addition to their intoxicating qualities, many alcoholic beverages may be highly nutritious. Some tribal people in South Africa suffered various dietary deficiencies when missionaries prohibited the brewing of native beer (Linton 1957:95).

Allan Holmberg provides a fascinating glimpse of drinking behavior among the Siriono that resembles American drinking behavior.

> Drinking bouts usually start informally. The man possessing the liquor invites a number of his male relatives to join him in consuming what beer he may have on hand. Bouts generally start in the afternoon, and, depending upon the quantity of liquor available, may last until far into the night or even be continued on the following day. The participants squat in a circle near the host's hammock and, as a calabash of mead is passed around, each in his turn drinks heavy draughts before passing it to the next person in the circle.

Elders of the Barabaig tribe in Tanzania at a beer drink. Circumcision of boys is an occasion where large quantities of home brewed beer (as much as 200 gallons) is consumed.

As a drinking feast progresses, the Siriono, who is a very uncommunicative fellow when sober, becomes an animated conversationalist, a performer, and a braggart. At the opening of the bout the talk usually turns to the merits of the liquor. One of my more poetic informants, Erésa-eánta (Strong-eyes), used to say, in describing the liquor at the start of almost every drinking feast: "Yesterday it was without force, like water or like earth, but today it has great strength." As the effects of the drinking begin to be felt, one or more of the participants breaks out in song, usually impromptu and related to some exploit of which he is particularly proud, such as the killing of a tapir or a harpy eagle. Another may be engaged in discussing the desirability of looking for a new wife (always a young one) or of casting out the shrew he now has. As the mood gets mellower everyone joins the singing, and when the party has reached an advanced stage almost everyone is singing a different tune at the same time.

The women are almost always in the background watching over their husbands, because they are quite certain from previous experience that the party will end in a brawl. This is always the case when there is sufficient liquor. A man deep in his cups will turn to another and insult him with some such phrase as "You are very lazy" or "You never bring me meat with any fat on it." He will be answered in the same vein, and a fight will soon break out. The Siriono do not fight with their fists at this time; physical aggression is expressed in the form of a wrestling match. Since the contestants are usually so drunk that they cannot stand up, these wrestling matches frequently terminate with both of them passed out on the floor, much to the merriment of the spectators (Holmberg 1960:93–95).

People in many different societies apparently drink intoxicating beverages for their pleasurable effects. Alcoholic beverages appear to have a broadly similar impact on a cross-cultural basis. They affect the nervous system and set aside many of the inhibitions of daily existence. The desire for such an effect is apparently widespread throughout the human species.

Sex

Sexual activities are recognized as a source of pleasure in most, but not all, human societies. Although Western social scientists like Havelock Ellis and Sigmund Freud wrote about human sexuality in the early part of the twentieth century, American social scientists avoided this topic until recently. Alfred Kinsey's publication of *Sexual Behavior of the Human Male* in 1948 actually established the scientific study of sexual behavior in America.

In anthropology, the study of human sexuality has a longer history. A major figure in this area of study, as well as in many other areas, was Bronislaw Malinowski. *The Sexual Life of Savages in North-Western Melanesia,* which Malinowski published in 1929, was one of the earliest full-scale descriptions of tribal sexual behavior. His comprehensiveness and intimacy of detail have rarely been duplicated in anthropological writing. Malinowski indicates that Trobriand sexual activities were private and that most of his information was derived from informants instead of from direct observation or experience. The following personal account given to Malinowski by a Trobriand informant indicates graphically the Trobriand attitude toward sex and sexual enjoyment.

When I sleep with Dabugera I embrace her, I hug her with my whole body, I rub noses with her. We suck each other's lower lip, so that we are stirred to passion. We suck each other's tongues, we bite each other's noses, we bite each other's chins, we bite cheeks and caress the armpit and the groin. Then she will say: "O my lover, it itches very much . . . push on again, my whole body melts with pleasure . . . do it vigorously, be quick, so that the fluids may discharge . . . tread on again, my body feels so pleasant" (Malinowski 1929:341).

Pornography and commercialized sex are among the fastest growing and most popular business enterprises in the U.S. today.

In many societies the sex act itself is not only a private matter, but it is also viewed with a great deal of ambivalence. The Cheyenne believe that sexual activity drains a man's power, which is one reason why berdache (half-men half-women) are taken on war parties. It is believed that the stored-up virility of these people will aid in the success of the war party. These ideas are most clearly developed among a number of New Guinea societies. Mae Enga believe that frequent copulation and loss of semen will dull a man's mind and leave his body withered (Lindenbaum 1972:244).

Obviously, Trobriand Islanders are not constrained by such a view of human sexuality. Beauty of women is an important part of their erotic life. Malinowski recorded an extensive vocabulary used to describe female breasts. He recorded at least eleven terms for the female breast ranging from *nutaviya* — a full

round and firm breast — to *nukaybwigwi* — a long thin breast like the roots of a tree (Malinowski 1929:301–302). Unfortunately, Malinowski failed to record equivalent terms used by Trobriand females to describe the male penis.

According to Malinowski, the most noteworthy aspect of Trobriand sexuality is the position used in sexual intercourse and their ethnocentric attitude toward European copulatory practices.

The woman lies on her back, the legs spread and raised, and the knees flexed. The man kneels against her buttocks, her legs resting on his hips. The more usual position, however, is for the man to squat in front of the woman and, with his hands resting on the ground, to move toward her or, taking hold of her legs, to pull her toward him. When the sexual organs are close to each other the insertion takes place. Again the woman may stretch her legs and place them directly on the man's hips, with his arms outside them, but the far more usual position is with her legs embracing the man's arms, and resting on the elbows.

No other positions are used. Above all, the natives despise the European position and consider it unpractical and improper. The natives, of course, know it, because white men frequently cohabit with native women, some even being married to them. But, as they say: "The man overlies heavily the woman; he presses her heavily downwards, she cannot respond."

Altogether the natives are certain that white men do not know how to carry out intercourse effectively. As a matter of fact, it is one of the special accomplishments of native cook-boys and servants who have been for some time in the employ of white traders, planters, or officials, to imitate the copulatory methods of their masters. In the Trobriands, Gomaya was perhaps the best actor in this respect. Gomaya's performance consisted in the imitation of a very clumsy reclining position, and in the execution of a few sketchy and flabby movements. In this the brevity and lack of vigor of the European performance were caricatured. Indeed, to the native idea, the white man achieves orgasm far too quickly; and there seems to be no doubt that the Melanesian takes a much longer time and employs a much greater amount of mechanical energy to reach the same result (Malinowski 1929:336–338).

Halfway around the world and at the other end of the sexual spectrum we find inhabitants of the Irish island of Inis Beag. John Messenger describes them as "one of the most sexually naive of the world's societies" (1969:109). They combine naivete with sexual repression and sexual puritanism. Urination and defecation are viewed with shame and the body is covered at all times. They avoid swimming because part of the body would be exposed. Premarital sexual activities apparently do not take place, and

sexual intercourse between married couples takes place quickly.

Asked to compare the sexual proclivities of Inis Beag men and women, one woman said, "Men can wait a long time for 'it,' but we can wait a lot longer." There is much evidence to indicate that the female orgasm is unknown or not experienced. A middle-aged bachelor, who has a reputation for making love to willing tourists during the summer, described the violent bodily reactions of a girl to his fondling and asked for an explanation; when told the "facts of life," he admitted not knowing that women also could achieve climax, although he was aware that some of them apparently enjoyed lovemaking. Inis Beag men feel that sexual intercourse is debilitating, and they will desist from it the night before they are to perform tasks which will require the expenditure of great energy.

Absolute privacy at night is sought by married couples when they copulate, and foreplay is limited to kissing and rough fondling of the lower body of the woman, especially her buttocks. Sexual activity invariably is initiated by the husband, and the wife is usually totally passive. Only the male superior position is employed, and intercourse takes place with underclothes not fully removed; orgasm for the man is achieved quickly, after which he falls asleep almost immediately. Whenever I talked with males of sexual practices other than those just described, my remarks were met with disbelief, or I was accused of "codding" my listeners (Messenger 1969:109–110).

Discussion of sex and any reference to nudity and reproduction are absent in Inis Beag. In contrast, Raymond Firth indicates that stories and jokes about sex permeate Tikopian conversations. A frequent theme in Tikopia sexual stories is the detachability of the genitalia. In these stories men obtain women's vulvas and women obtain men's penises, which can be used whenever desired. When Tikopian men congregate sexual jokings and accusations about sexual activity are common. A man may be greeted in the following manner, "Where did you sleep last night?", "He has an enormous penis, at it every night, every night" (Firth 1936:496).

Anthropologists are not always immune to sexual joking. H. Arlo Nimmo, who worked with the Bajau people of the Philippines, reports that the Bajau discuss sex frankly and in mixed company. He once overheard two women and a man discuss the probable size of his penis and the nature of his sex life. His assistant was asked the price of mangoes in a nearby town by two teenage Bajau girls. When he quoted the price, they told him it was very cheap compared to mangoes in Bajau. Nimmo writes, "My assistant was surprised at the high price and asked why. They responded that Bajau mangoes were bigger, sweeter, and lasted longer. The girls began giggling and my assistant finally realized that they were actually referring to the sexual favors of Bajau girls and not to mangoes" (Nimmo 1970:252–253).

Nimmo also describes a number of Bajau jokes.

> Once, when I was discussing the nature of the Bajau bride-price with a group of adults and children, one of the men told me jokingly that the bride-price was actually paid for the bride's vagina since that was the greatest asset a bride has to offer her husband. The household laughed heartily at the joke. On another interview occasion with several women, the nature of twins entered the discussion. One of the older women jokingly asked me if I knew how to make twins, and, if so, she wanted me to make some for her. All laughed without embarrassment and thought it a good joke (Nimmo 1970:252–253).

For many of us these jokes are not very humorous, but the Bajau find them a source of entertainment. Thus these jokes indicate the enormous difficulty of a cross-cultural under-standing of humor, jokes, and entertainment even on a topic as basic as sex.

From these few ethnographic examples, it is clear that the cultural variability in sexual practices and attitudes is immense. From puritanism to permissiveness, from danger to delight, sex remains an integral part of the human condition.

Games and Sports

Games are a source of recreation and pleasure in most societies. One cross-cultural study of games found that only one of a sample of fifty-six societies had no games at all (Roberts and Sutton-Smith 1962:166–185). In a previous cross-cultural study of games a group of researchers defined them in terms of five characteristics (Roberts, Arth, and Bush 1959:597):

1. organized play
2. competition
3. two or more sides
4. rules for determining a winner
5. agreed-upon rules of the game

For devotees of the multiple forms of solitaire and games designed to have no winners, this definition appears inadequate. We are faced, once again, with the traditional dilemma of anthropology — developing a definition that encompasses the varied manifestations of a human activity that intuition and common sense tell us belong together.

Using the above definition, John Roberts and his colleagues subdivided games into the following three major categories, based upon how the outcome is determined (1959:597):

1. *games of chance:* outcome determined by randomness and luck
2. *games of strategy:* outcome determined by logic and manipulation
3. *games of physical skill:* outcome determined by strength and skill

Roberts and his associates correlated these three categories of games with other aspects of culture such as political complexity, the nature of supernatural beings, environmental conditions, and the socialization of children. The interpretation developed by these researchers is based upon large-scale statistical analysis of material contained in the HRAF files (see Chapter 2). Games of physical skill are almost universal, and no significant correlations were found between this category of games and the aspects of culture investigated by Roberts and his co-workers. For games of chance and strategy, however, a number of intriguing results emerged.

Games of Chance

Games of chance that involve randomness and outcomes determined by the laws of probability are widely played. About half of the fifty-six societies studied by Roberts and his co-workers had such games. Games of chance are rarely complicated because the major interest in them appears to be gambling on the outcome. Dice, bingo, coin flipping, and roulette are some examples from American society.

Gambling is a common activity in many North American tribal groups. In the following account Malcolm McFee captures the excitement and strain of the "hand game," a popular gambling game of the Blackfoot Indians.

All that is required is space, two poles, planks, or timbers placed about three feet apart parallel to each other, two "bones," or short wooden cylinders about ½ inch in diameter and two inches long, one banded and the other plain, and some plain sticks to use as markers. Two teams line up facing each other behind each pole. One person starts the game by intently shuffling, showing, and after many flourishes hiding the bones, one in each hand. His team chants and drums with sticks on the pole in front of them to give him support and to confuse the opposition during the hiding. Finally he extends his hands so that one of the players on the other side can choose by one of several signs which hand holds the unmarked bone. If the "guesser" fails to choose correctly, his side forfeits one of their marker sticks and the "hider" tries again; if he guesses correctly, the bones and roles change sides. The game is over when one side wins all of the marker sticks. Bets between individuals, both participants and onlookers, are placed before the game begins and other bets are made frequently on the results of individual guesses. The drumming, chanting, joking, as well as the strain of waiting for the outcome of a game in which large sums of money are at stake, contribute to an exciting time (McFee 1972:80).

Rolling of dice and the casting of lots are mentioned in the Old Testament. Judaism is not the only sacred tradition that records the gambling activities of people. In the *Mahabharata,* one of the great epics of the Hindu religion, the main character, Arjuna, plays dice with an enemy king. All his worldly properties, his throne, and his wife were the stakes in this epic crap game. The game, however, was fixed: Arjuna lost everything. Subsequently the two enemy kings engaged in a massive battle in which Arjuna and his supporters emerged victorious.

In attempting to develop cross-cultural relations between games of chance and other aspects of culture, anthropologists discovered many curious associations. In societies where the ground plans of houses are circular or elliptical rather than rectangular, for example, games of chance tend to be found. What is even more curious is that in societies where games of chance occur frequently, houses are roofed with materials other than grass, leaves, brush, or thatch (Barry and Roberts 1972:296–308). Although these associations may appear to be strange, they may actually define important cultural circumstances that foster games of chance.

Societies with high levels of insecurity and uncertainty are also societies that tend to have games of chance. Uncertainty of food supply, prevalence of warfare, and child-care techniques such as restricted body movement for infants, a low frequency of contact between mother and child, infants sleeping apart from the mother, and generally a degree of infant isolation from the parents are factors that tend to be associated with games of chance. In colder climates, where the food supply is uncertain and socialization techniques emphasize infant isolation, leading to feelings of dependence and powerlessness, games of chance seem to be found frequently. Thus the correlation between circular houses built with substantial materials — wood, stone, ice — and games of chance may be an indirect connection between the uncertainty and insecurity of living in northern latitudes, the prevalence of games of chance, and the fact that strongly built round houses are easier to heat than rectangular or square houses (Barry and Roberts 1972:296–308).

Games of Strategy

Of the three categories of games, games of strategy are least commonly found. Most research links the existence of strategy games to social and cultural complexity. Strategic games tend to be found in societies with levels of political hierarchy, occupational specialization, and social classes. In many ways the society becomes a model for the game. People who acquire skill in the game are thought to represent individuals who acquire power and skill in the political, social, and economic arenas, where cunning, manipulation, and foresight are important qualifications. Chess, sometimes called "the royal game," represents hierarchy, specialization, and complex manipulation — all characteristics of India and Persia, considered to be the original home of this game.

This association between games of strategy and power may be seen in Audrey Richards's account of Baganda life (see Chapter 7). She describes two Baganda nobles playing a board game *(mweso)* while ignoring a cringing peasant seeking an audience. This game, relatively unknown in the West, is one of the most widely distributed games of strategy in the world. It is found throughout most of Africa, Madagascar, Sri Lanka, Indonesia, and the Western Pacific.

Within this vast band of territory variations of this board game have been described. Despite these variations, the game contains the following core elements and common characteristics (Townshend 1979:794–796):

1. The game involves two players or a team of players.
2. The game is characterized by lack of specialization of pieces and a lack of hierarchy.
3. Central to this game is an emphasis on the complex manipulation of moves and a strategy of planned and anticipated moves.
4. The playing surface consists of a number of pits or cup depressions. These cups vary in number and this constitutes one of the major variations in the game.
5. The game is played with small stones or seeds.
6. The object of the game is to capture your opponent's pieces and the play is characterized by speed.

In West Africa this board game is known as *"wari," "owari,"* or *"wayyo."*[1] W. Cardinall, who was a British colonial official in what is now Ghana, describes the Ashanti version of this game as follows:

> *Wari* can be played on mother earth. It is generally played on a specially constructed board. This takes the form of a small table

---

[1] In Africa this game is known by many names, but in the recent anthropological literature the name *mankala,* an Arabic word, is generally used to describe it as well as similar games.

Pokot men of East Africa play *wari* using scooped out pits in the ground as a playing board.

about three feet long and eight inches wide. The sides are each provided with six cups or hollowed-out squares, and at either end of the board is a larger receptacle. These last two do not enter into the actual play; they are merely to hold the counters or tokens captured. There are only two players and each has one of these receptacles for his use.

The two sides are allotted one to each player, who owns that nearest to him. In each cup there are placed four counters. These are usually stones, cowries or seeds. There are thus forty-eight counters in all, twenty-four on each side, at the beginning of the play.

The play, being purely one of mathematical calculation, lends itself to many variations; but the commonest is as follows. A player may move the contents of any one of the receptacles on his own side, which is the one nearest to him. He thus has six squares each containing four counters. He must take all the counters in one square, and then drop one counter into each successive square to his right, following across into the squares of his opponent if necessary. His opponent does likewise, and as soon as six counters — no more, no less — are in

one of his adversary's squares — the total of six being reached by his dropping one counter therein — he lifts those six from that square and puts them aside into his "prison" receptacle. If he makes six in one of his own squares, he cannot lift those.

The speed with which the game is played is extraordinary. Small children as well as adults indulge in it, and gambling over the result is only too frequent (Cardinall 1927: 253–254).

In Central Africa, among the Ba Ila of Zambia, this game is called *chisolo*. The Ba Ila have developed a number of variations for the game, although the procedures and strategy are the same as those described for the West African version. The ethnographers who studied the Ba Ila, Smith and Dale, point out that an average chisolo game may involve up to twenty-one moves, but they observed one game that took 117 moves (Smith and Dale 1920:232–237).

On the island of Madagascar, Ralph Linton describes the Tanala game of *katra* (1933:261–265). Its similarity to African chisolo and wari is obvious. Other versions of this game are found in the Western Pacific island of Yap, where it is called *kavil* (Muller 1917:204–206).

This game presents a typical anthropological problem. Where did it originate, and how did it spread? Despite the vast region involved, the numerous similarities in the game in all these regions denies the possibility of multiple or independent inventions of the same game. It is logical to assume instead that the game originated in a single locality and then was carried to other geographical zones. This type of geographical spread is called diffusion. Although we are unable to determine the center of origin of this game, a reasonable working hypothesis points to Southeast Asia as the possible place of origin. We know that Southeast Asian cultural items such as plantains, cowrie shells, and some musical instruments are found in Africa and that the Western Pacific also contains cultural elements from the same source. We also know that Malay-Indonesian voyagers were active in the Western Pacific and the East African coast, as well as the Madagascar area, and that it is possible that this board game derives from that source.[2]

Continuation of the diffusion process can be seen in the recent attempt to introduce this board game into American society. In 1978 one of the major manufacturers of board games produced a plastic version of the game modeled on the type of game played in West Africa. It was called *mandinka* and is obviously a spinoff from the widely acclaimed novel and television series, *Roots,* by Alex Haley. Mandinka unfortunately failed to capture the public's attention, and its manufacture has been discontinued.[3]

[2] Some anthropologists argue that the game originated in Ethiopia (Townshend 1979, 1980).

[3] A more complicated version called *owaree* is also produced in the United States.

Games of Physical Skill

Games of physical skill, or sports, are based upon the use of strength, agility, endurance, and muscular coordination. They constitute the most widely practiced form of game playing.

The variety of physical games can be demonstrated by some of the early accounts of the Maori of New Zealand. Many Maori activities were centered around water sports. Swimming, diving feet first, canoe racing, and surfing were common activities involving competition. The Maori also developed competitive games including boxing, wrestling, and tag games. Many games developed skills useful in warfare. One such game is described by Sir Peter Buck (1952:239):

> Ti rakau or touretua was played with rather thick sticks roughly two to three feet long. The players knelt in a circle with two sticks each. In time to a chant, they beat the sticks together and then threw first one and then the other to the neighbour on the right, sticks being thrown in a vertical position. Each threw the first stick in the right hand, caught the incoming stick with the empty hand, threw the second stick with the left hand and caught the incoming stick with that hand. The passing of sticks, first right then left, continued for some beats and then the two sticks were beaten together. The tempo of the chant was quickened and great dexterity in catching and passing had to be displayed to remain in the game. Those who dropped a stick fell out and the circle lessened until the last one left in was declared the victor. The game taught dexterity in catching with both hands and made the catching of a spear in battle not so difficult.

In addition to this game, which emphasizes dexterity and quickness, a number of games are more directly military in nature, such as spear throwing and stone throwing. Maori expertise at swordplay is described in an early account by Elsdon Best (1924:94). He describes

a mock sword contest between an elderly
Maori warrior and a British officer:

> A bout between Maori and British officer was
> then arranged. The octogenarian [80-year-old]
> gladiator commenced operations by a most
> grotesque war dance, accompanying his
> movements with a monotonous, croaking song,
> wielding the meanwhile his staff in exact mea-
> sure with his chant, and gradually nearing his
> opponent, who, on his part, stood firm, with his
> eye fixed on that of his adversary. From the
> manner in which the old man held his staff, we
> all imagined that his visitation [attack] would be
> in the shape of No. 5 or 6 of the broadsword
> exercise with the oar-shaped end of it, when
> suddenly, and with a vigour whereof he
> seemed quite incapable, Old Hooknose, elon-
> gating his left arm, and sliding the taika
> [wooden sword] through the same hand, gave
> his opponent the point, the staccato slighting
> on his ribs with an emphasis quite sufficient to
> prove that, had the tourney occurred twenty
> years ago, and been *à l'outrance* [to the bitter
> end], the white knight would have been – done
> brown and supped upon [killed, cooked and
> eaten].

Although throughout the colonial period of
New Zealand history the British and the Maori
fought a number of bitter wars; the British, nevertheless, had great admiration for these people. Perhaps this admiration was based upon
the sharing of certain cultural values, such as
bravery, a fierce sense of competition, and a
notion of "playing the game," for Maori games
reflected central cultural themes emphasizing
competition and warfare. This association of
competition, games, and warfare may be seen
in one historical event that occurred during the
Maori-British wars. A British detachment, surrounded by a group of Maori warriors, ran out
of ammunition and prepared to die to the last
man. The Maori war leader told the British,
however, that he was having so much fun that
he was willing to share half of his ammunition

**Men and women among the Sharanahua Indians of Peru
challenge each other in wrestling matches. This is one
of the few groups in which such a form of direct contest
on an individual basis takes place between the sexes.**

with them to continue the fight (Suggs
1960:203).

Many games of physical skill and strength
involve men; some games in which women
participate have been recorded, however.
Janet Siskind (1973:100) describes wrestling
matches between men and women of the
Sharanahua Indians of Peru. A man places a
rope around a woman's waist, and the woman
then places a rope around the man's shoulder
and under one arm. Each of them strains to
knock the other off balance and throw the opponent to the ground.

Games and Sports in the Modern World

In the modern world games have remained a major source of pleasure, amusement, and recreation. Differences between games in the modern world and games in the tribal world are clearly apparent, however.

One of the unique features of modern life is the sharp division between work and play. In Tikopia, as in most other tribal societies, such a distinction is unknown. The emergence of spectator sports on a massive scale is related to the complexity of modern society, the application of technology to sports, and the division between work and play.

The division between participants in professional sports as athletes and the people who observe these sports as spectators is related to the complexity of society. Professional athletes are not found in tribal societies; they emerge in societies in which such individuals can be supported by the wealth and food surpluses generated by the system. Thus ancient Rome with its gladiators, the Aztecs of Mexico with their teams of ball game players, and Japan with its famous wrestlers are examples of societies with professional athletes.

Games have become sports in the modern world and have also become big business and big politics. This phenomenon includes the different categories of games defined by Roberts and his co-workers. Gambling to a large degree has moved from an illegal and underworld activity to a legitimate industry in which the government itself is one of the major organizers of gambling enterprises. Off-track betting and the emergence of state lotteries are examples of this trend. Games of strategy have proliferated, becoming technologically more sophisticated as well as involving lengthy and complicated strategic and tactical rules. This includes the invention of electronic games as well as the development of historical simulation games in which participants can duplicate the great battles of the past as well as the futuristic battles of science fiction and space.

People as spectators take sports seriously. The following newspaper headlines illustrate this point:

1. One hundred soccer fans injured in riot in Dacca Stadium (Bangladesh).
2. Caserta, Italy: a general strike and three days of rioting and fighting took place in Caserta, Italy, when the local soccer team was demoted to bush league status.
3. British hooligans stage weekly riots as police step up fight on violence linked to soccer.
4. Six die as Mexicans celebrate team victory. One million fans poured into the streets of Mexico City for an all night celebration of Mexico's victory over the Belgian soccer team in the World Cup quarter-finals.

It is apparent from this small sample of headlines that modern sports command an incredible degree of loyalty and allegiance. It may even be suggested that violence may be more commonly associated with sports than with questions of politics and economics.

Why should sports command such allegiance and loyalty? We suggest that the organization of the world into nation-states serves as a model for international competition and warfare. This manifestation of sports may be seen in the Olympic games, which are organized on a national basis. Success in the games is a source of national pride and is often seen as an index of the superiority of competing social and economic systems. Thus when sportscasters report the results of Olympic games, they usually compare national standings in terms of medals won.

Another aspect of commitment to professional sport teams is that they can be seen as symbols of community and national unity. In a world is which different and often competing

Triumph! The enthusiastic reception that greeted the victory of the U.S. hockey team over their Russian opponents in the 1980 Olympics reveals the close relation between sports and politics in the contemporary world.

groups – racial, ethnic, religious, class – clash, sports may be one of the few arenas of common feeling. Thus one year after the worst urban riot of the 1960s, Detroiters joined in a massive celebration of the Tigers' World Series victory in 1968. In 1980 the unexpected victory of the United States Olympic hockey team over the Russian team again generated a surge of patriotism in the United States.

The social functions and the cultural meaning of professional sports go beyond national and local pride and politics. Professional athletes represent the appealing theme of rags to riches. The few athletes who succeed are not only well paid, but also are perceived as earning their reward through the merit of skill, dedication, training, and ability. It is truly an achieved status. Since many successful professional athletes are drawn from the lower social and economic segments of society, they reaf-

firm the central theme of the possibility of upward social mobility and opportunity. Social mobility is obviously not a realistic opportunity for most people in an industrial and bureaucratic world, but success in sports seems to validate the myth of social opportunity.

Games have usually been viewed as expressive rather than instrumental, or goal-directed, activities. In contemporary American society, however, many games and sports have become instrumental activities. Americans are told that they must jog, play tennis, and ride bicycles for good health and beauty. These activities are becoming a means rather than an end in themselves.

Gambling in the Modern World

The click of dice and the shuffling of cards are sounds familiar to most Americans. Gambling has always been part of American culture, and

The emergence of casinos in Atlantic City testifies to the growing legitimacy and continuing popularity of gambling in American society. On a daily basis, more than 10,000 gamblers visit this casino.

in recent years it has gained not only legal approval, but also governmental participation. Las Vegas as the gambling capital of the United States is currently being challenged by Atlantic City, and every indication points toward the imminent legalization of gambling in other parts of the United States.

Why has this shift in legal and cultural attitudes toward gambling taken place? One answer links gambling and the growing emphasis upon pleasure seeking and leisure in American society. Another perspective drawn from cross-cultural studies indicates that perhaps the American people now see their lives and their futures as beyond individual and rational control and at the mercy of forces and institutions beyond control or comprehension. In such a setting an individual's future appears more and more to depend upon chance and luck, a setting apparently conducive to gambling.

A more material, if not cynical, approach would emphasize the revenue-producing as-

pect of government control and supervision of gambling. Here the need for new sources of revenue might be considered as the major motivating force that bends the cultural pattern to its own end. Attitudes and morality, in other words, follow in the wake of material needs.

Games of Strategy in Modern Society

Monopoly is one of the most widely played games of strategy in American society. In recent years manufacturers of strategy games have introduced a tremendous variety of such games. Most of these games involve the manipulation of moves and strategic choices to determine the outcome. Some games, like Monopoly, may draw upon society as a model. Other games may attempt to duplicate as closely as possible historical events, such as particular wars or battles, allowing players to duplicate the feats and facts of history.

One of the more interesting and recent developments has been the use of computers in strategic game playing. Such computer games may range from chess to simulation of space flight. In most of these games the computer takes on the role of one of the players, and the object is to beat the computer.

Strategy games have become serious business. Military and political planners work out games or scenarios and then attempt to duplicate the possible moves and countermoves of contending forces. Even in the social sciences, games have been developed that simulate societal conditions. These games are often used in classrooms as teaching devices. SIMSOC (Simulated Society), for example, is a game used by sociologists to illuminate basic social processes in society.

Storytelling and Conversation

Storytelling and conversation are universal human pastimes. In tribal and peasant societies oral recitation is honed to a fine art. Individuals may compete with each other to gain prestige through their memorization and verbal abilities. One of the skills of a Yoruba Ifa diviner is the ability to memorize and recite thousands of verses. In rural Ireland, where storytelling is a keenly developed art, Messenger relates that one storyteller in County Kerry was able to recite from memory 186 different tales, almost 400 pages of printed text (1969:114). In peasant India, where writing has been part of the culture for over 3000 years, villagers still rely upon oral tradition. In Galipur adult men memorize very large segments of the religious epic, the "Ramayana," which is recited from beginning to end once a year. Each man memorizes the equivalent of twenty printed pages of verse, which must then be recited perfectly.

A similar pattern of an oral tradition was recorded by Roger Abrahams among Blacks living in Philadelphia. Stories about the legendary figure of Stackalee (or Staggerlee) are me-morized and recited. The best storytellers know numerous versions of this story and show great skill in recitation and memorization (1970).

As Firth points out for the Tikopians, "yarning" is a form of cultural amusement and entertainment for them (1936:55). This situation would appear to be true for most tribal societies that lack mechanical means of entertainment and written forms of communication.

Coyote: Storytelling Among the Apache

The Apache Indians of the Southwestern United States have a complex mythology explaining the origin of the world, the emergence of animals, and the existence of the Apache. One segment of this mythology relates the adventures of Coyote, a trickster figure. Coyote is responsible for many of the good things enjoyed by the Apache; he is also responsible for many of the bad things in life, however, such as

An Ivory Coast (Africa) storyteller enraptures his audience through his tales and his ability to make them live for the young listeners.

darkness and death. Death was made inevitable for humankind by Coyote throwing a stone into the water and declaring that if it sank, all living things must eventually die.

Coyote in Apache stories is best remembered, however, as a trickster figure, who violates the norms of Apache culture. Gluttony, theft, adultery, incest, and other faults of people were first introduced by Coyote. He runs around naked and engages in intercourse with his mother-in-law. Like the Navajo, the Apache practice strict avoidance between a man and his mother-in-law. Thus Coyote's sexual behavior with his mother-in-law is a source of continual amusement for the Apache.

Morris Opler, who has made detailed studies of Apache life, points out the educational functions of the Coyote myth cycle. Beyond these purposes, the stories are a source of entertainment and continual interest for Apache children and adults. Winter evenings were the most acceptable times for storytelling, and people stayed up all night to hear an experienced and renowned raconteur recite his repertoire of Coyote stories. One of Opler's informants captures the sense of excitement at storytelling time derived from the memories of his childhood.

> Sometimes in the evening we would all gather over at my grandmother's home. There would be my sister, my cousins, and myself. The old lady would tell us Coyote stories.
>
> It is not an easy task to learn these stories. You have to be patient when the stories are being told. You have to listen very closely. You have to sit up at night when it's very cold, no telling how long, sometimes all night. When a funny story comes along, everybody is laughing. And at all other times you have to listen very closely and be quiet. As much as I have sat up and listened to the stories, I have to be reminded of some of them in order to get it correctly the way I first heard it.
>
> When Coyote stories are being told, there is generally a big crowd present. The older people, before they told the Coyote stories, would say, "When you tell these stories, they make you very sleepy."
>
> Both old men and old women could tell the stories. Some of these stories are very funny, and many times the boys of about fourteen years of age would get together and go to some old man's home and say, "Tell us Coyote stories." (Opler 191:438–439)

Summary

Food, sex, games, and stories are major aspects of human enjoyment and recreation. In tribal societies where there is leisure time but few mechanical sources of entertainment, such activities are intrinsically woven into the fabric of everyday life. This point has been illustrated by Raymond Firth's description of a single day in the life of the Polynesian islanders of Tikopia. It is obvious from his account that work and play intermingle and that the dichotomy of weekend and work week is absent.

Everywhere human beings eat in order to live, but Dr. Johnson may have identified a unique characteristic of humanity: people cook and prepare their food. Consumption of food is a social as well as a gastronomic event. People are brought together to feast and have fun. As an integral element of culture, food is given value and meaning beyond that of merely sustaining life. Although few tribal menus would be classified as gourmet fare, in all societies there is the appreciation of the delicious and the delectable.

Although sexual activities are basic to the

continuity of any society, sexual attitudes and practices vary widely. At one extreme are societies that can be classified as prudish and puritanical and at the other extreme are societies that can be classified as permissive in their sexual practices and attitudes. For these latter societies, sex becomes an aspect of the pleasurable side of the human condition.

Anthropologists recognize three categories of games: physical skill, chance, and strategy. Of these three categories, games of physical skill are the most common. Games of chance and gambling appear to be associated with feelings of dependency, uncertainty, and powerlessness. Games of strategy tend to be associated with socially complex societies and involve the skills of manipulation, foresight, and planning.

In the modern world leisure has been separated from the domain of work. Sports and games have become organized, commercialized, and politicized, but the attraction of these activities appears almost irresistible to the majority of people in the world.

Before the invention of modern mass communications, humanity depended upon oral traditions for recreation, amusement, entertainment, and education. The capacity of storytellers for memorization appears incredible to those of us who depend upon writing and other means of recording.

Emphasis upon these four aspects of the pleasurable side of human existence provides a more reasonable image of humanity. Images of tribal and peasant people as locked in a continual battle for survival or as robotlike creatures of culture are distorted and one-sided. The ability to find enjoyment in activities that are ends in themselves may be the essential element in being human.

Key Terms and Concepts

humanism

diffusion

daily round

games of chance

games of physical

    skill

games of strategy

wari

Suggested Readings

Arnott, Margaret L., ed. *Gastronomy: The Anthropology of Food and Food Habits.* Chicago: Aldine, 1976. *A wide-ranging collection of papers that focus on the different ways food is prepared and eaten in human culture.*

Bates, Marston. *Gluttons and Libertines: Human Problems of Being Natural.* New York: Random House, 1971. *An entertaining and witty look at eating and sex in different societies.*

Goldstein, Jeffrey H., ed. *Sports, Games, and Play: Social and Psychological Viewpoints.* New York: Halsted Press, 1979. *A collection of papers dealing with games and sports. Concentrates largely on Western society.*

Kuper, Jessica, ed. *The Anthropologists' Cookbook.* New York: Universe Books, 1978. *Using the traditional format of the cookbook, anthropologists present a global gastronomy of recipes. More than just a listing of recipes, this volume provides insight into the cultural meaning of food, its preparation, and its consumption.*

Malinowski, Bronislaw. *Sexual Life of Savages in North-Western Melanesia.* New York: Harcourt, 1929. *Malinowski's classic account of sexuality in a non-Western tribal society.*

Marshall, Mac, ed. *Beliefs, Behaviors, and Alcoholic Beverages: A Cross-Cultural Survey.* Ann Arbor, Mich.: University of Michigan Press, 1979. *A cross-cultural look at the use and abuse of alcohol.*

Norbeck, Edward and Claire R. Ferrer, eds. *Forms of Play of Native North Americans.* American Ethnological Society, St. Paul, Minn.: West, 1979. *Nineteen essays describe and analyze games and play among North American Indian groups.*

Stevens, Jr., Phillip, ed. *Studies in the Anthropology of Play.* West Point: Leisure Press, 1978. *Two dozen papers focus on games, play, leisure, and recreation.*

Part III

Learning the System

Whatever disagreements may exist between anthropologists about the interpretation and analysis of human behavior, they all agree upon a central point — human beings *learn* their culture. It is this learning process that transforms raw humanity into cultural and social beings.

Socialization refers to the process of cultural acquisition and learning. Language is recognized as one mechanism for the transmission of culture. Social change, however, often makes a mockery of what we have learned. In this part, these complementary themes are joined. How we learn culture through language and other means and the problems of adapting to new situations are all part of learning the system.

Chapter 10 begins with a description of the techniques used by the Ngoni of Central Africa in bringing up their children and then looks at the influence of culture on personality formation and mental disorder. Chapter 11 focuses on language and reports how a fieldworker's son learned the Garo language; the rest of the chapter considers the relationship between language, thought, and culture. Chapter 12 opens with an account of Maori armed resistance to British domination in New Zealand. Because tribal and peasant cultures throughout the world have been fundamentally altered by European intrusion, we look at culture change as it is linked to five centuries of European colonial rule.

Among the Yanomamo of Brazil and Venezuela, young girls prepare for their future roles as mothers by taking care of their younger siblings. By the time she is ten years old, a Yanomamo girl will have learned most of the roles that will be expected of her as an adult.

Chapter 10

Learning the System: Socialization, Personality, and Mental Illness

Human infants are born without culture; they must be transformed into cultural and social persons. At birth human infants are endowed with a limited range of behavioral responses: they cry, eat, defecate, urinate, and sleep. As infants mature they learn and acquire the repertoire of their culture. This process of cultural acquisition is called *socialization.* Socialization is more than just the acquisition and learning of a culture. It plays a crucial role in the process of personality formation, and many anthropologists assume that a close relationship exists between culture and personality. During socialization individuals learn norms and roles appropriate to their culture. In all societies, however, there are individuals who do not conform to culturally defined standards of normality. Such individuals are often defined as mentally ill. Questions concerning the frequency, origin, and meaning of mental illness on a cross-cultural basis continue to intrigue both anthropologists and psychologists. In this chapter we explore three topics: socialization, culture and personality, and mental illness.

Learning to Be Ngoni

A vivid account of how the Ngoni of Malawi in Central Africa bring up their children is found in Margaret Read's book, *Children of Their Fathers* (1968). The Ngoni have a definite image of what it means to be a proper Ngoni. Characteristics such as respect for others, self-control, hard work, hospitality, generosity, and dignity are personality traits valued in an ideal Ngoni

The relationship between parent and child is fundamental to a child's development. The response of a San father to his small child's first playful exploration is an example of this relationship.

person. To a remarkable extent many Ngoni achieve this ideal. In order to develop these characteristics, Ngoni bring up their children in what would strike Americans as an unusual way.

Ngoni infants, rather than being cared for by their mothers, are placed in the care of young girls. A Ngoni child spends its first six or seven years of life in intimate contact with women, and affection, gratification, and nurturance are basic dimensions of child care. When a Ngoni baby is weaned, however, it is sudden, swift, and traumatic.

Since the Ngoni have different expectations for boys and girls, differentiation between the sexes begins at an early age. Young boys and girls have different play groups and play activities. There is a sexual element in this separation because the Ngoni frown on the sexual play of children. This separation is intensified by the institution of the boys' dormitory. At the age of six or seven, boys are removed from the comforting care of women; the harsh and masculine life of the boys' dormitory becomes their training ground. To the Ngoni this is an important institution in the education of young boys. For girls growing up is a gradual process. Girls model their behavior on older women, who remain the major figures in their social world.

"A NEW STRANGER HAS COME"

In these words the father's mother announced from the door of the hut that a child had been born. A nurse girl from outside the circle of relatives [was assigned] to care for a new infant. The nurse girl was chosen by the grandmother from among her dependent household staff, and was allotted to one particular baby. The girl, who was usually in her early teens and unmarried, was supervised by an older woman.

The nurse girl took charge of the baby in the early morning and kept it with her all day until nightfall, bringing it back to the mother at more or less regular intervals for suckling. The mother played with the baby if she felt like it, and sent for the nurse girl to bring it to her if strangers came and she wanted to display the child. When the baby cried, and it was not time to take him to his mother for suckling, the nurse girl jogged him up and down on her back, and walked to and fro with him endlessly, crooning little lullabies to soothe the baby.

WEANING

Studies of weaning in different cultures lay emphasis on the traumatic shock of separation from the mother. In the Ngoni pattern of nurse-girl care, it might seem that the actual

Among the Ngoni, young girls assume the responsibility for taking care of infants.

weaning was less of a shock than in cultural situations where the baby was with the mother all day, carried about by her and never refused the breast if it cried. Ngoni women, however, asserted that weaning was a shock to the child. The reasons for this shock were partly that it was done all in one morning at one fell swoop, and partly that the child was sent away from the mother at night.

The mother-in-law and the other senior women of the father's family took the initiative as well as assuming responsibility for deciding the moment for weaning. Those same senior women who had assisted at the birth of the child arrived one morning on the veranda of the mother's hut and announced, "We want to wean this child."

When the senior women announced that they had come to do the weaning, most young mothers meekly submitted, whatever their personal sentiments were. The senior women pounded chillies and put the hot paste on the mother's breasts, and held the child near enough to smell the chillies, even to touch them. They said to the child: "Leave it alone. This breast is now bad." While the child was howling with fright and frustration, the mother's breasts were covered with a cloth. The child was then picked up and carried away in its carrying cloth to the compound of its paternal grandmother [and] attended by its own nurse girl. The Ngoni women believed that if a weaned child was given cow's milk it would forget its mother's breasts quickly, but they admitted that it was a conventional belief and not always justified.

GROWING UP IN A WOMEN'S WORLD

The young Ngoni boy, up to the age of six or seven, grew up in a women's world. The care of a child, especially between the time of weaning and the coming of second teeth, was the concern of a number of women in addition to his own mother, from whom he was snatched away at weaning, and, for a time at least, kept away from her household for eating and sleeping.

For the small child, the whole superstructure of authority in the women's world built round his daily life a sense of security. The child's needs for food and sleep, washing and warmth, care when sick were taken care of primarily within his mother's household and in his grandmother's household.

The smallest children urinated and defecated wherever they happened to be. From the age of three or four, however, they were taught to tell someone if they wanted to defecate, and taken outside the hut. From the age of four or five small girls and boys went with their mothers and the other women to the section of the surrounding bush reserved for the women's toilet. At about the same age boys and girls were taught to withdraw from the public gaze when urinating. The Ngoni were extremely prudish about all physical acts connected with evacuating or sex, and began to demand correct behavior from children at an early age.

It was not considered proper for children to sleep in the same hut as their parents after the age of four or five, when they might become aware that intercourse was taking place. From this age, they went to sleep either with a widowed grandmother or senior helper.

This acquiring of habits, directed consciously by adults, was designed to give the child increasingly a sense of being part of a community which had certain standards of behavior. There were in this training some prohibitions which a child was expected to observe as soon as he could walk and talk. The most stringent was on any form of sex play between boys and girls. To avoid any likelihood of this, little boys and girls were early encouraged to form separate play groups. The elders kept an eye particularly on the boys, and if they showed any inquisitiveness in their play about the private parts of a girl playmate, they were beaten and told: "If you do this again, I shall tell your father." Any rudeness in speech or action towards parents or elders was corrected at once and the child was told: "That is not the Ngoni way."

Small Ngoni boys learning to dance. Imitation is an important learning procedure in socialization.

PLAY AND PLAYTHINGS

In spite of what appeared like a somewhat restrictive regime, Ngoni children were merry and busy all their waking hours. The small girls had "dolls" which they treated as little babies. Older girls made these dolls for the little ones, and showed them how to feed the doll from a tiny gourd and taught them lullabies to sing while they jogged the dolls on their back or nursed them on their lap.

Little boys had a wider range of toys. They made windmills [and] they had hoops of bamboo peelings. They had tops of wood and they were forever collecting scraps of iron. Many boys spent hours making clay figures, men, cattle, monkeys, dogs.

A perennial amusement among Ngoni boys of five to seven was playing at law courts. They sat around in traditional style with a "chief" and his elders facing the court, the plaintiffs and defendants presenting their case, and the counsellors conducting proceedings and cross-examining witnesses. In their high squeaky voices the little boys imitated their fathers whom they had seen in the courts, and they gave judgments, imposing heavy penalties, and keeping order in the court with ferocious severity.

THE BOYS' DORMITORY

There was no greater contrast for the small boy about the age of seven between life in the women's compound and his plunge into the life of the boys' dormitory. The hut known as the boys' dormitory and the whole system of living which it represented was a traditional feature of Ngoni village life. It was the place where boys slept and lived together, and where they learned to defend themselves and to obey authority. Once a boy went to sleep in a dormitory he never left it until he married, unless he was seriously ill.

Ngoni regarded dormitory life as an important coordinating factor in their young peoples' development. The first purpose was to remove boys from the influence of the women. Ngoni men were outspoken in condemning the effects of all women's influence on boys. The other main purpose of dormitory life in Ngoni culture was to mix up all the boys in the village and let the common life together teach them how to get on with their age-mates and knuckle under to their superiors in age. Age and strength were the only criteria for authority.

There was no doubt that this abrupt transition was a shock for many boys between six-and-a-half and seven-and-a-half. From having been impudent, well-fed, self-confident, and spoiled youngsters among the women many of them quickly became skinny, scruffy, subdued, and developed a hunted expression.

The dormitory was primarily a sleeping place, but through the group of boys who slept there the herding of cattle was organized and the off-duty amusements and occupations of the older boys were planned.

When the boys went to live in the dormitory they did not only escape from the women's world into a boys' circle; they entered the fringe of the men's world. They could sit on the edge of the men's group and listen to talk about men's affairs. The kinds of topics discussed included hunting, cases heard in the courts, the application of Ngoni law, [and] the organization of village affairs.

GIRLS' LIFE IN THE VILLAGE

When the girls had their second teeth and were acknowledged to have reached the new stage in their development, there was no abrupt transition for them. They continued as part of the women's world; they changed their occupations and their daily routine on the whole very little; and they went on sleeping in the hut of a widowed aunt or grandmother.

The Ngoni girls' circle was to some extent split into the households to which the girls belonged. There was no common residence or common eating place for all the group, to correspond with the boys' dormitory. Generally the girls continued to eat in their mothers' compound.

THE IDEAL NGONI PERSONALITY

Inherent in showing respect and being obedient and law-abiding was the much stressed quality of self-control. Early travelers remarked on the restrained, dignified, and courteous behavior in Ngoni villages. This kind of self-control was taught in a variety of contexts, from avoiding greedy and noisy eating as young children to putting up with being ordered about in the boys' dormitory, and from the insistence on the decorous forms of greeting and thanks to the suppression of an overt fear of pain at the puberty ceremonies.

Another quality emphasized in child training was generosity in sharing anything that a person had. It was a quality demanded of everyone, from the small child who was made to unclench his fist in which he was hiding three groundnuts and give two of them to his fellows, to the big chief whose duty at a feast was to see that everyone had enough and to send food from his own portion to anyone who looked hungry.

Competence in household management made many demands on a Ngoni young woman if she were to learn how to become on her marriage an ideal housewife. This included organizing food supplies, supervising cooking, and that supreme test of competence: dividing out the food so that all had a fair share. The same high standard of skill was expected in the general care and supervision of the compound, the children, and the household staff. Ngoni women, like their menfolk, were proud of being able to supervise other people and organize life around them, to control others satisfactorily, to hear complaints, and to pacify quarrels.

Boys and young men were expected to be physically strong, and tough in the sense of being able to do hard tasks, walk long distances, dance for hours on end, and put up with hardships without grumbling. The senior men hated to see idleness and set great store by young men working hard and persistently at any tasks undertaken.

Abiding by the law and obedience to authority were important values. "Respect" and "honoring" people established the value of human dignity, and the terrible effects of "losing face" when respect was not given.

Mutual aid and generosity were values extending far beyond the family and kinship circles and formed the basis of the open-handed hospitality. Related to these attitudes to other people was the emphasis in early and later childhood training on self-control. In spite of their warlike background and historical acts of agression in the past, the Ngoni in the villages admired the man who was "gentle," that is, "restrained," whose personal behavior in speech and action was under continuous control and who rejected all forms of excess.

Supporting the concept of the Ngoni ideal personality, and inherent in their emphasis on achievement, were three values taught and looked for in young people. Moral as well as physical strength was admired and praised in actions and attitudes. Persistence, thoroughness, and hard work were the essential requirements for achievement. Wisdom, contrasted with mere cleverness when considering people's needs and regulating the affairs of men, revealed knowledge, good judgment, ability to keep the peace, and skill in the use of speech (Read 1968:20, 24–27, 33–34, 39–43, 48–49, 51, 55, 81–83, 94).

Ngoni Socialization in Context

The Ngoni have a strong sense of their cultural identity. They continually differentiate themselves from non-Ngoni groups around them. To a large extent this distinctiveness has historical roots.

Originally, the Ngoni people were part of the Zulu Empire in southern Africa. In the early part of the nineteenth century they split away from the Zulu Empire and migrated as a unified group to their present homeland in Malawi. This migration required a march of over 1200 miles through hostile territory. When they arrived in what is now their present homeland, the Ngoni established their dominance over the local population through warfare. As a consequence they see themselves as superior to and separate from their neighbors.

Ngoni child-rearing practices seem to be a direct result of their desire to maintain a Ngoni identity. Ngoni perceive the boys' dormitory as an institution that "Ngon-izes" the boys and counteracts influences from non-Ngoni sources (Read 1968:49).

Although the Ngoni are no longer active militarily, many of the valued male traits, such as physical prowess, respect for authority, cooperation, and emphasis on achievement, are associated with a warfare pattern. They are ingredients for success in warfare and political domination. These traits also coincide with the cattle-herding activities of men. Ngoni women supervise large household units and are skilled in scheduling and organizing household activities. Thus both men and women develop supervisory, managerial, and organizational skills that Americans would recognize as some of the essential elements of successful administration.

Ngoni see a close relationship between the education and rearing of children and the development of a proper adult Ngoni. In 1879 a Ngoni chief refused to allow Christian missionaries to establish mission schools in his kingdom. He said, "If we give you our children to teach, your words will steal their hearts; they will grow up cowards, and refuse to fight for us when we are old; and knowing more than we do, they will despise us" (Read 1968:2).

Aspects of Ngoni child rearing and personality can be understood within the military, political, and economic contexts of Ngoni life as it developed in Central Africa. At the present time, Ngoni emphasis on education and achievement and their sense of leadership and responsibility provide advantages in accommodating to a changing world.

Socialization: The Humanizing Process

Socialization is the process of learning and acquiring culture. Some anthropologists find it convenient to differentiate socialization, the process of cultural transmission, from enculturation, the process of learning a particular culture (Williams 1972:1–2). For our purposes the term socialization will cover these similar and overlapping meanings.

Biological Basis of Socialization

A unique characteristic of the human species is the relatively long period of infantile dependency. During the early years of life children are directly dependent upon adults for their physical survival. This long period of dependency also sets the stage for the cultural transmission process, which continues throughout an individual's life.

No human infant is born with a genetic program for particular behavioral patterns. What is characteristic of human infants is a generalized capacity to learn, undoubtedly related to the significant growth in brain size that occurs in the first three years of life (Williams 1972:28). This generalized capacity enables the infant to acquire a particular cultural repertoire.

Processes of Socialization

Socialization is a learning process. Psychologists have developed theories designed to explain how we learn. Such theories use reward and punishment, reinforcement, imitation, and stimulus-response as fundamental concepts in explaining the learning process. A basic assumption of *learning theory* is that children do things on a random, trial-and-error basis. Parents and other authority figures, using the learning concepts referred to above, mold children's trial-and-error behavior into approved and accepted grooves. What is not entirely clear is how children internalize these demands; that is, incorporate them into their thinking and behaving.

Theories derived from the work of Sigmund Freud are concerned with the *internalization* of cultural norms. *Freudian theory,* in some respects, parallels learning theory. Seeking pleasure and avoiding pain, important principles in Freudian theory, parallel the learning theory emphasis upon reward and punishment. Identification with authority figures, usually parents, is an important part of Freudian theory. Such identification becomes the basis for transforming a child's inner drives into conformity with social and cultural requirements. In the Freudian model this conformity is not based upon the threat of external sanctions, but is internalized in terms of an inner censor, an individual's conscience or superego. Through this process of identification children acquire the standards of their culture. In American society, for example, as in all societies, there is an incest taboo. A Freudian analysis of the incest taboo identifies an internal censor rather than external sanctions that enforces conformity to this norm.

Although the learned and acquired quality

of culture has been recognized for over a century, no adequate theory of cultural transmission has been developed. In a survey of socialization theory, Thomas Williams states, "Currently available learning models are much too sparse for grasping the full richness and great complexity of what really occurs in the socialization process" (1972:63). A similar sentiment is expressed by Allan Tindall in a recent review of socialization studies (1976:198). We do not as yet totally understand how we become cultural beings.

Although socialization theories are generally inadequate, it is possible to describe a number of learning procedures that may be common to most societies. In Read's account of the Ngoni, four procedures are distinguishable: (1) imitation and play; (2) punishment and threat; (3) verbal admonitions; and (4) formal education.

Play activities of children are often modeled on adult behavior. The doll play of Ngoni girls duplicates the activities of nurse girls and their wards. Ngoni boys imitate their fathers when they play at being councillors. Proper Ngoni sexual behavior is fostered by threats of physical punishment, and proverbs and verbal admonitions express correct standards of Ngoni behavior. One of the most striking features of Ngoni socialization is the boys' dormitory, an institution of formal education where ideal Ngoni norms of behavior are consciously instilled.

Growing Up in Six Cultures

Anthropologists studying socialization in non-Western societies have made use of two major theoretical orientations: learning theory and Freudian theory. Although studies of socialization in different societies are valuable, they often differed in research methods, observations, and theoretical orientation. This factor made the cross-cultural study of socialization difficult, because research findings from different studies were not always comparable. The Six Cultures Project, which began in the 1950s, was specifically designed to avoid the pitfalls of the earlier studies. Instead of studying a single society, the project investigated six societies — the Gusii of Kenya, the Rajputs of Khalapur in India, the village of Taira in Okinawa, the Mixtecan Indians in the town of Juxtlahuaca, Mexico, the Tarong of the Philippines, and Orchardtown, a small New England community.

A field research guide was designed to collect comparable information about socialization and was used by each of the research teams studying the six communities. Fieldwork lasted from six to fourteen months. In each of the six societies research teams conducted interviews with twenty-four mothers who had children between three and ten years old. Observations of mothers and children were recorded according to behavioral categories defined in the field research guide.

The Six Cultures Project combines controlled comparison with statistical comparison. A single cultural practice, socialization, is systematically examined in a small number of societies drawn from the broadest possible spectrum of cultural diversity. These data, based upon interviews and observation, provide the basis for statistical analysis. This research effort was stimulated by the Human Relations Area Files (HRAF), which stressed comparability, cultural diversity, and statistical analysis.

To analyze data from this project, the researchers defined socialization in terms of five dimensions: nurturance, self-reliance, achievement, obedience, and responsibility for the socialization of children. Each of the six cultures was assessed and evaluated in terms of these dimensions.

Two general conclusions emerge from the Six Cultures Project. First, socialization practices vary markedly from society to society, and second, socialization practices were generally similar and widely shared in each community. The Gusii, for example, use fear and physical punishment in the training of their children, while Taira adults use praise to obtain desired behavior. In Tarong, teasing and scaring are used to discipline children. Tarong mothers are rated as warm and indulgent to their children, while Rajput mothers rarely cuddle or kiss their children.

A major area explored in this study concerned the role of fathers in the training of their children. At one extreme are the Gusii, where fathers and sons physically avoid one another. In other cultures fathers play a minimal role in the rearing of young children. Only in Orchardtown (New England) do the fathers spend considerable time with their young children. This pattern is probably related to the neolocal household characteristic of American society. American mothers generally have very little help in bringing up their children; fathers, therefore, play a more important part in the socialization of children. In the quarter century since this study was carried out, the socialization role of fathers in American households has become even more important. Employment of women outside the household, single parent families, and the demand for an egalitarian division of labor in the home have fostered increasing involvement of American fathers in the rearing of their children.

Although the Six Cultures Project represents a significant advance in the study of socialization, many issues remain unresolved and controversial. It is not clear what the impact and meaning of different child-rearing practices have upon learning, development, and personality. Different societies use very different techniques in the transmission of culture, and all of them appear to be equally effective. Many recent studies have emphasized the diversity of behavior and personality types found within a single culture. If there is indeed a shared pattern of child-training practices characteristic of a particular culture, the presence of varied personalities in the same culture can be used to question the primary significance attributed to child-rearing techniques in the formation of human personality.

Child Training: A Freudian Approach

Many studies of child-training practices use a Freudian model of biological and social stages of maturation: oral, anal, phallic, and latency stages. A Freudian model assumes that the human infant passes through these stages of development in becoming a social and cultural being. In Freudian terms, individuals who do not successfully pass from one stage to another are viewed as fixated at a lower level of maturation. Such fixations manifest themselves in an individual's personality.

At the *oral stage* an infant's primary source of pleasure and gratification, according to Freudian theory, is suckling at its mother's breast. There is considerable variation between cultures regarding suckling. In some societies children are breast-fed whenever they cry, an indulgent pattern; in other societies they are fed on fixed schedules, a rigid pattern. Mothers in some cultures may be inconsistent in the suckling of their babies. Breast-feeding may persist for five or six years, or it may be limited to the first few months of life. Weaning may be sudden, abrupt, and traumatic, or gradual and drawn out. Among the Ngoni the decision to wean is not made by the mother, but by senior women. A Ngoni child is physically removed from the mother and weaning is abrupt and immediate.

Progression from the oral stage leads to the *anal stage,* in which it is claimed that the child receives pleasure from bowel and bladder retention and release. Societies have varied practices concerning urination and defecation. Ngoni children begin their toilet training at the age of four or five, a relatively late age

Toilet training is part of the child rearing practices of every human society. Some anthropologists believe that techniques of toilet training affect adult personality.

compared to most societies. Cross-cultural surveys show that parents in most societies begin toilet training their children between the ages of one and one-half to two and one-half years.

For Freud the *phallic stage* is a period of physical growth among males, accompanied by pleasurable genital awareness. Feelings regarding incest, castration, and love for the mother — the Oedipal complex — make themselves felt. Malinowski, on the basis of his study of Trobriand Islanders, criticized Freud's assumption of the cultural universality of this stage.

At about the age of six a child enters the *latency period.* During this stage there is a lack of concern with sexuality, and children are supposed to be most receptive to learning and relatively well behaved. It is interesting that in Ngoni and American society formal education

begins at the age of six. Malinowski once again challenged the universality of the latency stage, however, by documenting the sexual interests of Trobriand children at the age when this period is expected to occur (Barnouw 1979:30).

Initiation Ceremonies

Initiation ceremonies, common in many societies, mark public recognition of the change from one status to another, especially from adolescence to adulthood (see Chapter 8). Female and male initiation ceremonies often separate individuals from the rest of the society and involve physical mutilations such as circumcision, clitorodectomy (removal of the female's clitoris), scarification, and removal of teeth. These cultural dramas are seen as effective means of instructing young people in cultural values.

An alternative interpretation of male initiation ceremonies has been advanced by John Whiting, R. Kluckholn, and A. Anthony (1958:359–370). They hypothesize that in societies where young boys are closely associated with their mothers, the boys develop a cross-sex identity, or a feminine identity. This is most likely to occur especially where boys sleep close to their mothers for an extended period of time. In many polygynous societies a husband and his wives sleep in separate quarters, the children staying with their mothers. In these societies close mother-son contact is likely. Whiting and his colleagues point out that where male dominance and superiority are important, a cross-sex identity among males is undesirable. Thus dramatic initiation ceremonies involving separation, endurance, themes of death and rebirth, and physical mutilation are employed to break the cross-sex identity and establish a strong masculine identity. Variations of this hypothesis have been tested cross-culturally and appear to be substantiated (Barnouw 1979:140).

Sex and Gender in Socialization

Ngoni girls, playing with dolls, learn the role appropriate for Ngoni women; Ngoni boys, playing with weapons and mimicking their fathers' performance as judges, learn the roles appropriate for men. Socialization of Ngoni children clearly points them toward appropriate male and female behavior patterns. From the age of six Ngoni boys and girls tread different paths. At the age of six Ngoni boys are removed from their parental households and take up residence in dormitories. Their training is primarily in the hands of older boys rather than their mothers and other women. Ngoni girls do not move into a dormitory, but remain with their parents or grandparents. Although boys and girls do share certain personality characteristics, the work they do, their domains of authority, and the roles they play are quite different. In these respects Ngoni share in a cultural universal — differences based upon sex. All societies have a sex-based division of labor and attribute inherent behavioral and psychological differences to the sexes.

Ngoni construct a set of behavioral roles for females and males based on the biological differences between the sexes. A growing area of controversy and research in anthropology concerns the degree to which male and female role allocations are based upon inherent biological differences. In one extreme position the differences between males and females in temperament, aptitude, and many areas of behavior are assumed to be biologically based. At the other extreme, differences in temperament,

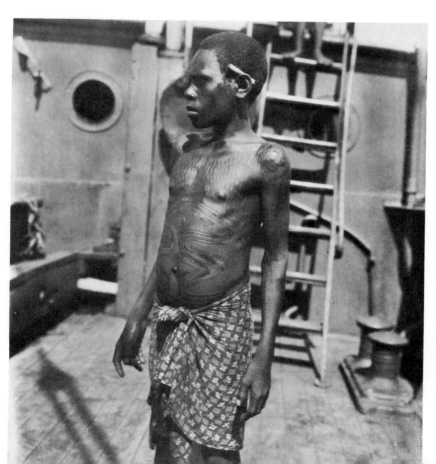

A New Guinea man showing the scarification on his face, chest, and abdomen acquired during a series of initiation ceremonies.

aptitude, and behavior are viewed as acquired during the process of socialization.

All societies use sex differences as a fundamental basis in role allocation. Certain activities appear to be linked to the biological differentiation of the human species. Care and rearing of young infants is primarily allocated to females. Mothers are the prime source of nutrition for their children. This connection, based upon a biological characteristic, sets the stage for the framework of female sex roles in cross-cultural perspective. Judith Brown (1970:1073–1078) points out that the subsistence role of women is related to their child-rearing commitment. According to Brown, if a subsistence activity does not interfere with the child-rearing activity, women can engage in both activities. The assumed incompatibility of particular subsistence activities, such as hunting and plowing, with child care responsibility explains the absence of women from these subsistence chores.

Much of the anthropological literature dealing with roles emphasizes the sex-based division of labor. Within many tribal and peasant societies, work responsibilities are divided into women's work and men's work; some activities are shared by both sexes. Nowhere are women the primary hunters of large game animals, nor do men usually have primary responsibility for the rearing of young children.

In a cross-cultural study of the division of labor by sex, Murdock and Provost (1973:203–225) distinguish three classes of activities related to sex. Hunting, manufacturing, mining, herding, trapping, and land clearing are primarily masculine tasks. Cooking, food preparation, laundering, fetching of water, gathering of fuel, and other domestic chores are primarily feminine tasks. Activities done by men in some societies and women in others include planting, harvesting, milking, basket weaving, and cloth making. Thus in a cross-cultural comparison we find some activities clearly related to sex, while others appear to be unrelated to sexual differences. We must point out, however, that this evidence is not proof of inherent biological differences between the sexes. It may, in fact, merely reflect the broad allocation of roles according to sex within the framework of broadly similar tribal and peasant societies.

The work of Murdock, Provost, and Brown concentrates upon economic activities. Most societies go beyond the allocation of economic roles by sex and build a set of male and female traits on the basis of sex differences. The Kaguru of East Africa, for example, associate firmness and order with men, while disorder and softness are attributed to women. A common belief in Mediterranean, Middle Eastern, and Indian cultures is that women cannot restrain their sexual impulses. In these cultures, therefore, male kin must control the sexual behavior of their women. The people of Colleíore assume that women suffer from the "long tongue," meaning that they are incorrigible gossips. In almost every society it is believed that differences in emotion, personality, and behavior are supposedly inherent for each sex. Usually the image of women is not only different from that of men, but also involves an evaluative component that places women in subordinate and low-valued status.

While recognizing the biological differences between females and males, the question becomes how far can these biological differences be used to account for the assumed gender differences in behavior, emotion, and personality? Martin and Voorhees, reviewing research data on aggression, indicate that young boys, ages three to six, are ". . . always more physically aggressive than their female agemates" (1975:45) Paralleling this finding, Beatrice and John Whiting, in an overall assessment of the material from the Six Cultures Project, document a number of sex-based uniformities that cut across cultural divisions: "At the three–five age period . . . boys engage

A scene from Collefiore, Italy. In rural Italy, young women are expected to use their spare time in useful and productive activity such as knitting and sewing. Young men have no such obligations and are free to pursue leisure activities such as loafing.

in more horseplay, rough and tumble physical contact; girls seek help or touch each other more frequently. . . . Nurturant behavior by girls increases rapidly as they grow older, while nurturance scores for . . . boys remain relatively constant" (1975:182). These findings suggest a genetic rather than a purely cultural basis for behavioral differences between males and females. Aside from these apparently biologically based differences, few patterns of behavior can be shown to have a genetic or hormonal basis, especially for temperament, aptitude, and personality.

Researchers have recently begun to investigate the hypothesis that many of the behaviors and characteristics attributed to females and males are not based on biological differences. Sex and gender roles are seen instead as a result of socialization, male dominance, and cultural definitions. Researchers have studied the Israeli kibbutzim to test these arguments concerning the influences of culture and biology on sex and gender roles. The European founders of these collective agrarian communities developed and thoroughly espoused an ideology of equality. In order to free women for participation in kibbutz economic, political, and military activities, the kibbutz assumes collective responsibility for the rearing of children and domestic chores. Infants and children are removed from their parents and reared in a collective dormitory. Women work in the fields alongside men and participate in the administration and management of kibbutz affairs.

A study by Nancy Datan finds that Israeli kibbutz women are beginning to take on a more feminine and motherly role (1977:326–343). Kibbutz women appear to desire greater femininity and sex appeal in their dress and voice strong desires to rear their own children. She also discovered that women are primarily engaged in domestic and service chores on the kibbutz and play a very minor role in productive and administrative activities.

This developing pattern of role differentiation between the sexes on Israeli kibbutzim appears to represent a return to traditional Western male and female roles. Why is this happening? One possible explanation is that inherent female tendencies, rooted in the biology of women, are reasserting themselves despite an ideology of sexual egalitarianism. An alternative explanation is that traditional Western cultural values regarding the proper role of females are more deeply rooted than commonly assumed and that they are reasserting themselves despite the ideological innovations introduced by the founders of the kibbutzim. Quite a different position is taken by Selma

Brandow (1979). She argues that there never was a true egalitarian ideology and that the growing femininity of kibbutz women is a continuation of male and female differences that are implicit in the kibbutz ideology. Brandow writes that the founders of kibbutz ideology

> did not really attempt to alter the existing sex stereotypes. Instead, both sexes appeared to continue to view men as responsible and rational, and women as weak and pliant. Taken all together then, the implicit aspects of the founders' ideology appear to have been much more powerful than those which were explicit (Brandow 1979).

Adult Socialization

From the preceding discussion, we might assume that socialization is a process restricted to infants and children. This is not true. Socialization is a process that continues throughout an individual's life and includes the acquisition of new statuses and their appropriate role behaviors during adulthood.

For Ngoni boys socialization into adult roles is a gradual and informal process beginning in childhood. For their American counterparts socialization into adult roles may require a different set of procedures. Few American adolescents directly observe and participate in the occupational roles of their fathers and mothers. In American society, furthermore, children may pursue occupations different from those of their parents. For most Americans occupational socialization occurs late in life, has few roots in childhood learning, and is primarily in the hands of nonkin.

One of the most abrupt and traumatic changes for Americans is career change: the movement into a new and different occupation. Women who leave their domestic chores as housewives for employment in business, industry, and government, as well as men and women who abandon one career for another, all face the difficulties of relinquishing one set of roles and norms for a new and different set. A new social personality must be developed in effect.

One of the most dramatic instances of adult socialization is described by Melford S. Weiss. He describes the training of paratroopers and

The tradition of tossing hats into the air at a West Point graduation represents initiation into the role of soldier and officer.

their initiation into this specialized segment of American culture. Paratroopers are separated from other members of the military during training. As paratrooper trainees they occupy a transitional state, and after successful completion of training they are incorporated into the group as full-fledged paratroopers. According to Weiss, successful completion of paratrooper training means a rebirth into a "new, select brotherhood and a new way of life." Bound to one another by training and pride, paratroopers see themselves as men who can "outdrink, outbrawl, and outwhore any other member of the armed forces" (Weiss 1967:23–26). The dramatic and demanding socialization of paratroopers is a consequence of this group's distinctiveness from the rest of society.

Dramatic transformations from one role to another are not unique to American society. Cheyenne Peace Chiefs must demonstrate many qualities and types of behavior that contrast sharply with those of a Cheyenne warrior (see Chapter 7). In order to become a Peace Chief, a Cheyenne man must demonstrate the qualities of bravery, aggression, and readiness to fight that are characteristic of a Cheyenne brave. As a Peace Chief, moderation, nonaggression, compassion, and avoidance of all hostility are part of this new role. It is not surprising that some men are unable and unwilling to make the transformation from warrior to Peace Chief.

Culture and Personality

Although anthropologists use a variety of definitions of culture, they all agree that culture is learned and shared by a group of people. Anthropologists assume that as individuals learn the content of their culture, they will grow up with behavioral and personality patterns distinctive to that culture. They hypothesize that individuals sharing similar cultural traditions will develop similar personality attributes. This

hypothesis concerning the relationship between culture and the individual is central to studies of culture and personality.

Cultural Diversity and Psychological Flexibility

Anthropology shares with psychology a common interest in the explanation and understanding of human behavior. Anthropologists use a comparative approach to emphasize the diversity of human behavior, while psychologists, because they lack a cross-cultural perspective, emphasize the uniformity of human behavior. This distinction between the two disciplines was probably more marked in the past than now, but it is a useful and still somewhat accurate way of presenting different orientations to the study of human behavior.

In the history of anthropology there has been fundamental disagreement between anthropologists and psychologists in three areas of human behavior: the Oedipal complex, adolescence, and normality.

Over half a century ago, Malinowski argued that the classic formulation of the *Oedipal complex* (see Chapter 5) as defined by Sigmund Freud was not applicable to the Trobriand Islanders and therefore could not be considered a *universal psychological dimension* of the human condition. Mead in her work among Samoan adolescent girls seriously questioned the notion accepted by most psychologists, that adolescent conflict and revolt are inherent stages in human maturation. Ruth Benedict argued that each culture developed its own standards and definitions of normality and abnormality. Benedict's position challenged many of the assumptions about abnormality developed from studies of mental illness in Western society. Although her position of *psychiatric relativism* is now questioned, she did force a reassessment of some of the assumed dimensions of normality and abnormality based upon a limited body of evidence.

Benedict's book, *Patterns of Culture* (1934), was an attempt to link individuals and culture through the concept of *ideal personality type.* Four cultures are used to illustrate her theory: the Dobuans of the South Pacific, the Zuni of the Southwestern United States, the Kwakiutl of the Northwest Coast of America, and the Plains Indians of the United States. She begins her argument by postulating that each culture is a unique and integrated configuration or pattern of cultural elements selected from the total range of possible human behavior. Each culture has a dominant drive that becomes the basis for selecting appropriate cultural elements; this drive permeates the entire cultural system. In growing up to be a Zuni, Dobuan, Kwakiutl, or Plains Indian, individuals attempt to model their behavior on explicit and implicit cultural definitions of the ideal human being. Zuni are expected to be moderate, cooperative, and submissive, dimensions that Benedict terms an Apollonian configuration. Dobuans are suspicious, distrustful, and feel persecuted, behavior that manifests their underlying "paranoid" configuration. Benedict calls the Kwakiutl "megalomaniacs" because of their stress upon pride, arrogance, and rank. Benedict considers the Plains Indians like the Cheyenne to be Dionysian, devoted to excess and seeking experiences that go beyond ordinary sensory capabilities. She cites the practices of self-torture, fasting, and the seeking of hallucinations as examples of a Dionysian configuration.

Benedict's approach poses a number of serious difficulties. Few cultures seem to be as integrated around a single dominant drive as she assumed. Critics of Benedict note that she avoided discussing behavioral patterns that did not conform to a particular society's major configurations. How the ideal personality is acquired is unclear in Benedict's model. In addition, Benedict overemphasized the uniformity of personality within a single culture; diversity of personality within a single culture appears to be both typical and common.

Although Benedict's work has been questioned and criticized, the contributions of Mead and Malinowski appear to have substantial support. Their work represents a significant and important aspect of the anthropological approach that testifies to the flexibility of the human psyche. Subject to the demands and constraints of culture, the human psyche exhibits considerable plasticity and pliancy.

Child Rearing and Personality

Basic to much of the culture and personality literature is the psychoanalytic approach pioneered by Sigmund Freud. An essential element in Freud's work is the assumption that the first few years of life are crucial in the formation of adult personality. How a child is raised as it proceeds through the maturation process becomes the foundation for its adult personality. Thus the weaning practices of the Ngoni, their toilet-training procedures, the shame and prudery inculcated in reference to sex, and the separation of young boys and girls are aspects of Ngoni socialization that a Freudian analyst would relate to their adult personality.

Using a Freudian approach, Ralph Linton, an anthropologist, and Abram Kardiner, a psychologist, in the late 1930s and early 1940s advanced a conceptual framework for the study of personality and culture (Kardiner 1939). They hypothesized that *child-training practices,* termed the *primary institution,* give rise to a *basic personality structure.* Linton and Kardiner argued that adults in a culture use a set of shared patterns and techniques to socialize their children. Following Freudian ideas, this hypothesis led to the conclusion that infants and children exposed to a common set of socialization practices will develop a common and shared personality type: the basic personality structure. This basic personality structure, in

Inconsistency and frustration appear to be part of Alorese child rearing practices and may be responsible for the temper tantrum of this Alorese child.

turn, influences and molds the other institutions of society, including religion, folklore, and art.

Cora DuBois's study of the people of Alor (1961) used Kardiner and Linton's approach. She found that inconsistency and uncertainty in Alorese child-training practices could be related to many forms of adult behavior. Alorese nursing mothers frustrate their children in a variety of ways. They may offer a breast when a child is not hungry, deny the breast when the child is hungry, and may or may not respond to crying fits and temper tantrums. An Alorese child is never sure of what response a mother will make. Alorese adults are described by DuBois as suspicious, distrustful, and fearful, which may be related to the frustrations they encounter during childhood. DuBois admits, however, that a connection between Alorese child-rearing practices, personality, and other institutions is neither clear nor direct (1961).

In studying the Alorese, DuBois used the Rorschach, or inkblot, test as a measure of Alorese personality. The Rorschach test, named after the Swiss psychologist who developed it, is a set of cards with inkblots on them. A person who is taking the test is presented with a card containing an inkblot and is asked to indicate what he or she sees. This technique assumes that an individual projects onto and into the inkblot major characteristics of his or her personality. Responses are then coded and interpreted in order to determine the dimensions of an individual's personality. Color and form are two important elements in interpreting the test. In a comparative study of American-born and foreign-born Chinese, for example, differences were noted in response to color and form. Chinese-born males and females responded to the form rather than the color of the inkblots, but American-born Chinese used color to determine form. These responses were interpreted as an indication that the foreign-born Chinese possessed greater emotional control (Abel and Hsu 1949).

Although much of the Freudian approach in anthropology emphasizes similarities in human personality, the work derived from Rorschach tests and field observations point to tremendous diversity in personality type within a single culture. In a reappraisal of her own work, DuBois indicates that diversity of Alorese personality types was more common than uniformity (1961:xx). Anthony Wallace studied the Tuscarora Indians of upstate New York (1952), using the Rorschach as a measure of personality. He discovered a wide diversity of personality types among them. Only a minority, about one-third of the Tuscarora, shared common personality dimensions (Wallace 1961). A consequence of this research and comparable findings in other societies is the recognition that there is more variability of personality within a culture than between cultures.

Subsistence and Personality

Early work in culture and personality emphasized the relationship between child rearing and personality. Some anthropologists subsequently attempted to link subsistence and economic patterns with certain personality attributes.

One of the most ambitious attempts to understand the relationship between subsistence and personality is found in the work of Walter Goldschmidt and his colleagues in East Africa in the early 1960s (Edgerton 1966, 1971; Goldschmidt 1976). Using the method of controlled comparison, they selected four tribal groups to study: the Kamba, the Hehe, the Sebei, and the Pokot. The Kamba and the Hehe are Bantu language family speakers; the Sebei and the Pokot speak languages that are part of the Kalenjin language group. Most importantly, within each of the four tribal groups there are separate populations engaged in horticulture and pastoralism. Each of the ethnographers in the project studied a particular tribe, but within each tribe they selected two communities: one horticultural and the other pastoral. In addition, members of the research team administered psychological tests, including Rorschachs, to representative groups in all four tribes and in

all eight communities. Thus it was possible to develop comparisons on the basis of language, tribe, and subsistence pattern.

Each of the two language groups has certain common elements, or a linguistic personality. Bantu speakers, regardless of tribe, believe in sorcery and witchcraft, place great value on land, desire sons, respect wealthy men, and their women look forward to old age. Kalenjin speakers, on the other hand, value cattle, desire both sons and daughters, respect prophets, and their women fear old age.

Each tribe, however, has a unique and consistent cluster of characteristics that distinguishes it from other tribes. Kamba fear poverty, restrain their emotions and impulses, and exercise male domination. Hehe are concerned with female authority, have a deep sense of mistrust and secrecy, and are characterized by impulsive aggression. Pokot have an intense interest in cattle, physical beauty, and sexual gratification, while Sebei fear disease, death, the malignant power of women, and have an overwhelming sense of jealousy and hostility.

Despite tribal and linguistic differences in culture and personality, communities with similar subsistence patterns were found to possess common personality characteristics. Horticulturalists, regardless of language and tribe, value hard work and cooperation, but are suspicious and hostile toward other members of the community. They are given to fantasy and abstraction, but also are anxious and less able to control and deal with their emotions and impulses. Pastoralists, in all four tribes, do not value hard work, act as individuals, are direct, open, realistic, and pragmatic. They control their emotions and their impulses (Edgerton 1965:446).

A conclusion that can be drawn from this study is that the sources of human personality are much more varied than suggested in the earlier literature, which focused primarily upon child rearing practices. There is obviously a tribal personality, a linguistic personality, and a subsistence personality. The emergence of a linguistic personality is particularly difficult to explain. The sharing of similar personality characteristics by members of the same language family could be the result of a common origin with traditions that have been carried from one generation to the next. There is also the possibility that the structure and grammar characteristic of a language family may affect an individual's responses to psychological tests. Economic pursuits clearly influence the values and dimensions of human character and personality.

Another attempt to determine the connection between economic conditions and personality characteristics is the concept of the *image of limited good* developed by George Foster (1965:293–315). Foster believes that a particular form of economy, peasant agriculture, leads to a common perception of the world. Peasants, he claims, view their world as composed of finite and limited resources. This view is not only applied to land, a scarce material resource, but also to health, love, honor, friendship, and sex. A person who increases his or her share of these scarce and valued resources is viewed as doing so at the expense of others. Any benefit for one is a loss for another. This basic orientation, in Foster's view, leads to particular personality and behavioral traits, including individualism, caution, reserve, secrecy, suspicion, mistrust, masculinity (machismo), respect, honor, and fear of change.

Foster's concept of the limited good has been widely criticized. Foster himself says, "I do not believe the image of Limited Good is characteristic only of peasant societies" (1965:311). If this orientation is found in other societies as well as under different economic systems, the personality and behavioral traits supposedly based upon it are not restricted to peasants.

A familiar situation from American student culture can be used to illustrate how an image of limited good can be established in a non-peasant society. When students are told by an instructor that grading in a course will be based upon a grading curve, they are faced with a situation of limited good. With a grading curve, only a small number of A's will be given and a small number of failing grades also must be given. It is unlikely that in such a setting student cooperation in studying and exam taking will emerge. Under these conditions, in fact, students will or should be suspicious, distrustful, individualistic, and secretive. In short, they will begin to resemble Foster's peasants.

Another problem with both the East African and the Foster studies concerns the meaning of personality assessment terms. The conclusions of the East African study were based upon the analysis of psychological tests, while Foster used ethnographic data. In neither case were exact definitions and meanings specified for the terms used. What do individualism, hard work, sexual aggression, and respect for authority really mean?

Culture and Mental Illness

Socialization transforms a human infant into a culturally defined human being. This transformation results, ideally, in individuals who are able to function effectively. Appropriate roles and behaviors are learned and integrated into a *normal* personality. Within the culturally specific definition of normality a wide diversity of personality traits and behavioral patterns are found. There are, however, certain behavioral patterns and personality traits that are defined as outside the range of normality. For some reason the process of socialization breaks down or is incomplete. Individuals exhibit levels of deviation and inappropriate behavior that mark them as *abnormal* or mentally ill.

In the comparative study of mental illness anthropologists often take two different approaches. One approach stresses a relativistic interpretation of mental illness; the other approach assumes that mental illness is a human affliction, largely independent of culture.

Over forty years ago, Ruth Benedict defined normality and abnormality in a purely relativistic manner. Each culture, according to Benedict, has its own definition of what is normal and abnormal. Normality in one culture may be viewed as abnormality in another culture.

Sociologists and psychologists more recently have advanced an interpretation of mental illness, called *labeling theory,* that draws heavily upon a relativistic approach (Murphy 1976:1019–1020). Labeling theorists argue that what becomes defined as mental illness is the consequence of labeling and categorizing vague and random forms of deviant behavior. An individual labeled as "mentally ill," "schizophrenic," or "depressive" begins to learn and accept the role of a mentally ill person. Once the stigmatized label is acquired, an individual's behavior is defined to fit the original diagnosis. In other words, labeling behavior as mental illness becomes a self-defining and self-fulfilling process.

An example of the self-fulfilling nature of the labeling process is illustrated by an experiment in which sane subjects voluntarily committed themselves to psychiatric hospitals (Rosenhan 1973). Once they were defined as having psychiatric problems, these subjects found that the interpretation of their behavior at the hospital justified the original diagnosis. If someone refused to write letters, for example, this behavior was interpreted as withdrawal, while someone who wrote many letters was seen as compulsive.

Labeling theory identifies the social perspective and situation of behavior as crucial to its definition and meaning. It could be argued that many people exhibit behavioral patterns on a daily basis that could be interpreted as aspects of mental illness if they took place in a mental hospital. In this relativistic approach, the label rather than the behavior draws the line between sanity and insanity.

At the time that Benedict and other anthropologists advanced the concept of cultural relativism, many psychiatrists and psychologists assumed a universalistic or non-relativistic definition of mental illness. This position is well stated by E. B. Forster, a psychiatrist with extensive experience in Ghana. He says,

> Psychiatric syndromes ... are similar in all races throughout the world. The mental reactions seen in our African patients can be diagnosed according to western textbook standards. ... Environment, constitutional and tribal cultural background merely modify the system. ... Basically, the disorders of thinking, feeling, willing and knowing are the same (Forster 1962:35).

In the last two decades many anthropologists have adopted this view of mental illness. Jane Murphy takes the position that notions of mental illness are found in every society, that behaviors defined as mental illness are broadly similar on a cross-cultural basis, that cross-cultural rates of mental illness tend to be the same, and that parallel forms of treatment are found in most societies (1976). Mental illness for her is "broadly distributed among human groups" and is "a type of affliction shared by virtually all mankind" (Murphy 1976:1027).

A limited body of cross-cultural data appears to support the position that psychiatric behavioral patterns are broadly similar in all societies. In Murphy's research among the Eskimo in the Arctic and the Yoruba of Nigeria, she discovered that both societies have a well-defined concept of insanity or mental illness. Called *Nuthkavihak* among the Eskimo, insanity manifests itself in such behaviors as talking to oneself, believing that one is an animal, refusing to talk, drinking urine, making strange grimaces, and threatening people. Yoruba identify *Were* or insanity as hearing voices, tearing off one's clothes, defecating in public and playing with the feces, hitting people, talking all the time or not talking at all, and throwing away food.

As part of the East Africa project, Edgerton investigated concepts of insanity held by members of four tribal groups (1966:408–425). He found that their ideas about psychotic behavior had a great deal in common and were not very dissimilar from concepts of insanity found in Western society or among the Eskimo or Yoruba. Psychotic behavior for these tribal groups is basically inexplicable, lacking reason or motivation. It includes nudity, eating dirt and feces, talking nonsense, inappropriate shouting and screaming, incest violation, solitary withdrawal, and acting like a child. In all four societies multiple causes for mental illness were recognized, including stress, worry, grief, poverty, and excessive drinking. As Edgerton points out (1966:415) this ambiguity about the causes of mental illness parallels the diagnosis of psychoses among Western psychiatrists and psychologists.

Murphy (1976:1027) summarizes the argument for cross-cultural similarity in mental illness by claiming "almost everywhere a pattern composed of hallucinations, delusions, disorientations, and behavior aberrations appears to identify the idea of 'losing one's mind.' " Edgerton identifies two distinct patterns of psychotic behavior: a mild and withdrawn pattern and a violent and aggressive pattern. As an example of the mild and withdrawn pattern Edgerton quotes an informant who describes one man with a mental illness:

> Old Eriyeza [a Sebei] is very mad indeed. He eats his own dung. He cannot even have intercourse with his wives. All day he hangs upside down from the roof of his house; he must be fed while he hangs this way. He has been made this way for about four years now. Recently, his son called for a Pokot doctor [a foreign specialist] to come in and treat him. This doctor came and

killed a bull, and squeezed some of its dung into some water. Eriyeza was made to drink this water but it did not help him . . . he still hangs upside down (1966:417).

To illustrate violent and aggressive behavior, Edgerton claims that "Kamba acts of violence can be violent indeed; a woman removed her husband's head with a large knife and kicked it around like a soccer ball for all to see . . ." (1966:417).

Murphy is a major proponent of the universalist position, but she recognizes that the particular content and symptoms of mental illness have a strong cultural component. Although Edgerton recognizes that psychotic behavior in the four East African tribes is broadly similar, there is a degree of tribal distinctiveness. Pokot are particularly given to arson, Kamba mention going naked more often than any other tribe, Hehe run away to the bush, and Sebei exhibit assaultive and violent behavior. It is this culturally specific aspect of mental illness that lends support to a relativist interpretation.

Culture-Specific Psychoses

In the anthropological literature there are a variety of mental illnesses that appear to be specific to particular people and places. Culturally specific psychoses may provide a basis for evaluating relativist and universalist interpretations of mental disorder. Descriptions of these disorders indicate that they reflect the general behavioral patterns described by Murphy and Edgerton for psychoses: hallucination, delusion, disorientation, and behavioral aberration. They also appear to be so distinctive, however, that they may reflect the overwhelming importance of unique cultural factors in their causation. Two of the best known culturally specific psychoses are *pibloktoq* and *running amok*.

Pibloktoq is a form of Arctic hysteria. Hysterical seizures have been noted for Eskimo groups, and similar syndromes have been described for the native populations of Siberia. Its

A Huli (New Guinea) man attempts to restrain his brother, who has been found demonstrating the behavior characteristic of running amok.

victims are principally women, but men also experience pibloktoq, and some observers claim that dogs can suffer from seizures of this disorder. Common behavioral characteristics of pibloktoq are running away, stripping off one's clothing, shouting, violent strength, compulsive body movements, and running around in the snow. These attacks apparently come on suddenly, may last up to a half hour or more, and leave its victims weak and spent. Reports indicate that pibloktoq sufferers may suddenly leap up, strip off their clothing, and run out naked onto the snow and ice fields. They do not assault others, but resist violently when someone tries to restrain them or bring them back to safety.

An intriguing psychosis, running amok, occurs in Malaysia, Indonesia, and New Guinea. Running amok is defined as wild man behavior, where a man goes berserk in a frenzy of aggression and destruction. There are apparently three stages in running amok: depres-

sion, withdrawal, and finally an outburst of destructive and aggressive behavior. In Indonesia and Malaysia, men running amok are often killed to put an end to their homicidal attacks on people. In New Guinea, however, amok sufferers are not harmed because they rarely attack anyone physically.

Pibloktoq and Amok: Universalist and Relativist Interpretations. One explanation for pibloktoq points to genetic causes; pibloktoq seizures resemble epileptic fits. A medical study of Siberian psychiatric patients identified 50 percent of them as epileptics. This study suggests that among Arctic populations, a genetic basis for epilepsy underlies attacks of pibloktoq. Anthony Wallace argues that inbreeding in these small and isolated Arctic populations may have resulted in a population in which a significant percentage of people have a genetic basis for epileptic or pibloktoq tendencies (Wallace 1961a:264). There are two basic problems with this explanation. As far as we know there is no firm evidence that pibloktoq seizures are actually epileptic seizures. In addition, the genetic basis of epilepsy and its genetic transmission have not been fully established. Thus a genetic explanation for pibloktoq still remains highly speculative.

Wallace has also advanced a nutritional or organic cause for pibloktoq, known as the calcium deficiency hypothesis (1961a). Wallace notes that dietary deficiencies, especially a reduced intake of calcium, result in a medical syndrome known as calcium tetany. Symptoms of calcium tetany strongly resemble attacks of pibloktoq. He hypothesizes that hysteria in Arctic populations may be the result of calcium deficiency. This hypothesis is appealing because Arctic diets are poor in calcium, and the lack of sunlight during much of the year would further aggravate this condition. This approach identifies pibloktoq as a medical and nutritional problem rather than a purely psychological one. Tests of this hypothesis have identified a tendency toward calcium deficiency in Eskimo populations, but the evidence is not conclusive (Foulks 1972:68).

Psychoanalytic explanations of mental disorders have been popular, and pibloktoq has been a major subject for psychoanalytic analysis. This interpretation has been universalist in nature, assuming basic impulses common to all humanity. A Freudian model of personality interprets the seizures as responses to frustration, the lack of love. Running away is seen as a seductive maneuver, an infantile desire to be pursued and loved (Wallace 1961:264; Freeman, Foulks, and Freeman 1978:203–210).

Cultural explanations have been common in the anthropological literature in explaining mental disorders. Unlike psychological theories, cultural theories focus upon particular cultural rules and situations as crucial in accounting for these culture-specific psychoses.

Cultural explanations focus on those aspects of Eskimo culture that stress passivity, cooperation, and inhibition of violence and anger in the process of interpersonal relationships. Jean Briggs's account of her difficulties with her Eskimo family when she spoke out openly and angrily is an excellent example of the personal and psychological inhibitions that Eskimo impose upon themselves (see Chapter 1). In addition, the intimacy of family life in small dwellings and the accommodation to others that this kind of life requires are an essential element of Eskimo life. Convulsive seizures and running away have been interpreted as responses to these living conditions. Because Eskimo are unable to express anger or aggression openly, pibloktoq becomes an alternative outlet.

The possible relationship between values of nonaggression and accommodation to small-scale social intimacy and hysterical attacks is intriguing. Evidence of such a relationship is provided in Joseph Louden's account of the people of Tristan da Cunha. Isolated in the middle of the South Atlantic, 2000 miles from South Africa, the 260 inhabitants of the Island of Tristan da Cunha occupy a territory of two square miles. Nonaggression and cooperation are highly valued aspects of this island culture. Louden reports that two psychological illnesses have a high incidence among these people. One takes the form of outbursts of epidemic hysteria; the other takes the form of severe frontal headaches. The explanation offered for these disorders is that the value placed on nonaggressive behavior is so great that anger toward others is displaced to the self, and that this displacement is the cause of epidemic hysteria and headaches (Louden 1970:292–332).

Amok has been described as an aggressive, wild, and destructive form of behavior. In Malaysia an individual running amok engages in a homicidal attack on other people. A slightly different pattern of running amok has been described by Philip Newman for the Gururumba of New Guinea (1965). Newman provides a cultural and contextual analysis of this pattern of behavior.

Running amok among the Gururumba consists largely of verbalized threats, mock attacks, demands for goods, and the taking of unimportant material objects. The onset of the attack is usually accompanied by sweating, a change in skin temperature, and trembling. In addition to these bodily changes, body movements are impaired, hearing and speech appear to be affected, and upon recovery the victim does not recollect the event. According to Newman, these attacks always occur in public and end by the individual running away into the bush for several days. Thus running amok for the Gururumba is much less disruptive and destructive than running amok in Malaysia.

Gururumba males from the ages of twenty-five to thirty-five, who are recently married, appear to be the only people who run amok in Gururumba society. This age, sex, and male role specificity is used by Newman to develop his relativist analysis of this behavioral pattern. Newman finds the sources of this psychosis in the social entanglements and pressures that surround this category of men. Recently married men incur bride-price debts that must be repaid. In addition, new marriages are often unstable, and divorce or separation can have a severe economic impact on these newly married men. At the same time they are being pressured into the complex and devious financial networks that are common in Highland New Guinea cultures. According to Newman, an individual announces his inability to participate fully in these social and financial entanglements by running amok. Newman thus concludes that running amok is not only generated by Gururumba social structure, but also communicates to others a message that modifies the image and expectations they have of such an individual.

Mental Illness in America: Economic Stress and Cultural Pattern.

Anthropologists may have retreated from the extreme relativism of Ruth Benedict, but they remain constant in their position that cultural factors play a crucial role in the genesis and pattern of mental disorders. This orientation can be seen in the cultural analysis of schizophrenia in American society. In a variety of research studies it has been found that the rates and symptoms of schizophrenia vary in different segments of the American population. Hollingshead and Redlich found social class differences in schizophrenia as well as other mental disorders (1958). They found that economically disadvantaged social classes suffered the highest frequency of mental illness. The conclusion could be drawn that the stresses and strains of economic deprivation and low self-esteem manifest themselves as mental problems. This position is substantiated by A. H. Leighton's work in Nova Scotia, where an economically deprived segment of the population also had high levels of mental illness (1961).

If social class in America is related to mental illness, it seems reasonable to assume that other sociocultural factors are also related to mental illness. Marvin Opler investigated the relationship between ethnic culture and patterns of schizophrenia (1959) by comparing Americans of Italian and Irish descent in a New York mental institution. He matched them for age, sex, religion, education, and I.Q. Comparison of these two groups showed two distinct ethnic patterns of schizophrenia. Irish schizophrenics felt guilty about sex, held rigid and systematic delusions, evidenced deeply repressed hostility to their mothers, and exhibited a generally withdrawn pattern of behavior. Italian schizophrenics, on the other hand, were much more likely to act out their schizophrenia in an excitable and aggressive manner. They were assaultive, suicidal, and destructive; they rejected authority, and they were given to temper tantrums and expressions of sexuality. From this study it appears clear that the cultural background of individuals has an enormous impact on the content and direction of their mental disorders.

Mental Disorders in Tribal Society. A popularly held notion in American society is that members of tribal societies, compared to people in American society, experience much lower levels of mental illness. This view is based to some extent upon a romanticized image of tribal societies, in which it is assumed that individuals do not face the stresses and strains common in complex urban-industrial society. Yet tribal people do not enjoy a trouble-free mental existence.

In a comparison of the prevalence of mental illness among Swedes, Eskimo, Yoruba, and Canadians, Jane Murphy found very similar rates of mental illness in these four populations (1976:1027). Murphy's research was based upon psychiatric surveys of the general population and was not limited to rates computed from hospital admissions. Comparative rates of mental illness computed from mental hospital admissions generally indicate low rates for tribal people. Such low rates are criticized as inaccurate, since few members of tribal society seek hospital care for mental disorders. Murphy's data can be interpreted as supporting the idea that mental illness is a fundamental affliction of the human species. Furthermore, if her findings are accurate, they indicate that in spite of the fact that different societies may vary in terms of how much stress they place upon their members it makes no difference in the rate of mental illness.

Treatment of Mental Illness

Labeling theorists have been highly critical of treatment procedures for the mentally ill in our society. Rosenhan's research indicates that once the staff of a psychiatric hospital diagnoses an individual as mentally ill, there is almost no way of reversing the diagnosis. Diagnosis and treatment of the patient, from the perspective of labeling theory, serve to socialize the individual into a mentally ill role. Based upon labeling theory approaches, criticism of

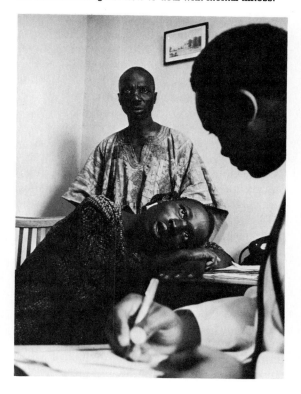

Nigeria's first psychiatrist, Dr. T. Adeoye Lambo, examines a patient in the presence of a native therapist who helps the British-trained psychiatrist in the analysis, with his own knowledge of how to deal with mental illness.

current treatment practices in American society has resulted in legislation that makes it difficult to commit patients to mental hospitals for long periods of time without their agreement (Murphy 1976:1027).

Marvin Opler, in a study of mental health in midtown Manhattan (1967:265–267), claims that 80 percent of the population suffers from some emotional disability. Based upon his study, he claims that almost a quarter of New York's population exhibit severe mental problems. Few of them, who were, according to Opler, as disturbed as patients in mental institutions, had ever received treatment.

If Opler's claims are valid, only a small percentage of the mentally ill in American society are placed under restraint. This factor might appear to justify the view stated earlier that mental illness is much more rampant in American society than in tribal society. The conclusion is not warranted, however. Murphy points out that there are four possible responses to the mentally ill that are found in all societies:

> If the behavior indicates helplessness, help tends to be given, especially in food and clothes. If the behavior appears foolish or incongruous, . . . laughter is the response. If the behavior is noisy and agitated, the response may be to try to quiet, sometimes by herbs and sometimes by other means. If the behavior is violent or threatening, the response is to restrain or subdue (Murphy 1976:1025).

Similar responses are found in American society. If individuals do not become violent or completely helpless, the most common response probably is to ignore their behavior. Finally, if we draw upon Edgerton's account of the Sebei man, old Eriyeza, the most powerful treatment for mental illness is a foreign specialist: a Pokot doctor. At one time the most powerful healer in American society for mental illness was also a foreign specialist: a Viennese-trained psychiatrist.

Summary

Socialization is the term used by anthropologists to describe the process of transforming human infants into cultural persons. Acquiring particular cultural values, allocating roles and behavior by sex, and developing a distinctive personality are part of this process, as we see in the way the Ngoni of Central Africa bring up their children. Among the Ngoni there is a clear conception of the ideal Ngoni human being. A variety of socialization techniques, including verbal precept, punishment and reward, imitation and play, and formal schooling, are used by the Ngoni to bring up their children to be proper Ngoni. Ideal Ngoni personality traits emphasizing achievement and hard work are related to their historical and political traditions.

Learning theory and Freudian theory are basic approaches to the explanation of how people are socialized. Learning theory emphasizes reward and punishment, imitation, and role models. Freudian theory emphasizes the internalization of cultural rules coupled with stages of maturation. These stages are oral, anal, phallic, and latency.

Many cross-cultural studies of socialization combine learning theory and Freudian theory. In the work of the Whitings and in the Six Cultures Project intensive fieldwork coupled with statistical comparison revealed the important role of different child-rearing practices in the formation of adult personality. Despite these and other studies, the impact and meaning of different child-rearing techniques are not entirely clear. An alternative approach to the understanding of personality formation is found in the work of Goldschmidt, Edgerton, and Foster, who identify an economic component in the formation of adult personality traits.

A controversial issue in contemporary anthropology is the impact of socialization on sex and gender roles. At the center of this controversy is the debate about the extent to which socialization reflects inherent biological differences between the sexes. In all cultures there is a division of labor based upon sex that can be linked to the reproductive role of women. Beyond this basic distinction, however, most societies attribute to both sexes fundamental differences in aptitude, temperament, and behavior. A number of anthropologists take the position that these differences are purely cultural products of the socialization process and do not reflect inherent biological differences.

Socialization involves not only the transmission of culture, but also the formation of individual personality. Culture and personality studies in anthropology focus upon the relationship between individuals and their culture. Recognition of cultural diversity led many anthropologists to stress the plasticity of behavior and personality. In the work of Linton and Kardiner, child-rearing practices leading to a basic personality structure were seen as primary institutions in a culture. Recently anthropologists have looked beyond child-rearing practices to other factors in personality development. Perhaps the most important finding in this area of anthropological research is the realization that differences in personality within a culture may be greater than differences between cultures.

Two divergent views of mental illness are now prevalent in anthropology. A relativist position drawing upon the work of Ruth Benedict defines normality and abnormality as cultural creations. A universalist view sees mental disorders as basically similar regardless of cultural content and causation. In recent years

many anthropologists have adopted this latter position.

Emergence of a universalist interpretation of mental disorder in anthropology rests upon comparative research. Cross-cultural studies by Edgerton and Murphy identify common definitions of insanity, similar patterns of psychotic behavior, comparable rates of psychoses, and parallel methods of treatment of the mentally ill.

A common definition of insanity focuses upon inexplicable behavior: people behave strangely for no apparent reason. Psychotic behavior is commonly accepted as falling into one of two general patterns: mild and withdrawn or violent and aggressive.

Limited data on rates of mental illness contradict the idea that high rates of mental illness are characteristic of urban and complex socie-ties. Mental disorders appear to occur as frequently in tribal societies as in our own society. Several patterns of treatment for the mentally ill are found in all societies: help, ridicule, tranquilization, and restraint.

Despite the widespread acceptance of a universalist explanation of mental illness, culturally specific psychoses are frequently explained in culturally specific terms. Thus while mental illness may be an affliction common to all humanity, particular cultural patterns and situations may have a significant impact upon who becomes ill and how the illness is manifested. Differential social class and ethnic patterns of schizophrenia among Americans support the idea that symptoms of mental illness are found in specific cultural situations and conditions.

Key Terms and Concepts

socialization
learning theory
internalization
Freudian theory
oral stage
anal stage
phallic stage
latency period
initiation ceremonies
Oedipal complex
psychiatric
    universalism
psychiatric
    relativism

ideal personality
    type
child training
    practices
primary institution
basic personality
    structure
image of the limited
    good
normality/abnormality
labeling theory
pibloktoq
running amok

Suggested Readings

Barnouw, Victor. *Culture and Personality*, 3rd ed. Homewood, Ill.: Dorsey Press, 1979. *A compre-hensive introduction to the field of psychological anthropology.*

Edgerton, Robert B. *Deviance: A Cross-Cultural Perspective.* Menlo Park, Calif.: Cummings, 1976. *A brief, cross-cultural survey that looks at people who steal, cheat, murder, lie, and just simply make trouble for others.*

Read, Margaret. *Children of Their Fathers: Growing up Among the Ngoni of Malawi.* New York: Holt, Rinehart and Winston, 1968. *A study of the Ngoni of Central Africa that focuses on the socialization practices of these people.*

Scheper-Hughes, Nancy. *Saints, Scholars, and Schizophrenics: Mental Illness in Rural Ireland.* Berkeley, Calif.: University of California Press, 1979. *A study that combines anthropological and psychological approaches to mental illness in an Irish village.*

Thompson, Richard A. *Psychology and Culture.* Dubuque, Iowa: Wm. C. Brown, 1975. *A concise overview of cognition, socialization, and culture and personality.*

Chapter 11

Language and Culture

Socialization is the process of converting a human infant into a culture-bearing person; language is a basic vehicle through which culture is learned and expressed. Human culture without language is both unthinkable and impossible. Whether culture is regarded as a learned system of behavior or as the domain of ideas and values, the importance of language remains undiminished.

From its inception cultural anthropology has included the study of language. In the early days of American anthropology many anthropologists were also students of language. They were especially interested in recording the languages of native Americans. The work of Boas and his students with American Indians, in fact, established the foundation for a branch of linguistics called descriptive linguistics. Descriptive linguistics involves the recording of non-written languages and an analysis of their grammar. Studies of the languages of tribal people, in conjunction with the comparative and historical study of languages with a documented history, were the foundation of linguistics as a specialized and distinct field of study. The development of linguistics as a study in itself created particular research methods, concepts, and theories.

Although linguistics is a specialized and distinct discipline, linguists and cultural anthropologists continue to share a common interest. Learning a language is basic to learning a culture, and therefore an understanding of the process of gaining linguistic competence is a central issue for both linguists and cultural anthropologists. Both linguists and anthropologists recognize that language is more than a device for the transmission of culture. Language and culture are inextricably linked, and the nature, meaning, and impact of this linkage are controversial and widely debated topics in both disciplines. In this chapter we will look at both the process of learning a language and the relationship between language and culture.

Learning Garo: A Fieldworker's Child in India

In 1954 Robbins Burling, with his wife and young son Stephen, arrived in the Garo Hills of Assam, India, where he planned to do field research among the Garo people for two years. Stephen was slightly more than one year old when they arrived. Because he was exposed to Garo speakers, and also in intimate contact with the Burlings' Garo-speaking servants, Stephen rapidly acquired fluency in the Garo language. Burling's record of his son's acquisition and development of Garo and English documents

Breaking the barriers of cross-cultural communication is one of the most delightful human experiences. An anthropologist's son and a San friend understand each other without spoken language.

the process of learning two languages simultaneously. It also illustrates some of the methods and terms used by linguists in the accurate recording of linguistic data.

Burling introduces a number of technical terms into his account: phoneme, morpheme, phonology, morphology, syntax, and lexical. *Phonemes* are the smallest units of sound recognized by the speakers of a language. *Phonology* is the system of sounds characteristic of a language. *Morphemes* are the smallest units of meaning in a language and usually contain more than one phoneme. *Morphology* is the systematic combination of morphemes to form words. *Syntax* is the system of rules underlying word order and the construction of sentences. *Lexical* refers to the vocabulary of a language. Burling uses these terms to designate the different aspects of the Garo language — sounds,

meaning, words, sentences, and vocabulary — that his son mastered. We will look at these terms in greater detail in our discussion of the structure of language.

Burling points out that his young son's babbling soon conformed to the sounds of both English and Garo. At first Stephen used a single set of sounds for both languages, but after some time he developed distinctive sound systems for each language. Although he learned both languages, Garo was the dominant one. His linguistic skill was demonstrated by his ability to translate freely from one language to the other and his fluent use of both languages, known as bilingualism. After leaving the Garo Hills and losing contact with Garo speakers, Stephen stopped using the language and apparently forgot it. Stephen's refusal to use Garo reflects the social context of speaking.

Stephen Burling with his Garo playmates.

LEARNING SOUNDS — PHONEMICS

When we arrived, Stephen was one year and four months old and was just beginning to attach meanings consistently to some of the vocal activity that he had been emitting in profusion for many months. His first few words were English, but he immediately came into regular contact with Garo speakers and soon added Garo words to his vocabulary; in fact, for the greater part of the time we were there, his Garo was significantly more fluent than his English.

Stephen began to use Garo words within a few weeks of our arrival, but his English vocabulary grew steadily and it was several months before Garo became clearly predominant. The eventual triumph of Garo was aided by a protracted hospitalization of his mother which removed him from close contact with his most important single English model. At this time, I spoke to him frequently in Garo, which diluted the effectiveness of the second major English source. Even after this the continued illness of his mother forced him into greater contact with Garos than might otherwise have been the case. The result was steady progress in the Garo language, which I believe he learned in much the same way as any Garo child.

When we arrived in the Garo Hills, Stephen had a total vocabulary of a mere dozen words, but even those required a considerable phonemic inventory. He had then three vowels, five consonants, and a distinction of voice and aspiration.

At this time all of his words were of the form CV or CVCV [C = consonant; V = vowel]; if the latter, the two syllables were always identical. The first progress after our arrival came at one year and five months when he learned suddenly and decisively to use two different syllables in the same word, including either different vowels or different consonants. "Kitty" was then pronounced as *kiti*

rather than as the earlier *kiki* and one of his first Garo words was *babi* (standard Garo *ba-bir-si*) "cook," his name for our cook.

At least until early in his third year, however, his speech was most efficiently described as a single phonemic system. It was an approximation to Garo, with the addition of a few phonemic distinctions which are not found in that language. Even at the age of 2:7 his Garo was clearly better than his English, and he could still be described as speaking a variety of Garo that happened to have a great many English loanwords. Some of the phonemes of his speech were found only in these loanwords, but there was no indication that he recognized these words, or these phonemes, as having any special status. Other English phonemes were interpreted by him according to Garo speech patterns.

By 2:8 and 2:9 I felt that Garo and English were becoming differentiated as phonemic systems. Many English vowels now seemed to be becoming fixed in positions slightly different from the nearest Garo vowels, although since the differences were often small and since there was so much free variation in his speech, it was not easy to specify exactly the moment of separation.

In other words, in the two months from 2:7 to 2:9 a systematic separation of the two vowel systems took place, and it was impossible to continue to describe them as one system.

LEARNING WORD ORDER — SYNTAX

[When Stephen was] one year and seven months, I began to notice a few utterances which, from an adult point of view consisted of more than one morpheme. He would say *cabo* (<Garo, *ca?-*"eat" and *-bo,* the imperative suffix); *galaha* (<Garo *gar-*"fall" and *-a-ha* "past"); *kukigisa* (Garo *cookie ge-sa*) "one cookie"; *guboi* "good boy." Gradually he acquired more such forms, particularly combinations of verb bases with one or another of

the principal verb suffixes which indicate such things as tense. He regularly used the suffix which he heard most often with the verb, as the imperative forms of "eat" and "get dressed" and the past of "fall," since "falling" was most often discussed after it happened.

Then on the first day of May, at one year and eleven months, I was sure for the first time that he could use suffixes freely and add any one of several suffixes to any verb. This was a decisive step and after that, he constantly produced new forms. On virtually the same day, he also was able to form syntactical constructions with a noun subject and a verb. Both morphological and syntactical constructions came at the same time and once the initial ability to make substitutions was gained, he went forward rapidly with more and more complex constructions.

Soon after his use of subject-verb sentences, he started to use verbs with nouns in other cases. My first recorded example is on May 17, two and one half weeks after his first construction: *papaci reaŋna* "go to Papa." On June 4, I recorded two three-word sentences (four and five morphemes respectively): *aŋa tolet naŋa,* "I need toilet," and *lala bi taleŋa* "Emula is preparing the bed." In both these examples one word was derived from English, though the word order, morphology and phonology were all completely Garo. This assimilation of English words into Garo was characteristic of his speech for as long as we were in the Garo Hills.

VOCABULARY AND MEANING

At 2:9 Stephen began for the first time to ask explicitly about words. He would occasionally start to speak, pause, point to something, and ask *wats dis;* receiving an answer, he would proceed to use the word in his sentence. He asked such questions equally well in both English and Garo. He also talked about words,

though it was difficult to know how well he grasped the sense of the sentences he used. For instance, he would point to his nose and say *in English it is nose,* or *in Gawo it is giŋtiŋ,* but he would sometimes get these reversed and call a Garo word English or vice versa. When he was two years and ten months old, I was able to interest him in playing a game with me. I would ask him a question such as "What does hand mean," and he would promptly supply the Garo equivalent; or, if I supplied him with a Garo word, he would return the English. He gave no indication that he noticed which language I presented him with, but consistently gave the opposite one. When I asked for the meaning of the word "table" however, for which the Garos use a word borrowed from English which is phonetically similar to the original, Stephen paused only briefly and then supplied the translation "dining room table." At 2:9 also, he started using the word *said* and its Garo equivalent *a-gan-a* correctly and with understanding in direct speech — another indication of his growing awareness of speech as a phenomenon that can be talked about. In either Garo or English he was able to say such things as *I said "sit down!"*

BILINGUALISM

As early as the age of 1:6, not quite two months after our arrival, I recorded what then seemed to me like translation. If we asked him if he wanted milk, he would unhesitatingly indicate the affirmative with the Garo equivalent *dut* "milk." However, six months later I could still find no evidence that he was really aware of the existence of two different languages in his environment. As in the case of *milk* and *dut* he did recognize that there were two words for certain things and sometimes he would say them together, one after the other, clearly recognizing that they were equivalents. But all his constructions at that time were completely Garo, the only significant English influence being lexical.

We spent about two months from the middle of July to the middle of September (2:1 to 2:3) in Gauhati, Assam, away from the Garo Hills, where Stephen came into contact with several English speakers, as well as numerous Assamese speakers. He continued to be cared for to a great extent by his Garo "ayah" [nursemaid], who even sought out the companionship of other Garos, so his contact with that language was never broken. But while we were in Gauhati, I began to feel that he really recognized the existence of the separate languages. He quickly learned who did not speak Garo and rarely attempted to speak to them. He was always more shy with them than with Garo speakers. By 2:3 he could understand a considerable amount of English, but spoke little. He then showed a facility for translating exactly what was said in English into idiomatic Garo. If I asked him a question in English, he was likely to give an immediate and unhesitating reply in Garo.

After returning to the Garo Hills, life was somewhat more normal. He had more continuous and intimate contact with his mother than he had had for some months. This finally resulted at the end of 1955, when he was two and one half years old, in an explosive expansion of his ability in English. Though his English never caught up with his Garo as long as we stayed in the Garo Hills, he developed a taste for speaking English with native English speakers and to my chagrin he came to prefer to speak English with me. Occasionally, when I failed to understand his still very foreign English, he would with obvious condescension translate into Garo, which, being said more correctly, was easier to understand. He translated without hesitation and with no apparent difficulty in switching from one language to the other. He frequently spoke to me in idiomatic English and immediately repeated it in just as idiomatic Garo for someone else's benefit.

THE LOSS OF GARO

When we left the [Garo Hills], there was still no doubt that Garo was his first language (when he spoke in his sleep, it was in Garo) but English had become a flexible means of expression as well. We spent about a month traveling across India. At first he attempted to speak Garo with every Indian he met, but by the end of the month was learning that this was futile. I tried to speak Garo with him from time to time, but he rarely used full Garo sentences even then.

The last time he ever used an extensive amount of Garo was on the plane leaving Bombay. He sat next to a Malayan youth who was racially of a generalized southern mongoloid type, so similar to many Garos that he could easily have passed for one. Stephen apparently took him for a Garo, recognizing the difference between him and the Indians that had failed to understand his language in the past weeks. A torrent of Garo tumbled forth as if all the pent-up speech of those weeks had been suddenly let loose. I was never again able to persuade him to use more than a sentence or two at a time. For a couple of months he would respond to Garo when I spoke to him, but he refused to use more than an occasional word. After this, he began failing even to understand my speech, though it was frequently difficult to know just how much was really lack of understanding and how much was deliberate refusal to cooperate. Certainly at times he would inadvertently give some sign that he understood more than he meant to, but increasingly he seemed genuinely not to understand, and within six months of our departure, he was even having trouble with the simplest Garo words, such as those for the body parts, which he had known so intimately (Burling 1959:45–47, 53–54, 56, 58, 61–63).

Context of Bilingualism

Bilingualism is the ability to speak two languages fluently. It includes, as illustrated in Stephen's case, the ability to translate easily between the two languages. There are two major situations in which bilingualism is common. The first is migration: speakers of one language move into another speech community. Although these migrants may acquire some competence in the new language, usually it is their children who become true bilinguals. These children can, like Stephen, switch back and forth between the two languages, keeping them phonemically and idiomatically distinct. The other situation in which bilingualism occurs is in communities where more than one language is spoken. This situation is found most frequently in linguistic border areas. Certain areas of Switzerland, Belgium, Scotland, and Wales are European examples of this phenomenon. In India, where fourteen different regional languages are spoken, bilingualism is common. R. F. Salisbury describes a situation in the Highlands of New Guinea where people speak not only two or three dialects of their own language, but also dialects from a totally different language family (1962). Many American Indian children also become bilingual, learning and using their Indian language at home while learning English in school.

Stephen's bilingualism was unusual, for it involved neither migration nor a bilingual speech community. Another exceptional aspect of this case is that his father, a linguistic anthropologist, carefully recorded his utterances and acquisition of both languages. Although many fieldworkers acquire a certain level of fluency in the language of the people they study, few, if any, systematically record their process of language acquisition.

Despite the somewhat unusual circumstances of Stephen's bilingualism, his acquisition of language followed a known pattern experienced by all normal human infants, whether *monolingual* (speaking a single language), *bilingual* (speaking two languages), or even *multilingual* (speaking three or more languages).

Stephen arrived in the Garo Hills at the age when infants begin to learn language. If he had been ten or twelve years old, his response to the Garo language would certainly have been different. As his father notes, he was on the threshold of meaningful speech, and he had already mastered about a dozen English words. Before this time he was babbling and vocalizing a range of sounds. Part of the initial step in language acquisition is the transformation of infant vocalizations into recognizable phonemic utterances. Stephen initially used a single sound system for both English and Garo words, but he subsequently developed two distinct phonemic systems.

Acquisition of language is based upon social interaction with adult speakers of a particular language. As a child, Stephen's English language models were his mother and father, while his Garo nursemaid and other Garo speakers were his Garo language models. The dominance of Garo over English can be attributed to the illness of his mother at a crucial time in his life. For a number of months his most intensive language contact was with his Garo nursemaid.

Studying bilingual children provides an opportunity for examining the social use of language, an issue that may not be as overtly visible with monolingual children. It is clear from Burling's account that Stephen, even as a young child, was acutely sensitive to the social context of language use. He clearly distinguished between Garo and English speakers, and he felt more comfortable in the presence of Garo speakers. Although his father spoke Garo, Stephen did not identify him with Garo speakers and used English when conversing with him.

There are two possible explanations for Stephen's unwillingness to speak Garo with his father. As an adult learning a language late in life, Burling probably retained an English phonemic system when speaking Garo; that is, he spoke Garo with an accent. He may not have achieved the linguistic skill that Stephen appeared to have attained, especially Stephen's idiomatic bilingualism. To Stephen, therefore, his father may have been an unskilled Garo speaker. An alternate explanation is that Stephen identified the Garo language with a class of speakers who shared distinctive physical characteristics. His attempts to speak Garo to Indians and later to a Malaysian youth who resembled the Garo physical type could be interpreted as the evidence for this position. Perhaps his unwillingness to speak Garo to his father occurred because his father did not look like a Garo.

The most dramatic aspect of this account is the total extinction of Garo from Stephen's speech patterns within a very short time. After leaving the Garo Hills, because he was unable to find Garo speakers his utterances in Garo were unrecognized and elicited no response. This lack of positive response was instrumental in extinguishing Garo as a means of communication for Stephen.

Language and Culture in Comparative Perspective

Linguists estimate that there are between 3000 and 8000 different languages spoken in the world today (Fromkin and Rodman 1978:329). The majority of these languages are unwritten. Early linguistic fieldworkers faced the problem of obtaining accurate and adequate data from the spoken utterances of their language informants. In response to this problem linguistic anthropologists developed the field of descriptive linguistics. Descriptive linguistics is primarily concerned with the identification and description of the discrete units of language, ranging from individual sounds (phonology) to sentence formation (syntax).

One of the first results to emerge from intensive research on languages spoken by tribal people was the recognition that there is no such thing as a "primitive" language. All languages have a system of sounds, words, and sentences that can adequately communicate the content of the culture. In addition, the grammatical structure of many tribal languages is exceedingly complex and complicated. Although languages vary greatly in their vocabulary, or lexicon — tribal people obviously had no words for steam engine or rifle — every human language can create new words and forms to describe new situations and objects.

In many ways, language resists the numerous forms of analysis that can be applied to other human activities. Cross-cultural comparison of economic, political, marital, and household systems indicates either some degree of evolutionary change or correlation with other aspects of a culture. This change or correlation is not generally true for language. Aside from the obvious fact that a vocabulary of a language may reflect the interests and material inventory of a culture, there seems to be no correlation between a language's complexity, structure, or grammar and other aspects of a culture. Technologically simple hunting and gathering groups may possess exceedingly complicated languages that are extremely difficult to learn. Paralleling this lack of correlation between language and other aspects of culture is the clear lack of any evolutionary sequence of languages from simple to complex. Language, while part of culture, appears in many respects to be separate from culture.

In recent years some linguists have shifted their interests away from language description and analysis. Many contemporary linguists and anthropologists now examine as major issues the definition of language, the components of language, the acquisition of language, the uniqueness of language as a human form of communication, the relation of language to thought, the cultural context of speaking, and the impact of language on behavior.

What Is Language?

St. Augustine, in commenting on the subject of time, said that he knew what time was as long as no one asked him to explain it. Language can be described in the same way. Each of us has a notion of what we mean by the term language, but we have difficulty in formulating a comprehensive definition. Linguists, who are professional students of language, apparently face the same problem.

James Spuhler, in a recent survey of linguistics, documents the inability of linguists to agree on a definition of language (1977:513–514). Some definitions emphasize the structure of language (grammar), while others emphasize the functions of language (information and communication). A major controversy swirls around the uniqueness of language. Some definitions consider language unique to humanity; others do not. As Spuhler points out, one definition of language, a "system of communication," grants language to insects. At the other extreme, Noam Chomsky, a major figure in contemporary linguistics, takes the position that language is "the human essence . . . unique to man" (1972).

A reason for this widespread disagreement is the recognition that communication exists among other animal species, and human language is only one form of communication. Bees have evolved complex dance and movement patterns that communicate the location of pollen. Great apes (chimpanzees and gorillas) use a variety of sounds, gestures, and expressions to communicate sexual receptivity, excitement, aggressive behavior, and fear. The essential problem is how to distinguish language as a distinct form of communication.

Two linguists, Victoria Fromkin and Robert Rodman, provide a minimal definition of language as consisting of sounds produced by an individual that signify certain meanings which can be shared and produced by others (1978:1–2). This definition, however, does not identify some of the vital criteria of language. A basic characteristic of human language is the purely arbitrary nature of its sounds and their meanings. Most linguists agree that no human language uses all of the potential sounds that can be generated by the human vocal tract. In addition, the most distinctive attribute of human language is the purely arbitrary nature of meaning given to words. When Stephen Burling used the Garo word *dut* as well as the English word *milk* to refer to the same white liquid obtained from cows and other animals, he demonstrated the arbitrary nature of words and sounds in language. There is no inherent connection between words in any language and what they represent. This symbolic and learned nature of language may make it a unique form of communication found only among human beings.

Structure of Language

Every verbal language consists of a set of sounds. Linguists divide the study of sound into two categories: phonetics and phonemics.

Phonetics is the study of the physical attributes of the sounds we make. These sounds can be measured and described by linguists using a commonly agreed-upon notational sys-

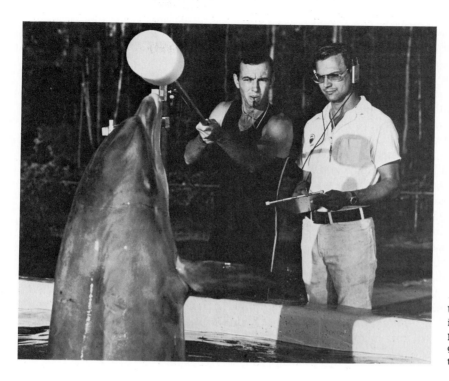

Underwater accoustical studies are being conducted with porpoises to explore the language that these animals use to communicate.

tem, called the International Phonetic Alphabet. Carol Eastman points out, for example, that to the linguist the [p][1] sounds in the words *pen* and *sleep* represent two distinct phonetic sounds (1975:6). The [p] in *pen* is pronounced with a puff of air, while the [p] in *sleep* is not. In terms of the physical manner in which they are produced, they are different sounds.

Phonemics is the study of the sounds in a language that are recognized and distinguished by its speakers. A *phoneme* is the smallest unit of sound that can be altered to change the meaning of words. Thus the three words *pin, tin, sin* have distinct meanings in English and are recognized as different by English speakers. The phonemes are /p/, /t/, and

/s/. Despite the phonetic distinctions between the [p] in *sleep* and in *pen*, they are phonemically the same for English speakers.

Sounds are combined into larger units called *morphemes*. A morpheme is the smallest combination of sounds that has meaning and cannot be broken into smaller meaningful units. Words can be composed of one or more morphemes, but not all morphemes are words. The word *like*, for example, is a single morpheme. *Dislike* and *unlike* are words composed of two morphemes. However *dis* and *un*, although morphemes, cannot stand alone. Most of the parts of speech called prefixes and suffixes in English are morphemes that must be combined with other morphemes to form words. For this reason they are called bound morphemes.

Morphemes in the form of words must be combined into larger utterances, either

---

[1] Linguists use brackets [ ] to enclose phonetic sounds and slashes / / to enclose phonemes.

phrases or sentences. These larger utterances are the forms of normal speech. There are complicated and complex sets of rules learned by every normal speaker of a language that permit the combination of morphemes into meaningful utterances. In linguistics the set of rules that determines the meaningful organization of words into sentences and phrases is called syntax. In English word order affects meaning, but this may not be true in other languages. The three morphemes, *you, are, there*, can be combined in three different ways. Thus *you are there, there you are*, and *are you there?* are all meaningful but different sentences in English. While *you there are, there are you*, and *are there you?* all contain meaningful morphemes, they are meaningless when presented in this order. In English they are syntactically unacceptable. Since different languages use different word orders and different techniques of sentence structure literal, or word for word, translations often appear bizarre and lack meaning.

In Latin, for example, word order is generally irrelevant to meaning. The English sentence "The father loves his son" can be expressed in many different ways in Latin. The Latin sentence that duplicates the word order of English is: *Pater amat filium*, "the father loves (his) son." The following sentences, with literal English translations, are all permissible in Latin: *Pater filium amat*, "the father (his) son loves"; *amat filium pater*, "loves (his) son the father"; *amat pater filium*, "loves the father (his) son"; *filium pater amat*, "(his) son the father loves"; *filium amat pater*, "(his) son loves the father." When translated word for word into English these sentences sound strange and confusing, but in Latin they all have the same meaning: "the father loves his son." In Latin the meaning is determined by endings — suffixes — added to words. In order to change the meaning of the above sentence to "the son loves his father," *filium* would have to be changed to *filius*, "the

son," and *pater* to *patrem*, "his father." Then you could write *patrem amat filius*, "the son loves his father."

Native speakers of a language cannot memorize all the possible sentences that can be created in their language. What is incredible about language is the ability of native speakers of a language to generate and understand completely new, unique, and correct sentences or phrases in their language. They obviously have learned syntactic rules that underlie the creative aspect of language. This aspect of language is one of the intriguing and controversial areas of contemporary linguistics.

How the "correct," that is grammatical, sentences of a language are generated is central to the work of Noam Chomsky. His work has led to the development of a theory of language known as *transformational–generative grammar* (1957). This theory postulates that the propensity for language and grammar is a basic attribute of all humanity and that there is a universal grammar underlying every human language. According to this theory all languages reflect logical structures of the mind, distinguishing basic syntactic components and categories. These components and categories constitute a syntactic base that generates deep structure and transformational rules.

Deep structure is the underlying grammatical form of the sentence that is transformed by a set of rules, the transformational rules, into the actual utterance or surface structure. Thus this theory seeks to uncover and make explicit the complex rules that human beings acquire unconsciously and implicitly in the process of language socialization.

Proponents of transformational–generative grammar represent a shift away from descriptive linguistics. Instead of ascertaining the units of language, these theorists are primarily interested in the rules that underlie linguistic performance. The sentence is the core element in their analysis of language.

The transformational-generative grammar theory is making a major impact upon cultural anthropology. Anthropologists who favor cognitive and structural theories draw upon transformational–generative theory in their analysis of behavior. They are interested in uncovering the hidden rules that lie beneath the diversity of cultural acts.

Acquiring and Learning Language

How children actually learn a language is not entirely clear. Obviously children acquire phonemic, morphological, and syntactic competency as they mature, but the mechanisms of learning are not well understood. Chomsky believes that children are inherently capable of developing transformational–generative grammars that provide the basis for the creation of meaningful utterances.

Some of these processes can be seen in Stephen Burling's acquisition of Garo and English. His first sounds were babbles, and eventually these were transformed into sounds that were not distinctive for the two languages. His first sound was /a/, a vowel that appears to be a child's first vowel whatever the language (Greenberg 1975: 92). Burling notes that his son began to form morphemes by duplicating sets of consonants and vowels in such words as *papa* and *kiki*. A word like *kiki* (kitten) was subsequently transformed into *kiti*. By the age of two and one-half Stephen was forming sentences in both Garo and English as his language repertoire and linguistic skill expanded.

Stephen's acquisition of Garo and English tends to be consistent with research findings in the study of child language. Studies of infants indicate that they generate phonemic utterances at an early age. By the end of the first year of life some of these phonemes are combined into morphemes. Morphemic usage shows a dramatic increase in the first few years of life. From about three morphemes used at the age of one, the average American child uses about 2500 morphemes by the age of six. The combination of morphemes into simple sentences also begins at about two years of age (Williams 1972:259–260). Recent studies of infant language indicate that very young children develop a grammar of their own. This language is usually referred to as "baby talk," even though it is not a simplified version of adult grammatical usages. Children attempt to systematize and regularize their own simple utterances. Grammatical overregularization is a process generally recognized in children's language acquisition. Young children who have learned grammatical rules tend to use them in all situations. Thus children who "know" the general rule for constructing the past tense in English, the addition of -*ed* to verbs, also use this rule for irregular verbs. As a consequence, they form words such as *gived, taked, hitted,* and *runned.* Children also overregularize in the construction of plurals, generating such delightful words as *mouses, foots,* and *tooths.* This tendency toward overregularization is not restricted to English-speaking children but occurs with all children. Overregularization suggests that children have in some manner acquired basic grammatical rules and apply them to new utterances.

Acquisition of language is a long and complex process. It is generally assumed that human beings are born with a capacity for language learning. Children are so expert in acquiring language proficiency, in fact, that it seems as though their brains are in some manner programmed for language learning (Fromkin and Rodman 1978:254). Yet, children must have adult speakers in order to translate their inborn tendencies for language into reality. This view is reinforced by studies of institutionalized children who are not exposed to competent adult speakers and whose langauge skills and proficiency are severely retarded.

Is Language Unique to Human Beings?

A question confronting cultural anthropologists, linguists, and psychologists is the degree to which culture and language are unique to human beings. Part of the problem stems from the lack of agreed-upon definitions of language and culture. Recent studies of nonhuman primates document their ability to make and use tools, a task considered to be diagnostic of culture (Lancaster 1975). Some primate behavior also appears to represent a learned and continuous social tradition, which is another diagnostic feature of culture (Lancaster 1975:51). These capabilities, no matter how limited, are considered manifestations of culture by some anthropologists. Other anthropologists consider the so-called cultural traits of the great apes to be so limited that they continue to see a great gap between human culture and primate behavior. It does seem evident, however, that some aspects of great ape behavior have a cultural component. To the extent that anthropologists are willing to accept these behaviors as cultural, culture is no longer an absolutely unique attribute of humanity.

Language remains the solitary barrier separating human beings from the great apes. None of the great apes has a spoken language, and the vocal sounds they make appear to have no symbolic content. Even this barrier appears to have been breached, however, by recent experiments that have succeeded in teaching a form of human language to chimpanzees and gorillas.

In the late 1960s a wife and husband team of psychologists, Beatrice and R. Allen Gardner, conducted an experiment that challenged the idea of the uniqueness of human language and the limited capacity of great apes for symbolic activity. The Gardners realized that earlier attempts to teach verbal language to chimpanzees failed because of the chimpanzee's physiological inability to produce the kinds of sounds that humans make in their language. They argued that this physical limitation did not reflect the true mental capacity that chimpanzees have for symbolic learning and communication. Instead of teaching a chimpanzee to speak, the Gardners taught a chimpanzee named Washoe the sign language used by deaf Americans, AMESLAN (Gardner and Gardner 1969).

AMESLAN (American sign language) is a language based upon symbols using finger, hand, and facial configurations and movements. This gesture based language has a structure comparable to the phonemes, morphemes, and syntax of verbal speech. The signs of AMESLAN are as arbitrary as the sounds of speech, and the full range of information available to sign users can be communicated through this language. Children acquiring AMESLAN go through developmental stages that are similar to the stages children go through in learning a verbal language. AMESLAN is a specific language and is different from sign languages used in other parts of the world. AMESLAN is also developing dialectical variations, which testify to its arbitrary and symbolic nature. Watching someone use AMESLAN is, for most people, comparable to listening to a foreign langauge.

Washoe proved to be an apt student of AMESLAN. She mastered 130 signs in a four-year period and regularly used AMESLAN to communicate with her human companions. At about the age of four, Washoe was transferred to a center for primate studies in Oklahoma, where she has continued to expand her use of AMESLAN.

The excitement generated by the Washoe experiment led to additional studies of the capacity of primates for learning to use symbols. By using plastic symbols and computer keyboards, as well as AMESLAN, researchers have shown, even on a preliminary basis, that chimpanzees possess the mental capacity for acquiring, using, and manipulating symbolic forms.

A direct descendant of the Washoe experiment is the work of Francine Patterson, who is teaching AMESLAN to a female gorilla, Koko. Patterson claims that Koko has mastered more than 600 AMESLAN signs and uses about 400 of them regularly in "conversation" with her human companions. In addition, Koko has been helping to teach AMESLAN to a young male gorilla, Michael.

Koko appears to be a sophisticated user of AMESLAN. She is able to argue with and insult people in this language, as well as create new words to express herself. The following argument between Koko and one of Patterson's assistants is an illustration of Koko's linguistic competence.

> The dispute began when Koko was shown a poster of herself that had been used during a fund-raising benefit. Manipulating hands and fingers, Cathy had asked Koko, "What's this?"
> "Gorilla," signed Koko.
> "Who gorilla?" asked Cathy.

"Bird," responded a bratty Koko, and things went downhill from there.
"You bird?" asked Cathy.
"You," countered Koko.
"Not me, you are bird," rejoined Cathy, mindful that "bird" can be an insult in Koko's lexicon.
"Me gorilla," asserted Koko.
"Who bird?" asked Cathy.
"You nut," replied Koko, resorting to another of her insults.
"Why me nut?" asked Cathy.
"Nut, nut," signed Koko.
"You nut, not me," Cathy replied.
Finally Koko gave up. Plaintively she signed, "Damn me good," and walked away signing, "Bad" (Patterson 1978:438, 440).

Koko not only uses AMESLAN to argue with and insult people, but she can lie as well. She uses lies to distort reality in order to avoid blame and punishment. Koko once broke a sink, and later when she was asked if she had

The chimpanzee Nim Chimpsky using sign language to ask trainer Laura Petitto for more to drink. Nim Chimpsky is one of the many primates being taught to use symbolic communication, a continuation of the Gardners' experiment with Washoe.

broken it, she used AMESLAN to accuse one of Patterson's human assistants of breaking the sink (Patterson 1978:459–460).

Research with chimpanzees and gorillas has demonstrated their ability to acquire some degree of competence in a human language. It is obvious that the mental and symbolic capacities of chimpanzees and gorillas are greater than previously assumed. Despite these research findings, many anthropologists and linguists do not accept the available evidence as conclusive proof that the great apes have mastered a human language. Chomsky defends the argument that language is unique to human beings by claiming that chimpanzees and gorillas have mastered only surface structure and a few transformational rules, but they lack the inborn capacity of deep structure, which is what generates language in human beings. "There's no reason to believe that whatever faculties apes use to solve language-like problems have any connection with the faculties humans use in human language" (Chomsky and Premack, 1979:8).

Language, Thought, and Culture

Language is more than a means of communication. For many years linguists and anthropologists have debated the relationship among language, thought, and culture. People speak and think in their language. Does this mean that people merely translate their thoughts into language, or is the very manner of human thought as well as what people think about determined by the language they use? This deterministic view of language raises the intriguing issue that the very process of thinking differs from language to language.

Language is also part of culture. It is learned, it is symbolic, and it is behavior. Language not only influences behavior, but social and cultural settings also influence what people say, how they say it, and what they intend to communicate. Body expressions and gestures are often more meaningful than the words people use. In addition, human beings have invented other forms of communication, such as sign languages and writing and, recently, computer languages.

Language and Thought

Cultural relativism dominated American anthropology in the first four decades of this century (see Chapter 2). At the same time a similar notion of relativism was found in linguistics. *Linguistic relativism* postulates that each language and the speakers of that language categorize and perceive the world differently. More recently, there has been a retreat from the relativistic position in linguistic theory. Chomsky's claim that there is an underlying universal grammar is a rejection of linguistic and grammatical relativism.

In its extreme form linguistic relativism is known as the Sapir–Whorf hypothesis, which takes its name from two eminent linguists, Edward Sapir and Benjamin Whorf. This hypothesis assumes that the language we speak determines our perception of reality. From the perspective of the *Sapir–Whorf hypothesis,* the statement "as we think, so we speak" is reversed to read "as we speak, so we think," meaning that members of different language communities think about their world in their own particular and unique way.

The idea that different languages represent alternative views of reality is seen in the work of Dorothy Lee. Analyzing linguistic data gathered by Malinowski from the Trobriand Islanders, she concludes that they lack notions of cause and effect. According to her interpretation, Trobriand Islanders see the world in configurations or in patterns rather than as a sequence of related events (Lee 1950:89–97).

Perhaps this relativist view can be illustrated by comparing Navajo and English statements about death. If someone is dying, an

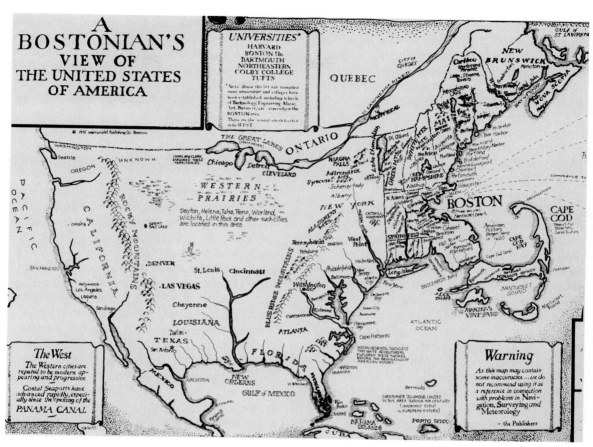

A cartoonist's representation of how Bostonians view their relationship to the rest of the United States. Bostonians, who speak of their city as the Hub of the Universe, do in fact think of it that way.

English speaking person would say, "John is dying," whereas a Navajo would say, "Dying is taking place with John." Analysis of these statements suggests that English speakers and Navajo speakers have different world views. English as a language requires its speakers to picture the world as active and dominated by human forces. John is doing the dying. On the other hand, the Navajo utterance has been in-terpreted as representing a world view that stresses passivity and dominance of nature over man; dying (an outside force) is happening to John.

It is almost inconceivable to think of an English verbal utterance that does not assume a time setting for the speaker. Events must take place in the past, present, or future, and it can be assumed that most English speakers believe that this is the way the world really exists. A time framework is built into the verbal structure of the English language. Linguistic analysis of non-Western languages indicates that such time settings may be irrelevant or nonexistent in the verbal structures of these languages. Non-Western language can express time — all languages can in one way or another express the statements of other languages — but the concept of a time setting may not be built into all of these languages. Whorf notes, for example, that Hopi verbs distinguish three different kinds of information — observation, reporting, and expectation — instead of time or duration (Whorf 1956:113).

Whorf's hypothesis about the influence of language upon thought and perception was based on Hopi linguistic data. He assumed that the Hopi view of reality was determined by the verbal structure of their language. Because time frameworks are not an integral part of Hopi verbs, Whorf took the position that time was not an important component in Hopi reality (1956:57–58). Much of the early work in evaluating the Sapir–Whorf hypothesis, in fact, used this indirect and analogous approach to infer world view and cognitive processes rather than using direct experimentation. More recently, however, empirical tests relating language to cognition and thinking have been developed.

John B. Carroll and Joseph B. Casagrande (1958:18–31) attempted to determine the influence of linguistic categories on Navajo-speaking Indian children and English-speaking American children. In the Navajo language verbs are categorized according to the form of an object. Carroll and Casagrande hypothesized that Navajo children would therefore classify objects by form instead of by color. It was assumed that American children would use color for categorizing objects. In an experiment designed to test this hypothesis, Navajo-speaking and English-speaking children were shown a yellow stick and a blue rope. The children were then given a yellow rope and asked to place it with one of the two other objects. The Navajo children tended to group objects according to form rather than color, placing the yellow rope with the blue rope. English-speak-

ing American children also placed the yellow rope with the blue rope, however. Based on this experiment, it appears that children use form rather than color in categorizing objects, and that language categories are relatively unimportant as a basis for classification. This experiment, as well as other experiments designed to investigate the relationship between language and cognition, was inconclusive as to the role and impact of language upon perception.

Recent research, however, suggests that certain forms of categorization may be built into the human species. The work of Brent Berlin and Paul Kay (1969) takes this position and challenges the Sapir–Whorf hypothesis. Berlin and Kay conducted an extensive cross-cultural study of basic color terms and color perception. Although they found that languages differ in many of the color terms and color categories recognized, people who spoke different languages located the color represented by a term in the same part of the color spectrum. This finding suggests that human beings share similar perceptions of color and color distinctions despite differences in color terminology from one language to another. Recent research indicates that there may be a neurophysiological basis for color vision in human beings and that people everywhere generally see and distinguish the same color categories, no matter what the linguistic color categories of their language are. In this research, however, it was also found that culture does have an influence on the way in which people in particular cultures indicate color prefences and perceive color categories (Wattenwyl and Zollinger 1979: 279–288).

Color categorization terms may not be the best basis for investigating the impact of language upon thought. In a study comparing Chinese and English speakers, Alfred Bloom found a relationship between linguistic categories and abstract thought (1979:585–586). Bloom points out that English, unlike Chinese, contains a linguistic category he calls "counterfactual." *Counterfactual statements* postulate hypothetical and nonfactual situations and then derive logical possibilities and implications from these "unreal" situations. "If John were to have gone to the library, he would have seen Mary" is a simple counterfactual statement that cannot, according to Bloom, be made in Chinese. His hypothesis is that because Chinese speakers lack a counterfactual category in their language, they would have great difficulty in understanding such statements and in deriving logical implications on the basis of such statements.

Using a variety of procedures, Bloom tested the abilities of Chinese speakers and American English speakers to understand counterfactual statements. In a study conducted in Hong Kong, Bloom found that "Chinese subjects consistently reacted to such questions as 'If the Hong Kong government had passed such a law, how would you have reacted?' by declaring, 'It didn't' or 'It won't,' and by branding such questions and the logic they imply as 'unnatural,' 'un-Chinese,' and even 'Western' " (Bloom 1979:585).

Bloom then compared English and Chinese language speakers as a further means of testing his hypothesis. He presented the following statement to English and Chinese language speakers: "If all circles were large and this small triangle were a circle, would it be large?" (1979:585). Twenty-five percent of the Chinese subjects answered yes, as compared with 83 percent of the English speakers. Many of the Chinese speakers were confused by the statement and commented, "No! How can all the circles be large? How can a triangle be a circle? What do you mean?" (Bloom 1979:585). Americans generally accepted the counterfactual premise that a small triangle could be a circle and drew logical conclusions from it.

An interesting finding of Bloom's study is that bilingual Chinese were more likely to use counterfactual logic when presented with the statement in English. This finding implies that bilingual speakers not only keep bilingual phonological and syntactic systems separate, but that they also keep apart the cognitive systems of the languages they have learned.

Bloom relates language and linguistic classifications to the higher and more abstract realms of thought rather than to the perception of ordinary reality such as color and form. Bloom, in fact, generalizes his experimental findings to suggest that the lack of interest in Chinese history and culture in theory building in philosophy, science, and theology may be linked to the lack of a counterfactual category in the Chinese language (1979:586).

As originally formulated, the Sapir–Whorf hypothesis was a theory of *linguistic determinism:* language determines thought. Anthropologists and linguists have retreated from this extreme position and merely recognize the impact of language and culture on thought and cognition. Bloom's work follows this direction, identifying abstract representation as particularly susceptible to linguistic categorization. This latter view reformulates the Sapir–Whorf hypothesis in a less extreme or "weak" version.

Language in Social and Cultural Context

Linguistic analysis has focused primarily on the formal study of language and the relation of language to thought and culture. Linguists have recorded diverse languages and investigated their grammatical systems. In the last two decades, both linguists and anthropologists have broadened their areas of research and now examine the social and cultural context of language behavior. In this development two closely related areas of research have emerged: sociolinguistics and the ethnography of speaking. *Sociolinguistics* is the study of the social context of language; the *ethnography of speaking* focuses on the analysis of speech events in specific social settings. Both approaches share a similar interest, the role of language in human behavior.

Sociolinguistics. Sociolinguists study the relationship between language and social structure. One aspect of this relationship is found in the existence of social and class dialects. William Labov (1964, 1966, 1968) studied speech patterns in New York City. He found that not only do speech patterns vary with class, but also the speech patterns of the higher classes have greater prestige value. He specifically noted the use and nonuse of /r/ as a marker of class and position. *Watta* instead of *water,* for example, indicates lower-class usage in New York.

A very controversial study linking speech patterns and social class was conducted by Basil Bernstein (1964), who examined the speech patterns of working-class and middle-class English schoolboys. Not only did he find differences in their speech patterns, but he also claimed that working-class speech patterns used a restricted code, while middle-class speech patterns used an elaborated code. Bernstein defined a restricted code as a range of speech forms that severely limits communication, learning, and social–economic mobility. The implications of Bernstein's conclusion have led to controversy. If his findings are correct, they indicate that the restricted speech patterns learned by lower-class children cannot be overcome by schooling or educational opportunity. Thus education does not serve as a means of social mobility for the working class.

Social class is the setting for social dialects for both Labov and Bernstein. In American society language also has an ethnic aspect. In the 1960s the issue of Black English became an educational, linguistic, and political question. One question was whether Black English is a dialect of English or a separate language. Linguists argued this question using phonology, morphology, and syntax as the basis for their positions. Whether it is a dialect of English or a separate language, most linguists attack the view that Black English is simply an incorrect and inferior version of Standard American English. Black English has its own phonological, morphological, and syntactic rules that make it as "logical" a language as any other.

Sex is as much a part of social structure as social class and ethnicity, and it is not surprising to find gender differences in language use. Many people feel that the use of certain words that express gender differences – *chairman, mailman, mankind* – give the appearance of male superiority or sexism. For many people the conversion of chairman to chairperson, mailman to letter carrier, and mankind to humankind appears to be frivolous and lacking in fundamental importance. But if we subscribe to the Sapir–Whorf hypothesis, that the way we speak determines or influences how we think, then eliminating sexism from language, if successful, may indeed change thinking in regard to gender and gender differences.

Proponents of these changes in English vocabulary have as their goal equality and openness. Language, however, can be used to hide, cover up, and blunt reality. George Orwell in his novel *1984* advanced the argument that in the totalitarian state of the future the authorities will control and define language in such a manner as to inhibit any thought that could be threatening to their totalitarian rule. In his book Orwell relates language to politics and thought control and describes an extreme version of the Sapir–Whorf hypothesis. He assumes that if a language contains no category for certain kinds of thought then those thoughts cannot be expressed.

Although at the present time no society appears to have reached this point, there can be little question of the widespread use, or mis-

Heavily armed, mounted riot police maintain order during a language demonstration by Flemish (Dutch) speaking people in Belgium in Schaarbeek borough.

use, of language, from advertising to politics, for miscommunicating and concealing reality. In World War II the mass murder of millions of Jews by the Nazis was referred to as "the final solution." Also during World War II Japanese-Americans were forcibly removed from their homes and placed in "relocation centers." In Vietnam, bombing attacks were defined as "protective reaction strikes." During the Watergate episode in the early 1970s burglary was redefined as "surreptitious entry capability." What these examples illustrate is the use of language to obscure rather than clarify reality.

Language and politics, however, can go beyond propaganda and misdirection. In societies where more than one language is spoken, language may become a political and social issue. Language and politics in such societies may involve stark and violent encounters between the members of different linguistic communities.

In India, for example, the decision to establish Hindi as the national language touched off violent controversies that still persist. In the streets of Bombay, Marathi and Gujarati speakers have slaughtered each other over the language chosen for street signs. Although the official policy of the Indian government at the time of independence in 1947 was not to establish states based upon linguistic boundaries, thirty years after independence almost all states within India do follow linguistic boundaries.

The Indian experience is not unusual. One of the factors underlying the secession of East Pakistan, now the independent nation-state of Bangladesh, was the desire of Bengali speakers to have their own nation independent of Urdu-speaking West Pakistan. Language conflict is not restricted to the multilingual states created by the European colonial powers. Language riots in Belgium between Flemish and

French speakers threatened to destroy that nation's integrity. In Canada the French-speaking segment of the population is demanding linguistic and political autonomy. Basque speakers in Spain, Breton speakers in Brittany, Gaelic speakers in Ireland, and Welsh speakers in Wales consider themselves linguistic minorities seeking political recognition as separate and independent entities. In the United States Spanish-speaking Americans are demanding greater recognition as a political, social, and linguistic unit.

The ethnography of speaking. Ethnographers of speech apply traditional anthropological research methods to the study of different speech behaviors. They focus on the social use of language and the functions of language in everyday life and carefully record speech acts and language use (Bauman and Sherzer 1974:8).

One analytic approach attempts to determine the basic rules that underlie speech performances. Following a transformational–generative model, verbal acts such as greetings and jokes are analyzed in terms of the rules available to speakers for these specific speech situations. Judith Irvine analyzed various strategies used by the Wolof of West Africa when they greet each other (1974:167–191). Problems and relations of status are involved in Wolof greetings. Among the Wolof a greeting must take place if the individuals know each other, but individuals who initiate a greeting are considered to be of lower status. A speech strategy for elevating a person's status is to take the role of respondent — that is, speaking as if the other person opened the conversation — rather than as initiator in the greeting encounter. Irvine notes that encounters among the Wolof can be awkward because both individuals may attempt to assume the role of respon-

A greeting is a cultural performance combining verbal and nonverbal communication, as well as considerations of status and role. A French grandmother remains seated while being greeted by her family.

dent (1974:178). Long periods of silence and avoidance of eye contact may be broken by one person saying, "Why didn't you greet me?" a delightful attempt to finess the situation by both initiating the greeting and still attempting to appear not to, thus avoiding the stigma of lower status.

The ethnography of speaking, like other ethnographic endeavors, provides a framework for the collection of diverse information. This framework is composed of a number of elements, including speech varieties available to members of the community, the cultural rules for speaking, the goals and strategies involved in verbal interaction, the interpretation of speech by members of the community, and the performance of individuals in the context of speaking. From this perspective speaking becomes, like economics, politics, religion, and marriage, a distinguishable cultural system in a society (Bauman and Sherzer 1974:7).

Nonverbal Communication

Thus far we have equated language with speech, but there are additional forms of human communication that do not depend upon sound. Sign language, for example, is one form of nonverbal communication that represents an extreme development of specific and standardized body gestures for communication. Recent anthropological and linguistic research has focused on the study of body movements — kinesics — and body space — proxemics — as means of communication. Another form of nonverbal communication — writing — has been of long-standing interest to linguists and anthropologists.

Kinesics. Kinesics is the study of how people use gestures, facial expressions, posture, body movements, eye contact, and touching to communicate their thoughts and feelings. Body language, as well as verbal language, shows marked cultural, sexual, and class differences.

People from the Mediterranean (Spain, Italy, and Greece) often use hand gestures along with verbal communication. North Europeans (English and Scandinavians), in contrast, do not tend to use hand and body movements when they speak.

Of all parts of the body, the face is the most expressive nonverbal communicator of feeling and thought. Smiling, scowling, grimacing, and raising one's eyebrows are aspects of facial language. For the Tuareg of North Africa use of facial expressions as language is limited. Tuareg men, but not women, wear a veil that covers all parts of their face except their eyes. Robert Murphy, who studied the Tuareg, notes

For a veiled Tuareg man, communication by facial expression is limited. Tuareg men become expert at reading the meaning of every expression of the eyes.

New Yorkers on a crowded subway train respond to invasion of their intimate body space by retreating into their private worlds and avoiding all social contact.

that they are eye watchers rather than mouth watchers, and during conversations with them his eyes were fixed by the steady stare of Tuareg men. He writes, "Everything is watched and used as a cue, the position of the eyelids, the lines and wrinkles of the eyes and nose, the set of the body, and the tone of the voice ..." (Murphy 1964:1265). A major point in his analysis is that the wearing of the veil by men increases social distance between individuals and fosters privacy and remoteness.

Proxemics. Allied to the language of the body is the concept of body space. *Proxemics* is the study of how people in different cultures define proper body space, both its use and its meaning. Edward and Mildred Hall (1971) studied the use and meaning of body space and identified four distinguishable space zones: intimate, personal, social, and public. The distance and meaning of these space zones vary from culture to culture. To the middle-class American contact with another person within a distance of six to eighteen inches is defined as an intimate zone. Between males and females this space may have strong sexual overtones; between individuals of the same sex and strang-

ers of either sex it may be sensed as disturbing. Americans in crowded elevators may respond to invasions of their intimate zone by evading eye contact and maintaining silence, thus avoiding any social interaction.

Writing. Many different writing systems have been developed, and they appear to represent an evolutionary sequence of development. The earliest forms of visual representation were pictograms, the direct representation of an object. Such forms of writing have no relationship to the spoken language, since they represent objects, not language sounds. Although picture writing may be the most ancient form of written communication, pictograms are now widely used in contemporary society. It is their separation from spoken language that makes them useful. Using pictures or symbols of a knife, fork, and spoon along the highways of the world, international road signs attempt to communicate the availability of dining facilities across the boundaries of language. English speakers, French speakers, and Italian speakers all have different words for these objects; however, their pictorial representation communicates the same meaning in all languages.

True writing occurs only when an arbitrary relationship develops between the visual form and that which it represents. True writing is the transcription of sounds or meanings of a language into a visual form. Unlike verbal language, writing is not a universal form of communication. Three types of true writing systems have been developed: word writing, syllable writing, and alphabet writing.

In word writing a written symbol represents an entire word. Invented by the Sumerians of southern Mesopotamia over 5000 years ago, it was taken over by the Babylonians and the Assyrians, who simplified it by using the forms to represent the sounds of syllables rather than entire words.

This syllable system was borrowed by the ancient Greeks. The Greek language, however, contained a complex polysyllabic structure that made the use of syllabic writing extremely cumbersome (Fromkin and Rodman 1974:363). The Greeks modified the writing system they borrowed so that the symbols stood for the phonemic sounds (consonants and vowels) of their language. Their modification created true *alphabetic writing*. A phonemic alphabet uses a relatively small number of visual symbols to represent the sounds of a language. Over 400,000 words in English can be represented by a combination of twenty-six vowels and consonants. If new words are invented, available symbols can be used to represent them.

Writing appears to be related to the emergence of complex society. When Samuel Noah Kramer deciphered the earliest cuneiform tablets of ancient Sumer, he did not find love poems, ethical treatises, scientific discourses, or great literature (1959). What he deciphered were warehouse receipts recording the delivery and collection of grain and wool by administrative overseers. This connection between writing and agricultural productivity and commercial activity raises the fundamental question of the function of writing. Ancient Sumer represents the earliest emergence of a state system with urban centers. It was based upon high levels of agricultural production that supported a political, military, and administrative elite. Kramer's work suggests that writing was developed by this elite as a device to record the vast forms of wealth they controlled, administered, and allocated.

From this point of view writing is an information storage and retrieval system. This function is seen by some anthropologists as the basis for verbal language. In comparing our ancient ancestors with nonhuman primates, anthropologists suggest that the demands of scavenging, hunting, foraging, social cooperation, and the use and making of tools were driving forces behind the emergence and evolution of human language. A learned social tradition,

International road signs attempt to transcend the limits of one particular language. Pictorial signs direct travelers to telephones and mechanical help for their automobiles, as well as alert them to possibly dangerous driving conditions and pedestrian crossings.

culture vital to the survival of the species, could be shared and communicated to succeeding generations linguistically. Language thus becomes the library of social and technological tradition as well as a transmission device.

In recent decades the information explosion in science, government, and industry has begun to overwhelm traditional means of storage and retrieval. Although the printing press and library were adequate storage and retrieval systems for over 500 years, neither printing nor the traditional library can now cope with the growing output and demand for information. As a consequence computers, computer languages, and miniaturized electronic storage devices are now being used for storage and retrieval. These devices, the inventions of contemporary society, must be recognized as part of the continuing evolution of symbolic communication.

Summary

Immediately after birth human babies make sounds that soon become babbles. Such babbling is the basis for phonemically distinctive sound systems that are the basis of every human language.

Burling's account of his son's acquisition of Garo and English illustrates some of the fundamental processes involved in language acquisition as well as fundamental properties of language. Stephen's babbles were transformed into recognizable phonemes. Although initially he spoke Garo and English with the same phonemic system, soon he began to distinguish the phonemic systems of the two languages. From a limited linguistic inventory, in a few months Stephen dramatically increased his linguistic competence and repertoire. Analysis of Stephen's language acquisition in terms of phonemes, morphemes, syntax, and lexicon reveals these elements as fundamental features of all languages.

Language is a form of communication that may be unique to human beings. Most linguists stress the purely arbitrary and symbolic nature of language. No language utilizes all the potential sounds that can be generated by the human vocal tract. A language is composed of selected sounds or phonemes. Phonemes are grouped into morphemes or words, and the meaning of morphemes is purely arbitrary. Languages combine morphemes into sentences and phrases according to syntactic rules. These rules of word order vary from language to language. Linguists traditionally studied and analyzed languages in terms of these concepts, which were designed to describe the grammar of a language.

A recent development in linguistics, identified with the work of Noam Chomsky, considers language as uniquely human and part of the inborn capacity of all normal human beings. This inborn capacity provides the creative and generative features of language and is used by Chomsky to explain the explosive growth in linguistic competence of children as well as their ability to regularize their utterances in terms of unconscious rules of grammar. Through this approach he seeks to uncover the universal forms of grammar common to all languages.

The notion that language is specific to the human species has been challenged by the successful teaching of nonverbal language, especially AMESLAN, to great apes. The questions of the uniqueness of human language and an agreed-upon definition of language remain controversial and unresolved issues at the present time.

In addition to the formal study of language,

linguists and anthropologists explore the relationship among language, culture, and thought. One of the first statements defining this relationship was the Sapir–Whorf hypothesis. This hypothesis, based upon a position of extreme linguistic relativism, assumes that the categories of a language determine the thinking patterns and perception of the speakers of that language. Experimental studies have failed to confirm the validity of this hypothesis, especially in reference to the concrete and visible aspects of reality. Recent research, however, supports the hypothesis that linguistic classifications may exercise considerable influence upon abstract thinking and high level concepts.

Linguists and anthropologists have recently developed two new areas of research, sociolinguistics and the ethnography of speaking, which focus on the social use of language in everyday life. Sociolinguists investigate the use of language in relationship to social organization and structure. Language use varies systematically by social class, gender, ethnicity, and other social attributes. The ethnography of speaking concentrates upon actual speech acts and attempts to understand the language rules used by the members of a speech community.

Spoken language is not the only form of human communication. Deaf people have developed a language of their own, AMESLAN, based on finger and hand movements as well as facial expressions. AMESLAN is a full-fledged language, comparable to spoken language. Body language (kinesics) and the use of space (proxemics), on the other hand, are modes of communication that supplement spoken language. Their use and understanding are often implicit, nonconscious, and vary cross-culturally.

Writing is the transcription of a spoken language into a graphic form. It appears to be associated with complex societies and is a recent historical development. Writing systems

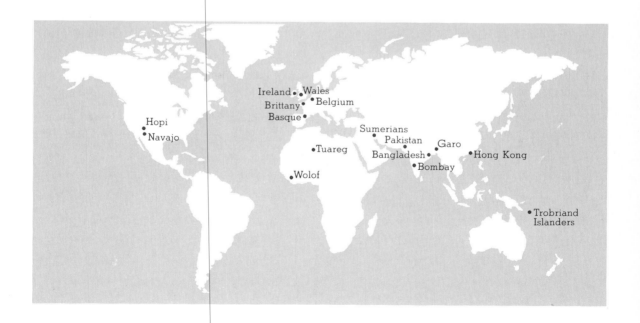

appear to follow an evolutionary sequence: pictographs, word writing, syllabic writing, and alphabet writing. Alphabetic writing transcribes the phonemic sounds of a language, and as a result a small number of symbols can be used to represent thousands of words.

Writing, like verbal language, can also be viewed as a library of information as well as a device that transmits knowledge. At the present time the information explosion is forcing the development of new and more efficient means of symbolic communication, storage, and retrieval. This is most evident in the computer revolution.

Key Terms and Concepts

phoneme
phonology
morpheme
morphology
syntax
lexical
monolingual
bilingual
multilingual
phonetics
phonemics
transformational-
    generative
    grammar

deep structure
AMESLAN
linguistic relativism
Sapir–Whorf
    hypothesis
counterfactual
    statements
sociolinguistics
ethnography of
    speaking
kinesics
proxemics
alphabetic writing

Suggested Readings

Burling, Robbins. *Man's Many Voices: Language in Its Cultural Context.* New York: Holt, Rinehart and Winston, 1970. An excellent introduction to language in culture that focuses on the social aspects of language.

Fromkin, Victoria, and Robert Rodman. *An Introduction to Language,* 2nd ed. New York: Holt, Rinehart and Winston, 1978. A clearly written, well-organized textbook introduction to language and linguistics.

Hall, Edward T. *The Silent Language.* New York: Doubleday, 1973. An introduction to nonverbal communication.

Linden, Eugene. *Apes, Men, and Language.* New York: Penguin, 1976. Written for a nonprofessional audience, this volume summarizes the data on chimpanzee language learning with a special focus on Washoe.

Orwell, George. *1984.* New York: New American Library, 1971. A powerful novel of the totalitarian state of the future where language is designed to prohibit the thinking of subversive thoughts.

Stross, Brian. *The Origin and Evolution of Language.* Dubuque, Iowa: Wm. C. Brown, 1976. An introductory book that focuses on the emergence and evolution of language.

Thorne, Barrie, and Nancy Henley, eds. *Language and Sex: Difference and Dominance.* Rowley, Mass.: Newbury House, 1975. A series of papers that focus on the role of sex and gender in language.

Chapter 12

When Systems Change

A paradox of the human condition is that as people learn the norms and roles of their society, these fundamental aspects of culture change. Such change may be slow and gradual, even imperceptible to the people experiencing it. If change is slow and gradual, people are not faced with the problem of discarding their old beliefs and behavioral patterns. If change is rapid and abrupt, however, people must adapt to new situations and learn new bahavior.

The most dramatic instance of swift and disturbing change is the confrontation between Western and non-Western societies, where change is rapid, pervasive, and frequently destructive. The reaction of tribal societies to the impact of Western society takes a variety of forms. One response is a *revitalization movement.* This movement combines religious, political, military, and economic elements from the traditional society as well as Western culture in an attempt to construct a new and viable social reality. These movements represent one of the most basic responses to cultural change.

Revitalization movements appear to occur when cultural distortion and stress are extreme. In the past 500 years tribal and peasant life throughout the world has been irreversibly changed; sometimes even completely destroyed. Many of the events and situations described in this text no longer exist. The Cheyenne no longer ride their ponies or hunt buffalo; the Kabaka is gone from his palace; the Tlingit no longer use potlatches to resolve their disputes. This transformation of tribal and peasant culture has taken place within the framework of the colonial experience — the political, military, economic, and cultural domination of the world by Western society. The 500 years of colonial and imperial rule have defined the dimensions of modern social change. Our own world, with its problems, conflicts, and accomplishments, is in large part a creation of the colonial experience. To comprehend the world we live in today we must understand the historical process of change called the colonial experience.

Hau Hau: A Maori Revitalization Movement

During the European age of discovery, exploration, and settlement (approximately 1500 to

Tribal people all over the world have been introduced to Western ideas and objects of material culture. Nanook, hero of "Nanook of the North," one of the greatest ethnographic films of the Eskimo ever made, is shown listening to a phonograph for the first time.

1900) hostilities between European and native people were common. Nowhere was this conflict more evident than in New Zealand, where the British and the Maori inhabitants engaged in intermittent warfare for over twenty years. The Hau Hau revitalization movement is more than a story of military conflict between the Maori and the British. Violence was part of the

Hau Hau movement, but its central elements were an amalgamation of Christian, Maori, and Old Testament beliefs into a religious movement. This religious aspect of the movement sets it apart from a merely military confrontation. Revitalization movements are clues to the human capacity for culture change, the massive impact of European contact, and the cultural processes that may be required to construct a new way of life from the wreckage of the past.

A prophet, Te Ua Haumene (also known by his mission name of Horopapera Tuwhakararo, which means John Zerubbabel) arose. Te Ua, who belonged to the Taranaki tribe, had learned the magic arts of a Maori *tohunga,* or priest, but he had also studied with Wesleyan missionaries. He claimed that the Angel Gabriel had spoken to him in a vision. Since Maoris took the Bible literally and were ready not only to adopt its injunctions, but also to apply Old Testament stories to their own circumstances, Te Ua's claims were accepted.

Te Ua was given the credit for causing a British ship, the *Lord Worsley,* to be drawn on to the Taranaki coast and, although his injunction that the ship should not be looted was not heeded, his fame as a prophet began to spread. Stories about him grew. He was said, in a story that recapitulates that of Abraham, to have maimed his son, and prepared to sacrifice him at the Angel Gabriel's behest, and then, at the angel's intercession, to have healed the boy's broken leg. The importance of Te Ua was an inspiration in the Maori struggle with the *pakeha* [white people]. Three coadjutors were quickly appointed for the new faith, Tahutaki, Hepanaia, and Wi Parana, who acquired divine blessing by inhaling the smoke of Te Ua's pipe. Tahutaki and Hepanaia persuaded their associates to undertake an expedition to Ahuahu, prophesying that some *pakehas* would be delivered

into their hands. A small company of troops was discovered, and quickly overcome, and the head of its officer, Captain T. W. J. Lloyd, who was decapitated, became thereafter the object through which Te Ua received the instructions of the Angel Gabriel. This military success established the credibility of the new religion, which was now quickly propagated.

On Gabriel's instructions, Te Ua now ordered that a *niu,* or post, be set up as a flagpole (the first was part of the mast of the *Lord Worsley,* on which flags were rigged. The assembled company marched around it, with raised hands, chanting incantations. The majority of the chants were unintelligible even to the Maoris, but the word "Hau," which occurred at the end of many lines of the chants, was a word for the vital spark, referring literally to the wind, [and to] angels of the wind, who descended from the ropes left dangling from the *niu.* A typical chant included English words, particularly words drawn from church services and from military activity, and the chants were intoned while the naked throng of men, women, and children touched the preserved heads of *pakeha* who had been killed, which were then believed to utter words of prophecy. Shivering, frenzy, and catalepsy occurred during the marching, and the marchers sometimes manifested glossalalia [speaking in tongues or babbling nonmeaningful speech]. Te Ua called the new faith *Pai-marire,* which means "good and faithful," and composed a shout to be used at all meetings: "Hapa! Pai-marire, hau" — "pass over, good and faithful." The formula was supposed to ward off bullets.

Te Ua declared victory over the *pakeha* to be near at hand. Gabriel would protect them, and the Virgin Mary was constantly with them. those who failed to follow the movement and to become Hau Hau believers would be ruined [the Hau Hau leaders claimed that]:

When the last Pakeha had perished in the sea, all the Maoris who had perished since the beginning of the world would leap from their graves with a shout, and stand in the presence of Zerubbabel, the Great Prophet. . . . The deaf would hear, the blind see, the lame walk; every species of disease would disappear; all would become perfect in their bodies as in their spirits. Men would be sent from heaven to teach the Maoris all the arts and sciences now known to Europeans.

The inspiration of the books of Revelation and Isaiah is evident. The Hau Hauists saw themselves as kin with the Jews, and there was some idea of their being the lost tribes. They expected Joshua and his legions to descend to help them, once all Maoris were converted. Thus distinct millennial and resurrectionist elements fused with the promise of active military assistance in the Maori struggle against the *pakeha* for the possession of the land. The Maoris said that the missionaries had taught them to turn their eyes to heaven, while the missionaries had turned *their* eyes to the land.

Te Ua's attempt to rally the tribes led to some premature engagements against the whites. Hepanaia led an attack on the Sentry Hill Redoubt in April 1864, and was repulsed with losses. Other Hau Hauists under Matene fought in the following month. Te Ua disowned the two prophets as disobedient and thus explained their failure to gain the promised immunity to bullets which the upraised hand would ensure when the battle was joined at the proper time. He now sent two groups of emissaries on new routes to arouse the tribes. It was on one of these excursions that in March 1865, Kereopa, one of the delegates, whose daughters had been burned to death by the British soldiers when they razed a village, wrought his vengeance on the inno-

Body tatooing was a traditional practice among the Maori of New Zealand. British soldiers and settlers often faced such tatooed warriors during the Maori-British wars of the nineteenth century.

cent Reverend Carl Sylvanus Volkner, killing him and subsequently eating his eyes in traditional Maori fashion, and using his blood for communion. The Hau Hauists, who identified with the Jews, set free the captain of the ship on which they captured the Rev. Volkner, because he, Captain Levy, was a Jew. The [Hau Hau] emissaries converted many natives, but a swift campaign [by British soldiers], on both the east and west coasts and in the interior, saw the defeat of the Maoris. Te Ua was captured early in 1866. He renounced his teachings, and he and Patara were freed; Kereopa was hanged, and several hundreds were deported to the Chatham Islands [isolated islands 450 miles from New Zealand] (Wilson 1973:247–250).

Historical Context of Hau Hau

To understand the emergence and meaning of the Hau Hau movement we must look at the history of Maori–British contact. Christian missionary activity began in New Zealand in 1814. By 1824 missionaries succeeded in converting some of the Maoris to Christianity, and in the following two decades approximately half of the Maori population became Christian. Once conversion began the Maori took their new religion seriously and accepted the Bible in its literal sense. In the 1820s the Maoris acquired European firearms, which raised traditional Maori intertribal warfare, already brutal, to new levels of bloodshed and horror. Thus the first sustained phase of Maori–white contact (1820–1840) was characterized by a rapid absorption of at least two elements of European culture — God and guns. In this first phase of contact, dramatic changes were grafted onto the existing Maori culture and traditional patterns of warfare were magnified, but no serious disruption of Maori culture occurred.

Maori acceptance of Christianity may have been based on their perception that European material wealth was a consequence of European religious beliefs and practices. This belief might explain Te Ua's statement that men would be sent from heaven to teach the Maoris the arts and sciences of the Europeans.

Beginning in the 1840s the Maoris faced a process of severe economic, political, and social disruption. After Britain proclaimed sovereignty over New Zealand in 1840, European settlers began to arrive in large numbers. Between 1840 and 1860 the population of European settlers rose from under 1000 to 100,000. This massive growth in European population was accompanied by confiscation and purchase of vast tracts of Maori land. In this phase the Maori population declined as a result of diseases introduced by Europeans as well as intertribal warfare. Land that had been sold to the British government at low prices was resold to European settlers at twenty times the original purchase price (Wilson 1973:250). Maoris who sold land felt cheated. In addition, the Maoris began to grow disenchanted with Christianity as practiced by Europeans. In converting to Christianity the Maoris modeled their behavior on Christian doctrine. As long as their Christian models were upright missionaries, the Maori had no reason to question the faith they had adopted. The vast number of European settlers with whom they now had contact, however, were Christians in name only. Not only did they steal Maori land, but they also gambled, drank, did not attend religious services, and violated most of the ten commandments.

Responses to the growing impact of Europeans upon Maori society were the development of Maori land leagues and attempts to establish large-scale political alliances between separate Maori tribes. Land leagues were formed to halt the loss of land. Political alliances were designed to integrate the warring Maori tribes into a single political unit capable of withstanding European domination. Both of these attempts to deal with the European presence failed. Intertribal jealousies and conflict doomed a unified political approach, and the government supported purchases and confiscation of Maori lands.

One index of the growing disintegration of Maori culture was the breakdown of internal social control. Chiefs had great difficulty enforcing their authority, and roving bands of young warriors, who were often drunk, terrorized the countryside.

By the late 1850s fighting between the Maoris and the British became widespread. On both sides warfare was accompanied by an escalation of terror and atrocity. Decapitation of

British prisoners, the burning of Maori villages, and the killing of women and children were common occurrences. Warfare between the Maoris and the British occurred intermittently for the next twenty years.

Within the context of the growing disarray of Maori culture and the escalating horrors of war, Hau Hau emerged in the 1860s. It represented a new faith in a time of trouble, the support of a heavenly power when the familiar world had collapsed, a belief in final victory, and ultimate opposition to the white man. Followers of the Hau Hau movement were initially victorious in encounters with small British forces. Such victories enhanced the credibility of the new religion and helped recruit additional adherents. The Hau Hauists were ultimately defeated, however, and the movement

disintegrated. Many of the followers of the Hau Hau movement became adherents of a new faith, the Ringatu Church. Unlike the aggressive and activist Hau Hau movement, this faith preached a combination of Maori and Christian beliefs that emphasized passivity and accommodation to white rule (Wilson 1973:401–402). A response of withdrawal and pacifism is not an unusual end for a revitalization movement.

Unless a revitalization movement becomes the dominant religious and political institution, its members face two alternatives. If they continue to offer military resistance to superior forces they may be completely exterminated. The more usual choice, as we have seen with the Hau Hau movement, is to accept defeat and accommodate to the dominant power as a withdrawn and pacifistic sect.

Social Change in Comparative Perspective

Revitalization movements such as Hau Hau take place in all parts of the world. These movements are among the most dramatic manifestations of social and cultural change, and a comparative study of them provides insight into the dynamics of change during periods of stress and disruption. Revitalization movements, however, are not the only manifestations of change. Anthropologists recognize that other processes of change operate in all cultures, and they are useful in understanding how and why cultural systems change. Examining the impact of Europeans on the Maoris was a vital ingredient in understanding the emergence of the Hau Hau movement. In the comparative study of social change, European exploration and colonialism are important elements in analyzing what happened in tribal and peasant societies throughout the world.

Revitalization Movements

There are many different types of revitalization movements. In some revitalization movements the major theme is a call for a return to the indigenous, or native, culture. The Ghost Dance religion of the western American Indians is an example of this type of movement. Participants believed that the dead would return, the buffalo would come back, and the white man would disappear. Other movements reject the indigenous culture and attempt to incorporate, through imitation, elements of the European culture that has engulfed their culture. Followers of such movements may consciously reject and destroy traditional paraphernalia and customs. In the Vailala Madness of Papua, New Guinea, reported by F. E. Williams, traditional religious and social customs were attacked and prohibited (1923). Participants in this movement acted out their perceptions of European culture. Tables were set in European fashion and decorated with flowers, cult temples resembling mission churches were constructed, and flagpoles, possibly imitations of wireless masts, were erected. Despite this imitation of European culture, the Vailala Madness was characterized by antiwhite feeling.

Cargo Cults

One of the common features of revitalization movements in New Guinea and Melanesia is an emphasis upon the acquisition of European trade goods, or cargo. For this reason many of these movements have been called *cargo*

Members of a New Hebrides (South Pacific) revitalization movement worship a cross in the belief that this will bring a return of the ancestors and give them access to the material goods of Western civilization.

cults. Basic to cargo cults is the belief that European goods are made by the ancestors of the tribal group. The members of these cults believe that these goods are supposed to come to the tribal people, but that they are intercepted by the Europeans, who keep them for their own selfish purposes. Members of the cargo cult believe that there will be a massive upheaval and cataclysm within the near future; the Europeans will be destroyed, the ancestors will return, and the cargo will arrive. In response to such beliefs many Melanesian groups build docks, runways, radio towers, and warehouses to receive the ships and planes carrying the cargo. In expectation of a new creation, gardens are abandoned, pigs are killed, and all work activities cease.

Theodore Schwartz investigated a cargo cult movement on the island of Manus in 1960, and his research documents the important role of European goods in these movements (1976).

The members of this cult group wrote an "order" for an enormous quantity of material goods and presented it to the European district commissioner, along with fifty dollars as a bribe, and they asked him to send this order to the source of the cargo. The order contained some ninety-three items listed in three columns, including the item number, quantity, and the item itself. It included 500 pistols with cartridges, 5 bicycles, 10 motorbikes, 10 tractors, 1,000,000 sheets of iron, 500 pieces of window glass, 500 window shades, 10 mattresses, 18 mosquito nets, 8000 bags of cement, 2,000,000 timbers, 500 boxes of tools, 28,000 chairs, 17,000 cases of nails in assorted sizes, 30,000 tablecloths, 16,000 radios, 14,000 refrigerators, 8 storage batteries, 3 workshop buildings, 40,000 drums of kerosene, 40,000 drums of fuel, 4000 warships, 5000 cargo boats, 10,000 bags of rice, sugar, and flour, 10,000 pigs, 60,000 pens, 2000 lawn mowers, 4900 sewing machines, and 9000 razor blades.

The list indicates both a deep desire on the part of this population to acquire European goods and a pathetic lack of understanding of the sources of European material wealth. A misunderstanding of European culture has frequently fostered the idea that special religious and magical skills possessed by Europeans are basic to their material wealth. Such themes integrating material goods and supernatural power and knowledge are fundamental in these revitalization movements.

Stages in Revitalization Movements

Interpretations of these dramatic manifestations of social change are found in the work of Anthony Wallace (1956, 1966) and Peter Worsley (1957). Wallace bases his approach on his research on the historic Handsome Lake Movement of the Iroquois Indians of upstate New York. Worsley derives his explanation from the analysis of Melanesian cargo cults.

In the 1790s the Iroquois were a battered and wrecked people, and their culture was in disarray. They had supported the British in the American Revolutionary War and suffered the consequences of being on the losing side. Iroquois social disintegration could be seen in the drinking, homicide, and physical assaults that became common among this once-proud people. Handsome Lake, an Iroquois chief, took part in this dissolute life-style. Then he experienced a revelation: messengers from God brought him a message to be preached to the Iroquois. The doctrine he preached was that traditional Iroquois habits and customs, such as the matrilineage, medicine societies, and female horticultural labor, must be abandoned. He denounced alcoholism, homicide, assault, and witchcraft. Handsome Lake urged his people to copy American agricultural and familial practices. The Iroquois were encouraged to go to school and to acquire the skills of American society. As Wallace notes, "The code of Handsome Lake met with outstanding success. The Iroquois became widely known for their sobriety [and] the new pattern of agricultural living . . ." (1966:32).

Based on this movement, Wallace postulates five stages in the life of a revitalization movement (1966:155–165):

1. *The steady state:* Slow process of change, no major cultural disorganization or individual stress.
2. *Period of increased stress:* Growing period of disorganization marked by increase in social deviance and individual pathology.
3. *Period of cultural distortion:* Major disorganization of the system. Increased individual alienation and despair.
4. *Period of revitalization:* Emergence of a prophet and a new utopian image of the good society. Message is spread and accepted. Major behavioral and organizational changes occur.

5. *The new steady state:* A new equilibrium is attained as the new religion develops into a conservative and organized institution.

Peter Worsley's analysis of Melanesian cargo cults parallels and supplements Wallace's analysis (1957). Worsley believes that cultural change resulting from European contact sets the stage for these movements. He suggests that the supernatural and religious elements of such cults are initial responses of tribal people to the strange and bewildering advent of European culture.

In addition, Worsley points out the importance of the subordination and humiliation often experienced by tribal people under European colonial control. Treated with contempt and condemned by European racial prejudice, native peoples were relegated to menial and poorly paid jobs in the European-dominated commercial economy. Subordination was often more than economic and political. Once-proud warriors were reduced to a dependent status. Young men were converted into household servants by their European overlords, and the term *houseboy,* used for domestic servants, contains within it all of the negative and personally demeaning elements of their subordinate position.

Worsley argues that religiously oriented revitalization movements emerge from the colonial social situation. He claims, however, that eventually they are replaced by political movements that are secular in nature. Increasing sophistication and awareness of European culture become the basis for opposition to colonial rule. Although the Hau Hau movement and the Handsome Lake movement ended in what Wallace would call the steady state of a conservative religion, other movements have developed into organized and effective independence movements. One aspect of revitalization movements, noted by Worsley, is the degree to which they attempt to integrate and unite pre-viously hostile and separate tribal entities. This process of amalgamation sets the stage for future political developments. Worsley believes that as political movements emerge, religious groups retreat into passive sects and unassertive congregations. Religious activism declines, emphasis is placed upon individual salvation, and the date for the coming of Utopia recedes into the distant future. This development has already taken place in Africa and Melanesia; cults became nonpolitical and were replaced by political parties, trade unions, and cooperatives. Worsley's interpretation adds an additional dimension to Wallace's analysis: the transformation of religiously based revitalization movements into secular political and economic organizations.

Processes of Change

Throughout history change has been a constant element in human culture. Anthropologists who direct much of their attention to the study of culture change identify the following processes of change: independent invention, diffusion, acculturation, and culture contact.

Independent Invention

Independent invention is the emergence of identical or similar practices in two or more societies without any contact or connection between them.

Nineteenth-century anthropologists emphasized independent invention as a fundamental process of culture change. The basic premise of cultural evolution was the progressive and sequential development of stages of human cultural development. A fundamental aspect of this theoretical position was the concept of the "psychic unity of mankind." Based on this concept evolutionists argued that all people thought in much the same way and that given similar circumstances, people would invent similar cultural practices and beliefs.

Nineteenth-century evolutionism has been discarded in contemporary cultural anthropology, although some contemporary theoretical positions emphasize the importance of independent invention. Stewart's multilinear evolutionary approach and Lévi-Strauss's structuralism assume the significance of this process of culture change.

One of the most important contemporary theories emphasizing independent invention is cultural ecology. Ecologists argue that the same set of ecological conditions leads to the emergence of similar cultural inventions. Carneiro's theory of state origins (Chapter 7) presents a theoretical argument for the emergence of the state under similar ecological conditions. In a similar fashion, Harris's argument about warfare, population, and infanticide (Chapter 6) is based upon the idea that the same conditions and circumstances independently give rise to similar solutions.

Diffusion

Diffusion is a process of cultural borrowing, the geographical spread of cultural items from their place of origin to other cultures.

Although nineteenth-century evolutionists recognized the role of diffusion in change, they minimized its importance in favor of independent invention. In the first three decades of the twentieth century, American anthropologists, led by Franz Boas, vehemently rejected evolutionary theory and elevated diffusion into the fundamental process of change. Any particular culture was viewed as composed of separate elements and traits borrowed from a variety of other cultures. This perspective is expressed by Ralph Linton in his classic description of the cultural elements that are part of the American way of life.

> There can be no question about the average American's Americanism or his desire to preserve this precious heritage at all costs. Never-theless, some insidious foreign ideas have already wormed their way into his civilization without his realizing what was going on. Thus dawn finds the unsuspecting patriot garbed in pajamas, a garment of East Indian origin; and lying in a bed built on a pattern which originated in either Persia or Asia Minor. He is muffled to the ears in un-American materials: cotton, first domesticated in India; linen, domesticated in the Near East; wool from an animal native to Asia Minor; or silk whose uses were first discovered by the Chinese.
>
> The American washes with soap invented by the ancient Gauls. Next he cleans his teeth, a subversive European practice which did not invade America until the latter part of the eighteenth century. He then shaves, a masochistic rite first developed by the heathen priests of ancient Egypt and Sumer. The process is made less of a penance by the fact that his razor is of steel, an iron-carbon alloy discovered in either India or Turkestan. Lastly, he dries himself on a Turkish towel.
>
> He puts on close-fitting tailored garments whose form derives from the skin clothing of the ancient nomads of the Asiatic steppes and fastens them with buttons whose prototypes appeared in Europe at the close of the Stone Age. He ties about his neck a strip of bright-colored cloth which is a vestigial survival of the shoulder shawls worn by seventeenth-century Croats. He gives himself a final appraisal in the mirror, an old Mediterranean invention, and goes downstairs to breakfast.
>
> His fork is a medieval Italian invention and his spoon a copy of a Roman original. He will usually begin the meal with coffee, an Abyssinian plant first discovered by the Arabs. He will probably sweeten it with sugar, discovered in India; and dilute it with cream, both the domestication of cattle and the technique of milking having originated in Asia Minor.
>
> Breakfast over, he places upon his head a molded piece of felt, invented by the nomads of Eastern Asia, and, if it looks like rain, puts on outer shoes of rubber, discovered by the ancient Mexicans, and takes an umbrella, invented in India. At the station he pauses for a

moment to buy a newspaper, paying for it with coins invented in ancient Lydia. Once on board he settles back to inhale the fumes of a cigarette invented in Mexico, or a cigar invented in Brazil. Meanwhile, he reads the news of the day, imprinted in characters invented by the ancient Semites by a process invented in Germany upon a material invented in China. As he scans the latest editorial pointing out the dire results to our institutions of accepting foreign ideas, he will not fail to thank a Hebrew God in an Indo-European language that he is a 100 percent (decimal system invented by the Greeks) American (from Americus Vespucci, Italian geographer) (Linton 1937:427–429).

Linton's description testifies to the overwhelming importance of diffusion in the development of American material culture. Every item described by Linton was invented outside the United States. Diffusionists, like Linton, were not particularly interested in the process of invention. Instead they were interested in documenting the center of origin for an item, discovering its routes of spread, and determining its acceptance in other cultures. A conclusion that can be drawn from most diffusionist studies is that for any single culture, most of its cultural elements were invented elsewhere and borrowed from these sources.

Culture history is in many respects the study of diffusion and its impact. The great religions of the world, Buddhism, Christianity, Islam, and Judaism, for example, began in specific places and then spread to other regions of the world. Most people know that Christianity spread from its origin in the Middle East, although few people are aware of the diffusion of Buddhism. Originating in northern India, Buddhism then spread throughout all of India, Southeast Asia (Burma, Thailand, Vietnam, Indonesia), and East Asia (China, Tibet, Japan, Korea). In its homeland, India, it virtually disappeared, but it survives in the lands to which it was carried. In human history the diffusion of

San children being introduced to the intricacies of the internal combustion engine.

major world religions has been a major factor in the transformation of many cultures.

Diffusion is not a simple process. It is rare for a society to borrow cultural elements without changing them in some way. Reinterpretation of borrowed items to fit into the fabric of an ongoing cultural system is a common phenomenon. Anthropologists recognize that in the diffusion process, borrowed items may be reinterpreted in form, function, and meaning. The pajamas on Linton's list of borrowed items were invented in India and are used as everyday street clothes in that country. Americans adapted them for use as sleepwear. In many revitalization movements Christian doctrines taught by missionaries were reinterpreted by native converts.

Not all cultures are open to cultural borrowing. The Zuni and Hopi, Indians of the Southwestern United States, are noted for their unwillingness to accept many customs of American culture. They retain their own religion, clan and familial organization, and their distinctive ethnic and cultural identity. Suspicion of outsiders and of foreign influence is basic to the maintenance and integrity of their own way of life. In the nineteenth century, the Ghost Dance originated among the Paiute Indians of Nevada and diffused to many American Indian tribes. Yet the Navajo rejected it because the message of the Ghost Dance stated that the dead would rise. Fear of the dead is a significant part of the Navajo world view, and the Ghost Dance message ran counter to their basic philosophy.

Acculturation and Culture Contact

Diffusion and independent invention are terms that describe the outcome of previous instances of change, where the process of change has not been directly observed. Acculturation and culture contact are processes of change that can be observed and documented by anthropologists. *Acculturation* was defined in American anthropology in the 1930s as the process of change that takes place when two or more cultures come into contact (Redfield, Linton, Herskovits 1936). British anthropologists used the phrase *culture contact* that was identical in meaning to the concept of acculturation.

Development of these concepts arose from the impact of Western culture on non-Western people and cultures. Although the concepts of acculturation and culture contact imply that change is a two-way process, in reality most acculturation and culture contact studies focused on changes occurring in tribal society as the result of the Western cultural presence. Thus when American anthropologists write about acculturated American Indians, they describe Indians who have taken over American behavioral norms and personality characteristics. British culture contact studies were also one-sided in their study of change. Little attention was paid to what was happening to European culture as the result of contact with native cultures.

A. Irving Hallowell, one of the pioneers in the study of the psychological acculturation of American Indians, recognized this bias in many acculturation studies. He attempted to counter this one-sided view by pointing out the impact American Indian cultures had upon American culture and society.

> In America we faced the Indian on receding frontiers for a long period; but outside the frontier there was the shadow of the Indian. This shadow is still upon us. We still mouth words and idioms that reflect intimate contacts with the aborigines of our land. We still make use of plants originally cultivated by them. We wear derivative forms of the footgear they wore. We have collected objects made by them in our homes and in our museums. Our artists have found inspiration in their artistic modes of expression. We constantly see the Indian sweep past our eyes on the movie screen. He persists in our historical novels and westerns (Hallowell 1959:470).

Acculturation and culture contact were more than new concepts designed to map the distribution of cultural elements. American anthropologists believed that studies of acculturation would reveal the laws of culture. This would be done by actually observing the agents of change, the items borrowed, the process of reinterpretation, and the modes of adjustment required by the adoption of new cultural items.

British culture contact studies focused primarily upon the practical uses of anthropological studies of changing native societies. British anthropologists were supported in many instances by colonial administrators who believed that the results of anthropological research could be useful in the governing of native populations. For their part, anthropologists saw themselves as aiding tribal societies through the difficult process of change and adjustment.

Many anthropologists involved in acculturation and culture contact studies unfortunately failed to realize that they, along with the groups they studied, were part of a unique experience — *colonialism,* the domination of most of the world by Western society (Asad 1973). Although the Greeks, Romans, Arabs, and Chinese, among others, had founded empires, none of them rivaled the scope and intensity of European world domination. Recognition of this one-sided bias in the use of acculturation and culture contact concepts in the study of change may have been one reason for their disappearance from the vocabulary of anthropologists. By the early 1960s the more general term *social change* replaced acculturation and culture contact.

The Colonial Experience

Culture change, as a result of independent invention and diffusion, is characteristic of all peoples and cultures. Prior to European world domination, these processes played themselves out in a limited geographical arena and generally involved a gradual process of change. European conquest and control introduced new factors into these processes of change. The conquering Spanish, for example, shattered the political systems of the Inca and the Aztec. Neither of these groups had the opportunity to work out their own destinies. By the same token we will never know what developments would have occurred in the Americas if Columbus had arrived 500 years later.

Imposition of European colonial domination meant that the world was divided into two camps: the dominant European culture and the subjugated tribal and peasant cultures of the world. Western missionaries, traders, plantation owners, and administrators became the major agents of change. What is most significant is that many tribal and peasant areas were brought into the commercial economy of European capitalism. By the time intensive fieldwork became an integral part of cultural anthropology, the tribal and peasant world had been fundamentally altered by the colonial experience. Thus change in the tribal and peasant world in the past 500 years has taken place within the framework of European colonialism.

European colonialism began in a small and seemingly insignificant manner with a few frail Portuguese ships sailing down the west coast of Africa in the last half of the 1400s. Five centuries later, at the end of World War II (1945), no more than two or three countries in the world could claim cultural and political independence from Europe. These five centuries encompassed a period of profound historical and cultural transformation. In the three decades following World War II (1945–1975) the European colonial empires collapsed. This change did not mean the end of European influence upon the world, however. Every tribal and peasant group mentioned in this text has in some way been a part of this process. European exploration and colonialism existed worldwide and fundamentally altered every society it touched.

Age of Exploration and Trade

Many historians have called the opening phases of European expansion the *Vasco da Gama era* (Cipolla 1965; Panikkar 1961). Da Gama was the Portuguese sailor who rounded the tip of South Africa (Cape of Good Hope) and reached India in 1498. The Portuguese subsequently defeated an Arab fleet in the Indian Ocean, established trading posts throughout the East Indies and Southeast Asia, and gained control of the spice trade of the Indies. Oceanic exploration by the Portuguese was later followed by Spanish, Dutch, English, and French exploration. A combination of oceanic sailing vessels, movable sails, and ship-mounted cannons gave the European naval powers domination over the oceans of the world. These first centuries of European expansion and domination were limited to control of strategic coastal areas. European domination rested upon the control of trade routes and, therefore, of trade itself.

In the early years of exploration and trade, the Europeans were well aware of the connection between control of trade and political domination. In the 1600s Sir Walter Raleigh wrote, "Whosoever commands the sea commands trade; whosoever commands the trade of the world commands the riches of the world, and consequently the world itself" (1978:6).

Ferdinand Magellan's circumnavigation of the globe between 1519 and 1522 signaled the worldwide scope of European expansion. This Portuguese sailor demonstrated that European technology, in the form of sailing vessels, now brought the entire world within the reach of European commercial and mercantile interests. From this time the European exploration and discovery of new places and strange peoples became part of world history.

In the succeeding two centuries, Dutch, French, Spanish, and English fleets explored the rest of the world. Since trade was their central interest, these powers established control over strategic localities and founded trading posts. With few exceptions, this phase did not involve the establishment of imperial regimes with settlement of large numbers of colonists. Thus a map of European overseas possessions at this time would have shown scattered settlements and trading posts along the coasts of Africa, India, and among the islands of the Pacific.

A major exception to this pattern was the experience of the Spanish in the New World. The Aztec and Inca civilizations of Mexico and Peru were cut short by the Conquistadores, and relatively small numbers of Spanish settlers were able to establish themselves with the labor and agricultural productivity of the Indian masses they had conquered. Within a few decades the Spanish established a plantation economy based on African slave labor. Thus Columbus's discovery of the New World led to the establishment of the first overseas European empire.

Age of Imperial Rule

By the middle of the eighteenth century, the *age of imperial rule,* the various European powers had established land empires throughout the world, a process that continued into the nineteenth century.

African coasts had been known to the Europeans since the 1470s. The interior of the "dark continent," as it was called, remained a mystery. The African interior was first intensively explored during the nineteenth century by such men as David Livingstone, John Speke, Richard Burton, Hugh Clapperton, and Henry Stanley. Strategic competition between the European powers led to the "scramble for Africa" in the latter part of the nineteenth century as the European powers carved up the continent into various colonial territories.

The social and political climate of New Zealand during the period of the Hau Hau movement is testimony to the expansion of European power and population into the distant corners of the non-Western world. This process of European political control, land acquisition, and immigration of European settlers into New Zealand was repeated through a significant portion of the non-Western world. Although op-

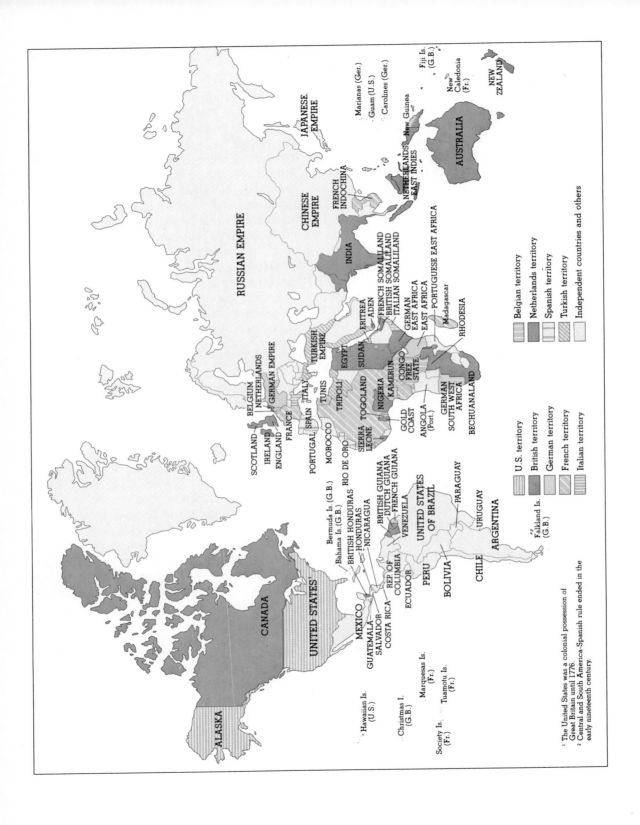

ALASKA

Hawaiian Is. (U.S.)

Christmas I. (G.B.)

Marquesas Is. (Fr.)

Tuamotu Is. (Fr.)

Society Is. (Fr.)

CANADA

UNITED STATES¹

MEXICO
GUATEMALA
SALVADOR
COSTA RICA
HONDURAS
NICARAGUA
BRITISH HONDURAS
Bahama Is. (G.B.)
Bermuda Is. (G.B.)

REP. OF COLUMBIA
ECUADOR
VENEZUELA
BRITISH GUIANA
DUTCH GUIANA
FRENCH GUIANA

PERU
BOLIVIA

UNITED STATES OF BRAZIL

PARAGUAY

CHILE

ARGENTINA

URUGUAY

Falkland Is. (G.B.)

SCOTLAND
IRELAND
ENGLAND
FRANCE
PORTUGAL
SPAIN
BELGIUM
NETHERLANDS
GERMAN EMPIRE
ITALY

RUSSIAN EMPIRE

CHINESE EMPIRE

JAPANESE EMPIRE

FRENCH INDOCHINA

INDIA

TURKISH EMPIRE

MOROCCO
RIO DE ORO
TUNIS
TRIPOLI
EGYPT
SUDAN

ERITREA
ADEN
FRENCH SOMALILAND
BRITISH SOMALILAND
ITALIAN SOMALILAND

SIERRA LEONE
GOLD COAST
TOGOLAND
NIGERIA
KAMERUN
CONGO FREE STATE

ANGOLA (Port.)

GERMAN EAST AFRICA
BRITISH EAST AFRICA
PORTUGUESE EAST AFRICA
Madagascar
RHODESIA

GERMAN SOUTH WEST AFRICA

BECHUANALAND

NETHERLANDS EAST INDIES

New Guinea

Marianas (Ger.)
Guam (U.S.)
Carolines (Ger.)

AUSTRALIA

Fiji Is. (G.B.)

New Caledonia (Fr.)

NEW ZEALAND

U.S. territory

British territory

German territory

French territory

Italian territory

Belgian territory

Netherlands territory

Spanish territory

Turkish territory

Independent countries and others

¹ The United States was a colonial possession of Great Britain until 1776.

² Central and South America-Spanish rule ended in the early nineteenth century.

position to European domination and hostilities were common between Europeans and native populations, a map of the world in 1900 shows its domination by European powers (see Figure 12.1). The British, French, Portuguese, Dutch, German, Italians, Belgians, and Spanish had far-flung overseas empires. The Russians under the Czar had extended their imperial rule to Siberia and Central Asia, and the United States had possessions in the Pacific. Even the few countries that could claim formal political independence were under the economic and commercial control of European powers.

The reasons for European expansion and supremacy are not entirely clear and have been widely debated by historians. An undeniable reason is technological superiority. Ship-mounted cannon, effective firearms, as well as well-organized fighting forces were the ultimate basis for European supremacy. For the tribal populations and peasant societies of the world these were irresistible forces, and the imposition of European political and administrative control rarely involved sustained and lengthy hostilities.

Impact of European Domination

European domination took place over a period of 500 years, and different areas of the world experienced domination in different ways. There were common aspects to the experience, however: changes in population, exploitation, effects of missionary activities, and the impact of colonial administration.

Population. Changes in population were one of the most basic consequences of European

domination. Conquered populations were sometimes exterminated. Many tribal groups initially suffered declines in population, although in this century increases in tribal populations became common. People were often moved from place to place. The sustained growth of European populations may have been related to the dominant position enjoyed by the peoples of Europe. In addition, migration and resettlement of Europeans and other people into conquered and colonized areas were among the most dramatic population shifts under imperial rule.

Destruction and genocide of tribal populations was one result of European domination in many parts of the world. In 1676 the Indian survivors of King Philip's War in New England were sold as slaves in the North African and West Indian slave markets. A brutal example of extermination of a tribal population occurred in Tasmania in the early nineteenth century. Not only did disease and alcohol decimate the indigenous population, but white settlers also actively hunted the Tasmanians as if they were animals, and shot men, women, and children as a form of sport (Oliver 1961). As a consequence the Tasmanians became extinct in the 1870s (Bonwick 1870). This pattern of population decimation, although it did not always lead to extermination, was also common throughout the Pacific Islands. Initial contact between Europeans and natives was also often punctuated by hostilities. Sailors and explorers introduced European diseases and alcohol. Firearms, introduced by Europeans and used in native warfare, also had an enormous impact upon the population. In the Marquesas Islands, in the Pacific, the native population in the eighteenth century was estimated to be about 80,000 people. Through a combination of disease, whiskey, and guns, the population of these islands fell to no more than 2000 by the beginning of the twentieth century (Oliver 1961:208–210).

Another consequence of European world

Figure 12.1. European powers divided up the world during the period of colonial expansion. A map of the world in 1900 shows the extent of their domination.

domination was large-scale movement and migration of people from one place to another. Native Americans (Indians) were forced westward by both settlers and the United States government. European expansion also involved the wholesale movement of European settlers to the Americas, South Africa, East Africa, Australia, and New Zealand.

European domination involved not only the movement of people, but also the transportation of domesticated plants and animals. During the Vasco da Gama era, Europeans became agents of diffusion on a worldwide scale. Introduction of new plants and animals had a dramatic impact upon both tribal and European populations and cultures. The introduction by the Spanish of domesticated animals into the New World, especially the horse, dramatically altered the pattern of life of many American Indian tribes. Before the introduction of the

horse, the plains of the United States were inhabited by simple horticulturists living in river valleys and by small bands of roving hunters and gatherers. With the introduction of the horse, mounted buffalo hunters could successfully exploit the resources of this region. Large numbers of American Indian tribes moving out onto the plains gave rise to a classic American Indian cultural pattern.

Another example testifying to the important role that Europeans played as agents of diffusion and change is seen in New Guinea. In Highland New Guinea societies like the Bomagai-Angoiang depend upon sweet potato cultivation. Sweet potatoes, initially domesticated in South America, grow in high altitudes and temperate climatic conditions — conditions found in Highland New Guinea. Spanish explorers in the sixteenth and seventeenth centuries may have introduced the sweet potato into New Guinea. If this is true, it means that the Highland cultures of New Guinea are to some degree the consequence of the diffusionary role of European explorers.

Worldwide distribution and introduction of new food crops have had important conse-

Nyanda (the short woman in the foreground) under arrest in Salisbury, South Rhodesia, in 1897. Accused by the British of instigating violence against white settlers, she was tried, convicted, and hanged.

quences. It can be argued that the introduction of potatoes and corn, domesticated by American Indians, into Europe was the basis of the population growth that began about 1650. This growth in population in turn became a driving force behind continuing European overseas expansion.

Centuries of population decline and stagnation in the tribal world have been followed by rapid population increase in this century. Public health measures, famine control, cessation of tribal warfare, and disease eradication programs introduced by Europeans have been instrumental in causing this increase. Along with increases in the numbers of tribal people, there has been an enormous population explosion in traditional peasant societies. At the time of European contact the populations of peasant societies were significantly larger than those of tribal groups. Peasant societies did not experience the population declines that were so prominent in tribal societies following European contact. Diseases that were lethal to tribal peoples posed little threat to the people of India, China, Southeast Asia, and the Middle East, where such diseases were already widespread. In addition, during the early contact period peasants were not viewed as subhuman savages to be hunted and shot down. This vicious and negative attitude toward tribal people was well expressed in 1867 in an article in the Topeka, Kansas, newspaper *Weekly Leader*. The article characterized Indians as "a set of miserable, dirty, lousy, blanketed, thieving, lying, sneaking, murdering, graceless, faithless, gut-eating skunks as the Lord ever permitted to infect the earth, and whose immediate and final extermination all men, except Indian agents and traders, should pray for" (Hallowell 1959:449).

Exploitation. Although greed was not the only motivation behind European expansion and control, it was certainly important. In the drive for financial gain, tribal and peasant societies were fundamentally altered and reshaped. In fact, the only societies that avoided this aspect of European domination were those that had nothing to offer in the way of turning a profit. Tikopia, described by Firth in the 1920s as a relatively untouched paradise, was untouched because it had little to offer Europeans looking for economic opportunities.

In the history of European expansion, no example of audacity and greed is as dramatic as that of the Spanish Conquistadores who destroyed the Aztec and Inca empires. Small bands of Spaniards toppled highly complex state systems. Although their horses and firearms helped, it was their greed for gold that drove them. No act of villainy was too great and no feat too difficult to deter them in their insatiable quest for wealth and power. Francisco Pizarro, with an army of no more than 180 men, marched into the Inca Empire in 1532 and seized the Inca monarch before an Indian army of thousands. Although the Inca monarch filled a room seventeen feet by twenty feet to a depth of nine feet with gold as a ransom, Pizarro executed him and divided up the country and the Indians among the Spanish conquerors and settlers.

Exploitation is a constant theme of colonialism. In the early period of colonialism trade monopolies and labor exploitation were common. Trade monopolies were based on military superiority and control of trade and trade routes. The Portuguese, for example, monopolized the spice trade in the sixteenth century by controlling the Indian Ocean and establishing a small number of fortified positions along the coasts of India, Southern Arabia, and East Africa. Labor exploitation frequently meant slavery, serfdom, and forced migration for many non-Western people. These forms of exploitation in effect turned much of the world's population into poorly paid producers of commodities for the European economy. Europe's growing prosperity during this period was directly related to this emerging world economy (Wallerstein 1974).

Exploitation was not restricted to economic and political domains; cultural exploitation occurred as well. Its most common manifestation was the devaluation of native cultures as worthless and inferior. Closely allied to these claims of European cultural superiority were theories of racial inferiority applied to native people. Arguments of racial inferiority of tribal people were a major ideological justification and excuse for slavery, the destruction of native cultures, and the imposition of colonial rule.

Slavery. Slavery existed in many parts of the world before European intrusion, but its growth and expansion were consequences of European economic activities. Demand for labor in the mines and plantations of the New World were met by the African slave trade.

From the earliest years of contact the Portuguese developed the African slave trade. The discovery of America and the emergence of the plantation economy gave an enormous impetus to the slave trade that involved the forced migration of millions of Africans to the New World. On a smaller scale, Europeans transported Hindu laborers to Fiji and Melanesian workers to Australia and to other Pacific Islands.

West Africa and parts of Central Africa became major sources of slaves. Slavery led to the emergence of powerful West African Kingdoms such as Dahomey, Benin, and Ashanti, which were built upon warfare, firearms, and the slave trade. Introduction of European firearms raised the level and intensity of warfare. A consequence of this warfare, in addition to slave-raiding expeditions, was the sale of defeated populations in the expanding slave

markets. Such sales generated more firearms, more European goods, and more warfare.

Importation of slaves into the New World resulted in the development of a new type of economy — the plantation. This productive system depended upon cheap slave labor and production of a single crop such as sugar or cotton on a plantation for an overseas cash market. Generating enormous profits, plantations growing tea, coffee, rubber, and cotton emerged in other parts of the world — India, Indonesia, and the Pacific. Worked by contract labor, these plantations gave rise to a rural, poverty-stricken labor force. In the postslavery economy of the New World, freed slaves also became dependent and impoverished rural workers. Throughout many parts of the Caribbean, slaves were replaced by indentured laborers recruited from India (Klass 1980).

Commodities and the cash market. Production of commodities such as tea, sugar, rubber, and cotton on a worldwide scale had enormous implications for native people. Many individuals became poorly paid laborers, sometimes no better than servants or slaves. In New Guinea large numbers of men migrated to work on European-owned mines and plantations. The lack of able-bodied men in rural areas meant that women, children, and the few remaining men were unable to grow enough food for their needs.

Production of a single cash crop for export put workers at the mercy of the world market. A slight fluctuation in price could mean disaster for producers. Often the brunt of economic decline fell most heavily upon laborers who were thrown out of work and who rarely had any economic alternatives. In many colonized areas control of prices rested in the hands of the dominant European power that owned the colony; for example, the British East India Company exercised direct control over all cash

One of the consequences of colonialism was the emergence of a plantation economy producing goods for the world market and worked by slaves or poorly paid laborers. In the American South, poorly paid Blacks worked as pickers in cotton plantations.

commodities produced in India. In the Netherlands East Indies (Indonesia) the Dutch restricted the production of spices by destroying some plants in order to keep prices high. If a small elite controls both political and economic power, the people at the bottom of the economic and political pyramid usually suffer the worst economic consequences.

Incorporation of non-Western society into a European-dominated commercial economy had far-reaching consequences. French and English traders in Northeast America opened a brisk trade in beaver skins with Indian groups. As the local fur-bearing animals were hunted out, Indian groups attempted to gain possession of the regions around the Great Lakes, where fur-bearing animals still abounded. Armed by their European trading partners, a series of Indian intertribal wars broke out in the eastern and Great Lake regions of North America over control of the market for beaver pelts. In this example, we see another facet of European exploitation. In order to satisfy the luxury demand for fashionable pelts in European society, American Indian groups engaged in intertribal warfare and a valuable resource was hunted almost to extermination.

In one sense the problem of endangered species, an issue that confronts the entire world at the present time, has deep historic roots and is still part of a worldwide commerce and commodity oriented economic system.

All of these exploitive activities had a single goal, the provision of commodities for the European market. The world was ransacked to satisfy these demands not only for gold, silver, furs, spices, cotton, and sugar, but also for such frivolous items as sweet-smelling sandalwood, mother-of-pearl, ivory, and bird-of-paradise feathers. To meet these demands tribal societies and their populations paid a terrible price.

European domination not only meant commodity and trade exploitation, but also the expropriation of land from native populations. In New Zealand, the British assumed political control in 1840, and by 1860, 100,000 Europeans had arrived and were actively acquiring land from the Maori inhabitants. Massive European settlement and native displacement occurred in North America, South America, Australia, South Africa, Rhodesia, East Africa, and some Pacific Islands. In some instances, as in Tasmania, the native populations were exterminated. More often, however, the natives who survived the initial confrontation with Europeans were reduced in population and relegated to out-of-the-way tribal reservations. The native population was almost always reduced to political and economic subordination and was expected to accommodate itself to the dominant European culture.

Agents of Change: Missionaries and Administrators

Many changes in tribal and peasant society were the unplanned and accidental consequence of the European pursuit of profit, land, power, or strategic advantage. Native society adapted, accommodated, resisted, or disappeared, but most Europeans were not very concerned about these changes. This lack of concern was not true for missionaries and administrators. Although many of their actions had unforeseen consequences, both missionaries and administrators had clear goals. In one case it was conversion and salvation of heathen souls; in the other case it was the establishment of law and order and the implementation of orderly administration. In both cases missionaries and administrators were the major agents of change in the non-Western world.

Missionaries. Today it is difficult to realize that Christian missionaries were among the most pervasive and determined agents of change in the tribal and peasant world. The earliest explorers were accompanied by missionaries, and the conversion of natives, who were considered "heathens," was almost as important as capturing their gold. In the early phases of contact and up to the end of the nineteenth century, the Christian missionary was a major agent of culture change.

It is not easy for anthropologists to assess objectively the impact of missionary activities on tribal society. The premises of missionary work are directly opposite to those of anthropology. As cultural relativists, anthropologists begin with the assumption that any cultural system is as good or bad as any other system. Missionaries begin with the ethnocentric view

Roman Catholic missionaries celebrate mass among the Tiwi of Australia. The young boys dressed in white are new graduates of the mission school.

that *their* religion is the true path to salvation. Almost all Christian missionaries assumed the superiority of European customs and the inferiority and backwardness of native customs. In the history of European domination, religious missionaries attempted to remold tribal society in the image of a Christian and European world.

Conversion to Christianity was the major objective of missionary work. Conversion often involved the destruction of native beliefs and rituals. One of the crudest, but most effective, techniques for proving the inferiority of native deities was the desecration of native shrines, temples, and holy places. Missionaries in the Pacific are known to have urinated and defecated on native shrines to demonstrate graphically that their god was superior to native deities. Not only were missionaries concerned with converting so-called heathens to their particular denomination of Christianity, but they also suppressed many native customs — plural marriage, dancing, sexual permissiveness, and nakedness — that they considered abhorrent and sinful. The shapeless Mother Hubbard dress introduced by missionaries to the islanders of the Pacific is an example of the overwhelming prudery of some missionaries. In Australia the Tiwi marriage system of infant bestowal and polygyny was suppressed by missionaries. These cases are only two examples of the way in which missionaries attacked a wide array of tribal customs and institutions.

Although many aspects of missionary activity had negative and destructive effects upon tribal cultures, other aspects of missionary work were beneficial. One of the most important consequences of early missionary activity was the suppression of some of the destructive aspects of early European contact. In the first phases of European exploration and discovery, native populations were often exposed to the worst elements of European society. These rogues and rascals included traders, beachcombers, whalers, escaped convicts, adventurers, runaway sailors, and slavers who were interested in fun and profit. Slavery, sexual exploitation and debauchery of native women, intensification of native warfare, the introduction of whiskey, guns, and diseases, and the shooting of natives for sport were some of the activities of Europeans in the early phases of contact. Missionaries attacked and in many areas successfully halted these excesses and depredations. In addition, some missionaries became spokesmen for native populations and attempted to defend their rights.

In the pursuit of converts missionaries introduced schools into many tribal societies. The founder of the Maori Hau Hau movement, Te Ua, had been educated by Wesleyan missionaries. In many ways education of native people by missionaries became the basis for future independence movements. Leaders of national independence movements were frequently educated in mission schools, and mission-funded schools and colleges became one of the major vehicles for exposing native people to the entire spectrum of Western culture. Thus the efforts of missionaries in suppressing the brutal excesses of European contact and the introduction of education must be considered a credit to these men and women.

In most cases the missionaries' sincerity cannot be doubted, and many were martyred in what they considered a noble calling and enterprise. Most anthropologists, however, remain ambivalent about missionaries and the impact of their activities. Douglas Oliver's assessment of missionaries in the Pacific portrays this ambivalent attitude:

> Great things have undoubtedly been done: cannibalism suppressed and areas made safe for trader and official; infanticide discouraged; islanders shielded for a while from the totally selfish exploitation of nonmissionary whites; and a smattering of education dispersed to help islanders compete in the white man's world. But there is a debit side, too.

Evangelism came along and sought to revolutionize native religions, putting in their place Western systems of belief and practice radically unsuited to Oceania. Some native cultures went to pieces under the impact; few of them survived as integrated systems, and in those that did, Christianity would hardly be recognized as such (Oliver 1961:177–178).

Centuries of missionary activity resulted in the conversion of most native populations to Christianity. By the time anthropological fieldworkers appeared in the tribal world, many of the excesses of missionary zeal had played themselves out. In the process tribal society was fundamentally altered, and few if any "untouched" societies remained to be studied by anthropologists.

Administrators. If missionaries brought the word of God, administrators brought the word of man. Emergence of land empires in the eighteenth and nineteenth centuries depended upon military and political rule. In order to exploit their territorial empires, European nation-states needed to have law and order. Local administrators became the agents of an extensive colonial system. They were responsible for the administration of justice, the imposition of peace, the collection of taxes, labor recruiting, and, in some cases, the allocation of land. Some colonial administrators had authority for vast areas and hundreds of thousands of native inhabitants.

In the earliest phases of contact private trading companies were given charters to trade in particular areas. Such private trading companies were found in Indonesia, India, South Africa, West Africa, and parts of the Pacific. Private trading companies, however, were more interested in turning a profit than in effectively governing territories. In some cases, especially the Belgian Congo (now the country of Zaire), the rapaciousness of private trading companies became an embarrassment to the European powers. In the Belgian Congo forced labor, severe beatings, and brutal exploitation of native populations were practiced by Europeans seeking to gain the most profit in the shortest period of time. For these and other reasons, toward the end of the nineteenth century the responsibility for the administration of colonial territories was taken away from private companies and placed in the hands of colonial governments.

With some exceptions, colonial administrators provided efficient and orderly government with a minimum of corruption and terror. An overriding concern of all colonial administrations was the avoidance of rebellion and revolt. One solution involved incorporating indigenous political institutions and political leaders into the colonial administration hierarchy. This action solved two problems. Colonial administrators were limited in terms of manpower and money; by using tribal leaders they were able to get an inexpensive staff. At the same time administrators avoided antagonizing the people who were most likely to organize and lead revolts. One anthropologist working in Central Africa once defined an African tribal chief as the only member of the colonial bureaucracy who did not take his vacation in England.

Unlike missionaries, colonial administrators did not interfere with or attempt to change many aspects of native culture such as kinship, marriage, religion, and local political institutions. They did, however, suppress customs that interfered with the imposition of law and order or were defined as repugnant and uncivilized. Native warfare was, of course, outlawed. In addition, infanticide, human sacrifice, cannibalism, headhunting, witchcraft accusations, and slavery were suppressed.

Colonial rule brought about significant changes. New legal systems were grafted onto traditional norms and customs. Implementation of administrative policies involved the establishment of new political and judicial institutions. Boundaries and territories established during imperial rule were possibly the most

Sir William E. Maxwell (seated on the left), governor of the Gold Coast colony (now Ghana) in 1895, with his aides and a contingent of African police. Use of local people in the police force was common throughout the British Empire.

important consequence of European colonialism; in time they became the basis for the modern nation-states of the Third World.

Heritage of Colonialism

Although the Age of Empire has ended, the consequences of European domination and culture persist. Europeans discovered a world of tribes, small states, and peasant societies. They left behind a world of nation-states. The territorial and political organization of the contemporary world is a heritage of European colonialism.

Despite the severing of colonial ties, many newly created nation-states have modeled their internal political institutions upon European prototypes. Constitutions, legal codes, and parliaments are common political institutions throughout Third World countries. Political ideas about freedom, voting, and civil rights have taken root in many former colonial territories. The practice of democracy is often violated, but most national leaders pay homage to this political philosophy.

Economic Dependence

One of the most far-reaching consequences of colonial rule was the economic transformation of the tribal and peasant world. Imposition of peace throughout the imperial realms provided a safe environment for economic and commercial investment. Cheap native labor and protected trade policies made such investments immensely profitable. In the space of a few decades the face of the tribal and peasant world was changed. Roads, railroads, and harbors were built; mines, commercial establishments, and factories were established. New urban areas emerged, and everywhere labor migration by tribesmen and peasants became a common phenomenon. All of these activities were tied to the growth of European industrialization. Tribal and rural areas provided raw materials, cheap labor, and potential markets for European industrial production.

Incorporation of tribal and peasant populations into a worldwide commercial and industrial economy had devastating effects upon these people. It involved a shift from the independence of a local subsistence economy to dependence upon a world economy. In this process tribesmen and peasants acquired new skills and jobs, new goods, and access to money. These gains, however, were coupled with the loss of economic and political independence. The new standard of living was now dependent upon decisions made in world capitals like London, New York, Paris, and Berlin. In the 1930s, as a result of the worldwide depression, thousands of African miners and workers in Central Africa were thrown out of work. The economic depression also had a devastating effect upon plantation workers in the South Pacific. Few of these workers understood what had happened, and it was no longer possible for them to withdraw into the security of a peasant or tribal economy. Copra producers in Melanesia, cocoa farmers in West Africa, and rubber workers in Indonesia and Malaysia were all at the mercy of fluctuating world economic conditions during these years.

It is possible that the industrial and commercial economy that the Europeans introduced into their colonies could become the basis for further economic development in Third World nations. Political leaders in the Third World are committed to the idea of economic development and a constantly rising standard of living. The populations of these new nations seek employment as well as the material products of industrialization. The enormous and difficult problems of economic growth for Third World countries have raised arguments about the actual independence of former European colonies. Some anthropologists claim that political dependence has been replaced by economic dependence, which makes development unlikely. With their economies dominated by commodity production established during the colonial period, many former European colonies operate at a severe economic disadvantage. Recent attempts by commodity producers, especially in oil and coffee, to set high world prices are attempts to redirect the flow of wealth. As one American government official commented during the 1973 Arab oil embargo and massive price increase, "This is their revenge for the nineteenth century."

Some anthropologists argue that one consequence of the colonial experience has been the amassing of huge wealth and control of the world economy by the West. This theory, known as the *dependency theory,* argues that despite their political independence Third World countries are not only dependent upon the West, but also fail to share and obtain an equitable distribution of the world's resources, production, and wealth. Proponents of dependency theory argue that the underdeveloped areas of the world are becoming more and more impoverished at the present time. They see multinational corporations replacing colonial regimes as the major institutions controlling the wealth and resources of the world.

Cultural Influences

Cultural influences first introduced by Europeans continue to manifest themselves throughout the Third World. Educational systems established by missionaries and colonial regimes have been maintained and are generally modeled after their European counterparts. In some African countries, for example, college students may learn more about the Latin language and Latin poetry than the languages and literature of their own country. Spanish, French, Portuguese, and English, all the languages of conquest and colonization, are the dominant languages of the world.

In the postcolonial era political and economic elites have emerged in Third World countries. Many of these elites look to Euro-American culture for their inspiration. Their children are often educated in Europe or America, creating a cosmopolitan and international group that shares ideas and values derived from Western experience and culture.

In the contemporary world, mass communication systems have become the chief means of disseminating Western cultural values and items on a world-wide scale. Many items of Western mass culture — blue jeans, disco music, and soft drinks — replace local cultural traditions. The appeal of Western culture is not limited to material items. Social movements and innovative values that have emerged in Western society — women's liberation, abortion, gay rights — are quickly transmitted all over the world. For example, when Cohen studied Collefiore, Italy, in the mid-sixties, the villagers knew little about the United States; none had ever been there. Yet, many of the changes they saw in the village — women working outside the home, short skirts, teenage dating — were called "the American way." They viewed these changes as inevitable, and they shared with rural people all over the world a grudging admiration for the new. In many ways we can see in this example a form of cultural imperialism, in which American and Western mass culture is accorded a superior status.

Westernization and Western influence continue to affect many nations. When Nehru was prime minister of India, he said he would like to see Indian society selectively adopt those aspects of Western culture that would be most advantageous. Other leaders have voiced similar sentiments. Complete control over the processes, selection, and direction of culture change, however, seems to be beyond human grasp. Limitation of the social and cultural consequences of change is not yet possible.

Traditional and modern forms of transportation in Saudi Arabia. The contrast between traditional and modern is one index of the rapid and uneven pace of change in the non-Western world.

Summary

Cultural change is a fundamental component of human history and society. In modern society we see ourselves as living in a world characterized by rapid change and think of the tribal and peasant world as unchanging islands of stability. Change, however, is as characteristic of tribal and peasant people as it is of Western society. In the last 500 years, in fact, the experience of tribal and peasant people in their confrontation with Western culture has brought about fundamental and irreversible changes in their traditional ways of life. For tribal people, imposition of Western culture has involved severe cultural and social disruption.

Revitalization movements are one reaction to these situations. Interpretations of revitalization movements stress the combination of native and Western elements into a religiously formulated ideology. Ideologies such as Hau Hau not only express hostility and opposition to Western culture, but also are attempts to create a new culture out of the wreckage of the past. Wallace has delineated several stages in the development of revitalization movements: the steady state, a period of increased stress, a period of cultural distortion, a period of revitalization, and the new steady state. Worsley adds an additional element to this analysis, the conversion of religiously based revitalization movements into secular and pragmatic political organizations.

Diffusion and independent invention are major processes of culture change. Diffusion stresses historical connections and borrowing to account for the geographical distribution of cultural and social elements. Independent invention assumes that similar circumstances lead to similar cultural solutions and practices.

Acculturation and culture contact are processes of culture change that represent the transfer of cultural items from one society to another. Anthropologists believed that acculturation and culture contact investigations would lead to an understanding of cultural dynamics through the process of intercultural transmission. Critics of these studies of change pointed out that they were often one-sided, focusing primarily upon what native populations

took from Western society and ignoring the impact of native cultures upon Western society. Acculturation and culture contact studies were criticized for their failure to place the confrontation of Western and non-Western societies within the wider context of Western colonialism.

The colonial experience is the framework for the comprehensive study of social change in the contemporary world. Exploration and exploitation were the basis of the colonial experience. European explorers and empire builders used ocean-going vessels and superior weaponry to sweep aside all resistance. In the early phases of contact, called the Vasco da Gama era, Europeans limited their colonial activities to the possession of strategic locations and the worldwide control of trade.

The second phase of European control began with imperial rule: the development of extensive overseas empires, the conquest of native peoples, and the establishment of imperial regimes.

Population change is one of the most dramatic consequences of the colonial experi-

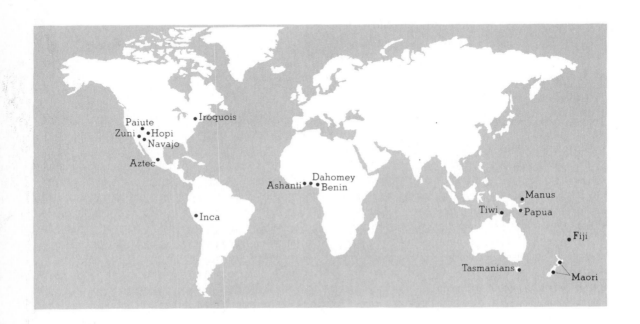

ence. Entire peoples and cultures disappeared and wholesale movement of populations involving both migration and slavery reshaped the distribution of people around the world.

Pursuit of financial and commercial gain was an important part of colonialism. In response to these demands the cultures of tribal and peasant peoples were fundamentally altered. Introduction of cash crops and the plantation economy reduced many populations to exploited and poorly paid laborers. Emergence of commodity production, exploitation of mineral resources, and development of overseas markets in colonial territories created urban areas where none had existed before. Colonialism created new cultural situations where traditional cultural practices could no longer be maintained.

Among the agents of change, missionaries and administrators stand out as key figures of directed change. Conversion of native populations to various denominations of Christianity meant the demise not only of traditional religious practices, but also many other customs deemed uncivilized, barbaric, and primitive. Administrators imposed Western notions of law, order, and government upon native societies and redrew the political map of the world. In this historical encounter — the colonial experience — the world was refashioned.

Although we now live in a postcolonial era, the impact of the colonial period on human history still continues. Westernization, especially among Third World elites and youths, appears to be a continuing process. Efforts to understand and control the direction of cultural change still elude even the most powerful economic and political leaders.

Key Terms and Concepts

revitalization
    movements
cargo cults
independent
    invention
diffusion
acculturation

culture contact
social change
Vasco da Gama era
colonialism
age of imperial rule
dependency theory

Suggested Readings

Allen, Charles, ed. *Plain Tales from the Raj.* London: Futura Publications, 1976. Based on more than sixty interviews with British men and women who lived in India when it was part of the British Empire, this book recounts the life of a bygone era.

Cipolla, Carlo M. *Guns, Sails, and Empires: Technological Innovation and the Early Phases of European Expansion 1400–1700.* New York: Pantheon, 1966. An eminent historian describes the technological basis for European domination in the early years of European exploration and discovery.

Diaz del Castillo, Bernal. *The True History of the Conquest of Mexico.* Ann Arbor, Mich.: Xerox University Microfilms, 1966 (reprint of 1800 ed.). An eyewitness account of the defeat and destruction of the Aztec Empire in 1520–1521 by a soldier who took part in Cortes's expedition.

Hemming, John. *Red Gold: The Conquest of the Brazilian Indians, 1500–1760.* An account of the defeat and destruction of the Indians of Brazil during three centuries of European colonialism.

Rodman, Margaret, and Matthew Cooper, eds. *The Pacification of Melanesia.* Ann Arbor, Mich.: University of Michigan Press, 1979. A collection of papers by anthropologists surveys the imposition of European colonial control throughout Melanesia and New Guinea. Useful as a detailed study of a complex and world-wide phenomenon.

Spindler, Louise S. *Culture Change and Modernization.* New York: Holt, Rinehart and Winston, 1977. An anthropological view of culture change using case studies and different models of change. An effective introduction to the difficult problem of understanding sociocultural change.

Woods, Clyde M. *Culture Change.* Dubuque, Iowa: Wm. C. Brown, 1975. A brief introduction to the anthropological study of change.

Part IV

Retrospect and Prospect

Describing and understanding behavior in different cultural settings was the goal in the first three parts of this book. Cultural anthropology with its particular methods, theories, and research findings was the means of accomplishing this goal. In this last part and final chapter, we turn our view toward cultural anthropology itself. This is not just a "history of anthropology" littered with names, dates, and events. Anthropology no less than horticulture, kinship, or war is a form of behavior and can be understood in much the same way as any other human endeavor. The emergence of anthropology and its growth, development, and future must be understood within the context of time and place.

In anthropology's first one hundred years, anthropologists took on the task of recording the traditional life ways of non-Western people that were generally ignored by other scholars. Today this particular task is less and less possible. Currently, many of the peasant and tribal people of the world are experiencing change on an unprecedented scale. The Western world has reached into the most remote areas of the planet, and no culture remains untouched. Tribal and peasant people have moved into urban centers, becoming part of the world-wide economic system. As a result, anthropologists can no longer restrict themselves to the small peasant village or tribal community. One consequence of this development has been the shift of anthropologists into new areas of research. Esther Newton's study of female impersonators — drag queens — that opens this final chapter is an illustration of the new frontiers of anthropology.

In recent years anthropologists have turned to the study of their own societies. Here a film is being made as part of a study project in a rural Mississippi community.

Chapter 13

Retrospect and Prospect

Up to this point the purpose of this book has been to describe the dimensions of cultural anthropology as well as to present its major conclusions and results. In this chapter, however, the perspective shifts to an introspective and historical view of cultural anthropology. Anthropology as a recognizable discipline emerged a little over a century ago, and since then it has undergone many developments and transformations. A description and understanding of these changes is valuable for several reasons. If we accept the basic anthropological maxim that the various parts of a culture are interrelated, we can see in the history of anthropology the changing circumstances and conditions of Western society of which anthropology is only a small part. Scientific disciplines do not develop in a vacuum; they are related to and respond to their social context. At the same time the particular history of anthropology has had a major influence on its future direction. Thus the focus of this chapter is on the history of anthropology and also its future prospects.

Fieldwork with Female Impersonators

The book began with accounts of fieldwork in tribal society or under conditions comparable to conditions in tribal society. The text closes with an account of fieldwork in an unlikely and unusual setting – a bar in the midwestern United States that features female impersonators, drag queens. This account is included to show that the problems faced by Esther Newton in her fieldwork with drag queens are comparable to the problems faced by anthropologists in more traditional settings.

Cooperation between third-world anthropologists and their American and European counterparts is one of the more recent developments of cultural anthropology. Allan Holmberg was the initial director of the Cornell University project in Vicos, Peru. He was first aided and then succeeded as director by Mario Vasquez, a Peruvian anthropologist.

The first drag show I saw was in a small bar on Chicago's Near North Side. I did not understand about half of the performance, and my reaction was one of mingled shock and fascination. The audience clearly found the performance exceedingly funny. Never having seen a man dressed in full female attire before, I was astounded to find performer and audience joined through laughter in the commission and witnessing of a taboo act. On the basis of that observation I hypothesized that I had witnessed a "cultural peformance" and decided to attempt to analyze it.

At this early stage the practical problem was to see more drag shows and to establish contact with a female impersonator to see if the study was feasible. I approached a female impersonator between shows in the bar in which he was working. I explained that I was

an anthropologist at the University of Chicago and that I would like to interview him. I stated that I was impressed with his performance and with the enthusiasm of the audience and that I wanted to question him about the profession of female impersonation. To my amazement, he replied that he had majored in anthropology in college and that he would willingly talk to me. Thereafter I interviewed this man seven times, at first in the bar and later at his home. He turned out to be my entree into the drag world and my best informant. He was a highly articulate, intelligent man who from the first was at least as dedicated to the study as I was. He had been performing professionally for about twelve years in several different parts of the country, and he knew the history and structure of the profession.

Between August and November, 1965, I interviewed four other female impersonators in their apartments. These interviews were set up for me by my original informant. In addition, I spent many evenings "hanging around" Chicago drag bars, seeing shows, and getting to know performers and audiences. The problem at this stage was in getting impersonators to talk to me at all. Above all they did not wish to be confronted by an unsympathetic person who would ask insensitive questions or show a condescending attitude. The fact that most of them did not really know what an anthropologist was, was helpful in avoiding preconceived hostility. But it is doubtful that they would have consented to talk to me without the enthusiastic endorsement of my original informant, who was a respected figure in the group. Second, in speaking with the potential informant to set up the interview, I made it plain that I had some familiarity with drag and that I was *not* interested in psychological problems.

My original informant left Chicago to take a job in Kansas City. He suggested that I come to Kansas City and that in his capacity as "boss" of the show, he would gain me admittance to the backstage, where I could meet the performers on a more sustained and less formal basis and could actually observe them in their natural habitat. Accordingly, I made three trips to Kansas City. Once the performers had accepted me as a fixture backstage and rapport had been established, I proceeded more or less as a field worker might. I lived in two different cheap hotels where performers lived. I spent time during the day with impersonators, both singly and in groups, and participated in their activities, including parties and outings. Most important, I spent every night in the two bars where the impersonators worked, either backstage, watching the show, or talking to the bar personnel and generally observing the bar life. I considered my own role to include a great deal of participation, which would have been difficult to avoid in any case. I not only listened and questioned, I also answered questions and argued. I helped out with the shows whenever I could, pulling curtains, running messages for the performers, and bringing in drinks and french fries from the restaurant across the street. When the performers half jokingly suggested that I should stand in for an absent stripper, however, I drew the line.

The most difficult methodological problem was not with performances per se but with audiences. Urban audiences are bound to present a problem; they are anonymous and transient. Drag audiences are worse, because there is an aura around drag shows that is at best risque, at worst sordid. This is particularly true of the straight audiences. Drag shows are subcultural events for many homosexuals, and the audiences are stable and drawn from a recognizable subculture. In Chicago and Kansas City, I came to know many of the "regulars" at gay drag shows and could question them about their relationship to female impersonators, both socially and as per-

Female impersonator, one of Ester Newton's key informants, in street clothes and in drag for performance.

formers. Straight audiences, on the other hand, are made up of people who have no or only very limited contact with female impersonators in a social sense, and who are entirely anonymous. Members of straight audiences do not wish to be questioned during or between performances by a roving anthropologist. Not only is their attendance at a drag show risque and probably slightly shameful, but they are generally out strictly "to have a good time." I would have been thrown out of the club immediately by the manager had any members of the straight audiences complained about me. After all, business is business. In this situation, the best I could do was to observe straight audiences again and again, and to consider them as entities, transient but with certain standard characteristics (Newton 1972:132–136).

To anthropologists of an earlier generation, this study might not be considered anthropology. Fieldwork in the drag world appears far removed from fieldwork in tribal and peasant societies. In many respects, however, Newton's account of her research and field problems parallels the experience of fieldworkers in non-Western cultures. There is the initial problem of gaining entrance to the world of the people being studied. In a fashion similar to the experiences of Hart, Briggs, Keiser, and Powdermaker, the contact person emerges as a vital element in Newton's anthropological fieldwork. In addition, Newton had to establish rapport, develop informants, carve out a suitable role and identity, and contend with the myriad problems of participation faced by a fieldworker in this "exotic" world.

Why might an older generation of anthropologists think that Newton's work is outside the limits of cultural anthropology? The first reason is that it is a study conducted in American society. In the 1930s when W. Lloyd Warner shifted his research interest from the Murngin of Australia to a New England town (Yankee City), he became a sociologist in the eyes of many anthropologists. Another reason is that Newton's research does not focus upon a culture, a society, or a community. Instead it focuses upon an occupational group that appears to represent an extreme level of deviance from mainstream American values.

Today few contemporary anthropologists would question the anthropological nature of Newton's study. In order to understand this shift in orientation from earlier conceptions of anthropology, we must look at historical developments in the discipline.

Retrospect: The Emergence of Anthropology

Although we have emphasized the crucial role of fieldwork in cultural anthropology, in the early period of the discipline (1860–1900) fieldwork was relatively uncommon. Historians of anthropology disagree about the date of anthropology's emergence as a discipline, but most agree that the work of Edward Tylor and Lewis Morgan in the 1860s and 1870s was crucial to the definition of cultural anthropology. Focusing upon tribal people as the subject matter for study and using the concept of culture to explain differences in behavior, Tylor and Morgan established the basic dimensions of cultural anthropology: a comparative perspective, nonbiological explanations for behavior, and an orientation toward non-Western society. They lacked a sense of rigor in the collection of their data, however. Content to rely upon the haphazard and often uncritical writings of explorers, administrators, traders, and missionaries, anthropologists of the nineteenth century constructed theoretical formulations based on inadequate and unreliable data. This factor may be one reason why this early period was characterized by interminable and insoluble theoretical arguments. Nineteenth-century anthropologists, for example, argued about whether matriarchy (rule by women) or patriarchy (rule by men) came first. It was a continuing controversy of this period. In many ways, there was a speculative and conjectural aspect to nineteenth-century anthropology that spun complicated and cumbersome theories on a frail foundation.

In the closing decades of the nineteenth century and the first two decades of the twentieth century, field research emerged as a core element in anthropology. At this point it became a technique for questioning nineteenth-century theoretical formulations. Malinowski's research in the Trobriand Islands during World War I added a dimension of depth to anthropological fieldwork. Fieldwork for the next half century became the basis for detailed descriptions of non-Western cultures. This apparently uncomplicated technique provided an empirical foundation for a multitude of different and often conflicting theoretical positions in cultural anthropology (see Chapter 2).

In cultural evolutionary theory of the nineteenth century, the stated goals were the discovery of the origin and development of cultural institutions using tribal societies to reconstruct the history of cultural development. With the benefit of historical hindsight, we can argue that the evolutionists' view of tribal society as representing earlier stages of human society served to justify and validate the expansion and domination associated with European colonialism and imperialism. For many evolutionists Western society, with its steam engines, factories, sexual mores, and monogamous marriage, represented the height of civilization and the advance of progress. By the beginning of the twentieth century growing emphasis upon fieldwork and the collection of more accurate data showed that the history of human cultures was far more complicated than the evolutionists had believed. The identification of contemporary tribal people as images of previous historical periods was erroneous. For this reason the institutions and behaviors of tribal people could not be used to reconstruct the history of cultural development.

Toward the close of the nineteenth century tribal groups in Africa, Melanesia, and the South Pacific were brought under colonial rule. In the United States the end of the nineteenth century saw the final defeat of the Indians in the West and their removal to tribal reservations. These changes in the circumstances of tribal people brought about corresponding changes in anthropology. Native peoples became an administrative concern, and in order to administer their native subjects, colonial officials realized that knowledge about the traditional culture could be useful. One consequence of this administrative concern was a partial convergence of colonial and anthropological interests, which was especially true in the British Empire. As a result colonial administrators and anthropologists supported by colonial governments wrote many accounts of tribal life. British colonial administrators employed anthropologists to investigate particular problems, while in other instances they financed general anthropological field research. Anthropologists were seen as experts in native life. In 1916, for example, an Australian governmental committee asked Malinowski to give evidence about native labor conditions in the Trobriand Islands (Malinowski 1918).

In American anthropology the placing of Indians on tribal reservations led many anthropologists to believe that the traditional Indian cultures were doomed to disappear in a relatively short time. American anthropologists in the early twentieth century undertook firsthand research on Indian reservations as one means of recording for posterity these traditional, but rapidly disappearing, Indian tribal customs and practices.

An instrumental and dominating figure in this process was Franz Boas. American anthropology was in many ways defined by Boas, who trained an entire generation of future anthropologists. Boas was opposed to cultural evolutionary theory and felt that the primary goals of anthropology should be the collection of descriptive cultural information and the careful reconstruction of the actual history of tribal groups insofar as the data permitted. His position has at some times been characterized as antitheoretical, but his position may also be interpreted as a reaction to the speculative excesses of nineteenth-century thinkers.

Another thread in the development of anthropology in the early twentieth century was the growing awareness of irrationality in human behavior. This view contrasts with the evolutionary theory of the nineteenth century, which emphasized the rational and intellectual faculties of humanity. Irrationality as a basis for human behavior became a common theme in several scientific disciplines. In psychology Sigmund Freud's psychoanalytic theory about the role of the unconscious and the sex drive as mainsprings for human behavior represents this trend.

Allied to this theme was a growing sense of disenchantment with Western culture. It is difficult to pinpoint with precision exactly when people in a culture alter their perspective about the world — when a culture changes its way of thinking. The brutal four years of World War I (1914–1918), dealt a shattering blow to the sense of optimism and naive belief in progress that was such an integral part of nineteenth-century thought in Western society. In 1914 the soldiers went to war accompanied by bands and waving crowds, but by 1918 disillusionment had set in. A civilization that mindlessly sent millions of young men to death and dismemberment in the mud and filth of the Western Front could no longer be held up as the last word in humanity's march to progress and perfection.

The historian Barbara Tuchman identifies World War I as one of the great turning points of Western society. "The Great War of 1914–18," she writes, "lies like a band of scorched earth dividing that time from ours. In wiping out so many lives, . . . in destroying beliefs, changing ideas, and leaving incurable wounds of disillusion, it created a physical as well as a psychological gulf between the two epochs" (Tuchman 1962:xiii).

Modern anthropology has its roots in this historical and social context. A growing sense of disenchantment permitted for the first time a widespread appreciation, if not admiration, for tribal cultures on the part of Western intellectuals. Field research, stimulated by Boas and Malinowski, became the badge of anthropological office. The field experience, rarely described in those days, became a form of personal initiation into tribal mysteries. To some degree anthropological theories gloried in the apparent irrationality of tribal society. Although anthropologists steadfastly denied differences in intelligence and behavior based upon physical and racial differences, they argued that the flexibility of humanity in the hands of culture was incredibly broad and varied.

When Western economists argued that economic behavior was guided by rational attempts to maximize economic self-interest and minimize economic losses, anthropologists pointed with undisguised pride at tribal people, who apparently danced to the drums of status and prestige rather than that of economic gain. Potlatch ceremonies of the Indians of the Northwest Coast of America, where property was given away or destroyed to elevate or validate the rank and prestige of important chiefs, became the dramatic representation of economic irrationality. Kwakiutl or Tlingit chiefs were portrayed as captives of their own cultural traditions.

Concepts such as the flexibility of human nature, cultural relativism, and the nonbiological basis for human behavior became dominant themes in American anthropology up to World War II. These themes were brought together in what has been the most widely read volume in anthropology, Ruth Benedict's *Patterns of Culture* (1934). Benedict set forth in this book the major thesis of cultural relativism: every society has its own distinct pattern that must be understood in its own terms. Each culture is integrated around its dominant theme and molds the basic character structure of all its members. Behavior defined as mental illness in one society can be a standard of normality in another society. These ideas were the anthropological versions of irrationality.

Although the intellectual and political developments of Western society influenced cultural anthropology, they were not the only influences on the discipline. Equally important were internal forces, especially the influence of three anthropologists — Boas, Malinowski, and Radcliffe-Brown — who exercised a dominant authority over the definition and direction of cultural anthropology.

We have already discussed Boas's anti-evolutionary position and his commitment to a nontheoretical and descriptive anthropology. At the same time Boas defined the very substance of anthropological interests. During the Boasian period of American anthropology (1900–1940), anthropologists were expected to be competent in all the subfields of the discipline: cultural anthropology, archaeology, physical anthropology, and linguistics. These subfields were seen as integral parts of a single discipline: anthropology, the study of humanity. In the 1930s the ideas of the British anthropologists Malinowski and Radcliffe-Brown began to have noticeable effect on American anthropology. Unlike American anthropologists, British anthropologists did not conceptualize the discipline as a general field with subfields. Social anthropology, the British equivalent (more or less) of cultural anthropology, was considered to be a separate and distinct science. This influence, in addition to the growing body of information and research techniques, tended to fragment the unity of Boas's general anthropology. By the 1940s subfield specialization had become a dominant theme in American anthropology, and today it is even more important.

Prospects: The Future of Anthropology

The future of any discipline is rooted in its past. Early anthropologists were not only concerned with stages of human cultural development, but also argued about the meaning of Greek myths, the origins of large stone monuments, and the relationships between race and cultural development. In many ways this wide range of humanistic, historical, and biological interests is still present in contemporary anthropology. Fieldwork, however, along with contextual and comparative analysis, is the basis for specialized developments in contemporary cultural anthropology. Although contemporary archaeologists, cultural anthropologists, linguists, and physical anthropologists are interested in each other's discoveries, it is nearly impossible for an anthropologist to be an expert in all these subfields. Specialization within subfields is now occurring, and this process appears to be a continuing and growing trend.

Geographical Specialization

Within cultural anthropology a trend developed after World War II emphasizing geographical area specialization. Cultural anthropologists now identify themselves on the basis of where they do research. In the jargon of anthropology there are Africanist, Oceanist, Europeanist, and Asian anthropologists. These terms refer to their geographic areas of specialization, not to where they were born or live. In addition, anthropologists with similar geographic interests tend to organize into groups. Thus at annual meetings of the major professional association of anthropologists, the American Anthropological Association, there are meetings of the Latin American Anthropology Group, Italianist Anthropologists, and the Middle East Research Group in Anthropology.

As with every other major trend in cultural

Sifting through garbage is a new method used by cultural anthropologists in studying the consumption practices of contemporary Americans.

anthropology, a variety of circumstances provided the context for this development. Foundations and government agencies that fund anthropological research often organize their funding programs by geographical area. It became apparent during and after World War II that specialists in the history, culture, language, and politics of particular world regions were needed. By organizing programs by geographical region, it became possible to identify more precisely the personnel and expertise needed. Universities responded by organizing area programs that brought together historians, geographers, linguists, anthropologists, political scientists, and other experts who shared an interest in a single region of the world. At Cornell University, for example, there are three separate Asian programs: Southeast Asian

(Burma, Thailand, Laos, Vietnam, Cambodia, Malaysia, Indonesia, Philippines), East Asian (China, Korea, Japan, Taiwan), and South Asian (India, Pakistan, Nepal, Sri Lanka), as well as the Latin American Studies Program. Other schools developed African, Middle Eastern, and East European programs.

Anthropologists who concentrated on the study of a particular culture found it necessary to understand the wider geographical setting in order to do contextual and comparative analysis. In the 1930s the advent of peasant studies required that anthropologists understand the larger society of which the peasant community was only one part. Familiarity with the history, literature, art, religion, and politics of a particular geographical region became necessary for an anthropologist.

All of these circumstances point in a single direction: further area concentration and research. As research information expands it becomes increasingly difficult for a single individual to develop real competence in more than one geographical area. Since more anthropologists are being trained now than ever before, and since they are generating significantly more information, the trend toward area concentration has become a way of handling the information explosion.

Topical Specialization

Except for missionaries and administrators, anthropologists were the only people who had a serious interest in tribal society. Thus the anthropological fieldworker had to be a jack-of-all-trades. Fieldworkers had to draw their own maps, describe the flora and fauna of the area, and investigate political, economic, kinship, and religious practices. As fieldwork developed anthropologists tended to concentrate on particular topics and for this reason, anthropologists can now be identified by their topical interest and specialization. Political anthropology, psychological anthropology, and educational anthropology are some of the current topical specializations in anthropology.

One of the earliest recognized specializations was psychological anthropology. Drawing upon psychological and psychoanalytic theory, anthropologists turned to tribal society as a laboratory for evaluating psychological hypotheses about human behavior. Margaret Mead's study of adolescent Samoan girls (1928) was one of the first attempts to test psychological generalizations in a tribal setting. Psychological anthropology may be the earliest example of anthropologists using the theories and findings of another discipline. Anthropologists soon realized, however, that theories derived from other disciplines could be helpful in analyzing their material. In order to accomplish this goal, anthropologists had to gain deeper knowledge of the analytic techniques and theories of other disciplines. This factor supported the growing trend toward topical specialization among anthropologists.

Topical specialization is a developing and continuing trend. Early specialization was oriented around major institutional topics — social organization, politics, economics, and religion. New specializations such as medical anthropology, legal anthropology, and educational anthropology have emerged recently, and it appears as if such topic specialization will continue. There are now such emerging specialties as the anthropology of the nation-state (Fallers 1974) and even extraterrestrial anthropology (Maruyama and Harkins 1975).

Theoretical Specialization

Before 1940 only a small number of individuals worked as anthropologists. As a result a few individuals could dominate the theoretical positions developed within the discipline. Morgan and Tylor were, as already mentioned, major figures in the nineteenth century. In early American anthropology Boas was the major figure, and the thinking of Radcliffe-Brown and Malinowski defined theoretical approaches in British anthropology in the 1930s and 1940s. After these men died (Boas and Malinowski in 1942, Radcliffe-Brown in 1955) their influence receded. Many of the ideas that they attacked — the role of history in culture, the importance of theory, the possibility of cultural evolution — once again became part of anthropology. These ideas provided a basis for the theoretical divergence characteristic of contemporary cultural anthropology. At the same time the great increase in the number of anthropologists made it much more difficult for a few individuals to dominate any theoretical position.

Many of the specializations in contemporary cultural anthropology are extensions of traditional anthropological interests. There are, however, a number of new frontiers in anthropology that represent departures from previous specializations. Among these new orientations are applied anthropology, urban anthropology, and the anthropology of complex societies.

Applied Anthropology

Applied anthropology is the application of anthropological knowledge to programs of planned social change. Use of anthropological knowledge in programs of directed change is a recent innovation, but its roots can be found in earlier decades. Malinowski and others saw the potential use and utility of anthropology for practical affairs. Although colonial regimes occasionally used the services of anthropologists, they were rarely convinced of the utility of anthropology in the administration of native people. As far back as 1884 the practical uses of anthropology were proclaimed. In that year Professor W. H. Flower, president of the

Anthropological Institute of London, pointed out the practical importance of ethnography to the rulers of other people. Conrad Reining, in reviewing this period, summarizes Professor Flower's position as follows:

> He urged that statesmen should not look upon human nature in the abstract, but should consider the special moral, intellectual, and social capabilities, wants, and aspirations of each particular race with which they have to deal. He pointed out that a knowledge of the special characteristics of native races and their relations to each other has a more practical object than the mere satisfaction of scientific curiosity, that such knowledge is vital to good administration, and may be the basis for the happiness and prosperity of millions of subject peoples (Reining 1962:598).

Professor Flower's appeal apparently had little effect, for cultural anthropology retreated from the practical world and appeared to have little relevance to the interests of statesmen and politicians. Although administrators used anthropologists to collect basic data about traditional cultures, until the 1930s anthropologists were not directly involved in the application of anthropology to problems of change and development.

In the 1930s the United States Bureau of Indian Affairs hired anthropologists to gather basic data about reservation life as part of a larger government policy of Indian development. Anthropologists assumed the role of experts and consultants in this project. The anthropologist neither defined the goals of change nor implemented them. One of the rare instances in which an anthropologist had control over all aspects of a development enterprise was the Vicos Project.

Vicos: A Case of Planned Change

In 1952 Allan Holmberg, who had studied the Siriono of Bolivia, was presented with an unusual opportunity. He and the university for which he worked, Cornell University, became the landlords of a Peruvian hacienda called Vicos. The 1700 Indian peasants of Vicos lived in conditions of poverty, illiteracy, subservience, and poor health. Holmberg and Cornell University decided to embark on a five-year program of planned social change designed to bring the people of Vicos, or Vicosinos, into the modern world as independent and free men and women.

Up until January 1952, Vicos was a manor or large estate, situated in a relatively small valley of Peru, about 250 miles north of the capital city of Lima. Vicos embraced an area of about 40,000 acres and had an enumerated population of 1,703 Quechua-speaking Indians, who had been bound to the land as serfs or peons since early colonial times.

At the head of the hierarchy [in Vicos] stands the renter or *patron,* always an outsider and non-Indian or Mestizo. He is the maximum authority within the system and all power to indulge or deprive is concentrated in his hands. Under his direction, if absentee, is an administrator, also an outsider and Mestizo, who is responsible to the renter for conducting and managing the day-to-day agricultural or grazing operations of the property.

Below and apart from this small non-Indian power elite stands the Indian society of peons, the members of which are bound to a soil they do not own and on which they have little security of tenure. The whole system is maintained by the application of sanctions ranging from brute force to the impounding of peon property. After thousands of years of use and inadequate care, however, the land had lost its fertility, seeds had degenerated, and the principal crops and animals were stunted and diseased. Per capita output was thus at a very low level, 80 percent of the population was infected with harmful parasites, and epidemics of such diseases as measles and whooping cough had been frequent over the years.

Several months prior to assuming the responsibilities of the power role at Vicos, a plan

Vicos — Shout of Reform. After buying their hacienda and their freedom, Vicosinos express their triumph by purchasing a new truck and emblazoning it with the slogan *Vicos — Grito de Reforma*.

of operations was drawn up which was focused on the promotion of human dignity rather than indignity and the formation of institutions at Vicos which would allow for a wide rather than a narrow shaping and sharing of values for all the participants in the social process. The principal goals of this plan thus became the devolution of power to the community, the production and broad sharing of greater wealth, the introduction and diffusion of new and modern skills, the promotion of health and wellbeing, the enlargement of the status and role structure, and the formation of a modern system of enlightenment through schools and other media.

In designing our program and a method of strategic intervention, we were very much aware of two, among many, guiding principles stemming from anthropological research: First, innovations are most likely to be accepted in those aspects of culture in which people themselves feel the greatest deprivations; and second, an integrated or contextual approach to value-institutional development is usually more lasting and less conflict-producing than a piecemeal one (Holmberg 1963:1–8).

Vicos: From 1952 to 1957

(1) Organization

1952. Vicos had an *hacienda*-type organization. Outside renters not only had free use of *hacienda peones* for labor and personal services, but also of their animals and tools. Power was concentrated in the hands of *patron*.

1957. *Hacienda* system and free services have been abolished; new system of community organization now is based on shared interests and local control.

(2) Land Ownership.

1952. No title to land, although Vicosinos

had tried on numerous occasions to purchase the land on which they had been living as *peones* for 400 years.

1957. Based on reports of development by the Cornell-Peru Project, the Institute of Indigenous Affairs asked the Peruvian Government to expropriate Vicos in favor of its indigenous population. This expropriation has now taken place.

(3) Local Authority.

1952. Under the *hacienda*-type organization there were no responsible secular authorities within the community.

1957. The Vicosinos have organized a board of their own delegates elected from each of six zones of the *hacienda*. They have the legal responsibility for the direction of community affairs.

(4) Income.

1952. The indigenous community of Vicos had no source of income of its own.

1957. Former *hacienda* lands are now farmed for the public good, providing a steady income for the payment of lands and the development of public service.

(5) Education.

1952. In the aspect of education Vicos had a very small school, with one teacher, 10–15 students.

1957. Vicos now possesses the most modern school in the whole region, recently made a *nucleo escolar,* with a capacity of 400 students. There are now 9 teachers and about 200 students, many of whom have had years of continuity in school.

(6) Production.

1952. Low economic production – each *hectare* of potato land produced a value of only $100.

1957. Each *hectare* of potato land is now producing a value of $400–$600.

(7) Health Facilities.

1952. There were no modern health facilities.

1957. A modern health center has been built by the Vicosinos and a neighboring community; a clinic is held twice a week and a public health program is underway (Holmberg 1958:12–16).

The impact and direction of social change at Vicos was not confined to this single peasant community. As knowledge regarding the changes at Vicos began to spread throughout the region, other depressed Indian communities also wished to improve their lives. The contagion of the Vicos project is summarized by Dobyns, Medrano, and Vasquez:

> The Indian peasants living in the immediate neighborhood of Vicos have viewed the social and economic results of project intervention with general enthusiasm. Their specific attitude is often one of jealousy of the Vicos Indians for having received special attention from the "gringos," and desire for equivalent programs for themselves. Since the direct intervention of Cornell University as administrator ceased in 1956, the community development and educational program of the Peruvian government carried on in Vicos has been extended to nine other adjacent communities, primarily through the functioning of the greatly enlarged Vicos school as a nucleus for a rural peasant school system.
>
> A number of communities have sent emissaries to Vicos to request technical advice, or small-scale financing, or both. The Vicos Indians have made small loans to finance communal agricultural enterprises like their own in communities unable to obtain bank financing.
>
> The Vicos Indians received requests for loans from the people of the *haciendas* Parash, Rurish and Uchusquillo in the Province of Huan on the eastern slope of the White Cordillera. Vicos fowl and egg vendors carried word of the new life in their community to these peasants.
>
> The case of Uchusquillo is far more dramatic than can be indicated here. The ten-year lease on that *hacienda* had expired, and the Uchusquillo Indians decided to follow the Vicos example. With a loan from Vicos, they rented the estate themselves and so became free men. (Dobyns, Medrano, Vasquez 1966:67).

Anthropologists: Consultants, Advocates, and Interventionists

Rarely is an anthropologist in the position of Holmberg and his associates at Vicos. It is more likely for an anthropologist to be hired to provide expert advice and to do research on particular problems of interest to a planning agency. Formulation of goals and implementation of change are not usually in the hands of anthropologists.

In World War II anthropologists were used as consultants. Politicians and military authorities decided that the Japanese–Americans on the West Coast posed a threat to national security. Because of this policy decision thousands of Japanese–Americans were relocated to camps throughout the United States. A number of anthropologists were hired to aid in the administration of these camps. It was assumed that anthropologists, as students of culture, would provide the practical information required for effective camp administration. During World War II anthropologists were employed to analyze Japanese and German culture in order to aid military and intelligence activities, and there were also attempts to utilize anthropological knowledge in diverting American food preferences away from scarce foods.

More recently anthropologists have been hired as consultants for the Peace Corps. They are primarily involved in the training of Peace Corps volunteers who are going to Third World countries to implement change, especially in such fields as education and agriculture. This consultant position has become the dominant approach in applied anthropology.

Anthropologists are almost always employed as consultants and experts by institutions and agencies that plan change for others. In recent years many anthropologists have become critical of this arrangement and have sought a greater voice for the people who will

experience the impact of change. This position is called an *interventionist or advocacy approach.* We can trace this position to the nineteenth century anthropologist Morgan, who successfully interceded as a lawyer in 1847 on behalf of Iroquois Indians in a land case. He also spoke out for the Sioux after they had massacred Custer and his troops. As a New York State legislator, Morgan introduced legislation on behalf of the Iroquois and advocated that two states be established and set aside for the Indian population of America (Leacock 1963:Id–IVi; Ii–IXX).

Today more and more anthropologists view the people they study as oppressed and powerless. As a result some anthropologists become self-appointed representatives for these people and assume an interventionist position. Using knowledge that they have acquired as anthropologists, they may become effective mediators between the people they study and the larger institutions of society that may be indifferent to the people's needs.

An example of this interventionist approach can be seen in the experience of Lisa Peattie in a neighborhood (barrio) called La Laja in a Venezuelan city (Peattie 1970). She was initially hired by a group of planners who were responsible for an urban development project, but Peattie soon found herself involved in controversy. As part of an overall plan of urban development, a sewer pipe and outlet were to be built near the neighborhood Peattie was studying. The local people opposed its construction, and it was Peattie's presence that allowed their concerns and opposition to be heard in the higher reaches of the Venezuelan bureaucracy and government. As a result of her intervention, the agency changed its plans. Her role in what she calls the "great sewer controversy" was based on her emotional ties to this neighborhood where she had lived and studied for two years as well as her ability as an educated foreigner to contact planners in the

Lisa Peattie with some of her Venezuelan friends. Anthropologists often develop close ties with the people they study. The great sewer controversy led Lisa Peattie to intervene on behalf of the people of La Laja barrio.

upper levels of the planning and development agency. She writes:

> It will be clear from this account that my role in the "Great Sewer Controversy" was such as justly to infuriate the top Venezuelan staff of the planning and development agency. I think that it was such, also, as to make it reasonable to look squarely at the accusation of some staff members that I was in some large sense responsible for what happened — that the issue would never have emerged if it had not been for "Doctora" Peattie. In general, I believe that this accusation is correct.
>
> Looking at the process by which the sewer became an issue, I think it would be fair to summarize as follows: my role in the first stage, that of generating dissatisfaction, was negligible; my role in the second, of organizing the dissatisfaction, was peripheral or secondary to that of various community leaders, but my role in the communicating of the dissatisfaction was crucial. It seems quite unlikely that La Laja's dissatisfaction with the sewer would ever have become such an issue had it not been for my presence. The fact that La Laja's opposition to the sewer became a major subject of discussion, a big issue, in the Caracas office of the Corporación de Guayana was directly traceable to my intervention (Peattie 1970:85–86).

Peattie's involvement in urban planning is illustrative of the role of applied anthropology in the decades following World War II. The emergence of development and modernization policies by the American government brought about anthropological involvement in many programs of directed cultural change. Much of this effort, which still continues, was directed toward "less developed" countries.

At the present time applied anthropology has come home. Two of the most recent and active areas of applied anthropology are education and medicine in American society. Delivery of health services, the meaning of illness and disease, and the hospital as a social entity are studied by anthropologists in the same manner as a tribal or peasant community is studied. The schoolroom, the school system, student populations, and the structure of education can all be investigated in the traditional manner of fieldwork, context, and comparison.

Applied anthropology promises to be one of the future areas of growth for anthropologists. In recent years it has become evident that the production of professional anthropologists will far exceed the number of academic positions available in American universities and colleges. Estimates show that 50 percent or more of all professional anthropologists will be engaged in nonacademic anthropology by the end of the twentieth century. A major area of nonacademic employment is the application of anthropological knowledge to the myriad problems and issues of contemporary society.

Urban and Complex Societies

When anthropology first emerged it was defined as the study of tribal society. In the 1930s, with the work of Robert Redfield (see Chapter 3), anthropology extended its subject matter to include the peasants of the world. Esther Newton's fieldwork with drag queens illustrates the new frontiers of anthropological fieldwork: urban anthropology and the anthropology of complex society.

Urban Anthropology

Urban anthropology is the study of the impact of urban environments upon human behavior. Interest in urban study has been stimulated by many factors. Redfield, who pioneered the study of peasants in anthropology, also influenced the trend toward urban studies. In his book *The Folk Culture of Yucatan* (1941) he compared four communities in the Yucatan peninsula of Mexico. They ranged in size from a relatively small and isolated community to a large coastal town. As part of his interest in the

The comparative study of urban poor is a major interest of urban anthropologists. These women in the black township of Soweto, South Africa, sift through garbage seeking items to supplement their meager incomes.

peasant community, he turned to the study of the city. Not only was the city the home of elites who commanded the institutions – political, economic, religious – of peasant society, but it was also the origin of the cultural traditions and values that penetrated into the peasant community.

In the 1920s Robert and Helen Lynd studied an American city in the Middle West using anthropological field methods (1929). They applied anthropological fieldwork techniques to an urban setting. William Lloyd Warner, who studied the Murngin of Australia between 1926 and 1929, used anthropological field techniques in his study of a small New England city (1963). Both the Lynd and Warner studies led to the growth of a literature dealing with urban life in America that is referred to as the community study approach.

As anthropologists studied tribal and peasant communities, they became aware that migration to urban areas was becoming a significant component of life in these communities. The study of rural migrants soon led to the investigation of migrants living in cities. A. L. Epstein's studies of urban life in the copper belt towns of Zambia (see Chapter 5), are an example of this growing interest in urban migration by anthropologists (Epstein 1953; 1958; 1964). Oscar Lewis, while studying the Mexican village of Tepotzlan, was impressed by the number of peasants who had migrated to Mexico City. He followed them into the city and described their way of life in their new urban environment. One of the major consequences of his work was a questioning of many of the generally accepted notions about the impact of urbanization upon migrants advanced by sociologists who had based their theories on North American urban studies. Lewis's research showed that the migrants he studied did not experience familial breakdown, or the increases in crime and violence, and the social

pathologies usually associated with urban life (1952). The field of urban anthropology was launched from these studies, and at the present time, it is one of the fastest growing specializations in cultural anthropology.

What can anthropology contribute to an understanding of urban life? The answer to this fundamental question can be found in the unique characteristics of the anthropological enterprise: fieldwork, context, and comparison.

The traditional form of anthropological field research can be adapted to any dimension of urban life that an anthropologist may wish to study. Esther Newton obviously could not establish herself in the group she was studying as Hart did with the Tiwi and Briggs did with the Eskimo. Participant observation, the development of rapport, and the use of key informants, however, result in data comparable in context and meaning to the data gathered by anthropologists in a tribal setting. By using participant observation and the interviewing of informants, urban anthropologists have studied migrants, ethnic groups, skid row alcoholics, bars, longshoremen, cult groups, hippie communes, schools, the elderly, the unemployed, cocktail waitresses, and street corner gangs (Eames and Goode, 1977). In all these studies, the establishment of social relations between the researcher and the people being studied permits both a contextual understanding of behavior and contact with the reality of urban existence.

One of the finest examples of urban anthropological research is Elliot Liebow's study of a group of black men who hang out on a street corner in a Washington, D.C., ghetto (1967). The following excerpt shows how Liebow takes a relatively simple event and uses it to illustrate the problems and realities of urban life, especially the uncertainty of life for urban Blacks. Most of the ethnographic description in Liebow's book documents this uncertainty.

In many instances, it is precisely the streetcorner man's orientation to the future — but to a future loaded with "trouble" — which not only leads to a greater emphasis on present concerns ("I want mine right now") but also contributes importantly to the instability of employment, family and friend relationships, and to the general transient quality of daily life.

Let me give some concrete examples. One day, after Tally had gotten paid, he gave me four twenty-dollar bills and asked me to keep them for him. Three days later he asked me for the money. I returned it and asked why he did not put his money in a bank. He said that the banks close at two o'clock. I argued that there were four or more banks within a two-block radius of where he was working at the time and that he could easily get to any one of them on his lunch hour. "No, man," he said, "you don't understand. They close at two o'clock and they closed Saturday and Sunday. Suppose I get into trouble and I got to make it [leave]. Me get out of town, and everything I got in the world layin' up in that bank? No good! No good!" (Liebow 1967:68–69).

The comparative approach is a vital part of anthropological research. Lewis's study of migrants in Mexico City, for example, contradicted the conclusions drawn from North American studies of urban migrants. Thus it can be seen that cross-cultural comparisons are essential in understanding urban life. In urban anthropology the use of controlled comparison has become an important analytic technique. M. Estellie Smith compared and contrasted Portuguese migrants in two New England towns (1975). Her analysis indicates that the differences in the economic prosperity of the two towns were reflected in the economic position of the Portuguese migrants. Smith concludes that urban social and economic structure may be more relevant to success than the content of the immigrant culture.

Bernard Wong, in a comparative study of Chinese in Lima, Peru, and New York City, discovered very different rates of cultural assimilation for the Chinese migrant groups (1978). The Chinese of New York form a tightly knit, unassimilated, and endogamous ethnic enclave that is a world unto itself. The Chinese of Lima, however, are full participants in Peruvian society. In a conclusion that parallels the findings of Smith, Wong found that differences between New York and Lima Chinese can be explained on the basis of structural and cultural features of the two societies. The Chinatown of New York City is an adaptation to the racist and discriminatory practices of American society. Because these discriminatory features are absent in Peru, no equivalent of the New York Chinatown is found. In addition, the godparenthood complex (see Chapter 5) of Peru permits Chinese to accept Peruvian godfathers and establish close ties with them. These two studies indicate the importance of comparative research and analysis in urban anthropology.

The Anthropology of Complex Society

Anthropology of complex societies is the study of the complex social systems that characterize the modern world. One of the major consequences of European colonial domination is the emergence of the nation-state as a basic political entity of modern life. Paralleling this political development is the emergence of the industrial-bureaucratic society (see Chapter 3). Since the vast majority of the world's population now lives in nation-states characterized by a bureaucratic type of organization, anthropologists have begun to study and analyze these complex societies.

Three major dimensions characterize complex society — worldwide economic interconnection and interrelationship, the growing absence of a local aspect to many of the institutions and values that dominate modern life, and stratification or social and economic inequality.

These three factors result in the creation of specific cultural forms. Thus it is possible to identify a growing international and cosmopolitan leadership that cuts across national, cultural, and even ideological boundaries. These leaders control vast economic resources, make major political decisions, staff the power positions of the world bureaucracies — corporate and governmental — and create, package, and distribute an emerging world culture. The most visible manifestation of the complex society is the emergence of the multinational corporation. No longer tied to a national base, the multinational corporation is truly international in scope. Thus American bankers give billions in loans to East European communist countries, the Ford Motor Company publicizes its latest model as the world car, and Western manufacturing concerns compete to build industrial plants in the People's Republic of China.

The technological revolution in communication has created a worldwide mass culture transmitted by movies, television, newspapers, and radio. What is communicated is a life-style that includes dress, recreation, food, personal values, and language. Glittering and efficient packaging of mass culture items is effectively eroding local traditions. Discotheques in New York, London, Moscow, Rio de Janeiro, Hong Kong, Tokyo, or New Delhi are indistinguishable from each other. The music is the same, the dances are almost identical, and aside from physical differences, the dancers are interchangeable. The most visible manifestation of mass culture may be the famous golden arches that tower in every city of the capitalist world.

Industrialism has created vast wealth, but the benefits of this world affluence have been unevenly distributed. Some anthropologists identify a culture of poverty characterizing

A slum area in Rio de Janeiro is one example of the poverty faced by rural migrants who have recently moved into urban areas.

Italian migratory workers at the Stuttgart railroad station going home for a vacation at Christmas.

people who do not benefit from this growth in wealth. Poverty-stricken groups are found in every nation and region of the world. Fieldwork with economically deprived groups is a major arena of recent anthropological research (Eames and Goode 1973). Many of these studies are used to test the two alternative theoretical positions developed to explain the behavior of the poor. One position, set forth by Oscar Lewis, argues that poverty is accompanied by characteristic cultural behaviors — a *culture of poverty* — that lock a population into a cycle of economic deprivation. Once such a culture of poverty emerges, it is transmitted from generation to generation and is largely immune to changing external circumstances and conditions. An opposing position defines the behavior of the poor as a direct and instrumental

strategy designed to meet the conditions of poverty. If these conditions change, it is argued, the behavior of the poor will change correspondingly.

Differences in wealth between regions of the world also exist. Many theorists assume that growth in economic wealth in one region is based upon exploitation and impoverishment of other regions. Thus a characteristic of complex society is the emergence of economic and political disparities between regions of the world that may be maintained and enhanced by the functioning of complex society.

An example of this new area of anthropological interest is a study of international labor migration in Europe and its relationship to economic development (Rhoades 1978). Using information from a variety of community studies, his own research, and historical and statistical data, Robert E. Rhoades questions the conclusion of economists that migration benefits both receiving and sending countries.

> The research findings presented in this paper point unavoidably to one conclusion: the primary beneficiaries of intra-European migration are receiving nation employers. German firms have found it desirable to recruit and transport foreign workers instead of instituting labor-saving technologies, or transferring production and employment to labor-exporting regions. Intra-European migration functions not for the "benefits" of migrant-sending regions or the German-working populations – as proclaimed at official levels – but for the purpose of maintaining high levels of labor input at minimum cost. Although "guest workers" and their families may benefit financially over the short run, there is no evidence that fundamental structural changes have taken place in labor-sending regions. After a hundred years of labor export, peripheral zones of outmigration have decayed [and] Europe's structural inequality characterized by growth in the core and poverty in the periphery is maintained by various mechanisms, including cyclical migration (1978:568–569).

Rhoades's investigation of the functioning of complex society and economic development uses migration as the basis and boundary of his research. Carol Smith, on the other hand, uses the nation-state for her analysis of economic development and underdevelopment in Guatemala (1978). Guatemala is one of the major coffee-producing nations of the world. Smith notes that the world demand for coffee has resulted in new modes of production based on a capitalistic economy. Within Guatemala certain areas and certain segments of the population have reaped the benefits of this new economy. She demonstrates, however, that there are many peripheral areas in Guatemala that have been unaffected or have even suffered economic decline as a result of capitalistic commodity production of coffee. In some instances, Indian subsistence farmers were converted into a plantation labor force and on occasion forced labor was practiced (1978:574–617).

Complex society poses a new challenge to anthropologists. Because context is an essential element in anthropological analysis, the existence of complex society requires a broader contextual framework than the traditional approaches used in the study of small tribal and peasant communities. In their study of an upstate New York community (Springdale) Arthur Vidich and Joseph Bensman demonstrated that the local community can be understood only when it is viewed as part of mass society (1958). What Springdalers wear, what they think, what they do, as well as their economic fate, are all crucially dependent upon institutions outside of and often unknown to the local community.

As anthropologists develop their investigations into complex society, they will depend increasingly upon data from other disciplines, such as demography, political science, economics, sociology, and history. Retaining the small-scale approach of ethnography and a perspective grounded in cross-cultural research, we can expect that anthropologists will question and criticize the accepted wisdom of these disciplines.

Third World Anthropologists

Although cultural anthropology has included in its ranks a number of individuals who were drawn from tribal society, its personnel have largely come from Western society and culture. This situation is now slowly beginning to change. Many men and women from tribal populations are becoming anthropologists. Although these anthropologists are trained and educated within a Western educational system, they bring a different and often critical perspective to anthropology.

Criticism of Western anthropology and

anthropologists is a central theme in the writings of many Third World anthropologists. According to many Third World anthropologists, Western anthropologists are often insensitive and inaccurate (Owusu 1978; Chilungu 1976). The use of terms such as nonliterate, primitive, savage, and uncivilized by Western anthropologists is seen by Third World anthropologists as evidence of prejudice, bias, and ethnocentrism on the part of Western observers. A more telling criticism involves the accusation that some anthropological work, including the renowned classics of the field, are replete with inaccuracies and mistakes. Many of these errors are attributed to poor research methods and lack of knowledge of the indigenous language (Chilungu 1976). An important contribution made by indigenous anthropologists working in their own societies is the correction of past errors that have too often become part of the folklore of anthropology.

A related issue that strikes at the heart of anthropology is: can an outsider really understand another culture? Some Third World anthropologists would say no. Many of them believe that only insiders studying their own culture and community can ever understand its true nature (Morauta 1979:564).

Third World anthropology can be more than the study of an anthropologist's own tribal group or community. It should include within its orbit of interest the study of Western society. One anthropologist who has chosen to study a group beyond his own community is Victor Uchendu. He is a Nigerian anthropologist who has written about his own people, the Igbo (1965), and who has also worked among the Navajo Indians of the Southwestern United States. As an Igbo living with the Navajo, he found his tribal heritage helpful in his fieldwork.

Because of the "social visibility" of my skin color, I could not play a covert role in the Navajo country. To most Navajo with whom I came into initial contact, I was just another Negro. The English-speaking Navajo refer to people of my race (Negroes) as "colored guys"; and the Navajo words *Nakaii lizhinii* — a term applied to my race, which means "Black Mexican" — indicate where the Navajo put me in their racial genealogy.

When the weather permitted, I put on my African robes, to emphasize my "African-ness" as I had been advised. (But the windy weather which sweeps Navajo country in summer proved an enemy to my robes!) Although I seemed to have passed unnoticed in my robes at the initial contacts, it became clear from information reaching me and from the comments of those who became my Navajo friends, that my embroidered robes were commented upon as "items of beauty." The perennial question was: How much did it cost?

The younger Navajo workers felt that I shared a common bond of "colonial" culture with them. The frequent questions asked of me were how the white man treated Africans and whether Africans lived on reservations. My answer to the latter question drew not only laughter but serious doubt: The following is an excerpt of the conversation:

"Do you live on reservation?" one Navajo friend asked.

"No. It is the white man who lives on reservation," I answered.

"How did you do this?" another asked unbelievingly.

"The mosquito did it for us," I grinned in reply.

The fact that I bear not only a tribal culture but share a common colonial experience with Navajo provided a common basis for identification with them, minimized Navajo suspicions, aroused their curiosity about Africa and improved rapport. As bearers of tribal cultures we were able to "trade" some exotic information with each other. The Navajo recorded my Igbo folk songs, proverbs, and riddles in exchange for their own songs and myths, and what was most important to me, they "helped me out" with the information I needed (Uchendu 1973:232–233, 236).

Most Third World anthropologists unfortunately suffer severe restraints in expanding their anthropological research endeavors. Lack of funding often restricts them to the inexpensive study of their own communities. Another reason for concentrating upon local research is the widespread demand by many Third World anthropologists and governments for a close relationship between research, political action, and social change. Governments of Third World countries want to use the expertise of indigenous anthropologists to further their individual national goals of development and change.

Many of these points can be illustrated by the development of anthropology in India. Anthropology was introduced into Indian education over fifty years ago by the British. Early Indian anthropologists, however, received their graduate and professional training in England. After India gained its independence in 1947, Indian universities began to offer full professional training in anthropology.

Before 1947 most Indian anthropologists studied tribal people in India. Only within the last thirty years have Indian anthropologists shifted the focus of their research from tribal people to the study of rural villages and urban centers. Today most Indian anthropologists do their field research in India, which is partly the result of funding policies established by the government to encourage social change and development in rural India. Government funding agencies are concerned with projects allied to Indian development programs and are interested in financing research linked to these goals rather than overseas research into problems that do not appear to be of direct concern to the problems of India.

In this overview of Indian anthropology we can see some of the numerous problems encountered by Third World anthropologists. Although some training in anthropology may have been instituted at a relatively early date, professional training could be acquired only in a Western country. Research funds for Third World anthropologists are generally limited. For this reason as well as government interest in local and national problems most Third World anthropologists concentrate their research efforts in their home communities and countries. In time, however, Third World anthropologists may extend their research interest to other people and societies.

Summary

In the century since its emergence, cultural anthropology has undergone change and transformation. Once defined as the study of tribal society, it now includes the study of Western culture and complex society. Esther Newton's research with American female impersonators testifies to this change.

Cultural anthropology was grounded initially in evolutionary theory. Most of these theories viewed the tribal world as a contemporary representation of a prior level of human existence. Boas in America and Radcliffe-Brown and Malinowski in England challenged the basis of evolutionary theory. They introduced fieldwork, new theoretical approaches, and trained a future generation of anthropologists. Twentieth-century anthropology reflected basic and fundamental changes in Western society and culture. The ethnocentric attitudes and assumed superiority of nineteenth-century European culture over other cultures were replaced by a growing sense of disenchantment, a recognition of irrationality in the behavior of people, and a new appreciation of tribal cultures.

Cultural anthropology shares with many other scientific disciplines the trend toward specialized fields of interest. This specialization has taken various forms. Geographical area, topic, and theoretical specialization are among the more important specialties. Although anthropologists still emphasize the basic unity of their discipline, the process of specialization is likely to continue. In many ways the trend toward complete fragmentation is countered and inhibited by the continuing emphasis upon fieldwork, contextual analysis, and cross-cultural comparison.

Three of the most significant specializations in contemporary anthropology are applied anthropology, urban anthropology, and the anthropology of complex societies. Applied anthropology is a culmination of the traditional anthropological interest in social change. Urban anthropology and the anthropology of complex society are reflections of basic changes that have taken place in the social, economic, and political structure of the world.

The emergence of Third World anthropol-

ogists is a recent development in anthropology. Although trained in the traditions of Western anthropology, these anthropologists are vocal in their criticism of Western anthropology as insensitive and inaccurate in the portrayal of tribal cutlure. Because of limited funding and government programs directed toward national problems, the majority of Third World anthropologists study their own cultures and societies. In time they will probably extend their research into other societies, including Western society. Uchendu's experience with the Navajo illustrates the advantages of an anthropologist with a tribal background. An anthropology based upon a non-Western perspective adds another dimension to the understanding of the human condition, and may be the most vital contribution of Third World anthropologists.

Although several major specializations in contemporary and future anthropology have been identified in this chapter, their separation is merely pedagogical. In the practice of applied anthropology a combination of specialties

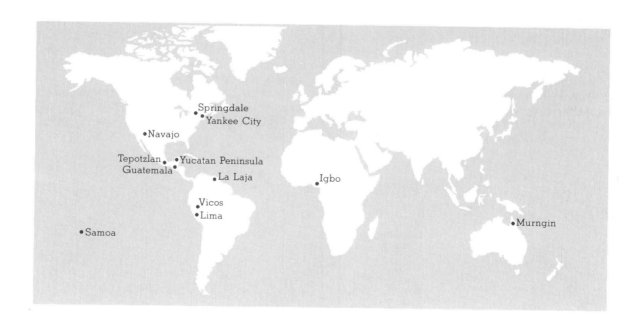

may be used — an anthropologist may specialize in economic studies, in a particular region of the world, in an urban center, and may use a particular theoretical perspective. If anthropology is to remain a living discipline, it must adapt itself to the conditions of the real world. The specializations identified in this chapter are part of the process of adaptation and change.

The behavior of human beings, however, is still the central concern of cultural anthropologists. The techniques first developed in the study of the so-called strange and exotic tribal societies are, with modification, still useful in the emerging world, which in its own way is both strange and exotic.

Key Terms and Concepts

anthropological specialization
applied anthropology
advocacy/interventionist anthropology

urban anthropology
anthropology of complex societies
culture of poverty
third-world anthropology

Suggested Readings

Arens, W., and Susan P. Montague, eds. *The American Dimension.* Port Washington, N.Y.: Alfred Publishing, 1976. From Star Trek to soap operas and from bagels to bootlegging, sixteen anthropologists look at native American culture.

Barnes, John. *Who Should Know What? Social Science, Privacy and Ethics.* New York: Cambridge University Press, 1980. A survey of the ethical and political responsibilities of social scientists.

Eames, Edwin, and Judith Granich Goodie. *An-thropology of the City.* Englewood Cliffs, N.J.: Prentice-Hall, 1977. A comprehensive textbook introduction to urban anthropology.

Foster, George. *Applied Anthropology.* Boston: Little, Brown, 1969. A comprehensive discussion of applied anthropology by a leading expert in the field.

Goldschmidt, Walter, ed. *The Uses of Anthropology.* Washington, D.C.: American Anthropological Association, 1980. A collection of essays relating anthropology to practical and everyday uses.

Liebow, Elliot. *Tally's Corner.* Boston: Little, Brown, 1967. An ethnographic study of Black street corner men in a Washington, D.C. ghetto. A classic example of urban anthropology.

Nash, June. *We Eat the Mines and the Mines Eat Us.* New York: Columbia University Press, 1979. A gripping portrayal of the life of Bolivian tin miners. Explores the dependency and exploitations of workers in a developing nation.

Newton, Esther. *Mother Camp: Female Impersonators in America.* Englewood Cliffs, N.J.: Prentice-Hall, 1972. An ethnographic study of female impersonators in the mid-western United States.

Glossary

Acculturation: the process of change that occurs when two or more cultures come into contact.

Achieved status: a status or position earned through individual effort and merit.

Advocacy/interventionist anthropology: a position taken by some anthropologists that requires them to represent the people they study and to intervene on their behalf.

Affinal kin: individuals who are related by marriage.

Age-grade: a grouping of individuals in terms of their age. Responsibilities, rights, and obligations of individuals change as they progress through different age-grades.

Age of Imperial Rule: the phase of European colonialism characterized by the establishment of land empires.

Agriculture: intensive cultivation of land based on the use of animal power, the plow, and effective soil fertilization techniques such as manuring and irrigation.

Alliance theory: the theory that the formation of alliances between different groups is the underlying reason for exogamous marriage.

Alphabetic writing: writing in which symbols stand for the phonemic sounds of the language.

Ambilineal descent: a form of descent in which relationships can be traced through either the male or female line.

Ameslan: American Sign Language. A gesture language used by deaf and hearing-impaired persons.

Amok: a form of mental illness found in Indonesia, Malaysia, and New Guinea in which men run wild in a frenzy of aggression.

Anal stage: a stage in the Freudian model of human maturation where pleasure is received from bowel and bladder retention and release.

Animism: a term used by E. B. Tylor to designate the belief in souls or spirits, which he held to be the origin of religious belief.

Anthropology: the scientific study of human beings and human behavior.

Anthropology of complex societies: the study of societies that are complex and characterized by the emergence of the nation-state and bureaucratic industrialism.

Anti-structure: a concept developed by V. W. Turner to describe a world without statuses, roles, and norms.

Applied anthropology: the application of anthropological knowledge to the resolution of practical problems.

Archeology: a subfield of anthropology that focuses on past human cultures.

Ascribed status: a status or position that an individual acquires at birth because of caste, class, sex, age, or other inherited characteristics.

Association: a nonkin group that is organized to perform the same purpose as a kin group.

At the bottom: one of the dimensions of Turner's theory of anti-structure. This category refers to those individuals who have a low status and lack social, political, and economic power.

Avoidance relationship: a relationship between individuals in which limited contact is culturally prescribed and expected.

Avunculocal residence: a pattern of residence in which a newly married couple lives with the groom's mother's brother.

Band: the basic unit of social organization found in simple political systems; typically found among foraging peoples.

Basic personality structure: the common set of personality features shared by individuals in a culture as a result of being socialized through a similar set of child training practices.

Berdache: in some North American Indian

groups, a man who dresses and acts like a woman and is thought to possess supernatural powers.

Betwixt and between: one of the dimensions of Turner's concept of anti-structure. This category refers to individuals and events that fall between social and cultural classifications.

Bilateral descent: a principle of descent in which relationships are traced through both male and female lines.

Bilineal descent (or double descent): a type of unilineal descent in which an individual is affiliated with matrilineal kin for some purposes and with patrilineal kin for others.

Bilingual: able to speak two languages fluently.

Bilocal residence: a pattern of residence in which a newly married couple may choose to live with or near either the bride's or groom's relatives.

Biocultural theory: a theory that examines the effect of biological inheritance on particular cultural patterns.

Bride-price: goods and property given to the bride's family by the groom's family.

Calendrical ritual: religious ritual that celebrates the transition from one season or time to another.

Cargo cult: a type of revitalization movement common throughout Melanesia and New Guinea in which the people believe that vast quantities of European material goods will be delivered, the Europeans will disappear, the ancestors will return, and a utopian paradise will emerge.

Caste: a group of people whose membership is determined by birth and that is assigned a particular place in the social and occupational hierarchy.

Chiefdom: an intermediate form of political organization in which several components of political power are present but they are not organized into a centralized and coercive system.

Child-training practices: the techniques used in a society to socialize children. Some anthropologists believe that these practices are the fundamental basis for adult personality.

Circumscription: the presence of physical boundaries that severely limit the expansion of a population, thus leading to conflict, warfare, and the eventual emergence of the state.

Clan: a unilineal kin group consisting of individuals who claim to be related to a common ancestor, but are unable to document their exact relationship.

Classificatory kinship: a relationship where different kin types are classified under a single kin term.

Coercive power: the ability to reward and punish others; the power is usually based on the control of police and military forces.

Coercive theories of the state: theories that attribute the origin of the state to force and warfare as one political group defeats and subjugates others.

Cognitive anthropology: an approach that focuses upon the maps or rules in people's minds that underlie their behavior.

Colonialism: a system of political rule in which a nation extends its control over other countries and peoples, usually denying them the right to fully participate in the political process.

Communitas: a term used in Turner's theory of anti-structure to describe a group of human beings linked only by the bonds of their humanity.

Comparative method: (*see* Cross-cultural analysis).

Complex political organization: a form of political organization in which all the components of power are found together and where coercive power is controlled by a central political authority.

Complex society: the form of society in the modern world organized in terms of the nation-state and bureaucratic industrialism.

Consanguineal kin: individuals who are related by birth and descent.

Contact person: an individual used by an anthropologist to establish initial contact with the group being studied.

Contagious magic: a principle of magical technique based on the assumption that things once in contact can still magically influence each other when separated.

Contextual analysis: the explanation of particular events by relating them to a broader setting.

Controlled comparison: a form of the comparative method in which a small number of societies sharing many social and cultural features are compared.

Counterfactual statements: statements that postulate nonfactual situations and then derive logical possibilities from them.

Couvade: a custom in some societies that strictly limits a father's usual activities after the birth of his child.

Cross-cousins: children of siblings of the opposite sex; one's cross-cousins are mother's brother's children and father's sister's children.

Cross-cultural analysis: the interpretation of human behavior based on comparisons between different cultures.

Crow kinship terminology: a unilineal kinship system associated with matrilineal descent.

Cultural anthropology: the study and analysis of the varied manners, customs, and beliefs of different groups of people throughout the world.

Cultural relativism: the position that the behavior and customs of a society must be understood in terms of that society's culture.

Culture: the way of life of a particular group of people — their shared set of learned manners, customs, and beliefs.

Culture and personality school: an area of anthropological study investigating the hypothesis that individuals who share cultural tradition will develop similar personality characteristics.

Culture contact: (*see* Acculturation).

Culture of poverty: a theory advanced by Oscar Lewis that poverty is accompanied by characteristic cultural behaviors that lock a population into a cycle of economic deprivation.

Curvilinear hypothesis: a hypothesis that relates household type to level of social complexity.

Daily round: an ethnographic account of a typical day in the life of a people that provides a comprehensive picture of community life.

Debtara: a magician-healer among the Amhara of Ethiopia.

Deep structure: a concept in Noam Chomsky's transformational-generative theory of language. Deep structure is the underlying grammatic structure of a sentence that is transformed into an actual utterance by transformational rules.

Dependency theory: a theory that holds that newly independent Third World nations are still economically dependent on the West.

Descent theory: the theory that marriage is a recruitment institution designed to maintain the cultural and biological continuity of a social group.

Diffusion: a process of cultural change involving the geographical spread and borrowing of cultural items.

Divination: a magical practice through which a diviner is said to be able to understand and predict the workings of the supernatural world.

Divorce: the legal dissolution of marriage.

Domesticated food economy: a subsistence system based on the growing of food crops and the herding of domesticated animals.

Dowry: goods and property given to the groom's family by the bride's family.

Duolocal residence: a pattern of residence in which a married couple live apart from each other.

Ecological theory: a theory that identifies human beings, culture, and physical environment as mutually related interacting components of a single ecosystem.

Ecological theory of warfare: a theory that interprets warfare as one aspect of an entire ecological system; warfare is seen as a means of keeping population and resources in balance.

Emic point of view: the interpretation of customs in a specific culture as seen by the participants or insiders.

Enculturation: the process of learning a particular culture.

Endogamy: a rule specifying that marriage take place within a specified group.

Eskimo kinship terminology: a kinship system often associated with bilateral descent. The terminology reflects the absence of unilineal descent and the importance of the nuclear family.

Ethnic group: a group sharing a common tribal heritage, culture, and language that sets it apart as a distinctive group.

Ethnocentrism: the interpretation and evaluation of other cultures in terms of the values and customs of one's own culture.

Ethnography: a description of the way of life or culture of a particular people.

Ethnography of speaking: the study and analysis of speech behaviors.

Etic point of view: the interpretation of customs in a specific culture as seen by observers or outsiders.

Evil eye: the belief that some people possess the supernatural power to injure or kill merely by looking at the victim.

Evolutionary theory (nineteenth century): an interpretation of human culture in terms of fixed stages of cultural development.

Exogamy: a rule requiring that a person marry outside one's own group.

Family: a social group related through blood and marriage.

Feuding: fighting between small groups of the same society, usually as revenge or retaliation.

Fictive kinship: a relationship between individuals who are not related by consanguineal or affinal ties.

Fieldwork: the basic technique of data collection used by cultural anthropologists. Involves living with the people being studied and participating in their activities.

Foraging: a subsistence system dependent upon the hunting of animals and the gathering of wild foods.

Fraternal polyandry: the marriage of a woman to two or more brothers.

Freudian theory: a theory that emphasizes identification with parents, the seeking of pleasure coupled with the avoidance of pain, and the internalization of cultural standards as important principles of cultural acquisition.

Frustration-aggression hypothesis: a hypothesis that claims expressions of aggression are generated when legitimate interests of individuals are frustrated.

Functional theory: a theory of culture and society that stresses the integration of culture and its continuity.

Functional theories of warfare: theories that assume warfare contributes to the social cohesion and continuity of society.

Games of chance: games where the outcome is determined by randomness and luck.

Games of physical skill: games where the outcome is determined by skill and strength.

Games of strategy: games where the outcome is determined by logic and manipulation.

Gardening: (see Horticulture).

Ghotul: a village dormitory for boys and girls found among the Muria of central India.

Godparenthood complex: a system whereby individuals named at a child's birth or baptism are given the responsibility of caring for the child should he or she be orphaned.

Hawaiian kinship terminology: an extremely classificatory kinship terminological system that reflects generational and sex differences.

Head man: a political position found in simple and intermediate forms of political organization that involves little power or authority.

Herding: (see Pastoralism).

Holism: the use in anthropology of different scientific disciplines as part of the total study of humanity.

Horticulture: a subsistence system using a relatively simple technology to grow food crops.

Household: a social group of individuals related by blood and marriage that is also a residential unit.

Human Relations Area Files (HRAF): a systematic collection of ethnographic data for societies throughout the world.

Humanism: a traditional part of cultural anthropology that stresses that a concern with humanity and a close relationship to people in another culture is as vital as the scientific part of anthropology.

Human nature theories of aggression: theories that attribute human aggression and warfare to inborn tendencies of humanity.

Hunting and gathering: (see Foraging).

Ideal personality type: a concept developed by Ruth Benedict that assumes individuals in a specific culture strive to model their behavior and personality on a type that is ideal in their culture.

Image of limited good: a concept developed by George Foster to describe the personality of peasants living in a situation of finite and limited resources.

Imitative magic: a principle of magical technique based on the notion that performing magic on one item will have the same effect on an item similar to it.

Incest taboo: the prohibition of sexual relations between mother and son, father and daughter, and brother and sister.

Independent household: a household established by a married couple independent of their kin.

Independent invention: a principle of culture change that states that similar circumstances in separate places will give rise to similar or identical items.

Industrialism: the systematic application of varied energy sources to the production process, resulting in high levels of productivity and a shift in the labor force from primary production (food) to manufacturing, service, and administrative activities.

Infanticide: the killing of newly born infants, a practice that appears to be a form of population control in areas with limited food resources.

Informants: persons knowledgeable about their own cultures who communicate their knowledge to the anthropologist.

Initiation ceremony: a rite that marks the public recognition of the change from one status to another, especially from adolescence to adulthood.

Intermediate political system: a form of political organization combining the various components of political power but lacking the centralization of coercive power.

Internalization: the process whereby individuals incorporate the norms and values of their society into their own thoughts and behaviors.

Iroquois kinship terminology: the most common unilineal kinship terminological system, which distinguishes members of an individual's lineage from other lineages.

Jajmani system: a system of economic exchange found in rural Indian communities. Based on reciprocity, the system links different caste groups into a network of shared obligations.

Joint household: a household created by the common residence and cooperation of two or more married couples.

Joking relationship: relationship between individuals where joking and teasing are permitted and expected.

Kindred: a kinship group based upon bilateral descent which includes relatives on both father's and mother's side.

Kinesics: the study of gestures, facial expressions, and body movements as means of communication; also known as body language.

Kingdom: a common form of state political organization in which power and authority are vested in a monarch or single authoritative ruler.

Kin term: a name for a particular relative or set of relatives. A single kin term is often used for different basic types.

Kin type: a particular and separate kin status or position. Different kin types are often classified under the same kin term.

Kula ring: a reciprocal trading complex of shell armbands and necklaces that involves the Trobriand Islanders and their island neighbors.

Labeling theory: a theory of mental illness that attributes mental disorder to the defining and labeling of ambiguous behavior as deviant behavior.

Latency period: a stage in the Freudian model of human maturation in which children are supposed to be most receptive to learning and well-behaved.

Law: the application of rules, ultimately backed by force, for the resolution of disputes and application of sanctions.

Learning theory: a theory that attempts to understand how children acquire and learn culture.

Level of political integration: the degree to which various units of a political system are integrated into a larger system.

Levirate: a widely practiced custom whereby a man is obliged to marry the wife of his deceased brother.

Lexical: relating to the vocabulary of a language.

Life-cycle ritual: a ceremony that celebrates a key event in an individual's life cycle.

Liminality: an aspect of Turner's theory of anti-structure that refers to the period of transition between statuses.

Lineage: a kinship group that consists of individuals who can trace their exact relationship to one another and to their common founding ancestor.

Linguistic determinism: a theory that language determines thought.

Linguistic relativism: a theory that speakers of different languages perceive and organize their worlds differently.

Linguistics: the scientific study of language.

Lumping it: the choice made when an individual decides to do nothing about a legal grievance he or she has.

Magic: a set of techniques – spells, formulas, and rituals – designed to control and manipulate supernatural powers and beings.

Managerial theory of the state: a theory advanced by Karl Wittfogel that attributes the emergence of state systems in Asia to the need for organizing and managing vast hydraulic projects required for the production of food.

Manioc: a starchy food plant originally domesticated by South American Indians and now grown throughout the tropical world; also called cassava.

Market exchange: a principle of economic exchange based upon buying and selling goods and services at prices determined by supply and demand.

Marriage: the socially recognized union of two or more individuals who are usually, but not always, of the opposite sex.

Mating: the sexual union of a couple.

Matriarchy: a society dominated by females.

Matrilocal residence: a pattern of residence in which a newly married couple lives with or near the bride's parents.

Matrilineal descent: a form of descent in which individuals trace their relationships through females only.

Modern evolutionary theory (general): a version of evolutionary theory that seeks to establish sequences of cultural development in the areas of politics and economics.

Moiety: a term applied to large-scale kin groups when a society is divided into only two such groups.

Monogamy: the marriage of one man to one woman at the same time.

Morpheme: the smallest unit of meaning in a language.

Morphology: the systematic combination of morphemes to form words.

Monolingual: able to speak only a single language.

Multilinear evolutionary theory: a modern theory of evolutionary development that compares cultural developments in separate, but environmentally similar, regions.

Multilingual: able to speak three or more languages fluently.

Multiplex relationships: a characteristic of tribal societies, according to Gluckman, where individuals are linked to each other through varied and multiple ties.

Neolocal residence: a pattern of residence in which a newly married couple lives apart from the parents or kin of both spouses.

Normality/abnormality: a culturally specified range of behavior from individuals who function effectively to individuals who exhibit inappropriate behavior.

Norms: rules that define and regulate acceptable behavior in a culture.

Nuclear family: a married couple and their children living as a separate unit; a type of independent household.

Oblique social protest: opposition to established authority expressed through indirect and nonviolent means.

Oedipal complex: Freud's theory that a son's hostility toward his father is caused by his unconscious incestuous feelings for his mother.

Omaha kinship terminology: a unilineal kinship terminological system found in association with patrilineal descent.

Oral stage: a stage in the Freudian model of human maturation in which an infant's primary source of pleasure is suckling at its mother's breast.

Outline of Cultural Materials (OCM): a classification scheme for categorizing the ethnographic data on a single society.

Outside structure: one of the dimensions of Turner's concept of anti-structure. This category consists of an invisible world of spiritual beings and power as well as individuals and groups who live beyond a community's cultural and social boundary.

Parallel cousins: children of siblings of the same sex; one's parallel cousins are mother's sister's children and father's brother's children.

Participant-observation: a method of fieldwork in which the anthropologist participates physically and emotionally in the culture being studied, while at the same time observing it scientifically.

Particularizing kinship system: a kinship terminology system that uses separate kin terms for each different kin type.

Pastoralism: a subsistence system based upon the herding of domesticated animals.

Patriarchy: a society dominated by males.

Patrilineal descent: a form of descent in which individuals trace their relationships through males only.

Patrilocal residence: a pattern of residence in which a newly married couple lives with or near the groom's parents.

Peasants: rural dwellers who produce not only their own food but food for the rest of a complex agricultural society.

Peasant society: a society based upon peasants and agriculture that is clearly differentiated into a hierarchy of superior statuses (urban dwellers) and inferior statuses (rural peasants).

Personality: the distinctive way an individual thinks, feels, and acts.

Phallic stage: a stage in the Freudian model of human maturation in which a male's awareness of his genitals brings about feelings about incest, castration, and love for his mother.

Phoneme: the smallest unit of sound recognized by the speakers of a language.

Phonemics: the study of sounds in a language that are recognized and distinguished by the speakers of the language.

Phonetics: the study of the physical attributes of sounds people make when they speak.

Phonology: the system of sounds characteristic of a language.

Phratry: a large-scale kin group composed of a large number of clans.

Physical anthropology: the scientific study of human biology, focusing upon the biological make-up of human populations and the origin and evolution of humankind.

Pibloktoq: a form of Arctic hysteria. Common symptoms of this mental disorder include running away, compulsive body movements, shouting, and stripping off one's clothing.

Political authority: the right of political rulers to exercise power.

Political centralization: the concentration of political power in the hands of a single ruler or a small political elite.

Political elite: the small group of individuals who occupy political offices and exercise political power.

Political role (or office): a defined position in a society where an individual makes decisions, controls the means of violence, and rules over followers.

Political theory of warfare: a theory that warfare is a consequence of the political supremacy engaged by a society.

Polyandry: the marriage of one woman to two or more men at the same time.

Polygyny: the marriage of one man to two or more women at the same time.

Potlatch: an important ceremony among northwest Pacific coast Indians in which goods were given away to gain prestige and resolve disputes.

Priest: a full-time religious specialist who is a member of an organized religious group.

Primary institution: a set of shared child training practices found in a society that are believed to be fundamental in shaping basic personality structures.

Problem-centered research: anthropological research projects that focus on particular theoretical or practical problems.

Proxemics: the study of how people in different cultures define the use and meaning of body space.

Psychiatric relativism: the theory that each culture has its own standards of normality and abnormality.

Psychiatric universalism: a theory of mental illness that assumes all mental disorders are the same regardless of cultural definitions of normality and abnormality.

Psychic unity of mankind: a concept used by

nineteenth century anthropologists that expressed the idea that all people in similar circumstances thought in much the same way.

Raiding: fighting directed at outside groups where the primary objective is to plunder and obtain booty.

Ramage: a descent group based upon ambilineal descent; frequently, a ramage is a residential or household group.

Reasonable man: a legal concept developed by Max Gluckman who claimed that all societies decide legal questions on the basis of what a reasonable person would do in a particular situation.

Reciprocity: a principle of economic exchange in which both parties attempt to maintain balance in the give-and-take exchange; sometimes called *gift exchange*.

Redistribution: a form of economic exchange in which goods are collected by a central authority who redistributes them to followers and clients.

Reliability: the degree to which different researchers or research techniques duplicate previously obtained information.

Religion: belief in the supernatural – an existence beyond the ordinary and understandable physical world.

Revitalization movement: a social movement combining religions, political, military, and economic elements from the traditional society as well as from Western culture in an attempt to create a new and viable social reality.

Rites of passage: rituals that mark the events in an individual's life cycle as he or she moves from one status to another.

Ritual: a repetitive and patterned procedure usually associated with religious practices.

Ritual warfare: a form of warfare in which the sportive aspects of fighting are dominant.

Role: a set of behaviors associated with a particular position or status in a society.

Running amok: (*see* Amok).

Sanction: the means used to enhance compliance with a society's laws and norms.

Sapir-Whorf hypothesis: an extreme statement of the linguistic relativism position arguing that the language we speak determines our perception of reality.

Secular religions: belief systems that reject traditional beliefs in the supernatural, but perform social and individual functions similar to traditional religions.

Sex-based group: a social group organized on the basis of sex.

Sexual division of labor: allocation of roles and statuses in a society on the basis of sex.

Shaman: a part-time religious specialist who is not a member of an organized religious group; a shaman has special powers to contact the supernatural.

Sharecropping: a system found in many peasant societies in which tenant farmers rent land from the landowners and pay their rent with a percentage of their harvest.

Simple political organization: a form of political organization in which small and autonomous communities are not integrated into a larger political system.

Symplex relationships: relationships in a complex society where individuals are linked by only a single tie.

Slash and burn cultivation: a horticultural technique in which trees and foliage are cut down, allowed to dry, and are burned, providing fertilizer for the next crop of plants.

Social anthropology: a term often used to describe British anthropology with its focus on society and social relationships.

Social change: the general term for the process of change as individuals in society modify their social organization and cultural behavior. Sources of social change may be either internal or external.

Social control: the varied mechanisms used to maintain conformity with a society's laws, values, and norms.

Social networks: an individually based set of linkages and relationships. Members of a network are often unknown to each other, but are linked by an individual who has relationships with all of them.

Social stratification: the division of society into a number of social classes that differ in their economic wealth, political power, life-style, and prestige.

Socialization: the process of acquiring culture.

Society: a group sharing a common territory, language, and social identity.

Sociobiology: a recent theory that claims a biological basis for human social behavior.

Sociolinguistics: the study of the social context of language.

Sororate: a custom whereby a man marries his deceased wife's sister.

Spirit possession: the taking over of human bodies by supernatural beings.

Stateless system: a political system without a centralized political institution.

State system: a political system with a complex and centralized political institution that organizes and controls the use of power.

Statistical comparison: the use of statistical methods to assess the relationship between variables in a large sample of cultures.

Status: a position or office in a society.

Structuralism: a theory of culture associated with Claude Lévi-Strauss that attempts to uncover the basic structure of human thinking that underlies cultural diversity.

Structure: a concept in Turner's theory of religion that refers to the organization of society in terms of statuses, roles, and norms.

Subsistence system: the techniques, technology, resources, and work activities used to produce food.

Sudanese kinship terminology: the most particularizing kinship terminological system, usually found in association with patrilineal descent in complex societies.

Supernatural: an existence beyond the ordinary and understandable physical world.

Swidden cultivation: (see slash and burn cultivation).

Symbiotic relationship: a mutually beneficial relationship between different species and organisms.

Synchronic: analyzing social and cultural events without reference to an historical or time dimension.

Syntax: the system of rules that underlie word order and the construction of sentences in a language.

Third World anthropology: a position advocated by some Third World anthropologists that only insiders studying their own cultures can understand their true nature.

Third-World nations: the nations that emerged from the European colonial empires.

Transformational-generative grammar: a theory of language developed by Noam Chomsky that postulates a universal grammar underlying all human languages.

Tribe: a group depending on foraging, horticulture, or pastoralism for subsistence.

Trouble cases: a concept developed by Llewellyn and Hoebel that assumes that law is in tribal societies only when a norm is violated.

Unilineal descent: a principle of descent in which relationships are traced through only one side of the family.

Urban anthropology: the study of the impact of urban environments on human behavior using traditional anthropological research techniques.

Validity: the accuracy of information obtained in the research process.

Vasco da Gama Era: the opening phase of European expansion, discovery, exploration, and control over strategic locations.

Voluntaristic theories of the state: theories that attribute the origin of state systems to a community's voluntary renunciation of political power to obtain the advantages of a large political unit.

Warfare: sustained and organized combat between recognized groups.

Wari: a game of strategy played throughout much of Africa, Madagascar, Indonesia, and the Western Pacific; also called mankala, mweso, chisolo, and katra.

Witchcraft: the belief that some people are able to use supernatural means to injure and kill people.

Bibliography

Abel, T. M., and Hsu, F. L. K. 1949. "Some Aspects of Personality as Revealed by the Rorschach Test." *Rorschach Research Exchange and Journal of Projective Techniques* 13:285–301.

Aberle, David F. 1961. "Navaho." In *Matrilineal Kinship,* edited by David M. Schneider and Kathleen Gough, pp. 96–201. Berkeley: University of California Press.

Abrahams, Roger D. 1970. *Deep Down in the Jungle.* Chicago: Aldine.

Aginsky, Burton. 1940. "An Indian Soliloquy." *American Journal of Sociology* 46:43–44.

Ardrey, Robert, 1966. *The Territorial Imperative.* New York: Atheneum.

———. 1964. *African Genesis.* New York: Dell.

Asad, Talal, ed. 1973. *Anthropology and the Colonial Encounter.* New York: Humanities Press.

Barnouw, Victor. 1979. *Culture and Personality.* 3rd ed. Homewood, Ill.: Dorsey Press.

Barry, Herbert, III; and Roberts, John M. 1972. "Infant Socialization and Games of Chance." *Ethnology* 11:296–308.

Bascom, William. 1977. "Some Yoruba Ways with Yams." In *The Anthropologists' Cookbook,* edited by Jessica Kuper, pp. 82–85. New York: Universe Books.

———. 1969. *Ifa Divination: Communication Between Gods and Men in West Africa.* Bloomington, Ind.: Indiana University Press.

Bauman, Richard, and Sherzer, Joel. 1974. *Explorations in the Ethnography of Speaking.* Cambridge: Cambridge University Press.

Beals, Alan. 1970. "Gopalpur, 1958–1960." In *Being an Anthropologist: Fieldwork in Eleven Cultures,* edited by George Spindler, pp. 32–57. New York: Holt, Rinehart & Winston.

Beattie, John. 1965. *Understanding an African Kingdom: Bunyoro.* New York: Holt, Rinehart & Winston.

Beckerman, Stephen. 1979. "The Abundance of Protein in Amazonia: A Reply to Gross." *American Anthropologist* 81:533–560.

Beidelman, T. O. 1971. *The Kaguru.* New York: Holt, Rinehart & Winston.

Benedict, Ruth. 1934. *Patterns of Culture.* Boston: Houghton Mifflin.

Berlin, Brent, and Kay, Paul. 1969. *Basic Color Terms: Their Universality and Evolution.* Berkeley: University of California Press.

Bernstein, Basil. 1964. "Elaborated and Restricted Codes: Their Social Origins and Some Consequences." *American Anthropologist* 66, 6:55–69.

Berreman, Gerald. 1972. "Social Categories and Social Interaction in Urban India." *American Anthropologist* 74:567–587.

Best, Elsdon. 1924. *The Maori.* Polynesian Society Memoirs 5. Wellington, New Zealand.

Bloom, Alfred H. 1979. "The Impact of Chinese Linguistic Structure on Cognitive Style." *Current Anthropology* 20:585–586.

Bohannan, Laura. 1977. "An Adaptation of Tiv Sesame Chicken." In *The Anthropologists' Cookbook,* edited by Jessica Kuper, pp. 87–88. New York: Universe Books.

Bohannan, Paul. 1958. "Extra-Processual Events in Tiv Political Institutions." *American Anthropologist* 60:1–12.

Bonwick, James. 1870. *The Last of The Tasmanians; or the Black War of Van Diemen's Land.* London: Sampson, Low, Son & Marston. 1970. Reprint. New York: Johnson Reprint Corp.

Brandow, Selma K. 1979. "Illusion of Equality." *International Journal of Women's Studies* 2:268–286.

Briggs, Jean L. 1970. "Kapluna Daughter: Adopted by the Eskimo." In *Women in the Field,* edited by Peggy Golde, pp. 19–44. Chicago: Aldine.

Brown, Judith K. 1970. "A Note on the Division of Labor by Sex." *American Anthropologist* 72:1073–1078.

Buck, Sir Peter (Te Rangi Hiroa). 1952. *The Coming of the Maori.* 2nd ed. Wellington, New Zealand: Whitcombe & Tombs.

Burling, Robbins. 1974. *The Passage of Power.* New York: Academic Press.

———. 1959. "Language Development of a Garo and English Speaking Child." *Word* 15:45–65.

Burton, Sir Richard Francis. 1864. *A Mission to Gelele, King of Dahomé.* London: Tinsley Bros. 1966. Reprint. New York: Praeger.

Buxton, Jean. 1958. "The Mandari of the Southern Sudan." In *Tribes without Rulers,* edited by John Middleton and David Tait, pp. 67–96. London: Routledge & Kegan Paul.

Cardinall, A. W. 1927. *In Ashanti and Beyond.* Philadelphia: J. B. Lippincott. 1970. Reprint. Westport, Conn.: Negro Universities Press, Affil. Greenwood Press.

Carneiro, Robert. 1970. "A Theory of the Origin of the State." *Science* 169:733–738.

Carroll, John B., and Casagrande, Joseph. 1958. "The Function of Language Classification in Behavior." In *Readings in Social Psychology,* 3rd ed., edited by E. E. Maccoby, T. H. Newcomb, and E. L. Hartley, pp. 18–31. New York: Holt, Rinehart & Winston.

Chagnon, Napoleon A. 1979. *Studying the Yanomamo.* New York: Holt, Rinehart & Winston.

Chilungu, Simeon W. 1976. "Issues in the Ethics of Research Method: An Interpretation of the Anglo-American Perspective." *Current Anthropology* 17:457–481.

Chomsky, Noam. 1972. *Language and Mind.* New York: Harcourt Brace Jovanovich.

_____. 1957. *Syntactic Structures.* The Hague, Netherlands: Mouton Publishers.

Chomsky, Noam, and Premack, David. 1979. "Encounter: Species of Intelligence." *The Sciences* 19:6–11, 23.

Cipolla, Carlo M. 1965. *Guns, Sails, and Empires.* New York: Pantheon Books.

Clarke, William. 1971. *Place and People: An Ecology of a New Guinean Community.* Berkeley: University of California Press.

Cohen, Abner, 1969. *Custom and Politics in Urban Africa.* London: Routledge & Kegan Paul.

Cohen, Mark N. 1977. *The Food Crisis in Prehistory: Overpopulation and Origins of Agriculture.* New Haven, Conn.: Yale University Press.

Cohen, Ronald. 1967. *The Kanuri of Bornu.* New York: Holt, Rinehart & Winston.

Cohn, Bernard S. 1980. "History and Anthropology." *Comparative Studies in Society and History* 22:2, 198–221.

Cole, Donald Powell. 1975. *Nomads of the Nomads.* Chicago: Aldine.

Collier, Jane F. 1975. "Legal Processes." *Annual Review of Anthropology,* edited by B. J. Siegel, A. R. Beals, and S. A. Tyler, Palo Alto: Annual Reviews Inc. 4:121–144.

Coon, Carleton S. 1971. *The Hunting Peoples.* Boston: Atlantic-Little, Brown.

_____. 1956. *A Reader in General Anthropology.* New York: Henry Holt.

Coser, Lewis. 1956. *The Functions of Social Conflict.* New York: Free Press.

Datan, Nancy. 1977. "Ecological Antecedents and Sex-Role Consequences in Traditional and Modern Israeli Sub-cultures." In *Sexual Stratification,* edited by Alice Schlegel, pp. 326–343. New York: Columbia University Press.

Denich, Bette. 1970. "Migration and Network Manipulation in Yugoslavia." In *Migration and Anthropology,* pp. 133–148. Seattle: University of Washington Press.

Dentan, Robert. 1970. "Living and Working with the Semai." In *Being an Anthropologist: Fieldwork in Eleven Cultures,* edited by George Spindler, pp. 85–112. New York: Holt, Rinehart & Winston.

Dobyns, Henry; Medrano, Carlos M.; and Vasquez, M. C. 1966. "A Contagious Experiment." In *A Casebook of Social Change,* edited by Arthur H. Niehoff, pp. 67–76. Chicago: Aldine.

DuBois, Cora. 1961. *The People of Alor.* Orig. published 1944. Reprint. Minneapolis: University of Minnesota Press.

Eames, Edwin, and Goode, Judith Granich. 1977. *Anthropology of the City.* Englewood Cliffs, N.J.: Prentice-Hall.

_____. 1973. *Urban Poverty in Cross-Cultural Context.* New York: Free Press.

Eames, Edwin, and Robboy, Howard. 1969. "Oblique Social Protest: Bureaucratic Entrapment and America's Everyman." Presented at Second International Congress of Social Psychiatry, August, 1969, London, England.

Eastman, Carol M. 1975. *Aspects of Language and Culture.* San Francisco: Chandler & Sharp.

Edgerton, Robert B. 1971. *The Individual in Cultural Adaptation: A Study of Four East African Peoples.* Berkeley: University of California Press.

_____. 1966. "Conceptions of Psychosis in Four East African Societies." *American Anthropologist* 68:408–425.

_____. 1965. "'Cultural' vs. 'Ecological' Factors in the Expression of Values, Attitudes, and Personality Characteristics." *American Anthropologist* 67:442–447.

Ekvall, Robert. 1968. *Fields on the Hoof.* New York: Holt, Rinehart & Winston.

Elwin, Verrier, 1947. *The Muria and Their Ghotul.* Bombay: Oxford University Press.

Epstein, A. L. 1969. "The Network and Urban Social Organization." In *Social Networks in Urban Situations,* edited by J. C. Mitchell, pp. 77–116. Manchester: Manchester University Press.

_____. 1964. "Urban Communities in Africa." In *Closed Systems and Open Minds: The Limits of Naivety in Social Anthropology,* edited by Max Gluckman, pp. 83–102. Edinburgh: Oliver & Boyd.

_____. 1958. *Politics in an Urban African Community.* Manchester: Manchester University Press.

_____. 1953. *The Administration of Justice and the Urban African: A Study of Urban Native Courts in Northern*

Rhodesia. London: HMSO The British Government Publisher.

Evans-Pritchard, Edward Evans. 1940. *The Nuer: A Description of the Modes of Livelihood and Political Institutions of a Nilotic People.* Oxford: Clarendon Press.

———. 1937. *Witchcraft, Oracles, and Magic among the Azande.* 1976. Reprint, abridged. Oxford: Clarendon Press.

Fallers, Lloyd A. 1974. *The Social Anthropology of the Nation-State.* Chicago: Aldine.

Firth, Raymond. 1960. "A Polynesia Aristocrat." In *The Company of Man,* edited by Joseph B. Casagrande, pp. 1–40. New York: Harper & Row.

———. 1936. *We the Tikopia.* London: George Allen & Urwin Ltd.

Forde, Daryll. 1950. "Double Descent among the Yakö." In *African Systems of Kinship and Marriage,* edited by A. R. Radcliffe-Brown and Daryll Forde, pp. 289–332. London: Oxford University Press.

Forster, E. B. 1962. "The Theory and Practice of Psychiatry in Ghana." *American Journal of Psychotherapy* 16:7–51.

Fortes, Meyer. 1950. "Kinship and Marriage among the Ashanti." In *African Systems of Kinship and Marriage,* edited by A. R. Radcliffe-Brown and Daryll Forde, pp. 252–284. London: Oxford University Press.

Fortes, Meyer, and Evans-Pritchard, E. E., eds. 1940. *African Political Systems.* London: Oxford University Press.

Foster, George. 1965. "Peasant Society and the Image of Limited Good." *American Anthropologist* 67:293–315.

Foulks, Edward F. 1972. *The Arctic Hysterias.* Anthropological Studies, 10. Washington, D.C.: American Anthropological Association.

Fox, Robin. 1978. *The Tory Islanders.* Cambridge: Cambridge University Press.

———. 1967. *Kinship and Marriage.* Baltimore: Penguin Books.

Frazer, Sir James G. 1959. *The New Golden Bough.* New York: New American Library.

Freeman, Daniel, M.A.: Foulks, Edward F.; and Freeman, Patricia A. 1978. "Child Development and Arctic Hysteria in the North Alaskan Eskimo Male." *Journal of Psychological Anthropology* 1:203–210.

Freud, Sigmund. 1930. *Civilization and Its Discontents.* New York: Jonathan Cope and Harrison Smith.

Fried, Morton; Harris, M.; and Murphy, R., eds. 1968. *The Anthropology of Armed Conflict and Aggression.* New York: Natural History Press.

Friedl, Ernestine. 1964. *Vasilika.* New York: Holt, Rinehart & Winston.

Fromkin, Victoria, and Rodman, Robert. 1978. *An Introduction to Language.* 2nd ed. New York: Holt, Rinehart & Winston.

Gardner, R. A., and Gardner, B. T. 1969. "Teaching Sign Language to a Chimpanzee." *Science* 165:664–672.

Gennep, Arnold Van. 1960. *The Rites of Passage.* Translated by Monika B. Vizedom and Gabrielle L. Chaffee. London: Routledge & Kegan Paul.

Gibbs, James L., Jr. 1964. "Social Organization." In *Horizons of Anthropology,* edited by S. Tax, pp. 160–170. Chicago: Aldine.

———. 1963. "The Kpelle Moot: A Therapeutic Model for the Informal Settlement of Disputes." *Africa* 33:1–11.

Gluckman, Max. 1961. "Anthropological Problems Arising from the African Industrial Revolution." In *Social Change in Modern Africa,* edited by Aidan Southall, pp. 67–82. London: Oxford University Press.

———. 1955. *The Judicial Process Among the Barotse of Northern Rhodesia.* Manchester: Manchester University Press.

———. 1950. "Kinship and Marriage among the Lozi of Northern Rhodesia and the Zulu of Natal." In *African Systems of Kinship and Marriage,* edited by A. R. Radcliffe-Brown and Daryll Forde, pp. 166–206. London: Oxford University Press.

———. 1940. "Analysis of a Social Situation in Modern Zululand." *Bantu Studies* 14, June, March, 1 and 2, 1–31, 147–175. 1958. Reprint. *Rhodes-Livingstone Papers, 28.* Manchester: Manchester University Press.

———. 1940a. "The Kingdom of the Zulu in South Africa." In *African Political Systems,* edited by M. Fortes and E. E. Evans-Pritchard, pp. 25–55. London: Oxford University Press.

———, ed. 1969. *Ideas and Procedures in African Customary Law.* London: Oxford University Press.

Gmelch, George, 1971. "Baseball Magic." *Transaction* 8,8.

Goldschmidt, Walter, 1977. "Anthropology and the Coming Crisis: Autoethnographic Appraisal." *American Anthropologist* 79:293–308.

———. 1974. "The Economics of Bride Price among the Sebei and in East Africa." *Ethnology* 13:4, 311–331.

Goldschmidt, Walter, with the assistance of Goldschmidt, Gale. 1976. *The Culture and Behavior of the Sebei: A Study in Continuity and Adaptation.* Berkeley: University of California Press.

Goody, J., and Tambiah, S. J. 1973 *Bridewealth and Dowry.* Cambridge: Cambridge University Press.

Gough, Kathleen. 1959. "The Nayars and the Definition of Marriage." *Journal of the Royal Anthropological Institute* 89:23–34.

Gould, Richard. 1969. *Yiwara: Foragers of the Australian Desert.* New York: Scribner.

Greenberg, J. 1975. "Research on Language Universals." In *Annual Review of Anthropology,* 4, edited by B. J. Siegel, A. R. Beals, and S. A. Tyler. Palo Alto: Annual Reviews, Inc.

Grivetti, Lewis Evans. 1978. "Culture, Diet, and Nutrition: Selected Themes and Topics." *BioScience* 28:171–176.

Haley, Alex. 1976. *Roots.* Garden City, N.Y.: Doubleday.

Hall, Edward, and Hall, Mildred. 1971. "The Sounds of Silence." *Playboy* 18: 6, 139–140, 148, 204, 206.

Hall, Edward. 1966. *The Hidden Dimension.* New York: Doubleday.

Hallowell, A. Irving. 1959. *The Backwash of the Frontier: The Impact of the Indian on American Culture.* Publication 4368. Washington, D.C.: Smithsonian Institution.

Hallpike, C. R. 1973. "Functionalist Interpretations of Warfare." *Man* 8:451–470.

Harner, Michael J., ed. 1973. *Hallucinogens and Shamanism.* New York: Oxford University Press.

_____. 1973*b*. "The Role of Hallucinogenic Plants in European Witchcraft." In *Hallucinogens and Shamanism,* edited by Michael J. Harner, pp. 125–150. New York: Oxford University Press.

_____. 1972. *The Jivaro: People of the Sacred Waterfalls.* Garden City, N.Y.: Doubleday/Natural History Press.

Harner, Michael J. 1973*a*. "The Sound of Rushing Water." In *Hallucinogens and Shamanism,* edited by Michael J. Harner, pp. 15–27. New York: Oxford University Press.

Harris, Marvin. 1977. *Cannibals and Kings.* New York: Random House.

_____. 1968. *The Rise of Anthropological Theory.* New York: Thomas Y. Crowell.

Harris, Marvin, and Wilson, E. O. 1978. "The Envelope and the Twig." *The Sciences* 18:8, 10–15, 27.

Hart, C. W. M. 1970. "Fieldwork among the Tiwi 1928–1929." In *Being an Anthropologist: Fieldwork in Eleven Cultures,* edited by George Spindler, pp. 142–163. New York: Holt, Rinehart & Winston.

Hart, C. W. M. and Pilling, Arnold. 1960. *The Tiwi of North Australia.* New York: Holt, Rinehart & Winston.

Heider, Karl. 1979. *Grand Valley Dani.* New York: Holt, Rinehart & Winston.

_____. 1970. *The Dugum Dani.* Viking Fund Publications in Anthropology, no. 49. New York: Wenner-Gren Foundation for Anthropological Research, Inc.

Hobbes, Thomas. 1651. *Leviathan.* 1958. Reprint. New York: Liberal Arts Press.

Hoebel, E. Adamson. 1978. *The Cheyennes.* 2nd ed. New York: Holt, Rinehart & Winston.

Hogbin, Ian. 1957. "Anthropology as Public Service and Malinowski's Contribution to It." In *Man and Culture,* edited by Raymond Firth, pp. 245–264. London: Routledge & Kegan Paul.

Hollingshead, August B., and Redlich, Frederick C. 1958. *Social Class and Mental Illness: A Community Study.* New York: John Wiley & Sons Inc.

Holmberg, Allan. 1965. "The Changing Values and Institutions of Vicos in the Context of National Development." *American Behavioral Scientist* 8:3–8.

_____. 1958. "The Research and Development Approach to the Study of Change." *Human Organization* 17:12–16.

_____. 1950. *Nomads of the Long Bow.* Washington, D.C.: Smithsonian Institution. 1969. Reprint. American Museum Science Books. Garden City, N.Y.: Natural History Press.

Honigman, John J. 1976. *The Development of Anthropological Ideas.* Homewood, Ill.: Dorsey Press.

Hopkins, Keith. 1980. "Brother-Sister Marriage in Roman Egypt." *Comparative Studies in Society and History* 22:3, pp. 303–354.

Howarth, David. 1978. *The Men-of-War.* The Seafarers. Alexandria, Va.: Time-Life Books.

Irvine, Judith. 1974. "Strategies of Status Manipulation in the Wolof Greeting." In *Explorations in the Ethnography of Speaking,* edited by R. Bauman and J. Sherzer, pp. 167–191. London: Cambridge University Press.

Kardiner, Abram. 1939. *The Individual and His Society.* New York: Columbia University Press.

Karp, Ivan. 1976. "The Myth of Field Research Methods." Presented at American Anthropological Association, Annual Meeting, November, 1976, Washington, D.C.

Keiser, R. Lincoln. 1970. "Fieldwork Among the Vice Lords of Chicago." In *Being an Anthropologist: Fieldwork in Eleven Cultures,* edited by George D. Spindler, pp. 200–273. New York: Holt, Rinehart & Winston.

Kinsey, Alfred C.; Pomeroy, W.; and Martin, C. 1948. *Sexual Behavior in the Human Male.* Philadelphia: The Saunders Press.

Klass, Morton. 1980. "Ecology and Family in Two Caribbean East Indian Communities." In *The New Ethnics,* edited by P. Saran and E. Eames, pp. 48–60. New York: Praeger Publishers.

Kluckhohn, Clyde, and Kelly, W. H. 1945. "The Concept of Culture." In *The Science of Man in the World Crisis,* edited by R. Linton, pp. 78–105. New York: Columbia University Press.

Kluckhohn, Clyde, and Leighton, Dorothea. 1946. *The Navaho.* 1962. Reprint. New York: Doubleday.

Kottak, Conrad. 1972. "Ecological Variables in the Origin and Evolution of African States: The Buganda Example." *Comparative Studies in Society and History* 14, 3:351–380.

Kramer, Samuel Noah. 1959. *History Begins at Sumer.* New York: Doubleday.

Kressel, Gideon M. 1977. "Bride-Price Reconsidered." *Current Anthropology* 18:3, 441–450.

Kroeber, A. L., and Kluckhohn, Clyde. 1952. *Culture: A Critical Review of Concepts and Definition.* Papers of the Peabody Museum of American Archaeology and Ethnology, Harvard University, vol. 47, no. 1. Cambridge, Mass.

Kuper, Hilda. 1963. *The Swazi: A South African Kingdom.* New York: Holt, Rinehart & Winston.

Kuper, Jessica, ed. 1977. *The Anthropologists' Cookbook.* New York: Universe Books.

Kupferer, Harriet. J. K. 1965. "Couvade, Ritual or Real Illness." *American Anthropologist* 67:99–102.

Labov, William. 1968. "The Reflection of Social Processes in Linguistic Structures." In *Readings in the Sociology of Language,* edited by Joshua A. Fishman, pp. 240–251. The Hague: Mouton.

———. 1966. *The Social Stratification of English in New York City.* Center for Applied Linguistics, Washington, D.C.

———. 1964. "Phonological Correlates of Social Stratification." *American Anthropologist* 66, 6:164–176.

Lancaster, Jane B. 1975. *Primate Behavior and the Emergence of Human Culture.* New York: Holt, Rinehart and Winston.

Leach, Marianne, and Leach, Terry. 1977. "Meydiha's Kisir: A Wheat Dish from Southern Turkey." In *The Anthropologists' Cookbook,* edited by Jessica Kuper, pp. 61–68. New York: Universe Books.

Leacock, Eleanor. 1877. Introduction to *Ancient Society,* by L. H. Morgan. 1963. Reprint. New York: Meridian Books, World Publishing Co.

Lee, Dorothy. 1950. "Lineal and Nonlineal Codifications of Reality." *Psychosomatic Medicine* 12:89–97.

Lee, Richard. 1968. "What Hunters Do for a Living, or How to Make Out on Scarce Resources." In *Man the Hunter,* edited by R. B. Lee and I. DeVore, pp. 30–48. Chicago: Aldine.

Leighton, A. H. 1961. "The Stirling County Study: Some Notes on Concepts and Methods." In *Comparative Epidemiology of the Mental Disorders,* edited by Paul H. Hoch and Joseph Zubin, pp. 24–31. New York: Grune and Stratton.

Levi-Strauss, Claude. 1969. *The Elementary Structures of Kinship.* Boston: Beacon Press.

Lewis, I. M. 1970. "A Structural Approach to Witchcraft and Spirit Possession." In *Witchcraft, Confessions and Accusations,* edited by Mary Douglas, pp. 293–309. London: Tavistock Publications.

Lewis, Oscar. 1961. *The Children of Sanchez.* New York: Random House.

———. 1952. "Urbanization without Breakdown." *Scientific Monthly* 75:31–41.

———. 1951. *Life in a Mexican Village.* Urbana, Ill.: University of Illinois Press.

Liebow, Elliot. 1967. *Tally's Corner.* Boston: Little, Brown and Co.

Lindenbaum, Shirley. 1972. "Sorcerers, Ghosts, and Polluting Women: An Analysis of Religious Belief and Population Control." *Ethnology* 11:241–253.

Linton, Ralph. 1957. *The Tree of Culture.* New York: Alfred Knopf.

———. 1937. "One Hundred Percent American." *The American Mercury.* 40:427–429.

———. 1933. *The Tanala: A Hill Tribe of Madagascar.* Field Museum of Natural History, Anthropological Series, 22:1–334.

Little, Kenneth. 1965. *West African Urbanization: A Study of Voluntary Associations in Social Change.* Cambridge: Cambridge University Press.

Llewellyn, K. N., and Hoebel, E. A. 1941. *The Cheyenne Way: Conflict and Case Law in Primitive Jurisprudence.* Norman, Okla.: University of Oklahoma Press.

Lorenz, Konrad. 1966. *On Aggression.* New York: Harcourt, Brace and World.

Louden, J. B. 1970. "Teasing and Socialization on Tristan da Curha." In *Socialization: The Approach from Social Anthropology,* edited by Philip Mayer, pp. 293–337. London: Tavistock Publications.

Lynd, Robert S., and Lynd, Helen M. 1929. *Middletown.* New York: Harcourt Brace.

McFee, Malcolm. 1972. *Modern Blackfeet.* New York: Holt, Rinehart & Winston.

Malinowski, Bronislaw. 1967. *A Diary in the Strict Sense of the Term.* New York: Harcourt, Brace and World.

———. 1944. *A Scientific Theory of Culture.* 1960. Reprint. New York: Oxford University Press.

———. 1929. *The Sexual Life of Savages in North-West Melanesia.* London: Routledge & Kegan Paul.

———. 1927. *Sex and Repression in Savage Society.* London: Routledge & Kegan Paul.

———. 1922. *Argonauts of the Western Pacific.* 1961. Reprint. New York: E. P. Dutton.

———. 1918. *Evidence by B. Malinowski, 27 October, 1916, on Pacific Labour Conditions.* British and Australian Trade in the South Pacific, Report 66, F13489. Melbourne: Parliament of the Commonwealth of Australia.

Maloney, Clarence, ed. 1976. *The Evil Eye.* New York: Columbia University Press.

Marriott, McKim. 1966. "A Feast of Love." In *Krishna: Myths, Rites, and Attitudes,* edited by Milton Singer, pp. 200–213. Chicago: University of Chicago Press.

Marshall, Lorna. 1967. "Kung Bushman Bands." In *Comparative Political Systems,* edited by Ronald Cohen and

John Middleton, pp. 15–43. Garden City, N.Y.: Natural History Press.

Martin, M. Kay, and Voorhies, Barbara. 1975. *Female of the Species.* New York: Columbia University Press.

Maruyama, Magoroh, and Harkins, Arthur, eds. 1975. *Cultures Beyond the Earth.* New York: Vintage Press.

Mayer, A. L. 1966. "The Significance of Quasi-Groups in the Study of Complex Societies." In *The Social Anthropology of Complex Societies,* edited by M. Banton, pp. 97–122. London: Tavistock Publications.

Mead, Margaret. 1935. *Sex and Temperament in Three Primitive Societies.* New York: Dell.

———. 1928. *Coming of Age in Samoa: A Psychological Study of Primitive Youth for Western Civilization.* New York: William Morrow.

Meggitt, Mervyn. 1979. "Reflections Occasioned by Continuing Anthropological Field Research Among the Enga of Papua New Guinea." In *Long-Term Field Research in Social Anthropology,* edited by G. M. Foster, T. Scudder, E. Colson, and R. V. Kemper, pp. 107–126. New York: Academic Press.

———. 1977. *Blood Is Their Argument: Warfare Among the Mae Enga Tribesmen of the New Guinea Highlands.* Palo Alto, Calif.: Mayfield Publishing Co.

Menen, Aubrey. 1953. "My Grandmother and the Dirty English." In *Dead Man in the Silver Market.* Westport, Conn.: Greenwood Press.

Messenger, John. 1969. *Inis Beag.* New York: Holt, Rinehart & Winston.

Middleton, John. 1970. "Africa." In *A Handbook of Method in Cultural Anthropology,* edited by Raoul Naroll and Ronald Cohen, pp. 225–229. New York: Columbia University Press.

Miner, Horace. 1956. "Body Ritual Among the Nacirema." *American Anthropologist* 58:503–507.

Minturn, Leigh; Grosse, Martin; and Haider, Santoah. 1969. "Cultural Patterns of Sexual Beliefs and Behavior." *Ethnology* 8:3, 301–318.

Mischel, Walter, and Mischel, Frances. 1958. "Psychological Aspects of Spirit Possession." *American Anthropologist* 60:249–260.

Mitchell, J. Clyde. 1974. "Perceptions of Ethnicity and Ethnic Behavior: An Empirical Exploration." In *Urban Ethnicity,* edited by A. Cohen, pp. 1–35. London: Tavistock Publications.

———. 1970. "Africans in Industrial Towns in Northern Rhodesia." In *Peasants in Cities,* edited by William Mangin, pp. 160–169. Boston: Houghton Mifflin.

Morauta, Louise. 1979. "Indigenous Anthropology in Papua New Guinea." *Current Anthropology* 20:561–576.

Müller, Wilhelm. 1917. *Yap.* Edited by G. Thilenius. Hamburg: Erg. der Sudsee Expedition, 1908–10.

Murdock, George. 1967. *Ethnographic Atlas.* Pittsburgh: University of Pittsburgh Press.

———. 1950. "Family Stability in Non-European Cultures." *Annals of the American Academy of Political and Social Science* 272:195–201.

———. 1949. *Social Structure.* New York: Macmillan.

———. 1934. *Our Primitive Contemporaries.* New York: MacMillan.

Murdock, George, and Provost, Caterina. 1973. "Factors in the Division of Labor by Sex: A Cross-Cultural Analysis." *Ethnology* 12:203–224.

Murphy, Jane M. 1976. "Psychiatric Labeling in Cross-Cultural Perspective." *Science* 191:1019–1028.

Murphy, Robert. 1967. "Tuareg Kinship." *American Anthropologist* 69:163–170.

———. 1964. "Social Distance and the Veil." *American Anthropologist* 66:1257–1274.

Nadel. S. F. 1952. "Witchcraft in Four African Societies." *American Anthropologist* 54:18–29.

Nader, Laura, and Todd, Harry F., Jr., eds. 1978. *The Disputing Process — Law in Ten Societies.* New York: Columbia University Press.

Nader, Laura, and Todd, Harry F., Jr. 1978a. Introduction to *The Disputing Process — Law in Ten Societies,* edited by L. Nader and H. F. Todd, Jr., pp. 1–40. New York: Columbia University Press.

Newman, Philip. 1965. *Knowing the Gururumba.* New York: Holt, Rinehart & Winston.

Newton, Esther. 1972. *Mother Camp: Female Impersonators in America.* Englewood Cliffs, N.J.: Prentice-Hall.

Nimmo, H. Arlo. 1970. "Bajau Sex and Reproduction." *Ethnology* 9:251–262.

Ohnuki-Tierney, Emiko. 1973. "The Shamanism of the Ainu of the Northwest Coast of Southern Sakhalin." *Ethnology* 12:15–30.

Oliver, Douglas. 1961. *The Pacific Islands.* Rev. ed. Garden City, N.Y.: Anchor Books/Doubleday.

Opler, Marvin K. 1967. *Culture and Social Psychiatry.* New York: Atherton Press.

———. 1959. "Cultural Differences in Mental Disorders: An Italian and Irish Contrast in the Schizophrenias — U.S.A." In *Culture and Mental Health,* edited by Marvin K. Opler, pp. 425–442. New York: Atherton Press.

Opler, Morris. 1941. *An Apache Life Way.* Chicago: University of Chicago Press.

Orwell, George. 1949. *1984.* New York: Harcourt, Brace and Co.

Owusu, Maxwell. 1978. "Ethnography of Africa: The Usefulness of the Useless." *American Anthropologist* 80:310–334.

Panikkar, K. M. 1953. *Asia and Western Dominance.* 1961. Reprint. London: W. H. Allen & Co. Ltd.

Pasternak, Burton. 1976. *Introduction to Kinship and Social Organization.* Englewood Cliffs, N.J.: Prentice-Hall.

Patterson, Francine. 1978. "Conversations with a Gorilla." *National Geographic* 154, 4:438–466.

Peattie, Lisa. 1970. *The View from the Barrio.* Ann Arbor, Mich.: University of Michigan Press.

Pelto, Pertti J. 1978. *Anthropological Research.* 2nd ed. New York: Harper & Row.

Peterson, Len. 1954. "Stand-in for a Murderer." In *The Ways of Mankind,* edited by Walter Goldschmidt, pp. 11–17. Boston: Beacon Press.

Pitt-Rivers, Julian. 1961. *The People of the Sierra.* Chicago: University of Chicago Press.

Pospisil, Leopold. 1971. *Anthropology of Law: A Comparative Theory of Law.* New York: Harper & Row.

Powdermaker, Hortense, 1966. *Stranger and Friend.* New York: W. W. Norton & Co.

Raleigh, Sir Walter. Quoted in Howarth, 1978.

Read, Margaret. 1968. *Children of Their Fathers: Growing Up among the Ngoni of Malawi.* New York: Holt, Rinehart & Winston.

Redfield, Robert. 1941. *The Folk Culture of Yucatan.* Chicago: University of Chicago Press.

Redfield, Robert; Linton, R.; and Herskovits, M. 1936. "Memorandum on the Study of Acculturation." *American Anthropologist* 37:149–152.

Redfield, Robert, and Rojas, Alfonso Villa. 1934. *Chan Kom, A Maya Village.* Washington: Carnegie Institution of Washington.

Reining, Conrad C. 1962. "A Lost Period of Applied Anthropology." *American Anthropologist* 64:593–600.

Reisman, Paul. 1971. "Defying Official Morality: The Example of Man's Quest for Woman among the Fulani." *Cahiers d'Études Africaines* 11:602–613.

Reminick, Ronald. 1974. "The Evil Eye Belief among the Amhara of Ethiopia." *Ethnology* 8:279–292.

Rhoades, Robert E. 1978. "Foreign Labor and German Industrial Capitalism 1871–1978: The Evolution of a Migration System." *American Ethnologist* 5:553–573.

Richards, Audrey. 1964. "Authority Patterns in Traditional Buganda." In *The King's Men,* edited by L. A. Fallers, pp. 256–293. London: Oxford University Press.

Rivers, W. H. R. 1906. *The Toda.* New York: Macmillan.

Roberts, John M. 1976. "Belief in the Evil Eye in World Perspective." In *The Evil Eye,* edited by Clarence Maloney. New York: Columbia University Press.

Roberts, John M.; Arth, M. J.; and Bush, R. R. 1959. "Games in Culture." *American Anthropologist* 61:597–605.

Roberts, John M.; and Sutton-Smith, B. 1962. "Child Training and Game Involvement." *Ethnology* 1:166–185.

Rosenhan, D. 1973. "On Being Sane in Insane Places." *Science* 179:250–258.

Rousseau, Jean-Jacques. 1938. *The Social Contract.* Translated by G. D. H. Cole. New York: Dutton (orig. publ. 1762).

Ruffino, Julio L. 1978. "Disputing over Livestock in Sardinia." In *The Disputing Process – Law in Ten Societies,* edited by L. Nader and H. F. Todd, Jr., pp. 209–246. New York: Columbia University Press.

Sahlins, Marshall D. 1961. "The Segmentary Lineage: An Organization of Predatory Expansion." *American Anthropologist* 63:322–345.

Salisbury, R. F. 1962. "Notes on Bilingualism and Linguistic Change in New Guinea." *Anthropological Linguistics* 4, 7:1–13.

Schwartz, Theodore. 1976. "The Cargo Cult: A Melanesian Type Response to Change." In *Responses to Change: Society, Culture, and Personality,* edited by George deVos, pp. 157–206. New York: Van Nostrand.

Service, Elman. 1971. *Primitive Social Organization.* 2nd ed. New York: Random House.

_____. 1966. *The Hunters.* Englewood Cliffs, N.J.: Prentice-Hall.

Simmel, Georg. 1955. *Conflict and the Web of Group Affiliations.* New York: Free Press.

Simmons, William S. 1971. *Eyes of the Night: Witchcraft among a Senegalese People.* Boston: Little, Brown and Co.

Siskind, Janet. 1973. *To Hunt in the Morning.* London: Oxford University Press.

Slater, Mariam Kreiselman. 1959. "Ecological Factors in the Origin of Incest." *American Anthropologist* 61:1042–1059.

Smith, Carol. 1978. "Beyond Dependency Theory: National and Regional Patterns of Underdevelopment in Guatemala." *American Ethnologist* 5:574–617.

Smith. E. W., and Dale, A. 1920. *The Ila-Speaking Peoples of Northern Rhodesia.* 2 vols. London: MacMillan.

Smith, M. Estellie. 1975. "A Tale of Two Cities: The Reality of Historical Differences." *Urban Anthropology* 4:61–72.

Southall, Aidan. 1976. "Nuer and Dinka Are People: Ecology, Ethnicity, and Logical Possibility." *Man* 11:4, 465–491.

_____. 1974. "State Formation in Africa." In *Annual Review of Anthropology,* edited by B. J. Siegel, A. P. Beals, and S. A. Tyler, 3: 153–165. Palto Alto, Calif.: Annual Reviews, Inc.

Speke, John Hanning. 1864. *Journal of the Discovery of the Source of the Nile.* New York: Harper.

Spuhler, James. 1977. "Biology, Speech, and Language." In *Annual Review of Anthropology,* edited by B. J. Siegel, A. R. Beals, and S. A. Tyler, 6: 509–562. Palo Alto, Calif.: Annual Reviews, Inc.

Steward, Julian. 1955. *Theory of Culture Change.* Urbana, Ill.: University of Illinois Press.

Suggs, Robert. 1960. *The Island Civilizations of Polynesia.* New York: The New American Library.

Suttles, Gerald. 1968. *The Social Order of the Slum.* Chicago: University of Chicago Press.

Tindall, B. Allan. 1976. "Theory in the Study of Cultural Transmission." In *Annual Review of Anthropology,* 5, edited by B. J. Siegel, A. R. Beals, and S. A. Tyler. Palo Alto, Calif.: Annual Reviews, Inc.

Townshend, Philip. 1979. "African Mankala in Anthropological Perspective." *Current Anthropology* 20:794–796.
———. 1980. "Mankala in Eastern and Southern Africa: A Distributional Analysis." *Azania* 14.

Tuchman, Barbara, 1962. *The Proud Tower.* New York: Macmillan.

Tuden, Arthur, and Marshall, Catherine. 1972. "Political Organization: Cross-Cultural Codes 4." *Ethnology* 11, 4:436–464.

Turnbull, Colin M. 1972. *The Mountain People.* New York: Simon & Schuster.
———. 1962. *The Forest People: A Study of the Pygmies of the Congo.* New York: Simon & Schuster.

Turner, Victor W. 1969. *The Ritual Process: Structure and Anti-Structure.* Chicago: Aldine.
———. 1968. *The Drums of Affliction.* Oxford: Clarendon Press.
———. 1967. *The Forest of Symbols.* Ithaca, N.Y.: Cornell University Press.

Tylor, Edward B. 1889. "On a Method of Investigating the Development of Institutions; Applied to Laws of Marriage and Descent." *Journal of the Royal Anthropological Institute* 18:245–269.

Uchendu, Victor. 1973. "A Navaho Community." In *A Handbook of Method in Cultural Anthropology,* edited by Raoul Naroll and Ronald Cohen, pp. 230–237. New York: Columbia University Press.
———. 1965. *The Igbo of Southeast Nigeria.* New York: Holt, Rinehart & Winston.

Vayda, Andrew, 1961. "Expansion and Warfare among Swidden Agriculturalists." *American Anthropologist* 63:346–358.

Vidich, Arthur, and Bensman, Joseph. 1958. *Small Town in Mass Society.* Princeton: Princeton University Press.

Wallace, Anthony. 1966. *Religion: An Anthropological View.* New York: Random House.
———. 1961. *Culture and Personality.* New York: Random House.
———. 1961a. "Mental Health, Biology and Culture." In *Psychological Anthropology,* edited by F. Hsu, pp. 255–295. Homewood, Ill.: Dorsey Press.
———. 1956. "Revitalization Movements." *American Anthropologist* 58:264–281.
———. 1952. *The Modal Personality Structure of the Tuscarora Indians, as Revealed by the Rorschach Test.* Bulletin 150. Washington D.C.: Bureau of American Ethnology.

Wallerstein, Immanuel. 1974. *The Modern World-System: Capitalist Agriculture and the Origins of the European World-Economy in the Sixteenth Century.* New York: Academic Press.

Walter, Eugene V. 1969. *Terror and Resistance.* London: Oxford University Press.

Warner, W. Lloyd. 1958. *A Black Civilization.* Rev. ed. New York: Harper Bros.

Warner, W. Lloyd, ed. 1963. *Yankee City.* Abridged ed. New Haven, Conn.: Yale University Press.

Watson, James. 1974. "Restaurants and Remittances: Chinese Emigrant Workers in London." In *Anthropologists in Cities,* edited by G. Foster and R. Kemper, pp. 201–222. Boston: Little, Brown and Co.

Wattenwyl, André von, and Zellinger, Heinrich. 1979. "Color-Term Salience and Neurophysiology of Color Vision." *American Anthropologist* 81:279–288.

Weiss, Melford S. 1967. "Rebirth in the Airborne." *Transaction* 4 (May): 23–26.

White, Isobel. 1977. "The Natives Eat Well." In *The Anthropologists' Cookbook,* edited by Jessica Kuper, pp. 216–220. New York: Universe Books.

White, Leslie A. 1949. *The Science of Culture.* New York: Grove Press.

Whiting, Beatrice, 1950. *Paiute Sorcery.* New York: Viking Fund Publications in Anthropology, 15.

Whiting, John; Kluckhohn, R.; and Anthony, A. 1958. "The Function of Male Initiation Ceremonies at Puberty." In *Readings in Social Psychology,* 3rd ed., edited by Eleanor E. Maccoby, Theodore M. Newcomb, and Eugene L. Hartley, pp. 359–370. New York: Henry Holt.

Whorf, B. L. 1956. *Language, Thought and Reality.* Boston: MIT Press.

Whyte, Martin. 1978. "Cross-Cultural Codes Dealing with the Relative Status of Women." *Ethnology* 17:211–237.

Williams, F. E. 1923. *The Vailala Madness and the Destruction of Native Ceremonies in Papua.* Territory of Papua, Anthropological Reports, 4: Port Moresby.

Williams, Thomas. 1972. *Introduction to Socialization: Human Culture Transmitted.* St. Louis: C. V. Mosby.

Wilson, Bryan R. 1973. *Magic and the Millennium.* New York: Harper and Row.

Wilson, Edward O. 1975. *Sociobiology.* Cambridge: Harvard University Press.

Wilson, Monica. 1950. "Nyakyusa Kinship." In *African Systems of Kinship and Marriage.* Edited by A. R. Radcliffe-Brown and Daryll Forde, pp. 111–139.

Winch, Robert F., and Blumberg, Rae Lesser. 1972. "Societal Complexity and Familial Complexity." *American Journal of Sociology* 77:898–920.

Wittfogel, Karl. 1957. *Oriental Despotism.* New Haven, Conn.: Yale University Press.

Wong, Bernard, 1978. "A Comparative Study of the Assimilation of the Chinese in New York City and Lima, Peru." *Comparative Studies in Society and History* 20:335–358.

Worsley, Peter. 1957. *The Trumpet Shall Sound.* London: MacGibbon and Kee.

Wright, Henry. 1977. "Recent Research on the Origin of the State." In *Annual Review of Anthropology,* edited by B. S. Siegel, A. R. Beals, and S. A. Tyler, 6: 379–397. Palo Alto, Calif.: Annual Reviews, Inc.

Wylie, Laurence. 1957. *Village in the Vaucluse.* Cambridge, Mass.: Harvard University Press.

Yoshida, Teigo. 1981. "The Stranger as God: The Place of the Outsider in Japanese Folk Religion." *Ethnology* 15, 2:87–99.

Young, Andrew. 1979. "Top Honor Is Awarded to Dr. Mead." *Philadelphia Inquirer,* 21 Jan. 1979.

ACKNOWLEDGMENTS (continued)

Edwin Eames and Howard Robboy, "Frustration and Indirect Aggression: Healthy Response in a Sick Society," speech presented in 1969 to the Second International Congress of Social Psychiatry, London, England.

A. L. Epstein, abridged from "Network and Urban Social Organization," in *Rhodes Livingstone Institute Journal* (June 1961). Reprinted by permission of University of Zambia Publishers and A. L. Epstein.

E. E. Evans-Pritchard, abridged from *The Nuer,* published by Oxford University Press (1940), by permission of the publisher.

Raymond Firth, abridged from *We the Tikopea,* published by George Allen & Unwin (Publishers) Ltd. (1936), reprinted by permission of George Allen & Unwin Ltd. and American Book Company.

Max Gluckman, abridged from "Analysis of a Social Situation in Modern Zululand," in *Rhodes Livingstone Institute Journal* No. 28. Reprinted by permission of University of Zambia Publishers and Mrs. Max Gluckman.

Marvin Harris and Edward Wilson, from "The Envelope and the Twig," in *The Sciences* vol. 18, no. 8 (October 1978). © 1978 by The New York Academy of Sciences. Reprinted by permission.

C. W. M. Hart, abridged from "Fieldwork Among the Tiwi: 1928–1929," in *Being an Anthropologist: Fieldwork in Eleven Cultures* edited by George D. Spindler. Copyright © 1970 by Holt, Rinehart and Winston, Inc. Reprinted by permission of Holt, Rinehart and Winston and George D. Spindler.

C. W. M. Hart and Arnold R. Pilling, abridged from *The Tiwi of North Australia.* Copyright © 1960 by Holt, Rinehart and Winston, Inc. Reprinted by permisson of Holt, Rinehart and Winston.

Allan R. Holmberg, abridged from "The Research and Development Approach to the Study of Change," in *Human Organization* vol. 17 (1958), published by The American Anthropological Association.

Allan R. Holmberg, the complete version of this article appeared under the title "The Changing Values and Institutions of Vicos in the Context of National Development" by Allan R. Holmberg published in *American Behavioral Scientist* Vol. 8, No. 7 (March 1965) pp 3–8 by permission of the publisher, Sage Publications, Inc.

Allan R. Holmberg, abridged from *Nomads of the Long Bow.* Copyright © 1969 by Laura H. Holmberg, executrix of the estate of Allan R. Holmberg. Reprinted by permission of Doubleday & Company, Inc.

R. Lincoln Keiser, abridged from "Fieldwork Among the Vice Lords of Chicago," in *Being an Anthropologist: Fieldwork in Eleven Cultures* edited by George D. Spindler. Copyright © 1970 by Holt, Rinehart and Winston, Inc. Reprinted by permission of Holt, Rinehart and Winston and George D. Spindler.

Marianne Leach and Jerry Leach, "Meydiha's Kisir:

A Wheat Dish from Southern Turkey," in *The Anthropologists' Cookbook* edited by Jessica Kuper. Copyright © 1977 by the Royal Anthropological Institute. Reprinted by permisson of the publishers, Universe Books Publishers and Routledge & Kegan Paul Ltd.

Ralph Linton, abridged from "One Hundred Percent American," in *American Mercury Magazine* vol. 40 (1937).

Bronislaw Malinowski, abridged from *The Sexual Life of Savages,* New York: Harcourt Brace Jovanovich, Inc. (1929). Reprinted by permission of Routledge & Kegan Paul Ltd. and Paul R. Reynolds, Inc.

McKim Marriott, abridged from "The Feast of Love," in *Krishna: Myths, Rites, and Attitudes* edited by Milton Singer, published by East West Center Press, Honolulu, Hawaii. (1966). Reprinted by permission.

Mervyn Meggitt, abridged from *Blood Is Their Argument,* by permission of Mayfield Publishing Company. Copyright © 1977 by Mervyn Meggitt.

Aubrey Menen, from "My Grandmother and the Dirty English," in *Dead Man in the Silver Market.* Copyright, 1953, by Aubrey Menen. Reprinted by permission of William Morris Agency, Inc., on behalf of the author.

Walter Mischel and Frances Mischel, from "Psychological Aspects of Spirit Possession," in *American Anthropologist* vol. 60, no. 2 (April 1958), published by The American Anthropological Association. Reprinted by permission.

Esther Newton, abridged from *Mother Camp: Female Impersonators in America,* published by Prentice-Hall, Inc. (1972). Reprinted by permisson of Esther Newton.

Len Peterson, abridged from "Stand-in for a Murderer," in *The Ways of Mankind* edited by Walter Goldschmidt, published by Beacon Press (1954). Reprinted by permission of Len Peterson and Walter Goldschmidt.

Hortense Powdermaker, abridged from *Stranger and Friend, the Way of an Anthropologist,* by permission of W. W. Norton & Company, Inc. Copyright © 1966 by Hortense Powdermaker.

Margaret Read, abridged from *Children of Their Fathers: Growing Up Among the Ngoni of Malawi.* Copyright © 1968 by Holt, Rinehart and Winston, Inc. Reprinted by permission of Holt, Rinehart and Winston.

William S. Simmons, abridged from *Eyes of the Night: Witchcraft Among a Senegalese People,* published by Little, Brown and Company (1971). Reprinted by permission of William S. Simmons.

John Hanning Speke, abridged from *Journal of the Discovery of the Source of the Nile,* published by Harper & Brothers, Publishers (1864).

Victor C. Uchendu, abridged from "A Navajo Community," in A *Handbook of Method in Cultural Anthropology* edited by R. Narroll and R. Cohen. Copyright © 1970 by Raoul Narroll and Ronald Cohen. Reprinted by permission of Doubleday & Company, Inc.

Bryan R. Wilson, abridged from *Magic and the Millennium.* Copyright © 1973 by Bryan Wilson. Reprinted by permission of Harper & Row, Publisher, Inc. and Heinemann Educational Books Ltd.

Photo Credits

Part I: Page 2, Richard Lee/Anthrophoto.

Chapter 1: Page 4, John Collier, Jr., courtesy of the Cornell University Archives and the Holmberg family; page 7, Arnold Pilling; page 9, Hortense Powdermaker Estate/The Lowry Museum; page 13, Lincoln Keiser, Reprinted with permission of Holt, Rinehart & Winston; page 16, Richard Harrington; page 24, Frank Arensberg/Earthwatch; page 25, Joan Pasternak/Earthwatch; page 32 top, Arnold Pilling; page 32 bottom, Malinowski, reprinted with the permission of Routledge & Kegan Paul, Ltd.; page 33, John Collier, Jr., courtesy of the Cornell Archives and the Holmberg family.

Chapter 2: Page 42, The Institute for Intercultural Studies; page 46, The University of Zambia; page 47, The University of Zambia; page 55 Allen Smith; page 57 left, Gardiner/*Peoples and Problems of the Pacific;* page 57 right, Tattersall/*Peoples and Problems of the Pacific;* page 60 left. UPI; page 60 right, Frank Siteman/Picture Cube; page 64, Niels Fock; page 68, The Alcala de Henares polyglot Bible/The N. Y. Public Library Rare Book Division.

Part II: Page 78, Klaus Francke/Peter Arnold Inc.

Chapter 3: Page 80, Dr. J. F. E. Bloss/Anthrophoto; page 83, University of California/*People and Place;* page 84, University of California/*People and Place;* page 91, Laurence K. Marshall; page 96, Kenneth Mallory/Anthrophoto; page 97, Gene Cohen; page 98, Edwin Eames; page 99, #102–LH–1056/The National Archives; page 103, Tony Leeds; page 104, Edwin Eames.

Chapter 4: Page 112, Peter Menzel; page 115, Arnold Pilling; page 119, Ralph Gates/Woodfin Camp; page 123, Oxford University Press/The

Muria and Their Ghotul; page 125, Couples, Inc.; page 127, Paul Hockings; page 131, Frank Siteman; page 136, Robert Azzi/Woodfin Camp.

Chapter 5: Page 142, Eric Kroll/Taurus; page 145, Smithsonian Institute, page 152, Brown Bros.; page 162, Napoleon Chagnon, page 163, Alan Carey/Image Works; page 165, American Museum of Natural History; page 166, Eric Kroll/Taurus.

Chapter 6: Page 172, the Bettmann Archive, Inc.; page 174, Historic Picture Service Inc., Chicago; page 177, Robert Glasse; page 185, Karl Heider/ The Film Study Center; page 187, The British Library; page 190, *Pax Britannica*/Harcourt, Brace & World; page 193, James Gibbs; page 194, Laboratory of Anthropology at Santa Fe; page 198, Robert Glasse.

Chapter 7: Page 202, Historic Picture Service Inc., Chicago, page 205, Speke and Mutesa (from *Journey to Discover the Source of the Nile*); page 211, Jerome Montegue; page 212, UPI; page 215, DeVore/Anthrophoto; page 218, Pitt River Museum; page 220, Dixon/The Museum of New Mexico; page 223, Hilda Kuper; page 227, Culver Pictures; page 228, Culver Pictures.

Chapter 8: Page 232, M. Etter/Anthrophoto; page 236, Edwin Eames; page 240, Edwin Eames; page 243, Brown Bros.; page 247, Michael Harner; page 249, Mimi Nichter/Anthrophoto; page 251, Edith Turner, University of Virginia; page 252, New Orleans Tourist Commission; page 256, Roy Rappaporte, reprinted by permission of Yale University Press; page 257, Dr. Wm. Bascom; page 258, Allen Smith; page 261, Museum of the American Indian.

Chapter 9: Page 266, Tom Pix/Peter Arnold, Inc.; page 269, Dr. Raymond Firth; *The Barabaig*, Klima, reprinted with permission, of Holt, Rhinehart & Winston; page 280, Allen Smith; page 285, Kenneth Mallory/Anthrophoto; page 287, *To Hunt in the Morning*, Janet Siskind, by permission of Oxford University Press; page 289, Globe Photo

Library; page 290 Resorts International; page 291, Marc and Evelyne Bernheim/Woodfin Camp.

Part III: Page 296, Courtesy of the Anthropology Resource Center.

Chapter 10: Page 296, Richard Lee/Anthrophoto; page 298, from *Children of Their Fathers*, by Margaret Read, reprinted with permission of Holt, Rhinehart & Winston; page 300, from *Children of Their Fathers*, by Margaret Read, reprinted with permission of Holt, Rhinehart & Winston; page 308, Marsha Fall Stuart/Global Focus; page 309, Museum of Natural History; page 311, Eugene Cohen; page 312, West Point Military Academy; page 315, Cora DuBois; page 320, Robert Glasse; page 323, Marc and Evelyne Bernheim/Woodfin Camp.

Chapter 11: Page 328, Richard Lee/Anthrophoto; page 330, Robbins Burling; page 337, Sea World; page 341, H. Terrace/Anthrophoto; page 347, UPI, page 348, Mark Antman/Image Works; page 350, Photo Researchers.

Chapter 12: Page 356, The Robert and Francis Flaherty Study Center, Claremont School of Theology; page 359, The Peabody Museum/Salem; page 362, Kal Muller/Woodfin Camp; page 366, Richard Lee/Anthrophoto; page 372, *Pax Britannica*, Harcourt, Brace & World; page 375, Culver Pictures; page 376, Arnold Pilling; page 379, The Peabody Museum of Salem; page 381, Azzi/ Woodfin Camp.

Part IV: Page 384, Dave Corbell/The Southern Folklore Center

Chapter 13: Page 366, John Collier Jr./Courtesy of the Cornell Archives and the Holmberg family; page 389, courtesy Dr. Esther Newton; page 394, Christie Moore/Odyssey; page 397, John Collier Jr./Courtesy of the Cornell archives and the Holmberg family; page 400, Lisa Peattie; page 401, © Alon Reininger, 1978, Contact; page 404, Anthony Leeds; page 405, Pictorial Parade.

Index